WORD PICTURES OF THE NEW TESTAMENT

Volume One

THE GOSPEL ACCORDING TO
MATTHEW

THE GOSPEL ACCORDING TO
MARK

THE UPDATED CLASSIC WORK BY
A. T. ROBERTSON

WORD PICTURES OF THE NEW TESTAMENT

Volume One

THE GOSPEL ACCORDING TO
MATTHEW

THE GOSPEL ACCORDING TO
MARK

Revised and Updated by
Wesley J. Perschbacher

Kregel
Academic & Professional

Word Pictures of the New Testament, Volume 1:
The Gospel According to Matthew
The Gospel According to Mark

© 2004 by Wesley J. Perschbacher

Published by Kregel Publications, a division of Kregel, Inc., P.O. Box 2607, Grand Rapids, MI 49501.

ISBN 0-8254-3640-0

Printed in the United States of America

04 05 06 07 08 / 5 4 3 2 1

CONTENTS

Preface to the Revised Edition

The original edition of A. T. Robertson's *Word Pictures in the New Testament* was published over seventy years ago. It has had a long and profitable ministry to pastors, missionaries, and students of the New Testament.

The revision of Robertson's work updates some information and adds new formatting.

The material has been newly typeset and includes the following changes:

1. The text has been updated and edited, with references changed to the New American Standard Bible (1995 ed.), except as noted, rather than to the Canterbury Version used by A. T. Robertson. The editorial revision includes changing British to American spellings.
2. Each page identifies the book, chapter, and verse being considered.
3. The Greek alphabet is used, rather than transliteration. Transliterated Greek was originally used because of the difficulty of printing the Greek text.
4. Alternate New International Version translations frequently are provided in the notes following each chapter.
5. The Greek is a generic text, with variants indicated when appropriate, pointing out different readings from the 1881 critical Greek text of Brooke Foss Westcott and Fenton John Anthony Hort (abbreviated WH), Majority Text (Maj.T), Textus Receptus (TR), and readings from Beza (TRb) and Stephanus (TRs).
6. Certain abbreviations have been spelled out—N.T. is New Testament, O.T. is Old Testament—while other abbreviations remain the same, such as MSS for manuscripts in footnotes and LXX for Septuagint.
7. Roman numbers have been replaced with Arabic numbers.

Preface to the 1930 Edition

It has now been forty years (1890) since Dr. Marvin R. Vincent wrote his most useful series of volumes entitled *Word Studies in the New Testament*. They are still helpful for those for whom they were designed, but a great deal of water has run under the mill in these years. More scientific methods of philology are now in use. No longer are Greek tenses and prepositions explained in terms of conjectural English translations or interchanged according to the whim of the interpreter. Comparative grammar has thrown a flood of light on the real meaning of New Testament forms and idioms. New Testament writers are no longer explained as using one construction "for" another. New light has come also from the papyri discoveries in Egypt. Unusual Greek words from the standpoint of the literary critic or classical scholar are here found in everyday use in letters and business and public documents.

The New Testament Greek is now known to be not a new or peculiar dialect of the Greek language, but the very lingo of the time. The vernacular Κοινή, the spoken language of the day, appears in the New Testament as in the scraps of Oxyrhynchus and Fayum papyri. There are specimens of the literary Κοινή in the papyri as also in the writings of Luke, the Epistles of Paul, the Epistle to the Hebrews. A new Greek-English lexicon of the New Testament will come in due time which will take note of the many startling discoveries from the Greek papyri and inscriptions first brought to notice in their bearing on the New Testament by Dr. Adolf Deissmann, then of Heidelberg, now of Berlin. His *Bible Studies* (translation by Alexander Grieve, 1901) and his *Light from the Ancient East* (revised edition translated by L. R. M. Strachan, 1927) are accessible to students unfamiliar with the German originals.

There is no doubt of the need of a new series of volumes today in the light of the new knowledge. Many ministers have urged me to undertake such a task and finally I have agreed to do it at the solicitation of my publishers. The readers of these volumes are expected to be primarily those who know no Greek or comparatively little and yet who are anxious to get fresh help from the study of words and phrases in the New Testament, men who do not have

9

access to the technical books required, like Moulton and Milligan's *Vocabulary of the Greek Testament.*

The critical student will appreciate the more delicate distinctions in words. But it is a sad fact that many ministers, laymen, and women who took courses in Greek at college, university, or seminary have allowed the cares of the world and deceitfulness of riches to choke off the Greek that they once knew. Some, strangely enough, have done it even in the supposed interest of the very gospel, whose vivid messages they have thus allowed to grow dim and faint. If some of these vast numbers can have their interest in the Greek New Testament revived, these volumes will be worthwhile. Some may be incited, as many have been by my volume, *The Minister and His Greek New Testament,* to begin the study of the Greek New Testament under the guidance of a book like Davis's *Beginner's Grammar of the Greek New Testament.* Others who are without a turn for Greek or without any opportunity to start the study will be able to follow the drift of the remarks and use it to profit in sermons, in Sunday school lessons, or for private edification.

The six volumes will follow this order: volume 1, the Gospel according to Matthew and Mark; volume 2, the Gospel according to Luke; volume 3, Acts; volume 4, the Pauline Epistles; volume 5, the Gospel according to John and the Epistle to the Hebrews; volume 6, the General Epistles and the Revelation of John. For purely exegetical and expository development, a more chronological order would be required. These volumes do not claim to be formal commentary. Nowhere is the whole text discussed, but everywhere those words are selected for discussion which seem to be rich for the needs of the reader in the light of present-day knowledge. A great deal of the personal equation is thus inevitable. My own remarks will be now lexical, now grammatical, now archaeological, now exegetical, now illustrative—anything that the mood of the moment may move me to write that may throw light here and there on the New Testament words and idioms. Another writer might feel disposed to enlarge upon items not touched upon here. But that is to be expected even in the more formal commentaries, useful as they are. To some extent it is true of lexicons. No one man knows everything, even in his chosen specialty, or has the wisdom to pick out what every reader wishes explained. But even diamonds in the rough are diamonds. It is for the reader to polish them as he will. He can turn the light this way and that. There is a certain amount of repetition at some points, part of it on purpose to save time and to emphasize the point.

I have called these volumes *Word Pictures in the New Testament* for the obvious reason that language was originally purely pictographic. Children love to read by pictures, either where it is all picture or where pictures are interspersed with simple words. The Rosetta Stone is a famous illustration. The Egyptian hieroglyphics come at the top of the stone, followed by the Demotic Egyptian language with the Greek translation at the bottom. By means of this stone the secret of the hieroglyphs or pictographs was unraveled. Chinese characters are also pictographic. The pictures were first for ideas, then for words, then for syllables, then for letters. Today in Alaska there are Indians who still use pictures alone for communicating their ideas. "Most words have been originally metaphors, and metaphors are continually falling into the rank of words" (Professor Campbell). Rather is it not true that words are metaphors, sometimes with the pictured flower still blooming, sometimes with the blossom blurred? Words have never gotten wholly away from the picture stage.

These old Greek words in the New Testament are rich with meaning. They speak to us out of the past with lively images to those who have eyes to see. It is impossible to translate all of one language into another. Much can be carried over, but not all. Delicate shades of meaning defy the translator. But some of the very words of Jesus we have still, as He said: "The words that I have spoken unto you are spirit and are life" (John 6:63). We must never forget that in dealing with the words of Jesus we are dealing with things that have life and breath. That is true of all the New Testament, the most wonderful of all books of all time. One can feel the very throb of the heart of Almighty God in the New Testament if the eyes of his own heart have been enlightened by the Holy Spirit. May the Spirit of God take of the things of Christ and make them ours as we muse over the words of life that speak to us out of the New Covenant that we call the New Testament.

—A. T. ROBERTSON
Louisville, Kentucky
The Gospel According to Matthew

THE GOSPEL ACCORDING TO
MATTHEW

Introduction to Matthew

There have been questions as to who actually wrote the *Greek* Matthew. Papias records, as quoted by Eusebius, that Matthew wrote the *Logia* of Jesus in Hebrew (Aramaic). Is our present Matthew based upon a Greek translation of the Aramaic *Logia* along with Mark and other sources, as modern scholars tend to think? If so, was the translator the Apostle Matthew or some other disciple? There is no way to reach a clear decision in the light of known facts. There is no real reason why Matthew could not have written both the Aramaic *Logia* and our Greek Matthew, unless one believes that Matthew and parts of Mark were redacted into one work by someone who placed Mark on a par with Matthew. Mark's book rests primarily on the preaching of Simon Peter. Scholfield in 1927 published *An Old Hebrew Text of St. Matthew's Gospel.* Such work must be based on conjecture. We know quite too little of the origin of the Synoptic Gospels to say dogmatically that the apostle Matthew was not in any real sense the author.

If the book is genuine, as I believe, the date becomes a matter of interest. Here again there is nothing absolutely decisive to be gained from textual research, save that Matthew was written after the Gospel according to Mark and apparently uses Mark. If Mark is given an early date, then Matthew's book could be relatively early. Many place its appearance between 70 and 80. It is not certain whether Luke wrote after Matthew, though that is quite possible. No definite use of Matthew by Luke can be shown. One guess is as good as another, and each decides by his own predilections. My own view that Matthew was written in about 60 is as good as any.[1]

In the Gospel itself, we find "Matthew the tax collector" (Matt. 9:9; 10:3; cf. 9:9) though Mark (2:14) and Luke (5:27) call him "Levi." Evidently, therefore, he had two names (one Greek and one Hebrew), as did John Mark. It is significant that Jesus called this man from so disreputable a business to follow him. There is no indication that Levi was a disciple of John the Baptist. He was specially chosen by Jesus to be one of the twelve apostles, a businessman like the fishermen James, John, Andrew, and Simon. In lists of the apostles he comes seventh or eighth. Nothing definite is told about him in the Gospels,

15

apart from the fact that he was in the circle of the twelve and that he gave a feast for his fellow publicans in honor of Jesus.

Matthew was in the habit of keeping accounts and it is quite possible that he took notes of the sayings of Jesus as he heard them. At any rate, he gives much attention to the teachings of Jesus as, for instance, the Sermon on the Mount in chapters 5–7, the parables in chapter 13, the denunciation of the Pharisees in chapter 23, and the great eschatological discourse in chapters 24–25. As a Rome-collaborating tax-gatherer in Galilee, he was not a narrow Jew, so we do not expect a book prejudiced in favor of the Jews. He does go to some lengths to show that Jesus is the Jewish Messiah and national hope and makes frequent quotations of the Old Testament to confirm and illustrate Jesus' messianic position. However, one finds no narrow nationalism in Matthew. Jesus is both Messiah of the Jews and Savior of the world.

Ten parables in Matthew are not in the other Gospels: (1) the tares; (2) the hidden treasure; (3) the Net; (4) the Pearl of Great Price; (5) the Unmerciful Servant; (6) the Laborers in the Vineyard; (7) the Two Sons; (8) the Marriage of the King's Son; (9) the Ten Virgins; and (10) the Talents. The only miracles found only in Matthew are those of the two blind men (9:27–31) and the coin in the mouth of the fish (17:24–27). The story of Bartimaeus is given with the added detail that a second blind man with him also was healed (20:29–34). But Matthew gives the narrative of the birth of Jesus from the standpoint of Joseph, while Luke tells that wonderful story from the perspective of Mary. Some details of the death and Resurrection are given by Matthew alone.

The book follows the same general chronological plan as that in Mark, but groups certain material—such as the miracles in chapters 8 and 9, and the parables in chapter 13.

The style is free from Hebraisms and has few individual peculiarities. The author is fond of the phrase *the kingdom of heaven* and pictures Jesus as the Son of Man, but also as the Son of God. He sometimes abbreviates Mark's statements and sometimes expands them to be more precise.

Alfred Plummer shows the broad general plan of both Mark and Matthew to be:

Introduction to the Gospel: Mark 1:1–13 = Matthew 3:1–4:11.
Ministry in Galilee: Mark 1:14–6:13 = Matthew 4:12–13:58.
Ministry in the neighborhood: Mark 6:14–9:50 = Matthew 14:1–18:35.
Journey through Perea to Jerusalem: Mark 10:1–52 = Matthew 19:1–20:34.
Last week in Jerusalem: Mark 11:1–16:8 = Matthew 21:1–28:8.

The Gospel of Matthew comes first in the New Testament, though it is not so in all of the Greek manuscripts. Because of its position, it is the most widely read and the most influential writing in the New Testament. Such honor is appropriate, although Matthew was written after Mark and it is not so beautiful as Luke nor so profound as John. It gives a just and straightforward portrait of the life and teachings of Jesus Christ as Lord and Savior. The author persuasively shows that Jesus fulfills the Old Testament messianic hope, so it is a good bridge from Old Testament prophecy to introduce the New Testament fulfillment.

THE TITLE

The Textus Receptus has "The Holy Gospel according to Matthew" (τὸ κατὰ Ματθαῖον ἅγιον Εὐαγγέλιον), though the Elzevirs omit "holy," not agreeing here with Stephanus, Griesbach, and Scholz. Only minuscules (cursive Greek manuscripts and all late) have the adjective. Other minuscules and nine uncials, including W (the Washington Codex of the fifth century), C of the fifth century (the palimpsest manuscript) and Delta of the ninth century, together with most Latin manuscripts, have simply "Gospel according to Matthew" (Εὐαγγέλιον κατὰ Ματθαῖον). Aleph and B, the two oldest Greek uncials of the fourth century, have only "According to Matthew" (Κατὰ Ματθαῖον; note double θ, theta). The Greek uncial D of the fifth or sixth century follows Aleph and B, as do some of the earliest Old Latin manuscripts and the Curetonian Syriac. It is clear, therefore, that the earliest form of the title was simply "According to Matthew." It may be doubted if Matthew (or the author, if not Matthew) had any title at all. The use of "according to" makes it plain that the meaning is not "the Gospel of Matthew," but the Gospel as given by Matthew, *secundum Matthaeum,* to distinguish the report by Matthew from that by Mark, by Luke, by John. Least of all is there any authority in the manuscripts for saying "Saint Matthew," a Roman Catholic practice observed by some Protestants.

The word *gospel* (εὐαγγέλιον) comes to mean "good news" in Greek, though originally it referred to a reward for good tidings, as in Homer's *Odyssey* 14.152 and in the LXX in 2 Kings 4:10. In the New Testament it is the good news of salvation through Christ. The English word *gospel* probably comes from the Anglo-Saxon *godspell,* "story or narrative of God," the life of Christ. It was confused with the Anglo-Saxon *gospell,* "good story," which seems like a translation of the Greek εὐαγγέλιον. But primarily the English word means the God story as seen in Christ, which is the best news that the world has ever had. One thinks at once of the use of *word* (λόγος) in John 1:1, 14. So then it is, according to the Greek, not the "Good News of Matthew," but the "Good News of God," brought to us in Christ the Word, the Son of God, the Image of the Father, the Message of the Father. We are to study this story first as presented by Matthew. The message is God's and it is as fresh to us today in Matthew's record as when he first wrote it.

NOTES

1.   Editor's note: Much research has helped date the New Testament autographs since A. T. Robertson wrote his introduction, including discovery of the Dead Sea Scrolls and other manuscript evidence. Those who would downgrade the historicity of the Gospels have strived unsuccessfully to find evidence to place Matthew after the first century. There is more evidence to place it even earlier, possibly in the 40s or early 50s.

Matthew: Chapter 1

1:1. *The record*[1] ($\beta \iota \beta \lambda o\varsigma$). There is no article in the Greek,[2] but the genitives following $\beta \iota \beta \lambda o\varsigma$ make it definite. This Greek term originally referred to the papyrus plant, from which the inner bark or rind was used to make sheets of writing material. The English *paper* derives from $\pi \alpha \pi \upsilon \rho o\varsigma$ (papyrus). Pieces of papyrus were beaten together to form a flat writing surface. Papyri could be purchased in rolls of varying lengths, according to the writer's need. This word is found in the New Testament ten times with the meaning "book or scroll."[3] $\beta \iota \beta \lambda \iota o\nu$ is a diminuitive of $\beta \iota \beta \lambda o\varsigma$, but in the NT does not have the diminuitive force, and is a synonym of $\beta \iota \beta \lambda o\varsigma$.[4] The plural form of this word is $\beta \iota \beta \lambda \iota \alpha$. from which we get the English term *Bible*.[5] $T\grave{\alpha}$ $\beta \iota \beta \lambda \iota \alpha$ was used by early Christians to refer to the Old and New Testament books. Matthew is not applying the word *book* to the Old Testament, nor to his own book. He refers to *the genealogy*[6] of Jesus Christ ($\beta \iota \beta \lambda o\varsigma$ $\gamma \epsilon \nu \acute{\epsilon} \sigma \epsilon \omega \varsigma$ $\text{'}I\eta \sigma o\hat{\upsilon}$ $X\rho \iota \sigma \tau o\hat{\upsilon}$). Moffatt translates it "the birth roll of Jesus Christ." We have no means of knowing where the writer obtained the data for this genealogy. It differs radically from that in Luke 3:23–38. One can give only his own theory of the difference. Apparently in Matthew we have the actual genealogy of Joseph, which would be the legal pedigree of Jesus according to Jewish custom. In Luke we apparently have the actual genealogy of Mary, which would be the real line of Jesus, which Luke naturally gives as he is writing for the Gentiles.

Jesus the Messiah[7] ($\text{'}I\eta \sigma o\hat{\upsilon}$ $X\rho \iota \sigma \tau o\hat{\upsilon}$). The absence of the articles here is common in titles of books. Both names, *Jesus Christ*, are used. The first is the name *Jesus* ($\text{'}I\eta \sigma o\hat{\upsilon}\varsigma$), given by the angel to Joseph (Matt. 1:21), which describes the mission of the child. The second was originally a verbal adjective ($X\rho \iota \sigma \tau \acute{o}\varsigma$) meaning *anointed*, from the verb *to anoint* ($X\rho \iota \omega$). It was used often in the Septuagint (referred to hereafter as LXX) as an adjective like "the anointed priest" (1 Kings 2:10 LXX = 1 Sam. 2:10 in canonical Scripture) and then as a substantive to translate the Hebrew word *Messiah* ($M\epsilon \sigma \sigma \iota \alpha \varsigma$). So Andrew said to Simon: "'We have found the Messiah,' (which translated means Christ)" (John 1:41). In the Gospels, it is sometimes *the Anointed One, the*

Messiah, or it is a proper name with title, as here, *Jesus Christ.* Paul in his later epistles usually has it Christ Jesus.

The son of David,[8] *the son of Abraham* (υἱοῦ Δαυὶδ[9] υἱοῦ Ἀβραάμ). Matthew proposes to show that Jesus Christ is on the human side the son of David, as the Messiah was to be, and the son of Abraham. He was not merely a Jewish heir of Abrahamic promises; rather he fulfilled the promise made to Abraham. So Matthew begins the messianic line with Abraham while Luke traces Christ's lineage back to Adam. The Hebrew and Aramaic often used the word *son* (בֵּן) to refer to someone's quality or character, but here the idea is literal blood descent. Christians are called sons of God because Christ has bestowed this dignity upon us (Rom. 8:14; 9:26; Gal. 3:26; 4:5–7). Verse 1 is the description of the list in verses 2–17. The names are given in three groups: First, Abraham to David (2–6); second, David to Babylon removal (6–11); third, Jechoniah to Jesus (12–16). The removal to Babylon (μετοικεσίας βαβυλῶνος) occurs at the end of verse 11, the beginning of verse 12, and twice in the résumé in verse 17. This great event is used to mark off the two last divisions from each other. It is a good illustration of the genitive as the case of genus or kind. The Babylon removal could mean either "to Babylon" or "from Babylon," or indeed, the removal "of Babylon." But Jewish readers would know the facts from the Old Testament. Matthew means the deportation "to Babylon."[10] Then verse 17 makes a summary of the three lists, fourteen names in each by counting David twice and omitting several names, a common sort of mnemonic device. Matthew does not mean to say that there were only fourteen in actual genealogy. The names of the women (Tamar, Rahab, Ruth, and Bathsheba the wife of Uriah) are likewise not counted. But it is a most interesting list.

1:2. *Was born*[11] (ἐγέννησεν). This word comes, like some of the early chapters of Genesis, with regularity through verse 16, until the birth of Jesus is reached when there is a sudden change. The word itself does not always mean immediate parentage, but merely direct descent. The article occurs here each time with the object of ἐγέννησεν, but not with the subject of the verb to distinguish sharply the proper names. Indeclinable (uninflected) proper names usually have the article if the case would not otherwise be clear. Note here that the nominatives have no article, but the accusatives do. Thus, the article emphasizes the distinction between the subject and the object. The conjunction δὲ functions here as a mere copulative rather than in opposition.[12]

1:2–16. *Jesse was the father of [the] David the king. . . . Jacob was the father of [the] Joseph. . . .* (Ἰεσσαὶ δὲ ἐγέννησεν τὸν δεανὶδ τὸν βασιλέα.

...Ἰακὼβ δὲ ἐγέννησεν τὸν Ἰωσήφ. ...). In the case of David the king (1:6) and Joseph the husband of Mary (1:16), the article is repeated showing apposition. The mention of the brethren of Judah (1:2) and of both Phares and Zara (1:3) may show that Matthew was not copying a family pedigree but making his own table.

Bathsheba who had been the wife of Uriah (ἐκ τῆς τοῦ Οὐρίου). In verse 6, the double article illustrates the genitive of relationship. The feminine τῆς refers to the wife of τοῦ Οὐρίου. The words, *who had been the wife of Uriah,*[13] are indicated in the Greek by the article τῆς. Thus, the English translation requires a paraphrase or expansion of the article in order to be understood (see 2 Sam. 11–12). The spelling of these Hebrew names in English is usually according to the Hebrew form, not the Greek. In the Greek itself the Hebrew spelling is often observed in violation of Greek rules for the ending of words with no consonants save ν, ρ, or ς. Greek spelling of names often differs from the Hebrew spelling. One of the reasons is that Greek is limited in the use of the *h* sound to the rough breathing mark at the beginning of a word, or to the double consonants χ ("ch"), θ ("th"), and ϕ ("ph"). Thus *Abram* or *Abraham* is always spelled in Greek as "Ἀβραάμ," without an *h* sound. Another example is Βηθλέεμ (2:1ff.) where both Hebrew and English would have the *h* sound in the last syllable. Also, the ending of a Greek word could only be with a vowel, a diphthong, or the consonants ν or " plus double consonants ξ and ψ. Thus names adapted into the Greek language would be altered. For example, *Judah* would become *Judas* (Ἰούδας or Ἰούδα) because Greek had no *h* sound for the ending. When Greek proper nouns end in letters other than a vowel, diphthong, ν or " or double consonants, it usually indicates that a foreign name has been transliterated into Greek. Most of these proper names are indeclinable.

1:16. *Joseph the husband of Mary, by whom Jesus was born, who is called the Messiah* (τὸν Ἰωσὴφ τὸν ἄνδρα Μαρίας, ἐξ ἧς ἐγεννήθη Ἰησους ὁ λεγόμενος Χριστός).[14] All the Greek manuscripts give verse 16 as above save the Ferrar Group of minuscules, which are supported by the Sinaitic Syriac Version. This group reads: "Jacob begat Joseph; Joseph, to whom was betrothed Mary the virgin, begat Jesus, who is called the Christ." But a closer study of this reading shows that the scribe did not mean to deny the virgin birth of Jesus. In the very sentence Mary is called the virgin and the passage about Joseph (Matt. 1:18–25) is left intact wherein the supernatural birth of Jesus is definitely affirmed. Probably all that this reading of "begat" means is that Joseph was the "putative (i.e. supposed, reputed, commonly considered) father of Jesus," as Moffatt in his New Translation of the New Testament so translates it. It is remarkable that the oldest scrap of papyrus (P') of any portion of the New Testament contains the ordinary Greek text of Matthew 1:16.[15]

1:18. *Now the birth of Jesus Christ* (τοῦ δὲ ᾽Ιησοῦ Χριστοῦ ἡ γένεσις[16]). A new topic may be introduced by δέ in entire harmony with the preceding discussion. In the Greek *Jesus Christ* comes before *birth* as the important matter after 1:16.[17] But it is plain that the story of the birth of Jesus Christ is to be told briefly. It "was as follows" (οὕτως), the usual Greek idiom. The oldest manuscripts have the same word *genealogy* (γένεσις) used in 1:1, not the word *begotten* for birth, as in 1:16 (ἐγέννησεν). "It is in fact the word Genesis. The evangelist is about to describe, not the genesis of the heaven and the earth, but the genesis of Him who made the heaven and the earth, and who will yet make a new heaven and a new earth."[18]

When His mother Mary had been betrothed to Joseph (μνηστευθείσης[19] τῆς μητρὸς αὐτοῦ Μαρίας τῷ ᾽Ιωσήφ).[20] Matthew proceeds to explain his statement in 1:16, which had implied that Joseph, though the legal father of Jesus in the royal line, was not the biological father of Mary's son. Betrothal was a serious matter among the Jews, not lightly entered into and not lightly broken. "The man who betrothed a maiden was legally husband (Gen. 29:31; Deut. 22:23–28) and an informal cancelling of betrothal was impossible."[21] Though they did not live together as husband and wife until actual marriage, breach of faithfulness on the part of the betrothed was treated as adultery and punishable by death.[22] Matthew uses the genitive absolute construction here, a very common Greek idiom.[23]

By the Holy Spirit (ἐκ πνεύματος ἁγίου).[24] The discovery that Mary was pregnant was inevitable and it is plain that she had not told Joseph.

She was found to be with child (εὑρέθη ἐν γαστρὶ ἔχουσα). This way of putting it, the usual Greek idiom, plainly shows that it was the discovery that shocked Joseph. He did not as yet know what Matthew plainly asserts that the Holy Spirit, not Joseph and not any other man, was responsible for the pregnancy of Mary. The virgin birth of Jesus has been a disturbing fact to some through all the ages and remains a difficulty to those who do not believe in the preexistence of Christ, the Son of God, before His Incarnation. This is the primal fact about the birth of Christ. The Incarnation of Christ is clearly stated by Paul (2 Cor. 8:9; Phil. 2:5–11; and involved in Col. 1:15–19) and by John (John 1:14; 17:5). One who frankly admits the actual preexistence of Christ and the real Incarnation has taken the longest and most difficult step in the matter of the supernatural birth of Christ. That being true, no merely human birth, without the supernatural element, can possibly explain the facts. Incarnation is far more than the indwelling of God by the Holy Spirit in the human heart. To admit real incarnation and also full human birth, both father and mother, creates a greater difficulty than to admit conception by the Holy Spirit. Only Matthew and Luke tell the story of the supernatural birth of Jesus, although John 1:14 seems to refer to it. Mark has nothing whatever concerning the birth and childhood of Jesus and so cannot be used as a witness on the subject. Matthew and Luke insist that Jesus had no human father. There is such a thing in nature as parthenogenesis among animals in the lower orders of life. But that scientific fact has no bearing here. We see God sending his Son into the world to be the world's Savior. He gave him a human mother, but not a human father, so that Jesus Christ is both Son of God and Son of man—the God-Man. Matthew tells the story of the birth of Jesus from the view of Joseph, as Luke gives it from the standpoint of Mary. The two narratives harmonize. One credits these birth narratives according to what is accepted about the love and power of Almighty God to do what he wills. There is no miracle with God who has all power and all knowledge. The laws of nature simply express God's will, but he has not revealed all his will in the laws we discover. God is Spirit. He is Person. He holds in his own power all life. John 3:16 is called the "Little Gospel" because it puts briefly the love of God for men in sending his own Son to live and die for us.

1:19. *Being a righteous man*[25] (δíκαιος ὤν), or just. The same adjective is used of Zacharias and Elizabeth (Luke 1:6) and Simeon (Luke 2:25).[26] He had the Jewish conscientiousness for observing the Law, which would have sentenced Mary to death by stoning (Deut. 22:23). "As a good Jew he would have shown his zeal if he had branded her with public disgrace."[27] Though Joseph was upright, he would not do that.

And not wanting[28] (καὶ μὴ θέλων). So we must understand καὶ here, "and yet." Matthew makes a distinction here between "willing" (θέλων) and "wishing" (ἐβουλήθη).[29] The distinction between "purpose" (θέλω) and "desire" (βούλομαι) is not always drawn, but it is present here. His purpose was not "to disgrace her" (δειγματίσαι),[30] from the root (δείκνυμι, "to show"), a rare word (see its use in Col. 2:15).[31] The substantive (δειγματισμός) occurs on the Rosetta Stone in the sense of *verification*. There are a few instances of the verb in the papyri, although the meaning is not clear.[32] The compound form appears (παραδειγματίζω) in Hebrews 6:6. Curiously, there are earlier instances of the compound than of the simple form, but new examples of the simple verb may turn up as more early texts are found.[33] Joseph planned to put her away secretly.[34] He could give her a bill of divorcement (ἀπολῦσαι), the *gêt* laid down in the Mishna, without a public trial. He had to give her the writ (*gêt*) and pay the fine (Deut. 24:1). So he proposed to do this *privately* (λάθρᾳ)[35] to avoid as much scandal as was possible. One is obliged to respect Joseph and sympathize with his motives. He evidently loved Mary and was appalled to find her untrue. It is impossible to ascribe Jesus' parentage to Joseph according to the narrative of Matthew without saying that Matthew produced a legend to cover up the illegitimate birth. The Talmud openly charges Mary with this sin. Joseph had "a short but tragic struggle between his legal conscience and his love."[36]

1:20. *An angel of the Lord appeared to him in a dream* (ἄγγελος κυρίου κατ᾽ ὄναρ ἐφάνη αὐτῷ). This expression (ἄγγελος κυρίου) always occurs without the article in the New Testament, except when, as in 1:24, there is reference to a previously mentioned angel. This is an anaphoric article. Sometimes in the Old Testament, Yahweh himself is represented by this phrase. Surely Joseph needed God's help if ever a man did. If Jesus was really God's Son, Joseph was entitled to know this supreme fact, so that he might be just to both Mary and her child. Help came in a dream, but the message was distinct and decisive for Joseph. He is called "son of David"[37] as had been shown by Matthew in 1:16. Mary is called "his wife" (τὴν γυναῖκά σου).[38]

"Do not be afraid to take Mary as your wife" (μὴ φοβηθῇς παραλαβεῖν Μαρίαν τὴν γυναῖκά σου). "Do not be afraid" is the second person singular ingressive first aorist passive deponent subjunctive in prohibition, μὴ φοβηθῇς. "To take" (παραλαβεῖν)[39] is ingressive aorist active infinitive. Verse 20 explains that "he had planned" (αὐτοῦ ἐνθυμηθέντος), genitive absolute again (from ἐν *and* θύμος) to send her away with a writ of divorce. He had pondered and had planned as best he knew, but now God had called a halt. He had to decide whether he was willing to shelter Mary by marrying her and take upon himself whatever stigma might attach to her. Joseph was told that the child was begotten of the Holy Spirit and that Mary was innocent of any sin. But who would believe it now if he told it of her? Mary knew the truth and had not told him because she could not expect him to believe it.

1:21. *"You shall call His name Jesus"* (καλέσεις τὸ ὄνομα αὐτοῦ Ἰησοῦν).[40] The rabbis named six whose names were given before birth: "Isaac, Ishmael, Moses, Solomon, Josiah, and the name of the Messiah, whom may the Holy One, blessed be His name, bring in our day." Joseph learned that this child was to be named *Jesus*. Jesus is the same as Joshua, a contraction of Jehoshuah (Num. 13:16; 1 Chron. 7:27), signifying in Hebrew, "Jehovah is helper," or

"Help of Jehovah."[41] Jesus is the Greek form of Joshua (Heb. 4:8). He is another Joshua to lead the true people of God into the Promised Land. The name itself was common enough. Josephus speaks of numerous "Joshuas" in the first century. "Yahweh is salvation" was seen in the leading of Joshua out of the wilderness for the Hebrews and in Jesus for all believers. "The meaning of the name, therefore, finds expression in the title *Savior* as applied to our Lord (Luke 1:47; 2:11; John 4:42)."[42]

"For He will save" ($\sigma\acute{\omega}\sigma\epsilon\iota$) his people from their sins and so be their Savior ($\sigma\omega\tau\acute{\eta}\rho$). He will be Prophet, Priest, and King, but *Savior* sums it all up in one word. The explanation is carried out in the promise, for he is the one who ($\alpha\grave{\upsilon}\tau\acute{o}\varsigma$)[43] will save ($\sigma\acute{\omega}\sigma\epsilon\iota$ with a play on the name Jesus) "his people from their sins." Paul will later explain that by the covenant people, the children of promise, God means spiritual Israel, all who believe whether Jews or Gentiles. This wonderful word touches the very heart of the mission and message of the Messiah. Jesus himself will show that the kingdom of heaven includes all those and only those who have the reign of God in their hearts and lives.

"From their sins" ($\grave{\alpha}\pi\grave{o}$ $\tau\hat{\omega}\nu$ $\grave{\alpha}\mu\alpha\rho\tau\iota\hat{\omega}\nu$ $\alpha\grave{\upsilon}\tau\hat{\omega}\nu$), both sins of omission and of commission. The substantive ($\grave{\alpha}\mu\alpha\rho\tau\acute{\iota}\alpha$) is from the verb ($\grave{\alpha}\mu\alpha\rho\tau\acute{\alpha}\nu\epsilon\iota\nu$) and means "missing the mark," as with an arrow. Jesus will save those who fall "away from" ($\grave{\alpha}\pi\acute{o}$), as well as "out of" ($\grave{\epsilon}\kappa$) their sins. In Christ, sins will be cast into oblivion and he will cover them up out of sight.

1:22. *All this took place to fulfill* ($\tau o\hat{\upsilon}\tau o$ $\delta\grave{\epsilon}$ $\acute{o}\lambda o\nu$ $\gamma\acute{\epsilon}\gamma o\nu\epsilon\nu$ $\acute{\iota}\nu\alpha$ $\pi\lambda\eta\rho\omega\theta\hat{\eta}$). Alford says that "it is impossible to interpret $\acute{\iota}\nu\alpha$ in any other sense than *in order that*."[44] That was the old notion, but modern grammarians recognize the nonfinal use of this particle in the Koiné and even the consecutive like the Latin *ut*. Some even argue for a causal use. If the context called for result, one need not hesitate to say so, as in Mark 11:28, John 9:36, 1 John 1:9, and Revelation 9:20; 13:13.[45] Here it refers to purpose—God's purpose. Matthew reports the angel as saying, "spoken by" ($\grave{\upsilon}\pi\acute{o}$, immediate agent) the Lord "through" ($\delta\iota\acute{\alpha}$, intermediate agent) the prophet. When $\delta\iota\acute{\alpha}$ is added to $\grave{\upsilon}\pi\acute{o}$, a distinction is made between the intermediate and the mediate agent.

Now all this took place ($\tau o\hat{\upsilon}\tau o$ $\delta\grave{\epsilon}$ $\acute{o}\lambda o\nu$ $\gamma\acute{\epsilon}\gamma o\nu\epsilon\nu$, third person singular present perfect active indicative). It stands on record as historical fact. But the virgin birth of Jesus is not due to this interpretation of Isaiah 7:14. It is not necessary to maintain[46] that Isaiah himself saw anything more in his prophecy than that a woman then a virgin would bear a son and that in the course of a few years Ahaz would be delivered from the king of Syria and Israel by the coming of the Assyrians. This historical illustration finds its richest fulfillment in the birth of Jesus from Mary. "Words of themselves are empty. They are useful only as vessels to convey things from mind to mind."[47] The Hebrew word for young woman is translated by παρθένος in Greek; in English by "virgin." But it is not necessary to conclude that Isaiah himself contemplated the supernatural birth of Jesus. We do not have to say that the idea of the virgin birth of Jesus came from Jewish sources. Certainly it did not come from the pagan myths that were utterly foreign to this environment, atmosphere, and spirit. It is far simpler to admit the supernatural fact than try to explain the invention of the idea as a myth to justify the deification of Jesus. The birth, life, and death of Jesus throw a flood of light on the Old Testament narrative and prophecies for the early Christians. In Matthew and John in particular, we often see "that the events of Christ's life were divinely ordered for the express purpose of fulfilling the Old Testament."[48]

1:23. *They shall call* (καλέσουσιν).[49] Men, people, will call his name Immanuel,[50] "God (is) with us."[51] "The interest of the evangelist, as of all New Testament writers, in prophecy, was purely religious."[52] But surely the language of Isaiah has had marvelous illustration in the incarnation of Christ. This is Matthew's explanation of the meaning of Immanuel, a descriptive appellation of Jesus Christ and more than a mere motto designation. God's help, Jesus = the Help of God, is thus seen. Jesus said to Philip: "He that has seen Me has seen the Father" (John 14:9).

1:24. *Took Mary*[53] *as his wife* (παρέλαβεν[54] τὴν γυναῖκα αὐτοῦ). The angel had told him not to be afraid to take to his side Mary his wife (1:20). So when he awoke from his sleep, he promptly obeyed the angel and "took his wife home" (Moffatt).[55] One can only imagine the relief and joy of Mary when Joseph nobly rose to his high duty toward her.[56]

1:25. *But kept her a virgin until she gave birth to a Son*[57] (καὶ οὐκ ἐγίνωσκεν αὐτὴν ἕως οὗ ἔτεκεν υἱόν). Note the imperfect tense, continuous or linear action. Joseph lived in continence with Mary until the birth of Jesus. Ἕως οὗ ("until") with an aorist indicative is used when an actual event is recorded, ἔτεκεν ("she gave birth"). Matthew does not say that Mary bore no other children than Jesus. "Her firstborn" is not genuine here, but it is part of the text in Luke 2:7. The perpetual virginity of Mary is not taught. Jesus had brothers and sisters, and the natural meaning is that they were younger children of Joseph and Mary and not children of Joseph by a previous marriage.

[Joseph] *called His name Jesus* (ἐκάλεσεν[58] τὸ ὄνομα αὐτοῦ Ἰησοῦν)[59] as the angel had directed and the child was born in wedlock. Joseph showed that he was an upright man in a most difficult situation.

NOTES

1. NASB (1978) has "book."
2. A. T. Robertson states: Titles of books may be without the article, being already specific enough. *A Grammar of the Greek New Testament in the Light of Historical Research* (Nashville: Broadman, 1934), 793.
3. Book of Moses (Mark 12:26), book of Psalms (Luke 20:42; Acts 1:20), book of the prophets (Acts 7:42), book of the words of Isaiah (Luke 3:4), book of the genealogy of Jesus Christ (Matt. 1:1), book of life (Phil. 4:3; Rev. 3:5; 20:15), and the books of magical arts (Acts 19:19).
4. Βίβλος is used in Luke 3:4 to refer to the words of Isaiah, and βιβλίον in Luke 4:17 refers to the writings of Isaiah.
5. The Greek βιβλία was transliterated into the Latin term *biblia,* which was transliterated into the Old French *bible,* which was transliterated into the English *Bible.*
6. Robertson gives his own translation here, "genealogical table." "The specific reference is to the discussion of the birth of Jesus in chapters 1 and 2. Some apply it only to 1:1–17. Cf. Genesis 5:1, 'The book of the generations of Adam.' This English word, *generation,* like the Greek in the original, is ambiguous, but *lineage* is the most probable rendering; 'The book of the lineage of Jesus Christ.'" *Commentary on the Gospel According to Matthew* (New York: Macmillan, 1911), 51.
7. NIV has "Jesus Christ," a transliteration of the Greek. NASB gives the Hebrew meaning.
8. "Not merely Davidic descent; *the son of David* was a Messianic term (Matt. 21:9; cf. also 9:27; 15:22; 20:30f.; 22:42). Jesus Himself made no claim to his Davidic descent, probably because He would have been understood as claiming a political kingdom." Robertson, *Commentary on Matthew,* 51–52.
9. Δαυίδ in Nestle/Aland; Δαυείδ in WH; Δαβίδ in the TR and Maj.T.
10. Robertson's translation, "the removal (of the Jews) to Babylon." NIV has "the exile to Babylon."
11. NASB (1978) translates an active verb in Greek with a passive verb, "was born." The NIV and NASB (1995) have "was the father of."
12. In classical Greek, δέ, calling attention to the second of two things, may mean (1) "in the next place," or (2) "on the other hand." The first of these uses is the original one and is copulative. The second is adversative.
13. The NIV has "whose mother had been Uriah's wife." NASB (1995) inserts the name *Bathsheba,* although the name is not found in the Greek text.
14. The NIV and NASB (1978 edition) have *"who is called Christ."*

15. Robertson discusses the problem in Chapter 14 of *Studies in the Text of the New Testament* (repr. ed., Joplin, Mo.: College Press, 1969), 162–73.

16. Γένεσις in GNT/NA and WH: TR and Maj.T have γέννησις.

17. It is not certain whether "Jesus" is here a part of the text as it is absent in the old Syriac and the Old Latin while the Washington Codex has only "Christ." The Vatican Codex has "Christ Jesus." NIV has "this is how the birth of Jesus Christ came about." Note that NASB (1995 edition) translates Χριστοῦ as Christ not Messiah as in 1:1.

18. James Morison, *A Practical Commentary on the Gospel According to St. Matthew* (London: Hodder and Stoughton, 1899), 8.

19. TR and Maj.T include the conjunction γάρ after μνηστευθείσης.

20. NIV has "His mother Mary was pledged to be married to Joseph."

21. Alan Hugh McNeile, *The Gospel According to St. Matthew: The Greek Text with Introduction, Notes, and Indices* (repr. ed., Grand Rapids: Baker, 1980), 7.

22. *New Testament in Braid Scots* actually has "mairry't till Joseph." for "betrothed to Joseph."

23. A noun or pronoun and an anarthrous (without an article) participle in the genitive case often function as a grammatical unrelated or subordinate clause to the main clause. The genitive noun or pronoun functions as the subject of the genitive participle.

24. NIV has "through the Holy Spirit."

25. "The ground (or cause) of action in the principal verb may be suggested by the participle. Cf. δίκαιος ὢν καὶ μὴ θέλων αὐτὴν δειγματίσαι ἐβουλήθη." Robertson, *Grammar,* 1128. NIV correctly gives a causal sense, "because Joseph her husband was a righteous man."

26. "An upright man," *New Testament in Braid Scots* has it.

27. McNeile, *Matthew,* 7.

28. NIV has "did not want."

29. NIV has "he had in mind."

30. NIV has "to expose her to public disgrace." TR and Maj.T have παραδειγματίσαι, GNT/NA and WH have δειγματίσαι.

31. The Latin Vulgate has it *traducere,* the Old Latin *divulgare*, Wycliff *pupplische* (publish), Tyndale *defame:* Moffatt *disgrace*, Braid Scots: *Be i the mooth o' of the public.*

32. James Hope Moulton and George Milligan, *The Vocabulary of the Greek Testament* (London: Hodder and Stoughton, 1952), 138.

33. The papyri examples mean to furnish a sample (P Tebt. 5:75), "to make trial of" (P. Ryl. I. 28.32). The substantive means "exposure" in (P Ryl. I. 28.70).

34. NIV has "he had in mind to divorce her quietly." NASB (1978 edition) has ". . . desired. . . ."

35. GNT/NA, WH and Maj.T have λάθρᾳ; TR does not have the iota subscript, λάθρα.

36. NcNeile, *Matthew*, 8.

37. ATR states: "This fact confirms the interpretation of the genealogy above as that of Joseph and merely the legal genealogy of Jesus." *Commentary on Matthew*, 58.

38. Both the NASB and the NIV have "as your wife." However, Mary was already considered legally to be his wife even before he took her home. The same structure and word order are found in 1:19, "Joseph her husband."

39. NIV has "do not be afraid to take Mary home."

40. NIV has "you are to give him the name Jesus."

41. John A. Broadus, *Commentary on Matthew* (repr. ed., Grand Rapids: Kregel, 1990), 10.

42. Marvin R. Vincent, *Word Studies in the New Testament*, Vol. 1, *The Synoptic Gospels* (repr. ed., Grand Rapids: Eerdmans, 1946), 16.

43. NASB (1978) has an appropriate emphasis: "It is He who will save. . . ."

44. Henry Alford, *The Greek Testament, with a Critically Revised Text*, 4 vols. in 2 vols.; Vol. 1, *The Four Gospels*, rev. by Everett F. Harrison (Chicago: Moody, 1958), 8.

45. See discussion in Robertson, *Grammar*, 997–99.

46. Broadus, *Commentary on Matthew*, 11.

47. Morison, *Practical Commentary*, 11.

48. McNeile, *Matthew*, 11. See also Matt. 2:15–18; 4:12–17; 8:17; 12:17–21; 13:13–15; 21:4f; John 12:38f.; 13:18; 19:24, 28, 36–37.

49. GNT/NA, WH and TRs have καλέσουσιν, TRb and Maj.T do not include the moveable ν, καλέσουσι.

50. *Immanuel* is a transliteration of the Hebrew spelling; *Emmanuel* is a transliteration of the Greek spelling.

51. "The word of itself does not imply incarnation. In the instance in Isaiah 7:14 it was a visitation of God with power in connection with the incident. But here much more is put into the phrase because a real incarnation of God has taken place in the person of Jesus." Robertson, *Commentary on Matthew*, 60.

52. Alexander Balmain Bruce, *The Expositor's Greek Testament*, Vol. 1, *The Synoptic Gospels* (Grand Rapids: Eerdmans, 1951, 68.

53. Both NIV and NASB (1995 edition) include the name *Mary*. Mary is clearly implied but not explicit in the Greek text.

54. GNT/NA, WH and TRs have παρέλαβεν, TRb and Maj.T do not include the moveable ν, παρέλαβε.

55. NIV has "took Mary home as his wife." Moffatt's translation is better.

56. Mary's problems have been sketched in A. T. Robertson, *Mary the Mother of Jesus: Her Problems and Her Glory* (New York: Doran, 1925).

57. NIV has "But he had no union with her until she gave birth to a son."

58. GNT/NA, WH and TRs have ἐκάλεσεν, TRb and Maj.T do not have the moveable ν, ἐκάλεσε.

59. NIV has "And he gave him the name Jesus."

Matthew: Chapter 2

2:1. *Now after Jesus was born*[1] (Τοῦ δὲ Ἰησοῦ γεννηθέντος). The fact of the birth of Jesus is stated by the genitive absolute construction (first aorist passive participle of the same verb γεννάω used twice already of the birth of Jesus, 1:16, 20, and used in the genealogy, 1:2–16). Matthew does not propose to give biographic details of the supernatural birth of Jesus, wonderful as it was and disbelieved as it is by some today who actually deny that Jesus was born at all or ever lived, men who talk of "the Jesus Myth," or "the Christ Myth." "The main purpose is to show the reception given by the world to the new-born Messianic King. Homage from afar, hostility at home; foreshadowing the fortunes of the new faith: reception by the Gentiles, rejection by the Jews."[2]

In Bethlehem of Judea (ἐν Βηθλέεμ τῆς Ἰουδαίας[3]). There was a Bethlehem in Galilee seven miles northwest of Nazareth.[4] This Bethlehem (the name means "house of bread") of Judah was the scene of Ruth's life with Boaz (Ruth 1:1f.; Matt. 1:5) and the home of David, descendant of Ruth and ancestor of Jesus (Matt. 1:5). David was born here and anointed king by Samuel (1 Sam. 17:12). The town came to be called "the city of David" (Luke 2:11). Jesus, who was born in this "House of Bread," called himself "the bread of life" (John 6:35), the true Manna from heaven. Matthew assumes the knowledge of the details of the birth of Jesus in Bethlehem that are given in Luke 2:1–7 or did not consider them germane to his purpose. Joseph and Mary went to Bethlehem from Nazareth because it was the ancestral home for both of them. The first enrollment by the Emperor Augustus, as the papyri show, was "by families" (κατ᾽ οἰκίαν). Possibly Joseph had delayed the journey for some reason. Now he had to go, and the time for the birth of the child approached.

In the days of Herod the king[5] (ἐν ἡμέραις Ἡρῴδου τοῦ Βασιλέως[6]). This is the only date for the birth of Christ given by Matthew. Luke 2:1–3 gives a more precise date. It was the time of the first enrollment by Augustus and while Cyrenius was ruler of Syria (see discussion in volume on Luke). Matthew tells that Jesus was born while Herod was king. This *Herod* sometimes is

31

called "Herod the Great," who died in 4 B.C.[7] He was appointed governor of Galilee in 47 B.C. but was elevated to king of Judea in 37 under Antony and Octavius. He was great in sin and in cruelty and had won the favor of the emperor.[8] The story in Josephus is a tragedy.[9] It is not made plain by Matthew how long before the death of Herod Jesus was born. The once-accepted date of A.D. 1, is certainly wrong, as Matthew shows. It seems plain that the birth of Jesus cannot be put later than B.C. 5. The data supplied by Luke probably calls for B.C. 7 or 6.

Magi from the east (μάγοι ἀπὸ ἀνατολῶν). The etymology of *magi* is quite uncertain. It may come from the same Indo-European root as μέγας, though some identify a Babylonian origin. Herodotus speaks of a tribe of magi among the Medians. Among the Persians there was a priestly caste of magi like the Chaldeans in Babylon (Dan. 1:4). Daniel was head of such an order (Dan. 2:48). The English word *magician* derives from this term. It sometimes carried the idea of magic, as in the case of Simon Magus (Acts 8:9, 11) and of Elymas Barjesus (Acts 13:6, 8). In Matthew the idea seems to be rather that the magi were astrologers. Babylon was the home of astrology, but we only know that the men were from the east, whether Arabia, Babylon, Persia, or elsewhere. The notion that they were kings arose from an interpretation of Isaiah 60:3; Revelation 21:24. The idea that they were three in number is due to the mention of three kinds of gifts (gold, frankincense, myrrh), but that is no proof at all. Legend has added to the story that their names were Caspar, Balthasar, and Melchior and that they represented Noah's sons Shem, Ham, and Japheth. A casket in the Cologne Cathedral has been supposed to contain the skulls of the three. The phrase translated "from the east," ἀπὸ ἀνατολῶν, means "from the risings" (of the sun).

2:2. *"Where is He who has been born King of the Jews?"*[10] (Ποῦ ἐστιν ὁ τεχθεὶς βασιλεὺς τῶν Ἰουδαίων;) The magi claim that they had seen his star, which was either a miracle or a combination of bright stars or a comet. These men may have been Jewish proselytes and may have known of the messianic hope, for even Virgil, who lived from 70 to 19, had caught a vision of it. The whole world was on tiptoe in expectancy for something. James Hope Moulton[11] refers to the magian belief that a star could be the counterpart or "angel" (cf. Matt. 18:10) of a great man.[12] They came to worship the newly born King of the Jews. Seneca[13] tells of magians who came to Athens with sacrifices to Plato after his death. They had somehow concluded that the star they had seen pointed to the birth of this messianic king. Cicero (*De Divin.* i. 47) refers to the constellation from which, on the birth night of Alexander, magians foretold that the destroyer of Asia was born.[14] Alford[15] is convinced that Matthew is not saying that the magi believed a miracle had occurred in the night sky. But one must be allowed to say that the birth of Jesus as God's only Son become incarnate is the greatest of all miracles. Even the methods of astrologers need not disturb those who are sure of this fact.

"For we saw His star in the east"[16] (εἴδομεν γὰρ αὐτοῦ τὸν ἀστέρα ἐν τῇ ἀνατολῇ). This does not mean that they saw a star that stood in the east. If they had followed an eastern star, they would not have gone to Judea. The words *in the east* are probably to be taken with *we saw*, i.e., "We were in the east when we saw it," or more likely, "We saw His star at its rising." Moffatt puts it "when it rose." The singular form τῇ ἀνατολῇ does sometimes mean "east" (see Rev. 21:13), though the plural is more common, as in Matthew 2:1. In Luke 1:78 the singular means "dawn," as the verb ἀνέτειλεν does in Matthew 4:16.

2:3. *He was troubled, and all Jerusalem with him*[17] (ἐταράχθη καὶ πᾶσα Ἱεροσόλυμα μετ᾽ αὐτοῦ). Those familiar with the story of Herod the Great can well understand why the city would be unnerved by reports of a troubled king.[18] Herod in his rage over his family's rivalries and jealousies, put to death the two sons of Mariamne (Aristobulus and Alexander), Mariamne herself, and Antipater, another son and once his heir, besides the brother and mother of Mariamne (Aristobulus, Alexandra) and her grandfather John Hyrcanus. He made will after will and was now suffering from what would be a fatal illness. He was furious over the question of the magi. He showed his excitement, and the whole city was upset. The people knew only too well what he could do when in a rage over the disturbance of his plans. "The foreigner and usurper feared a rival, and the tyrant feared the rival would be welcome."[19] Herod was a hated Idumaean.

2:4. *He inquired of them where the Messiah was to be born*[20] (ἐπυνθάνετο παρ᾽ αὐτῶν ποῦ ὁ Χριστὸς γεννᾶται). The prophetic present (γεννᾶται) is given, the very words of Herod retained by Matthew's report. The third person singular imperfect active indicative (ἐπυνθάνετο) suggests that Herod inquired repeatedly, probably of one and another of the leaders gathered together, both Sadducees (chief priests) and Pharisees (scribes). Alan McNeile[21] doubts that Herod actually called together all the Sanhedrin because he had begun his reign with a massacre of the Sanhedrin. "He could easily ask the question of a single scribe."[22] Still, his murder of the elders had been thirty years before, and now Herod was desperately in earnest to learn what the Jews really expected concerning the coming of the Messiah. "Elders" are not mentioned, so Herod probably did not convene the Sanhedrin, but called in leaders among the chief priests and scribes. This would have been a free assembly for conference, not a formal meeting. He had evidently heard of this expected king, and he would swallow plenty of pride in order to compass the defeat of these hopes.

2:5. *They said to him* (οἱ δὲ εἶπαν αὐτῷ).[23] Whether the ecclesiastics had to search the Scriptures, they give the common Jewish opinion that the Messiah was to come from Bethlehem of the seed of David (John 7:42). They quoted Micah 5:2 in "a free paraphrase" as Henry Alford calls it, for it is not precisely like either the Hebrew or LXX texts.[24] It may have come from a collection of *testimonia* made familiar by the research of J. Rendel Harris. Herod consulted the experts and heard their answer: "Bethlehem of Judah is the place." The use of the third person singular perfect passive indicative (γέγραπται) is the common form in quoting Scripture, "it stands written."

2:6. *"Who will shepherd"*[25] (ὅστις ποιμανεῖ). The Authorized Version had "shall rule," but "shepherd" is correct. "Homer calls kings 'the shepherds of the people.'"[26] In Hebrews 13:20 Jesus is called "the great shepherd of the sheep." Jesus calls Himself "the good shepherd" (John 10:11). Peter calls Christ "the shepherd and guardian of your souls" (1 Peter 2:25). "The Lamb in the center of the throne shall be their shepherd" (Rev. 7:17). Jesus told Peter to "shepherd" the lambs (John 21:16). The English word *pastor* means "shepherd."

2:7. *Then Herod secretly called the magi*[27] (Τότε Ἡρῴδης λάθρᾳ[28] καλέσας τοὺς μάγους). Surely Herod did not tell his Jewish experts why he was concerned about the Messiah. Likewise, he conceals his motives from the magi. And yet he "determined from them"[29] (ἠκρίβωσεν παρ᾽ αὐτῶν), "learned exactly" or "accurately." He was anxious to see if the Jewish prophecy of the birthplace of the Messiah agreed with the indications of the star to the magi.

The exact time the star appeared (τόν χρόνον τοῦ φαινομένου ἀστέρος) is not "the time when the star appeared," but the age of the star's appearance.[30]

2:8. *And he sent them to Bethlehem and said* (καὶ πέμψας αὐτοὺς εἰς Βηθλέεμ[31] εἶπεν). Simultaneous aorist participle, "sending said."

"Search carefully"[32] (ἐξετάσατε ἀκριβῶς)[33] concerning the child.

"Report to me, so that I too may come and worship Him" (ἀπαγγείλατέ μοι, ὅπως κἀγὼ ἐλθὼν προσκυνήσω αὐτῷ). The deceit of Herod seemed plausible enough and might have succeeded but for God's intervention to protect His Son from the jealous rage of Herod.

2:9. *Went on before them*[34] (προῆγεν αὐτούς), third person singular imperfect active indicative, "kept on in front of them," not as a guide to the town, since they now knew that, but to the place where the child was, in a house according to 2:11.[35]

2:10. *They rejoiced exceedingly with great joy*[36] (ἐχάρησαν χαρὰν μεγάλην σφόδρα), third person singular second aorist passive indicative with cognate accusative. Their joy was due to the success of the search.

2:11. *Opening their treasures* (ἀνοίξαντες τοὺς θησαυροὺς αὐτῶν). Here treasures means "caskets." The Greek is from the verb (τίθημι), a receptacle for valuables. In the ancient writers, it meant "treasury," as in 1 Maccabees 3:29. It is a "storehouse" in Matthew 13:52. It means "the things laid up in store," "treasure" in heaven (Matt. 6:20), in Christ (Col. 2:3). In their "caskets" the magi had gold, frankincense, and myrrh, all available at that time from Arabia, though gold was found in Babylon and elsewhere.

2:12. *Having been warned by God in a dream*[37] (χρηματισθέντες κατ᾽ ὄναρ). The verb means "to transact business" (χρηματίζω from χρῆμα and that from χράομαι), "to use." Then "to consult," "to deliberate," "to make answer," as of magistrates or an oracle, "to instruct," "to admonish." In the LXX and the New Testament, it occurs with the idea of being warned by God and has the same meaning in the papyri.[38] Wycliff puts it here: "An answer taken in sleep."

2:13. *"For Herod is going to search for the Child to destroy Him"*[39] (μέλλει γὰρ Ἡρώδης ζητεῖν τὸ παιδίον τοῦ ἀπολέσαι αὐτό[40]). The magi had been warned in a dream not to report to Herod, and now Joseph was warned in a dream to take Mary and the child away. The above Greek statement gives a vivid picture of the purpose of Herod.

2:15. *He remained there until the death of Herod*[41] (ἕως τῆς τελευτῆς Ἡρώδου). In Egypt Joseph was to keep Mary and Jesus until the death of Herod the monster. Matthew quotes Hosea 11:1 to show that this fulfilled God's purpose to call His Son out of Egypt.[42] He may have quoted again from a collection of *testimonia*, rather than from the LXX. There is a Jewish tradition in the Talmud that Jesus "brought with him magic arts out of Egypt in an incision on his body"[43] "This attempt to ascribe the Lord's miracles to Satanic agency seems to be independent of Matthew, and may have been known to him, so that one object of his account may have been to combat it."[44]

2:16. *Slew all the male children who were in Bethlehem* (ἀνεῖλεν πάντας τοὺς παῖδος τοὺς ἐν Βηθλέεμ).[45] The flight of Joseph was justified, for Herod was "violently enraged" (ἐθυμώθη λίαν) that he had been mocked or deluded (ἐνεπαίχθη) by the magi.[46] Herod did not know, of course, how old the child was, so he took no chances and included "all the little boys" (πάντας τοὺς παῖδας, masculine article) in Bethlehem two years old and under, perhaps fifteen or twenty. It is no surprise that Josephus makes no note of this small item in Herod's chamber of horrors. It was another fulfilment of the prophecy in Jeremiah 31:15.

2:18. *"A voice was heard in Ramah, weeping and great mourning, . . . because they were no more"* (Φωνὴ ἐν ʿΡαμὰ ἠκούσθη, κλαυθμὸς καὶ ὀδυρμὸς πολύς, . . . ὅτι οὐκ εἰσίν). The quotation from Jeremiah 31:15 seems to be from the LXX. It was originally written of the Babylonian captivity but it has a striking illustration in this case. Macrobius[47] notes that Augustus said that it was better to be Herod's sow (ὗς) than his son (υἱός), for the sow had a better chance of survival.

2:20. *"For those who sought the Child's life are dead"*[48] (τεθνήκασιν γὰρ οἱ ζητοῦντες τὴν ψυχὴν τοῦ παιδίου[49]). Only Herod had sought to kill the young child, but it is a general statement of a particular fact, as in the idiom, "They say. . . ." The idiom may be suggested by Exodus 4:19: "For all the men who were seeking your life are dead."

2:22. *Then after being warned by God in a dream*[50] (χρηματισθεὶς δὲ κατ' ὄναρ). He was already afraid to go to Judea because Archelaus[51] was reigning (ruling, though not technically king—βασιλεύει). In a fret shortly before his death, Herod had changed his will again and put Archelaus, the worst of his living sons, in the place of Antipas. So Joseph went to Galilee. Matthew has said nothing about the previous dwelling of Joseph and Mary in Nazareth. We learn that from Luke who tells nothing of the flight into Egypt. The two narratives supplement one another and are in no sense contradictory.

2:23. *"He shall be called a Nazarene"*[52] (Ναζωραῖος κληθήσεται). Matthew says to fulfill what was spoken through the prophets[53] (ὅπως πληρωθῇ τὸ ῥηθὲν διὰ τῶν προφητῶν). It is the plural and no single prophecy exists that the Messiah was to be called a Nazarene.[54] It may be that this term of contempt (John 1:46; 7:52) is what is meant, and that several prophecies are to be combined like Psalms 22:6, 8; 69:11, 19; Isaiah 53:2, 3, 4. The name *Nazareth* means "a shoot or branch," but it is by no means certain that Matthew has this in mind. See Broadus for the various theories.[55] But, despised as Nazareth was at that time, Jesus has exalted its fame. The lowly Nazarene he was at first, but it is our glory to be the followers of the Nazarene. Bruce says that "in this case, therefore, we certainly know that the historic fact suggested the prophetic reference, instead of the prophecy creating the history."[56] The parallels drawn by Matthew between the history of Israel and the birth and infancy of Jesus are not mere fancy. History repeats itself, and writers of history find frequent parallels. Surely Matthew is not beyond the bounds of reason or of fact in illustrating in his own way the birth and infancy of Jesus by the providence of God in the history of Israel.

NOTES

1. NIV has "After Jesus was born."
2. Alexander Balmain Bruce, *The Expositor's Greek Testament*, Vol. 1, *The Synoptic Gospels* (Grand Rapids: Eerdmans, 1951), 69. See Joshua 19:15.
3. GNT/NA and Maj.T have Βηθλέεμ, WH and TR accent the ultima (last syllable) Βηθλεέμ.
4. Josephus, *Antiquities of the Jews*, 19.15.
5. NIV has "during the time of King Herod."
6. GNT/NA, WH, and Maj.T have the iota subscript, Ἡρῴδου, TR does not, Ἡρώδου.
7. Josephus, *Antiquities of the Jews*, 17.6.
8. Robertson calls him "Herod the Great Pervert" in *Some Minor Characters in the New Testament* (repr. ed., Nashville: Broadman & Holman, 1976), 25.
9. Josephus, *Antiquities of the Jews*, 14–18. Harold W. Hoehner, *Herod Antipas: A Contemporary of Jesus Christ* (Grand Rapids: Zondervan, 1972), 269–76, mentions six different wills of Herod the Great that affected the succession after his death, which he knew was not far off. Robertson states, "He was an Idumean, a friend of the Romans, fond of Greek customs, hated by the Pharisees and the Jews generally for his innovations and cruelties, but a man of great vigor and force of character. He had rebuilt (or begun to rebuild, rather) the temple. His will had been changed several times because of suspicions towards and jealousies between his various sons and his wives, mother, sister, and mother-in-law. Even now he was in poor health and abnormally sensitive about any question." A. T. Robertson, *Commentary on the Gospel According to Matthew* (New York: Macmillan, 1911), 62.
10. NIV has "Where is the one who has been born king of the Jews?"
11. James Hope Moulton in *Journal of Theological Studies* (1902): 524.
12. Alan Hugh McNeile, *The Gospel According to St. Matthew: The Greek Text with Introduction, Notes, and Indices* (repr. ed., Grand Rapids: Baker, 1980), 14.
13. Epistle 58.
14. McNeile, *Matthew*, 14.
15. Henry Alford *The Greek New Testament, with a Critically Revised Text*, 4 vols. in 2 vols. (Chicago: Moody, 1958), 1.10.
16. NIV has "We saw his star in the east."

17. NIV has "He was disturbed."
18. Josephus, *Antiquities of the Jews*, 14–15.
19. Bruce, *Expositor's*, 71.
20. NIV has "He asked them where the Christ was to be born."
21. McNeile, *Matthew*, 15.
22. Josephus, *Antiquities of the Jews*, 14.9.4.
23. NIV has "They replied" in response to Herod's question. GNT/NA and WH have εἶπον, TR and Maj.T have a different spelling for the same verb, εἶπον.
24. Alford, *Greek New Testament*, 1.13.
25. NIV has "Who will be the shepherd."
26. Marvin R. Vincent, *Word Studies in the New Testament*, Vol. 1, *The Synoptic Gospels* (repr. ed., Grand Rapids: Eerdmans, 1946), 20.
27. NIV has "Then Herod called the Magi secretly."
28. GNT/NA, WH, and Maj.T have the iota subscript in both words, Ἡρῴδης λάθρᾳ, TR omits the iota subscript in both words, Ἡρώδης λάθρα.
29. NIV has "found out from them."
30. NASB has "the exact time the star appeared." NIV has "the exact time the star had appeared."
31. See footnote on Βηθλέεμ in 2:1.
32. NIV has "make a careful search."
33. GNT/NA and WH have ἐξετάσατε ἀκριβῶς. TR and Maj.T have the words in reverse order, ἀκριβῶς ἐξετάσατε.
34. NIV has "went ahead of them." Robertson, *Commentary on Matthew*, 66, states: "We can hardly suppose that the star had disappeared after its rising till now. Probably all that is meant is that the star kept moving on before them."
35. A. T. Robertson, *Word Pictures in the New Testament*, 6 vols. (New York: Richard R. Smith, 1930–1933), 1.19, speaks of "the inn according to Luke 2:7. Justin Martyr says that it was in a cave. The stall where the cattle and donkeys stayed may have been beneath the inn in the side of the hill." However, Matthew 2:11 speaks of a house where the child was found. It is unlikely that they would have stayed in an inn for up to two years. They evidently moved to a more permanent residence.
36. NIV has "they were overjoyed."
37. NIV has "having been warned in a dream."
38. G. Adolph Deissman, *Bible Studies: Contributions, Chiefly from Papyri and Inscriptions, to the History of the Language*, 2d ed., trans. A. Grieve (Edinburgh: T. & T. Clark, 1923), 122.
39. NIV has "for Herod is going to search for the child to kill him."

40. GNT/NA, WH, and Maj.T have the iota subscript, whereas TR omits it, Ἡρώδης.

41. NIV has "where he stayed until the death of Herod."

42. Robertson, *Commentary on Matthew*, 67, states: "There is, however, no prophecy here, but an allusion to the historical fact that God had led the children of Israel (often called God's son or servant) out of Egypt. It is a typical use of the well-known event, a designed coincidence according to the author, who sees striking parallels between the history of Israel and the life of Jesus."

43. *Shabb*, 104b. Robertson, states: "Jesus was in Egypt only as an infant and had no opportunity to be influenced by the magical arts practised there. Celsus has needlessly brought this charge against Christ." *Commentary on Matthew*, 67.

44. McNeile, *Matthew*, 19.

45. See footnote in 2:1. NIV has "he gave orders to kill all the boys in Bethlehem."

46. Vulgate *illusus esset*. NASB has "had been tricked." NIV has "had been outwitted."

47. *Sat.* 2.4.11.

48. NIV has "for those who were trying to take the child's life are dead."

49. GNT/NA and WH have the moveable ν in Τεθνήκασιν, whereas TR and Maj.T omit it, τεθνήκασι.

50. NIV has "having been warned in a dream."

51. Robertson, *Commentary on Matthew*, 69, states: "When Joseph had left Judea, Herod's will was for Antipas to succeed him. At the last moment he changed his will again (Josephus, *Antiquities of the Jews*, 18.8–11) so that Ἀρχέλαος was to rule over Judea and Samaria while Antipas was to be tetrarch of Galilee and Perea and Philip tetrarch of Iturea and Τραχηονιτὸ. This was all news to Joseph when he reached the borders of Judea. Ἀρχέλαος was a much worse man than Antipas. Hence Joseph hesitated to expose the child to the fury of another man of the temper of Herod the Great."

52. NIV has "He will be called a Nazarene."

53. NIV has "so was fulfilled what was said through the prophets."

54. It is assumed from the outset that it says "which was written." But it does not say so! It says "which was spoken." The fact is, some prophecies were written down and never spoken. Some were both written and spoken; while others were spoken and never written. This is in the latter class. There is great difference between τὸ ῥηθέν, "which was spoken," and ὅ γέγραπται, "which stands written"! E. W. Bullinger, *Figures of Speech Used in the Bible* (repr. ed., Grand Rapids: Baker, 1968), 710–11.

55. John A. Broadus, *Commentary on Matthew* (repr. ed., Grand Rapids: Kregel, 1990), 28.
56. Bruce, *Expositor's*, 78.

■ ■ ■ ■ ■ ■

Matthew: Chapter 3

3:1. *Now in those days John the Baptist came* (Ἐν δὲ ταῖς ἡμέραις ἐκείναις παραγίνεται Ἰωάννης[1] ὁ βαπτιστὴς). Here the synoptic narrative begins with the baptism of John (cf. Mark 1:2; Luke 3:1) as given by Peter in Acts 1:22: "beginning with the baptism of John until the day that He was taken up from us."[2] Matthew does not indicate the date when John appeared, as Luke does in chapter 3 (the fifteenth year of Tiberius's reign). It was some thirty years after the birth of John, precisely how long after the return of Joseph and Mary to Nazareth we do not know. Moffatt translates the verb παραγίνεται "came on the scene," but it is the historical present and calls for a vivid imagination on the part of the reader. There he is as he comes forward, makes his appearance. His name *John* means "Gift of Jehovah" (cf. German *Gotthold*) and is a shortened form of Johanan. He is described as "the Baptist," "the Baptizer," for that is the rite that distinguishes him. The Jews had proselyte baptism, as I. Abrahams shows,[3] but this rite was meant for Gentiles who accepted Judaism. John is treating the Jews as Gentiles in demanding baptism at his hands on the basis of repentance.

Preaching in the wilderness of Judea (κηρύσσων ἐν τῇ ἐρήμῳ τῆς Ἰουδαίας).[4] It was the rough region in the hills toward the Jordan and the Dead Sea. There were some people scattered over the barren cliffs. Here John came in close touch with the rocks, the trees, the goats, the sheep, and the shepherds, the snakes that slipped before the burning grass over the rocks. He was the Baptizer, but he was also the preacher, heralding his message out in the barren hills at first where few people were, but soon his startling message drew crowds from far and near.

3:2. *"Repent"* (μετανοεῖτε). Broadus used to say that this is the worst translation in the New Testament. The trouble is that the English word *repent* means "to be sorry again," from the Latin *repoenitet* (impersonal). John did not call on the people to be sorry, but to change (think afterwards) their mental attitudes (μετανοεῖτε) and conduct. The Vulgate has "do penance," and Wycliff follows that. Better is the Old Syriac, "Turn ye." The French (Geneva) has it "Amendez vou." This is John's great word,[5] and it has been hopelessly

41

mistranslated. The tragedy is that no one English word reproduces the meaning and atmosphere of the Greek. The Greek has a word meaning to "be sorry" ($\mu\epsilon\tau\alpha\mu\epsilon\lambda o\mu\alpha\iota$). This corresponds to the English *repent*. This is the word used of Judas (Matt. 27:3). John was a new prophet, and he returned to the call of the old prophets: "Turn ye" (Isa. 55:7; Ezek. 33:11, 15; Joel 2:12).

"For the kingdom of heaven is at hand" ($\check{\eta}\gamma\gamma\iota\kappa\epsilon\nu^6$ $\gamma\grave{\alpha}\rho$ $\dot{\eta}$ $\beta\alpha\sigma\iota\lambda\epsilon i\alpha$ $\tau\hat{\omega}\nu$ $o\dot{\upsilon}\rho\alpha\nu\hat{\omega}\nu$).[7] Note the position of the verb and the present perfect tense. It was a startling word that John thundered over the hills, and it echoed throughout the land. The Old Testament prophets had said that it would come some day in God's own time. As herald of the new day, John proclaims that it has drawn near. How near, he does not say, but he evidently means *very* near—near enough to see the signs and the proof. He does not explain what he means by "the kingdom of heaven." The other Gospels use "the kingdom of God," as Matthew does sometimes. However, Matthew speaks of "the kingdom of heaven" more than thirty times. John means "the reign of God," not the political or ecclesiastical organization that the Pharisees expected. His words would be understood differently by different groups. Jewish apocalypses connected numerous eschatological images to "the kingdom of heaven." It is not clear what sympathy John had with these eschatological features. He employs vivid language, but we do not have to confine John's intellectual and theological horizon to that of the rabbis of his day. He was an original student of the Old Testament in his wilderness environment. No evidence demands that he was in contact with the Essenes, who also lived in the desert. His voice is a new one that strikes terror among the perfunctory theologians of the temple and of the synagogue. It is the fashion of some critics to deny to John any conception of the spiritual content of his words. This is a wholly gratuitous criticism.

3:3. *For this is the one referred to by Isaiah the prophet*[8] ($o\hat{\upsilon}\tau os$ $\gamma\grave{\alpha}\rho$ $\dot{\epsilon}\sigma\tau\iota\nu$ $\dot{o}$ $\rho\eta\theta\epsilon\iota s$ $\delta\iota\grave{\alpha}$ $H\sigma\alpha i o\upsilon^9$ $\tau o\hat{\upsilon}$ $\pi\rho o\phi\acute{\eta}\tau o\upsilon$). Matthew interprets the mission and message of the Baptist through Isaiah 40:3, where "the prophet refers to the return of Israel from the exile, accompanied by their God."[10] He applies it to the work of John as "the voice of one crying in the wilderness" for the people to make ready the way of the Lord who is now near. He was only a voice, but what a voice. He can be heard yet across the centuries.

3:4. *Now John himself* ($A\dot{\upsilon}\tau\grave{o}s$ $\delta\grave{\epsilon}$ $\dot{o}$ $I\omega\acute{\alpha}\nu\nu\eta s^{11}$). Matthew thus introduces the man and draws a vivid sketch of his dress (note $\epsilon\iota$, imperfect tense), his habits, and his food. Such an uncouth figure might not have fit the pulpit, but in the wilderness it did not matter. His lifestyle was probably a matter of necessity, not an affectation, though it was the garb of the original Elijah.

Elijah wore rough sackcloth of camel hair (2 Kings 1:8). Alfred Plummer holds that "John consciously took Elijah as a model."[12]

3:6. *And they were being baptized* (καὶ ἐβαπτίζοντο). The imperfect tense shows the repetition of the act as the crowds from Judea and the surrounding country kept going out to him (ἐξεπορεύετο), imperfect tense again, a regular stream of folks going forth. Moffatt takes it as causative middle, "got baptized," which is possible. "The movement of course was gradual. It began on a small scale and steadily grew till it reached colossal proportions."[13] It is a pity that baptism is now such a matter of controversy. Let Plummer, the great Church of England commentator on Matthew, speak here of John's baptizing these people who came in throngs: "It is his office to bind them to a new life, symbolized by immersion in water."[14] That is correct, symbolized, not caused or obtained. The word *river* is the correct reading, "the river Jordan." They were baptized "as they confessed their sins" (ἐξομολογούμενοι), probably each one confessing just before baptism, "making open confession" (Weymouth). It was a never to be forgotten scene here in the Jordan. John was calling a nation to a new life. They came from all over Judea and even from Perea on the other side of El Ghor (the Jordan Gorge). Mark adds that finally all Jerusalem came.

3:7. *The Pharisees and Sadducees* (τῶν Φαρισαίων καὶ Σαδδουκαίων). These two rival parties do not often take common action, but they unite against John and again against Jesus (see Matt. 16:1). "Here a strong attraction, there a strong repulsion, made them for the moment forget their differences."[15] John saw these rival ecclesiastics "coming for baptism" (ἐρχομένους ἐπὶ τὸ βάπτισμα). Alford speaks of "the Pharisees representing hypocritical superstition; the Sadducees carnal unbelief.[16] One cannot properly understand the theological atmosphere of Palestine at this time without learning about these greatly differing movements.[17] John clearly grasped the significance of the ecclesiastics who had followed the crowds to the Jordan. He exposed their hypocrisy before the people.

"You brood of vipers" (Γεννήματα ἐχιδνῶν). Jesus will use the same language against the Pharisees (Matt. 12:34; 23:33). Broods of snakes were often seen by John in the rocks. When these snakes sensed fire they would scurry (φυγεῖν) to their holes for safety.

"The wrath to come" (τῆς μελλούσης ὀργῆς) was not just for Gentiles as the Jews supposed, but for all who were not prepared for the kingdom of heaven (1 Thess. 1:10). No doubt the Pharisees and Sadducees winced under the sting of this powerful indictment.

3:8. *"Fruit in keeping with repentance"* (καρπὸν ἄξιον τῆς μετανοίας). John demands proof from these men of the new life before he administers baptism to them. "The fruit is not the change of heart, but the acts which result from it."[18] John was bold indeed to challenge as unworthy the very ones who posed as ethical lights and leaders. "Anyone can do acts externally good but only a good man can grow a crop of right acts and habits."[19]

3:9. *"And do not suppose that you can say to yourselves"* (καὶ μὴ δόξητε λέγειν ἐν ἑαυτοῖς). John touched the tender spot of ecclesiastical pride. They felt that the merits of the fathers, especially of Abraham, were enough for all Israelites. The reformer made clear that a breach existed between him and the religious leaders over the value of race before God.

"From these stones" (ἐκ τῶν λίθων τούτων).[20] "Pointing, as he spoke to the pebbles on the beach of the Jordan."[21]

3:10. *"The axe is already laid at the root of the trees"*[22] (ἤδη δὲ ἡ ἀξίνη πρὸς τὴν ῥίζαν τῶν δένδρων κεῖται). This verb κεῖται is used as the present passive of τίθημι. But the idea really is, "the axe lies at (πρός, "before") the root of the trees." It is there ready for business. The prophetic present occurs also with "is cut down" and "thrown."

3:11. *"Mightier than I"*[23] (ἰσχυρότερός μού). Ablative after the comparative adjective. His baptism is water baptism, but the Coming One "will baptize you with the Holy Spirit and fire." "Life in the coming age is in the sphere of the Spirit. Spirit and fire are coupled with one preposition as a double baptism."[24] Broadus[25] takes "fire" in the sense of separation like the use of the fan. As the humblest of servants John felt unworthy to take off the sandals of the Coming One. Regarding βαστάζω, see on Matthew 8:17.

3:12. *"He will burn up the chaff with unquenchable fire"*[26] (κατακαύσει πυρὶ ἀσβέστῳ). Note the perfective use of κατά. The threshing floor, the fan, the wheat, the garner, the chaff (ἄχυρον, chaff, straw, stubble), the fire furnish a lifelike picture. The "fire" here is probably the coming Messiah's judgment, just as in verse 11. The Messiah "will thoroughly clear His threshing floor"[27] (διακαθαριεῖ τὴν ἅλωνα αὐτοῦ [28]). He will sweep from side to side to make it clean.

3:13. *Then Jesus arrived* (Τότε παραγίνεται ὁ Ἰησοῦς). The same historical present is used in Matthew 3:1. He comes all the way from Galilee to Jordan "to be baptized by him"[29] (τοῦ βαπτισθῆναι ὑπ' αὐτοῦ). The genitive articular infinitive of purpose, a very common idiom. The fame of John had reached Nazareth, and the hour has come for which Jesus has waited.

3:14. *But John tried to prevent Him*[30] (ὁ δὲ Ἰωάννης διεκώλυεν αὐτὸν[31]). It is the conative[32] imperfect. The two men of destiny are face-to-face, possibly for the first time. The Coming One stands before John and he recognizes him, even before the attesting sign is given.

3:15. *"To fulfill all righteousness"* (πληρῶσαι πᾶσαν δικαιοσύνην). The explanation of Jesus satisfies John and he baptizes the Messiah, who has no sins to confess. It was "fitting" (πρέπον) to do so, or else the Messiah would seem to hold aloof from the forerunner. Thus the ministries of the two are linked.

3:16. *He saw the Spirit of God descending as a dove* (εἶδεν[33] [τὸ] πνεῦμα [τοῦ] θεοῦ καταβαῖνον ὡσεὶ περιστεράν). It is not certain whether Matthew means that the Spirit of God took the form of a dove or came upon Jesus as a dove comes down. Either makes sense, but Luke 3:22 has it "in bodily form like a dove" (σωματικῷ εἴδει ὡς περιστεράν), and that is probably the idea here. Christians have considered the dove to be a symbol of the Holy Spirit.

3:17. *A voice out of the heavens* (φωνὴ ἐκ τῶν οὐρανῶν). This was the voice of the Father to "My beloved Son" (ὁ υἱός μου ὁ ἀγαπητός). Thus each person of the Trinity (Father, Son, Holy Spirit) is represented at this formal entrance of Jesus upon his messianic ministry. John heard the voice, of course, and saw the dove. It was a momentous occasion for John and for Jesus and for the whole world. The words are similar to Psalm 2:7 and the voice at the Transfiguration (Matt. 17:5). The good pleasure of the Father is expressed by the timeless aorist (εὐδόκησα).

NOTES

1. GNT/NA, Maj.T, and TR has Ἰωάννης, whereas WH has a single ν, Ἰωάνης.
2. A. T. Robertson, *Commentary on the Gospel According to Matthew* (New York: Macmillan, 1911), 72, states: "As is common in many ancient writers, there is a wide gap here between the incident of the return of Joseph to Nazareth and the appearance of John the Baptist as a preacher. The writer means that while Jesus lived in Nazareth, John the Baptist began his work."
3. I. Abrahams, *Studies in Pharisaism and the Gospels* (repr. ed., New York: Ktav, 1967), 37.
4. NIV has "preaching in the Desert of Judea."
5. Alexander Balmain Bruce, *The Expositor's Greek Testament*, Vol. 1, *The Synoptic Gospels* (Grand Rapids: Eerdmans, 1951), 79.
6. GNT/NA and WH have the moveable ν, ἤγγικεν, whereas TR and Maj.T omit it, ἤγγικε.
7. NIV has "the kingdom of heaven is near."

8.   NIV has "This is he who was spoken of through the prophet Isaiah."

9.   GNT/NA, TR, and Maj.T have the diaresis in Ἡσαίου, whereas WH omits it, Ἡσαίου.

10. Alan Hugh McNeile, *The Gospel According to St. Matthew: The Greek Text with Introduction, Notes, and Indices* (repr. ed., Grand Rapids: Baker, 1980), 25.

11. See footnote in 3:1 concerning the spelling of Ἰωάννης.

12. Alfred Plummer, *An Exegetical Commentary on the Gospel According to Saint Matthew* (repr. ed., Grand Rapids: Eerdmans, 1956), 27.

13. Bruce, *Expositor's*, 81.

14. Plummer, *Matthew*, 28.

15. McNeile, *Matthew*, 26.

16. *Greek Testament*, 1.22.

17. There are numerous books and articles in Bible dictionaries. Robertson pictured the Pharisees in the first Stone Lectures (1916) at Princeton University. This series was reprinted as *The Pharisees and Jesus* (New York: Scribner, 1920).

18. McNeile, *Matthew*, 27.

19. Bruce, *Expositor's*, 83.

20. NIV has "out of these stones."

21. Marvin R. Vincent, *Word Studies in the New Testament*, Vol. 1, *The Synoptic Gospels* (repr. ed., Grand Rapids: Eerdmans, 1946), 24.

22. NIV has "The ax is already at the root of the trees."

23. NIV has "more powerful than I."

24. McNeile, *Matthew*, 29.

25. John A. Broadus, *Commentary on Matthew* (repr. ed., Grand Rapids: Kregel, 1990), 51–52.

26. NIV has "burning up the chaff with unquenchable fire."

27. NIV has "He will clear his threshing floor."

28. Attic future of -ιζω and note δια-.

29. NIV has "to be baptized by John." However, the name *John* is not found in the Greek text.

30. NIV has "But John tried to deter him."

31. See footnote 1 for this chapter concerning the spelling of Ἰωάννης.

32. Conative means attempted or contemplated but yet incompleted action.

33. GNT/NA and WH have the moveable ν, εἶδεν, whereas TR and Maj.T omit it, εἶδε.

Matthew: Chapter 4

4:1. *To be tempted by the devil* (πειρασθῆναι ὑπὸ τοῦ διαβόλου). Matthew locates the temptation at a definite time, "then" (τότε) and place, "into the wilderness" (εἰς τὴν ἔρημον). It is the same general region in which John was preaching. It is not surprising that Jesus was tempted by the Devil immediately after the baptism that signified his formal entrance into the messianic work. That is a common experience with those who step out into the open for Christ. Matthew says that "Jesus was led up into the wilderness by the Spirit to be tempted by the devil." Mark 1:12 puts it more strongly, that the Spirit "drives" (ἐκβάλλει) Christ into the wilderness. It was a strong impulsion by the Holy Spirit that led Jesus into the wilderness to think through the full significance of the great step he had now taken. That step opened the door for the Devil and involved inevitable conflict with the Slanderer (τοῦ διαβόλου). This term is applied to Judas (John 6:70), to men (2 Tim. 3:3; Titus 2:3), and to women ("she devils," 1 Tim. 3:11) who do the work of the arch Slanderer. There are those today who do not believe that a personal Devil exists, but they do not offer an adequate explanation of the existence of sin. Certainly Jesus did not discount or deny the reality of the Devil's presence. The word *tempt* (πειράζω) here and in 4:3 means originally "to test, to try." That is its usual meaning in the ancient Greek and in the Septuagint. A bad sense of the word (in the form ἐκπειράζω) is found in 4:7 and in LXX Deuteronomy 6:16. Hence it comes to mean, as often in the New Testament, "to solicit to sin." "It is difficult to understand how Jesus as the Son of God could be tempted. But it is just as difficult to see how as a human he could escape temptation. Clearly the purpose of God in this and all the temptations of Christ was to fit Jesus to be a sympathizing Savior by reason of actual experience (Heb. 2:10, 18; 4:15; 5:7–9). The reality of temptation does not imply sin in the nature of Jesus. He felt the temptation all the more because he resisted to the uttermost. He was a real man, though free from sin."[1] The evil sense comes from its use for an evil purpose.

4:2. *After He had fasted*[2] (νηστεύσας). No perfunctory ceremonial fast but abstention from food during a time of communion with the Father. Moses had such a fast during forty days and forty nights (Exod. 34:28). "The period of the fast, as in the case of Moses was spent in a spiritual ecstasy, during which the wants of the natural body were suspended."[3]

He then became hungry[4] (ὕστερον ἐπείνασεν) at the close of the forty days.

4:3. *"If You are the Son of God"* (Εἰ υἱὸς εἶ τοῦ θεοῦ). More exactly, "If You are Son of God," for there is no article with "Son." However, the Devil is alluding to the words of the Father to Jesus at the baptism: "This is My Son the Beloved." He challenges this address by a condition of the first class. He assumes the condition to be true and deftly calls on Jesus to exercise his power as Son of God to appease his hunger. Such actions will prove to himself and to all others that he really is what the Father called him.

"Become bread" (ἄρτοι γένωνται). Literallly, "that these stones (round smooth stones which possibly the Devil pointed to or even picked up and held) become loaves" (each stone a loaf). It was all so simple, obvious, easy. It would satisfy the hunger of Christ and was quite within his power.

4:4. *"It is written"* (γέγραπται). Third person singular perfect passive indicative, "it stands written and is still in force." Each time Jesus quotes Deuteronomy to repel the subtle temptation of the Devil. Here it is Deuteronomy 8:3 from the LXX. Bread is a mere detail[5] in dependence upon God.

4:5. *Then the devil took Him* (Τότε παραλαμβάνει αὐτὸν ὁ διάβολος). Matthew is fond of the temporal adverb τότε (see already 2:7; 3:13; 4:1, 5). Note the vivid imagery of the historic present. Luke puts this temptation third, organizing them by geographical order. Alford believes that the person of Christ was allowed to be at the disposal of the Devil.[6]

On the pinnacle of the temple (ἐπὶ τὸ πτερύγιον τοῦ ἱεροῦ). Literally "wing." The English *pinnacle* is from the Latin *pinnaculum*, a diminutive of *pinna* (wing). "The temple" (τοῦ ἱεροῦ) here includes the whole temple area, not just the sanctuary (ὁ ναός), the Holy Place, and Most Holy Place. It is not clear what place is meant by "wing." It may refer to Herod's royal portico, which overhung the Kedron Valley and looked down some four hundred and fifty feet, a dizzying height.[7] This was on the south of the temple court. Hegesippus says that James the Lord's brother was thrown down from the wing of the temple.

4:6. *"Throw Yourself down"* (βάλε σεαυτὸν κάτω). The appeal to hurl himself down into the abyss would intensify the nervous dread that most people feel at such a height. The Devil urged presumptuous reliance on God and quotes

Scripture to support his view (Ps. 91:11f). In so doing, he omits a clause and misinterprets the Word of God to trip the Son of God. If the populace should see him sailing down as if from heaven, they would believe that Jesus was the Messiah. This would be a sign from heaven in accord with popular messianic expectation. The angels would be a spiritual parachute for Christ.

4:7. *"'You shall not put the Lord your God to the test'"*[8] (Οὐκ ἐκπειράσεις κύριον τὸν θεόν σου). Jesus quotes Deuteronomy again (6:16) to show that the Devil has wholly misapplied God's promise of protection.

4:8. *And showed Him* (καὶ δείκνυσιν αὐτῷ). This wonderful panorama had to be partially mental and imaginative, since the Devil caused to pass in review "all the kingdoms of the world and their glory." But this fact does not prove that all phases of the temptations were subjective or that the Devil was not truly there. Here again we have the vivid historical present (δείκνυσιν). The Devil now has Christ upon a very high mountain—whether the traditional Quarantania or some other. From Nebo's summit, Moses caught the vision of the land of Canaan (Deut. 34:1–3). Luke (4:5) says that the whole panorama was "in a moment of time," so it clearly had an element of vision.

4:9. *"All these things I will give You"*[9] (Ταῦτά σοι πάντα δώσω). The Devil claims to rule the world, even that outside Palestine or the Roman Empire. Jesus does not dispute his claim. "The kingdoms of the cosmos" (4:8) were under his sway. Κόσμου brings out the orderly arrangement of the universe while ἡ οἰκουμένη presents the inhabited earth. Whether Satan can deliver on his promise, Jesus spurns the condition[10] that he must "fall down and worship me"[11] (πεσὼν προσκυνήσῃς μοι). Luke (4:7) puts it, "worship before me" (προσκυνήσῃς ἐνώπιον ἐμοῦ), which is less offensive language but still ultimately implies worship of the Devil. The ambition of Jesus is thus appealed to at the price of recognition of the Devil's primacy in the world. This compromise would have involved surrender of the Son of God to the world ruler of this darkness. "The temptation was threefold: to gain a temporal, not a spiritual, dominion; to gain it at once; and to gain it by an act of homage to the ruler of this world, which would make the self-constituted Messiah the vice-regent of the devil and not of God."[12]

4:10. *"Go, Satan!"*[13] (Ὕπαγε, Σατανᾶ). The words "behind Me" (ὀπίσω μου) belong to Matthew 16:23, not here. This temptation is the limit of diabolical suggestion and argues for the logical order in Matthew. *Satan* means "Adversary," and Christ so identifies the Devil. Jesus quotes Deuteronomy 6:13 to repel the infamous suggestion by Scripture quotation. Jesus will warn men against trying to serve God and mammon (Matt. 6:24). The Devil, as lord of the evil world, constantly tries to win men to his service. The word in Matthew 4:10 for serve is λατρεύσεις from λάτρις, "a hired servant," one who works for hire.

4:11. *Then the devil left Him* (Τότε ἀφίησιν αὐτὸν ὁ διάβολος). Note the use of *then* (τότε) again and the historical present. The movement is swift.

And behold (καὶ ἰδού), as so often in Matthew, carries on the scene.

Angels came and began to minister to Him[14] (ἄγγελοι προσῆλθον καὶ διηκόνουν αὐτῷ). Προσῆλθον is a constative aorist, third person plural aorist active indicative. Διηκόνουν describes picturesque imperfect, linear action. The victory was won in spite of the fast of forty days and the repeated onsets of the Devil, who had tried every avenue of approach. The angels could cheer him in the inevitable nervous and spiritual reaction from the strain of conflict, and probably also with food, as in the case of Elijah (1 Kings 19:6f.). The issues at stake were of vast import, as the champions of light and darkness grappled for mastery. Luke (4:13) adds that the Devil left Jesus only "until a good opportunity" (ἄχρι καιροῦ).

4:12. *Now when [Jesus]*[15] *heard* (Ἀκούσας δέ). The reason for Christ's return to Galilee is that John had been imprisoned. The Synoptic Gospels skip from the temptation of Jesus to the Galilean ministry, a whole year. But for John 1:19–3:36, we should know nothing of the "year of obscurity."[16] Christ's work in Galilee began after the close of the active ministry of the Baptist, who lingered on in prison for a year or longer.

4:13. *He came and settled in Capernaum*[17] (ἐλθὼν κατῴκησεν εἰς Καφαρναούμ). Jesus went first to Nazareth, his old home, but he was rejected there (Luke 4:16–31). In Capernaum (probably the archaeological site of Tell Hum) Jesus was in a large town, one of the centers of Galilean political and commercial life, including a fish mart. Many Gentiles came to Capernaum. Here the message of the kingdom would have a better chance than in Jerusalem, with its ecclesiastical prejudices, or in Nazareth, with its local jealousies. So Jesus "made His home" (κατῴκησεν) here.

4:16. *"Saw a great Light"*[18] (φῶς εἶδεν μέγα). Matthew refers to Isaiah 9:1–5 and applies the words about the deliverer from Assyria to the Messiah. "The same district lay in spiritual darkness and death and the new era dawned when Christ went thither."[19]

Light sprang up on "those who were sitting in the land and shadow of death" (ἐν χώρᾳ καὶ σκιᾷ θανάτου). Death is personified.

4:17. *Jesus began to preach* (ἤρξατο ὁ Ἰησοῦς κηρύσσειν) in Galilee. He had been preaching for over a year elsewhere. His message carries on the words of the Baptist about "repentance" and the "kingdom of heaven" (Matt. 3:2) being at hand. The same word for "preaching," (κηρύσσειν) from κῆρυξ, *herald*, is used of Jesus as of John. Both proclaimed the good news of the kingdom. Jesus is more often described as the Teacher, (ὁ διδάσκαλος) who taught (ἐδίδασκεν) the people. He was both herald and teacher.

4:18. *Casting a net into the sea*[20] (βάλλοντας ἀμφίβληστρον εἰς τὴν θάλασσαν). The term used refers to a casting net (compare ἀμφιβάλλω in Mark 1:16, casting on both sides). The net was thrown over the shoulder and spread into a circle (ἀμφί). In 4:20 and 21 another word, δίκτυα, refers to nets of any kind. The large dragnet (σαγήνη) appears in Matthew 13:47.

4:19. *"Fishers of men"* (ἁλιεῖς ἀνθρώπων). Andrew and Simon were fishermen by trade. They had already become disciples of Jesus (John 1:35–42), but now they are called upon to leave their business and to follow Jesus in his travels and work. These two brothers promptly (εὐθέως) accepted the call and challenge of Jesus.

4:21. *Mending their nets*[21] (καταρτίζοντας τὰ δίκτυα αὐτῶν). These two brothers, James and John, were getting their nets ready for use. The verb (καταρτίζω) means to adjust, to articulate, to men if needed (Luke 6:40; Rom. 9:22; Gal. 6:1). So they promptly left their boat and father and followed Jesus. They had also already become disciples of Jesus. Now there are four who follow him steadily.

4:23. *Was going throughout all Galilee*[22] (περιῆγεν ἐν ὅλῃ τῇ Γαλιλαίᾳ). Literally Jesus "was going around (imperfect) in all Galilee." This is the first of the three tours of Galilee made by Jesus. This time he took the four fishermen he had called to personal service. The second time he took the twelve. On the third visit he sent the twelve on ahead by twos. He was teaching and preaching the gospel of the kingdom in the synagogues chiefly and on the roads and in the streets where Gentiles could hear.

Healing every kind of disease and every kind of sickness (θεραπεύων πᾶσαν νόσον καὶ πᾶσαν μαλακίαν). The occasional sickness is called μαλακίαν, the chronic or serious disease νόσον.

4:24. *The news about Him spread throughout all Syria*[23] (ἀπῆλθεν ἡ ἀκοὴ αὐτοῦ εἰς ὅλην τὴν Συρίαν). Rumor (ἀκοή) carries things almost like the wireless or radio. Gentiles all over Syria to the north heard what was going on in Galilee. The result was inevitable. Jesus had a moving hospital of patients from all over Galilee and Syria.

All who were ill (τοὺς κακῶς ἔχοντας), literally "those who had it bad," cases that the doctors could not cure.

Suffering with various diseases and pains (ποικίλαις νόσοις καὶ βασάνοις συνεχομένους). "Held together" or "compressed" is the idea of the participle. The same word is used by Jesus in Luke 12:50 and by Paul in Philippians 1:23 and of the crowd pressing on Jesus (Luke 8:45). They brought these difficult and chronic cases (present tense of the participle) to Jesus, "various" (ποικίλαις) health problems such as fever, leprosy, blindness. The adjective means literally "many colored" or "variegated," like flowers, paintings, or jaundice. Some had "torments" (βασάνοις), a term of oriental origin that meant a touchstone for testing gold because pure gold rubbed on it left a peculiar mark. Then it was used for examination by torture. Sickness was often regarded as torture. These diseases are described "in a descending scale of violence"[24] as "demoniacs, lunatics, and paralytics" as Moffatt puts it, "demoniacs, epileptics, paralytics" as Weymouth has it (δαιμονιζομένους καὶ σεληνιαζομένου· καὶ παραλυτικούς). The English "lunatic," from the Latin *luna* (moon), carries the same picture as the Greek σεληνιάζομαι, from σελήνη (moon). Once even epileptics were called "lunatics" or "moonstruck" because the seizures supposedly followed the phases of the moon[25] (see this use in Matt. 17:15). The English *paralytics* transliterates the Greek word with the same meaning. These diseases are called "torments."

4:25. *Large crowds followed Him* (ἠκολούθησαν αὐτῷ ὄχλοι πολλοί). Note the plural, not just one crowd but crowds. And from all parts of Palestine including Decapolis, the region of the Ten Greek Cities east of the Jordan. No political campaign could have matched this outpouring of people to hear and be healed by Jesus.

NOTES

1. A. T. Robertson, *Commentary on the Gospel According to Matthew* (New York: Macmillan, 1911), 83.
2. NIV has "After fasting."
3. Henry Alford, *The Greek Testament, with a Critically Revised Text*, 4 vols. in 2 vols.; Vol. 1, *The Four Gospels*, rev. by Everett F. Harrison (Chicago: Moody, 1958), 28.
4. NIV has "He was hungry."
5. Alexander Balmain Bruce, *The Expositor's Greek Testament*, Vol. 1, *The Synoptic Gospels* (Grand Rapids: Eerdmans, 1951), 89.
6. Alford, *Greek Testament*, 29.
7. Josephus, *Antiquities of the Jews,* 15.11.5.
8. NIV has "Do not put the Lord your God to the test."

9. NIV has "All this I will give you." GNT/NA and WH have Ταῦτά σοι πάντα δώσω, but TR and Maj.T have a different word order, Ταῦτα πάντα σοι δώσω.

10. Ἐάν and aorist subjunctive, second class undetermined with likelihood of determination.

11. NIV has "Bow down and worship me."

12. Alan Hugh McNeile, *The Gospel According to St. Matthew: The Greek Text with Introduction, Notes, and Indices* (repr. ed., Grand Rapids: Baker, 1980), 41.

13. NIV has "Away from me, Satan."

14. NIV has "and attended him."

15. The name *Jesus* is not found in the Greek text of GNT/NA and WH. Rather, the pronoun is used as in NASB (1978 edition). However, ὁ Ἰησοῦς is found in TR and Maj.T.

16. James Stalker, *The Life of Christ* (New York: Revell, 1891), 49–53.

17. NIV has "He went and lived in Capernaum." TR and Maj.T have a different spelling for the city, Καπερναούμ.

18. NIV has "have seen a great light." GNT/NA, WH, and Maj.T have with the moveable ν, whereas TR has εἶδεν without the moveable ν.

19. McNeile, *Matthew*, 44.

20. NIV has "lake" for sea.

21. NIV has "preparing their nets."

22. NIV has "went throughout Galilee." GNT/NA and WH have ἐν ὅλῃ τῇ Γαλιλαία, whereas TR and Maj.T have ὅλην τὴν Γαλιλαίαν.

23. NIV has "spread all over Syria."

24. McNeile, *Matthew*, 48.

25. Bruce, *Expositor's*, 94.

Matthew: Chapter 5

5:1. *He went up on the mountain*[1] (ἀνέβη εἰς τὸ ὄρος). Not *a* mountain as the Authorized Version has it. The Greek article is poorly handled in most English versions. We do not know what mountain it was. It was the one where Jesus and the crowds were. "Delitzsch calls the Mount of Beatitudes the Sinai of the New Testament."[2] He apparently went up to get in closer contact with the disciples, "when Jesus saw the crowds." Luke 6:12 says that he went off to the mountain to pray, Mark 3:13 that he went up and called the twelve. All three purposes are true. Luke adds that, after a whole night in prayer and after the choice of the twelve, Jesus came down to a level place on the mountain and spoke to the multitudes from Judea to Phoenicia. The crowds are great in Matthew and in Luke. There is no real difficulty with identifying the Sermon on the Mount in Matthew with the Sermon on the Plain in Luke.[3]

5:2. *Began to teach them* (ἐδίδασκεν αὐτούς). Inchoative (inceptive) imperfect. He sat on the mountainside in the manner of the Jewish rabbis, instead of standing. It was a most impressive scene, as Jesus spoke loudly enough to be heard by the great throng. The newly chosen twelve apostles were there, "a large crowd of His disciples, and a great throng of people" (Luke 6:17).

5:3. *"Blessed"* (Μακάριοι). The English word *blessed* more precisely translates the Greek verbal εὐλαγητοί, as in Luke 1:68 (in Zacharias's praise to God); or the perfect passive participle εὐλογημένος, as in Luke 1:42 (in Elizabeth's greeting of Mary) and Matthew 21:9 (the shout as Jesus enters Jerusalem). Both forms come from εὐλογέω, "to speak well of" (εὖ λόγος). Μακάριοι is an adjective that means "happy." The word *happy* in English etymology goes back to *hap*, referring to chance or good luck. This derivation can be found in *haply, hapless, happily,* and *happiness.* "Blessedness is, of course, an infinitely higher and better thing than mere happiness," according to Weymouth. English has thus ennobled *blessed* to a higher rank than *happy.* But "happy" is what Jesus said, and the *Braid Scots New Testament* dares to say "Happy" each time, as does the *Improved Edition of the American Bible Union Version.*[4] The Greek word is as old as Homer and Pindar and was used of the Greek gods and also of men, but largely of outward prosperity. It is

54

applied to those who died in the Lord in Revelation 14:13. The LXX Old Testament uses it of moral quality. "Shaking itself loose from all thoughts of outward good, it becomes the express symbol of a happiness identified with pure character. Behind it lies the clear cognition of sin as the fountain-head of all misery, and of holiness as the final and effectual cure for every woe. For knowledge as the basis of virtue, and therefore of happiness, it substitutes faith and love."[5] Jesus puts this word *happy* in a rich environment. "This is one of the words which have been transformed and ennobled by New Testament use; by association, as in the Beatitudes, with unusual conditions, accounted by the world miserable, or with rare and difficult."[6] It is a pity that we have not kept the word *happy* on the high and holy plane where Jesus placed it. "If you know these things, happy (μακάριοι) are you if you do them" (John 13:17). "Happy (μακάριοι) are those who have not seen and yet have believed" (John 20:29). Paul applies this adjective to God, "according to the gospel of the glory of the happy (μακάριοι) God" (1 Tim. 1:11, au trans.; see also Titus 2:13). The term *beatitude* (Latin *beatus*) comes close to the meaning of Christ here by μακάριοι. It will pay one to make a careful study of all the "beatitudes" in the New Testament where μακάριοι is employed. It occurs nine times in Matthew 5:3–11, although the beatitudes in verses 10 and 11 are very much alike. The copula is not expressed in these nine occurences. In each case a reason is given for the beatitude, "for" (ὅτι). This shows the spiritual quality involved. Some of the phrases employed by Jesus here occur in the Psalms; some are even in the Talmud, a Jewish rabbinical document originating later than the New Testament. That is of small moment. "The originality of Jesus lies in putting the due value on these thoughts, collecting them, and making them as prominent as the Ten Commandments. No greater service can be rendered to mankind than to rescue from obscurity neglected moral commonplaces."[7] Jesus probably repeated his sayings many times, as great teachers do, but this sermon has unity, progress, and consummation. It does not contain all that Jesus taught, but it stands out as the greatest single sermon of all time in its penetration, pungency, and power.

"The poor in spirit" (οἱ πτωχοὶ τῷ πνεύματι). Luke has only "the poor," but he seems to mean the same as this form in Matthew, "the pious in Israel, for the most part poor, whom the worldly rich despised and persecuted."[8] The word used, πτωχός, is applied to the beggar Lazarus in Luke 16:20, 22. Derived from πτώσσω, "to crouch, to cower," it suggests spiritual destitution. The alternative noun for "poor," πένης, is from πένομαι, "to work for one's daily bread." The reference is to one who works for a living. Πτωχός is more

frequent in the New Testament and implies deeper poverty than does πένης. "The kingdom of heaven" here means the reign of God in the heart and life. This is the *summum bonum*—what matters most.

5:4. *"Those who mourn"* (οἱ πενθοῦντες). This is another seeeming paradox. This verb "is most frequent in the LXX for mourning for the dead, and for the sorrows and sins of others."[9] "There can be no comfort where there is no grief."[10] Sorrow should make us look for the heart and hand of God and so find the comfort latent in grief.

5:5. *"The gentle"*[11] (οἱ πραεῖς). Wycliff has "Blessed be mild men." The ancients used the word for outward conduct. They did not rank it as a virtue. It was a mild equanimity that could be negative or positive. But Jesus lifted the word to a nobility. The Beatitudes assume a new heart, for the natural man does not find happiness in the qualities mentioned here by Christ. The English word *meek* has lost its reference to a fine blend of spiritual poise and strength—as was meant by the Master. He calls himself "gentle and humble in heart" (Matt. 11:29) and Moses is also called meek (Num. 12:3). It is the gentleness of strength, not effeminacy. By "the earth" (τὴν γῆν) Jesus seems to mean the Land of Promise (Ps. 37:11) though Bruce[12] thinks that it is the whole earth. Can it be the solid earth as opposed to the sea or the air?

5:6. *"Those who hunger and thirst for righteousness"* (οἱ πεινῶντες καὶ διψῶντες τὴν δικαιοσύνην). Jesus turns one of the elemental human instincts to spiritual use. There is in all men hunger for food, for love, for God. It is passionate hunger and thirst for goodness, for holiness. The word for "satisfied," χορτασθήσονται, means to feed or to fatten cattle. It is derived from the words for fodder or green grass used in Mark 6:39, χλωρὸς χόρτος.

5:7. *"They shall receive mercy"*[13] (ἐλεηθήσονται), *"Sal win pitie theirels"* (*Braid Scots*). "A self-acting law of the moral world."[14] "What is sometimes true of men is the law of the kingdom of heaven."[15]

5:8. *"They shall see God"*[16] (αὐτοὶ τὸν θεὸν ὄψονται). Without holiness no man will see the Lord (Heb. 12:14). The beatific vision is only possible here on earth to those with pure hearts. No other can see the King now. Sin befogs and beclouds the heart, so that one cannot see God. Purity has here its widest sense and includes everything.

5:9. *"The peacemakers"* (οἱ εἰρηνοποιοί). Not merely "peaceable men" (Wycliff) but "makkers up o' strife" (*Braid Scots*). It is hard enough to keep the peace. It is still more difficult to bring peace where it is not. "The perfect peacemaker is the Son of God (Eph. 2:14f.)"[17] Thus we shall be like our Elder Brother.

5:10. *"Those who have been persecuted for the sake of righteousness"*[18] (οἱ δεδιωγμένοι ἕνεκεν δικαιοσύνης). Sometimes people try to gain attention and pity by acting as if they are being persecuted. The kingdom of heaven belongs to those who suffer because they are following Christ without compromise, people who are guilty of no wrong.

5:11. *"Falsely . . . because of Me"* ([ψευδόμενοι] ἕνεκεν ἐμοῦ). Codex Bezae changes the order of these last beatitudes, but that is irrelevant to meaning. Two criteria are set for receiving a martyr's crown and great reward (μισθός) in heaven. The bad things said of Christ's followers must be untrue and the slander must be borne for Christ's sake. No prize awaits one who deserves the evil opinion of others.

5:13. *"If the salt has become tasteless"*[19] (ἐὰν δὲ τὸ ἅλας μωρανθῇ). The verb is from μωρός ("dull, sluggish, stupid, foolish") and means to play the fool, to become foolish. Here it refers to salt that has become tasteless or insipid (Mark 9:50). It is common in Syria and Palestine to see salt scattered in piles on the ground because it has lost its flavor, or as the Braid Scots New Testament puts it, "hae tint its tang." It has become the most worthless thing imaginable. Jesus may have used here a current proverb.

5:15. *"Put it under a basket"*[20] (τιθέασιν αὐτὸν ὑπὸ τὸν μόδιον). Not *a* bushel, but *the* bushel. "The figure is taken from lowly cottage life. There was a projecting stone in the wall on which the lamp was set. The house consisted of a single room, so that the tiny light sufficed for all."[21] It was not put under the bushel (the only one in the room) save to put it out or to hide it. The bushel was an earthenware grain measure.

"The lampstand" (τὴν λυχνίαν), not "candlestick." It is lamp stand in each of the twelve examples in the Bible. There was the one lamp stand for the single room.

5:16. *"Even so"*[22] (οὕτως). The adverb points backward to the lamp stand. Thus men are to let their lights shine, not to glorify themselves but "your Father who is in heaven." Light shines to see others by, not to call attention to itself.

5:17. *"I did not come to abolish, but to fulfill"* (οὐκ ἦλθον καταλῦσαι ἀλλὰ πληρῶσαι). The verb *abolish* means to "loosen down" as of a house or tent (2 Cor. 5:1). *Fulfill* means to "fill full" or complete. This Jesus did to the ceremonial law, which pointed to him. He also kept the moral law. "He came to fill the law, to reveal the full depth of meaning that it was intended to hold."[23]

5:18. *"The smallest letter or stroke"*[24] (ἰῶτα ἓν ἢ μία κεραία). "Not an iota, not a comma" (Moffatt), "not the smallest letter, not a particle"

(Weymouth). The iota is the smallest Greek vowel, which Matthew here uses to represent the Hebrew *yod* (jot), the smallest Hebrew letter. "Tittle" is from the Latin *titulus,* which came to mean the stroke above an abbreviated word, then any small mark. It is not certain here whether κεραία means a little horn, the mere point which distinguishes some Hebrew letters from others or the "hook" letter *Vau*. Sometimes *yod* and *vau* were hardly distinguishable. "In *Vay.* R. 19 the guilt of altering one of them is pronounced so great that if it were done the world would be destroyed."[25]

5:19. *"Whoever keeps and teaches"*[26] (ὃς δ᾽ ἂν ποιήσῃ καὶ διδάξῃ). Jesus puts practice before preaching. The teacher must live the doctrine before teaching it to others. The scribes and Pharisees were men who "say and do not" (Matt. 23:3), who preach but do not perform. This is Christ's test of greatness.

5:20. *"Surpasses"* (περισσεύσῃ . . . πλεῖον). Overflow like a river out of its banks. Then Jesus adds "more" followed by an unexpressed ablative (genitive, τῆς δικαιοσύνης), brachylogy (brevity). A daring statement on Christ's part that they had to be better than the rabbis. They must excel the scribes, the small number of regular teachers (5:32–48), and the Pharisees (6:1–18), who were the separated ones, the orthodox pietists.

5:22. *"But I say to you"*[27] (ἐγὼ δὲ λέγω ὑμῖν). Jesus assumes a tone of superiority over the Mosaic regulations and their interpreters in six examples. He goes further than does the Law into the very heart. "He finds the principle behind the precept and indorses that."[28]

"'You good-for-nothing' . . . 'You fool'" (Ῥακά . . . Μωρέ). The first is probably an Aramaic word meaning "empty, simpleton or blockhead,"[29] used to express contempt for someone. The second word is Greek ("dull, stupid") and is a fair equivalent of "raca." It is urged by some that μωρέ is a Hebrew word, but Field (*Otium Norvicense*) objects to that idea. "'Ῥακά expresses contempt for a man's head = you stupid! Μωρέ expresses contempt for his heart and character = you scoundrel."[30]

"The fiery hell"[31] (τὴν γέενναν τοῦ πυρός), "the Gehenna of fire." The genitive case (τοῦ πυρός) is the genus case describing gehenna as marked by fire. Gehenna is the Valley of Hinnom where fire burned continually. Here idolatrous Jews once offered their children to Molech (2 Kings 23:10). Jesus finds one cause of murder to be abusive language. Gehenna should be carefully distinguished from hades (ᾅδης), which is never the place of punishment. Hades is the place of departed spirits, without reference to moral condition.[32] The place of torment is in hades (Luke 16:23), but so is the place of blessing—"paradise."

5:24. *"Go; first be reconciled"*[33] (ὕπαγε πρῶτον διαλλάγηθι), second person singular second aorist passive imperative: "get reconciled" (ingressive aorist, "take the initiative"). This is the only example of this compound in the New Testament. Usually καταλλάσσω occurs with it.[34] A prodigal son, Longinus, writes to his mother, Nilus: "I beseech thee, mother, be reconciled (διαλάγητι) with me." The boy is a poor speller, but with a broken heart he uses the identical form that Jesus does. "The verb denotes mutual concession after mutual hostility, an idea absent from καταλλάσσω," according to Lightfoot. This is because of διά ("two; between two").

5:25. *"Make friends quickly with"*[35] (ἴσθι εὐνοῶν), a present periphrastic active imperative. The verb is from εὔνοος (friendly, kindly disposed). "Mak up wi' yere enemy" (*Braid Scots New Testament*). Compromise is better than prison where no principle is involved, but only personal interest. It is so easy to see principle where pride is involved.

"The officer" (τῷ ὑπηρέτῃ). Ὑπό, "under," and ἠρέσσω, "to row." This word originally referred to a galley slave who was the "under rower" or bottom rower on a ship with several ranks of rowers. It came to mean any servant, including the attendant in the synogogue (Luke 4:20). Luke so describes John Mark in his relation to Barnabas and Saul (Acts 13:5). He applies it to "servants of the word" in Luke 1:2.

5:26. *"The last cent"*[36] (τὸν ἔσχατον κοδράντην), a Latin word, *quadrans*, one-fourth of an *as* (ἀσσάριον), or two mites (Mark 12:42), a vivid picture of inevitable punishment for debt. This is emphasized by the strong double negative οὐ μὴ with the aorist subjunctive.

5:27. *"You shall not commit adultery"*[37] (Οὐ μοιχεύσεις). These quotations (vv. 21, 27, 33) from the LXX Decalogue (Exod. 20 and Deut. 5) use οὐ and the second person singular future active indicative (volitive future, common Greek idiom). In 5:43, the positive (or affirmative) form, volitive future, occurs (ἀγαπήσεις). In verse 42, the second person (δός) singular second aorist active imperative is used. In verse 38, no verb occurs.

5:28. *"In his heart"* (ἐν τῇ καρδίᾳ αὐτοῦ). The inner man, including the intellect, affections, and will. It is not just the center of the blood circulation, though it means that, nor just the emotional nature. This word is exceedingly common in the New Testament and always should be noted for careful study. It is from a root that means "to quiver or palpitate." Jesus locates adultery in the eye and heart before the outward act. Wunsche (*Beitrage*) quotes two pertinent rabbinical sayings as translated by Bruce: "The eye and the heart are the two brokers of sin."[38] Hence the peril of lewd pictures and plays to the pure.

5:29. *"Makes you stumble"* (σκανδαλίζει σε). This is far better than the Authorized Version, "offend thee." *Braid Scots New Testament* has it rightly "ensnare ye." It is not the notion of giving offence or provoking but of setting a trap. The substantive (σκάνδαλον, from σκανδαλήθρον) means the stick in the trap that springs and closes the trap when the animal touches it. Pluck out the eye when it is a snare, cut off the hand, even the right hand. These vivid pictures are not to be taken literally, but powerfully plead for self-mastery. It is not mutilating of the body that Christ enjoins, but control of the body against sin. The man who plays with fire will get burnt. Modern surgery finely illustrates the teaching of Jesus. The tonsils, teeth, or appendix, if left diseased, will destroy the whole body. Cut them out in time and the life will be saved. "Spiritual surgery is what Jesus has in mind."[39] Dr. Marvin R. Vincent notes that "the words scandal and slander are both derived from σκάνδαλον."[40] And Wycliffe renders, "if thy right eye *slander* thee." Certainly slander is a scandal and a stumbling block, a trap, and a snare.

5:31. *"A certificate of divorce"* (ἀποστάσιον), "a divorce certificate" (Moffatt), "a written notice of divorce" (Weymouth). The Greek is an abbreviation of βιβλίον ἀποστασίου (Matt. 19:7; Mark 10:4). Vulgate has here *libellum repudii.* The papyri use συγγραφὴ ἀποστασίου in commercial transactions as "a bond of release."[41] The written notice (βιβλίον) was a protection to the wife against an angry whim of the husband who might send her away with no paper to show for it.

5:32. *"Except for the reason of unchastity"*[42] (παρεκτὸς λόγου πορνείας). An unusual phrase that perhaps means "except on the ground of unchastity" (Weymouth), "except unfaithfulness" (Goodspeed), and is equivalent to μὴ ἐπὶ πορνείᾳ in Matthew 19:9. McNeile denies that Jesus made this exception, because Mark and Luke do not give it.[43] He claims that the early Christians made the exception to meet a pressing need. However, one fails to see the force of this charge against Matthew's report of the words of Jesus. It looks like criticism to meet modern needs.

5:34. *"Make no oath at all"*[44] (μὴ ὀμόσαι ὅλως), more exactly "not to swear at all" (indirect command, and aorist infinitive). Certainly Jesus does not prohibit oaths in a court of justice, for he himself answered Caiaphas on oath (Matt. 26:63–64). Paul made solemn appeals to God (1 Cor. 15:31; 1 Thess. 5:27). Jesus prohibits all forms of profanity. The Jews were masters in the art of splitting hairs about allowable oaths or forms of profanity—just as modern Christians excuse a great variety of vernacular "cuss words."

5:38. *"An eye for an eye, and a tooth for a tooth"* (Ὀφθαλμὸν ἀντὶ ὀφθαλμοῦ καὶ ὀδόντα ἀντὶ ὀδόντος).[45] Note ἀντί with the notion of exchange or substitution. Like divorce, this *lex talionis* (law of retaliation) is a restriction upon unrestrained vengeance. "It limited revenge by fixing an exact compensation for an injury."[46] A money payment is allowed in the Mishna. The law of retaliation exists in some countries today.

5:39. *"Do not resist an evil person"* (μὴ ἀντιστῆναι τῷ πονηρῷ). Here again it is the infinitive (second aorist active) in indirect command. But is it "the evil man" or the "evil deed"? The dative case is the same form for masculine and neuter. Weymouth puts it, "not to resist a (the) wicked man"; Moffatt, "not to resist an injury"; Goodspeed, "not to resist injury." The examples will go with either view. Jesus protested when smitten on the cheek (John 18:22). And Jesus denounced the Pharisees (Matt. 23) and fought the Devil always. The language of Jesus is bold and picturesque and is not to be pressed too literally. The purpose of expressions that seem to be paradoxical is to startle us and make us think. We are expected to fill in the other side of the picture. One thing certainly is meant by Jesus: Personal revenge is taken out of our hands. Aggressive or offensive war by nations is also condemned, but not necessarily defensive war or defence against robbery and murder. Professional pacifism may be mere cowardice.

5:40. *"Your shirt . . . your coat"*[47] (τὸν χιτῶνά σου. . . καὶ τὸ ἱμάτιον). The "tunic" is really a sort of shirt or undergarment and would be demanded at law. A robber would seize first the outer garment or cloke (one coat). If one loses the undergarment at law, the outer one goes also (the more valuable one). "Better let him have the costly outer garment also. One will save his temper, save the lawyer's fee, and perhaps shame the aggressor in the suit."[48]

5:41. *"Whoever forces you"*[49] (ὅστις σε ἀγγαρεύσει). The Vulgate has *angariaverit*. The word is of Persian origin and means public couriers or mounted messengers (ἄγγαροι), who were stationed at fixed points with horses ready for use to carry royal messages. A traveler passing such a post station could be accosted by an official, who might rush out and compel him to go back to another station to do an errand for the king. This was called "impressment into service." This very thing was done to Simon of Cyrene, who was thus compelled to carry the cross of Christ (Matt. 27:32, ἠγγάρευσαν).

5:42. *"Do not turn away"* (μὴ ἀποστραφῇς). Second person singular second aorist passive subjunctive in prohibition. "This is one of the clearest instances of the necessity of accepting the spirit and not the letter of the Lord's commands (see vv. 32, 34, 38). Not only does indiscriminate almsgiving do little but injury to society, but the words must embrace far more than almsgiving."[50] Recall that Jesus is a popular teacher who expects hearers to understand his paradoxes.

5:43. *"And hate your enemy"* (καὶ μισήσεις τὸν ἐχθρόν σου). This phrase is not in Leviticus 19:18. It is a rabbinical inference that Jesus repudiates bluntly. The Talmud says nothing of love for enemies. Paul in Romans 12:20 quotes Proverbs 25:22 to prove that we ought to treat our enemies kindly. Jesus taught us to pray for our enemies and did it himself even when he hung upon the cross. Our word *neighbor* is from "nigh-bor," one who is nigh or near. The Greek word πλησίον here has the same connotation. But proximity often means strife and not love. Those who have adjoining farms or homes may be positively hostile in spirit. The Jews came to look on members of the same tribe or Jews everywhere as their neighbors. But they hated the Samaritans, who were half Jews and lived between Judea and Galilee. Jesus taught men how to act as neighbors by the parable of the Good Samaritan (Luke 10:29–37).

5:48. *"Therefore you are to be perfect"*[51] (Ἔσεσθε οὖν ὑμεῖς τέλειοι). Τέλειοι comes from τέλος, meaning "end, goal, limit." It is the goal before us, the absolute standard of our heavenly Father. The word is used also for relative perfection, as of adults compared with children.

NOTES

1. NIV has "He went up on a mountainside."
2. Marvin R. Vincent, *Word Studies in the New Testament*, Vol. 1, *The Synoptic Gospels* (repr. ed., Grand Rapids: Eerdmans, 1946), 33.
3. See full discussion in A. T. Robertson, *Harmony of the Gospels for Students of the Life of Christ* (New York: Harper and Row, 1922), 273–76.
4. Philadelphia: American Baptist Publication Society, 1883. Phillips, Jerusalem Bible, and Today's English Version are among several late-twentieth-century English translations and paraphrases that use the translation "happy."
5. Vincent, *Word Studies*, 1.35.
6. Alexander Balmain Bruce, *The Expositor's Greek Testament*, Vol. 1, *The Synoptic Gospels* (Grand Rapids: Eerdmans, 1951), 97.
7. Ibid., 96.
8. Alan Hugh McNeile, *The Gospel According to St. Matthew: The Greek Text with Introduction, Notes, and Indices* (repr. ed., Grand Rapids: Baker, 1980), 50.
9. Ibid., 50.
10. Bruce, *Expositor's*, 98.

11. NIV has "The meek."
12. Bruce, *Expositor's*, 98.
13. NIV has "They will be shown mercy," literally, "They will be mercied."
14. Bruce, *Expositor's*, 1.99.
15. A. T. Robertson, *Commentary on the Gospel According to Matthew* (New York: Macmillan, 1911), 94.
16. NIV has "They will see God."
17. McNeile, *Matthew*, 53.
18. NIV has "those who are persecuted because of righteousness."
19. NIV has "If the salt loses its saltiness."
20. NIV has "put it under a bowl."
21. Bruce, *Expositor's*, 1.102.
22. NASB (1978 edition) does not include this.
23. McNeile, *Matthew*, 58.
24. NIV has "The smallest letter, not the least stroke of a pen."
25. McNeile, *Matthew*, 59.
26. NIV has "Whoever practices and teaches."
27. NIV has "But I tell you."
28. Robertson, *Commentary on Matthew*, 98.
29. Ibid., 99.
30. Bruce, *Expositor's*, 107.
31. NIV has "fire of hell."
32. Vincent, *Word Studies*, 40.
33. NIV has "First go and be reconciled."
34. Adolph Deissmann, *Light from the Ancient East* (repr. ed., Grand Rapids: Baker, 1978), 187, gives an A.D. second-century papyrus example.
35. NIV has "Settle matters."
36. NIV has "The last penny."
37. NIV has "Do not commit adultery."
38. Bruce, *Expositor's*, 108.
39. Robertson, *Commentary on Matthew*, 100.
40. Vincent, *Word Studies*, 1.41.
41. James Hope Moulton and George Milligan, *The Vocabulary of the Greek Testament* (London: Hodder and Stoughton, 1952), 69.
42. NIV has "except for marital unfaithfulness."
43. McNeile, *Matthew*, 66.
44. NIV has "Do not swear at all."
45. From Exodus 21:24; Deuteronomy 19:21; Leviticus 24:20.

46.   McNeile, *Matthew*, 69.
47.   NIV has "Your tunic . . . your cloak."
48.   Robertson, *Commentary on Matthew*, 102.
49.   NIV has "If someone forces you."
50.   McNeile, *Matthew*, 70.
51.   NIV has "Be perfect, therefore."

Matthew: Chapter 6

6:1. *"Beware"*[1] (Προσέχετε), "hold the mind on a matter," "take pains," "take heed." The Greek idiom is ancient and occurs in the LXX at Job 7:17. In the New Testament the substantive νοῦς is understood.

"Righteousness" (τὴν δικαιοσύνην[2]) is the correct text in this verse. "Jesus has discussed the theory of righteousness in contrast with that of the scribes. He now turns to the practice of righteousness in contrast with that of the Pharisees."[3] Three specimens of Pharisaic "righteousness" are given (alms, prayer, fasting).

"To be noticed by them"[4] (πρὸς τὸ θεαθῆναι αὐτοῖς), first aorist passive infinitive of purpose. Our word *theatrical* is derived from this word, which referred to a spectacular performance.

"With your Father" (παρὰ τῷ πατρὶ ὑμῶν). Literally "beside your Father," standing by his side, as he looks at it.

6:2. *"Do not sound a trumpet before you"*[5] (μὴ σαλπίσῃς ἔμπροσθέν σου). Is this literal or metaphorical? No actual instance of such conduct has been found in the Jewish writings. Alan McNeile suggests that it may refer to the blowing of trumpets in the streets on the occasion of public fasts.[6] Marvin R. Vincent suggests the thirteen trumpet shape of the chests in the temple treasury that received contributions (Luke 21:2).[7] At the Winona Lake, Indiana, conference center one summer, a missionary from India named Levering stated that he had seen Hindu priests do this very thing to get a crowd to see their beneficences. The rabbis could have done it also; certainly it was in keeping with their love of praise. Jesus expressly says that hypocrites (οἱ ὑποκριταὶ) do this. "Hypocrite" comes from ὑποκρίνομαι "to answer in reply," the word for actor, interpreter, or one who impersonates another. The Attic form was ἀποκρίνομαι, "to pretend, feign, dissemble, act the hypocrite, or wear a mask." This is the harshest word that Jesus uses to characterize any class of people. He employs it for these pious pretenders who pose as perfect.

"They have their reward in full"[8] (ἀπέχουσιν τὸν μισθὸν αὐτῶν). Ἀποχή means "receipt." This related verb is common in the papyri for receiving a receipt. "They have their receipt in full," all the reward that they will get. With

65

this public notoriety, "they can sign the receipt of their reward."[9] So also in verse 5.

6:4. *"In secret"* (ἐν τῷ κρυπτῷ). The TR and the Maj.T have the additional words ἐν τῷ φανερῷ (openly) at the end of this verse and also at the end of 6:6. These readings are not genuine. Jesus does not promise a *public* reward for private piety.

6:5. *"They love to stand and pray in the synagogues and on the street corners"* (ἐν ταῖς συναγωγαῖς καὶ ἐν ταῖς γωνίαις τῶν πλατειῶν ἑστῶτες προσεύχεσθαι). Synagogues were the usual places of prayer, and crowds stopped for business or to talk on street corners. If the hour of prayer overtook a Pharisee here, he would strike his attitude of prayer. A Muslim bowing face down on the sidewalk to say prayers would be a similar example.

6:6. *"Go into your inner room"* (εἴσελθε εἰς τὸ ταμεῖόν σου).[10] The word for "inner room" is a late syncopated form of ταμεῖον, from ταμίας, "steward," and the root ταμ- from τέμνω, "to cut." The meaning is a storehouse, a private apartment, chamber, closet, or "den" where one can withdraw and shut the world out to commune with God.

6:7. *"Do not use meaningless repetition"* (μὴ βατταλογήσητε).[11] Used of stammerers who repeat the words, then mere babbling or chattering, empty repetition. The etymology is uncertain, but it is probably onomatopoetic (nouns whose sounds reinforce their meaning), like the English word "babble." Worshipers of Baal on Mount Carmel (1 Kings 18:26) and of Diana in the amphitheatre at Ephesus, who yelled for two hours (Acts 19:34), engaged in repetitive babbling. The Syriac Sinaitic has it: "Do not be saying idle things." Certainly Jesus does not mean to condemn all repetition in prayer, since he himself prayed three times in Gethsemane "saying the same thing once more" (Matt. 26:44). "As the Gentiles do," clarifies Jesus. "The Pagans thought that by endless repetitions and many words they would inform their gods as to their needs and weary them (*fatigare deos*) into granting their requests."[12] "But the point of the Pharisees was not to gain the ear of God, but the eye of men."[13]

6:9. *"Pray, then, in this way"*[14] (Οὗτος οὖν προσεύχεσθε ὑμεῖς). "You" is in contrast with "the Gentiles." This should be called the "model prayer" rather than the "Lord's Prayer." Thus pray as he gives them a model. He himself did not use it as a liturgy (cf. John 17). There is no evidence that Jesus meant it for liturgical use by others. In Luke 11:2–4, practically the same prayer though briefer is given at a later time by Jesus to the apostles in response to a request that he teach them how to pray. McNeile argues that the form in Luke is the original, to which Matthew has made additions: "The tendency of liturgical formulas is towards enrichment rather than abbreviation."[15] But there is no evidence whatever that Jesus designed this prayer to be a set formula. There is no real harm in a liturgical formula if one likes it, but no one sticks to just one formula in prayer. There is good and not harm in children learning and saying this noble prayer.

"'Our Father'" (Πάτερ ἡμῶν). Some people are disturbed over the words "Our Father." They say that no one who has not been "born again" has a right to call God "Father." But that is to say that an unconverted sinner cannot pray until he is converted, an absurd contradiction. God is the Father of all people in one sense: recognition of him as "Father" in the full sense is the first step in coming back to him in regeneration and conversion.

"'Hallowed be Your name'" (ἁγιασθήτω τὸ ὄνομά σου). In the Greek the verb comes first, as in the petitions in verse 10. They are all aorist imperatives, action expressing urgency.

6:11. *"'Give us this day our daily bread'"*[16] (τὸν ἄρτον ἡμῶν τὸν ἐπιούσιον δὸς ἡμῖν σήμερον). This adjective "daily" (ἐπιούσιον) coming after "Give us this day" (δὸς ἡμῖν σήμερον) has given expositors a great deal of trouble. The effort has been made to derive it from ἐπί and ὤν (οὖσα). It clearly comes from ἐπί and ιὼν (ἐπί and εἰμι) like τῇ . . . ἐπιούσῃ ("on the coming day, the next day," Acts 16:11). But the adjective ἐπιούσιος is rare. Origen said it was made by the Evangelists Matthew and Luke to reproduce the idea of an Aramaic original. Moulton and Milligan wrote in 1919, "The papyri have as yet shed no clear light upon this difficult word (Matt. 6:11; Luke 11:3), which was in all probability a new coinage by the author of the Greek Q to render his Aramaic Original."[17] Deissmann claims that only about fifty purely New Testament or "Christian" words can be admitted out of the more than five thousand used. "But when a word is not recognizable at sight as a Jewish or Christian formation, we must consider it to be an ordinary Greek word until the contrary is proved. Ἐπιούσιος has all the appearance of a word that originated in the trade and traffic of everyday life.[18] This opinion has been confirmed by Albert Debrunner's discovery[19] of ἐπιούσιος in an ancient housekeeping book."[20] It is not a word coined by the Evangelist or "Q" to express an Aramaic original. The word occurs also in three late MSS after 2 Maccabees 1:8, τοὺς ἐπιουσίους after τοὺς ἄρτους. The meaning, in view of the kindred participle (ἐπιούσῃ) in Acts 16:11, seems to be "for the coming day," a daily prayer for the needs of the next day. Every housekeeper, including the one who wrote the words discovered by Debrunner, has understood this concept.[21]

6:12. *"'Forgive us our debts'"* (ἄφες ἡμῖν τὰ ὀφειλήματα ἡμῶν). Luke 11:4 has "sins" (ἁμαρτίας). In the ancient Greek ὀφείλημα is common for actual legal debts, as in Romans 4:4, but here it is used of moral and spiritual debts to God. "Trespasses" is a mistranslation made common by *The Book of Common Prayer* of the Church of England. It fits verse 14 in Christ's argument about prayer, but it is not the word used in the model prayer itself. In Matthew 18:28, 30, Christ again pictures sin "as debt and the sinner as a debtor."[22] We are described as having wronged God. The word ὀφειλή for moral obligation once was supposed to be peculiar to the New Testament, but it has been found to be commonly used in that sense in the papyri.[23] We ask forgiveness "in proportion as" (ὡς) we *also* have forgiven those in debt to us, a most solemn reflection. "Jesus assumes that the man who asks God forgiveness has already done that towards those in debt to Him."[24] Ἀφήκαμεν is one of the three κ (kappa) aorists, ἔθηκα, ἔδωκα, and ἧκα. It means to send away, to dismiss, to wipe off.

6:13. *"'And do not lead us into temptation'"*[25] (καὶ μὴ εἰσενέγκῃς ἡμᾶς εἰς πειρασμόν). "Bring" or "lead" bothers many people. It seems to present God as an active agent in subjecting us to temptation, a thing specifically denied in James 1:13. The word here translated "temptation" (πειρασμόν) means "trial" or "test," as in James 1:2. Vincent takes it so here.[26] *Braid Scots* has it: "And lat us no be siftit." But God does test or sift us, though he does not tempt us to evil. No one understood temptation so well as Jesus, for the Devil tempted him by every avenue of approach to all kinds of sin, but without success. In the Garden of Gethsemane Jesus will say to Peter, James, and John: "Pray that you may not enter into temptation" (Luke 22:40). That is the idea here. Here we have what grammarians call a "permissive imperative." The idea is, "Do not allow us to be led into temptation." There is a way out (1 Cor. 10:13), but it is a terrible risk.

"'Deliver us from evil'"[27] (ῥῦσαι ἡμᾶς ἀπὸ τοῦ πονηροῦ). The ablative case in the Greek obscures the gender. We have no way of knowing whether the form derives from ὁ πονηρός (the Evil One) or τὸ πονηρόν (the evil thing). If the form is masculine and so ὁ πονηρός, it can either refer to the Devil as *the* Evil One or to a spirit of evil that lies within a person who seeks to do us ill. The word πονηρός has a curious history coming from πόνος (toil) and πονέω (to work). It reflects the idea either that work is bad or that *this particular* work is bad. The bad idea drives out the good in work or toil, an example of human depravity.

The doxology is placed in the margin or brackets in modern English versions because it is wanting in the oldest Greek manuscripts. The earliest forms vary much, some shorter, some longer. The use of a doxology arose when this prayer began to be used as a liturgy, to be recited or chanted in public worship. Evidently, it was not part of the model prayer as given by Jesus.

6:14. *"If you forgive others for their transgressions"*[28] (Ἐὰν γὰρ ἀφῆτε τοῖς ἀνθρώποις τὰ παραπτώματα αὐτῶν). This is not part of the prayer. The word *transgressions* literally is "falling to one side," a lapse or deviation from truth or uprightness. The ancients sometimes used it of intentional falling or attack upon one's enemy, but "slip" or "fault" (Gal. 6:1) is the common New Testament idea. Παράβασις (Rom. 5:14) is a positive violation, a transgression, conscious stepping aside or across.

6:16. *"A gloomy face"* (σκυθρωποί).[29] Only here and Luke 24:17 in the New Testament. It is a compound of σκυθρός (sullen) and ὄψις (countenance). These actors or hypocrites "put on a gloomy look" (Goodspeed) and, if necessary, even "disfigure their faces"[30] (ἀφανίζουσιν . . . τὰ πρόσωπα αὐτῶν), that they may look like they are fasting. It is this pretence of piety that Jesus so sharply ridicules. There is a play on the Greek words ἀφανίζουσιν (disfigure) and φανῶσιν (figure). They conceal their real looks that they may seem to be fasting, conscious and pretentious hypocrisy.

6:18. *"In secret"* (ἐν τῷ κρυφαίῳ).[31] Here, as in verses 4 and 6, TR has the additional phrase ἐν τῷ φανερῷ ("in the open; openly"), but it is not genuine. The word κρυφαῖος is here alone in the New Testament. It occurs four times in the LXX.

6:19. *"Do not store up for yourselves treasures"* (μὴ θησαυρίζετε ὑμῖν θησαυρούς). Do not have this habit (μη and the present imperative). See on Matthew 2:11 for the word *treasure*. Here there is a play on the word θησαυροὺς. "Treasure not for yourselves treasures." The same sort of wordplay is in verse 20 with the cognate accusative. In both verses ὑμῖν is dative of personal interest and is not reflexive but the ordinary personal pronoun. Wycliff has it: "Do not treasure to you treasures." *"Where moth and rust destroy"* (ὅπου σὴς καὶ βρῶσις ἀφανίζει). Something that "eats" (βιβρώσκω) or "gnaws" or "corrodes."

"Break in"[32] (διορύσσουσιν). Literally "dig through." It was easy to dig through the mud walls or sun-dried bricks. The Greeks called a burglar a "mud digger" (τοιχόρυχος). Steel safes are not fully safe, even if their armor is a foot thick.

6:22. *"If your eye is clear"*[33] (ἐὰν οὖν ᾖ ὁ ὀφθαλμός σου ἁπλοῦς). Ἁπλοῦς is used of a marriage contract in which the husband was to repay the dowry "pure and simple" (τὴν φερνὴν ἁπλήν) in the case of divorce. In case he does not do so promptly, he is to pay interest.[34] There are various instances of such usage. Here and in Luke 11:34 the eye is called "single" in a moral sense. The word means "without folds," like a piece of cloth unfolded—*simplex* in Latin. Bruce considers this parable of the eye difficult. "The figure and the ethical meaning seem to be mixed up, moral attributes ascribed to the physical eye which with them still gives light to the body. This confusion may be due to the fact that the eye, besides being the organ of vision, is the seat of expression, revealing inward dispositions."[35] The "evil" eye (πονηρός) may be diseased and is used of stinginess in the LXX. So ἁπλοῦς may refer to liberality, as Hatch argues.[36] The passage may be elliptical, with something to be supplied. If our eyes are healthy, we see clearly and with a single focus (without astigmatism). If the eyes are diseased (bad, evil), they may even be cross-eyed or cockeyed. We see double and are confused by our vision. We keep one eye on the hoarded treasure of earth and roll the other proudly up to heaven. Seeing double is doublemindedness, as is shown in verse 24.

6:24. *"No one can serve two masters"* (Οὐδεὶς δύναται δυσὶ κυρίοις δουλεύειν). Many try it, but failure awaits them all. Men even try "to be slaves to God and mammon" (θεῷ δουλεύειν καὶ μαμωνᾷ). Mammon is a Chaldee, Syriac, and Punic word like *Plutus* for the money god (or devil). The slave of mammon will obey mammon while pretending to obey God. When the guide is blind and leads the blind, both fall into the ditch. The man who cannot tell road from ditch sees falsely.

"He will be devoted to one" (ἑνὸς ἀνθέξεται). The word means to line up, face-to-face (ἀντί), with one man against the other.

6:25. *"Do not be worried about your life"* (μὴ μεριμνᾶτε τῇ ψυχῇ ὑμῶν).[37] This is as good a translation as the Authorized Version was poor: "Take no thought for your life." The old English word "thought" meant anxiety or worry, as Shakespeare says in Hamlet (3.1.92–93):

> The native hue of resolution
> Is sicklied o'er with the pale cast of thought.

Once someone might have said that a poor soul "died with thought and anguish." But words change with time and now this passage is actually quoted "as an objection to the moral teaching of the Sermon on the Mount, on the ground that it encouraged, nay, commanded, a reckless neglect of the future."[38] We have narrowed the meaning of *thought* to mere planning, without any notion of the anxiety inherent in the Greek. The verb μεριμνάω is from μερίς, μερίζω, because care or anxiety distracts and divides. The word occurs in Christ's rebuke to Martha for her excessive solicitude about something to eat (Luke 10:41). The notion of proper care and forethought appears in 1 Corinthians 7:32; 12:25; Philippians 2:20. It is here the present imperative with the negative, a command not to have the habit of petulant worry about food and clothing. The command is to stop such worry or not to begin indulging in it. In verse 31 Jesus repeats the prohibition with the second person plural ingressive aorist active subjunctive: "Do not become anxious;" "Do not grow anxious."

"About your life" (τῇ ψυχῇ). Here ψυχή stands for the life principle common to man and beast, which is embodied in the σῶμα: The former needs food; the latter clothing.[39] Σῶμα in the Synoptic Gospels occurs in three senses.[40] First, it is the life principle, as here, which can be killed (Mark 3:4). Second, it is the seat of the thoughts and emotions, on a par with καρδία and διανοία (Matt. 22:37) and πνεῦμα (Luke 12:46; cf. John 12:27, 13:21). Third, it is something higher, which makes up the real self (Matt. 10:28, 16:26). In Matthew 16:25 (Luke 9:24) ψυχή appears in two senses, saving the physical life and losing the higher, more important one.

"What you will eat . . . what you will drink . . . what you will put on" (τί φάγητε [ἢ τί πίητε] . . . τί ἐνδύσησθε). Here the direct question with the deliberative subjunctive occurs with each verb (φάγωμεν, πίωμεν, περιβαλώμεθα). This deliberative subjunctive of the direct question is retained in the indirect question employed in verse 25. Different verbs for clothing occur in verses 25 and 31, both in the indirect middle. Περιβαλώμεθα, "fling round ourselves," in verse 31 is in apposition to ἐνδύσησθε, "put on yourselves," in verse 25).

6:27. *"To his life"* (ἐπὶ τὴν ἡλικίαν αὐτοῦ). The word ἡλικίαν is used either of height (stature) or length of life (age). Either makes good sense here, though probably "stature" suits the context best. Certainly anxiety will not help either kind of growth. This is no plea for idleness, for even the birds are diligent and the flowers grow.

6:28. *"The lilies of the field"* (τὰ κρίνα τοῦ ἀγροῦ). The meaning extends beyond lilies to other wildflowers.[41]

6:29. *"Not even Solomon . . . clothed himself"*[42] (οὐδὲ Σολομὼν . . . περιεβάλετο). Middle voice and so "did not clothe himself," "did not put around himself."

6:30. *"The grass of the field"* (τὸν χόρτον τοῦ ἀγροῦ). The common grass of the field. This heightens the comparison. "The dry grass is still used in Palestine to make fires to bake bread."[43]

6:33. *"But seek first His kingdom"* (ζητεῖτε δὲ πρῶτον τὴν βασιλείαν... αὐτοῦ). This in answer to those who see in the Sermon on the Mount only ethical comments. Jesus in the Beatitudes drew the picture of the man with the new heart. He places the kingdom of God and righteousness before temporal food and clothing.

6:34. *"Do not worry about tomorrow"* (μὴ οὖν μεριμνήσητε εἰς τὴν αὔριον). The last resort of the anxious soul when all other fears are allayed. The ghost of tomorrow stalks out, with all its hobgoblins of doubt and distrust. "After all one is more anxious about imaginary ills than about the actual ills."[44]

NOTES

1. NIV has "Be careful."
2. TR and Maj.T have τὴν ἐλεημοσύνην.
3. A. T. Robertson, *Commentary on the Gospel According to Matthew* (New York: Macmillan, 1911), 104.
4. NIV has "to be seen by them."
5. NIV has "do not announce it with trumpets."
6. Alan Hugh McNeile, *The Gospel According to St. Matthew: The Greek Text with Introduction, Notes, and Indices* (repr. ed., Grand Rapids: Baker, 1980), 74.
7. Marvin R. Vincent, *Word Studies in the New Testament*, Vol. 1, *The Synoptic Gospels* (repr. ed., Grand Rapids: Eerdmans, 1946), 43.
8. NIV has "they have received their reward in full."
9. Deissmann, *Bible Studies*, 229. See also Adolph Deissmann, *Light from the Ancient East* (repr. ed., Grand Rapids: Baker, 1978), 110f.
10. NIV has "into your room."
11. NIV has "Do not keep on babbling."
12. Alexander Balmain Bruce, *The Expositor's Greek Testament*, Vol. 1, *The Synoptic Gospels* (Grand Rapids: Eerdmans, 1951), 119.
13. Robertson, *Commentary on Matthew*, 106.
14. NIV has "This is how you should pray."
15. McNeile, *Matthew*, 76.
16. NIV has "Give us today our daily bread."
17. Moulton and Milligan, *Vocabulary*, 242.
18. See Deissmann's hints in *Neutestamentliche Studien Georg Heinrici Dargebracht* (Leipzig, 1914), 118f.

19. Albert Debrunner, *Theol. Lit. Ztg.* (1925), col. 119.

20. Deissmann, *Light from the Ancient East*, New ed. (1927), 78, n 1.

21. Albert Debrunner, *A Greek Grammar of the New Testament and Other Early Christian Literature* (rev. ed., Chicago: University of Chicago Press, 1961), ß 123.1.

22. Vincent, *Word Studies*, 1.43.

23. Deissmann, *Bible Studies*, 221 and *Light from the Ancient East*, new ed., 331.

24. Robertson, *Commentary on Matthew*, 108.

25. NIV has "and lead us not into temptation."

26. Vincent, *Word Studies,* 1.43–44.

27. NIV has "deliver us from the evil one."

28. NIV has "if you forgive men when they sin against you."

29. NIV has "look somber."

30. NASB has "neglect their appearance."

31. This is the reading of the text in GNT and WH. TR and Maj.T have the reading ἐν τῷ κρυπτῷ, the same as in 6:9.

32. NIV has "break in."

33. NIV has "If your eyes are good."

34. Moulton and Milligan, *Vocabulary,* 58.

35. Bruce, *Expositor's*, 124.

36. Hatch, *Essays in Biblical Greek*, 80.

37. NIV has "Do not worry about your life."

38. Vincent, *Word Studies*, 1.48.

39. McNeile, *Matthew*, 86.

40. Ibid.

41. Ibid., 89.

42. NIV has "not even Solomon . . . was dressed."

43. Robertson, *Commentary on Matthew*, 112.

44. Ibid., 113.

Matthew: Chapter 7

7:1. *"Do not judge"* (Μὴ κρίνετε), the habit of censoriousness, sharp, unjust criticism. The English word *critic* is from this word. It means to separate, distinguish, discriminate.

7:3. *"The speck"* (τὸ κάρφος). Not dust but a piece of dried wood or chaff, splinter (Weymouth, Moffatt), a very small particle that may irritate.

"The log"[1] (δοκόν). A log on which planks in the house rest (so papyri), joist, rafter, plank (Moffatt), a pole sticking out grotesquely from the eye. Jesus may have quoted a current proverb similar to "people who live in glass houses shouldn't throw stones." Tholuck quotes an Arabic proverb: "How seest thou the splinter in thy brother's eye, and seest not the cross-beam in thine eye?"[2]

7:5. *"You will see clearly"* (διαβλέψεις), only here and Luke 6:42 and Mark 8:25 in the New Testament: "Look through, penetrate," in contrast to βλέπεις, "to gaze at," in verse 3. Get the log out of your eye and you will see clearly how to help the brother get the splinter out (ἐκβαλεῖν) of his eye.

7:6. *"Do not give what is holy to dogs"*[3] (Μὴ δῶτε τὸ ἅγιον τοῖς κυσίν). It is not clear to what "the holy" refers, whether to earrings or to amulets. Whatever is holy does not appeal to dogs. Richard Trench says that the reference is to meat offered in sacrifice, which must not be flung to dogs: "It is not that the dogs would not eat it, for it would be welcome to them; but that it would be a profanation to give it to them, thus to make it a σκύβαλον, Exodus 22:31."[4] The yelping dogs would jump at it. Dogs are kin to wolves and infest the streets of oriental cities.

"Your pearls before swine"[5] (τοὺς μαργαρίτας ὑμῶν ἔμπροσθεν τῶν χοίρων). The word *pearl* we have in the name *Margarita* (or Margaret). Pearls look a bit like peas or acorns and would deceive the hogs until they discovered the deception. Wild boars trample with their feet and rend with their tusks anything that angers them.[6]

7:9. *"Loaf*[7] *... stone"* (ἄρτον ... λίθον). Some stones look like loaves of bread. So the Devil suggested that Jesus make loaves out of stones (4:3).

7:10. *"Fish ... snake"* (ἰχθὺν ... ὄφιν). Fish are a common article of food,

74

and water snakes could be substituted. Anacoluthon in this sentence in the Greek.

7:11. *"How much more"* (πόσῳ μᾶλλον). Jesus is fond of the *a fortiori* argument from the less to the greater.[8]

7:12. *"You want them to treat you"* (ἵνα ποιῶσιν ὑμῖν οἱ ἄνθρωποι). Luke (6:31) puts the Golden Rule parallel with Matthew 5:42. The negative form is in Tobit 4:15, "Do to no one what you yourself dislike." It was used by Hillel, Philo, Isocrates, Confucius. "The Golden Rule is the distilled essence of that 'fulfilment' (5:17) which is taught in the sermon."[9] Jesus puts it in positive form.

7:13. *"Through the narrow gate"* (διὰ τῆς στενῆς πύλης). The Authorized Version "at the strait gate" misled those who did not distinguish between "strait" and "straight." The figure of the two ways had a wide circulation in Jewish and Christian writings (cf. Deut. 30:19; Psalm 1; Jer. 21:8).[10] "The narrow gate"[11] is repeated in verse 14, with τεθλιμμένη added. The way is "compressed," narrowed as in a defile between high rocks, a tight place like στενοχωρία in Romans 8:35. "The way that leads to life involves straits and afflictions."[12] Vincent quotes the Pinax or Tablet of Cebes, a contemporary of Socrates:[13] "Seest thou not, then, a little door, and a way before the door, which is not much crowded, but very few travel it? This is the way that leadeth unto true culture." "The broad way" (εὐρύχωρος) is in every city, town, village with the glaring lights that lure to destruction.

7:15. *"False prophets"* (τῶν ψευδοπροφητῶν). There were false prophets in the time of the Old Testament prophets. Jesus predicts the coming of "false Christs and false prophets" (Matt. 24:24) who will lead many astray. They came in due time posing as angels of light like Satan. They included Judaizers (2 Cor. 11:13ff.) and proto-Gnostics (1 Tim. 4:1; 1 John 4:1). Already false prophets were on hand when Jesus spoke on this occasion (cf. Acts 13:6; 2 Peter 2:1). In outward appearance they look like sheep, but within they are "ravening wolves" (λύκοι ἅρπαγες), greedy for power, gain, self. It is a tragedy that such men and women reappear through the ages and always find victims. Wolves are more dangerous than dogs and hogs.

7:16, 20. *"You will know them by their fruits"*[14] (ἀπὸ τῶν καρπῶν αὐτῶν ἐπιγνώσεσθε αὐτούς). The verb *know* (γινώσκω) has ἐπί added, "fully know." The illustrations from the trees and vines have many parallels in ancient writers.

7:21. *"Not . . . but"* (Οὐ … ἀλλ'). Sharp contrast between the mere talker and the doer of God's will.

7:22. *"'Did we not prophesy in Your name?'"* (οὐ τῷ σῷ ὀνόματι

$\dot{\epsilon}\pi\rho o\phi\eta\tau\epsilon\dot{\nu}\sigma\alpha\mu\epsilon\nu$[15]). The use of $o\dot{\nu}$ in the question expects the affirmative answer. They claim to have prophesied or preached in Christ's name and to have done many miracles. But Jesus will tear off the sheepskin and lay bare the ravening wolf.

7:23. *"'I never knew you'"* ($O\dot{\nu}\delta\dot{\epsilon}\pi o\tau\epsilon$ $\ddot{\epsilon}\gamma\nu\omega\nu$ $\dot{\nu}\mu\hat{\alpha}\varsigma$). "I was never acquainted with you" (experimental knowledge). Success, as the world counts it, is not a criterion of one's knowledge of Christ and relation to him. "I will profess unto them" ($\dot{o}\mu o\lambda o\gamma\dot{\eta}\sigma\omega$ $\alpha\dot{\nu}\tau o\hat{\iota}\varsigma$), the very word used of profession of Christ before men (Matt. 10:32). This word Jesus will use for public and open announcement of their doom.

7:24. *"And acts on them"*[16] ($\kappa\alpha\dot{\iota}$ $\pi o\iota\epsilon\hat{\iota}$ $\alpha\dot{\nu}\tau o\dot{\nu}\varsigma$). That is the point in the parable of the wise builder, "who dug deep and laid a foundation on the rock" (Luke 6:48).

7:25. *"Had been founded"*[17] ($\tau\epsilon\theta\epsilon\mu\epsilon\lambda\dot{\iota}\omega\tau o$). Third person singular past perfect indicative passive state of completion in the past. It had been built upon the rock and it stood. No argument.

7:26. *"And does not act on them"*[18] ($\kappa\alpha\dot{\iota}$ $\mu\dot{\eta}$ $\pi o\iota\hat{\omega}\nu$ $\alpha\dot{\nu}\tau o\dot{\nu}\varsigma$). The foolish builder put his house on sand that could not hold in the storm. One is reminded of the words of Jesus at the beginning of the sermon in 5:19 about the one "who does and teaches." Hearing sermons is a dangerous business if one does not put them into practice.

7:28. *The crowds were amazed at His teaching* ($\dot{\epsilon}\xi\epsilon\pi\lambda\dot{\eta}\sigma\sigma o\nu\tau o$ $o\dot{\iota}$ $\ddot{o}\chi\lambda o\iota$ $\dot{\epsilon}\pi\dot{\iota}$ $\tau\hat{\eta}$ $\delta\iota\delta\alpha\chi\hat{\eta}$ $\alpha\dot{\nu}\tau o\hat{\nu}$). They listened spellbound and were left amazed. Note the imperfect tense, a buzz of astonishment. The verb means literally "were struck out of themselves."

7:29. *And not as their scribes*[19] ($\kappa\alpha\dot{\iota}$ $o\dot{\nu}\chi$ $\dot{\omega}\varsigma$ $o\dot{\iota}$ $\gamma\rho\alpha\mu\mu\alpha\tau\epsilon\hat{\iota}\varsigma$ $\alpha\dot{\nu}\tau\hat{\omega}\nu$).[20] They had heard many sermons before from the rabbis in the synagogues. Specimens of these discourses are preserved in the Mishna and Gemara, the Jewish Talmud. These comprise an amazing collection of dry, dull, disjointed comments covering every conceivable problem in history. The scribes quoted the rabbis before them and were afraid to express an idea without bolstering it up by some predecessor. Jesus spoke with the authority of truth, the reality and freshness of the morning light, and the power of God's Spirit. This sermon, which made such a profound impression, ended with the tragedy of the fall of the house on the sand like the crash of a giant oak in the forest. There was no smoothing over the outcome.

NOTES

1. NIV has "the plank."
2. Quoted in Marvin R. Vincent, *Word Studies in the New Testament*, Vol. 1, *The Synoptic Gospels* (repr. ed., Grand Rapids: Eerdmans, 1946), 49.
3. NIV has "do not give dogs what is sacred."
4. Richard Trench, *Exposition of the Sermon on the Mount drawn from the Writings of St. Augustine*, 4th rev. ed. (London: Kegan Paul, Trench & Co., 1886), 301–2, n 4.
5. NIV has "your pearls to pigs."
6. A passage in which chiasmus helps the interpretation is "Do not give dogs what is sacred; do not throw your pearls to pigs, if you do, they may trample them under their feet and then turn and tear you to pieces" (NIV). The NIV has both the dogs and pigs trampling the sacred things under their feet and attacking the person. The TEV unravels the chiasmus so that only the dogs attack while the pigs trample underfoot.
7. NIV has "bread."
8. A. T. Robertson, *Commentary on the Gospel According to Matthew* (New York: Macmillan, 1911), 115.
9. Alan Hugh McNeile, *The Gospel According to St. Matthew: The Greek Text with Introduction, Notes, and Indices* (repr. ed., Grand Rapids: Baker, 1980), 93.
10. See Didache 1–6; Barnabas 18–20.
11. NIV has "narrow the road" and NASB has "the way is narrow."
12. McNeile, *Matthew*, 94.
13. Vincent, *Word Studies*, 50.
14. NIV has "by their fruit you will recognize them."
15. So reads GNT/NA and WH. TR and Maj.T have προεφητεύσαμεν.
16. NIV has "puts them into practice."
17. NIV has "it had its foundation."
18. NIV has "Does not put them into practice."
19. NIV has "And not as their teachers of the law."
20. TR and Maj.T omit the pronoun αὐτῶν.

■ ■ ■ ■ ■

Matthew: Chapter 8

8:2. *"Lord, if You are willing"* (Κύριε ἐὰν θέλῃς). The leper knew that Jesus had the power to heal him. His doubt was about his willingness. "Men more easily believe in miraculous power than in miraculous love."[1] This is a condition of the third class (undetermined but with a prospect of being determined). The leper had a hopeful doubt. Jesus accepted his challenge with the assurance that "I am willing." The command to "tell no one" was to suppress excitement and prevent hostility.

8:5. *A centurion came to Him* (προσῆλθεν αὐτῷ ἑκατόνταρχος). Dative in spite of the genitive absolute εἰσελθόντος αὐτοῦ[2] as in verse 1, a not infrequent Greek idiom, especially in the Koiné.

8:6. *"Fearfully tormented"*[3] (δεινῶς βασανιζόμενος). Nominative singular masculine present passive participle from the root βάσανος (see on Matt. 4:24). The boy (παῖς), slave (δοῦλος, Luke 7:2), was bedridden (βέβληται, perfect passive indicative of βάλλω), a chronic paralytic.[4]

8:7. *"I will come and heal him"*[5] (Ἐγὼ ἐλθὼν θεραπεύσω αὐτόν). First person singular future active indicative, not a deliberative subjunctive in question.[6] The word here for "heal," θεραπεύσω, means first "to serve with medical attention," then "to cure or restore to health." In verse 8, the centurion uses the more definite word for healing (ἰαθήσεται) as Matthew does in verse 13 (ἰάθη). Luke (9:11), like a physician, says that Jesus healed (ἰᾶτο) those in need of treatment (θεραπείας), but the distinction is not always observed. In Acts 28:8 Luke uses ἰάσατο of the miraculous healings in Malta by Paul. In 28:9 he employs ἐθεραπεύοντο, apparently of the practice of Luke the physician (so William M. Ramsay). Matthew represents the centurion himself as speaking to Jesus, while Luke has it that two committees from the centurion brought the messages, which is apparently a more detailed narrative. What one does through others he does himself, as Pilate "scourged Jesus" by ordering that He be scourged.

8:9. *"For I also am a man under authority"*[7] (καὶ γὰρ ἐγὼ ἄνθρωπός εἰμι ὑπὸ ἐξουσίαν). "Also" is in the text, though καί here can mean "even." If that is the intent, the sense would be, "Even I in my subordinate position have

78

soldiers under me." As a military man, he had learned obedience to his superiors and so expected instant obedience to his commands (aorist imperatives and aoristic present indicatives). Hence his faith in Christ's authority over the illness of the boy caused him to assume that Jesus had only to say the word, and it would be done.

8:10. *"Such great faith"* ($\tau o \sigma a \acute{u} \tau \eta \nu$ $\pi \acute{\iota} \sigma \tau \iota \nu$). The belief shown by a Roman centurion was greater than the faith shown by any of the Jews. In like manner, Jesus expressed surprise at the great faith shown by the Canaanite woman (see on 15:22–28).

8:11. *"Recline at the table"*[8] ($\dot{a}\nu a \kappa \lambda \iota \theta \acute{\eta} \sigma o \nu \tau a \iota$), recline at table on couches as Jews and Romans did. Hence Leonardo da Vinci's famous picture of the Last Supper is an anachronism, with all seated in chairs.

8:12. *"But the sons of the kingdom"*[9] ($o \grave{\iota}$ $\delta \grave{\epsilon}$ $u \grave{\iota} o \grave{\iota}$ $\tau \hat{\eta} s$ $\beta a \sigma \iota \lambda \epsilon \acute{\iota} a s$), a favorite Hebrew idiom similar to "a son of hell" (23:15) and "sons of this age" (Luke 16:8). The Jews felt that they had a right to the privileges of the kingdom because of their descent from Abraham. But mere natural birth did not bring spiritual sonship, as John the Baptist had taught (Matt. 3:9).

"Into the outer darkness"[10] ($\epsilon \grave{\iota} s$ $\tau \grave{o}$ $\sigma \kappa \acute{o} \tau o s$ $\tau \grave{o}$ $\dot{\epsilon} \xi \acute{\omega} \tau \epsilon \rho o \nu$). A comparative adjective like "farther out." Reference is to the darkness outside the limits of the lighted palace, a metaphor for hell or punishment (25:30). The repeated article makes it bolder and more impressive, "the darkness the outside," there where the wailing and gnashing of teeth is heard in the thick blackness of night.

8:14. *Lying sick in bed with a fever*[11] ($\beta \epsilon \beta \lambda \eta \mu \acute{\epsilon} \nu \eta \nu$ $\kappa a \grave{\iota}$ $\pi \upsilon \rho \acute{\epsilon} \sigma \sigma o \upsilon \sigma a \nu$), two participles, "bedridden" (accusative singular feminine perfect passive of $\beta \acute{a} \lambda \lambda \omega$) and "burning with fever" (accusative singular feminine present active). We are not told how long she burned with the fever, but it may have been sudden and must have been severe (Mark 1:30), since they tell Jesus about her as he reaches the house of Peter. Fever itself was considered a disease. "Fever" is from German *feurer* (fire) like the Greek $\pi \hat{\upsilon} \rho$.

8:15. *He touched her hand* ($\mathring{\eta} \psi a \tau o$ $\tau \hat{\eta} s$ $\chi \epsilon \iota \rho \grave{o} s$ $a \mathring{\upsilon} \tau \hat{\eta}$), in loving sympathy as the Great Physician.

Waited on Him[12] ($\delta \iota \eta \kappa \acute{o} \nu \epsilon \iota$ $a \mathring{\upsilon} \tau \hat{\wp}$).[13] She "began to minister" (conative or inceptive imperfect) at once to Jesus in gratitude and love.

8:16. *When evening came* ('O$\psi \acute{\iota} a s$ $\delta \grave{\epsilon}$ $\gamma \epsilon \nu o \mu \acute{\epsilon} \nu \eta s$), a genitive absolute. Matthew draws a beautiful sunset scene at the close of the Sabbath day, as does Mark 1:32. Crowds came to Jesus as he stood in the door of Peter's house (Matt. 8:16; see also Mark 1:33). All the city gathered there with "all those who had it bad" (see on Matt. 4:24), and he healed them "with a word" (λόγῳ). It was a never-to-be-forgotten memory for those who saw it.

8:17. *"He Himself took our infirmities and carried away our diseases"*[14] (Αὐτὸς τὰς ἀσθενείας ἡμῶν ἔλαβεν καὶ τὰς νόσους ἐβάστασεν), a quotation from Isaiah 53:4. It is not clear in what sense Matthew applies the words in Isaiah, whether in the precise sense of the Hebrew or in an independent manner. Moffatt translates it: "He took away our sicknesses, and bore the burden of our diseases." Goodspeed puts it: "He took our sickness and carried away our diseases." Deissmann thinks that Matthew has made a free interpretation of the Hebrew, has discarded the translation of the LXX, and has transposed the two Hebrew verbs. In such a case, Matthew means: "He took upon himself our pains, and bore our diseases."[15] Alfred Plummer holds that "It is impossible, and also unnecessary, to understand what the Evangelist understood by 'took' (ἔλαβεν) and 'bare' (ἐβάστασεν). It at least must mean that Christ removed their sufferings from the sufferers. He can hardly have meant that the diseases were transferred to Christ."[16] Βαστάζω occurs freely in the papyri with the sense of lift, carry, endure, carry away (the commonest meaning).[17] In Matthew 3:11 we have the common vernacular use "to take off sandals." The Attic Greek did not use it in the sense of carrying off. "This passage is the cornerstone of the faith-cure theory (health and wealth gospel), which claims that the atonement of Christ includes provision for *bodily* no less than for spiritual healing, and therefore insists on translating 'took away.'"[18] We have seen that the word βαστάζω will possibly allow that meaning, but I agree with McNeile: "The passage, as Matthew employs it, has no bearing on the doctrine of the atonement." But Jesus does show his sympathy for us. "Christ's sympathy with the sufferers was so intense that he really felt their weaknesses and pains."[19] In our burdens Jesus steps under the load with us and helps us to carry on.

8:19. *A scribe* (εἷς γραμματεύς). One (εἷς) = "a," indefinite article. Already a disciple as shown by "another of the disciples" (ἕτερος δὲ τῶν μαθητῶν [αὐτοῦ]) in 8:21. He calls Jesus "Teacher" (διδάσκαλε), but he seems to be a "bumptious" brother, full of self-confidence and self-complacency. "Even one of that most unimpressionable class, in spirit and tendency utterly opposed to the ways of Jesus."[20] Yet Jesus deals gently with him.

8:20. *"The foxes have holes"* (Αἱ ἀλώπεκες φωλεοὺς ἔχουσιν), a lurking hole, burrow.

"The birds of the air have nests" (τὰ πετεινὰ τοῦ οὐρανοῦ κατασκηνώσεις). "Roosts, i.e. leafy, σκηναί for settling at night (*tabernacula, habitacula*), not nests."[21] The verb (κατασκηνόω) is in LXX Psalm 103:12 (104:12) of birds.

"The Son of Man" (ὁ υἱος τοῦ ἀνθρώπου). This remarkable expression, which Jesus often applied to himself, appears here for the first time in Matthew. Much study has been devoted to its nuances of meaning. "It means much for the speaker, who has chosen it deliberately, in connection with private reflections, at whose nature we can only guess, by study of the many occasions on which the name is used."[22] Often it means the "representative man." It may sometimes stand for the Aramaic *barnasha,* "the man," but in most instances this idea will not do. Jesus uses it as a concealed messianic title. It is possible that this scribe would not understand the phrase at all. Bruce thinks that here Jesus means "the unprivileged Man," who is worse off than the foxes and the birds.[23] Jesus spoke Greek as well as Aramaic. It is inconceivable that the Gospels should never call Jesus "the Son of Man" and always credit it to him as his own words if he did not so term himself. The term is used in the Gospels about eighty times, thirty-three in Matthew. Jesus in his early ministry, except at the very start in John 4, abstains from calling himself Messiah. This term suited his purpose exactly to get the people used to his special claim as Messiah when he is ready to make it openly.

8:21. *"Lord, permit me first to go and bury my father"*[24] (Κύριε, ἐπίτρεψόν μοι πρῶτον ἀπελθεῖν καὶ θάψαι τὸν πατέρα μου). The first man was an enthusiast. This one is overcautious. It is by no means certain that the father was dead. Tobit urged his son Tobias to be sure to bury him: "Son, when I am dead, bury me."[25] The probability is that this disciple means that, after his father is dead and buried, he will then be free to follow Jesus. "At the present day, an Oriental, with his father sitting by his side, has been known to say respecting his future projects: 'But I must first bury my father!'"[26] Jesus wanted first things first. Even if the man's father was not actually dead, service to Christ comes first.

8:22. *"Allow the dead to bury their own dead"*[27] (ἄφες τοὺς νεκροὺς θάψαι τοὺς ἑαυτῶν νεκρούς). The spiritually dead are always on hand to bury the physically dead, if one's real duty is with Jesus. Chrysostom says that, while it is a good deed to bury the dead, it is a better one to preach Christ.[28]

8:24. *But Jesus Himself was asleep*[29] (αὐτὸς δὲ ἐκάθευδεν), third person singular imperfect active indicative, was sleeping, a picturesque scene. The Sea of Galilee is 680 feet below the Mediterranean Sea. These sudden squalls come down from the summit of Hermon with terrific force (σεισμὸς μέγας) like an earthquake. Mark 4:37 and Luke 8:23 call it a "whirlwind" (λαῖλαψ) in furious gusts.

8:25. *"Save [us], Lord; we are perishing"*[30] (Κύριε, σῶσον, ἀπολλύμεθα).[31]

More precisely, "Lord, save us at once (aorist); we are perishing (present linear)."

8:27. *"Even the winds and the sea obey Him"*[32] (καὶ οἱ ἄνεμοι καὶ ἡ θάλασσα αὐτῷ ὑπακούουσιν). A nature miracle. Even a sudden drop in the wind would not at once calm the sea. "J. Weiss explains that by 'an astonishing coincidence' the storm happened to lull at the moment that Jesus spoke!"[33] Some minds are easily satisfied by their own stupidities.

8:28. *The country of the Gadarenes*[34] (τὴν χώραν τῶν Γαδαρηνῶν).[35] This is the correct text in Matthew, while in Mark 5:1 and Luke 8:26 it is "country of the Gerasenes." Dr. Thompson discovered by the lake the ruins of Khersa (Gerasa). This village is in the district of the city of Gadara some miles southeastward so that it can be called after Gerasa or Gadara.[36] So Matthew speaks of "two demoniacs," while Mark and Luke mention only the leading one.

The tombs (τῶν μνημείων) were chambers cut into the mountainside. On the eastern side of the lake the precipitous cliffs are of limestone formation and full of caves. It is one of the proofs that one is a maniac that he haunts the tombs. People shunned the region as dangerous because of the madmen.

8:29. *"Son of God"* (υἱὲ τοῦ θεοῦ). The recognition of Jesus by the demons is surprising. The whole subject of demonology is difficult. Some hold that it is merely the ancient way of describing disease. But that does not explain such situations as this. Jesus is described as treating the demons as real beings. He separates their existence from that of the human personality. Missionaries have sometimes claimed to have seen demons cast out. The Devil knew Jesus clearly and it is not strange that Jesus was recognized by the Devil's agents. They know that there is nothing in common between them and the Son of God (ἡμῖν καὶ σοί, ethical dative) and they fear torment "before the time"[37] (πρὸ καιροῦ). Usually τὰ δαιμόνια is the word in the New Testament for demons, but in verse 31 we have οἱ δαίμονες, the only example of this precise term in the New Testament. Δαιμόνιον is a diminutive of δαίμων. In Homer, δαίμων is used synonymously with θεός and θεά. Hesiod employed δαίμων of men of the golden age as tutelary deities. Homer has the adjective δαιμόνιος usually in an evil sense. Empedocles considered the demons both bad and good. They were thus used to relieve the gods and goddesses of much rascality. George Grote notes that the Christians were thus by pagan usage justified in calling idolatry the worship of demons[38] (See 1 Cor. 10:20–21; 1 Tim. 4:1; Rev. 9:20; 16:13–14). In the Gospels, demons are equated with unclean spirits (Mark 3:22, 30; 5:12, 15; Luke 4:33). The demons are disturbers of the whole life of man (Vincent; Matt. 12:45; Mark 5:2–5; 7:25; Luke 13:11, 16).

8:32. *The whole herd rushed down the steep bank* (ὥρμησεν πᾶσα ἡ ἀγέλη κατὰ τοῦ κρημνοῦ), down from the cliff (ablative case) into the sea, a constative aorist. The influence of mind on matter is now understood better than formerly, but we have the mastery of the mind of the Master on the minds of the maniacs, the power of Christ over the demons, over the herd of hogs. Difficulties in plenty exist for those who see only folklore and legend, but it is plain enough if we take Jesus to be true Lord and Savior. The incidental destruction of the hogs need not trouble us when we are so familiar with nature's tragedies which we cannot comprehend.

8:34. *They implored Him to leave their region*[39] (παρεκάλεσαν ὅπως μεταβῇ ἀπὸ τῶν ὁρίων αὐτῶν). The whole city was excited over the destruction of the hogs and begged Jesus to leave. They forgot the healing of the demoniacs in their concern over the loss of property. They cared more for hogs than for human souls.

NOTES

1. Alexander Balmain Bruce, *The Expositor's Greek Testament*, Vol. 1, *The Synoptic Gospels* (Grand Rapids: Eerdmans, 1951), 137).

2. TR and Maj.T have a dative absolute Εἰσελθόντι αὐτῷ here rather than the genitive absolute.

3. NIV has "in terrible suffering."

4. A. T. Robertson, *Commentary on the Gospel According to Matthew* (New York: Macmillan, 1911), 121.

5. NIV has "I will go and heal him."

6. Alan Hugh McNeile, *The Gospel According to St. Matthew: The Greek Text with Introduction, Notes, and Indices* (repr. ed., Grand Rapids: Baker, 1980), 104.

7. NIV has "For I myself am a man under authority."

8. NIV has "Take their places."

9. NIV has "But the subjects of the kingdom."

10. NIV has "into the darkness."

11. NIV has "lying in bed with a fever."

12. NIV has "began to wait on him."

13. TR has αὐτοῖς rather than the singular form.

14. NIV has "He took up our infirmities and carried our diseases."

15. Deissmann, *Bible Studies*, 192f.

16. Alfred Plummer, *An Exegetical Commentary on the Gospel According to Saint Matthew* (repr. ed., Grand Rapids: Eerdmans, 1956), 128.

17. James Hope Moulton and George Milligan, *The Vocabulary of the Greek Testament* (London: Hodder & Stoughton, 1952), 106.

18. Marvin R. Vincent, *Word Studies in the New Testament*, Vol. 1, *The Synoptic Gospels* (repr. ed., Grand Rapids: Eerdmans, 1946), 53.

19. McNeile, *Matthew*, 108.

20. Bruce, *Expositor's*, 142.

21. McNeile, *Matthew*, 109.

22. Bruce, *Expositor's*, 142.

23. Ibid.

24. NIV has "Lord, first let me go and bury my father."

25. Tobit 4:3.

26. Plummer, *Matthew*, 130, n 1.

27. NIV has "Let the dead bury their own dead."

28. *The Nicene and Post-Nicene Fathers*, Vol. 10, "The Works of St. Chrysostom," Homily 27 (New York: Christian Literature Company, 1894), 188.

29. NIV has "Jesus was sleeping." The proper noun Ἰησοῦς is not found in the Greek text, but the pronoun Αὐτός is, which clearly refers to Jesus.

30. NIV has "Lord, save us! We are going to drown."

31. TR and Maj.T include the pronoun, "Save us," (σῶσον ἡμῶν), whereas GNT/NA and WH do not include the pronoun.

32. NIV has "Even the winds and the waves obey him!"

33. McNeile, *Matthew*, 111.

34. NIV has "The region of the Gadarenes."

35. GNT/NA and WH have Γαδαρηνῶν, whereas TR and Maj.T have Γεργεσηνῶν.

36. William M. Thompson, *The Land and the Book* (Grand Rapids: Baker, 1954), 375.

37. NIV has "before the appointed time."

38. George Grote, *History of Greece* (New York: American Book Exchange, 1881), 255–56.

39. NIV has "They pleaded with him to leave their region."

Matthew: Chapter 9

9:1. *[Jesus] came to His own city*[1] (ἦλθεν εἰς τὴν ἰδίαν πόλιν). Capernaum has become the home of Jesus[2] (4:13; Mark 2:1).

9:2. *They brought to Him a paralytic*[3] (προσέφερον αὐτῷ παραλυτικόν). The imperfect "were bringing" sets a graphic scene. Details in Mark 2:1–4 and Luke 5:17 make it even more vivid.

Lying on a bed[4] (ἐπὶ κλίνης βεβλημένον). Stretched on a couch, an accusative singular masculine perfect passive participle. Κλινίδιον refers to a little bed or couch in Luke 5:19; it is "a pallet" (κράβαττος) in Mark 2:4, 9, 11.

"Your sins are forgiven" (ἀφίενταί[5] σου αἱ ἁμαρτίαι). Third person singular present passive indicative (aoristic present). Luke (5:21) has ἀφεῖναι, Doric and Ionic perfect passive indicative for the Attic ἀφεῖνται, one of the dialectical forms appearing in the Κοινή.

9:3. *"This fellow blasphemes"*[6] (Οὗτος βλασφημεῖ). Notice the sneer indicated by "this fellow." "The prophet always is a scandalous, irreverent blasphemer from the conventional point of view."[7]

9:6. *"So that you may know"* (ἵνα δὲ εἰδῆτε). Jesus accepts the challenge in the thoughts of the scribes and performs the miracle of healing the paralytic, who so far only had his sins forgiven. Physical healing became a sign to prove his messianic power on earth to forgive sins even as God does. The word ἐξουσία may mean either power or authority. He had both as a matter of fact. Note the same word in 9:8.

Then He said to the paralytic (τότε λέγει τῷ παραλυτικῷ). These words, of course, were not spoken by Jesus. Curiously Matthew interjects them right in the midst of the sayings of Jesus in reply to the scorn of the scribes. Still more remarkable is the fact that Mark (2:10) has precisely the same words in the same place, save that Matthew adds τότε, of which he is fond. Mark, as we know, largely reports Peter's words and sees with Peter's eyes. Luke (5:24) has the same idea in the same place without the vivid historical present λέγει (εἶπεν παραλελυμένῳ) with the participle in place of the adjective. This is one of the many proofs that both Matthew and Luke use Mark's Gospel.

85

"Pick up your bed"[8] (ἆρόν σου τὴν κλίνην). Pack up at once (second person singular aorist active imperative) the rolled-up pallet.

9:9. *He saw a man . . . sitting in the tax collector's booth*[9] (εἶδεν ἄνθρωπον καθήμενον ἐπὶ τὸ τελώνιον). The tax office or customhouse of Capernaum collected taxes from the boats going across the lake outside of Herod's territory or from people going from Damascus to the coast. This was a caravan route.

Called Matthew[10] (Μαθθαῖον λεγόμενον). Here and in 10:3, Matthew is named as one of the twelve apostles. He had two names, as was common. Mark 2:14 and Luke 5:27 call him Levi. The publicans (τελῶναι) get their name in English from the Latin *publicanus* (a man who did public duty). It was not a very accurate designation. They were detested because they practiced graft. Even Gabinius, the proconsul of Syria, was accused by Cicero of stealing legitimate tax money from Syrians and Jews. Already Jesus had spoken of the publican (5:46) in a way that shows the public disfavor in which they were held.

9:10. *Many tax collectors and sinners*[11] (πολλοὶ τελῶναι καὶ ἁμαρτωλοί), often coupled together in common scorn and in contrast with the righteous (δίκαιοι in 9:13). It was a strange medley at Levi's feast—Jesus and the four fisher disciples along with Nathanael and Philip; Matthew Levi and his former companions, publicans and sinners. Pharisees with their scribes or students were onlookers, along with disciples of John the Baptist who were fasting at the very time Jesus was feasting with this crowd. The Pharisees criticize sharply "your Teacher" for such a social breach of "reclining" together with publicans at Levi's feast.

9:12. *"But those who are sick"*[12] (ἀλλ'[13] οἱ κακῶς ἔχοντες). Probably a current proverb about the physician. As a physician of body and soul, Jesus was bound to come in close touch with the social outcasts.

9:13. *"But go and learn"* (πορευθέντες δὲ μάθετε). With biting sarcasm Jesus bids these preachers to learn the meaning of Hosea 6:6. It is repeated in Matthew 12:7. Second person plural ingressive aorist active imperative (μάθετε).

9:14. *The disciples of John*[14] (οἱ μαθηταὶ Ἰωάννου[15]). One is surprised to find disciples of the Baptist in the role of critics of Christ along with the Pharisees. But John was languishing in prison, and they perhaps blamed Jesus for doing nothing about it. John would not have gone to Levi's feast on a Jewish fast day. "The strict asceticism of the Baptist (11:18) and of the Pharisaic rabbis (Luke 18:12) was imitated by their disciples."[16]

9:15. *"The attendants of the bridegroom"*[17] (οἱ υἱοὶ τοῦ νυμφῶνος). It is a late Hebrew idiom for the wedding guests, "the friends of the bridegroom and all the sons of the bridechamber"[18] (cf. John 2:29).

9:16. *"Unshrunk cloth"* (ῥάκους ἀγνάφου), an unfulled, raw piece of woollen cloth that will shrink when wet and tear a hole bigger than the damage it was to repair. Thus, "a worse tear results"[19] (χεῖρον σχίσμα γίνεται). Compare with the English word *schism*. The "filling up" patch (τὸ πλήρωμα) thus does more harm than good.

9:17. *"Old wineskins"* (ἀσκους παλαιούς), goatskins with the rough part inside. "Our word *bottle* originally carried the true meaning, being a bottle of leather. In Spanish *bota* means a leather bottle, a boot, and a butt. In Spain wine is still brought to market in pig-skins."[20] The new wine will ferment and crack the dried-up old skins. "The wine pours out"[21] (ὁ οἶνος ἐχεῖται).

9:18. *"My daughter has just died"* (Ἡ θυγάτηρ μου ἄρτι ἐτελεύτησεν), aorist tense with ἄρτι and so better, "just now died," "just dead" (Moffatt). Mark 5:23 has it, "at the point of death," Luke (8:42) "was dying." It is not always easy even for physicians to tell when death has come. Jesus in 9:24 pointedly said, "The girl has not died, but is asleep," meaning that she did not die to stay dead.

9:20. *[She] touched the fringe of His cloak*[22] (ἥψατο τοῦ κρασπέδου τοῦ ἱματίου αὐτοῦ), the hem or fringe of a garment, a tassel or tuft hanging from the edge of the outer garment according to Numbers 15:38. It was made of twisted wool. Jesus wore the common outer garment of the day, with these fringes at the four corners. The Jews actually counted the words *Yahweh One* from the numbers of the twisted white threads, a refinement that would not have concerned Jesus. This poor woman had an element of superstition in her faith as many people have, but Jesus honors her faith and cures her.

9:23. *The flute-players* (τοὺς αὐλητάς). The girl had just died, but already "a crowd in noisy disorder"[23] (τὸν ὄχλον θορυβούμενον) had gathered in the outer court with wild wailing and screaming. Such mourners were "brought together by various motives, sympathy, money, desire to share in the meat and drink going at such a time."[24] Besides the several flute players (voluntary or hired), there probably were "some hired mourning women (Jer. 9:17) *praeficae*, whose duty it was to sing *naenia* in praise of the dead."[25] These, when put out by Jesus, began laughing at him[26] (κατεγέλων αὐτοῦ), in a loud and repeated (imperfect) guffaw of scorn. Jesus overcame this repellent environment.

9:27. *As Jesus went on from there* (παράγοντι ἐκεῖθεν τῷ Ἰησοῦ), associative instrumental case with ἠκολούθησαν. It was the supreme opportunity of the two blind men. Note two demoniacs in 8:28 and two blind men in 20:30. See the same word παράλων used of Jesus in 9:9.

9:29. *He touched their eyes* (ἥψατο τῶν ὀφθαλμῶν αὐτῶν). The men had faith (9:28) and Jesus rewards their faith, yet he touched their eyes as he sometimes did with kindly sympathy.

9:30. *Their eyes were opened.*[27] *And Jesus sternly warned them*[28] (ἠνεώχθησαν[29] αὐτῶν οἱ ὀφθαλμοί. Καὶ ἐνεβριμήθη αὐτοῖς ὁ Ἰησοῦς). Ἐνεβριμήθη is a difficult word, a compound of ἐν and βριμάομαι (to be moved with anger). It is used of horses snorting,[30] of men fretting or angry (Dan. 11:30). It is found only here in Matthew.[31] It occurs twice in Mark (1:43; 14:5) when Matthew omits it. John 11:33 has it. Here it has the notion of commanding sternly, a sense unknown to ancient writers. Most manuscripts have the middle ἐνεβριμήσατο,[32] but Aleph and B have the passive ἐνεβριμήθη, which WH accepts, but without the passive sense (cf. ἀπεκρίθη). "The word describes rather a rush of deep feeling which in the synoptic passages showed itself in a vehement injunctive and in John 11:33 in look and manner."[33] Bruce translates Euthymius Zigabenus on Mark 1:32: "Looked severely, contracting His eyebrows, and shaking His head at them as they are wont to do who wish to make sure that secrets will be kept."[34]

"See that no one knows about this" (Ὁρᾶτε μηδεὶς γινωσκέτω). Note elliptical change of persons and number in the two imperatives.

9:32. *A mute . . . man* (ἄνθρωπον κωφόν),[35] literally blunted in tongue as here and so dumb, in ear as in Matthew 11:5 and so deaf. Homer used it of a blunted dart.[36] Others applied it to mental dullness.

9:34. *"By the ruler of the demons"*[37] (Ἐν τῷ ἄρχοντι τῶν δαιμονίων), demons, not devils. The codex Bezae omits this verse, but it is probably genuine. The Pharisees are becoming desperate. Unable to deny the reality of the miracles, they seek to discredit them by trying to connect Jesus with the Devil himself, the prince of the demons. They will renew this charge later (12:24) when Jesus will refute it with biting sarcasm.

9:35. *Jesus was going through*[38] (καὶ περιῆγεν ὁ Ἰησοῦς), an imperfect tense descriptive of this third tour of all Galilee.

9:36. *They were distressed and dispirited*[39] (ἦσαν ἐσκυλμένοι[40] καὶ ἐρριμμένοι), periphrastic past perfect with imperfecdt indicative. It was a sad and pitiful state the crowds were in, rent or mangled as if by wild beasts. Σκύλλω occurs in the papyri in the sense of "plunder, concern, vexation." "Used here of the common people, it describes their religious condition. They were harassed, importuned, bewildered by those who should have taught them; hindered from entering into the kingdom of heaven (23:13), laden with the burdens which the Pharisees laid upon them (v. 3). Ἐρριμμένοι denotes men cast down and prostrate on the ground, whether from drunkenness,[41] or from mortal wounds."[42] This perfect passive participle is from ῥίπτω, to throw down. The masses were in a state of mental dejection that moved Jesus with compassion (ἐσπλαγχνίσθη).

9:38. *"To send out workers"* (ὅπως ἐκβάλῃ ἐργάτας). Jesus turns from the figure of the shepherdless sheep to the harvest field ripe and ready for the reapers. The verb ἐκβάλλω really means to drive out, to push out, to draw out with violence or without. Prayer is the remedy offered by Jesus in this crisis of the lack of teachers. How seldom do we hear prayers for more preachers.

NOTES

1. NIV has "Jesus came to his own town." The proper noun Ἰησοῦς is not found in the Greek text, however, the subject obviously refers to Jesus.
2. A. T. Robertson, *Commentary on the Gospel According to Matthew* (New York: Macmillan, 1911), 130.
3. NIV has "Some men brought to him a paralytic."
4. NIV has "lying on a mat."
5. TR and Maj.T have ἀφέωνται, 3 pers. pl. perf. pass. indic.
6. NIV has "This fellow is blaspheming."
7. Bruce, *Expositor's,* 149.
8. NIV has "Take your mat."
9. NIV has "He saw a man . . . sitting at the tax collector's booth."
10. NIV has "named Matthew." GNT/NA and WH spell it in the Greek with a double theta (θθ), whereas TR and Maj.T have Ματθαῖον.
11. NIV has quotes around "sinners."
12. NIV has "But the sick."
13. GNT/NA, Maj.T, and TR have ἀλλ᾽, whereas WH has ἀλλά.
14. NIV has "John's disciples."
15. Only WH spell "John" with one ν, (Ἰωάνου).
16. Alan Hugh McNeile, *The Gospel According to St. Matthew: The Greek Text with Introduction, Notes, and Indices* (repr. ed., Grand Rapids: Baker, 1980), 120.
17. NIV has "The guests of the bridegroom."
18. *Tos. Berak. ii.10.*
19. NIV has "making the tear worse."
20. Marvin R. Vincent, *Word Studies in the New Testament*, Vol. 1, *The Synoptic Gospels* (repr. ed., Grand Rapids: Eerdmans, 1946), 55.

21. NIV has "the wine will run out."
22. NIV has "[She] touched the edge of his cloak."
23. NIV has "the noisy crowd."
24. Bruce, *Expositor's*, 127.
25. Ibid.
26. NIV has "laughed at him."
27. NIV has "their sight was restored."
28. TR and Maj.T have the spelling $\dot{\alpha}\nu\epsilon\dot{\omega}\chi\theta\eta\sigma\alpha\nu$.
29. NIV has "warned them sternly."
30. Aeschylus, *Theb.* 461.
31. McNeile, *Matthew*, 97.
32. Including TR and Maj.T.
33. McNeile, *Matthew*, 127.
34. Bruce, *Expositor's*, 1.155.
35. NIV has "man who . . . could not talk." WH do not include $\ddot{\alpha}\nu\theta\rho\omega\pi\sigma\nu$.
36. *Iliad* 11.390.
37. NIV has "by the prince of demons."
38. NIV has "Jesus went through."
39. NIV has "They were harassed and helpless."
40. TR has $\dot{\epsilon}\kappa\lambda\epsilon\lambda\nu\mu\dot{\epsilon}\nu\sigma\iota$.
41. Polybius, 5.48.2.
42. Willoughby G. Allen, *A Critical and Exegetical Commentary on the Gospel According to Matthew*, International Critical Commentary (Edinburgh: T. & T. Clark, 1912), 99.

Matthew: Chapter 10

10:1. *His twelve disciples* (τοὺς δώδεκα μαθητὰς αὐτοῦ). At Matthew's first mention of the group of "learners," he uses the article to show that the group already is established (see on Mark 3:14–17). They were chosen before the Sermon on the Mount, but Matthew did not mention it. Mark (3:13–19) and Luke (6:12–16) state that Jesus chose or appointed them after a night of prayer and came down with them to deliver His Sermon on the Mount (Luke 6:17).

Gave them authority (ἔδωκεν αὐτοῖς ἐξουσίαν). "Power" (Moffatt, Goodspeed). One may be surprised that here only the healing work is mentioned, though Luke (9:2) has it "to proclaim the kingdom of God and to perform healing." And Matthew says (10:7), "and as you go, preach." Hence it is not fair to say that Matthew knows only the charge to heal the sick, important as that was as a sign that Jesus was Christ. The physical distress was great, but the spiritual even greater. Power is more likely the idea of ἐξουσία here. The healing ministry attracted attention and did much good. Today we have hospitals and skilled physicians and nurses, but we should not deny the power of God to bless these agencies and to cure disease as He wills. Jesus is still Master of soul and body, but intelligent faith does not abstain from seeking the help of qualified physicians.

10:2. *The names of the twelve apostles* (τῶν δὲ δώδεκα ἀποστόλων τὰ ὀνόματά). Apostleship is the disciples' official function, corresponding to their work as missionaries. Simon's name always appears first on the lists, including the list of those gathered in the upper room in Acts 1:13. He was foremost until the beginning of the church at Pentecost (Acts 2–3). Judas Iscariot comes last each time until his death is reported in Acts 1:15–18 and he is replaced (vv. 20–26). Matthew calls him the betrayer (ὁ παραδούς). *Iscariot* usually is thought to mean "man of Kerioth," referring to a town near Edom referred to in Joshua 15:25. Philip comes fifth and James son of Alphaeus ninth. *Bartholomew* is another name for Nathanael. *Thaddaeus* is another name for Judas the brother of James. Simon Zelotes also is called Simon the Canaanean (*zealot* is from a Hebrew word). This is apparently their first preaching and

91

healing tour without Jesus. He sends them by twos (Mark 6:7). Matthew names them in pairs, probably as they were sent out.

10:5. *These twelve Jesus sent out* (Τούτους τοὺς δώδεκα ἀπέστειλεν ὁ Ἰησοῦς). The word for "sent out," ἀπέστειλεν, comes from the same root as that for "apostles." This word reappears in verse 16.

"Way of the Gentiles"[1] (ὁδὸν ἐθνῶν), objective genitive, way leading to the Gentiles. This prohibition against going among the Gentiles and Samaritans applied only to this initial venture. They were to give the Jews first opportunity and not get involved with interracial tensions that might prejudice their cause at this stage. Later Jesus sent them to disciple all the Gentiles (28:19).

10:6. *"The lost sheep of the house of Israel"* (τὰ πρόβατα τὰ ἀπολωλότα οἴκου Ἰσραήλ), the sheep, the lost ones, mentioned here first by Matthew. Jesus expresses pity, not blame.[2] John Bengel notes that Jesus says "lost" more frequently than "led astray."[3] "If the Jewish nation could be brought to repentance the new age would dawn."[4]

10:7. *"As you go, preach"* (πορευόμενοι κηρύσσετε), present participle and present imperative. They were itinerant preachers—"heralds" (κῆρυξ) proclaiming good news. The summary message is that of the Baptist (3:2), which had so startled the country: "The kingdom of heaven is at hand." That sermon had echoed up and down the Jordan Valley. Now they are to shake Galilee with it, as Jesus had (4:17).[5]

10:9. *"Do not acquire gold"*[6] (Μὴ κτήσησθε χρυσόν). It is not, "Do not possess" or "own," but "do not procure" for yourselves, second person plural indirect middle aorist subjunctive. Gold, silver, brass (copper) are given in a descending scale of value, which also covers the most insignificant metal, bronze.

"For your money belts"[7] (εἰς τὰς ζώνας ὑμῶν). In your girdles or belts used for carrying money.

10:10. *"No bag"* (μὴ πήραν). This can mean a traveling bag of possessions or a place for travelers to keep bread. Deissman finds that πήρα refers to a beggar's collecting bag in an inscription on a monument at Kefr Hanar in Syria: "While Christianity was still young the beggar priest was making his rounds in the land of Syria on behalf of the national goddess."[8] Deissman also quotes a pun in the Διδασκαλία[9] about some itinerant widows who said that they were not so much χῆραι (spouseless) as πῆραι (pouchless). He cites also Shakespeare[10] "Time hath, my lord, a wallet at his back, wherein he puts alms for oblivion."[11]

"For the worker is worthy of his support"[12] (ἄξιος γὰρ ὁ ἐργάτης τῆς τροφῆς αὐτοῦ).[13] Luke quotes the same words in recording Jesus' charge to

the seventy (Luke 10:7), only with the term meaning "reward," μισθοῦ, instead of "food," τροφῆς. In 1 Timothy 5:18, Paul quotes Luke's form as Scripture (ἡ γραφή) or a commonplace saying. The word for "workman," ἐργάτης is used by Jesus when he tells his followers to pray for laborers (Matt. 9:38). The patristic writing *Didache* shows that in the second century, leaders still were careful about receiving pay for preaching. Traveling sophists also threw the work of itinerant teachers into disrepute.[14] The wisdom of these restrictions was justified in Galilee at this time. Mark 6:6–13 and Luke 9:1–6 vary slightly from Matthew in some details of the instructions of Jesus.

10:13. *"If the house is worthy"*[15] (ἐὰν μὲν ᾖ ἡ οἰκία ἀξία), a third class condition. What makes a house worthy? "It would naturally be readiness to receive the preachers and their message."[16]

10:14. *"Shake the dust off"* (ἐκτινάξατε τὸν κονιορτόν). "Shake out," a vigorous gesture of disfavor. The Jews had violent prejudices against the smallest particles of Gentile dust. The issue was not that there were germs in the dust. Such things were not known. Rather, the Jews regarded anything associated with the Gentiles as contaminated with the putrescence of death. If the apostles were mistreated, they were to treat the merciless householders as if they were Gentiles (cf. 18:17; Acts 18:6). Again the instruction was for this tour, with its peculiar perils.

10:15. *"More tolerable"*[17] (ἀνεκτότερον). The papyri use this adjective of a convalescent. In the rural United States, people once described themselves as feeling "tolerable," with similar meaning. The Galileans had far more opportunities to hear the truth than had Sodom and Gomorrah.

10:16. *"As sheep in the midst of wolves"*[18] (ὡς πρόβατα ἐν μέσῳ λύκων). The presence of wolves was a fact then and now. Some of these very sheep of Israel (v. 6) would turn out to be wolves crying for Christ's crucifixion. The situation called for wisdom and courage.

"So be shrewd as serpents and innocent as doves" (γίνεσθε οὖν φρόνιμοι ὡς οἱ ὄφες καὶ ἀκέραιοι ὡς αἱ περιστεραί). The serpent symbolized wisdom or shrewd, keen intellect (Gen. 3:1; Ps. 58:5), the dove was a symbol of simplicity (Hos. 7:11). This was a proverb, referring to a difficult combination of virtues to master. Either without the other leads to trouble. The first clause with ἄρνας for πρόβατα is in Luke 10:3.[19] The combination of wariness and innocence is necessary for the protection of the sheep and the discomfiture of the wolves. For "innocent" (ἀκέραιοι) Moffatt and Goodspeed have "guileless." The word means "unmixed (α privative and κεράννυμι), unadulterated, simple, or unalloyed."

10:17. *"Beware of men"*[20] (προσέχετε ἀπὸ τῶν ἀνθρώπων), ablative case with ἀπό: "Hold your mind [noun understood] away from." The article with ἀνθρώπων points back to λύκων (wolves) in verse 16.

"To the courts"[21] (εἰς συνέδρια), the local courts of justice in every Jewish town. The word is used by Herodotus for a deliberative body (*concilium*). It became synonymous with the "Sanhedrin" in Jerusalem.

"In their synagogues" (ἐν ταῖς συναγωγαῖς αὐτῶν). The body rather than the place of worship. Jesus refers to the synagogue as an assembly exercising ecclesiastical discipline. An example is the man born blind who was cast out of the synagogue for defending Jesus (John 9:35). After the Babylonian Exile, synagogues were the centers of community anywhere Jews lived.

10:19. *"Do not worry"* (μὴ μεριμνήσητε), an ingressive aorist subjunctive in prohibition. "Do not become anxious" (6:31). "Self-defence before Jewish kings and heathen governors would be a terrible ordeal for humble Galileans. The injunction applied to cases when preparation of a speech would be impossible."[22] "It might well alarm the bravest of these simple fishermen to be told that they would have to answer for their doings on Christ's behalf before Jewish councils and heathen courts."[23] Christ is not advising pastors that they should not prepare sermons.

"In that hour"[24] (ἐν ἐκείνῃ τῇ ὥρᾳ), if not before. The Spirit of your Father will speak to you and through you (10:20). Here is the difference between *posing* as martyr or courting a martyr's crown and authentic faith in which full loyalty to Christ induces real heroism.

10:22. *"You will be hated"*[25] (ἔσεσθε μισούμενοι), periphrastic future passive, linear action, with a timeless sense. It will go on through the ages.

"Because of My name"[26] (διὰ τὸ ὄνομά μου). In the Old Testament as in the Targums and the Talmud, "the name" as here stands for the person (Matt. 19:29; Acts 5:41; 9:16; 15:26).

"The one who has endured to the end"[27] (ὁ ὑπομείνας εἰς τέλος). This is an effective aorist participle with future indicative following.

10:23. *"Until the Son of Man comes"*[28] (ἕως ἂν ἐλθῇ ὁ υἱὸς τοῦ ἀνθρώπου[29]). Moffatt puts it "before the Son of man arrives," as if Jesus referred to this special tour of Galilee. Jesus could overtake them. Possibly so, but it is by no means clear. Exegetes have connected Jesus' words to the Transfiguration, to the coming of the Holy Spirit at Pentecost, and to the Second Coming. A few have argued that Matthew has put the saying in the wrong context or even that Jesus was mistaken, a very serious charge. Use of ἕως with an aorist subjunctive for a future event is a good Greek idiom.

10:25. *"Beelzebul"*[30] (Βεεζεβουl according to B;[31] Βεελζεβοὺλ[32] by most Greek MSS; *Beelzeboub*[33] by many non-Greek MSS). The etymology of the word is unknown. It is a term of reproach, whether it means "lord of a dwelling" with a pun on "master of the house" (οἰκοδεσπότην) or "lord of flies" or "lord of dung" or "lord of idolatrous sacrifices." It is "an opprobrious epithet; exact form of the word and meaning of the name have given more trouble to commentators than it is all worth"[34] (see on Matt. 12:24).

10:26. *"Therefore do not fear them"*[35] (μὴ οὖν φοβηθῆτε αὐτούς). Repeated in verses 28 and 31 (μὴ φοβεῖσθε present middle imperative here in contrast with an aorist passive subjunctive in the preceding prohibitions). Note also the accusative case with the aorist passive subjunctive, transitive though passive. The same construction is used in Luke 12:5. In Matthew 10:28 the construction is with ἀπό and the ablative, a translation Hebraism found in Luke 12:4.[36]

10:28. *"Destroy both soul and body in hell"* (καὶ ψυχὴν καὶ σῶμα ἀπολέσαι ἐν γεέννῃ). *Soul* here means the eternal spirit, not just life in the body. *Destroy* is not annihilation, but eternal punishment in gehenna, the real hell (see on 5:22). Bruce thinks that the Devil as tempter is here meant, not God as the judge,[37] but his reasoning is unpersuasive. There is a tendency to avoid contemplating the fear of God, and nothing is more important to learn.

10:29. *"Two sparrows"* (δύο στρουθία). The diminutive of στρουθός means any small bird, sparrows in particular.

"For a cent"[38] (ἀσσαρίου), genitive of price, is found only here and Luke 12:6 in the New Testament. It is a diminutive of the Roman monetary denomination the *as*.

"Apart from your Father"[39] (ἄνευ τοῦ πατρὸς ὑμῶν). The Father who knows about sparrows knows and cares about us.

10:31. *"Than many sparrows"* (πολλῶν στρουθίων), ablative case of comparison with διαφέρετε.

10:32. *"Who confesses Me,*[40] . . . *I will also confess him"*[41] (ὅστις ὁμολογήσει ἐν ἐμοὶ . . . ὁμολογήσω κἀγὼ ἐν αὐτῷ). This is an Aramaic idiom, not Hebrew (see also Luke 12:8). Literally this Aramaic idiom reproduced in the Greek means "confess in me," indicating a sense of unity with Christ and of Christ with the man who takes the open stand for him.

10:33. *"Whoever denies Me"*[42] (ὅστις δ᾽ ἂν ἀρνήσηταί με), a third person singular aorist middle subjunctive here with ὅστις, though a third person singular future active indicative ὁμολογήσει above. Note the accusative as the case of extension. Saying no to Christ leads to a complete breach. This cleavage by Christ of one who repudiates him is a solemn law, not a mere social disconnection. It is public and final.

10:34. *"I did not come to bring peace, but a sword"* (οὐκ ἦλθον βαλεῖν εἰρήνην ἀλλὰ μάχαιραν). This is a bold and dramatic climax. The aorist infinitive means a sudden hurling of the sword where peace was expected. Christ does bring peace, but not as the world gives, for his peace comes in conquest over enmity, not through compromise with evil. This is the triumph of the cross over Satan. Meanwhile, Christ's cause inevitably means division in families, in communities, in states. It is no namby-pamby sentimentalism that Christ preaches, no peace at any price. The cross of Christ is the answer to the Devil's offer of compromise in world dominion. For Christ the kingdom of God is virile righteousness, not mere emotionalism.

10:35. *"To set"*[43] (διχάσαι), literally divide in two, δίχα. Jesus uses Micah 7:1–6 to describe the same rottenness of the age that Micah had condemned. Family and social ties forged in this context cannot bar the way to loyalty to Christ and righteous living.

"A daughter-in-law" (νύμφην), literally bride, the young wife who often lives in the house and under the rule of her mother-in-law. It is a tragedy to see a father or mother step between the child and Christ.

10:38. *"Does not take his cross"* (οὐ λαμβάνει τὸν σταυρὸν αὐτοῦ). This is the first mention of "cross" in Matthew. Criminals were crucified outside Jerusalem. It was the custom for the condemned person to carry his own cross, as Jesus did until Simon of Cyrene was impressed for the purpose. The Jews had been familiar with crucifixion since the days of Antiochus Epiphanes or before. One Maccabean ruler, Alexander Jannaeus, had crucified eight hundred Pharisees. It is not certain that Jesus was thinking of his own coming crucifixion when he used this figure. The disciples would hardly think of that outcome unless some of them had remarkable foresight.

10:39. *"Will lose it"* (ἀπολέσει αὐτήν). This seeming paradox appears in four forms according to Willoughby Allen:[44] (1) Mark 8:35 = Matthew 16:25 = Luke 9:24; (2) Matthew 10:39; (3) Luke 17:33; (4) John 12:25. *The Wisdom of Sirach* (Hebrew text) in 51:26 has: "He that gives his life finds [wisdom]." Christ repeats this profound sayings on multiple occasions. Plato[45] says something similar though not so sharply put. The article and aorist participles (ὁ εὑρῶν, ὁ ἀπολέσας) are timeless in themselves, just like ὁ δεχόμενος in verses 40 and 41.

10:41. *"In the name of a prophet"*[46] (εἰς ὄνομα προφήτου). In Oxyrhynchus Papyrus 37 (A.D.) we find ὀνόματι ἐλευθέρου in virtue of being free-born.

"He that receives a prophet from no ulterior motive, but simply *qua* prophet (*ut prophetam*, Jer.) would receive a reward in the coming age equal to that of his guest."[47] Εἰς here is simply ἐν with the same meaning. It is not correct that εἰς has to be translated "into." Besides these examples of εἰς ὄνομα in verses 41 and 43, see 12:41, εἰς τὸ κήρυγμα Ἰωνα.[48]

10:42. *"To one of these little ones"* (ἕνα τῶν μικρῶν τούτων). The "little ones" are simple believers who are neither apostles, prophets, or particularly righteous. They are just learners "in the name of a disciple"[49] (εἰς ὄνομα μαθητοῦ). Alford thinks that children were present (cf. Matt. 18:2–6).[50]

NOTES

1.   NIV has "among the Gentiles."
2.   Alexander Balmain Bruce, *The Expositor's Greek Testament*, Vol. 1, *The Synoptic Gospels* (Grand Rapids: Eerdmans, 1951), 159.
3.   John Albert Bengel, *New Testament Word Studies*, vol. 1 (repr. ed., Grand Rapids: Kregel, 1971), 156.
4.   Alan Hugh McNeile, *The Gospel According to St. Matthew: The Greek Text with Introduction, Notes, and Indices* (repr. ed., Grand Rapids: Baker, 1980), 134.
5.   Bruce, *Expositor's*, 159.
6.   NIV has "do not take along any gold."
7.   NIV has "in your belts."
8.   Adolph Deissmann, *Light from the Ancient East* (repr. ed., Grand Rapids: Baker, 1978), 108f.
9.   Διδασκαλία is equal to *Const. Apost.* 3.6.
10. *Troilus and Cressida* 3.3.145.
11. Deissmann, *Light from the Ancient East*, 109.
12. NIV has "for the worker is worth his keep."
13. TR and Maj.T make the verb ἐστιν explicit, whereas GNT/NA and WH leave it implicit or elliptical.
14. *Didache* 13.
15. NIV has "if the home is deserving."
16. McNeile, *Matthew*, 136.
17. NIV has "more bearable."
18. NIV has "like sheep among wolves."
19. Bernard P. Grenfell and Arthur S. Hunt, eds., *New Sayings of Jesus and Fragment of a Lost Gospel from Oxyrhynchus* (New York: Oxford University Press, 1904).

20. NIV has "be on your guard against men."
21. NIV has "to the local councils."
22. McNeile, *Matthew*, 140.
23. Alfred Plummer, *An Exegetical Commentary on the Gospel According to Saint Matthew* (repr. ed., Grand Rapids: Eerdmans, 1956), 152.
24. NIV has "At that time."
25. NIV has "all men will hate you."
26. NIV has "because of me."
27. NIV has "he who stands firm to the end."
28. NIV has "before the Son of Man comes."
29. WH does not include $\check{\alpha}\nu$.
30. NIV has "Beelzebub."
31. So WH.
32. So GNT/NA, TRs, and Maj.T.
33. So TRb.
34. Bruce, *Expositor's*, 1.165.
35. NIV has "so do not be afraid of them."
36. See A. T. Robertson, *A Grammar of the Greek New Testament in the Light of Historical Research* (Nashville: Broadman, 1934), 577.
37. Bruce, *Expositor's*, 1.166.
38. NIV has "for a penny."
39. NIV has "apart from the will of your Father."
40. NIV has "whoever acknowledges me."
41. NIV has "I will also acknowledge him."
42. NIV has "whoever disowns me."
43. NIV has "to turn."
44. *Matthew*, 111.
45. *Gorgias* 512.
46. NIV and Moffatt have "because he is a prophet."
47. McNeile, *Matthew*, 150.
48. Robertson, *Grammar*, 593.
49. NIV has "because he is a disciple."
50. Henry Alford, *The Greek Testament, with a Critically Revised Text*, 4 vols. in 2 vols.: Vol. 1, *The Four Gospels*, rev. by Everett F. Harrison (Chicago: Moody, 1958), 112.

Matthew: Chapter 11

11:1. [And it happened] *when Jesus had finished* (Καὶ ἐγένετο ὅτε ἐτέλεσεν ὁ Ἰησοῦς). Five times in Matthew, 7:28; 11:1; 13:53; 19:1; and 26:1, the transition from great discourses back to the narrative follows the formula, "And it happened when Jesus had finished . . . that. . . ."[1] The chapter division should not be here, for 11:1 belongs with the preceding section.

Giving instructions[2] (διατάσσων, complementary participle with ἐτέλεσεν), means giving orders in detail (δια-). Note both "teach and preach," as in 4:23. Where did Jesus go? Did He follow behind the twelve as he did the seventy (Luke 10:1)? Bruce holds with Chrysostom that Jesus avoided the places where they were, giving them room and time to do their work.[3] But, if Jesus himself went to the chief cities of Galilee, he would necessarily visit many of the same points. Jesus likely would have followed at some distance. The apostles came back together in Capernaum to tell Jesus all that they had done and taught (Mark 6:30). Matthew follows the general outline of Mark, but the events are not grouped in chronological order. We are told that "He departed from there to teach and preach"[4] (μετέβη ἐκεῖθεν τοῦ διδάσκειν καὶ κηρύσσειν).

11:2. *Now when John, while imprisoned, heard*[5] (Ὁ δὲ Ἰωάννης ἀκούσας ἐν τῷ δεσμωτηρίῳ[6]). This probably coincides with the raising of the son of the widow of Nain (Luke 7:18). The word for "prison," δεσμωτήριον, is the place where one was kept bound (Acts 5:21, 23; 16:26; see Matt. 4:12). It was in Machaerus east of the Dead Sea, which at this time was under the rule of Herod Antipas.[7] John's disciples had access to him. So he sent a question "by" (διά) them to Jesus, not "by two" (δύο), as in Luke 7:19.

11:3. *"Are You the Expected One?"*[8] (Σὺ εἶ ὁ ἐρχόμενος[;]). This phrase refers to the Messiah (Ps. 118:26; Dan. 7:13; Mark 11:9; Luke 13:35; 19:38; Heb. 10:37). Some rabbis applied the phrase to some forerunner of the kingdom.[9] Was there to be "another"[10] (ἕτερον) after Jesus? John had been in prison "long enough to develop a prison mood."[11] Once it had been clear to him, but his environment was depressing, and Jesus had done nothing to get him out of Machaerus.[12] John longed for reassurance.

11:4. *"What you hear and see"* (ἃ ἀκούετε καὶ βλέπετε). This symbolical message was for John to interpret, not for them.

11:5. *"The dead are raised up"* (νεκροὶ ἐγείρονται). The son of the widow of Nain had been raised. Did he raise the dead also on this occasion? "Tell John your story over again and remind him of these prophetic texts"[13] (cf. Isa. 35:5; 61:1). The items were convincing and clearer than mere eschatological symbolism. "The poor" in particular have the gospel, a climax.

11:6. *"He who does not take offense at Me"*[14] (ὃς ἐὰν μὴ σκανδαλισθῇ ἐν ἐμοί[15]). Indefinite relative clause with first aorist passive subjunctive. This beatitude is a rebuke to John for his doubt though he was in prison. Doubt is not a proof of superior intellect, scholarship, or piety. John was in the fog, and that is the time not to make serious decisions. "In some way even the Baptist had found some occasion of stumbling in Jesus."[16]

11:7. *As these men were going away*[17] (Τούτων δὲ πορευομένων), present participle genitive absolute. The eulogy of Jesus was spoken as the two disciples of John were going away. Is it a matter of regret that they did not hear this wondrous praise of John that they might cheer him with it? "It may almost be called the funeral oration of the Baptist, for not long afterwards Herodias compassed his death."[18]

"A reed shaken by the wind?"[19] (κάλαμον ὑπὸ ἀνέμου σαλευόμενων;). Κάλαμος (Latin *calamus*) refers to reeds that grew in plenty in the Jordan Valley where John preached. It is used of a staff made of a reed (Matt. 27:29), a writer's pen (3 John 13), or a measuring rod (Rev. 11:1). The reeds by the Jordan River bent with the wind, but not so John.

11:9. *"And one who is more than a prophet"* (καὶ περισσότερον προφήτου). Ablative of comparison. Περισσότερον is itself comparative, meaning "exceeding, surrounded by, or overflowing." John had all the great qualities of a true prophet, "vigorous moral conviction, integrity, strength of will, fearless zeal for truth and righteousness."[20] He also was forerunner of the Messiah (Mal. 3:1).

11:11. *"Yet the one who is least"* (ὁ δὲ μικρότερος). The article with the comparative was becoming an acceptable form of superlative in vernacular Κοινή. In Modern Greek, it is the only idiom for the superlative.[21] Papyri and inscriptions show the same construction. This statement seems paradoxical. John is greater (μείζων) than all others in character, but a qualitative shift in the kingdom has come. Now each believer in God will share a greater position and privilege. John is at the end of one age (see v. 14), and the new era is dawning. All those that come after John stand upon his shoulders. John is the mountain peak between the old and the new.

11:12. *"Suffers violence"*[22] (βιάζεται). This verb occurs only here and in Luke 16:16 in the New Testament. It seems to be middle voice in Luke. Deissmann quotes an inscription "where βιάζομαι is without doubt reflexive and absolute," as in Luke 16:16.[23] But in numerous papyri examples, it is passive.[24] "There seems little that promises decisive help for the difficult *Logion* of Matthew 11:12 = Luke 16:16." In Matthew 11:12, the form can be either middle or passive, and either makes sense, though the respective meanings are not the same. The passive idea is that the kingdom is stormed or taken by men of violence[25] (βιασταὶ ἁρπάζουσιν αὐτήν). It is like a conquered city. The middle voice may mean "experiences violence" or "forces its way," like a rushing mighty wind. These difficult words of Jesus mean that the preaching of John "has led to a violent and impetuous thronging to gather round Jesus and his disciples."[26]

11:14. *"John himself is Elijah"*[27] (αὐτός ἐστιν Ἡλίας[28]). Jesus here identifies John as the promised "Elijah" of Malachi. The people understood Malachi 4:1 to mean that Elijah himself would return. John denied that he was Elijah reborn (John 1:21). But Jesus affirms that John filled the Elijah role (Matt. 17:12). He emphasizes the point: "He who has ears to hear, let him hear."

11:16. *"It is like children sitting in the market places"*[29] (ὁμοία ἐστὶν παιδίοις καθημένοις ἐν ταῖς ἀγοραῖς[30]). This parable of the children playing in the marketplace is given also in Luke 7:31–32. Had Jesus as a child in Nazareth played games with the children? He must have watched them often since he showed a keen interest in them. Jesus really created the modern child's world. He rejected the indifference previously shown to children. These metaphors in the Gospels are vivid. Children would not play wedding or funeral in a peevish fret. The ἀγορά was originally the assembly, then the forum or public square where the people gathered for trade or for talk (Acts 17:17). The Roman forum served as a marketplace, and bazaars still can be found along streets, though not so much in public squares. The English word *cheap* originally referred to the market bartering. Not until modern times did it come to mean items of inferior quality that are accepted at a lower price. The word translated "mourn," ἐκόψασθε, means "to beat the heart." It is direct middle, after the fashion of Eastern funeral lamentations.

11:19. *"Wisdom is vindicated by her deeds"*[31] (ἐδικαιώθη ἡ σοφία ἀπὸ τῶν ἔργων[32] αὐτῆς), a timeless aorist passive.[33] *Vindicated* means "set right." Luke 7:35 has "by all her children," a phrase added in Matthew in some MSS, presumably to conform Matthew to Luke. These words are difficult, but understandable. God's wisdom has planned the different conduct of both John and

Jesus. He does not wish all to be just alike in everything. "This generation" (v. 16) is childish, not childlike, and full of whimsical inconsistencies in their fault-finding. They exaggerate. John did not have a demon and Jesus was not a glutton or a winebibber. "And, worse than either, for $\phi \acute{\iota} \lambda o \varsigma$ is used in a sinister sense and implies that Jesus was the comrade of the worst characters, and like them in conduct. A malicious nickname at first, it is now a name of honor: the sinner's lover."[34] Cf. Luke 15:2. The plan of God is justified by results.

11:20. *Most of His miracles* ($\alpha \acute{\iota} \pi \lambda \epsilon \hat{\iota} \sigma \tau \alpha \iota \delta \nu \nu \acute{\alpha} \mu \epsilon \iota \varsigma \alpha \dot{\nu} \tau o \hat{\nu}$). Literally, "His very many mighty works" if elative as usual in the papyri.[35] But the usual superlative makes sense here as the Canterbury translation has it. This word $\delta \acute{\nu} \nu \alpha \mu \iota \varsigma$ for "miracle" presents the notion of power, as the English word *dynamic*. The word $\tau \acute{\epsilon} \rho \alpha \varsigma$ is "wonder or portent." It is *miraculum* (miracle), as in Acts 2:19. It occurs only in the plural and always with $\sigma \eta \mu \epsilon \hat{\iota} \alpha$. The word $\sigma \eta \mu \epsilon \hat{\iota} o \nu$ means "sign" (Matt. 12:38) and is common in John's Gospel alongside $\ddot{\epsilon} \rho \gamma o \nu$, "work," as in John 5:36. Other words used are $\pi \alpha \rho \acute{\alpha} \delta o \xi o \varsigma$, which is related etymologically to *paradox* (Luke 5:26); $\ddot{\epsilon} \nu \delta o \xi o \varsigma$, "glorious" (Luke 13:17); and $\theta \alpha \nu \mu \acute{\alpha} \sigma \iota o \varsigma$, "wonderful" (Matt. 21:15).

11:21. *Chorazin*[36] ($X o \rho \alpha \zeta \acute{\iota} \nu$[37]) is mentioned here and in Luke 10:13. What little has been learned of this town indicates the "meagerness of our knowledge of Judaism in the time of Christ"[38] and of the many things not told in our Gospels (John 21:25). We know something of Bethsaida and more about Capernaum as places of privilege.

11:22. *Nevertheless*[39] ($\pi \lambda \acute{\eta} \nu$). Neither of these cities repented and changed their conduct. Note condition of the second class, determined as unfulfilled in verses 21 and 23.

11:25. *At that time Jesus said* (Ἐν ἐκείνῳ τῷ καιρῷ ἀποκριθεὶς ὁ Ἰησοῦς εἶπεν). Jesus spoke to his Father in an audible voice. The time and place we do not know, but we catch a glimpse of Jesus in worship. "It is usual to call this golden utterance a prayer, but it is at once prayer, praise, and self-communing in a devout spirit."[40] Critics are disturbed because this passage from the *Logia* of Jesus or "*Q*" of Synoptic criticism (Matt. 11:25–30 = Luke 10:21–24) is so manifestly Johannine in spirit and language, "the Father" (ὁ πατήρ), "the Son" (ὁ υἱός). The fourth Gospel was not written till the close of the first century, and whatever *Logia* may have existed was written before the Synoptic Gospels. The only satisfying explanation lies in the fact that Jesus had a strain of teaching that is preserved in John's Gospel. Here he is in precisely the same mood of elevated communion with the Father that is reflected in John 14 to 17. Even Adolf Harnack is disposed to accept this *Logion* as a genuine saying of Jesus. "Thank" (ὁμολογοῦμαι) is better rendered "praise" (Moffatt). Jesus praises the Father "not that the σοφοί were ignorant, but that the νήπιοι knew."[41]

11:26. *"Was well-pleasing in Your sight"*[42] (εὐδοκία ἐγένετο[43] ἔμπροσθέν σου). "For such has been thy gracious will" (Weymouth).

11:27. *"All things have been handed over to Me by My Father"*[44] (Πάντα μοι παρεδόθη ὑπὸ τοῦ πατρός μου). This sublime claim is not to be whittled down or away by explanations. It is the timeless aorist, like ἐδόθη in 28:28, and "points back to a moment in eternity, and implies the pre-existence of the Messiah."[45] The messianic consciousness of Christ is clearly stated in this moment of high fellowship. Note ἐπιγινώσκει twice for "fully know." Note also βούληται = "wills; is willing." The Son retains the power and will to reveal the Father.

11:28. *"Come to Me"* (Δεῦτε πρός με). Verses 28 to 30 are not in Luke and are among the special treasures of Matthew's Gospel. This call of Jesus to the toiling and the burdened is sublime. The ones called are in a state of weariness (Πεφορτισμένοι), nominative plural masculine perfect passive participle.

"And I will give you rest" (κἀγὼ ἀναπαύσω ὑμᾶς). Here is rejuvenation, not just rest. The English slang expression "rest up" is close to the idea of the Greek compound ἀνα-παύω. It is causative active voice.

11:29. *"Take My yoke upon you and learn from Me"* (ἄρατε τὸν ζυγόν μου ἐφ᾿ ὑμᾶς καὶ μάθετε ἀπ᾿ ἐμοῦ). The rabbis used the term *yoke* for school. The English word *school* is related etymologically to the Greek σχολή, "leisure." But Jesus offers refreshment (ἀνάπαυσιν) in his school and promises to make the burden light, for he is a meek and humble teacher. Humility seemed servile to the ancients; it was no virtue. Jesus has made a virtue of this vice. He glorified this attitude. Paul urges, "with humility of mind regard one another as more important than yourselves" (Phil. 2:3). In portions of the world, people still use shoulder yokes to make burdens easier to carry. Jesus promises that we shall find that his yoke greatly lightens the burden. "Easy" is a poor translation of χρηστός; Moffatt puts it "kindly." That is the meaning of the term when the LXX uses it in the Old Testament. We have no adjective that quite carries the notion of "kind and good." The yoke of Christ is useful, good, and kindly (cf. Song 1:10).

11:30. *"For My yoke is easy"* (ὁ γὰρ ζυγός μου χρηστὸς). "The rabbis called the yoke of the law heavy. It was a burden no one could bear. Jesus makes demands that are light in comparison."[46]

NOTES

1. Alan Hugh McNeile, *The Gospel According to St. Matthew: The Greek Text with Introduction, Notes, and Indices* (repr. ed., Grand Rapids: Baker, 1980), 99.

2. NIV has "instructing."

3. Alexander Balmain Bruce, *The Expositor's Greek Testament*, Vol. 1, *The Synoptic Gospels* (Grand Rapids: Eerdmans, 1951), 169.

4. NIV has "he went on from there to teach and preach."

5. NIV has "When John heard in prison."

6. WH has only one ν, Ἰωάνης.

7. Josephus, *Antiquities of the Jews*, 18.5.2.

8. NIV has "Are you the one who was to come."

9. McNeile, *Matthew*, 151.

10. NIV has "someone else."

11. Bruce, *Expositor's*, 169.

12. See A. T. Robertson, *John the Loyal: Studies in the Ministry of John the Baptist* (Nashville: Broadman, 1977), chap. 9.

13. Bruce, *Expositor's*, 170.

14. NIV has "the man who does not fall away on account of me."

15. WH has the variant ἄν.

16. Alfred Plummer, *An Exegetical Commentary on the Gospel According to Saint Matthew* (repr. ed., Grand Rapids: Eerdmans, 1956), 161.

17. NIV has "As John's disciples were leaving."

18. Plummer, *Matthew*, 161.

19. NIV has "A reed swayed by the wind?"

20. Bruce, *Expositor's*, 172.

21. A. T. Robertson, *A Grammar of the Greek New Testament in the Light of Historical Research* (Nashville: Broadman, 1934), 668.

22. NIV has "has been forcefully advancing."

23. *Bible Studies*, 258.

24. James Hope Moulton and George Milligan, *The Vocabulary of the Greek Testament* (London: Hodder and Stoughton, 1952), 109.

25. NIV has "forceful men lay hold of it."

26. Fenton John Anthony Hort, *Judaistic Christianity: A Course of Lectures* (London: Macmillan, 1894), 26.

27. NIV has "he is the Elijah." NASB adds the name "John" although not in the Greek text.

28. WH has a different spelling, Ἠλείας, and TRb has the rough breathing Ἡλίας.

29. NIV has "They are like children sitting in the marketplaces."
30. Maj.T has a different word order plus different spellings, ἐστὶ παιδίοις ἐν ἀγοπαῖς καθημένοὶ; TRs has the moveable $ν$ in ἐστὶν and παιδίοις ἐν ἀγοραῖς καθημένοις; TRb has ἐστὶ παιδαρίοις καθννένοις.
31. NIV has "Wisdom is proved right by her actions."
32. TR and Maj.T have τέκνων rather than ἔργων.
33. Robertson, *Grammar*, 836f.
34. Bruce, *Expositor's*, 175.
35. Moulton and Milligan, *Vocabulary*, 1.79, and Robertson, *Grammar*, 670.
36. NIV has "Korazin."
37. WH has a different spelling, Χοραζείν.
38. Plummer, *Matthew*, 164.
39. NIV has "but."
40. Bruce, *Expositor's*, 177.
41. McNeile, *Matthew*, 161.
42. NIV has "your good pleasure."
43. TR and Maj.T have a different word order which does not affect the translation, ἐγένετο εὐδοκία.
44. NIV has "All things have been committed to me by my Father." This claim is the same as that made to the disciples after the Resurrection (Matt. 28:18).
45. Plummer, *Matthew*, 168.
46. A. T. Robertson, *Commentary on the Gospel According to Matthew* (New York: Macmillan, 1911), 155.

■ ■ ■ ■ ■

Matthew: Chapter 12

12:1. *At that time* (ἐν ἐκείνῳ τῷ καιρῷ), a general statement with no clear idea of specific time (so also 14:1). This paragraph begins with the same time frame indication as 11:25. The word καιρός means that this happened at a definite and particular time, but we cannot fix it.

Through the grainfields on the Sabbath (τοῖς σάββασιν διὰ τῶν σπορίμων[1]). The fields were of wheat or barley, the only grain crops. The plucking of grain by travelers was a custom. It was not considered stealing (Deut. 23:25).[2]

12:2. *"Your disciples do"*[3] (οἱ μαθηταί σου ποιοῦσιν). These critics are waiting for a chance, and they jump at this violation of the Pharisaic rules of Sabbath observance. The disciples were plucking the heads of grain and rubbing them between their hands to separate the kernel from the chaff. Pharisees regarded these actions as reaping and threshing (Luke 6:1), respectively. "Reaping" of any sort on the Sabbath is forbidden in the Talmud.[4]

12:3. *"What David did"* (τί ἐποίησεν Δαυίδ[5]), from the necessity of hunger. Christ appeals to the conduct of David (1 Sam. 21:6). David and those with him did "what was not lawful" (ὃ οὐκ ἐξὸν ἦν), which was precisely the charge made against the disciples (ὃ οὐκ ἔξεστιν) in verse 2. "All the arguments used by Jesus turn on the real significance of the day as one of rest and worship. It is not meant to be a bondage, but a blessing. . . . In the case of David appeal is to an historical example where necessity overcomes the rules of worship."[6]

12:6. *"Something greater than the temple"*[7] (τοῦ ἱεροῦ μεῖζόν[8]), ablative of comparison, τοῦ ἱεροῦ. What is greater? Jesus may mean himself as Christ. It may be he means "the work of Christ and His disciples was of more account than the Temple."[9] "If the temple was not subservient to Sabbath rules, how much less the Messiah!"[10]

12:7. *"The innocent"* (τοὺς ἀναιτίους). Ἀν + αἴτιος, there is "no ground against; no accusation." The same term, common in ancient Greek, is used in verses 5 and 7. Jesus quotes Hosea 6:6 here as he did in Matthew 9:13. This is a pertinent prophecy that had escaped the notice of the sticklers for ceremonial literalness and the letter of the law. "Ever in the Old Testament the real

106

worship was more important than the forms of worship. This the Pharisees did not understand."[11]

12:8. *"For the Son of Man is Lord of the Sabbath"* (κύριος γάρ ἐστιν[12] τοῦ σαββάτου ὁ υἱὸς τοῦ ἀνθρώπου). Jesus' claim that the Son of Man is master of the Sabbath, and so above the Pharisaic regulations, naturally angered them in the extreme. With the phrase *Son of Man*, Jesus involves the claim of messiahship, and as the representative Man he affirms his solidarity with the human race, "standing for the human interest."[13]

12:10. *"Is it lawful to heal on the Sabbath?"* (Εἰ ἔξεστιν τοῖς σάββασιν θεραπεῦσαι[14]). The use of εἰ in direct questions is elliptical and seems an imitation of the Hebrew.[15] See also 19:3. It is not translated in English.

12:12. *"How much more valuable then is a man than a sheep!"* (πόσῳ οὖν διαφέρει ἄνθρωπος προβάτου). Here is another of Christ's pregnant questions that goes to the root of things. It is an a fortiori argument: "By how much does a human being differ from a sheep? That is the question which Christian civilization has not even yet adequately answered."[16] The poor Pharisees are left in the pit.

12:13. *"Stretch out your hand"* (Ἔκτεινόν σου τὴν χεῖρα[17]). Probably the arm was not withered, though that is not certain. But he did the impossible. "He stretched it out," straight, I hope, toward the Pharisees who were watching Jesus (Mark 3:2).

12:14. *Conspired against Him*[18] (συμβούλιον ἔλαβον κατ᾽ αὐτοῦ). An imitation of the Latin *concilium capere* and found in papyri of the A.D second century.[19] This incident marks a crisis in the hatred of the Pharisees toward Jesus. They bolted out of the synagogue and actually conspired with their hated rivals the Herodians as to how to put Jesus to death (Mark 3:6 = Matt. 12:14 = Luke 6:11). By "destroy" (ἀπολέσωσιν), they meant "kill."

12:15. *Aware of this* (γνούς), nominative singular masculine second aorist active participle of γινώσκω. Jesus read their very thoughts, which were plain to anyone who saw their angry countenances.

12:17. *This was to fulfill* (ἵνα[20] πληρωθῇ). This final use of ἵνα refers to all the healing works of Christ through this time, as they are summarized in verse 16. The passage quoted is Isaiah 42:1–4, "a very free reproduction of the Hebrew with occasional side glances at the Septuagint,"[21] possibly from an Aramaic collection of *Testimonia*.[22] Matthew applies the prophecy about Cyrus to Christ.

12:18. *"My Beloved"*[23] (ὁ ἀγαπητός μου). This phrase reminds one of Matthew 3:17, the Father's words at Christ's baptism.

12:20. *"A battered reed"*[24] (κάλαμον συντετριμμένον). "A crushed reed He will not break," a picture of compassion. The curious augment in κατεάξει (third person singular future active indicative) is to be noted. The copyists kept the augment where it did not belong in this verb,[25] even in Plato.

"A smoldering wick"[26] (λίνον τυφόμενον), the wick of a lamp, smoking and flickering and going out. Only here in the New Testament. Flax is found in Exodus 9:31. Vivid images that picture Jesus in the same strain as his own great words in Matthew 11:28–30.

12:23. *"This man cannot be the Son of David, can he?"*[27] (Μήτι οὗτός ἐστιν ὁ υἱος Δαυίδ;[28]). The form of the question expects the answer "no," but they put it so because of the Pharisaic hostility towards Jesus. The multitudes were amazed[29] or "stood out of themselves" (ἐξίσταντο), imperfect tense, vividly portraying the situation. They were almost beside themselves with excitement.

12:24. *But when the Pharisees heard this* (οἱ δὲ Φαρισαῖοι ἀκούσταντες). Matthew 9:32–34 set out the charge that Jesus was in league with the prince of demons, though the incident may be later than this one. See on 10:25 about "Beelzebub." The Pharisees feel that the excited condition of the crowds and the manifest disposition to believe that Jesus the Messiah (the Son of David) demands a strenuous response. They can't deny the fact of the miracles, for the blind and dumb man both sees and speaks (12:22). In desperation they suggest that Jesus uses the power of Beelzebub the prince of the demons.

12:25. *And knowing their thoughts Jesus said to them*[30] (εἰδὼς δὲ τὰς ἐνθυμήσεις αὐτῶν εἶπεν αὐτοῖς[31]). They now find out what a powerful opponent Jesus is. By parables, by a series of conditions (first class), by sarcasm, by rhetorical question, by merciless logic, he lays bare their hollow insincerity and the futility of their arguments.

12:26. *"If Satan casts out Satan, he is divided against himself"* (εἰ ὁ Σατανᾶς τὸν Σατανᾶν ἐκβάλλει, ἐφ᾽ ἑαυτὸν ἐμερίσθη). Satan does not cast out Satan. Note the timeless aorist passive ἐμερίσθη, matching the aorist passive ἔφθασεν from φθάνω in verse 28 (see Phil. 3:16). The alternatives are set out by the aorists. Either Satan has become divided against Satan, or the kingdom of God has arrived.

12:29. *"How can anyone enter the strong man's house and carry off his property . . . ?"* (ἢ πῶς δύναταί τις εἰσελθεῖν εἰς τὴν οἰκίαν τοῦ ἰσχυροῦ καὶ τὰ σκεύη αὐτοῦ ἁρπάσαι . . . ;). Christ is engaged in deathless conflict with Satan the strong man. "Property"[32] (σκευή) means house gear, house furniture, or equipment, as in Luke 17:36 and Acts 27:17, the tack line of the ship.

12:30. *"He who is not with Me"* (ὁ μὴ ὢν μετ᾽ ἐμοῦ). With these solemn words Jesus draws the line of cleavage between himself and his enemies, then and now. Jesus still has his enemies who hate him, as they hate all words and deeds of the Spirit. These words and actions sting the rebellious conscience of one who hates God and pour fuel onto the fire of fury. Each unbeliever may have the choice. We either gather with (συνάγων) Christ or scatter (σκορπίζει) to the four winds. Christ is the magnet of the ages. He draws or drives away. "Satan is the arch-waster, Christ the collector, Saviour."[33]

12:31. *"But blasphemy against the Spirit"* (ἡ δὲ τοῦ πνεύματος βλασφημία), an objective genitive. This is the unpardonable sin.

12:32. *"Against the Holy Spirit"* (κατὰ τοῦ πνεύματος τοῦ ἁγίου). The shape of the unforgivable sin is made plainer. What is this blasphemy against the Holy Spirit? These Pharisees had attributed the works of the Holy Spirit, by whose power Jesus wrought his miracles (12:28), to the Devil. That was without excuse and would not be forgiven in their age or in the coming one (12:32). People often ask if they can commit the unpardonable sin. Probably some do who ridicule the manifest work of God's Spirit in people's lives and attribute the Spirit's work to the Devil.

12:34. *"You brood of vipers"* (γεννήματα ἐχιδνῶν). The Baptist had used these same terrible words to convict the Pharisees and Sadducees (Matt. 3:7). These Pharisees had taken Satan's side. Their charge that Jesus was in league with Satan reveals the evil heart within.

12:35. *"The good man brings out of his good treasure what is good. . . ."* (ὁ ἀγαθὸς ἄνθρωπος ἐκ τοῦ ἀγαθοῦ θησαυροῦ ἐκβάλλει ἀγαθά. . . .). The heart "spurts out" (ἐκβάλλει) good or evil according to the supply of treasure, θησαυροῦ, within. Verse 35 is like Matthew 7:17–19. Jesus repeated his crisp pungent sayings.

12:36. *"Every careless word"* (πᾶν ῥῆμα ἀργὸν). An ineffective, useless word (α privative and ἔργον). A word that does no good and so is pernicious. It is a solemn thought. Jesus, who knows our very thoughts (12:25), insists that our words reveal our thoughts and form a just basis for the interpretation of character (12:37). Here we have judgment by words as in 25:31–46, where Jesus presents judgment by deeds. Both are real tests of actual character. Homer spoke of "winged words" (πτερόεντα ἐπέα). Our words can be heard easily around the earth. Who knows where they stop?

12:38. *"A sign from You"*[34] (ἀπὸ σοῦ σημεῖον). One wonders at the audacity of scribes and Pharisees. They accused Jesus of casting out demons by being in league with Satan, then blandly asked for a "sign," as if the other miracles were not signs. "The demand was impudent, hypocritical, insulting."[35]

12:39. *"An evil and adulterous generation craves for a sign"*[36] (Γενεὰ πονηρὰ καὶ μοιχαλίς σημεῖον ἐπιζητεῖ). They were adulterous in that they had broken the marriage tie that had bound Israel to Jehovah.[37] See Psalm 73:27; Isaiah 57:3ff.; 62:5; Ezek. 23:27; James 4:4; Rev. 2:20.

12:40. *"The sea monster"* (τοῦ κήτους), a sea monster, a huge fish. In Jonah 2:1 the LXX has κήτει μεγαλῷ. "Three days and three nights" may simply mean three days in popular speech. Jesus rose "on the third day" (Matt. 16:21), not "on the fourth day." It is just a fuller form for "after three days" (Mark 8:31; 10:34).

12:41. *"At the judgment"* (ἐν τῇ κρίσει). In verses 41 and 42, Matthew speaks of "the judgment." In all other references, Matthew refers to the "day of judgment" (ἡμέρᾳ κρίσεως; see 10:15; 11:22, 24; 12:36). Luke 10:14 uses the phrase ἐν τῇ κρίσει.

"They repented at the preaching of Jonah; and behold, something greater than Jonah is here" (μετανόησαν εἰς τὸ κήρυγμα Ἰωνᾶ, καὶ ἰδοὺ πλεῖον Ἰωνᾶ ὧδε). The Ninevites repented, whereas the Pharisees are finding fault with Jesus. Note that here εἰς is equivalent to ἐν. Matthew uses the neuter πλεῖον for "something greater," not the masculine πλείων for "someone greater." The same idiom occurs in verses 6 and 48. Jesus is something greater than the temple, greater than Jonah, greater than Solomon. "You will continue to disbelieve in spite of all I can say or do, and at last you will put me to death. But I will rise again, a sign for your confusion, if not for your conversion."[38]

12:44. *" 'To my house' "*[39] (Εἰς τὸν οἶκόν μου). So the demon describes the man in whom he had dwelt. "The demon is ironically represented as implying that he left his victim voluntarily, as a man leaves his house to go for a walk."[40] "Worse than the first" is a proverb.

12:46. *His mother and brothers* (ἡ μήτηρ καὶ οἱ ἀδελφοὶ αὐτοῦ). Brothers of Jesus, younger sons of Joseph and Mary. The charge of the Pharisees that Jesus was in league with Satan was not believed by the disciples of Jesus, but some of his friends did think that he was beside himself (Mark 3:21) because of the excitement and strain. It was natural for Mary to want to take him home for rest and refreshment. So the mother and brothers are pictured standing outside the house (or the crowd). They send a messenger to Jesus.

12:47. Aleph, B, L, Old Syriac, omit this verse, as do WH.[41] It is genuine in Mark 3:32 = Luke 8:20. It was probably copied into Matthew from Mark or Luke.

12:49. *"Behold My mother and My brothers"*[42] (Ἰδοὺ ἡ μήτηρ μου καὶ οἱ ἀδελφοί μου). A dramatic wave of the hand towards his disciples (learners) accompanied these words. Jesus loved his mother and brothers, but they were not to interfere in his messianic work. The real spiritual family of Jesus encompassed all who follow him. But it was hard for Mary to go back to Nazareth and leave Jesus with the excited throng so great that he was not even stopping to eat (Mark 3:20).

NOTES

1. TRb and Maj.T omit the moveable ν, σάββασι.
2. A. T. Robertson, *Commentary on the Gospel According to Matthew* (New York: Macmillan, 1911), 155.
3. NIV has "your disciples are doing."
4. Robertson, *Commentary on Matthew*, 156.
5. WH spells the proper noun Δαυείδ, and TR and Maj.T spell it Δαβίδ.
6. Robertson, *Commentary on Matthew*, 156.
7. NIV has "one greater than the temple."
8. TR has μείζων, but the neuter is correct.
9. Alfred Plummer, *An Exegetical Commentary on the Gospel According to Saint Matthew* (repr. ed., Grand Rapids: Eerdmans, 1956), 173.
10. Willoughby G. Allen, *A Critical and Exegetical Commentary on the Gospel According to Matthew*, International Critical Commentary (Edinburgh: T. & T. Clark, 1912), 128.
11. Robertson, *Commentary on Matthew*, 157.
12. TR adds καί here.
13. Alexander Balmain Bruce, *The Expositor's Greek Testament*, Vol. 1, *The Synoptic Gospels* (Grand Rapids: Eerdmans, 1951), 183.
14. WH, TR, and Maj.T have the present infinitive θεραπεύειν.
15. A. T. Robertson, *A Grammar of the Greek New Testament in the Light of Historical Research* (Nashville: Broadman, 1934), 916.
16. Bruce, *Expositor's*, 184.
17. TR and Maj.T have the reverse order, Ἔκτεινον τὴν χεῖρά σου.
18. NIV has "plotted."
19. Deissmann, *Bible Studies*, 238.
20. TR and Maj.T have ὅπως in place of ἵνα.
21. Bruce, *Expositor's*, 185.
22. Alan Hugh McNeile, *The Gospel According to St. Matthew: The Greek Text with Introduction, Notes, and Indices* (repr. ed., Grand Rapids: Baker, 1980), 172.

23. NIV has "the one I love."
24. NIV has "a bruised reed."
25. Robertson, *Grammar*, 1212.
26. NIV has "a smoldering wick."
27. NIV has "Could this be the Son of David?"
28. TR and Maj.T have the spelling $\Delta\alpha\beta\text{ί}\delta$, and WH has the spelling $\Delta\alpha\upsilon\epsilon\text{ί}\delta$.
29. NIV has "were astonished."
30. NIV has "Jesus knew their thoughts and said to them." The name *Jesus* is found in the NIV and NASB and in the TR, but not in the Greek Text of WH and GNT/NA.
31. TR and Maj.T include ὁ Ἰησοῦς here.
32. NIV has "possessions."
33. Bruce, *Expositor's*, 188.
34. NIV has "a miraculous sign from you."
35. Bruce, *Expositor's*, 191.
36. NIV has "a wicked and adulterous generation asks for a miraculous sign." For proof of the wickedness of the age, see Josephus, *Wars of the Jews*, 5.10.5.
37. Plummer, *Matthew*, 182.
38. Bruce, *Expositor's*, 191.
39. NIV has "to the house."
40. McNeile, *Matthew*, 183.
41. It is included in brackets in GNT/NA. TR and Maj.T include this verse.
42. NIV has "Here are my mother and my brothers."

■ ■ ■ ■ ■

Matthew: Chapter 13

13.1. *That day*[1] (Ἐν τῇ ἡμέρᾳ ἐκείνῃ[2]). This group of parables is placed by Matthew on the same day as the blasphemous accusation and the visit of the mother of Jesus. It has been called "the busy day" because Matthew tells so much about it. It serves as a specimen of many filled with stress and strain.

Was sitting by the sea[3] (ἐκάθητο παρὰ τὴν θάλασσαν). The accusative case is no difficulty. Jesus came out of the stuffy house and took his seat on the shore. "Was sitting," ἐκάθητο, is third person singular imperfect middle/passive deponent indicative. The people stretched up and down along the shore in this picturesque scene.

13:2. *And the whole crowd was standing on the beach*[4] (καὶ πᾶς ὁ ὄχλος ἐπὶ τὸν αἰγιαλὸν εἰστήκει). Past perfect tense of ἵστημι with imperfect sense, "had taken a stand" and so "was standing." Note the accusative with ἐπί, "upon" the beach where the waves break one after the other. Αἰγιαλός is from ἅλς, "sea," and ἄγνυμι, "to break," or from ἀΐσσω, "to rush." Jesus had to sit in a boat to escape the crush.

13:3. *And He spoke many things to them in parables*[5] (καὶ ἐλάλησεν αὐτοῖς πολλὰ ἐν παραβολαῖς). This is the first time so many parables are recorded and of such length. A number are in Luke 12–18 and Matthew 24–25. Already Matthew has given Salt and Light (5:14–16), the Birds and the Lilies (6:26–36), the Splinter and the Beam (7:3–5), the Good and Bad Trees (7:17–19), the Wise and Foolish Builders (7:24–27), the Garment and Wineskins (9:16f.), and the Children in the Marketplace (11:16–17). It is not certain how many Jesus spoke on this occasion. Matthew mentions eight: the Sower, the Tares, the Mustard Seed, the Leaven, the Hidden Treasure, the Pearl of Great Price, the Net, and the Householder. Mark adds the Lamp (4:21 = Luke 8:16) and the Growing Seed (4:26–29). Mark 4:33 and Matthew 13:34 imply that there were others. The word *parable* (παραβολή from παραβάλλω) means "to place alongside for measurement or comparison like a yardstick." It illustrates spiritual or moral truth. The word occasionally is employed for sentence sayings or proverbs (Matt. 15:15; Mark 3:23; Luke 4:23; 5:36–39; 6:39) or a figure or type (Heb. 9:9; 11:19). Synoptics use parabolic comparisons such as the Sower

113

and noncomparative illustrations such as the Rich Fool and the Good Samaritan.[6] Middle Eastern speech "finds expression in a multitude of such utterances."[7] The Old Testament and the Talmud have parables, but those of Jesus are in a category of their own. Jesus held the mirror up to nature to throw light on truth. The fable describes things that could not be. A parable may not be fact, but it could be. It is in harmony with the nature of the case. The allegory ($\dot{\alpha}\lambda\lambda\eta\gamma o\rho\dot{\iota}\alpha$) is a speaking parable that is self-explanatory. John Bunyan's *The Pilgrim's Progress* is a classic example. All allegories are parables, but not all parables are allegories. The Prodigal Son is allegory, as is the Vine and Branches (John 15). Instead of the word *parable*, John refers to a $\pi\alpha\rho o\iota\mu\dot{\iota}\alpha$, "a saying by the way" (John 10:6; 16:25, 29). Each parable of Jesus illustrates one main point and the details usually are incidental. If details have meaning, Jesus explains them. Much heresy has come from fantastic attempts to read too much into parables. In the case of the Parable of the Sower (13:3–8), Jesus gives careful exposition (18–23). On the same occasion, Jesus gave his reason for using parables (9–17).

"*Behold, the sower went out to sow*"[8] ('Iδοὺ ἐξῆλθεν ὁ σπείρων τοῦ σπείρειν). Matthew is very fond of this exclamation ἰδοὺ ("behold"). It is "*the* sower," not "*a* sower." Jesus expects us to see the man as he steps forth to begin scattering with his hand. Parables of Jesus are vivid word pictures. To understand them, one must see them with the eyes of Jesus. Christ drew his parables from familiar objects.

13:4. "*As he sowed*"[9] (ἐν τῷ σπείρειν αὐτόν). Literally, "in the sowing as to him," a neat Greek idiom unlike our English temporal conjunction. Locative case with the articular present active infinitive.

"*Beside the road*"[10] (παρὰ τὴν ὁδόν). Access paths surround fields, and in more primitive agriculture, in which fields were not so clearly laid out or deeply plowed, people might make paths across a plowed field. Seed could easily come to lie upon a compacted, beaten track.

"*Ate them up*"[11] (κατέφαγεν αὐτά). Literally "ate them down," though the English equivalent is "ate up." Third person singular second aorist active indicative of κατεσθίω (a defective or deponent verb).

13:5. "*The rocky places*" (τὰ πετρώδη). In that limestone country, ledges of rock often jut out and are covered by thin layers of soil.

"*Immediately they sprang up*"[12] (εὐθέως ἐξανέτειλεν). "Shot up at once" (Moffatt). Double compound (ἐξ, out of the ground, ἀνα, up). Ingressive aorist of ἐξανατέλλω.

13:6. "*But when the sun had risen*"[13] (ἡλίου δὲ ἀνατείλαντος). The same verb as in verse 5, except for the absence of ἐξ, a genitive absolute of ἀνατέλλω. "The sun having sprung up."

13:7. *"Among the thorns, and the thorns came up[14] and choked them out"[15]* (ἐπὶ τὰς ἀκάνθας, καὶ ἀνέβησαν αἱ ἄκανθαι καὶ ἔπνιξαν[16] αὐτά). Not "sprang up" as in verse 5, for a different verb occurs meaning "came up" out of the ground. Seeds of the thorns were already in the soil. The thorns got a quick start, as weeds somehow do, and, literally, "choked them off" (ἔπνιξαν, the effective aorist of ἀποπνίγω; see on v. 22). Luke (8:33) uses ἀπεπνίγη of the hogs drowning.

13:8. *"Yielded a crop"* (ἐδίδου καρπόν). The tense changes to the imperfect of δίδωμι, "to give." There was ongoing fruitbearing.

"Some a hundredfold" (ὃ μὲν ἑκατόν). The hundredfold yield means that a hundred grains were harvested for each planted. This is not so great by modern standards, but it was very good for ancient agriculture in Palestine (cf. Gen. 26:12). Instances of hundredfold yields are given by Wetstein for Greece, Italy, and Africa. Herodotus says that in Babylonia grain yielded two hundredfold and even three hundredfold.[17] This, of course, was due to irrigation, as in the Nile Valley.

13:9. *"He who has ears, let him hear"* (ὁ ἔχων ὦτα ἀκουέτω[18]). So also in 11:15 and 13:43. Even Jesus had to exhort people to listen and understand his sayings, especially his parables. They require thought and are often enigmatic.

13:10. *"Why do You speak to them in parables?"[19]* (Διὰ τί[20] ἐν παραβολαῖς λαλεῖς αὐτοῖς). Already the disciples are puzzled over the meaning of this parable and the reason for teaching with these stories. So they asked. Jesus was used to questions and surpassed other teachers in his replies.

13:11. *"To know the mysteries"[21]* (γνῶναι τὰ μυστήρια). Second aorist active infinitive of γινώσκω. The word μυστήριον is from μυστῆς, "one initiated," and that from μυέω (μύω), "to close or shut" (Latin, *mutus*). Mystery religions of the East had all sorts of secrets and signs, as secret societies still do. But initiates knew them. So the disciples have been initiated into the secrets of the kingdom of heaven. Paul speaks of the mystery once hidden but now revealed or made known in Christ (Rom. 16:25; 1 Cor. 2:7). In Philippians 4:12, Paul says that he has learned or been initiated (μεμύημαι) into the secret of living in dependence on what God provides. Jesus explains that his parables are open to the disciples, but shut to the hostile Pharisees. In the Gospels, μυστήριον is used only here and in the parallels of Mark 4:11 and Luke 8:10.

13:13. *"Therefore I speak to them in parables"* (διὰ τοῦτο ἐν παραβολαῖς αὐτοῖς λαλῶ). Jesus can go on preaching the mysteries of the kingdom, but the Pharisees will never comprehend what he is saying. However, he is anxious that the disciples get personal knowledge ($\gamma\nu\hat{\omega}\nu\alpha\iota$, v. 11) of these same mysteries. So he explains in detail what he means to teach by the parable. Note the position of $\dot{\upsilon}\mu\epsilon\hat{\iota}\varsigma$. He appeals to them to listen as he explains.

"Because while seeing"[22] ($\ddot{o}\tau\iota$ $\beta\lambda\dot{\epsilon}\pi o\nu\tau\epsilon\varsigma$). In the parallel passages in Mark 4:12 and Luke 8:10, we find $\ddot{\iota}\nu\alpha$ with the subjunctive. This does not necessarily mean that in Mark and Luke $\ddot{\iota}\nu\alpha = \ddot{o}\tau\iota$ with the causal sense, though a few rare instances of such usage can be found in late Greek.[23] Matthew has "an adaptation of Isaiah 6:9f. which is quoted in full in verse 14f."[24] Matthew presents a seeming paradox: People see outwardly but not in reality (cf. John 9:41).[25] The idiom in Matthew gives no trouble save in comparison with Mark and Luke. The form $\sigma\upsilon\nu\iota o\hat{\upsilon}\sigma\iota\nu$ is an ω verb form ($\sigma\upsilon\nu\iota\omega$) rather than the $\mu\iota$ verb ($\sigma\upsilon\nu\iota\eta\mu\iota$) common in the Koινή.

13:14. *"Is being fulfilled"*[26] ($\dot{\alpha}\nu\alpha\pi\lambda\eta\rho o\hat{\upsilon}\tau\alpha\iota$). Third person singular aoristic present passive indicative. Jesus points out the fulfilment. The formula is not Matthew's usual $\ddot{\iota}\nu\alpha$ or $\ddot{o}\pi\omega\varsigma$ $\pi\lambda\omega\rho\dot{\eta}\theta\eta$ $\tau\dot{o}$ $\dot{\rho}\eta\theta\epsilon\nu$ ("so that the words might be fulfilled;" e.g., 1:22). The verb $\dot{\alpha}\nu\alpha\pi\lambda\eta\rho\dot{o}\omega$ occurs in the Pauline Epistles but nowhere else in the Gospels. It means "to fill up as a cup," "to fill another's place" (1 Cor. 14:16), or "to fill up what is lacking" (Phil. 2:30). Here it means that the prophecy of Isaiah 6:9–10 is satisfied in the conduct of the Pharisees. There are two ways of reproducing the Hebrew idiom (infinitive absolute), one by $\dot{\alpha}\kappa o\hat{\eta}$, the other by $\beta\lambda\dot{\epsilon}\pi o\nu\tau\epsilon\varsigma$. Note the strong negative $o\dot{\upsilon}$ $\mu\dot{\eta}$ with an aorist subjunctive.

13:15. *"Has become dull"*[27] ($\dot{\epsilon}\pi\alpha\chi\dot{\upsilon}\nu\theta\eta$). Third person singular aorist passive indicative. From $\pi\dot{\alpha}\chi\upsilon\varsigma$, "thick, fat, or stout." The meaning is that the heart is degenerated with callouses or even fat.

"With their ears they scarcely hear"[28] ($\tau o\hat{\iota}\varsigma$ $\dot{\omega}\sigma\dot{\iota}\nu$ $\beta\alpha\rho\dot{\epsilon}\omega\varsigma$ $\ddot{\eta}\kappa o\upsilon\sigma\alpha\nu$), another aorist. Literally, "they heard (or hear) heavily with their ears."

"They have closed their eyes" ($\tau o\dot{\upsilon}\varsigma$ $\dot{o}\phi\theta\alpha\lambda\mu o\dot{\upsilon}\varsigma$ $\alpha\dot{\upsilon}\tau\hat{\omega}\nu$ $\dot{\epsilon}\kappa\dot{\alpha}\mu\mu\upsilon\sigma\alpha\nu$). The epic and vernacular verb $\kappa\alpha\mu\mu\dot{\upsilon}\omega$, "to shut down." We say "shut up," meaning the mouth, but the eyes really shut *down*. The Hebrew verb in Isaiah 6:10 means to smear over. The eyes can be smeared with wax or cataract and thus closed. "Sealing up the eyes was an oriental punishment."[29] See Isaiah 29:10; 44:18.

"Otherwise" ($\mu\dot{\eta}\pi o\tau\epsilon$). This negative purpose as a judgment is left in the quotation from Isaiah. It is a solemn thought for all who read or hear the Word of God.

"And I would heal them" ($\kappa\alpha\dot{\iota}$ $\dot{\iota}\dot{\alpha}\sigma o\mu\alpha\iota$ $\alpha\dot{\upsilon}\tau o\dot{\upsilon}\varsigma$). The LXX changes to the future indicative rather than the aorist subjunctive, as before.

13:16. *"But blessed [happy] are your eyes"* (ὑμῶν δὲ μακάριοι οἱ ὀφθαλμοί). A beatitude for the disciples in contrast with the Pharisees. See on 5:3 for a discussion of "blessed" or "happy."

13:18. *"[You] hear then the parable"*[30] (Ὑμεῖς οὖν ἀκούσατε τὴν παραβολήν). Jesus has given in 13:13 one reason for his use of parables. The Pharisees have brought this judgment of nonunderstanding on themselves by their spiritual dullness.

13:19. *"When anyone hears"* (παντὸς ἀκούοντος). Genitive absolute present participle, "while everyone is listening and not comprehending" (μὴ συνιέντος, "not putting together" or "not grasping." Perhaps at that very moment Jesus observed a puzzled look on some faces.

"The evil one comes and snatches away" (ἔρχεται ὁ πονηρὸς καὶ ἁρπάζει). The birds pick up the seeds while the sower sows. The Devil is busy snatching or seizing like a bandit the word of the kingdom before it has time to sprout.

"What has been sown in his heart" (τὸ ἐσπαρμένον ἐν τῇ καρδίᾳ αὐτοῦ). Accusative singular neuter perfect passive participle of σπείρω, "sow."

"This is the one" (οὗτός ἐστιν ὁ). Matthew, as Mark, speaks of people who hear the words as the seed itself. That creates some confusion in this condensed form of what Jesus actually said, but his point remains clear.

"On whom seed was sown beside the road"[31] (ὁ παρὰ τὴν ὁδὸν σπαρείς), nominative singular masculine aorist passive participle. The seed in the heart is not responsible for this loss along the way. In human terms, fault lies with the one who lets the Devil snatch truth away.

13:21. *"Yet he has no firm root in himself"*[32] (οὐκ ἔχει δὲ ῥίζαν ἐν ἑαυτῷ), cf. ἐρριζωμένοι in Colossians 2:7 and Ephesians 3:17. The person lacks the stability of a well-rooted tree. There was overnight "mushroom growth," which endured a while (πρόσκαιρος). But what was quick to sprout was temporary, and the person stumbled (σκανδαλίζεται). This pictures some that intend to follow Christ in an emotional moment. They drop away overnight because there was no reality of saving faith.

"Affliction"[33] (θλίψεως). From θλίβω, to press, to oppress, to squeeze (cf. 7:14). The English word *tribulation*, used in some translations, is from the Latin *tribulum*, the roller used by the Romans for pressing wheat. "When, according to the ancient law of England, those who wilfully refused to plead had heavy weights placed on their breasts, and were pressed and crushed to death, this was literally θλίψις."[34]

13:22. *"Choke the word"* (συμπνίγει[35] τὸν λόγον). Matthew used ἔπνιξαν, "choked off" in verse 7. Here the term is συμπνίγει, "choke together." Both subjects are lumped together into the historical present singular. "Lust for money and care go together and between them spoil many an earnest religious nature,"[36] "thorns" indeed. The thorns flourish and the character sickens and dies, choked to death for lack of spiritual food, air, and sunshine.

13:23. *"Who indeed bears fruit"*[37] (ὃς δὴ καρποφορεῖ). Some in reality (δή) do bear fruit (cf. Matt. 7:16–20). The fruit reveals the character of the tree and the value of the stalk as wheat straw. A stalk that is nothing but chaff and straw is worthless. The first three classes have no fruit, showing that they are unsaved. Each person who belongs to the Sower is fruitful. The lesson of the parable as explained by Jesus is precisely this: the variety in the results of the seed sown according to the soil on which it falls. Every teacher and preacher knows how true this is. It is the teacher's task as the sower to sow the right seed, the word of the kingdom. The soil determines the outcome. Some critics today who scorn this interpretation of the parable by Jesus say that is too allegorical, with too much detail. The explanation probably was not that given by Jesus. One problem is that scholars are not agreed as to the main point being made. This parable was not meant to explain all the problems of human life; it makes a single point.

13:24. *[Jesus] presented another parable to them*[38] (Ἄλλην παραβολὴν παρέθηκεν αὐτοῖς). This introduction occurs again in verse 31. He placed another parable beside (παρά) the one already given and explained. The same verb, παραθεῖναι, occurs in Luke 9:16.

"May be compared"[39] (Ὡμοιώθη). Timeless aorist passive indicative and a common way of introducing these parables of the kingdom where a comparison is drawn (18:23; 22:2; 25:1). The case of ἄνθρωποι is associative instrumental.

13:25. *"While his men were sleeping"*[40] (ἐν τῷ καθεύδειν τοὺς ἀνθρώπους). Same use of the articular present infinitive with ἐν and the accusative, as in verse 4.

"Sowed tares"[41] (ἐπέσπειρεν[42] ζιζάνια). Literally "sowed upon," "resowed" (Moffatt). The enemy deliberately sowed "the darnes." Technically ζιζάνια does not refer to tares, but rather bearded darnel, a bastard wheat. The enemy sowed darnel "over," ἐπί, the good wheat. This darnel, *lolium temulentum*, is common in Palestine and resembles wheat, except that the grains are black. Before the grain matures, it is indistinguishable from the wheat, so it cannot be weeded out until near the harvest.

13:26. *"Then the tares became evident also"*[43] (τότε ἐφάνη καὶ τὰ ζιζάνια).

The darnel "became plain," ἐφάνη, third person singular second aorist passive indicative, effective aorist of φαίνω, "show."

13:29. *"You may uproot the wheat with them'"* (ἐκριζώσητε ἅμα αὐτοῖς τὸν σῖτον). Literally, "root out." Easy to do with the roots of wheat and darnel intermingled. So συλλέγοντες is not "gather up" but "gather together," here and verses 28 and 30. Note other compound verbs: "grow together" (σύαυξάνεσθαι); "burn up or incinerate" (κατακαῦσαι); "bring together" (συναγάγετε).

13:30. *"My barn"* (τὴν ἀποθήκην μου). See 3:12; 6:26. Granary, storehouse, place for putting things away.

13:31. *"Is like"* (Ὁμοία ἐστίν). Adjective for comparison with associative instrumental, as in verses 13, 44, 45, 47, 52.

"A mustard seed" (κόκκῳ σινάπεως), a single grain in contrast with the collective σπέρμα (17:20).

"A man took and sowed"[44] (λαβὼν ἄνθρωπος ἔσπειρεν). Vernacular phrasing, like Hebrew and all conversational style in Κοινή.

13:32. *"A tree"* (δένδρον). "Not in nature, but in size." "An excusable exaggeration in popular discourse."[45]

13:33. *"The kingdom of heaven is like leaven"*[46] (Ὁμοία ἐστὶν ἡ βασιλεία τῶν οὐρανῶν ζύμη), in its pervasive power. Curiously some people deny that Jesus here likens the expanding power of the kingdom of heaven to leaven, because, they say, leaven is the symbol of corruption. But the language of Jesus is not to be explained away by such exegetical jugglery. The Devil is likened to a lion (1 Peter 5:8), but Jesus is "the Lion that is from the tribe of Judah" (Rev. 5:5). The nature of leaven is to permeate the flour (ἀλεύρου) until the whole is leavened. There is no hidden symbolism in the fact that there are three measures. That was merely a common amount to bake. T. R. Glover suggests that Jesus may have remembered watching his mother using three measures of wheat flour in baking bread.[47] Some have looked for a reference to the Trinity here, which is quite far from the mark. The word for leaven, ζύμη, is from ζέω, "to boil or seethe." It was common to fermentation, another pervasive process.

13:35. *"I will utter"* (ἐρεύξομαι). To cast forth like a river, to gurgle, to disgorge, the passion of a prophet (from Pss. 19:2; 78:2). The psalmist claims to utter "things hidden from the foundation of the world," and Matthew applies this language to the words of Jesus. Certainly the life and teaching of Jesus threw a flood of light on the purposes of God, which had long been hidden (κεκρυμμένα).

13:36. *"Explain to us"* (Διασάφησαν[48] ἡμῖν). Aorist tense of urgency, also found in 18:31. "Make it thoroughly clear right now." The disciples waited until they were alone with Jesus in the house, then they asked for help with this parable about darnel in the wheat. Evidently they had less trouble with the parables of the Mustard Seed and the Leaven.

13:38. *"The field is the world"* (ὁ δὲ ἀγρός ἐστιν ὁ κόσμος). The article with both "field" and "world" in Greek means that subject and predicate are coextensive and so interchangeable. Both the good seed and the darnel are sown in the world, not in the kingdom, the church.

13:39. *"And the harvest is the end of the age"* (ὁ δὲ θερισμὸς συντέλεια αἰῶνός ἐστιν[49]). The separation comes at the consummation of the age, the harvest time. Meanwhile, all the seed grows together in the field, the world.

13:41. *"Out of His kingdom"* (ἐκ τῆς βασιλείας αὐτοῦ). Out from the midst of the kingdom, where God's rule extends and where the good and bad are found mixed together (cf. ἐκ μέσου τῶν δικαίων in v. 49, "from the midst of the righteous"). Just as wheat and darnel are mixed in the field until separated at harvest, so evil and good are mixed in the world until separated. Jesus does not mean to say that the bad seed "stumbling blocks" (τὰ σκάνδαλα) are actually members of the kingdom. Rather, they are simply mixed in the field with the wheat, and God leaves them until the separation comes. Their destiny is "the furnace of fire" (τήν κάμινον τοῦ πυρός, v. 42).

13:43. *"Then the righteous will shine forth as the sun"* (τότε οἱ δίκαιοι ἐκλάμψουσιν ὡς ὁ ἥλιος). Shine out as the sun comes from behind a cloud[50] and drive away the darkness after the separation has come (cf. Dan. 12:3).

13:44. *"And hid again"*[51] (ἔκρυψεν καί). The treasure was hidden again until the person had a right to it; this was not an issue of bad morality. "He may have hid it to prevent it being stolen, or to prevent himself from being anticipated in buying a field."[52] But even if it was a piece of sharp practice, that is not the point. The kingdom of God has enormous value, for which no sacrifice is too much to pay.

13:45. *"A merchant"* (ἐμπόρῳ). The type of merchant is a traveling broker, or possibly a door-to-door salesman of the type once referred to as a "drummer" because he would beat a drum to announce his coming as he approached an isolated frontier home.

13:46. *"He went and sold"*[53] (ἀπελθὼν πέπρακεν). Literally, "he has gone off and sold." The present perfect indicative, the dramatic perfect of vivid picture. Then he bought it. Present perfect, imperfect, and aorist tenses mix for lively action.

13:47. *"A dragnet"*[54] (σαγήνη). Latin, *sagena*, English, *seine*. The ends were stretched out and drawn together. The is the only use of the word in the New Testament. Just as the field is the world, so the dragnet catches all the fish that are in the sea. Separation comes afterwards. Marvin R. Vincent pertinently quotes Homer's *Odyssey* (22.384–89) where the slain suitors in the halls of Ulysses are likened to fish on the shore caught by nets with myriad meshes.[55]

13:48. *"Containers"*[56] (ἄγγη[57]). The only New Testament occurrence, though a similar term for a flask of oil, ἀγγεῖον, is found in 25:4.

13:52. *"Has become a disciple of the kingdom of heaven"*[58] (μαθητευθεὶς τῇ βασιλείᾳ[59] τῶν οὐρανῶν). Nominative singular masculine first aorist passive participle. The same verb is used in a transitive form in the Great Commission, 28:19. Here a scribe becomes a disciple in the kingdom. "The mere scribe, Rabbinical in spirit, produces only the old and stale. The disciple of the kingdom like the Master, is always fresh-minded, yet knows how to value all old spiritual treasures of Holy Writ, or Christian tradition."[60] This believing scribe has a special treasure, preserving what is worth saving of tradition (παλαιά) and replacing what is dated with things fresh (καινά). This person "brings out" (ἐκβάλλει) both sorts.

13:55. *"Is not this the carpenter's son?"* (οὐχ οὖτός ἐστιν ὁ τοῦ τέκτονος υἱός;). Joseph may have been the well-known, the leading, or even the only carpenter/stonemason in Nazareth until Jesus took up his craft. The people of Nazareth cannot comprehend how one from this respectable but undistinguished origin and environment could possess the wisdom that Jesus appeared to have in his teaching (ἐδίδασκεν). They knew Joseph, Mary, the brothers (four of them named) and sisters (names not given). Jesus passed here as the son of Joseph and these were younger brothers and sisters (technically half brothers and half sisters).

13:57. *And they took offense at Him* (καὶ ἐσκανδαλίζοντο ἐν αὐτῷ). Graphic imperfect passive. Literally, "they stumbled at Him," "they were repelled by him" (Moffatt), "they turned against him" (Weymouth). It was unpardonable for Jesus not to be as commonplace as they.

"A prophet is not without honor" (Οὐκ ἔστιν προφήτης ἄτιμος). This commonplace proverb has been found in the literature of Jewish, Greek, and Roman writers, as well as in the Logia of Jesus.[61]

13:58. *Many miracles* (δυνάμεις πολλάς). Literally, Jesus did not show "much power" in Nazareth. Jesus would not work miracles in the midst of such "disbelief" (ἀπιστίαν) among the townspeople.

NOTES

1. NIV has "That same day."
2. TR and Maj.T include δέ here.
3. NIV has "sat by the lake."
4. NIV has "while all the people stood on the shore."
5. NIV has "Then he told them many things in parables."
6. John A. Broadus, *Commentary on Matthew* (repr. ed., Grand Rapids: Kregel, 1990), 283.
7. Alan Hugh McNeile, *The Gospel According to St. Matthew: The Greek Text with Introduction, Notes, and Indices* (repr. ed., Grand Rapids: Baker, 1980), 185.
8. NIV has "A farmer went out to sow his seed."
9. NIV has "As he was scattering the seed."
10. NIV has "along the path."
11. NIV has "ate it up."
12. NIV has "It sprang up quickly."
13. NIV has "But when the sun came up."
14. NIV has "thorns, which grew up."
15. NIV has "choked the plants."
16. WH, TR, and Maj.T have the verb spelled ἀπέπνιξαν.
17. Herodotus, *History*, 1.93.
18. TR and Maj.T have ἀκούειν ἀκουέτω.
19. NIV has "Why do you speak to the people in parables?"
20. TR has Διατί.
21. NIV has "The knowledge of the secrets."
22. NIV has "though seeing."
23. For a discussion of the problem, see A. T. Robertson "*The Causal Use of* ἵνα," in *Studies in Early Christianity,* ed. S. J. Case (1928).
24. McNeile, *Matthew*, 190.
25. Ibid.
26. NIV has "is fulfilled."
27. NIV has "has become calloused."
28. NIV has "they hardly hear with their ears."
29. Marvin R. Vincent, *Word Studies in the New Testament*, Vol. 1, *The Synoptic Gospels* (repr. ed., Grand Rapids: Eerdmans, 1946), 79.
30. NIV has "Listen then to what the parable of the sower means."
31. NIV has "the seed sown along the path."
32. NIV has "But since he has no root."

33. NIV has "trouble."
34. Richard Trench, *Synonyms of the New Testament* (repr. ed., Grand Rapids: Baker, 1989), 202–4.
35. WH alone spells this word συνπνίγει.
36. Alexander Balmain Bruce, *The Expositor's Greek Testament*, Vol. 1, *The Synoptic Gospels* (Grand Rapids: Eerdmans, 1951), 197.
37. NIV has "He produces a crop."
38. NIV has "Jesus told them another parable." The name *Jesus* is not in the Greek text.
39. NIV has "is like."
40. NIV has "while everyone was sleeping."
41. NIV has "sowed weeds."
42. TRs has ἔσπειρεν, but TRb and Maj.T have ἔσπειρε.
43. NIV has "then the weeds also appeared."
44. NIV has "took and planted."
45. Bruce, *Expositor's*, 201.
46. NIV has "The kingdom of heaven is like yeast."
47. T. R. Glover, *Jesus of History* (London: Student Christian Movement, 1927), 27–28.
48. TR and Maj.T have Φράσον.
49. TR and Maj.T have τοῦ αἰῶνός ἐστιν.
50. Vincent, *Word Studies*, 81.
51. NIV has "He hid it again."
52. Alfred Plummer, *An Exegetical Commentary on the Gospel According to Saint Matthew* (repr. ed., Grand Rapids: Eerdmans, 1956), 197.
53. NIV has "he went away and sold."
54. NIV has "a net."
55. Vincent, *Word Studies*, 81.
56. NIV has "baskets."
57. TR and Maj.T have ἀγγεῖα.
58. NIV has "has been instructed about the kingdom of heaven."
59. TR and Maj.T have εἰς τὴν βασιλείαν.
60. Bruce, *Expositor's*, 204.
61. Oxyr, *Papyri* 1.3.

Matthew: Chapter 14

14:1. *Herod the tetrarch* (Ἡρῴδης ὁ τετραάρχης[1]). "Tetrarch (here) but 'king' in verse 9 as in Mark 6:14. *Tetrarch* was technically correct. It was a title inferior to *king*, and indicated a native ruler subject to Rome, but of considerable power."[2] Herod Antipas was ruler of Galilee and Perea, one-fourth of the dominion of Herod the Great.

Heard the news about Jesus[3] (ἤκουσεν ... τὴν ἀκοὴν Ἰησοῦ see on 4:24). This is a cognate accusative singular feminine. He "heard the hearing or rumor," followed by an objective genitive. It is rather surprising that he had not heard of Jesus before.

14:2. *Said to his servants*[4] (εἶπεν τοῖς παισὶν αὐτοῦ), literally "boys," but here the courtiers, not the menials of the palace.

"Miraculous powers are at work in him"[5] (δυνάμεις ἐνεργοῦσιν ἐν αὐτῷ). Ἐνεργέω is related to the English *energy* and *energize*. "The powers of the invisible world, vast and vague in the king's imagination."[6] Herod thought Jesus might be a reincarnation of John the Baptist. Though John wrought no miracles, one who had come back from death might be under the control of the unseen powers. So Herod argued, his fears quickened by a guilty conscience. Possibly he could still see the head of John on a charger. "The king has the Baptist on the brain."[7] Josephus told the story that the ghosts of Alexander and Aristobulus haunted the palace of Herod the Great after he murdered them.[8] There were many conjectures about Jesus as a result of His tour of Galilee, and Herod Antipas feared this one.

14:3. *In prison* (ἐν φυλακῇ). Literally, "in the guardhouse." Josephus tells that the prison fortress was named Machaerus.[9] It stood on a high hill where an impregnable fortress had been built. H. B. Tristram gives an early description of the site, describing remains of "two dungeons, one of them deep and its sides scarcely broken in" with "small holes still visible in the masonry where staples of wood and iron had once been fixed. One of these must surely have been the prison-house of John the Baptist."[10] "On this high ridge Herod the Great built an extensive and beautiful palace."[11] "The windows commanded

124

a wide and grand prospect, including the Dead Sea, the course of the Jordan, and Jerusalem."

Because of Herodias (διὰ Ἡρῳδιάδα[12]). The death of John had taken place some time before. The Greek aorists here (ἔδησεν, ἀπέθετο) are not used for past perfect. The Greek aorist simply narrates the event without drawing distinctions in past time. This Herodias was the unlawful wife of Herod Antipas. She was herself a descendant of Herod the Great and had married Herod Philip of Rome, not Philip the Tetrarch. She divorced Philip in order to marry Antipas after he had divorced his wife, the daughter of Aretas, king of Arabia. Her first husband was still alive, and marriage with a sister-in-law was forbidden to Jews (Lev. 18:16). Because John condemned the union, Herod Antipas had put John in prison at Machaerus. The bare fact is mentioned in Matthew 4:12 without the name of the place (see also on 11:2 for John's discouragement in the place of bondage, ἐν τῇ δεσμωτηρίῳ).

14:4. *For John had been saying to him* (ἔλεγεν γὰρ Ἰωάννης[13] αὐτω). Possibly the Pharisees may have put Herod up to inveigling John to Machaerus on one of his visits there to express an opinion concerning his marriage to Herodias, and the imperfect tense (ἔλεγεν) probably means that John said it repeatedly.[14] John's judgment on Herod and Herodias was blunt and brave. His uncompromising proclamation cost him his head, but it is better to have a head like John's and lose it than to have an ordinary head and keep it. Herod Antipas was a politician and curbed his resentment toward John because the people still held (third person plural imperfect active indicative) John to be a prophet.

14:6. *But when Herod's birthday came*[15] (γενεσίοις δὲ γενομένοις τοῦ Ἡρῴδου[16]). This is a locative of time (cf. Mark 6:21) without the genitive absolute. The earlier Greeks used the word γενεσία for funeral commemorations (birthdays of the dead), γενεθλία being the word for birthday celebrations of living persons. But that distinction seems to have disappeared over time, as shown in the papyri. Γενεσία in the papyri[17] is always a birthday feast, as it is in Matthew and Mark. Philo uses both words of birthday feasts. Persius, a Roman satirist, describes a banquet on Herod's Day.[18]

Danced before them[19] (ὠρχήσατο . . . ἐν τῷ μέσῳ). This was Salome, daughter of Herodias by her first marriage. The root of the verb means some kind of rapid motion. "Leaped in the middle," Wycliff puts it. It was a shameful exhibition of lewd dancing prearranged by Herodias to compass her purpose for John's death. Salome had stooped to the level of an *almeh*, or common dancer.

14:7. *Promised with an oath* (μεθ᾽ ὅρκου ὡμολόγησεν). Literally, "confessed with an oath." For this verb in the sense of promise, see Acts 7:17.

Whatever she asked (ὃ ἐὰν αἰτήσηται). Note middle voice of αἰτήσηται. Herod intended to give something the girl asked for herself (cf. Esther 5:3; 7:2).

14:8. *Having been prompted* (προβιβασθεῖσα). See Acts 19:33 for a similar verb (προβαλόντων), "pushing forward." "It should require a good deal of 'educating' to bring a young girl to make such a grim request."[20]

"Here" (ὧδε), on the spot, here and now.

"On a platter" (ἐπί πίνακι), dish, plate, platter.

14:9. *Grieved*[21] (λυπηθεὶς[22]). In verse 5 we read that Herod wanted (θέλων) to put John the Baptist to death (ἀποκτεῖναι). However, he shrank from the public relations problems of this dastardly display of brutality and bloodthirstiness. Men who do wrong always have some flimsy excuses for their sins. "Because of his oaths" (διὰ τοὺς ὅρκους), Herod committed a judicial murder of the most revolting type. "More like profane swearing than deliberate utterance once for all of a solemn oath."[23] He was probably maudlin with wine and befuddled by the presence of the guests.

14:10. *Had John beheaded* (ἀπεκεφάλισεν Ἰωάννην[24]). A causative active tense of a late verb ἀποκεφαλίζω, he took his head off.

14:11. *She brought it to her mother*[25] (ἤνεγκεν τῇ μητρὶ αὐτῆς). This is a gruesome picture as Herodias with fiendish delight witnesses the triumph of her implacable hatred of John for daring to reprove her for her marriage with Herod Antipas. Legend actually pictures Salome as sensually lusting for John, but there is no proof of this.

14:12. *And they went and reported to Jesus*[26] (καὶ ἐλθόντες ἀπήγγειλαν τῷ Ἰησοῦ). After they had buried John, the disciples told Jesus, who alone knew the full picture of how great John really was. The fate of John prefigured what Jesus would face. According to Matthew 14:13, Jesus learned of the murder, then withdrew to the desert alone. Jesus already needed rest after the strain of the recent tour.

14:13. *In a boat*[27] . . . *on foot* (ἐν πλοίῳ . . . πεζῇ). For πεζῇ, some MSS have πεζῷ. A contrast between the lake and the land route.

14:14. *Their sick* (τοὺς ἀρρώστους αὐτῶν). "Without strength," ῥώννυμι and α privative.

Felt compassion (ἐσπλαγχνίσθη), a deponent passive. The verb gives the traditional Jewish conception of the bowels (σπλάγχνα) as the seat of compassion.

14:15. *When it was evening*[28] (ὀψίας δὲ γενομένης). This is a genitive absolute. The Jewish marked sunset at about 6 P.M., as in 8:16 and 14:23, but "evening" began at 3 P.M.

"This place is desolate"[29] (Ἐρημός ἐστιν ὁ τόπος). To be alone, Jesus had wandered to a mountainside in an area that was relatively uninhabited, with no large towns near. Now a large number of people had joined him. There were "villages" (κώμας) where people could buy food, but they would have to walk to them. Thus, the disciples remarked that "the hour is already late"[30] (ἡ ὥρα ἤδη παρῆλθεν). Jesus should send the people on their way while they had time to find their supper.

14:16. *"You give them something to eat"* (δότε αὐτοῖς ὑμεῖς φαγεῖν). The emphasis is on ὑμεῖς in contrast (note position) with their "send away" (ἀπόλυσον). It is the urgent aorist of instant action (δότε). It was an astounding command. The disciples were to learn that "no situation appears to Him desperate, no crisis unmanageable."[31]

14:17. *They said to Him*[32] (οἱ δὲ λέγουσιν αὐτῷ), third person plural present active indicative as historical present. The disciples are quick to come up with obvious reasons why the task imposed by Jesus is impractical.

14:18. *And He said* (ὁ δὲ εἶπεν). Here is the contrast between the helpless doubt of the disciples and the confident courage of Jesus. He used "the five loaves and two fishes," which they had mentioned as a reason for doing nothing.

"Bring them here to Me" (Φέρετέ μοι ὧδε αὐτούς[33]). They had overlooked the power of Jesus in this emergency.

14:19. *To sit down on the grass* (ἀνακλιθῆναι ἐπὶ τοῦ χόρτου[34]). "Recline," of course, the word means, first aorist passive infinitive. A beautiful picture in the afternoon sun on the grass on the mountainside that sloped westward. The orderly arrangement in hundreds and fifties (Mark 6:40)[35] made it easy to count them and feed them. Jesus stood where all could see him breaking (κλάσας) the thin Jewish cakes of bread[36] then distributing them through the disciples. This is the only nature miracle recorded by all four Gospels. It was impossible for the crowds to misunderstand or be deceived about what was happening. If Jesus is really Lord of the universe (John 1:1–18; Col. 1:15–20), he who created has power to go on creating what he wills.

14:20. *Were satisfied* (ἐχορτάσθησαν), third person plural effective aorist passive indicative of χορτάζω. See Matthew 5:6. From the substantive χόρτος, "grass." Cattle were filled with grass and people usually with other food. They all were satisfied.

Broken pieces, twelve full baskets (τῶν κλασμάτων δώδεκα κοφίνους πλήρεις). Not the scraps upon the ground, but the pieces broken by Jesus and still in the "twelve baskets" (δώδεκα κοφίνους) and not eaten. Each of the twelve had a basketful left over (τὸ περισσεῦον). One hopes that the boy who had the five loaves and two fishes to start with (John 6:9) got some of the extra. Each of the Gospels uses the word for wicker baskets (κόφινος). Wycliff's translation used the term "coffins." Juvenal says that the grove of Numa near the Capenian gate of Rome was "let out to Jews whose furniture is a basket (*cophinus*) and some hay" (for a bed).[37] In describing the Feeding of the Five Thousand, Matthew and Mark use the word σπυρίς, referring to a sort of hamper or large provisions basket.

14:21. *Besides women and children* (χωρὶς γυναικῶν καὶ παιδίων). Perhaps on this occasion there were not so many women and children as usual because of the rush of the crowd around the head of the lake. Matthew adds this detail. He does not mean that the women and children were not fed, but simply that those "who ate" (οἱ ἐσθίοντες) included five thousand men (ἄνδρες), besides the women and children.

14:22. *Immediately He made the disciples get into the boat and go ahead of Him to the other side* (Καὶ εὐθέως ἠνάγκασεν τοὺς μαθητὰς[38] ἐμβῆναι εἰς τὸ πλοῖον καὶ προάγειν αὐτὸν εἰς τὸ πέραν). Literally, he "compelled" or "forced" (cf. Luke 14:23) the disciples to leave. The explanation for this strong word here and in Mark 6:45 is given in John 6:15. The excited crowd intended to take Jesus by force and make him their national king. This would have touched off political revolution and the defeat of Jesus. The disciples may have been swept along with this mob psychology, for they shared the Pharisaic hope of a political kingdom. Jesus may have sent the disciples out of the way to calm them and allow him to handle the crowd more easily.

While He sent the crowds away[39] (ἕως οὗ ἀπολύσῃ τοὺς ὄχλους). The use of the third person singular aorist active subjunctive with ἕως or ἕως οὗ is a common Greek idiom where the purpose is not yet realized (see also 18:30; 26:36). A translation sometimes might be "while." The subjunctive is retained after a past tense instead of the change to the optative of the ancient Attic. The optative is very rare anyhow, but Luke uses it with πρὶν ἤ in Acts 25:16.

14:23. *On the mountain*[40] (εἰς τὸ ὄρος). After dismissing the crowd, Jesus went up alone onto the mountain on the eastern side of the lake to pray as he often did. If ever he needed the Father's sympathy, it was now. The masses were out of control in their enthusiasm, and the disciples wholly misunderstood him. The Father alone could offer help.

14:24. *Battered by the waves*[41] (βασανιζόμενον ὑπὸ τῶν κυμάτων), like a man with demons (8:29). One can see, as did Jesus (Mark 6:48), the boat bobbing in the choppy sea.

14:25. *Walking on the sea*[42] (περιπατῶν ἐπὶ τὴν θάλασσαν[43]). This is another nature miracle. Some scholars actually explain it all away by urging that Jesus was only walking along the beach and not on the water, an impossible interpretation unless Matthew's account is myth. Matthew uses the accusative (extension) with ἐπί in verse 25 and the genitive (specifying case) in verse 26.

14:26. *They were terrified* (ἐταράχθησαν). This is stronger than "they were troubled" in the King James Version.

"A ghost" (Φάντασμα), "an apparition or specter." The noun is related to φαντάζω, "appear or make visible," and that from φαίνω, "shine or give light." They cried out "in fear" (ἀπὸ τοῦ φόβου). "A little touch of sailor superstition."[44]

14:28. *"On the water"* (ἐπὶ τὰ ὕδατα). Peter, as usual, is impulsive. Matthew alone gives this detail.

14:30. *But seeing the wind*[45] (βλέπων δὲ τὸν ἄνεμον). This is popular speech (cf. Exod. 20:18 and Rev. 1:12, "to see the voice," τὴν φωνήν). Peter saw the effect of the wind on the waves.[46] "It is one thing to see a storm from the deck of a stout ship, another to see it from the midst of the waves."[47] Peter was actually beginning to sink (καταποντίζεσθαι) into the sea, although he probably was a good swimmer as a fisherman.[48]

"Lord, save me!" (Κύριε, σῶσόν με). It was a dramatic moment that wrung from Peter the cry. With the aorist, his meaning was "Do it quickly." He could walk on the water until he saw the wind whirl the water round him.

14:31. *"Why did you doubt?"* (εἰς τί ἐδίστασας;). The verb is found only here and 28:17 in the New Testament. Ἐδίστασας is from διστάζω, which is related to δίς (twice). It means "pulled two ways." Peter's trust in the power of Christ gave way to dread of the wind and waves. Jesus, who was standing on the water, took hold of Peter (ἐπελάβετο, middle voice) and pulled him up.

14:32. *Stopped*[49] (ἐκόπασεν), from κόπος, toil. The wind grew weary or tired. It had exhausted itself in the presence of its Master (cf. Mark 4:39). It is no mere coincidence that the wind ceased at this moment.

14:33. *Worshiped Him* (προσεκύνησαν αὐτῷ). Jesus accepted the disciples' worship. They were growing in appreciation of the person and power of Christ from the attitude in 8:27. They will soon be ready for the confession of 16:16. Already they can say: "You are certainly God's Son!"[50] (Ἀληθῶς θεοῦ υἱὸς εἶ). The absence of the article allows it to mean a Son of God, as the centurian says in 27:54. But they probably meant "the Son of God," as Jesus claimed to be.

14:34. *Gennesaret* (Γεννησαρέτ), a rich plain four miles long and two miles broad on the western side of the lake.[51] The first visit of Jesus apparently stimulated the usual excitement at his cures.

14:36. *And as many as touched it were cured*[52] (καὶ ὅσοι ἥψαντο διεσώθησαν). Completely (δι-) healed. People were eager to touch the hem of Christ's mantle, as did the woman in 9:20. Jesus honored their superstitious faith.

NOTES

1. TR has ʿΗρῴδης; TR and Maj.T have ὁ τετράρχης.
2. A. T. Robertson, *Commentary on the Gospel According to Matthew* (New York: Macmillan, 1911), 175.
3. NIV has "heard the reports about Jesus."
4. NIV has "said to his attendants."
5. NIV has "miraculous powers are at work in him."
6. Alexander Balmain Bruce, *The Expositor's Greek Testament*, Vol. 1, *The Synoptic Gospels* (Grand Rapids: Eerdmans, 1951), 206.
7. Ibid.
8. Josephus, Jewish *Wars*, 1.30.7.
9. Josephus, *Antiquities of the Jews*, 17.5.2.
10. H. B. Tristram, *The Land of Moab: Travels and Discoveries on the East Side of the Dead Sea and Jordan* (New York: Harper & Brothers, 1873).
11. John A. Broadus, *Commentary on Matthew* (repr. ed., Grand Rapids: Kregel, 1990), 316.
12. TR has ʿΗρωδιάδα without the iota subscript.
13. WH has only one ν in Ἰωάνης.
14. Broadus, *Commentary on Matthew*, 317.
15. NIV has "On Herod's birthday."
16. TR has ʿΗρῴδου, without the iota subscript.
17. *Fayum Towns*, 114(20), 115(8), 119(30).
18. Persius, *Sat.* V. 180–83.
19. NIV has "danced for them."
20. Bruce, *Expositor's*, 207.
21. NIV has "distressed."
22. TR and Maj.T have ἐλυπήθη.
23. Bruce, *Expositor's*, 207.
24. TR and Maj.T include the article with the proper noun, τὸν Ἰωάννην; WH has only one ν with the proper noun, Ἰωάνην.

25. NIV has "who carried it to her mother."
26. NIV has "Then they went and told Jesus."
27. NIV has "by boat."
28. NIV has "As evening approached."
29. NIV has "This is a remote place."
30. NIV has "it's already getting late."
31. Bruce, *Expositor's*, 209.
32. NIV has "they answered."
33. TR and Maj.T have a different word order, αὐτοὺς ὧδε.
34. TR and Maj.T have a different case and number with the preposition, ἐπὶ τοὺς χόρτους.
35. Robertson, *Commentary on Matthew*, 178.
36. NIV has "broke."
37. Juvenal, *Satires* 3.14.
38. TR includes the specific subject of the verb and the personal pronoun, ἠνάγκασεν ὁ Ἰησοῦς τοὺς μαθητὰς αὐτοῦ; Maj.T includes the same as TR except for the personal pronoun, αὐτοῦ at the end.
39. NIV has "while he dismissed the crowd."
40. NIV has "on a mountainside."
41. NIV has "buffeted by the waves."
42. NIV has "walking on the lake."
43. TR and Maj.T have a different case with the preposition, ἐπὶ τῆς θαλάσσης.
44. Bruce, *Expositor's*, 210.
45. NIV has "when he saw the wind."
46. Robertson, *Commentary on Matthew*, 180.
47. Bruce, *Expositor's*, 211.
48. John Albert Bengel, *New Testament Word Studies*, vol. 1 (repr. ed., Grand Rapids: Kregel, 1971), 197.
49. NIV has "died down."
50. NIV has "Truly you are the Son of God."
51. Robertson, *Commentary on Matthew*, 180.
52. NIV has "and all who touched him were healed."

Matthew: Chapter 15

15:1. *Pharisees and scribes* (Φαρισαῖοι καὶ γραμματεῖς). It is unusual to see the Pharisees mentioned before the scribes. "The guardians of tradition in the capital have their evil eye on Jesus and co-operate with the provincial rigorists,"[1] if the Pharisees were not all from Jerusalem.

From Jerusalem (ἀπὸ Ἱεροσολύμων). Jerusalem is the headquarters of the conspiracy against Jesus, with the Pharisees as leading conspirators. Already the Herodians have joined with the Pharisees to put Jesus to death (12:14 = Mark 3:6 = Luke 6:11). Soon Jesus also will warn the disciples against the Sadducees (Matt. 16:6).

15:2. *"The tradition of the elders?"* (τὴν παράδοσιν τῶν πρεσβυτέρων;). This was oral law handed down by the elders of the past in *ex cathedra* fashion and later codified in the Mishna. Handwashing before meals is not a requirement of the Old Testament. It is, we know, a good thing for sanitary reasons, but the rabbis made it a mark of righteousness. This item was magnified at great length in the oral teaching. The washing (νίπτονται, middle voice) of the hands called for minute regulations. It was commanded to wash the hands before meals; it was one's duty to do it after eating. The more rigorous did it between courses. The hands must be immersed. Then the water itself must be "clean" and the cups or pots used must be ceremonially "clean." Vessels were kept full of clean water ready for use (see John 2:6–8). Thus a central issue is raised between Jesus and the rabbis, far more than a point of etiquette or hygiene. The rabbis held ritual uncleanness to be a mortal sin. The confrontation may have come to a head in a Pharisee's house.

15:3. *"You yourselves"*[2] (καὶ ὑμεῖς). Jesus admits that the disciples had transgressed the rabbinical traditions. Jesus treats it as a matter of no great importance. The real issue was putting the tradition of the elders in the place of the commandments of God. When the two clashed, the rabbis transgressed the commandment of God "for the sake of your tradition" (διὰ τὴν παράδοσιν ὑμῶν). The accusative with διά means for the sake of, not "by means of." Tradition is not good or bad in itself. It is merely what is handed on from one to another. Custom tended to make traditions as binding as law. The Talmud is

132

a monument to the struggle with tradition. There could be no compromise on this subject, and Jesus stands for real righteousness and spiritual freedom, not bondage to mere ceremony and tradition. The rabbis placed tradition (the oral law) above the law of God.

15:5. *"But you say"* (ὑμεῖς δὲ λέγετε). In sharp contrast to the command of God. Jesus had quoted the fifth commandment (v. 4; cf. Exod. 20:12; Deut. 5:16) with the penalty "to be put to death"[3] (θανάτῳ τελευτάτω), "go on to his end by death," in imitation of the Hebrew idiom. They dodged this command of God about the penalty for dishonoring one's father or mother by the tradition of *Korbaʾn* (Gk. Κορβᾶν, Mark 7:11). All one had to do to evade one's duty to father or mother was to say *"korbaʾn"* or "gift" (δῶρον), with the idea of using the money for God. By an angry oath of refusal to help one's parents, the oath or vow was binding. By this magic word one set himself free (οὐ μὴ τιμήσει, he shall not honor, v. 6) from obedience to the fifth commandment. Sometimes unfilial sons paid graft to the rabbinical legalists for such dodges. Were some of these very faultfinders guilty?

15:6. *"You invalidated the word of God"*[4] (ἠκυρώσατε τὸν λόγον τοῦ θεοῦ[5]). It was a stinging indictment that laid bare the hollow pretence of their quibbles about handwashing. Κύρος means "force or authority," so ἄκυρος means *"without* authority; null and void." It is a late verb, ἀκυρόω but in the LXX, Galatians 3:17, and in the papyri, the adjective, verb, and substantive occur in legal phraseology, as in canceling a will. Jesus charges that hairsplitting technicalities and immoral conduct have annulled the moral force of God's Law.

15:7. *"Rightly did Isaiah prophesy of you"*[6] (καλῶς ἐπροφήτευσεν[7] περὶ ὑμῶν Ἡσαΐας). There is sarcasm in this pointed application of Isaiah's words (LXX Isa. 29:13) to these rabbis. The portrait was to the very life "teaching as their doctrines the commandments of men." They were indeed far from God if they imagined that God would be pleased with such gifts at the expense of duty to one's parents.

15:11. *"This defiles the man"*[8] (τοῦτο κοινοῖ τὸν ἄνθρωπον). This word is from κοινός, which is used in two senses, either what is "common" to all and general, like the Κοινή Greek, or what is unclean and "common" ceremonially or in reality. The ceremonial "commonness" disturbed Peter on the housetop in Joppa (Acts 10:14; see also Acts 21:28; Heb. 9:13). One who is thus religiously common or unclean is cut off from doing religious acts. "Defilement" was a grave issue with the rabbinical ceremonialists. Jesus appeals to the crowd (v. 10): "Hear and understand"[9] (Ἀκούετε καὶ συνίετε). He draws a profound distinction. Moral uncleanness is what defiles or makes common.

That is to be dreaded, not to be glossed over. "This goes beyond the tradition of the elders and virtually abrogates the Levitical distinctions between clean and unclean."[10] One can see the pretenders shrivel under these withering words.

15:12. *"Were offended"* (ἐσκανδαλίσθησαν), third person plural first aorist passive indicative. "Were caused to stumble," "have taken offence" (Moffatt), "have turned against you" (Weymouth), "were shocked" (Goodspeed).[11] They took umbrage (resentment and displeasure) at the public rebuke, with its scorpian sting of truth. The glowering faces of the Pharisees made the disciples uneasy.

15:14. *"They are blind guides"* (τυφλοί εἰσιν ὁδηγοί[12]), a graphic picture. Once in Cincinnati a blind man introduced me to his blind friend. He said that he was "showing him the city." Jesus is not afraid of the Pharisees. Let them alone to do their worst. It is a proverbial expression that blind leaders and blind victims will land in the ditch.

15:15. *"Explain the parable to us"* (Φράσον ἡμῖν τὴν παραβολὴν [ταύτην]). They asked Him to explain the pithy saying in verse 11, not in verse 14. The disciples had been upset by Christ's powerful exposure of the *"korba'n"* duplicity and the words about "defilement" (v. 11).

15:16. *"Are you still lacking in understanding also?"*[13] (Ἀκμὴν καὶ ὑμεῖς ἀσύνετοί ἐστε;). Ἀκμήν is an adverbial accusative (classical αἰχμή, "point of a weapon") = ἀκμὴν χρονοῦ ("at this point of time, just now") = ἔτι. Ἀκμήν occurs in papyri and inscriptions, though condemned by grammarian traditionalists. Jesus was asking, "In spite of all My teaching, are you also, as the Pharisees, without spiritual insight and grasp?" One must never forget that the disciples lived in a Pharisaic environment. Their religious worldview was Pharisaic defined by the Pharisees. They were lacking in spiritual intelligence or sense, "totally ignorant" (Moffatt).

15:17. *"Do you not understand?"*[14] (οὐ νοεῖτε[;][15]). Christ expects us to make use of our νοῦς, intellect, not for pride but for insight. The mind does not work infallibly, but we should use it for its God-given purpose. Intellectual laziness or flabbiness is no credit to a devout soul.

15:18. *"Out of the mouth"* (ἐκ τοῦ στόματος). Spoken words come out of the heart and so are a true index of character. By "heart" (καρδίας), Jesus means not just the emotional nature, but the entire inward life of "evil thoughts" (διαλογισμοὶ πονηροί, v. 19) that issue in words and deeds. "These defile the man," not "eating with unwashed hands." The captious quibblings of the Pharisees, for instance, had come out of evil hearts.

15:22. *A Canaanite woman* (γυνὴ Χαναναία). Phoenicians were descended from the original Canaanite inhabitants of Palestine. They were Semitic pagans.

"Have mercy on me" ('Ελέησόν με). She identified herself with her daughter's case.[16]

15:23. "Because she keeps shouting at us"[17] (ὅτι κράζει ὄπισθεν ἡμῶν). The disciples disliked the public attention of this strange woman who cried after them. They did not show any concern as to whether the woman went away with her daughter healed or unhealed.

15:24. "I was sent only" (Οὐκ ἀπεστάλην), first person singular second aorist passive indicative of ἀποστέλλω. Jesus takes a new turn with this Phoenician by making a test case of her request. She represented the problem of the Gentile world. Jews were still "the lost sheep of the house of Israel," in spite of the conduct of the Pharisees.

15:27. "Even the dogs" (καὶ . . . τὰ κυνάρια). She took no offense that she was called a Gentile dog. Rather, with quick wit she turned Christ's very word for little dogs (κυνάρια) to her advantage. Little dogs eat of the little pieces of bread (ψιχίων, diminutive again) that fall from the little children's table (κυρίων).

15:28. "It shall be done for you as you wish"[18] (γενηθήτω σοι ὡς θέλεις). Her great faith and keen rejoinder won her case.

15:29. He was sitting there[19] (ἐκάθητο ἐκεῖ). He was sitting on the mountainside near the Sea of Galilee, possibly to rest and to enjoy the view but more likely to teach.

15:30. And they laid them down at His feet (καὶ ἔρριψαν αὐτοὺς παρὰ τοὺς πόδας αὐτοῦ[20]). A very strong word, which might be translated "flung them down." The sick were not deposited carelessly but in haste. So many were coming.[21] It was a great day for "they glorified the God of Israel."

15:32. "Three days" (ἡμέραι τρεῖς[22]). A parenthetic nominative plural feminine.[23]

"And have nothing to eat" (οὐκ ἔχουσιν τί φάγωσιν). This is an indirect question with the deliberative subjunctive retained. In the feeding of the five thousand, Jesus took compassion on the people and healed their sick (14:14). Here the hunger of the multitude moves him to compassion (σπλαγχνίζομαι, in both instances). He is unwilling (οὐ θέλω) to send them away hungry.

"They might faint" (ἐκλυθῶσιν). Unloosed, (ἐκλύω) exhausted.

15:33. The disciples said to Him[24] (καὶ λέγουσιν αὐτῷ οἱ μαθηταί[25]). Third person plural present active indicative as historical present. So soon they have forgotten the feeding of the five thousand (14:13–21). Jesus will remind them of both demonstrations of his power (16:9–10). They forgot both of them. Some scholars scoff at the idea of two miracles so similar, though both are narrated in detail by Mark and Matthew and both are later mentioned by Jesus. Jesus repeated points of teaching and performed many similar works of healing. Why shouldn't He use the same miraculous strategy to meet a similar need. He now is in the region of the Decapolis.

15:34. *"A few small fish"* (ὀλίγα ἰχθύδια), a diminutive again.

15:35. *On the ground* (ἐπὶ τὴν γῆν). In 14:19 the word used for "grace" or "blessing" is εὐλόγησεν. Vincent notes that Jewish custom was for the head of the house to say the blessing only if he shared the meal, unless the guests were his own household.[26] But we need not think of Jesus as bound by the Jewish customs.

15:39. *To the region of Magadan*[27] (εἰς τὰ ὅρια Μαγαδάν[28]). On the eastern side of the Sea of Galilee and so in Galilee again. Mark calls it Dalmunutha (8:10). Perhaps it is, after all, the same place as Magdala, as most manuscripts have it.

NOTES

1. Alexander Balmain Bruce, *The Expositor's Greek Testament*, Vol. 1, *The Synoptic Gospels* (Grand Rapids: Eerdmans, 1951), 212.
2. NIV has simply "you."
3. NIV has "must be put to death."
4. NIV has "you nullify the word of God."
5. TR and Maj.T have ἠκυρώσατε τὴν ἐντολὴν τοῦ θεοῦ.
6. NIV has "Isaiah was right when he prophesied about you."
7. TRs has προεφήτευσεν; TRb and Maj.T do not include the moveable ν; προεφήτευσε.
8. NIV has "that is what makes him unclean."
9. NIV has "Listen and understand."
10. Bruce, *Expositor's*, 214.
11. "War ill-pleased" (Braid Scots).
12. TRs has the reverse order, ὁδηγοί εἰσιν τυφλοί; TRb and Maj.T eliminate the moveable ν; εἰσι.
13. NIV has "Are you still so dull?"
14. NIV has "Don't you see?"
15. TR and Maj.T have οὔπω νοεῖτε.
16. NIV has "suffering terribly from demon-possession."
17. NIV has "for she keeps crying out after us."

18. NIV has "Your request is granted."
19. NIV has "sat down."
20. TR has παρὰ τοὺς πόδας τοῦ Ἰησοῦ.
21. Marvin R. Vincent, *Word Studies in the New Testament*, Vol. 1, *The Synoptic Gospels* (repr. ed., Grand Rapids: Eerdmans, 1946), 89.
22. TR has ἡμέρας τρεῖς.
23. A. T. Robertson, *A Grammar of the Greek New Testament in the Light of Historical Research* (Nashville: Broadman, 1934), 460.
24. NIV has "His disciples answered."
25. TR and Maj.T have the personal pronoun, οἱ μαθηταὶ αὐτοῦ.
26. Vincent, *Word Studies*, 90.
27. NIV has "to the vicinity of Magadan."
28. TR and Maj.T have the proper noun spelling, Μαγδαλά.

Matthew: Chapter 16

16:1. *The Pharisees and Sadducees* (οἱ Φαρισαῖοι καὶ Σαδδουκαῖοι). The first time that we have this combination of the two parties who disliked each other exceedingly. Hatred makes strange bedfellows. They hated Jesus more than they did each other. Their hostility has not decreased during the absence of Jesus, but rather increased.

Testing Jesus, they asked Him[1] (πειράζοντες ἐπηρώτησαν αὐτόν). Their motive was bad.

A sign from heaven (σημεῖον ἐκ τοῦ οὐρανοῦ). The scribes and Pharisees had already asked for a sign (12:38). Now this new combination adds "from heaven." What did they have in mind? They may not have had any definite idea to embarrass Jesus. The Jewish apocalypses did speak of spectacular displays of power by the Son of Man (the Messiah). The Devil had suggested that Jesus let the people see him drop down from the pinnacle of the temple, and the people expected the Messiah to come from an unknown source (John 7:27) who would do great signs (John 7:31). Chrysostum[2] suggests stopping the course of the sun, bridling the moon, or a clap of thunder.

16:2. *"Fair weather"* (Εὐδία). An old poetic word from εὐ and Ζεύς as the ruler of the air and giver of fair weather. So men today say "when the sky is red at sunset." It occurs on the Rosetta Stone and in a fourth-century Oxyrynchus papyrus for "calm weather" that made it impossible to sail the boat.[3]

16:3. *"Threatening"*[4] (στυγνάζων), a sky covered with clouds. It is used also of a gloomy countenance as of the rich young ruler in Mark 10:22. It is found nowhere else in the New Testament. This is the very sign of a rainy day that we use today. The word for "storm" (χειμών)[5] is the common one for winter and a storm.

"The signs of the times" (τὰ . . . σημεῖα τῶν καιρῶν). How little the Pharisees and Sadducees understood the situation. Soon Jerusalem would be destroyed and the Jewish state overturned. It is not always easy to "discern"[6] (διακρίνειν, "discriminate") the signs of our own time, but we ought not to be blind when others are gullible.

16:4. *"An evil and adulterous generation seeks after a sign"* (Γενεὰ πονηρὰ καὶ μοιχαλὶς σημεῖον ἐπιζητεῖ). The demand for a sign is precisely that found in Matthew 12, except that now Jesus' opponents want a sign "from heaven." So Jesus gives precisely the same response as in 12:39, one of the true doublets of Scripture. The only difference is that 16:4 leaves out the description of Jonah that he was "the prophet," τοῦ προφήτου.[7]

16:5. *Came*[8] (ἐλθόντες). This probably means "went," as in Luke 15:20 (in Latin, *ire*, not *venire*; so Mark 8:13, ἀπῆλθεν).

Had forgotten[9] (ἐπελάθοντο). Perhaps in the hurry to leave Galilee, probably in the same boat by which they came across from Decapolis.

16:7. *They began to discuss*[10] (διελογίζοντο). They kept it up, third person plural imperfect middle/passive deponent indicative. Pathetic was the incapacity of the disciples to understand Christ's parabolic warning against "the leaven of the Pharisees and Sadducees" (v. 6) after the collision with both parties in Magadan. It is "loaves" (ἄρτους) rather than "bread."[11]

16:8–11. *"Do you not yet understand or remember . . . ?"* (οὔπω νοεῖτε, οὐδὲ μνημονεύετε . . . ;). Jesus asks four pungent questions, critiquing the disciples' intellectual dullness. He refers to the feeding of the five thousand and uses the word κοφίνους for the baskets used to gather the leftover bread (v. 9; cf. 14:20). He refers to the larger baskets, σπυρίδας, used to gather leavings after the four thousand were fed (v. 10; cf. 15:37). After settling that misunderstanding, he repeats his warning to beware of the leaven of the scribes and Pharisees (v. 11). Teachers can understand that the patience of this Teacher must have been strained.

16:12. *Then they understood* (τότε συνῆκαν), third person plural first aorist active indicative of συνίημι, "to grasp or comprehend." They saw the point after this elaborate rebuke and explanation that by "leaven" Jesus meant "teaching."

16:13. *Caesarea Philippi* (Καισαρείας τῆς Φιλίππου). Up on a spur of Mount Hermon under the rule of Herod Philip.

He was asking[12] (ἠρώτα), began to question, inchoative or inceptive imperfect tense. He was giving them a test or examination. The first was for the opinion of men about the Son of Man.

16:14. *And they said*[13] (οἱ δὲ εἶπαν[14]). They were ready to respond, for they knew that popular opinion was divided on that point (14:1–2). They give four opinions. Jesus was not much concerned by their answers. He knew that the Pharisees and Sadducees were bitterly hostile to him. The masses were only superficially following, and they had vague expectations of him as a political

Messiah. He was more interested in the insights reached by the disciples and their developing faith.

16:15. *"But who do you say that I am?"* (Ὑμεῖς δὲ τίνα με λέγετε εἶναι;). This is what matters and what Jesus wanted to hear. Note the emphatic position of ὑμεῖς—"But *you*, who do *you* say that I am?"

16:16. *"You are the Christ, the Son of the living God"* (Σὺ εἶ ὁ Χριστὸς ὁ υἱὸς τοῦ θεοῦ τοῦ ζῶντος). Peter speaks for all. It was a noble confession, but not a new claim. Peter had made it before (John 6:69) when the multitude deserted Jesus in Capernaum. Since early in his ministry (John 4), Jesus had avoided the word *Messiah* because of its political connotations. But now Peter plainly calls Jesus "*the* Anointed One, *the* Messiah, *the* Son of the God *the* living one" (note the four articles). This great confession of Peter means that he and the other disciples believe in Jesus as the Messiah and were true in spite of the defection of the Galilean populace (John 6).

16:17. *"Blessed are you"* (Μακάριος εἶ), a beatitude for Peter. Jesus accepts the confession as true. Thereby Jesus on this solemn occasion solemnly claims to be the Messiah, the Son of the living God, his deity in other words. The disciples express positive conviction in the messiahship or Christhood of Jesus as opposed to the divided opinions of the populace. "The terms in which Jesus speaks of Peter are characteristic—warm, generous, unstinted. The style is not that of an ecclesiastical editor laying the foundation for church power, and prelatic pretentions, but of a noble-minded Master eulogizing in impassioned terms a loyal disciple."[15] The Father had helped Peter get this spiritual insight into the Master's person and work.

16:18. *"I also say to you"*[16] (κἀγὼ δέ σοι λέγω). "The emphasis is not on 'You are Peter' over against 'You are the Christ,' but on κἀγώ: 'The Father has revealed to you one truth, and I also tell you another.'"[17] Jesus calls Peter here by the name that he had said Peter would have (John 1:42). *Peter* (Πέτρος) is simply Greek for *Cephas* (Aramaic). Then it was prophecy, now it is fact. In verse 17 Jesus addresses him as "Simon Bar-Jonah," his full patronymic (Aramaic) name. But Jesus has a purpose now in using the nickname *Peter* that he himself gave to Simon. Jesus makes a remarkable play on Peter's name, a pun in fact that has caused volumes of controversy and endless theological strife.

"Upon this rock" (ἐπὶ ταύτῃ τῇ πέτρᾳ), a ledge or cliff of rock like that in 7:24 on which the wise man built his house. Πέτρος is usually a smaller detachment of the massive ledge. But too much must not be made of this point since Jesus probably spoke Aramaic to Peter, which draws no such distinction (Κηφᾶς).

"I will build My church" (οἰκοδομήσω μου τὴν ἐκκλησίαν). What did Jesus mean by this word-play? It is the figure of a building, and he uses the word ἐκκλησίαν, which usually refers to a local organization in the New Testament. However, it can take on a more general sense. The word originally meant "assembly" (Acts 19:39), but it came to be applied to an "unassembled assembly," as in Acts 8:3, where it refers to Christians who were persecuted by Saul from house to house. "And the name for the new Israel, ἐκκλησία, in His mouth is not an anachronism. It is an old familiar name for the congregation of Israel found in Deuteronomy (18:26; 23:2) and Psalms (22:36), both books well known to Jesus."[18] It is interesting to observe that in Psalm 89 most of the important words employed by Jesus on this occasion occur in the LXX text. So οἰκοδομήσω in 89:5; ἐκκλησία in verse 6; κατισχύω in verse 22; Χριστός in verses 39 and 52; ᾅδης in verse 49 (ἐκ χεῖρος ᾅδου). If one is puzzled over the connection of *building* with the word ἐκκλησία, 1 Peter 2:5a explains, "[You] are being built up as a spiritual house" (οἰκοδομεῖσθε οἶκος πνευματικός). Peter, the very one to whom Jesus is here speaking, is writing to Christians in the five Roman provinces in Asia (1:1). It is difficult to resist the impression that Peter is thinking of the words of Jesus. In verse 9, Peter speaks of these Christians as part of "a chosen race, a royal priesthood, a holy nation." Peter's spiritual building is general, not local. This is undoubtedly the picture in the mind of Christ in Matthew 16:18. The great spiritual house is Christ's Israel, not the Jewish nation. What is the rock on which Christ will build his vast temple? It was not on Peter alone. Peter by his confession furnishes the rock on which his church will rest. Jesus will build on the same kind of faith that Peter has confessed. The perpetuity of this church general is guaranteed.

"The gates of Hades will not overpower it"[19] (πύλαι ᾅδου οὐ κατισχύσουσιν αὐτῆς). Each word here creates difficulty. Hades is technically the unseen world, the Hebrew sheol, the land of the departed, that is death. Paul uses θάνατε in 1 Corinthians 15:55 in quoting Hosea 13:14 for ᾅδη. It is not common in the papyri, but it is common on tombstones in Asia Minor, "doubtless a survival of its use in the old Greek religion."[20] The ancient pagans divided Hades (α privative and ἰδεῖν, to see, abode of the unseen) into *Elysium* and *Tartarus*. The Jews identified the parts of sheol into *Abraham's bosom* and *gehenna* (cf. Luke 16:25). Christ was in hades (Acts 2:27, 31), not in gehenna. We have here the figure of two buildings. First there is the Church of Christ on its rock and second is the House of Death (hades). "In the Old Testament 'the gates of Hades' (sheol) never bears any other meaning (Isa. 38:10; cf. in the

apocrypha, Wisd. 16:3; 3 Macc. 5:51) than death," McNeile claims.[21] See also Psalm 9:13; 107:18; Job 38:17 (πύλαι θανάτου πυλῶροι ᾄδου). Christ does not speak of the possibility that hades will *attack* the church. Rather the issue is whether death can ever prevail or gain a possible victory over the church. "The ἐκκλησία is built upon the Messiahship of her master, and death, the gates of Hades, will not prevail against her by keeping Him imprisoned. It was a mysterious truth, which He will soon tell them in plain words (v. 21); it is echoed in Acts 2:24–31."[22] Christ's church will prevail and survive because he will burst the gates of hades and come forth conqueror. He will ever live and be the guarantor of the perpetuity of his people or church. The verb κατισχύω literally means "have strength against" (ἰσχύω from ἰσχύς and κατ'). It occurs also in Luke 21:36 and 23:23. It appears in the ancient Greek, the LXX, and in the papyri with the accusative and is used in the modern Greek with the sense of gaining the mastery over. The wealth of imagery in Matthew 16:18 makes it difficult to decide each detail, but the main point is clear: *The ἐκκλησία, which consists of those confessing Christ as Peter has just done, will not cease.* The gates of hades or bars of sheol will not close down on it. Christ will rise and will keep his church alive. "Sublime Porte" was what the Turks called their center of power, the city of Constantinople.

16:19. *"The keys of the kingdom"* (τὰς κλεῖδας τῆς βασιλείας). Here again we have the figure of a building with keys to open from the outside. The question is raised at once if Jesus does not here mean the same thing by "kingdom" that he did by "church" in verse 18. In Revelation 1:18 and 3:7, Christ the risen Lord has "the keys of death and of Hades." He has also "the keys of the kingdom of heaven," which he here hands over to Peter as "gatekeeper" or "steward" (οἰκονόμος), provided we do not understand it as a special and peculiar prerogative belonging to Peter. The same power here given to Peter belongs to every disciple of Jesus in all the ages. Advocates of papal supremacy insist on the primacy of Peter here and the power of Peter to pass on this supposed sovereignty to others. But this misses the mark. We shall soon see the disciples actually disputing again (Matt. 18:1) as to which of them is the greatest in the kingdom of heaven. They will still be at it on the night before Christ's death (20:21). Clearly neither Peter nor the rest understood Jesus to say that Peter was to have supreme authority. What follows clarifies matters. Peter held precisely the keys given to every preacher and teacher.

"Whatever you bind on earth shall have been bound in heaven" (ὃ ἐὰν δήσῃς ἐπὶ τῆς γῆς ἔσται δεδεμένον ἐν τοῖς οὐρανοῖς). In rabbinical language to "bind" is to forbid, to "loose" (λύσῃς) is to permit. Peter would be

like a rabbi who passes on many points. Rabbis of the school of Hillel *loosed* many things that the school of Shammai *bound*. The teaching of Jesus is the standard for Peter and for all preachers of Christ. Note the future perfect periphrastic participle ($\xi\sigma\tau\alpha\iota$ $\delta\epsilon\delta\epsilon\mu\acute{\epsilon}\nu\sigma\nu$, $\xi\sigma\tau\alpha\iota$ $\lambda\epsilon\lambda\nu\mu\acute{\epsilon}\nu\sigma\nu$), a state of completion. All this assumes, of course, that Peter's use of the keys will be in accord with the teaching and mind of Christ. The binding and loosing is repeated by Jesus to all the disciples (18:18). After the Resurrection, Christ will use this same language to all the disciples (John 20:23). Peter was only "first among equals," *primus inter pares*, in that on this occasion he spoke for the faith of all. It is a violent leap in logic to reason from the technical rabbinical language that Jesus employed to a claim that Peter was given power to forgive sins. Every believer who truly proclaims the terms of salvation in Christ uses the keys of the kingdom. The proclamation of these terms when accepted by faith in Christ has the sanction and approval of God the Father. The more personal we make these great words, the nearer we come to the mind of Christ. The more ecclesiastical we make them, the further we drift from him.

16:20. *That they should tell no one*[23] ($\H{\iota}\nu\alpha$ $\mu\eta\delta\epsilon\nu\grave{\iota}$ $\epsilon\H{\iota}\pi\omega\sigma\iota\nu$). Jesus had himself avoided this claim in public. He was the Messiah ($\acute{o}$ $X\rho\iota\sigma\tau\acute{o}\varsigma$), but the people did not understand what that meant. They inevitably saw the Messiah as a political figure. Jesus was plainly profoundly moved by Peter's great confession on behalf of the disciples. He was grateful and confident of the final outcome. But he foresaw peril to all. Peter had confessed him as the Messiah, and on this rock of faith thus confessed he would build his church or kingdom. They all would have and use the keys to this greatest of all buildings, but now was the time for silence.

16:21. *From that time Jesus began* ($A\pi\grave{o}$ $\tau\acute{o}\tau\epsilon$ $\H{\eta}\rho\xi\alpha\tau\sigma$ $\acute{o}$ $I\eta\sigma\sigma\hat{\upsilon}\varsigma$). It was a suitable time for the disclosure of the greatest secret of his death. A little over six months remained before the cross. The disciples must be readied. The great confession of Peter made this seem an appropriate time. He will stress the warnings (17:22–23; 20:17–19) that he now "began" to teach. They would understand only with great difficulty the necessity ($\delta\epsilon\hat{\iota}$, "must") of his suffering death at the hands of the Jerusalem ecclesiastics and his resurrection "on the third day" ($\tau\hat{\eta}$ $\tau\rho\acute{\iota}\tau\eta$ $\acute{\eta}\mu\acute{\epsilon}\rho\alpha$).[24] Dimly the shocked disciples grasped something of what Jesus said.

16:22. *Peter took Him aside* ($\pi\rho\sigma\sigma\lambda\alpha\beta\acute{o}\mu\epsilon\nu\sigma\varsigma$ $\alpha\grave{\upsilon}\tau\grave{o}\nu$ $\acute{o}$ $\Pi\acute{\epsilon}\tau\rho\sigma\varsigma$). Middle voice, "taking to himself," aside and apart, "as if by a right of his own. He acted with greater familiarity after the token of acknowledgment had been given. Jesus, however, reduces him to his level."[25] "Peter here appears in a new character; a minute ago speaking under inspiration from heaven, now under inspiration from the opposite quarter."[26] Syriac Sinaitic for Mark 8:32 has it "as though pitying him." But this exclamation and remonstrance of Peter was soon interrupted by Jesus.

"God forbid it, Lord! This shall never happen to You" ("Ἴλεώς σοι, κύριε· οὐ μὴ ἔσται σοι τοῦτο).[27] Supply εἴη or ἔστω ὁ θεός. The strongest kind of negation, as if Peter would not let it happen. Peter had perfect assurance.

16:23. But He turned[28] (ὁ δὲ στραφεὶς). Nominative singular masculine second aorist passive participle, quick ingressive action, away from Peter in revulsion, and toward the other disciples (Mark 8:33 has ἐπιστραφεὶς καὶ ἰδὼν τοὺς μαθητὰς αὐτοῦ).

"Get behind Me, Satan" ("Ὕπαγε ὀπίσω μου, Σατανᾶ). Peter had played the part of a rock in the noble confession and was given a place of leadership. Now he plays the part of Satan and is ordered to the rear. Peter was tempting Jesus not to go on to the cross, just as Satan had in the wilderness. "None are more formidable instruments of temptation than well-meaning friends, who care more for our comfort than for our character."[29] "In Peter the banished Satan had once more returned."[30]

"A stumbling block to Me" (σκάνδαλον εἶ ἐμοῦ[31]). Objective genitive. Peter was acting as Satan's catspaw, in ignorance but nonetheless truly. He had set a trap for Christ that would undo all his mission to earth. "You are not, as before, a noble block, lying in its right position as a massive foundation stone. On the contrary, you are like a stone quite out of its proper place, and lying right across the road in which I must go—lying as a stone of stumbling."

"You are not setting your mind"[32] (οὐ φρονεῖς). "Your outlook is not God's, but man's" (Moffatt). You do not think God's thoughts. Clearly the consciousness of the coming cross is not a new idea with Jesus. We do not know when he first foresaw this outcome any more than we know when first the messianic consciousness appeared in Jesus. He had the glimmerings of it as a boy of twelve, when he spoke of "My Father's house." He knows now that he must die on the cross.

16:24. "Take up his cross" (ἀράτω τὸν σταυρὸν αὐτοῦ), pick up at once, aorist tense. This same saying is in 10:38. But it is pertinent here in explaining Christ's rebuke of Peter. Christ's own cross faces him. Peter had dared to pull Christ away from his destiny. He would do better to face squarely his own cross and to bear it after Jesus. The disciples were familiar with cross-bearing as a figure of speech since criminals frequently were crucified outside Jerusalem.

"Follow" (ἀκολουθείτω), third person singular present active imperative. Keep on following.

16:25. *"Save his life"* (τὴν ψυχὴν αὐτοῦ σῶσαι). Paradoxical play on *life* or *soul*, using it in two senses. The same is true of *saving* and *losing* (ἀπολέσῃ).

16:26. *"Gains . . . forfeits"* (κερδήσῃ . . . ζημιωθῇ). Both third person singular aorist subjunctives (one active, the other passive), condition of third class, undetermined, but with prospect of determination, just a supposed case. The verb for "forfeit" occurs in the sense of being fined or penalized by money. So it is in the papyri and inscriptions.

"In exchange" (ἀντάλλαγμα), as an exchange, accusative in apposition with τί. The soul has no market price, though the Devil thinks so. "A man must give, surrender, his life, and nothing less to God; no ἀντάλλαγμα is possible."[33] This word ἀντάλλαγμα occurs twice in the *Wisdom of Sirach*: "There is no exchange for a faithful friend" (6:15). "There is no exchange for a well-instructed soul" (26:14).

16:28. *"Some of those who are standing here"* (τινες τῶν ὧδε ἐστώτων[34]). Does Jesus refer to the Transfiguration, the Resurrection, the Day of Pentecost, the Destruction of Jerusalem, or the Second Coming and Judgment? We know only that Jesus was certain of his final victory, which would be typified and symbolized in various ways. The apocalyptic eschatological symbolism employed by Jesus here does not dominate his teaching. He used it at times to picture the triumph of the kingdom, not to set forth the full teaching about it. The kingdom of God was already in the hearts of men. There would be climaxes and consummations.

NOTES

1. NIV has "tested him by asking him." The proper noun Ἰησοῦς is not found in the Greek text.
2. Chrysostom, *Homily* 53.
3. Aleph and B and some other MSS omit verses 2 and 3. W omits part of verse 2. These verses are similar to Luke 12:54–56. McNeile rejects them here. Alan Hugh McNeile, *The Gospel According to St. Matthew: The Greek Text with Introduction, Notes, and Indices* (repr. ed., Grand Rapids: Baker, 1980), 235. WH places them in brackets. Jesus often repeated his sayings. Theodor Zahn suggests that Papias added these words to Matthew. *Geschichte des neutestamentlichen Kanons* (Erlangen: 1888–92).
4. NIV has "overcast."
5. NIV has "stormy."

6. NIV has "interpret."
7. TR and Maj.T include τοῦ προφήτου; GNT/NA and WH do not include τοῦ προφήτου.
8. NIV has "went."
9. NIV has "forgot."
10. NIV has "they discussed."
11. Both NIV and NASB translate "bread."
12. NIV has "asked."
13. NIV has "They replied."
14. TR and Maj.T have Οἱ δὲ εἶπον.
15. Alexander Balmain Bruce, *The Expositor's Greek Testament*, Vol. 1, *The Synoptic Gospels* (Grand Rapids: Eerdmans, 1951), 223.
16. NIV has "And I tell you."
17. McNeile, *Matthew*, 240.
18. Bruce, *Expositor's*, 223–24.
19. NIV has "the gates of Hades will not overcome it."
20. James Hope Moulton and George Milligan, *The Vocabulary of the Greek Testament* (London: Hodder & Stoughton, 1952), 9.
21. McNeile, *Matthew*, 242.
22. Ibid.
23. NIV has "not to tell anyone."
24. "On the third day" and "after three days" are clearly equivalent. In free speech "after three days" may still be on the third day, but it cannot mean on the fourth day. See A. T. Robertson, *Commentary on the Gospel According to Matthew* (New York: Macmillan, 1911), 193.
25. John Albert Bengel, *New Testament Word Studies*, vol. 1 (repr. ed., Grand Rapids: Kregel, 1971), 214.
26. Bruce, *Expositor's*, 226.
27. NIV has "Never, Lord!"
28. NIV has "Jesus turned." The proper noun Ἰησοῦς is not found in the Greek text.
29. Bruce, *Expositor's*, 226.
30. Alfred Plummer, *An Exegetical Commentary on the Gospel According to Saint Matthew* (repr. ed., Grand Rapids: Eerdmans, 1956), 234.
31. TR and Maj.T have σκάνδαλόν μου εἶ.
32. NIV has "you do not have in mind."
33. McNeile, *Matthew*, 247.
34. TR has τινες τῶν ὧδε ἑστηκότων; Maj.T has τινες ὧδε ἑστῶτες.

Matthew: Chapter 17

17:1. *Six days later*[1] (μεθ᾽ ἡμέρας ἕξ). This could be on the sixth day, but as Luke (9:28) puts it "about eight days," we can say only that it was about one week. No attempt is made to be precise, since the precise number of days is irrelevant to the account.

Jesus took with Him (παραλαμβάνει ὁ Ἰησοῦς), literally, takes along. Note the historical present. These three disciples form an inner group. They have shown more understanding of Jesus. The same three would be at Gethsemane.

Led them up on a high mountain (ἀναφέρει αὐτοὺς εἰς ὄρος ὑψηλὸν), probably Mount Hermon again, though we do not know. "The Mount of Transfiguration does not concern geography," according to Holtzmann.

By themselves (κατ᾽ ἰδίαν); Mark 9:2 adds "alone" (μόνους).

17:2. *He was transfigured before them* (μετεμορφώθη ἔμπροσθεν αὐτῶν). The word is the same as the *metamorphoses*[2] of pagan mythology. Luke, speaking to Gentiles, does not use it. The idea is change (μετα-) of form (μορφή). It really presents the essence of a thing as separate from the σχῆμα (fashion), the outward accident. So in Romans 12:2, Paul uses both verbs, μὴ συσχηματίζεσθε ("be not conformed") and μεταμορφοῦσθε ("be transformed"). In 1 Corinthians 7:31, σχῆμα is used for the fashion of the world, while in 16:12 μορφή is used of the form of Jesus after his resurrection. The false apostles are described by μετασχηματίσομαι in 11:13–15. In Philippians 2:6 ἐν μορφῇ refers to the preincarnate state of Christ and μορφὴν δούλου to the incarnate state (2:7), while σχήματι ὡς ἄνθρωπος emphasizes his being found "in likeness of men." But it will not do in Matthew 17:2 to use the English transliteration *metamorphoses* because of its pagan associations. "Transfigured," from the Latin Vulgate *transfiguratus est* is better. "The deeper force of μεταμορφοῦσθαι is seen in 2 Corinthians 3:18 (with reference to the shining on Moses' face), Romans 12:2."[3] The word occurs in a second-century papyrus of the pagan gods who are invisible. Matthew guards against the pagan idea by adding and explaining about the face of Christ "as the sun" and his garments "as the light."

17:3. *Moses and Elijah appeared to them*[4] (ὤφθη αὐτοῖς Μωϋσῆς καὶ

'Ηλίας[5]). Third person singular aorist passive indicative with Moses (to be understood also with Elijah), but the participle συλλαλοῦντες is plural, agreeing with both. "Sufficient objectivity is guaranteed by the vision being enjoyed by all three."[6] The Jewish apocalypses reveal popular expectations that Moses and Elijah would reappear. Both had mystery connected with their deaths. One represented law, the other prophecy, while Jesus represented the gospel (grace). They spoke of his "decease" (Luke 9:31). The cross was the theme uppermost in the mind of Christ. The disciples did not comprehend, so Jesus receives needed comfort from fellowship with Moses and Elijah.

17:4. *Peter said to Jesus* (ἀποκριθεὶς δὲ ὁ Πέτρος εἶπεν τῷ Ἰησοῦ). "Peter to the front again, but not greatly to his credit."[7] It is not clear what Peter means by his saying: "It is good for us to be here" (καλόν ἐστιν ἡμᾶς ὧδε εἶναι). Luke 9:33 adds "not knowing what he said," as they "were heavy with sleep." So it is not well to take Peter too seriously on this occasion. At any rate he makes a definite proposal.

"I will make"[8] (ποιήσω[9]), first person singular future active indicative, though the aorist subjunctive has the same form.

"Three tabernacles"[10] (τρεῖς σκηνάς), booths. The Feast of Tabernacles was not far away. Peter may have meant that they should just stay on the mountain and not go to Jerusalem for the feast.

17:5. *A bright cloud overshadowed them*[11] (νεφέλη φωτεινὴ ἐπεσκίασεν αὐτούς). They were up in a cloud land that swept around and over them. See this verb used of Mary (Luke 1:35) and of Peter's shadow (Acts 5:15).

"This is My beloved Son"[12] (Οὗτός ἐστιν ὁ υἱός μου ὁ ἀγαπητός). At the baptism (3:17) these words were addressed *to* Jesus. Here the voice out of the bright cloud speaks to them *about* Jesus.

"Listen to Him" (ἀκούετε αὐτοῦ), even when he speaks about his death. It is a sharp rebuke to Peter for his consolation to Jesus about his death.

17:7. *Jesus came to them and touched them*[13] (καὶ προσῆλθεν ὁ Ἰησοῦς καὶ ἁψάμενος αὐτῶν[14]), tenderness in their time of fear.

17:8. *And lifting up their eyes*[15] (ἐπάροντες δὲ τοὺς ὀφθαλμοὺς αὐτῶν), after the reassuring touch of Jesus and his words of cheer.

They saw no one except Jesus Himself alone[16] (οὐδένα εἶδον εἰ μὴ αὐτὸν Ἰησοῦν μόνον[17]). Moses and Elijah were gone in the bright cloud.

17:9. *"Until the Son of Man has risen from the dead"*[18] (ἕως οὗ ὁ υἱὸς τοῦ ἀνθρώπου ἐκ νεκρῶν ἐγερθῇ). This conjunction is common with the subjunctive for a future event, his resurrection (ἐγερθῇ). Again they puzzled over his meaning (Mark 9:10). Jesus evidently hopes that this vision of Moses and Elijah and his own glory might stand them in good stead at his death.

17:10. *"Elijah must come first"* ('Ηλίαν[19] δεῖ ἐλθεῖν πρῶτον). So this piece of theology concerned them more than anything else. They had just seen Elijah, but Jesus the Messiah had come before Elijah. The scribes used Malachi 4:5. Jesus had also spoken again of his death and resurrection. They could not put it all together.

17:12. *"Elijah already came"*[20] ('Ηλίας[21] ἤδη ἦλθεν). Thus Jesus identifies John the Baptist with the promise in Malachi, though not the person Elijah (John 1:21).

"They did not recognize him" (οὐκ ἐπέγνωσαν αὐτόν), third person singular second aorist active of indicative of ἐπιγινώσκω, "to recognize." Just as they did not know Jesus (John 1:26), they had not known John. As a result, John had died, and Jesus soon would.

17:13. *Then the disciples understood* (τότε συνῆκαν οἱ μαθηταί). One of the three κ aorists. It was plain enough even for them. John was Elijah in spirit and had prepared the way for the Messiah.

17:15. *"He is a lunatic"*[22] (σεληνιάζεται). Literally it means "moonstruck." The symptoms of epilepsy were supposed to be aggravated by the changes of the moon (cf. 4:24).

"And is very ill"[23] (καὶ κακῶς πάσχει) as often in the Synoptic Gospels.

17:17. *"You unbelieving and perverted generation"*[24] ('Ω γενεὰ ἄπιστος καὶ διεστραννένη), distorted, twisted in two, corrupt. Nominative singular feminine perfect passive participle of διαστρέφω.

17:20. *"Because of the littleness of your faith"*[25] (Διὰ τὴν ὀλιγοπιστίαν ὑμῶν[26]), a good translation. It was less than "the size of a mustard seed"[27] (ὡς κόκκον σινάπεως, 13:31). They had no miracle faith. A. B. Bruce holds "this mountain" to be the Mount of Transfiguration, to which Jesus pointed.[28] Whether this is true, he is teaching in a parable. Our trouble is always with "this mountain" that confronts our path.

"'Move'" (Μετάβα[29]). A form of μετάβηθι, imperfect of μεταβαίνω, "change your location."

17:23. *And they were deeply grieved*[30] (καὶ ἐλυπήθησαν σφόδρα). They at last understood that he was talking about his own death and resurrection.

17:24. *Those who collected the two-drachma tax*[31] (οἱ τὰ δίδραχμα λαμβάνοντες). This temple tax amounted to an Attic drachma or the Jewish half shekel,[32] about one-third of a dollar. Every Jewish man twenty years of age and over was expected to pay it for the maintenance of the temple. But it was not a compulsory tax like that collected by the publicans for the government. "The tax was like a voluntary church-rate; no one could be compelled to pay."[33] The same Greek word occurs in two Egyptian papyri of the first century A.D. for the receipt for the tax for the temple of Suchus.[34] This tax for the Jerusalem temple was due in the month Adar (March) and it was now nearly six months overdue. But Jesus and the Twelve had been out of Galilee most of this time, hence the question of the tax collectors. The payment had to be made in the Jewish half shekel, so the money changers did a thriving business in charging a small premium for the Jewish coin. Their take amounting to an estimated forty-five thousand dollars a year. It is significant that they approached Peter rather than Jesus, perhaps not wishing to embarrass "Your Teacher," "a roundabout hint that the tax was overdue."[35] Evidently Jesus had been in the habit of paying Peter's.

17:25. *Jesus spoke to him first*[36] ($\pi\rho o\acute{\epsilon}\phi\theta\alpha\sigma\epsilon\nu$ $\alpha\mathring{v}\tau\grave{o}\nu$ $\acute{o}$ $'I\eta\sigma o\mathring{v}\varsigma$ $\lambda\acute{\epsilon}\gamma\omega\nu$). $\Pi\rho o\acute{\epsilon}\phi\theta\alpha\sigma\epsilon\nu$ is used only here in the New Testament. One example is found in a papyrus dated A.D. 161.[37] The old idiomatic use of $\phi\theta\acute{\alpha}\nu\omega$ with the participle survives in this example of $\pi\rho o\phi\theta\acute{\alpha}\nu\omega$ in verse 25, meaning "to anticipate, to get before one in doing a thing." The $Ko\iota\nu\acute{\eta}$ uses the infinitive with $\phi\theta\acute{\alpha}\nu\omega$, which has come to mean simply to arrive. Here the anticipation is made plain by the use of *pro-*.[38] The "prevent" of the Authorized Version was the original idea of *praevenire*, "to go before, to anticipate." Peter felt obliged to take the matter up with Jesus. But the Master had observed what was going on and spoke to Peter first.

"*Customs or poll-tax*"[39] ($\tau\acute{\epsilon}\lambda\eta$ $\mathring{\eta}$ $\kappa\mathring{\eta}\nu\sigma o\nu$). Customs or wares collected by the publicans (like $\phi\acute{o}\rho o\nu$, Rom. 13:7) and also the capitation tax on persons, indirect and direct taxation. $\kappa\mathring{\eta}\nu\sigma o\varsigma$ is like the Latin *census*, a registration for the purpose of appraising property, corresponding to $\acute{\eta}$ $\mathring{\alpha}\pi o\gamma\rho\alpha\phi\acute{\eta}$ in Luke 2:2; Acts 5:37. By this parable, Jesus as the Son of God claims exemption from the temple tax as the temple of his Father, just as royal families do not pay taxes but get tribute from the foreigners or aliens who are really subjects.

17:26. "*The sons are exempt*" ($\mathring{\epsilon}\lambda\epsilon\acute{v}\theta\epsilon\rho o\acute{\iota}$ $\epsilon\mathring{\iota}\sigma\iota\nu$ $o\acute{\iota}$ $\upsilon\acute{\iota}o\acute{\iota}$). Christ, of course, and the disciples also in contrast with the Jews. Thus a reply to Peter's prompt "Yes." "Logically" ($'A\rho\alpha$ $\gamma\epsilon$) they are free from the temple tax, but practically He will submit.

17:27. "*However, so that we do not offend them*"[40] ($\mathring{\iota}\nu\alpha$ $\delta\grave{\epsilon}$ $\mu\grave{\eta}$ $\sigma\kappa\alpha\nu\delta\iota\lambda\acute{\iota}\sigma\omega\mu\epsilon\nu$ $\alpha\mathring{v}\tau o\acute{v}\varsigma$). He does not wish to create the impression that he and the disciples despise the temple and its worship. Aorist tense here, though some MSS have present subjunctive (linear).

"A hook"[41] (ἄγκιστρον). The only example in the New Testament of fishing with a hook. From an unused verb ἀγκίζω, to angle, and that from ἄγκοκς, a curve (so also ἀγκάλη, the inner curve of the arm, Luke 2:38). This may have been a multiple-hook tackle, as Peter was to look at "the first fish that comes up"[42] (τὸν ἀναβάντα πρῶτον ἰχθὺν).

"A shekel"[43] (στατῆρα). Greek stater = four drachmae, enough for two persons to pay the tax.

"For you and Me"[44] (ἀντὶ ἐμοῦ καὶ σοῦ). Common use of ἀντὶ in commercial transactions, "in exchange for." Here we have a miracle of foreknowledge. Such instances have happened. Some try to get rid of the miracle by calling it a proverb or by saying that Jesus only meant for Peter to sell the fish and thus get the money, a species of nervous anxiety to relieve Christ and the Gospel of Matthew of the miraculous. "All the attempts have been in vain which were made by the older Rationalism to put a non-miraculous meaning into these words" according to B. Weiss. It is not stated that Peter actually caught such a fish, though that is the natural implication. Why provision is thus only made for Peter and Jesus, we do not know.

NOTES

1. NIV has "After six days."
2. Cf. Ovid.
3. Alan Hugh McNeile, *The Gospel According to St. Matthew: The Greek Text with Introduction, Notes, and Indices* (repr. ed., Grand Rapids: Baker, 1980), 249.
4. NIV has "there appeared before them Moses and Elijah."
5. TR and Maj.T have ὤφθησαν in place of ὤφθη.
6. Alexander Balmain Bruce, *The Expositor's Greek Testament*, Vol. 1, *The Synoptic Gospels* (Grand Rapids: Eerdmans, 1951), 229.
7. Ibid.
8. NIV has "I will put up."
9. TR and Maj.T have ποιήσωμεν.
10. NIV has "three shelters."
11. NIV has "a bright cloud enveloped them."
12. NIV has "This is my Son, whom I love."
13. NIV has "Jesus came and touched them."
14. TR and Maj.T have ἥψατο αὐτῶν.
15. NIV has "When they looked up."
16. NIV has "they saw no one except Jesus."

17. TR and Maj.T have τὸν Ἰησοῦν μόνον.

18. NIV has "Don't tell anyone what you have seen, until the Son of Man."

19. TRs has Ἡλίαν; WH has Ἠλείαν.

20. NIV has "Elijah has already come."

21. TRs has Ἡλίας; WH has Ἠλείας.

22. NIV has "he has seizures."

23. NIV has "and is suffering greatly."

24. NIV has "O unbelieving and perverse generation."

25. NIV has "Because you have so little faith."

26. TR and Maj.T have ἀπιστίαν.

27. NIV has "as small as a mustard seed."

28. Bruce, *Expositor's*, 233.

29. TR and Maj.T have Μετάβηθι.

30. NIV has "And the disciples were filled with grief."

31. NIV has "the collectors of the two-drachma tax."

32. Josephus, *Antiquities* 3.194.

33. Alfred Plummer, *An Exegetical Commentary on the Gospel According to Saint Matthew* (repr. ed., Grand Rapids: Eerdmans, 1956), 244.

34. James Hope Moulton and George Milligan, *The Vocabulary of the Greek Testament* (London: Hodder and Stoughton, 1952), 159.

35. Bruce, *Expositor's*, 234.

36. NIV has "Jesus was the first to speak."

37. Moulton and Milligan, *Vocabulary*, 556.

38. See A. T. Robertson, *A Grammar of the Greek New Testament in the Light of Historical Research* (Nashville: Broadman, 1934), 1120.

39. NIV has "duty and taxes."

40. NIV has "But so that we may not offend them."

41. NIV has "your line."

42. NIV has "the first fish you catch."

43. NIV has "a four-drachma coin."

44. NIV has "for my tax and yours."

Matthew: Chapter 18

18:1. *"Who then is greatest"*[1] (Τίς ἄρα μείζων ἐστίν). The ἄρα seems to point back to the tax-collection incident when Jesus had claimed exemption for them all as "sons" of the Father. But it was not a new dispute, for jealousy had been growing in their hearts. The wonderful words of Jesus to Peter on Mount Hermon (16:17–19) had evidently made Peter feel a fresh sense of leadership on the basis of which he had dared even to rebuke Jesus for speaking of his death (v. 22). And then Peter was one of the three, with James and John, who accompanied the Master up the Mount of Transfiguration. Peter on that occasion had spoken up promptly. And just now the tax collectors had singled out Peter as the one who seemed to represent the group. Mark 9:33 represents Jesus as asking them about their dispute on the way into the house, perhaps just after their question in Matthew 18:1. Jesus had noticed the wrangling. It will break out again (Matt. 20:20–28; Luke 22:24). Plainly no "primacy of Peter" was admitted by the others. Use of the comparative μείζων (so ὁ μείζων in v. 4), rather than the superlative μέγιστος, is quite in accord with the Κοινή idiom where the comparative is displacing the superlative.[2] But it is a sad discovery to find the disciples chiefly concerned about their own places (offices) in the political kingdom that they expected Jesus to establish.

18:2. *He called a child to Himself*[3] (προσκαλεσάμενος παιδίον[4]). Nominative singular masculine aorist indirect middle participle. It may have been Peter's "little child" (παιδίον), as it was probably in Peter's house (Mark 9:33).

Set him[5] (ἔστησεν αὐτό). Third person singular first aorist active indicative transitive, not intransitive second aorist, ἔστη.

Before them[6] (ἐν μέσῳ αὐτῶν). Luke adds (9:47) "by His side" (παρ᾽ ἑαυτῷ). Both statements can be true.

18:3. *"Unless you are converted and become like children"*[7] (ἐὰν μὴ στραφῆτε καὶ γένησθε ὡς τὰ παιδία). This is a third class condition, undetermined but with the prospect of determination. στραφῆτε is second person plural second aorist passive subjunctive, and γένησθε is second person plural second aorist middle subjunctive. They were headed in the wrong direction with their selfish ambition. "His tone at this time is markedly severe, as much

153

as when He denounces the Pharisaism in the bud He had to deal with."[8] The strong double negative οὐ μὴ εἰσέλθητε means that they will otherwise not get into the kingdom of heaven at all, let alone have big places in it.

18:4. *"This child"* (τὸ παιδίον τοῦτο). Jesus repeated this saying about humility a number of times (for example, 23:12). Probably Jesus pointed to the child by his side. The ninth-century story that the child was Ignatius is worthless. It is not that the child humbled himself, but that the child is humble from the nature of the case, in relation to older persons. That is true, however willful the child may be. Bruce observes that to humble oneself is "the most difficult thing in the world for saint as for sinner."[9]

18:5. *"In My name"* (ἐπὶ τῷ ὀνόματί μου). For "one such little child" (any believer in Christ), Luke (9:48) has "this little child" as a representative or symbol. "On the basis or ground of My name," "for My sake." Very much like εἰς ὄνομα in 10:41, which does not differ greatly from ἐν ὀνόματι (Acts 10:48).

18:6. *"These little ones"* (τῶν μικρῶν τούτων), in the same sense as "one such little one" above. The child is a type representing believers generally.

"A heavy millstone"[10] (μύλος ὀνικός), the large upper millstone that was turned by a donkey (ὄνος). There were no examples of the adjective ὀνικός (turned by a donkey) outside the New Testament until papyri revealed several references to stones or other loads that a donkey was needed to move. G. Adolf Deissmann notes papyri examples of the sale of a donkey and the tax on a donkey's burden of goods.[11]

"The depth of the sea"[12] (τῷ πελάγει τῆς θαλάσσης). "The sea of the sea." Πέλαγος is probably from πλήσσω, "to beat," and so the beating, splashing waves of the sea. "Far out into the open sea, a vivid substitute for εἰς τὴν θάλασσαν."[13]

18:7. *"Through whom"* (δι' οὗ). Jesus recognizes the inevitableness of stumbling blocks, traps, hindrances, the world being as it is, but he does not absolve those who set the traps (cf. Luke 17:1).

18:8–9. *"Into the eternal fire. . . . Into the fiery hell"* (εἰς τὸ πῦρ τὸ αἰώνιον. . . . εἰς τὴν γέενναν τοῦ πυρός). In verses 8–9 occurs one of the doublets in Matthew. For another that is almost the same, see 5:29–30. Jesus must have repeated variations of his pungent sayings many times. Instead of εἰς γέενναν in 5:29–30, 18:8 has εἰς τὸ πῦρ τὸ αἰώνιον, and verse 9 has εἰς τὴν γέενναν τοῦ πυρός.[14] Verse 8 is the first use in Matthew of αἰώνιος. He will use it again in 19:16, 29 with ζωή ("life"), in 25:41 with πῦρ ("fire"), and in 25:46 with κόλασιν ("punishment") and ζωήν. The word αἰώνιος means "without beginning" when applied to the gospel in Romans 16:25 and "ageless, without beginning or end" when applied to God in verse 26. Other places, such as this, it frequently means "without end." The effort to limit the meaning to the fire, but not to the enduring of punishment in the fire, must be applied to the parallel of life as well. If the punishment is limited, *ipso facto* the life is limited.

18:9. *"With one eye"* (μονόφθαλμον), literally "one-eyed." This Ionic compound in Herodotus is condemned by the Atticists, but it is revived in the vernacular Κοινή. Its only uses in the New Testament are here and in Mark 9:47.

18:10. *"Despise one of these little ones"*[15] (καταφρονήσητε ἑνὸς τῶν μικρῶν τούτων). Literally, "think down on," with the assumption of superiority.

"Their angels" (οἱ ἄγγελοι αὐτῶν). The Jews believed that each nation had a guardian angel (Dan. 10:13, 20f.; 12:1). Each of the seven churches in Revelation (1:20) have "angels," whether that means human or divine messengers. Does Jesus mean that each little child or child of faith is cared for by an angel who appears in God's presence and that with special intimacy these "see the face of My Father" (βλέπουσιν τὸ πρόσωπον τοῦ πατρός μου)? Or does he simply mean that the angels do take an interest in the welfare of God's people (Heb. 1:14)? There is comfort to us in that thought. Certainly Jesus means that the Father takes special care of his "little ones," who believe in Him. There are angels in God's presence (Luke 1:19).

18:11. This verse almost certainly is not genuine here, but it occurs in Luke 19:10.[16]

18:12. *"Does he not leave the ninety-nine on the mountains and go and search for the one that is straying?"*[17] (οὐχὶ ἀφήσει τὰ ἐνενήκοντα ἐννέα[18] ἐπὶ τὰ ὄρη καὶ πορευθεὶς ζητεῖ τὸ πλανώμενον;). "Will he not leave the ninety-nine upon the mountains, and going does he not seek (change to present tense) the wandering one?" On the high pastures where the sheep graze at will, one has wandered afield. See this parable in Luke 15:4–7. The English word *planet* is from πλανάομαι. They were called "wandering (or moving) stars" as opposed to "fixed stars," as is their relative appearance in the night sky.

18:14. *"It is not the will of your Father who is in heaven"*[19] (οὐκ ἔστιν θέλημα ἔμπροσθεν τοῦ πατρὸς ὑμῶν τοῦ ἐν οὐρανοῖς). Observe that WH read μου ("my") rather than ὑμῶν ("your") after B Sahidic Coptic. Either makes good sense, though the word *your* carries on the picture of God's care for each "one of these little ones" (ἓν τῶν μικρῶν τούτων) among God's children. The use of ἔμπροσθεν (lit. "before the face; in front of") with θέλημα is a Hebraism, as is ἔμπροσθέν σου in 11:26 with εὐδοκία, "good will, pleasure."

18:15. *"If your brother sins"*[20] ('Ἐὰν δὲ ἁμαρτήσῃ [εἰς σὲ[21]] ὁ ἀδελφός σου). Literally the form means "commits a sin," third person singular ingressive aorist active subjunctive of ἁμαρτάνω.

"Show him his fault" (ἔλεγξον αὐτόν). Private reproof is hard, but it is the way of Christ.

"You have won" (ἐκέρδησας). Second person singular aorist active indicative of κερδαίνω in conclusion of a third class condition, a sort of timeless aorist, a blessed achievement already made.

18:16. *"Take one or two more with you"*[22] (παράλαβε μετὰ σοῦ ἔτι ἕνα ἢ δύο). Take along (παρά) with (μετά) you (cf. Deut. 19:15).

18:17. *"He refuses to listen to them"* (παρακούσῃ αὐτῶν). The meaning is the same as Isaiah 65:12, in which God is the ignored one. There are many papyrus examples for "ignoring, disregarding, hearing without heeding, hearing aside (παρα-), hearing amiss, or overhearing" (Mark 5:36).

"The church" (τῇ ἐκκλησίᾳ). In view is the local assembly, not the general as in 16:18 (see discussion on). The problem here is whether Jesus has in mind an actual body of believers in existence or whether he is speaking prophetically of local churches as they will be organized after Pentecost. Some see this as evidence that the twelve apostles already constitute a local ἐκκλησία, a sort of moving church of preachers. That could be true only in essence, since they did not have a localized assembly. Alexander Bruce holds that they were "the nucleus" of a local church at any rate.[23]

18:18. *"Shall have been bound"*[24] (ἔσται δεδεμένα ἐν οὐρανῷ[25]). Third person plural future indicative with a nominative plural neuter perfect passive participle as a periphrastic construction as in "shall have been loosed"[26] (ἔσται λελυμένα). In 16:19 this same unusual form occurs. There the finding and the loosing seems addressed only to Peter, but it is here repeated for the church, or at least the disciples.

18:19. *"If two of you agree"* (ἐὰν δύο συμφωνήσωσιν ἐξ ὑμῶν). The English *symphony* is from this root. The word no longer means "a concord of voices, a chorus in harmony," though that would be an appropriate ideal for the church.

"By My Father" (παρὰ τοῦ πατρός μου), from the side of My Father.

18:20. *"I am there"*[27] (ἐκεῖ εἰμι). This blessed promise implies that those gathered are really disciples with the Spirit of Christ as well as disciples "in My name" (εἰς τὸ ἐμὸν ὄνομα). One of the Oxyrhynchus "Sayings of Our

Lord" is: "Wherever there are (two) they are not without God, and wherever there is one alone I say I am with him." Also this: "Raise the stone and there you will find me, cleave the wood and there am I."

18:21. *"Up to seven times?"* (ἕως ἑπτάκις). Peter thought that he was being generous in wondering if he should forgive a brother as many as seven times. The Jewish rule for forgiving someone was three times (Amos 1:6). The question is a natural extension of Matthew 18:15. "Against me" seems genuine here. "The man who asks such a question does not really know what forgiveness means."[28]

18:22. *"Up to seventy times seven"* (ἕως ἑβδομηκοντάκις ἑπτά). It is not clear whether this idiom means seventy-seven or 490 ("seventy times seven"). If ἑπτάκις occurred here, it would clearly be 490 times. The same ambiguity is seen in Geneses 4:24, where the LXX text, by omitting και makes Lamech's boasted revenge either seventy-seven or 490 times as great as the offense. In *Testament of the Twelve Patriarchs, Benjamin,*[29] it is used clearly in the sense of seventy times seven. The question is meaningless in Matthew 18:22. Jesus obviously means that forgiveness is to be unlimited, whichever number is used. "The unlimited revenge of primitive man has given place to the unlimited forgiveness of Christians."[30]

18:23. *"Who wished to settle accounts"* (ὃς ἠθέλησεν συνᾶραι λόγον), seen also in 25:19. Perhaps a Latinism, *rationes conferre.* First aorist active infinitive of συναίρω, to cast up accounts, to settle, to compare accounts with. Not in ancient Greek writers, but in two papyri of the second century A.D. in the very sense here. The substantive appears in an early-third-century Nubian ostracon.[31]

18:24. *"Ten thousand talents"* (μυρίων ταλάντων). One talent was the value equivalent of six thousand denarii, the equivalent of six thousand working days' pay or thirty years of work. A single talent was nearly a lifetime's income. The imperial taxes of Judea, Idumea, and Samaria for one year raised only 600 talents, while Galilee and Perea paid 200.[32]

18:25. *"He did not have the means to repay"*[33] (μὴ ἔχοντος δὲ αὐτοῦ ἀποδοῦναι). There is no "no means" in the Greek. This idiom is seen in Luke 7:42; 14:14; Hebrews 6:13. Genitive absolute though αὐτόν in the same clause as often found in the New Testament.

"To be sold" (πραθῆναι), first aorist passive infinitive of πιπράσκω. This was according to the law (Exod. 22:3; Lev. 25:39, 47). Wife and children were treated as property in those primitive times.

18:27. *"The debt"* (τὸ δάνειον). The term is common in the papyri in referring to a loan. The interest had increased the debt enormously. "This heavy oriental usury is of the scenery of the parable."[34]

18:28. *"Who owed him a hundred denarii"* (ὃς ὤφειλεν αὐτῷ ἑκατὸν δηνάρια). A denarius was worth about eight and a half pence. The hundred denarii here were equal to some "fifty shillings,"[35] "about four pounds,"[36] "twenty pounds" (Moffatt), "twenty dollars" (Goodspeed), "100 shillings" (Weymouth). These are various efforts to represent in modern language the small amount of this debt compared with the big one.

"He seized him"[37] (ἔπνιγεν). "Held him by the throat."[38] It is third person singular imperfect active indicative, probably inchoative (inceptive), "began to choke or throttle him." The Roman law allowed this indignity. Marvin R. Vincent quotes Livy,[39] who tells how the necks were twisted (*collum torsisset*), and how Cicero[40] says, "Lead him to the judgment seat with twisted neck (*collo aborto*)."

"What you owe" (εἴ τι ὀφείλεις[41]). Literally, "if you owe anything," however little. He did not even know how much it was, only that he owed him something. "The 'if' is simply the expression of a pitiless logic."[42]

18:30. *"But he was unwilling"*[43] (ὁ δὲ οὐκ ἤθελεν). Third person singular imperfect active indicative indicating persistent refusal.

"Until he should pay back" (ἕως ἀποδῷ[44]). This futuristic aorist subjunctive is the rule with ἕως for a future goal. He was to stay in prison until he should pay. "He acts on the instinct of a base nature, and also doubtless in accordance with long habits of harsh tyrannical behavior towards men in his power."[45] On debt imprisonment among the Greeks and Romans, see Deissmann.[46]

18:31. *"Reported"*[47] (διεσάφησαν), made wholly clear to the lord.

18:33. *"Should you not also"*[48] (οὐκ ἔδει καὶ σέ[;]). "Was it not necessary?" The king fits the cap on this wicked slave that he put on the poor debtor.

18:34. *"The torturers"*[49] (τοῖς βασανισταῖς). Not simply to prison, but to terrible punishment. The papyri give various instances of the verb βασανίζω, "to torture," which was applied to slaves and others. "Livy (ii.23) pictures an old centurion complaining that he was taken by his creditor, not into servitude, but to a workhouse and torture, showing his back scarred with fresh wounds."[50]

"Until he should repay all"[51] (ἕως οὗ ἀποδῷ πᾶν). Just as in verse 30, his very words. But this is not purgatorial but punitive, for he could never pay back that vast debt.

18:35. *"From your heart"* (ἀπὸ τῶν καρδιῶν ὑμῶν). No sham or lip pardon, and as often as needed.[52] This is Christ's full reply to Peter's question in 18:21.

NOTES

1.   NIV has "Who is the greatest."
2.   A. T. Robertson, *A Grammar of the Greek New Testament in the Light of Historical Research* (Nashville: Broadman, 1934), 667ff.
3.   NIV has "He called a little child."
4.   TR and Maj.T has προσκαλεσάμενος ὁ Ἰησοῦς παιδίον.
5.   NIV has "had him stand."
6.   NIV has "among them."
7.   NIV has "unless you change and become like little children."
8.   Alexander Balmain Bruce, *The Expositor's Greek Testament*, Vol. 1, *The Synoptic Gospels* (Grand Rapids: Eerdmans, 1951), 236.
9.   Ibid.
10. NIV has "a large millstone."
11. G. Adolf Deissmann, *Light from the Ancient East: The New Testament Illustrated by Recently Discovered Texts of the Graeco-Roman World*, trans. L. R. M. Strachan (rev. ed., Grand Rapids: Baker, 1965), 81.
12. NIV has "the depths of the sea."
13. Alan Hugh McNeile, *The Gospel According to St. Matthew: The Greek Text with Introduction, Notes, and Indices* (repr. ed., Grand Rapids: Baker, 1980) 261.
14. NIV has "into the fire of hell."
15. NIV has "look down on one of these little ones."
16. A. T. Robertson, *Commentary on the Gospel According to Matthew* (New York: Macmillan, 1911), 202.
17. NIV has "will he not leave the ninety-nine on the hills and go to look for the one that wandered off?"
18. TR has ἀφεις τὰ ἐννενηκονταεννέα; Maj.T has ἀφεις τὰ ἐννήκοντα ἐννέα.
19. NIV has "your Father in heaven is not willing."
20. NIV has "if your brother sins against you."
21. WH, based on Aleph B Sanhidic, does not include "against you" (εἰς σέ). "These words are possibly not genuine, but they correctly interpret the sense, as is plain from verse 21f.; also Luke 17:3f., where this logion occurs in another connection," Robertson, *Commentary on Matthew*, 202.
22. NIV has "take one or two others along."
23. Bruce, *Expositor's*, 1.240.

24. NIV has "will be bound."
25. TR and Maj.T have ἔσται δεδεμένα ἐν τῷ οὐρανῷ.
26. NIV has "will be loosed."
27. NIV has "there am I."
28. Alfred Plummer, *An Exegetical Commentary on the Gospel According to Saint Matthew* (repr. ed., Grand Rapids: Eerdmans, 1956), 255.
29. 7.4.
30. McNeile, *Matthew*, 268.
31. Deissmann, *Light from the Ancient East*, 117.
32. Josephus, *Antiquities*, 11.4.
33. NIV has "he was not able to pay."
34. McNeile, *Matthew*, 269.
35. Bruce, *Expositor's*, 243. All the equivalencies given in this volume refer to 1930s monetary value. Such figures vary radically, of course, mirroring the economics of the time.
36. McNeile, *Matthew*, 269.
37. NIV has "He grabbed him."
38. Willoughby G. Allen, *A Critical and Exegetical Commentary on the Gospel According to Matthew*, International Critical Commentary (Edinburgh: T. & T. Clark, 1912), 200.
39. 4.53.
40. *Pro cluentio*, 21.
41. TR has ὅτι ὀφείλεις.
42. Heinrich August Meyer, *Critical and Exegetical Hand-Book to the Gospel of Matthew*, Vol. 1 (repr. ed., Winona Lake, Ind.: Alpha, 1980), 333.
43. NIV has "But he refused."
44. TR and Maj.T have ἕως οὗ ἀποδῷ.
45. Bruce, *Expositor's*, 243.
46. Deissmann, *Light from the Ancient East*, 270, 330.
47. NIV has "told."
48. NIV has "shouldn't you."
49. NIV has "to be tortured."
50. Marvin R. Vincent, *Word Studies in the New Testament*, Vol. 1, *The Synoptic Gospels* (repr. ed., Grand Rapids: Eerdmans, 1946), 107.
51. NIV has "until he should pay back all."
52. "Cherished resentment is not forgiveness." Robertson, *Commentary on Matthew*, 205.

Matthew: Chapter 19

19:1. *He departed*[1] (μετῆρεν), literally, to lift up, change something to another place. It is transitive in the LXX and in a Cilician rock inscription. It is intransitive here and in 13:53, the only New Testament instances. Absence of ὅτι or καί after καὶ ἐγένετο makes this one of the clear Hebraisms in the New Testament.[2] This language is a sort of formula that Matthew sets at the close of important groups of λόγια, as in 7:28; 11:1; 13:53.

The region of Judea beyond the Jordan[3] (τὰ ὅρια τῆς Ἰουδαίας πέραν τοῦ Ἰορδάνου). This is a curious expression. It apparently means that Jesus left Galilee to go to Judea by way of Perea as the Galileans often did, to avoid passing through Samaria. Luke (17:11) expressly says that he passed through Samaria and Galilee when he left Ephraim in northern Judea (John 11:54). He was not afraid to pass through the edge of Galilee and down the Jordan Valley in Perea on this last journey to Jerusalem. McNeile is needlessly opposed to the trans-Jordanic or Perean aspect of this phase of Christ's work.[4]

19:3. *Some Pharisees came to Jesus, testing Him*[5] (προσῆλθον αὐτῷ Φαρισαῖοι πειράζοντες αὐτόν[6]). They "could not ask a question of Jesus without sinister motives."[7] See on 4:1 regarding the word πειράζω.

"For any reason at all"[8] (κατὰ πᾶσαν αἰτίαν). This clause is an allusion to the dispute between the two theological schools over the meaning of Deuteronomy 24:1. The school of Shammai took the strict and unpopular view of divorce for unchastity alone, while the school of Hillel took the liberal and popular view of easy divorce for any passing whim. The husband could divorce if he saw a more pleasing woman or if his wife burned his food. It was a dilemma and meant to divide Jesus' popularity with the people. There is no real trouble about the use of κατά here in the sense of because of.[9]

19:5. *"Be joined"*[10] (κολληθήσεται[11]). The third person singular future passive indicative verb means, "shall be glued to," the verb means.

"The two shall become one flesh" (ἔσονται οἱ δύο εἰς σάρκα μίαν). This use of εἰς after εἰμι is called a predicate accusative and is an imitation of the Hebrew, though a few examples occur in the older Greek and in the papyri. Its

161

frequency is due to Hebrew influence, and in such texts as this one and the LXX, the form is a direct translation of the Hebrew idiom.

19:6. *"What therefore God has joined together"* (ὃ οὖν ὁ θεὸς συνέζευξεν). Note "what," not "whom." The marriage relation God has made. "The creation of sex, and the high doctrine as to the cohesion it produces between man and woman, laid down in Genesis, interdict separation."[12] The word for "joined together" means "yoked together," a common verb for marriage in ancient Greek. It is the timeless aorist indicative (συνέζευξεν), true always.

19:7. *"A certificate"* (βιβλίον). A little βίβλος (see on 1:1), a scroll or document (papyrus or parchment). This was some protection to the divorced wife and a restriction on laxity.

19:8. *"Because of your hardness of heart"*[13] (πρὸς τὴν σκληροκαρδίαν ὑμῶν). Σκληροκαρδίαν evidently is strictly of biblical origin. It is found only in the LXX and the New Testament. The meaning is a heart dried up (οκληρός), hard and tough.

"But from the beginning it has not been this way"[14] (ἀπ᾽ ἀρχῆς δὲ οὐ γέγονεν οὕτως). Third person singular (present) perfect active indicative of γίνομαι is used to emphasize the permanence of the divine ideal. "The original ordinance has never been abrogated nor superseded, but continues in force."[15] "How small the Pharisaic disputants must have felt in the presence of such holy teaching, which soars above the partisan view of controversialists into the serene region of idea, universal, eternal truth."[16]

19:9. *"Except for immorality"*[17] (μὴ ἐπὶ πορνείᾳ). The marginal reading in WH (παρεκτὸς λόγου πορνείας) also adds "makes her an adulteress" (ποιεῖ αὐτὴν μοιχευθῆναι) and also these words: "and he that marries her when she is put away commits adultery" (καὶ ὁ ἀπολελυμένην γαμήσας μοιχᾶται). There seems to be a certain amount of assimilation in various manuscripts between this verse and the words in 5:32. But, whatever reading is accepted here, even the short one in WH (μὴ ἐπὶ πορνείᾳ, not for fornication), it is plain that Matthew represents Jesus in both places as allowing divorce for "fornication" (πορνεία), which is technically adultery (μοιχεία is a cognate noun from the verb μοιχάω or μοιχεύω). Here, as in 5:31–32, a group of scholars deny the genuineness of the exception given by Matthew alone. McNeile holds that "the addition of the saving clause is, in fact, opposed to the spirit of the whole context, and must have been made at a time when the practice of divorce for adultery had already grown up."[18] That in my opinion is gratuitous criticism that is unwilling to accept Matthew's report because it disagrees with the view Matthew expresses. He adds: "It cannot be supposed that Matthew wished to represent Jesus as siding with the school of Shammai." Why not, if Shammai on this point agreed with Jesus? Those who deny Matthew's report are those who are opposed to remarriage at all. Jesus by implication, as in 5:31, does allow remarriage of the innocent party, but not of the guilty one. Certainly Jesus has lifted the whole subject of marriage and divorce to a new level, far beyond the petty contentions of the schools of Hillel and Shammai.

19:10. *The disciples said to Him* ($\lambda\acute{\epsilon}\gamma o\upsilon\sigma\iota\nu$ $\alpha\dot{\upsilon}\tau\hat{\omega}$ $o\dot{\iota}$ $\mu\alpha\theta\eta\tau\alpha\dot{\iota}$ [$\alpha\dot{\upsilon}\tau o\hat{\upsilon}$]). "Christ's doctrine on marriage not only separated Him *toto caelo* from Pharisaic opinions of all shades, but was too high even for the Twelve."[19]

"The relationship"[20] ($\dot{\eta}$ $\alpha\dot{\iota}\tau\acute{\iota}\alpha$). The word may refer to the use in verse 3 "for every cause." It may have a vague idea here = *res*, condition. But the point clearly is that "it is not expedient to marry" ($o\dot{\upsilon}$ $\sigma\upsilon\mu\phi\acute{\epsilon}\rho\epsilon\iota$ $\gamma\alpha\mu\hat{\eta}\sigma\alpha\iota$) if such a strict view is held. If the bond is so tight, a man had best not commit matrimony. It is a bit unusual to have $\ddot{\alpha}\nu\theta\rho\omega\pi o\varsigma$ and $\gamma\upsilon\nu\acute{\eta}$ contrasted rather than $\dot{\alpha}\nu\acute{\eta}\rho$ and $\gamma\upsilon\nu\acute{\eta}$.

19:11. *"But only those to whom it has been given"* ($\dot{\alpha}\lambda\lambda$' $o\hat{\iota}\varsigma$ $\delta\acute{\epsilon}\delta o\tau\alpha\iota$). This is a neat Greek idiom, dative case of relation and third person singular perfect passive indicative. The same idea is repeated at the close of verse 12. It is a voluntary renunciation of marriage for the sake of the kingdom of heaven. "Jesus recognizes the severity of the demand as going beyond the capacity of all but a select number." It was a direct appeal to the spiritual intelligence of the disciples not to misconceive his meaning, as certainly the monastic orders have done.

19:13. *And the disciples rebuked them* ($o\dot{\iota}$ $\delta\grave{\epsilon}$ $\mu\alpha\theta\eta\tau\alpha\dot{\iota}$ $\dot{\epsilon}\pi\epsilon\tau\acute{\iota}\mu\eta\sigma\epsilon\nu$ $\alpha\dot{\upsilon}\tau o\hat{\iota}\varsigma$). No doubt people did often crowd around Jesus for a touch of his hand and his blessing. The disciples probably felt that they were doing Jesus a kindness. How little they understood children and Jesus. It is a tragedy to make children feel that they are in the way at home and at church. These men were the twelve apostles and yet had no vision of Christ's love for little children. Where children are protected, the reason usually is the influence of Christians and the words of Jesus.

19:14. *"Let"* ($\ddot{A}\phi\epsilon\tau\epsilon$). "Leave them alone," a second person plural second aorist active imperative.

"Do not hinder them" ($\mu\grave{\eta}$ $\kappa\omega\lambda\acute{\upsilon}\epsilon\tau\epsilon$ $\alpha\dot{\upsilon}\tau\acute{\alpha}$). The idiom of $\mu\acute{\eta}$ with the present imperative means "Stop hindering them."

"Such as these" ($\tau\hat{\omega}\nu$ . . . $\tau o\iota o\acute{\upsilon}\tau\omega\nu$), children and the childlike (see on 18:3–6).

19:16. *"What good thing"* ($\tau\acute{\iota}$ $\dot{\alpha}\gamma\alpha\theta\grave{o}\nu$). Mark (10:17) has the adjective "good" with "Teacher."

"I may obtain"[21] (σχῶ[22]). First person singular ingressive aorist active subjunctive, "may get or acquire."

19:17. *"Why are you asking Me about what is good?"* (Τί με ἐρωτᾷς περὶ τοῦ ἀγαθοῦ;[23]). He had asked Jesus in verse 16 "what good thing" he should do. He evidently had a light idea of the meaning of ἀγαθός. "This was only a teacher's way of leading on a pupil."[24] So Jesus explains that "One there is who is good," one alone who is really good in the absolute sense.

19:20. *"What am I still lacking?"*[25] (τί ἔτι ὑστερῶ;). The man suffers from what feels like a psychological paradox. He finds no fault in himself regarding the keeping of all these commandments, yet he has an uneasy conscience. Jesus called him to what he did not have. He thought of goodness as *quantitative* (a series of acts) and not *qualitative* (of the nature of God). Did his question reveal proud complacency or pathetic despair? Perhaps there was a bit of both.

19:21. *"If you wish to be complete"*[26] (Εἰ θέλεις τέλειος εἶναι). This is a condition of the first class, determined as fulfilled. Jesus assumes that the young man really desires to be perfect (see Matt. 5:48).

"Your possessions" (σου τὰ ὑπάρχοντα). "Your belongings." The Greek neuter plural participle used like the now antiquated English word *belonging*. "Your belongings." The Greek neuter plural participle used like the English word "belongings." It was a huge demand, for he was rich.

19:22. *He went away grieving*[27] (ἀπῆλθεν λυπούμενος). "Went away grieved." He felt that Jesus had asked too much of him. He worshiped money more than God when put to the test. Jesus, demand is not given as normative, except to those who are in the grip of materialism. Different persons are in the power of different sins. One sin is enough to keep one away from Christ.

19:23. *"It is hard"* (δυσκόλως), "with difficulty," an adverb from δύσκολος. This word has a range of meanings from "hard to find food, fastidious, and faultfinding" to the sense in which it is used here, "difficult."

19:24. *"It is easier for a camel to go through the eye of a needle"* (εὐκοπώτερόν ἐστιν κάμηλον διὰ τρυπήματος ῥαφίδος διελθεῖν[28]). Jesus, of course, means by this comparison, whether an Eastern proverb or not, to express the impossible. The efforts to explain it as a possibility are doomed, whether as referring to a ship's cable, κάμιλον, or ῥαφίς as a narrow gorge, or as some entrance gate that camels must kneel to go through. Jesus pointedly calls the thing "impossible" (v. 26). The Jews in the Babylonian Talmud did have a proverb that a man even in his dreams did not see an elephant pass through the eye of a needle.[29] The Qur'an speaks of the wicked finding the gates of heaven shut "till a camel shall pass through the eye of a needle." The Qur'an, however, copies many biblical allusions. The word for an ordinary needle is $\dot{\rho}\alpha\phi\dot{\iota}\varsigma$. Luke 18:25 employs $\beta\epsilon\lambda\acute{o}\nu\eta$, the medical term for a surgical needle not used elsewhere in the New Testament.

19:25. *Were very astonished*[30] ($\dot{\epsilon}\xi\epsilon\pi\lambda\acute{\eta}\sigma\sigma o\nu\tau o$). The third person plural imperfect passive indicative is descriptive of their blank amazement. They were literally "struck out."

19:26. *Looking at them*[31] ($\dot{\epsilon}\mu\beta\lambda\acute{\epsilon}\psi\alpha\varsigma$). Jesus saw their amazement.

19:27. *"What then will there be for us?"* ($\tau\acute{\iota}$ $\ddot{\alpha}\rho\alpha$ $\ddot{\epsilon}\sigma\tau\alpha\iota$ $\dot{\eta}\mu\hat{\iota}\nu;$). A pathetic question, showing a hopeless lack of comprehension.

19:28. *"In the regeneration"*[32] ($\dot{\epsilon}\nu$ $\tau\hat{\eta}$ $\pi\alpha\lambda\iota\gamma\gamma\epsilon\nu\epsilon\sigma\acute{\iota}\alpha$[33]). The new birth of the world is to be fulfilled when Jesus sits on his throne of glory. This word was used by the Stoics and the Pythagoreans. It is common also in the mystery religions.[34] It is found in the papyri also. We must put no fantastic ideas into the mouth of Jesus, but he did look toward the consummation of his kingdom. What is meant about the disciples also sitting on twelve thrones is not clear.

19:29. *"Many times as much"*[35] ($\dot{\epsilon}\kappa\alpha\tau o\nu\tau\alpha\pi\lambda\alpha\sigma\acute{\iota}o\nu\alpha$[36]). Eternal life is the real reward.

19:30. *"But many who are first will be last; and the last, first"*[37] ($\Pi o\lambda\lambda o\grave{\iota}$ $\delta\grave{\epsilon}$ $\ddot{\epsilon}\sigma o\nu\tau\alpha\iota$ $\pi\rho\hat{\omega}\tau o\grave{\iota}$ $\ddot{\epsilon}\sigma\chi\alpha\tau o\iota$ $\kappa\alpha\grave{\iota}$ $\ddot{\epsilon}\sigma\chi\alpha\tau o\iota$ $\pi\rho\hat{\omega}\tau o\iota$). This paradoxical enigma is probably in the nature of a rebuke to Peter and refers to rank in the kingdom. There are other possible applications, as the following parable illustrates.

NOTES

1. NIV has "he left."
2. A. T. Robertson, *A Grammar of the Greek New Testament in the Light of Historical Research* (Nashville: Broadman, 1934), 1042f.
3. NIV has "the region of Judea to the other side of the Jordan."
4. Alan Hugh McNeile, *The Gospel According to St. Matthew: The Greek Text with Introduction, Notes, and Indices* (repr. ed., Grand Rapids: Baker, 1980), 271.
5. NIV has "Some Pharisees came to him to test him." The NASB includes the name Jesus, which is not found in the Greek text, but definitely refers to him.
6. TR and Maj.T. have the article, $o\dot{\iota}$ $\Phi\alpha\rho\iota\sigma\alpha\hat{\iota}o\iota$.
7. Alexander Balmain Bruce, *The Expositor's Greek Testament*, Vol. 1, *The Synoptic Gospels* (Grand Rapids: Eerdmans, 1951), 245.
8. NIV has "for any and every reason."

9. Robertson, *Grammar*, 509.

10. NIV has "be united."

11. TR and Maj.T have προσκολληθήσεται.

12. Bruce, *Expositor's*, 246.

13. NIV has "because your hearts were hard."

14. NIV has "But it was not this way from the beginning."

15. Marvin R. Vincent, *Word Studies in the New Testament*, Vol. 1, *The Synoptic Gospels* (repr. ed., Grand Rapids: Eerdmans, 1946), 108.

16. Bruce, *Expositor's*, 246.

17. NIV has "except for marital unfaithfulness."

18. McNeile, *Matthew*, 274.

19. Bruce, *Expositor's*, 246.

20. NIV has "the situation."

21. NIV has "to get."

22. TR and Maj.T have the present tense verb, ἔχω.

23. TR and Maj.T have Τί με λέγειν ἀγαθόν;

24. Bruce, *Expositor's*, 249.

25. NIV has "What do I still lack?"

26. NIV has "If you want to be perfect."

27. NIV has "he went away sad."

28. TR and Maj.T have διελθεῖν. "Jesus meant the illustration to be taken literally. . . . It is an exaggeration, but designedly so. There was at that time no door in Jaffa Gate called 'Needle's eye.'" A. T. Robertson, *Commentary on the Gospel According to Matthew* (New York: Macmillan, 1911), 211.

29. Vincent, *Word Studies*, 109.

30. NIV has "were greatly astonished."

31. NIV has "looked at them."

32. NIV has "at the renewal."

33. WH has a different spelling, ἐν τῇ παλινγενεσίᾳ. "This word occurs only one other time in the New Testament (Titus 3:5) and then in the sense of personal regeneration." A. T. Robertson, *Commentary on the Gospel According to Matthew* (New York: Macmillan, 1911), 212.

34. Samuel Angus, *The Mystery Religions and Christianity: A Study in the Religious Background of Early Christianity* (London: J. Murray, 1925), 95ff.

35. NIV has "a hundred times as much."

36. WH reads πολλαπλασίονα, manifold.

37. NIV has "But many who are first will be last, and many who are last will be first."

Matthew: Chapter 20

20:1. *"For"* (γάρ). The parable illustrates the aphorism in 19:30.

"A landowner" (ἀνθρώπῳ οἰκοδεσπότῃ). As in the case of ἄνθρωποι βασιλεῖ in 18:23, we need not use the word *man* to literally translate ἄνθρωπος. The meaning is best rendered in English, simply "a landowner."

"Early in the morning" (ἅμα πρωΐ). A classic idiom. Ἅμα as an "improper" preposition is common in the papyri. Πρωΐ is just an adverb in the locative form. It refers to early dawn, break of day, country fashion for starting to work.

"To hire" (μισθώσασθαι). The middle voice aorist tense means to hire for oneself.

20:2. *"For a denarius for the day"* (ἐκ δηναρίου τὴν ἡμέραν). A normal day's wage (see on 18:28). The ἐκ with the ablative represents the agreement (συμφωνήσας) with the workmen (ἐργατῶν). "The day," the Greek has it, an accusative of extent of time.

20:3. *"Standing idle in the market place"*[1] (ἐστῶτας ἐν τῇ ἀγορᾷ ἀργούς). The marketplace was the place where day workmen and employers met. At Hamadan in Persia, Morier in *Second Journey Through Persia*, as cited by Richard Trench,[2] says: "We observed every morning, before the sun rose, that a numerous band of peasants were collected, with spades in their hands, waiting to be hired for the day to work in the surrounding fields."

20:4. *"Whatever is right"* (ὃ ἐὰν ᾖ δίκαιον). "Is fair,"[3] not anything he pleased, but a just proportionate wage. Indefinite relative with subjunctive ἐάν = ἄν.

20:6. *"Idle all day long"*[4] (ὅλην τὴν ἡμέραν ἀργοί). Extent of time (accusative) again. Ἀργοί is α privative and ἔργον, work, no work, is the problem of the unemployed.

20:10. *"But each of them also received a denarius"* (καὶ ἔλαβον [τὸ] ἀνὰ δηνάριον καὶ αὐτοί[5]). Literally, "themselves also a denarius apiece" (distributive use of ἀνά). Bruce asks if this householder was a humorist when he began to pay off the last first and paid each one a denarius according to agreement. False hopes were raised in those who came first until they got only what they had agreed to receive.[6]

20:11. *"They grumbled"*[7] (ἐγόγγυζον). Onomatopoetic word, the meaning suiting the sound. Our words murmur and grumble are similar. Probably here it is an inchoative (ingressive) imperfect, began to grumble. It occurs in old Ionic and in the papyri.

20:12. *"You have made them equal to us"* (ἴσους ἡμῖν αὐτοὺς ἐποίησας), associative instrumental case ἡμῖν after ἴσους. It was a protest against the supposed injustice of the householder.

"The burden and the scorching heat of the day"[8] (τὸ βάρος τῆς ἡμέρας καὶ τὸν καύσωνα). The last had worked one hour. Apparently they worked as hard as any while they were at it, but others of these sweat-stained men had stood the sirocco, the hot, dry, dust-laden east wind. This is the wind that had blasted the grain in Pharaoh's dream (Gen. 41:6), withered Jonah's gourd (Jonah 4:8), and blighted the vine in Ezekiel's parable (Ezek. 17:10). The complainers seemed to have a good case.

20:13. *"And said to one of them"*[9] (ἑνὶ αὐτῶν εἶπεν[10]). Evidently the spokesman of the group. "Friend" (Ἑταῖρε), "comrade." The landowner made a kindly reply to the one in place of addressing the whole crew. Εταῖρε survives in modern Greek.

20:14. *"Take"* (ἆρον), second person singular aorist active imperative of αἴρω. Pick up, as if he had saucily refused to take it from the table or had contemptuously thrown the denarius on the ground. If the first had been paid first and sent away, there would probably have been no murmuring, but "the murmuring is needed to bring out the lesson."[11]

"I wish"[12] (θέλω). The *will* of the landowner is the point of the parable.

20:15. *"What I wish with what is my own?"*[13] (ὁ θέλω . . . ἐν τοῖς ἐμοῖς[;]), in the sphere of my own affairs. There is in the Κοινή an extension of the instrumental use of ἐν.

"Is your eye envious?"[14] (ὁ ὀφθαλμός σου πονηρός ἐστιν . . . ;). See on 6:22–24 about the evil eye and the good eye. The complainer has a grudging eye while the landowner has a liberal or generous eye. See Romans 5:7 for a distinction between δίκαιος and ἀγαθός.

20:16. *"The last shall be first, and the first last"*[15] (ἔσονται οἱ ἔσχατοι πρῶτοι καὶ οἱ πρῶτοι ἔσχατοι). The adjectives change places as compared with 19:30. The point is the same, though this order suits the parable better. After all one's work does not rest wholly on the amount of time spent on it. "Even so hath Rabbi Bun bar Chija in twenty-eight years wrought more than many studious scholars in a hundred years."[16]

20:17. *Aside* (κατ᾽ ἰδίαν). This is the prediction in Matthew of the cross (16:21; 17:22; 20:17). "Aside by themselves" (Moffatt). The verb is παρέλαβεν. Jesus is having his inward struggle (Mark 10:32) and makes one more effort to get the Twelve to understand him.

20:19. *"And crucify"*[17] (καὶ σταυρῶσαι). The details fall on deaf ears, even the point of the Resurrection on the third day.

20:20. *Then* (Τότε). Surely an inopportune time for such a request, just after the pointed prediction of Christ's crucifixion. Perhaps their minds had been preoccupied with the words of Jesus (19:28) that they would sit on twelve thrones, taking these arrangements in a literal sense. The mother of James and John, probably Salome, possibly a sister of the Master's mother (John 19:25), apparently prompted her two sons because of the family relationship and now speaks for them.

Making a request[18] (αἰτοῦσά τι). "Asking something," "plotting perhaps when their Master was predicting."[19] The "something" put forward as a small matter was simply the choice of the two chief thrones promised by Jesus (19:28).

20:22. *"You do not know what you are asking"* (Οὐκ οἴδατε τί αἰτεῖσθε). Αἰτεῖσθε is second person plural indirect middle aorist, "ask for yourselves," "a selfish request."

"We are able" (Δυνάμεθα). This is amazing proof of their ignorance and self-confidence. Ambition had blinded their eyes. They had not caught the martyr spirit.

20:23. *"You shall drink"*[20] (πίεσθε), second person plural future middle indicative from πίνω. Christ's cup was martyrdom. James was the first of the Twelve to meet the martyr's death (Acts 12:2) and John the last if reports are true about him. How little they knew what they were saying.

20:24. *The ten became indignant*[21] (οἱ δέκα ἠγανάκτησαν), a strong word for angry resentment. The ten felt that James and John had taken advantage of their relation to Jesus.

20:25. *Called them to Himself*[22] (προσκαλεσάμενος), nominative singular masculine indirect middle aorist participle, calling to him. "They were all in sore need of more instruction about humility and service."[23]

20:26. *"Whoever wishes to become great"*[24] (ὃς ἐὰν θέλῃ ἐν ὑμῖν μέγας γενέσθαι). Jesus does not condemn the desire to become great. It is a laudable ambition. There are "great ones" (μεγαλοί) among Christians as among pagans, but they do not "lord it over" one another (κατακυριεύουσιν), a LXX word and very expressive, or "play the tyrant" (κατεξουσιάζουσιν), another suggestive word.

"Your servant" (ὑμῶν διάκονος). This word may come from διά and κόνις ("dust"), "to raise a dust by one's hurry," and so "to minister." It is a general word for servant and is used in a variety of ways, including the technical sense of our "deacon" in Philippians 1:1. More frequently it was applied in the New Testament church to ministers of the gospel (1 Cor. 3:5). The way to be "first" (πρῶτος), says Jesus, is to be your "servant" (δοῦλος). This reversed popular opinion then as now.

20:28. "A ransom for many" (λύτρον ἀντὶ πολλῶν). The Son of Man is the outstanding illustration of this principle of self-abnegation, in direct contrast to the self-seeking ambition of James and John. The word translated "ransom" is the one commonly employed in the papyri as the price paid for a slave who is then set free by the one who bought him, the purchase money for manumitting slaves.[25] There is the notion of exchange also in the use of ἀντί. Jesus gave his own life as the price of freedom for the slaves of sin. There are those who refuse to admit that Jesus held this notion of a *substitutionary* death because the word occurs only here and the corresponding passage in Mark 10:45 in the New Testament. But one cannot so easily get rid of passages that contradict a theological opinion. Jesus here rises to the full consciousness of the significance of his death for men.

20:29. *They were leaving Jericho*[26] (ἐκπορευομένων αὐτῶν ἀπὸ Ἰεριχώ[27]). Matthew and Mark 10:46 indicate that Jesus and the disciples were leaving Jericho, while Luke 18:35 places the incident as they were *drawing near* to Jericho (εἰς Ἰεριχώ). It is probably that Mark and Matthew refer to the old Jericho, the ruins of which have been discovered, while Luke alludes to the new Roman Jericho. This explanation places the two blind men between the two towns. In the state of Kentucky in the United States are two towns about a half mile apart, both called "Pleasureville" (one Old Pleasureville, the other New Pleasureville). Mark (10:46) and Luke (18:35) mention only one blind man, Bartimaeus (Mark).

20:30. *That Jesus was passing by*[28] (ὅτι Ἰησοῦς παράγει). "Two blind men were sitting by the road"[29] (δύο τυφλοὶ καθήμενοι παρὰ τὴν ὁδόν) at their regular stand. They heard the crowd yelling that Jesus of Nazareth was passing by (παράγει, third person singular present active indicative of direct discourse retained in the indirect). Now was their one opportunity. They had heard what he had done for other blind men. They hailed him as "the Son of David," a confession of his messiahship. By now, Jesus had healed many blind, and the multitude was impatient for something greater, so the people were impatient with the cries of these poor men that their eyes be "opened" (ἀνοίγωσιν, third person plural second aorist passive subjunctive).

20:34. *Touched their eyes* (ἥψατο τῶν ὀμμάτων[30] αὐτῶν). Ὀμμάτων is a synonym for ὀφθαλμῶν in Mark 8:23 and here alone in the New Testament. It is a common poetic word of Euripides and occurs in the LXX and the papyri. The verb ἅπτομαι is common in the Synoptic Gospels. The touch of Christ's hand would sooth the eyes as they were healed.

NOTES

1. NIV has "standing in the marketplace doing nothing."
2. Richard Trench, *Notes on the Parables*, 7th ed. (London: Parker and Son, 1857), 171.
3. Willoughby G. Allen, *A Critical and Exegetical Commentary on the Gospel According to Matthew*, International Critical Commentary (Edinburgh: T. & T. Clark, 1912).
4. NIV has "all day long doing nothing."
5. TR has a different word order καὶ ἔλαβον καὶ αὐτοὶ ἀνὰ δηνάριον.
6. Alexander Balmain Bruce, *The Expositor's Greek Testament*, Vol. 1, *The Synoptic Gospels* (Grand Rapids: Eerdmans, 1951), 254.
7. NIV has "they began to grumble."
8. NIV has "the burden of the work and the heat of the day."
9. NIV has "one of them."
10. TR has a different word order, εἶπεν ἑνὶ αὐτῶν.
11. Alfred Plummer, *An Exegetical Commentary on the Gospel According to Saint Matthew* (repr. ed., Grand Rapids: Eerdmans, 1956), 274.
12. NIV has "I want."
13. NIV has "with my own money."
14. NIV has "are you envious?"
15. NIV has "the last will be first, and the first will be last."
16. Jer. *Berak.* 2.5c.
17. NIV has "and crucified."
18. NIV has "asked a favor."
19. Bruce, *Expositor's*, 256.
20. NIV has "you will indeed drink."
21. NIV has "they were indignant."
22. NIV has "called them together."
23. A. T. Robertson, *Commentary on the Gospel According to Matthew* (New

York: Macmillan, 1911), 216.

24. NIV has "whoever wants to become great."

25. See examples in James Hope Moulton and George Milligan, *The Vocabulary of the Greek Testament* (London: Hodder and Stoughton, 1952), 382–83, and G. Adolf Deissmann, *Light from the Ancient East: The New Testament Illustrated by Recently Discovered Texts of the Graeco-Roman World*, trans. L. R. M. Strachan (rev. ed., Grand Rapids: Baker, 1965), 328f.

26. NIV has "As Jesus and his disciples were leaving Jericho." The words *Jesus and his disciples* are not found in the Greek text, but they are implicit.

27. TR spells Ἱεριχώ with a rough breathing; WH spells it Ἱερειχώ.

28. NIV has "that Jesus was going by."

29. NIV has "two blind men were sitting by the roadside."

30. TR and Maj.T have ὀφθαλμῶν.

Matthew: Chapter 21

21:1. *To Bethphage* (εἰς Βηθφαγή), an indeclinable Aramaic name used only here in Scripture (= Mark 11:1 = Luke 19:29). It means "house of unripe young figs." It apparently lay on the eastern slope of Olivet or at the foot of the mountain, a little farther from Jerusalem than Bethany. Both Mark and Luke speak of Christ's coming "to Bethphage and Bethany," as if Bethphage was reached first. It was apparently larger than Bethany.

At the Mount of Olives[1] (εἰς[2] τὸ Ὄρος τῶν Ἐλαιῶν). Matthew has thus three instances of εἰς with Jerusalem, Mount of Olives. Mark and Luke use πρός with Mount of Olives, the Mount of Olive trees (ἐλαιῶν from ἐλαία, olive tree), the mountain covered with olive trees.

21:2. *"Into the village opposite you"*[3] (εἰς τὴν κώμην τὴν κατέναντι[4] ὑμῶν), another use of εἰς. If it means "into" as translated, it could be Bethany right across the valley and this is probably the idea.

"And a colt with her"[5] (καὶ πῶλον μετ' αὐτῆς), the young of any animal. Here to come with the mother and the more readily so.

21:3. *"'The Lord'"* (Ὁ κύριος). It is not clear how the word would be understood here by those who heard the message though it is plain that Jesus applies it to himself. The word is from κύρος, power or authority. In the LXX it is common in a variety of uses. It appears in the New Testament for a "master" of the slave (Matt. 10:24), the harvest (9:38), or the vineyard (20:8). It refers to God (Matt. 11:25), or Jesus as the Messiah (Matt. 8:25; Acts 10:36). This is the only time in Matthew where the words ὁ κύριος are applied to Jesus except for a doubtful passage in 28:6.[6] Particularly in Egypt it was applied to "the Lord Serapis." Ptolemy and Cleopatra are called "the lords, the most great gods" (οἱ κύριοι θεοὶ μέγιστοι). Even Herod the Great and Herod Agrippa I are addressed as "Lord King." In the West, Roman emperors were not called "lords" until the time of Domitian. But Christians have always seen in this occurrence a reference to Jesus Christ. It seems that the disciples already were calling Jesus "Lord," and he accepted the appellative and used it, as here.

21:4. *Through the prophet* (διὰ τοῦ προφήτου). The first line is from Isaiah

62:11, the rest from Zechariah 9:9. John 12:14–16 makes it clear that Jesus did not quote the passage himself. In Matthew it is not so clear, but probably it is his own comment about the incident. It is not that Christ is artificially fulfilling the prophecy, but his conduct flows naturally into fulfillment.

21:5. *"The daughter of Zion"* (τῇ θυγατρὶ Σιών). The reference to Jerusalem is found in Isaiah 22:4. Similar language refers to Babylon (Isa. 47:1) and Tyre (Ps. 45:12).

"Mounted"[7] (ἐπιβεβηκώς), nominative singular masculine perfect active participle of ἐπιβαίνω, "having gone upon."

"Even on a colt, the foal of a beast of burden"[8] (ἐπὶ ὄνον καὶ ἐπὶ πῶλον υἱὸν ὑποζυγίου[9]). These words give trouble if καὶ is here taken to mean "and." Fritzsche argues that Jesus rode alternately upon either animal, a possible but needless interpretation. Here is common poetic Hebrew parallelism: "upon an ass, even upon a colt." The use of ὑποζυγίου (a beast of burden, under a yoke) for ass is common in the LXX and in the papyri.[10]

21:7. *And He sat on the coats*[11] (καὶ ἐπεκάθισεν ἐπάνω αὐτῶν). Mark 11:7 and Luke 19:35 show that Jesus rode the colt. Matthew does not contradict that. The garments (τὰ ἱμάτια) were put on the colt by "them" (αὐτῶν), not on both asses. The construction is somewhat loose, but intelligible. The garments thrown on the animals were the outer garments (ἱμάτια). Jesus "took his seat" (ἐπεκάθισεν, third person singular ingressive aorist active indicative) upon the garments.

21:8. *Most of the crowd*[12] (ὁ δὲ πλεῖστος ὄχλος). See 11:20 for this same idiom, article with superlative, a true superlative.[13]

In the road[14] (ἐν τῇ ὁδῷ). Most of the crowd did lay coats in the road. Note the change of tenses (constative aorist ἔστρωσαν, descriptive imperfects ἔκοπτον . . . καὶ ἐστρώννυον showing the growing enthusiasm of the crowd). When the colt had passed over their garments, they would pick the garments up and spread them again before.

21:9. *The crowds going ahead of Him, and those who followed* (οἱ δὲ ὄχλοι οἱ προάγοντες αὐτὸν[15] καὶ οἱ ἀκολουθοῦντες). Note the two groups with two articles and the present tense (linear action) and the imperfect ἔκραζον, "were shouting," as they went.

"Hosanna to the Son of David" (Ὡσαννὰ τῷ υἱῷ Δαυίδ[16]). Jesus now let them proclaim Him as the Messiah. "Hosanna" means "Save, we pray." They repeat words from the *Hallel* (Ps. 148:1), and one recalls the song of the angelic host when Jesus was born (Luke 2:14). "Hosanna in the highest" (heaven).

21:10. *All the city was stirred*[17] (ἐσείσθη πᾶσα ἡ πόλις). Shaken as by an earthquake. "Even Jerusalem frozen with religious formalism and socially undemonstrative, was stirred with popular enthusiasm as by a mighty wind or by an earthquake."[18]

21:12. *Drove out* (ἐξέβαλεν). Drove out, assumed authority over "the temple of God."[19] John 2:14 has a similar incident at the beginning of the ministry of Jesus. It is not impossible that Jesus should repeat this cleansing at its close. The same abuses still existed. The traffic went on in the court of the Gentiles. To a certain extent it served a legitimate purpose. Here the tables "of the money changers" (τῶν κολλυβιστῶν, from κολλυβός, a small coin) were overturned. See on 17:24 for the need of the change for the temple tax. The doves were the poor man's offering.

21:13. *"A robbers' den"*[20] (σπήλαιον λῃστῶν). Because they charged exorbitant prices. This quote is from the LXX of Isaiah 56:7.

21:15. *The children* (τοὺς παῖδας). This is masculine and refers probably to boys who had caught the enthusiasm of the crowd.

21:16. *"Do You hear"* (ἀκούεις. . . ;). In a rage at the desecration of the temple by the shouts of the boys, they try to shame Jesus, as responsible for it.

"You have prepared"[21] (κατηρτίσω). The quotation is from Psalm 8:3 (LXX). In Matthew 4:21 the same verb is used for mending nets. Here it is the timeless aorist middle indicative with the perfect use of κατα-. It was a stinging rebuke.

21:17. *To Bethany* (εἰς Βηθανίαν). The Hebrew means "house of depression or misery."[22] But the home of Martha and Mary and Lazarus was a house of solace to Jesus during this week of destiny.

Spent the night there[23] (ηὐλίσθη ἐκεῖ), whether at the Bethany home or out in the open air. It was a time of crises for all.

21:18. *He became hungry*[24] (ἐπείνασιν). Third person singular ingressive aorist active indicative, felt hungry (Moffatt). Possibly Jesus spent the night out of doors and so had no breakfast.

21:19. *A lone fig tree*[25] (συκῆν μίαν). "A single fig tree" (RV margin). The construction serves a purpose somewhat resembling that filled by the English indefinite article. Strictly speaking, Greek has no indefinite article, just as Latin has no definite article. Sometimes εἷς ("one, single, someone") or τὶς ("someone, something") is used like an indefinite article, although not here.

"No longer shall there ever be any fruit from you"[26] (Μηκέτι ἐκ σοῦ καρπὸς γένηται εἰς τὸν αἰῶνα). Strickly speaking this is a prediction, not a prohibition or wish as in Mark 11:14 (optative φάγοι). "On you no fruit shall ever grow again" (Weymouth). The double negative οὐ μή with the aorist subjunctive (or

future indicative) is the strongest kind of negative prediction. It sometimes amounts to a prohibition like οὐ and the future indicative.[27] The early figs start in spring before the leaves and develop after the leaves. The main fig crop was early autumn (Mark 11:13). There should have been figs on the tree with the crop of leaves. It was a vivid object lesson. Matthew does not distinguish between the two mornings as Mark does (Mark 11:12, 20) but says "all at once"[28] (παραχρῆμα) twice (21:19, 20). This word is a form of παρὰ τὸ χρῆμα like our "on the spot."[29] It occurs in the papyri in monetary transactions with immediate cash payment.

21:21. *"Do not doubt"* (μὴ διακριθῆτε), second person plural aorist passive subjunctive, third class condition. To be divided in mind, to waver, to doubt, the opposite of "faith" (πίστιν), trust, confidence.

"What was done to the fig tree" (τὸ τῆς συκῆς ποιήσετε). The Greek means "the matter of the fig tree," as if a slight matter in comparison with "this mountain" (τῷ ὄρει τούτῳ). Removing a mountain is a bigger task than blighting a fig tree. "The cursing of the fig tree has always been regarded as of symbolic import, the tree being in Christ's mind an emblem of the Jewish people, with a great show of religion and no fruit of real godliness. This hypothesis is very credible."[30] Alfred Plummer follows Theodor Zahn in referring it to the Holy City.[31] Certainly "this mountain" is a parable and one already reported in Matthew 17:20 (cf. Luke 17:6).

21:22. *"Believing"*[32] (πιστεύοντες). This is the point of the parable of the mountain, "faith in the efficacy of prayer."[33]

21:24. *"I will also ask you one thing"*[34] ('Ερωτήσω ὑμᾶς κἀγὼ λόγον ἕνα). Literally "one word" or "a word." The answer to Christ's word will give the answer to their query. The only human ecclesiastical authority that Jesus had came from John.

21:25. *"The baptism of John was from what source. . . ?"*[35] (τὸ βάπτισμα τὸ Ἰωάννου[36] πόθεν ἦν[;]). This represents his relation to Jesus, who was baptized by him. At once the ecclesiastical leaders find themselves in a dilemma created by their challenge of Christ.

Reasoning among themselves[37] (οἱ δὲ διελογίζοντο ἐν ἑαυτοῖς[38]). Picturesque imperfect tense describing their struggle with a hopeless quandary.[39]

21:29. *" 'I will not' "* (Οὐ θέλω).[40] Logically the "I, sir" ('Εγώ, κύριε) suits better for the second son (v. 30) with a reference to the blunt refusal of the first. So also the manuscripts differ in verse 31 between the first (Ὁ πρῶτος) and the last (ὁ ὕστερος or ἔσχατος).

"But afterward he regretted it and went" (ὕστερον δὲ μεταμεληθεὶς

ἀπῆλθεν). The one who actually did the will of the father is the one who "regretted it and went,"[41] μεταμεληθεὶς ἀπῆλθεν. Μεταμέλομαι really means "to repent, to be sorry afterwards." This must be distinguished sharply from the word μετανοέω, which is used thirty-four times in the New Testament (e.g., Matt. 3:2), and μετανοία, used twenty-four times (e.g., Matt. 3:8). The verb μεταμέλομαι occurs in the New Testament only five times (Matt. 21:29, 32; 27:3; 2 Cor. 7:8; Heb. 7:21). Paul distinguishes sharply between mere *sorrow* and the active *repentance* he calls μετάνοιαν (2 Cor. 7:9). In the case of Judas it was mere remorse (Matt. 27:3). In Jesus' story, the boy was sorry that he had stubbornly refused to obey his father and went and obeyed. Godly sorrow leads to repentance (μετανοίαν), but self-centered sorrow is not repentance.

21:31. *"Will get into the kingdom of God before you"*[42] (προάγουσιν ὑμᾶς εἰς τὴν βασιλείαν τοῦ Θεοῦ). "In front of you" (Weymouth). The publicans and harlots march ahead of the ecclesiastics into the kingdom of heaven. It is a powerful indictment of the complacency of the Jewish theological leaders.

21:32. *"In the way of righteousness"* (ἐν ὁδῷ δικαιοσύνης). In the path of righteousness. Compare the two ways in Matthew 7:13–14 and "the way of God" (22:16).

21:33. *"And put a wall around it"* (φραγμὸν αὐτῷ περιέθηκεν). Or fence as a protection against wild beasts.

"Dug a wine press in it" (ὤρυξεν ἐν αὐτῷ ληνόν), out of the solid rock to hold the grapes and wine as they were crushed.

"Built a tower"[43] (ᾠκοδόμησεν πύργον). This was for the vinedressers and watchmen (2 Chron. 26:10). Utmost care was thus taken. Note "a booth in a vineyard" (Isa. 1:8; see also Job 27:18; Isa. 24:20).

"Rented it out" (ἐξέδετο), for hire, the terms not being given. The lease allowed three forms, money-rent, a proportion of the crop, or a definite amount of the produce whether it was a good or bad year. Probably the last form is contemplated here.

21:34. *"His slaves"*[44] (τοὺς δούλους αὐτοῦ). These slaves are distinguished from the vine growers[45] (γεωργοῖς, "workers of the soil") or workers of the vineyard who had leased it from the householder before he went away. The conduct of the farmers toward the landowner's slaves portrays the behavior of the Jewish people and the religious leaders in particular toward the prophets and now toward Christ. The treatment of God's prophets by the Jews pointedly illustrates this parable.

21:37. *"They will respect my son"* (Ἐντραπήσονται τὸν υἱόν μου). Third person plural second future passive indicative from ἐντρέπω, to turn at, but used transitively here as though active or middle. It is the picture of turning with respect when one worthy of it appears.

21:38. "'Seize his inheritance'"[46] (σχῶμεν[47] τὴν κληρονομίαν αὐτοῦ), first person plural ingressive aorist active subjunctive (hortatory, volitive) of ἔχω. "Let us get his inheritance."

21:41. "He will bring those wretches to a wretched end" (Κακοὺς κακῶς ἀπολέσει αὐτούς). The paronomasia or assonance is very clear. A common idiom in literary Greek. "He will put the wretches to a wretched death" (Weymouth).

"Who" (οἵτινες). "Who or which," ones who are of a different character.

21:42. "The stone which" (Λίθον ὅν), inverse attraction of the antecedent into the case of the relative.

"The builders rejected" (ἀπεδοκίμασαν οἱ οἰκοδομοῦντες), from Psalm 118:22. These experts in building God's temple had rejected the cornerstone chosen by God for his own house. But God has the last word and sets aside the building experts and puts his Son as the Head of the corner.

21:43. "The kingdom of God will be taken away from you" (ἀρθήσεται ἀφ᾽ ὑμῶν ἡ βασιλεία τοῦ θεοῦ), third person singular future passive indicative of αἴρω. It was the death knell for the Jewish nation, with their hopes of political and religious world leadership.

21:44. "Will be broken to pieces" (συνθλασθήσεται). Some ancient manuscripts do not have this verse. But it graphically pictures the fate of the man who rejects Christ. The verb means to shatter. We are familiar with the ruin caused when an automobile crashes into a stone wall, a tree, or a train.

"Will scatter him like dust"[48] (λικμήσει αὐτόν). The verb was used of winnowing out the chaff and then of grinding to powder. This is the fate of any on whom this rejected stone falls.

21:45. Understood[49] (ἔγνωσαν), third person plural ingressive second aorist active indicative of γινώσκω. There was no mistaking the meaning of these parables. The dullest could see the point.

21:46. Considered Him to be a prophet[50] (εἰς προφήτην αὐτὸν εἶχον[51]), descriptive imperfect of ἔχω, to hold. This fear of the people was all that stayed the hands of the rabbis on this occasion. Murderous rage was in their hearts toward Jesus.

NOTES

1.   NIV has "on the Mount of Olives."
2.   TR and Maj.T have the preposition πρός instead of εἰς.

3. NIV has "to the village ahead of you."
4. TR and Maj.T have ἀπέναντι for κατέναντι.
5. NIV has "with her colt by her."
6. A similar usage is shown in James Hope Moulton and George Milligan, *The Vocabulary of the Greek Testament* (London: Hodder and Stoughton, 1952), 365–66, and in G. Adolf Deissmann, *Light from the Ancient East: The New Testament Illustrated by Recently Discovered Texts of the Graeco-Roman World*, trans. L. R. M. Strachan (rev. ed., Grand Rapids: Baker, 1965), 349–67.
7. NIV has "riding."
8. NIV has "on a colt, the foal of a donkey."
9. TR and Maj.T omit the second ἐπί.
10. G. Adolf Deissmann, *Bible Studies: Contributions, Chiefly from Papyri and Inscriptions, to the History of the Language, the Literature, and the Religion of Hellenistic Judaism and Primitive Christianity*, trans. A. Grieve. (Edinburgh: T.&T. Clark, 1901), 161.
11. NIV has "and Jesus sat on them." The name *Jesus* is not found in the Greek text but is implied in the context.
12. NIV has "A very large crowd."
13. A. T. Robertson, *A Grammar of the Greek New Testament in the Light of Historical Research* (Nashville: Broadman, 1934), 670.
14. NIV has "on the road."
15. TR and Maj.T omit αὐτόν.
16. TR and Maj.T spell the name Δαβίδ; WH spells it Δαυείδ.
17. NIV has "the whole city was stirred."
18. Alexander Balmain Bruce, *The Expositor's Greek Testament*, Vol. 1, *The Synoptic Gospels* (Grand Rapids: Eerdmans, 1951), 262.
19. TR and Maj.T have τὸ ἱερὸν τοῦ θεοῦ. Robertson comments that the correct text is probably with τοῦ θεοῦ, though it is the only example of the phrase.
20. NIV has "a den of robbers."
21. NIV has "you have ordained."
22. "It may mean 'house of dates.'" A. T. Robertson, *Commentary on the Gospel According to Matthew* (New York: Macmillan, 1911), 222.
23. NIV has "where he spent the night."
24. NIV has "he was hungry."
25. NIV has "a fig tree."
26. NIV has "May you never bear fruit again!"
27. Robertson, *Grammar,* 926f.

28. NIV has "Immediately."
29. Joseph Henry Thayer, *Greek-English Lexicon of the New Testament* (New York: American Door, 1889), 487.
30. Bruce, *Expositor's*, 264.
31. Alfred Plummer, *An Exegetical Commentary on the Gospel According to Saint Matthew* (repr. ed., Grand Rapids: Eerdmans, 1956), 291.
32. NIV has "If you believe."
33. Plummer, *Matthew*, 291.
34. NIV has "I will also ask you one question."
35. NIV has "John's baptism—where did it come from?"
36. WH has the spelling Ἰωάνου.
37. NIV has "They discussed it among themselves."
38. TR and Maj.T use a different preposition παρ᾽ ἑαυτοῖς.
39. "They saw at once the two horns of the dilemma. If they admitted the heavenly origin of John's baptism, the retort was too patent. If they denied it they would not injure Jesus with the people, but only hurt themselves. They are in a logical cul-de-sac" (Robertson, *Commentary on Matthew*, 225).
40. Many manuscripts read thus, though the Vatican manuscript (B) has the order of the two sons reversed.
41. NIV has "he changed his mind and went."
42. NIV has "are entering."
43. NIV has "built a watchtower."
44. NIV has "his servants."
45. NIV has "some farmers."
46. NIV has "take his inheritance."
47. TR and Maj.T have the verb κατάσχωμεν.
48. NIV has "will be crushed."
49. NIV has "knew."
50. NIV has "held that he was a prophet."
51. TR and Maj.T have ὡς προφήτην αὐτὸν εἶχον.

Matthew: Chapter 22

22:1. *Jesus spoke to them again in parables* (ὁ Ἰησοῦς πάλιν ἐν παραβολαῖς αὐτοῖς). Matthew has already given parables of the Two Sons and the Wicked Husbandmen. He alone records this parable of the Marriage Feast. It is similar to that of the Supper (Luke 14:16–23), but that is from another occasion. Some scholars consider this merely Matthew's version of the Lucan parable, only in the wrong place. Matthew does tend to group sayings of Jesus. But here the word πάλιν definitely locates this parable in a particular occasion. Some critics do not believe these words ever were spoken by Jesus. Rather they were the writer's effort to cover the sin and fate of the Jews, the calling of the Gentiles, and God's demand for righteousness. No evidence supports the allegation that the parable doesn't belong to this occasion or that it doesn't belong to Jesus. These parables fit the style of Jesus as storyteller and suit the occasion.

22:2. *"A wedding feast"*[1] (γάμους). The plural, as here (vv. 2, 3, 4, 9), is common in the papyri for wedding festivities. Several times of feasting might be held over a period of days. There were seven in Judges 14:17. A form of the phrase used here (γάμους ποιεῖν) occurs in the Doric of Thera, about 200 B.C. The singular γάμος is common in the papyri for the wedding contract, but Frederick Field[2] sees no difference between the singular here in 22:8 and the plural (see also Gen. 29:22; Esther 9:22; 1 Macc. 10:58).

22:3. *"To call those who had been invited"* (καλέσαι τοὺς κεκλημένους). "Perhaps an unconscious play on the words, lost in both the Authorized Version and the Revised Version, to call the called."[3] It was a Jewish custom to invite a second time those already invited (Esther 5:8; 6:14). The prophets of old had given God's invitation to the Jewish people. Now the Baptist and Jesus had given the second invitation that the feast was ready.

"And they were unwilling to come"[4] (καὶ οὐκ ἤθελον ἐλθεῖν). This negative imperfect characterizes the stubborn refusal of the Jewish leaders to accept Jesus as God's Son (John 1:11). This is "The Hebrew Tragedy."[5]

22:4. *"'My dinner'"* (τὸ ἄριστόν μου). It is breakfast, not dinner. In Luke 14:12 both ἄριστον (breakfast) and δεῖπνον (dinner) are used. This noon or midday meal, like the French breakfast at noon, was sometimes called δεῖπνον

181

μεσημβρινόν (midday dinner or luncheon). The regular dinner (δεῖπνον) came in the evening. The confusion arose from applying ἄριστον to the early morning meal and then to the noon meal (some not eating an earlier meal). In John 21:12, 15, ἀριστάω is used of the early morning meal: "Break your fast" (ἀριστήσατε). When ἄριστον was applied to luncheon, like the Latin *prandium*, ἀκράτισμα was the term for the early breakfast.

"*My fattened livestock*'"[6] (τὰ σιτιστά). Verbal from σιτίζω, to feed with wheat or other grain, to fatten. Fed-up or fatted animals.

22:5. "*They paid no attention*" (ἀμελήσαντες), literally, neglecting, not caring for. To neglect an invitation to a wedding feast is a gross discourtesy. They may even have ridiculed the invitation, but the verb does not say so.

"*One to his own farm [or field], another to his business*"[7] (ὃς μὲν εἰς τὸν ἴδιον ἀγρόν, ὃς δὲ ἐπὶ τὴν ἐμπορίαν αὐτοῦ[8]). This is the only example of ἐμπορίαν in the New Testament, from ἔμπορος, merchant, one who travels for traffic (ἐμπορεύομαι).

22:7. "*Armies*"[9] (στρατεύματα). Bands of soldiers, not grand armies.

22:9. "*The main highways*'"[10] (τὰς διεξόδους τῶν ὁδῶν). Διοδοί are cross streets, while διεξόδοι (double compound) seem to be main streets leading out of the city where also side streets may branch off, "byways."

22:10. "*The wedding hall*"[11] (ὁ γάμος). But WH rightly reads ὁ νυμφών, marriage dining hall. The same word in 9:15 means the "bride chamber."

22:12. "*Without wedding clothes*" (μὴ ἔχων ἔνδυμα γάμου). Μή is in the Κοινή, the usual negative with participles unless special emphasis on the negative is desired, as in οὐκ ἐνδεδυμένον. There is a subtle distinction between μή and οὐ, like our subjective and objective notions. Some hold that the wedding garment here is a portion of a lost parable separate from that of the wedding feast, but there is no evidence for that idea. Wunsche does report a parable by a rabbi of a king who set no time for his feast and some guests arrived properly dressed waiting at the door, while others came in their working clothes. The ones improperly dressed did not wait, but went off to work. When the summons suddenly came, they had no time to dress properly. They were made to stand and watch while the others partook of the feast.

"*And the man was speechless*" (ὁ δὲ ἐφιμώθη). He was muzzled, dumb from confusion and embarrassment. It is used of the ox (1 Tim. 5:18).

22:13. "*Throw him into the outer darkness*'"[12] (ἐκβάλετε αὐτὸν εἰς τὸ σκότος τὸ ἐξώτερον[13]). His darkness seemed all the blacker because he had experienced the brilliantly lighted banquet hall (see on 8:12).

"*In that place there will be weeping and gnashing of teeth*" (ἐκεῖ ἔσται ὁ κλαυθμὸς καὶ ὁ βρυγμὸς τῶν ὀδόντων). "The outer darkness" is "one of the most awful descriptions of hell."[14]

22:14. *"For many are called, but few are chosen"*[15] (πολλοὶ γάρ εἰσιν κλητοί, ὀλίγοι δὲ ἐκλεκτοί). This crisp saying of Christ occurs in various connections. He evidently repeated the saying frequently to draw a distinction between the *called* (κλητοί) and the *called out from the called* (ἐκλεκτοί).

22:15. *Then the Pharisees went*[16] (Τότε πορευθέντες οἱ Φαρισαῖοι). So-called deponent passive and redundant use of the verb as in 9:13: "Go and learn."

And plotted together[17] (συμβούλιον ἔλαβον). Like the Latin *consilium capere*, as in 12:14.

How they might trap Him in what He said[18] (ὅπως αὐτὸν παγιδεύσωσιν ἐν λόγῳ). Παγιδεύω, "to ensnare or trap," occurs only here in the New Testament. It is found in the LXX in 1 Kings 28:9; Ecclesiastes 9:12; and *Testament of the Twelve Patriarchs, Joseph* 7:1. This is a vivid picture of the effort to trip Jesus in his speech like catching a bird or beast in a snare.

22:16. *And they sent their disciples to Him* (καὶ ἀποστέλλουσιν αὐτῷ τοὺς μαθητὰς αὐτῶν), students, pupils of the Pharisees, as in Mark 2:18. There were two Pharisaic theological seminaries in Jerusalem, the schools of Hillel and Shammai.

Along with the Herodians (μετὰ τῶν Ἡρῳδιανῶν[19]), not members of Herod's family or Herod's soldiers, but partisans or followers of the Herod dynasty. The form -ιανος is a Latin termination, as in Χριστιανούς from Χριστιανός (Acts 11:26). The Herodians are mentioned also in Mark 3:6 as joining the Pharisees against Jesus.

"For You are not partial to any"[20] (οὐ γὰρ βλέπεις εἰς πρόσωπον ἀνθρώπων). Literally, You do not look on the face of men. Paying regard to appearance is the sin of partiality which is condemned in James 2:1, 9, when προσωπολημψίαις, προσωπολημπτεῖτε are used in imitation of the Hebrew idiom. This suave flattery implied "that Jesus was a reckless simpleton."[21]

22:19. *"Show Me the coin used for the poll-tax"*[22] (ἐπιδείξατέ μοι τὸ νόμισμα τοῦ κήνσου). Κῆνσος, the Latin census, was a head or *capitation* tax, *tributum capitis*, for which silver denarii were struck with the figure of Caesar and a superscription, e.g., "Τιβερίου Καίσαρος"[23] Νόμισμα is the Latin *numisma* and occurs here only in the New Testament. It is common in the old Greek, from νομίζω, "sanctioned by law or custom."

22:20. *"Whose likeness and inscription is this?"*[24] (Τίνος ἡ εἰκὼν αὕτη καὶ ἡ ἐπιγραφή;). It was probably a Roman coin because of the image (picture) on it. The earlier Herods avoided this practice because of Jewish prejudice, but the Tetrarch Philip introduced it on Jewish coins and he was followed by Herod Agrippa I. This coin was pretty certainly stamped in Rome with the image and name of Tiberius Caesar on it.

22:21. *"Render"*[25] (Ἀπόδοτε). "Give back" to Caesar what is already Caesar's. "The very inscription of the money was an acknowledgement of debt to Caesar. The tax was not a gift, but a debt for law, order, and roads. There is a duty to the state and a duty to God. Jesus had already indorsed the temple tax. The 'image and superscription' implied the authority of the emperor who had struck the coin. The two spheres are distinct, but both exist. The Christian is not to evade either."[26]

22:24. *"His brother as next of kin shall marry his wife"*[27] (ἐπιγαμβρεύσει ὁ ἀδελφὸς αὐτοῦ τὴν γυναῖκα αὐτοῦ). The Sadducees were "aiming at amusement rather than deadly mischief."[28] It was probably an old conundrum that they had used to the discomfiture of the Pharisees. This passage is quoted from Deuteronomy 25:5–6. The word appears here only in the New Testament and elsewhere only in the LXX. It is used of any connected by marriage, as in Genesis 34:9 and 1 Samuel 18:22. But in Genesis 38:8 and Deuteronomy 25:5 it is used specifically of levirate marriage, marrying one's brother's widow.

22:33. *They were astonished* (ἐξεπλήσσοντο). The third person plural descriptive imperfect passive indicative shows the continued amazement of the crowds.

22:34. *[Jesus]*[29] *had silenced the Sadducees* (ἐφίμωσεν τοὺς Σαδδουκαίους). He had muzzled the Sadducees. The Pharisees could not restrain their glee, though they were joining with the Sadducees in trying to entrap Jesus.

They gathered themselves together[30] (συνήχθησαν ἐπὶ τὸ αὐτό). Third person plural first aorist passive indicative, "were gathered together." Ἐπὶ τὸ αὐτό explains more fully συν- (see also Acts 2:47). They "mustered their forces" (Moffatt).

22:36. *"Which is the great commandment in the Law?"*[31] (ποία ἐντολὴ μεγάλη ἐν τῷ νόμῳ;). The positive adjective is sometimes as high in rank as the superlative. See μέγας in Matthew 5:19 in contrast with ἐλάχιστος. The superlative μέγιστος occurs in the New Testament only in 2 Peter 1:4. Possibly this scribe wishes to know which commandment stood first (Mark 12:28) with Jesus. "The scribes declared that there were 248 affirmative precepts, as many as the members of the human body; and 365 negative precepts, as many as the days in the year, the total being 613, the number of letters in the Decalogue."[32] But Jesus cuts through such hairsplitting to the heart of the problem.

22:42. *"What do you think about the Christ?"* (Τί ὑμῖν δοκεῖ περὶ τοῦ Χριστοῦ;) Jesus here assumes that Psalm 110 refers to the Messiah. By this pungent question about the Messiah as David's son and Lord, he forces the Pharisees to face the problem of the Christ's joint deity and humanity. "They held divergent views concerning the Messiah,"[33] and probably they had never faced this text before. They were unable to answer.

NOTES

1. NIV has "a wedding banquet."
2. Frederick Field, *Notes on the Translation of the New Testament* (repr. ed., Peabody, Mass: Hendrickson, 1994.
3. Marvin R. Vincent, *Word Studies in the New Testament*, Vol. 1, *The Synoptic Gospels* (repr. ed., Grand Rapids: Eerdmans, 1946), 119.
4. NIV has "but they refused to come."
5. C. R. Conder. *The Bible and the East* (Edinburgh: W. Blackwood, 1896).
6. NIV has "fattened cattle."
7. NIV has "one to his field."
8. TR and Maj.T have ὃ μὲν . . . ὃ δέ.
9. NIV has "army."
10. NIV has "the street corners."
11. NIV has "the wedding hall."
12. NIV has "throw him outside."
13. TR and Maj.T have ἄρατε αὐτὸν καὶ ἐκβάλετε εἰς τὸ σκότος τὸ ἐξώτερον.
14. A. T. Robertson, *Commentary on the Gospel According to Matthew* (New York: Macmillan, 1911), 229.
15. NIV has "For many are invited, but few are chosen."
16. NIV has "Then the Pharisees went out."
17. NIV has "and laid plans."
18. NIV has "to trap him in his words."
19. TR omits the iota subscript Ἡρωδιανῶν.
20. NIV has "because you pay no attention to who they are."
21. Alexander Balmain Bruce, *The Expositor's Greek Testament*, Vol. 1, *The Synoptic Gospels* (Grand Rapids: Eerdmans, 1951), 274.
22. NIV has "Show me the coin for paying the tax."
23. Alan Hugh McNeile, *The Gospel According to St. Matthew: The Greek Text with Introduction, Notes, and Indices* (repr. ed., Grand Rapids: Baker, 1980), 319.
24. NIV has "Whose portrait is this? And whose inscription?"

25. NIV has "Give."
26. Robertson, *Commentary on Matthew*, 231.
27. NIV has "his brother must marry the widow."
28. Bruce, *Expositor's*, 275.
29. The name *Jesus* is not explicit in the Greek text but implied.
30. NIV has "the Pharisees got together."
31. NIV has "which is the greatest commandment in the Law?"
32. Vincent, *Word Studies*, 122.
33. Robertson, *Commentary on Matthew*, 234.

Matthew: Chapter 23

23:2. *"The scribes and the Pharisees have seated themselves in the chair of Moses"*[1] (Ἐπὶ τῆς Μωϋσέως[2] καθέδρας ἐκάθισαν οἱ γραμματεῖς καὶ οἱ Φαρισαῖοι). This is the gnomic or timeless aorist tense, ἐκάθισαν, not the aorist for the perfect. The "seat of Moses" means the office of the interpreter of Moses. "The heirs of Moses' authority by an unbroken tradition can deliver *ex cathedra* pronouncements on his teaching."[3]

23:3. *"For they say things and do not do them"*[4] (λέγουσιν γὰρ καὶ οὐ ποιοῦσιν). "As teachers they have their place, but beware of following their example."[5]

"Do not do according to their deeds"[6] (κατὰ δὲ τὰ ἔργα αὐτῶν μὴ ποιεῖτε). Do not practice their practices. Jesus does not here disapprove of Pharisaic teaching as he does elsewhere. The point made here is that they do not practice what they teach as God sees it.

23:4. *"But they themselves are unwilling to move them with so much as a finger"*[7] (αὐτοὶ δὲ τῷ δακτύλῳ αὐτῶν οὐ θέλουσιν κινῆσαι αὐτά[8]). A picturesque proverb. They are taskmasters, not burden-bearers or sympathetic helpers.

23:5. *"But they do all their deeds to be noticed by men"*[9] (πάντα δὲ τὰ ἔργα αὐτῶν ποιοῦσιν πρὸς τὸ θεαθῆναι τοῖς ἀνθρώποις). In 6:1 this idiom occurs. Image regulates the conduct of the rabbis.

"For they broaden their phylacteries"[10] (πλατύνουσιν γὰρ τὰ φυλακτήρια[11]). Φυλακτήρια is an adjective from φυλακτήρ, φυλάσσω ("to guard"). The term refers to a fortified place or garrison, but in rabbinical use it meant a protective safeguard, like a charm or amulet. The rabbis wore *tephillin* or prayer-fillets, small leather cases with four strips of parchment on which were written the words of Exodus 13:1–10 on one strip and verses 11–16 on another, Deuteronomy 6:4–9 on a third, and 11:13–21 on the fourth. They took literally the words about "a sign unto your hand," "a memorial between your eyes," and "frontlets." That for the head was to consist of a box with four compartments, each containing a slip of parchment inscribed with one of the four passages. Each strip tied with a well-washed hair from a calf's tail. A thread

of fibers might become polluted with mildew. The phylactery of the arm was to contain a single slip, with the four texts written in four columns of seven lines each. The black leather straps by which they were fastened were wound seven times around the arm and three times around the hand. Rabbis held these talismans in as high a reverence as the Scriptures themselves. Scripture scrolls and these boxes were the only possessions that might be rescued from a fire that broke out on the Sabbath. They imagined that God wore the *tephillin.*[12] Jesus ridicules such minute concern for pretentious externalism and literalism. *Tephillin* are now worn on the forehead and left arm by ultraorthodox Jews at the daily morning prayer.[13] "The size of the phylacteries indexed the measure of zeal, and the wearing of large ones was apt to take the place of obedience."[14] Hence they were made "broad." The superstitious would wear them as mere charms to ward off evil.

"*Lengthen the tassels of their garments*"[15] (μεγαλύνουσιν τὰ κράσπεδα). In 9:20 we see that Jesus, like the Jews generally, wore a tassel or tuft, hem or border, a fringe on the outer garment according to Numbers 15:38. Here again the Jewish rabbi had minute rules about the number of the fringe threads and the knots (see on 9:20). They made a virtue of the size of the fringes. "Such things were useful as reminders; they were fatal when they were regarded as charms."[16]

23:6. "*They love the place of honor at banquets*" (φιλοῦσιν δὲ[17] τὴν πρωτοκλισίαν ἐν τοῖς δείπνοις). Literally, this is the first reclining place on the divan at the meal. The Persians, Greeks, Romans, and Jews differed in custom, but all wanted the place of honor at formal functions. The contemporary equivalent is seating at the head table. At the last Passover, just two days after this exposure of the Pharisees in the presence of the apostles, the apostles had an ugly snarl over this very point of precedence (Luke 22:24; John 13:2–11).

"*And the chief seats in the synagogues*"[18] (καὶ τας πρωτοκαθεδρίας ἐν ταῖς συναγωγαῖς). "An insatiable hunger for prominence."[19] These chief seats were on the platform looking to the audience and with the back to the chest in which were kept the rolls of Scripture. The Essenes had a different arrangement. People today pay high prices for front seats at the theatre, but at church prefer the rear seats.

23:7. "*And respectful greetings in the market places*"[20] (καὶ τοὺς ἀσπασμοὺς ἐν ταῖς ἀγοραῖς). Rabbis courted special public courtesy and notice. They wanted everyone to uphold their ministerial dignity, as some in professional ministry still do.

23:8. *"But do not be called Rabbi"*[21] (ὑμεῖς δὲ μὴ κληθῆτε, ῾Ραββί), an apparent aside to the disciples. Note the emphatic position of ὑμεῖς. Some regard verses 8–10 as a later addition or not part of this address to the Pharisees. In his twelfth-century commentary on the Gospels, the monk-exegete scholar Euthymius Zigabenus says: "Do not seek to be called (ingressive aorist subjunctive), if others call you this it will not be your fault." This is not far from the Master's meaning. Rabbi means "my great one," "my Master," apparently a comparatively new title in Christ's time.

23:9. *"Do not call anyone on earth your father"* (καὶ πατέρα μὴ καλέσητε ὑμῶν ἐπὶ τῆς γῆς).[22] In Gethsemane Jesus said: "Abba, Father" (Mark 14:36). Certainly the ascription of "Father" to pope and priest seems out of harmony with what Jesus here says. He should not be understood to be condemning the title to one's real earthly father. Jesus often leaves the exceptions to be supplied.

23:10. *"Do not be called leaders"*[23] (μηδὲ κληθῆτε καθηγηταί). This word occurs here only in the New Testament. It is found in the papyri for teacher (Latin, *doctor*). It is the modern Greek word for professor. "While διδάσκαλος represents *Rab*, καθηγητής stands for the more honorable Rabban, -βον."[24] Gustaf Dalman suggests that the same Aramaic word may be translated by either διδάσκαλος or καθηγητης.

"For One is your Leader, that is, Christ"[25] (ὅτι καθηγητὴς ὑμῶν ἐστιν εἷς ὁ χριστός[26]). The use of these words here by Jesus like "Jesus Christ" in his prayer (John 17:3) is held by some to show that they were added by the evangelist to what Jesus actually said, since the Master would not have so described himself. But he commended Peter for calling him "the Christ the Son of the living God" (Matt. 16:16f.). We must not empty the consciousness of Jesus too much.

23:12. *"Whoever exalts himself"* (ὅστις δὲ ὑψώσει ἑαυτόν). It is somewhat like 18:4; 20:26. It is given by Luke in other contexts (14:11; 18:14). This is characteristic of Christ.

23:13–14. *"Woe to you, scribes and Pharisees, hypocrites"*[27] (Οὐαὶ δὲ ὑμῖν, γραμματεῖς καὶ Φαρισαῖοι ὑποκριταί). Jesus uses the terrible word Οὐαὶ ("woe") in dramatic repetition in verses 13, 15, 16, 23, 25, 27, and 29.[28] The verb in the active (ὑποκρίνω) meant to separate slowly or slightly subject to gradual inquiry. The middle voice was "to make answer, to take up a part on the stage, to act a part." It came to mean "to feign or pretend, to wear a mask, to act the hypocrite, or to play a part." This hardest word falls on the religious leaders—scribes and Pharisees—who had justified this thunderbolt of wrath by their conduct toward their Messiah and their treatment of things high and holy. Alfred Plummer cites these seven woes as another example of Matthew's fondness for the number seven.[29] This seems to owe more to Plummer's fancy than to fact. Matthew's Gospel is not the Apocalypse of John. Note that all the woes are illustrations of Pharisaic *saying* but not *doing*.[30]

"*Because you shut off the kingdom of heaven from people*"[31] (ὅτι κλείετε τὴν βασιλείαν τῶν οὐρανῶν ἔμπροσθεν τῶν ἀνθρώπων). In Luke 11:52 the lawyers are accused of keeping the door to the house of knowledge locked and with flinging away the keys so as to keep themselves and the people in ignorance. These custodians of the kingdom by their teaching obscured the way to life. It is a tragedy to think how preachers and teachers of the kingdom of God may block the door for those who try to enter in (τοὺς εἰσερχομένοι, conative accusative plural masculine present middle/passive deponent participle). These doorkeepers of the kingdom slam it shut in people's faces, and they themselves are on the outside where they will remain. They hide the key to keep others from going in.

23:15. "*You make him twice as much a son of hell as yourselves*" (ποιεῖτε αὐτὸν υἱὸν γεέννης διπλότερον ὑμῶν). It is a convert to Pharisaism rather than Judaism that is meant by "one proselyte"[32] (ἕνα προσήλυτον), from προσέρχομαι, "newcomers, aliens." There were two kinds of proselytes: (1) of the gate, who were not actual Jews but God-fearers and well-wishers of Judaism, such as Cornelius; and (2) of righteousness, who received circumcision and became actual Jews. A very small percent of the latter became Pharisees. There was a Hellenistic Jewish literature (including the writings of Philo and Sibylline Oracles) that was designed to attract Gentiles to Judaism. But the Pharisaic missionary zeal to compass land and sea (περιάγετε, "go around") was a comparative failure. And success was even worse, Jesus says plainly. Διπλοῦς ("twofold, double") is common in the papyri. The comparative is used, as from διπλός. The comparative form also appears in Appian. Note the ablative of comparison ὑμῶν. The "son of Gehenna" means one fitted for and so destined for gehenna. "The more converted the more perverted," said H. J. Holtzmann. In a special sense, the Pharisees claimed to be sons of the kingdom (Matt. 8:12). They were more partisan than pious.

23:16. "*Woe to you, blind guides*" (Οὐαὶ ὑμῖν, ὁδηγοὶ τυφλοί). Note omission of "scribes and Pharisees, hypocrites" with this third woe. In 15:14 Jesus had already called the Pharisees "blind guides" (leaders). Jesus had explained in 5:33–37 that they split hairs in oaths, as in distinguishing between the temple and the gold of the temple.

"*Whoever swears by the gold of the temple is obligated*"[33] (ὃς δ' ἂν ὀμόσῃ ἐν τῷ χρυσῷ τοῦ ναοῦ, ὀφείλει). He owes or is bound by his oath. The Authorized Version wording "is guilty" is old English and has the obsolete sense of guilt as fine or payment.

23:17. *"You fools and blind men"*[34] (μωροὶ καὶ τυφλοί). In 5:22 Jesus had warned against calling a man μωρός in a rage, but here he describes the stupidity of the blind Pharisees as a class. "It shows that not the word but the spirit in which it is uttered is what matters."[35]

23:23. *"You tithe"*[36] (ἀποδεκατοῦτε). The tithe had to be paid upon "all the increase of your seed" (Lev. 27:30; Deut. 14:22). The English word *tithe* means "tenth." The small aromatic herbs mint (τὸ ἡδύοσμον, sweet smelling), anise or dill (τὸ ἄνηθον), and cummin (τὸ κύμινον, with aromatic seeds), show the Pharisaic scrupulous conscientiousness in tithing marketable commodities. "The Talmud tells of the ass of a certain Rabbi which had been so well trained as to refuse corn of which the tithes had not been taken."[37]

"These are the things you should have done without neglecting the others"[38] (ταῦτα [δὲ] ἔδει ποιῆσαι κἀκεῖνα μὴ ἀφιέναι[39]). Jesus does not condemn tithing. What he does condemn is doing it to the neglect of "weightier provisions of the law"[40] (τὰ βαρύτερα). The Pharisees were externalists (cf. Luke 11:39–44).

23:24. *"Who strain out a gnat"* (οἱ διυλίζοντες τὸν κώνωπα). By filtering through (διά), not the "straining at" in swallowing so crudely suggested by the poor wording in the Authorized Version.

"And swallow a camel" (τὴν δὲ κάμηλον καταπίνοντες). Gulping or drinking down the camel is Oriental hyperbole similar to that in 19:24. See also 5:29, 30; 17:20; 21:21. Both insects and camels were ceremonially unclean (Lev. 11:4, 20, 23, 42). According to the Rabbis, "he that kills a flea on the Sabbath is as guilty as if he killed a camel."[41]

23:25. *"But inside they are full of robbery and self-indulgence"*[42] (ἔσωθεν δὲ γέμουσιν ἐξ ἁρπαγῆς καὶ ἀκρασίας). A serious accusation. These observers of the external ceremonies did not draw the line at robbery (ἁρπαγῆς) and graft (ἀκρασίας) in their lack of control. This is a modern picture of wickedness in high places—both civil and ecclesiastical—where morality is ruthlessly trodden underfoot.

23:26. *"First clean the inside of the cup and of the dish, so that the outside of it may become clean also"* (καθάρισον πρῶτον τὸ ἐντὸς τοῦ ποτηρίου, ἵνα γένηται καὶ τὸ ἐκτὸς αὐτοῦ καθαρόν). The idea is for both the *outside* (ἐκτός) and the *inside* (ἐντός) of the cup and the platter (fine side dish) to be clean, but the inside is the more important. Note the change to singular in verse 26 as if Jesus in a friendlier tone pleads with a Pharisee to mend his ways.

23:27. *"You are like whitewashed tombs"* (παρομοιάζετε τάφοις κεκονιαμένοις). The dative plural masculine perfect passive participle is from κονιάω and that from κονία. Jesus is not speaking of rock-hewn tombs of the well-to-do but the sepulchres of the lower class, which dotted fields and road-sides. The white coloring came from dust or lime whitened with powdered lime dust. When Jesus spoke the sepulchres had been freshly whitewashed. Tombs were whitewashed a month before Passover so that travelers might see them and avoid being defiled by touching one (Num. 19:16). In Acts 23:3 Paul called the high priest a whitewashed wall.

23:29. *"You build the tombs of the prophets"*[43] (οἰκοδομεῖτε τοὺς τάφους τῶν προφητῶν). They were bearing witness against themselves (ἑαυτοῖς, v. 31; cf. Luke 11:48–52). "These men who professed to be so distressed at the murdering of the Prophets, were themselves compassing the death of Him who was far greater than any prophet."[44] There are four monuments that have popularly been called The Tombs of the Prophets at the base of the Mount of Olives. They have sometimes been identified with Zechariah, Absalom, Jehoshaphat, and the apostle James. Their true purpose has long been forgotten, but they date to about the first century. Conceivably, one or more of these might have been under construction at the time that Jesus spoke. The charges of this seventh and last woe applied to the entire Jewish nation, and not merely to the Pharisees.

23:32. *"Fill up, then, the measure of the guilt of your fathers"*[45] (καὶ ὑμεῖς πληρώσατε τὸ μέτρον τῶν πατέρων ὑμῶν). The keenest irony in this command has been softened in some manuscripts to the future indicative (πληρώσετε). "Fill up the measure of your fathers; crown their misdeeds by killing the prophet God has sent to you. Do at last what has long been in your hearts. The hour is come."[46]

23:33. *"You serpents, you brood of vipers"*[47] (ὄφεις γεννήματα ἐχιδνῶν). These blistering words are a climax reminiscent of similar words by the Baptist (3:17). Jesus made the same characterization in his exchange with the Pharisees after they accused him of being in league with Beelzebub (12:34). A curse in the Talmud is somewhat like this: "Woe to the house of Annas! Woe to their serpent-like hissings."

"How will you escape the sentence of hell?"[48] (πῶς φύγητε ἀπὸ τῆς κρίσεως τῆς γεέννης;) Deliberative subjunctive.

23:35. *"Zechariah, the son of Berechiah"*[49] (Ζαχαρίου υἱοῦ βαραχίου).

John Broadus gives the alternative explanations as to why the phrase "son of Berechiah" occurs here but not in Luke 11:51.[50] The usual explanation is that the reference is to Zachariah the son of Jehoiada the priest, who was slain in the court of the temple (2 Chron. 24:20ff.). How the words, "son of Berechiah," got into Matthew we do not know. In the case of Abel, a reckoning for the shedding of his blood was foretold (Gen. 4:10) and the same was true of the slaying of Zechariah (2 Chron. 24:22).

23:37. *"How often I wanted to gather your children together"*[51] (ποσάκις ἠθέλησα ἐπισυναγαγεῖν τὰ τέκνα σου). More exactly, how often did I long to gather to myself (double compound infinitive). The same verb (ἐπισυνάγει) is used of the hen with the compound preposition ὑποκάτω. In a culture where chickens roamed freely, it was not unusual to see a hen quickly gather chicks under her wings when she thought there might be danger. These words bring to mind Jesus' previous visits to Jerusalem, which are told more fully in John's Gospel.

NOTES

1. NIV has "The teachers of the law and the Pharisees sit in Moses' seat."
2. TR and Maj.T have the spelling Μωσέως; WH has Μωυσέως.
3. Alan Hugh McNeile, *The Gospel According to St. Matthew: The Greek Text with Introduction, Notes, and Indices* (repr. ed., Grand Rapids: Baker, 1980), 329.
4. NIV has "for they do not practice what they preach."
5. Alexander Balmain Bruce, *The Expositor's Greek Testament*, Vol. 1, *The Synoptic Gospels* (Grand Rapids: Eerdmans, 1951), 278.
6. NIV has "do not do what they do."
7. NIV has "but they themselves are not willing to lift a finger to move them."
8. TR and Maj.T have τῷ δέ δακτύλῳ αὐτῶν οὐ θέλουσιν κινῆσαι αὐτά.
9. NIV has "Everything they do is done for men to see."
10. NIV has "They make their phylacteries wide."
11. TR and Maj.T have δέ rather than γάρ.
12. Marvin R. Vincent, *Word Studies in the New Testament*, Vol. 1, *The Synoptic Gospels* (repr. ed., Grand Rapids: Eerdmans, 1946), 123.
13. McNeile, *Matthew*, 330.
14. Bruce, *Expositor's*, 279.
15. NIV has "the tassels on their garments long."
16. Alfred Plummer, *An Exegetical Commentary on the Gospel According to Saint Matthew* (repr. ed., Grand Rapids: Eerdmans, 1956), 314–19.
17. TR and Maj.T have τε in place of δέ.

18. NIV has "and the most important seats in the synagogues."

19. Bruce, *Expositor's*, 280.

20. NIV has "they love to be greeted in the marketplaces."

21. NIV has "But you are not to be called Rabbi."

22. Robertson had a far higher view of the term αββα than do most scholars. Quoting McNeile, *Matthew*, 331, at this point, Robertson writes: "Jesus meant the full sense of this noble word for our heavenly Father. 'Abba was not commonly a mode of address to a living person, but a title of honor for Rabbis and great men of the past.'" A number of ancient references to this term have turned up since Robertson wrote, confirming that the term was used in the Jewish family circle as a direct address corresponding loosely to the Greek πατήρ. It may be pushing the extent of its intimacy to say, as some do, that calling God αββα is tantamount to calling him "Daddy." Greek law, however, did deny use of the term to slaves in addressing their masters, on the grounds that it was disrespectful in its informality.

23. NIV has "Nor are you to be called Teacher."

24. McNeile, *Matthew*, 332.

25. NIV has "for you have one Teacher, the Christ."

26. TR and Maj.T have εἷς γὰρ ὑμῶν ἐστιν ὁ καθηγητὴς ὁ Χριστός.

27. NIV has "Woe to you, teachers of the law and Pharisees, you hypocrites."

28. Bruce, *Expositor's*, 280. TR and Maj.T had eight woes, adding verse 14. The Revised Version placed it in the margin. It is called verse 13 in WH and rejected on the authority of Aleph B D as a manifest gloss from Mark 12:40 and Luke 20:47. The MSS that insert it place it either before or after verse 13.

29. Plummer, *Matthew*, 316.

30. Willoughby G. Allen, *A Critical and Exegetical Commentary on the Gospel According to Matthew*, International Critical Commentary (Edinburgh: T. & T. Clark, 1912), 245.

31. NIV has "You shut the kingdom of heaven in men's faces."

32. NIV has "a single convert."

33. NIV has "if anyone swears by the gold of the temple, he is bound by his oath."

34. NIV has "You blind fools."

35. McNeile, *Matthew*, 334.

36. NIV has "You give a tenth."

37. Vincent, *Word Studies*, 124.

38. NIV has "You should have practised the latter, without neglecting the former."

39. TR and Maj.T omit δέ.

40. NIV has "the more important matters of the law."
41. Jer. *Shabb.* 107.
42. NIV has "but inside they are full of greed and self-indulgence."
43. NIV has "You build tombs for the prophets."
44. Plummer, *Matthew*.
45. NIV has "Fill up, then, the measure of the sin of your forefathers."
46. Bruce, *Expositor's*, 285.
47. NIV has "You snakes, you brood of vipers."
48. NIV has "How will you escape being condemned to hell?"
49. NIV has "Zechariah, son of Berekiah."
50. John A. Broadus, *Commentary on Matthew* (repr. ed., Grand Rapids: Kregel, 1990), 476–77.
51. NIV has "How often I have longed to gather your children together."

Matthew: Chapter 24

24:1. *Jesus came out from the temple*[1] (ἐξελθὼν ὁ Ἰησοῦς ἀπὸ τοῦ ἱεροῦ). Discourses since Matthew 21:23 have been in the temple courts (ἱερόν, the sacred enclosure). But now Jesus leaves it for good after the powerful denunciation of the scribes and Pharisees in chapter 23. His public teaching is over. It was a tragic moment.

And was going away (ἐπορεύετο, third person singular descriptive imperfect middle/passive deponent indicative). The disciples, as if to relieve the tension of the Master, came to him (προσῆλθον) to show (ἐπιδεῖξαι, ingressive aorist active infinitive) the buildings of the temple (τας οἰκοδομὰς τοῦ ἱεροῦ). They were familiar to Jesus and the disciples, but beautiful like a snow mountain.[2] The monument that Herod the Great had begun would not be complete until just a few years before its destruction (cf. John 2:20). Great stones were of polished marble.

24:2. *"Not one stone here will be left upon another"* (οὐ μὴ ἀφεθῇ ὧδε λίθος ἐπὶ λίθον), stone upon stone. The startling prediction shows the gloomy current of Jesus' thoughts, which were not changed by words of admiration for the temple.

24:3. *As He was sitting*[3] (Καθημένου δὲ αὐτοῦ), a genitive absolute. Jesus sits on the Mount of Olives looking down on Jerusalem and the temple he has just left. After the climb up the mountain, four disciples, Peter, James, John, Andrew, come to Jesus with questions raised by his solemn words. They ask about the destruction of Jerusalem and the temple, Christ's own second coming (παρουσία, presence, common in the papyri for the visit of the emperor), and the end of the world. Did they think that these events would all take place simultaneously? There is no way to know, but Jesus treats all three in this great eschatological discourse. This mixing of events and eras is raised as an issue by textual critics of the Synoptic Gospels. Modern theories have tended to impugn the knowledge of Jesus or of the writers or of both. It is sufficient for our purpose to see that Jesus uses the destruction of the temple and of Jerusalem as part of a complex of events leading to his own second coming

196

and ultimately to the end of the world or consummation of the age (συντελείας τοῦ αἰῶνος). In a painting the artist by skillful perspective may give on the same surface the inside of a room, the fields outside the window, and the sky far beyond. Certainly in this discourse Jesus blends in apocalyptic language the background of his death on the cross, the coming destruction of Jerusalem, his own second coming, and the end of the world. He now touches one, now the other. It is not easy for us to separate clearly the events clearly. The point Jesus is making in the whole picture is that we must be ready for his coming and the end. The destruction of Jerusalem in A.D. 70 came as he had foretold. Some date the Synoptic Gospels after 70 simply to avoid the predictive element. Such theorists want to limit the foreknowledge of Jesus to a merely human level. The word παρουσία occurs nowhere in the Gospels except verses 3, 27, 37, and 39. It turns up often in the Epistles, either of presence as opposed to absence (Phil. 2:12) or the second coming of Christ (2 Thess. 2:1).

24:4. *"See to it that no one misleads you"*[4] (Βλέπετε μή τις ὑμᾶς πλανήσῃ). This warning runs all through the discourse. Given Jesus' clarity here, the many eschatological deceptions through the ages are all the more amazing. The verb in the passive appears in 18:12 when the one sheep wanders astray. Here it is in the active voice with the causative sense to lead astray. The English word *planet* comes from this root.

24:5. *"For many will come in My name"* (πολλοὶ γὰρ ἐλεύσονται ἐπὶ τῷ ὀνόματί μου). They will arrogate to themselves false claims of messiahship in (on the basis of) the name of Christ himself.[5] Josephus gives false Christs as one of the reasons for the explosion against Rome that led to the city's destruction. Each new hero was welcomed by the masses, including Simon Bar-kokhba, "the desert Messiah" who ignited the second Jewish rebellion against Rome (132–35). "I am the Messiah," each would say. In the modern West, a variety of pseudomessiahs have arisen. For example, Annie Besant introduced a theosophical Messiah and Mary Baker Eddy founded the Church of Christ, Scientist, on claims that in effect placed her on a par with Jesus.

24:6. *"See that you are not frightened"*[6] (ὁρᾶτε, μὴ θροεῖσθε). This is asyndeton here, with two imperatives, as ὁρᾶτε βλέπετε in Mark 8:15.[7] Look out for wars and rumors of wars, but do not be scared out of your wits by them. θροέω means "to cry aloud, to scream," and in the passive "to be terrified by an outcry." Paul uses this very verb (μηδὲ θροεῖσθαι) in 2 Thessalonians 2:2 as a warning against excitement over false reports that he had predicted the immediate second coming of Christ.

"But that is not yet the end"[8] (ἀλλ᾽ οὔπω ἐστὶν τὸ τέλος). It is curious how people overlook these words of Jesus as they proceed to set dates for the immediate end. That happened continually during the twentieth century.

24:8. *"But all these things are merely the beginning of birth pangs"*[9] (πάντα δὲ ταῦτα ἀρχὴ ὠδίνων). The Jews used the very phrase for sufferings of the Messiah that were to come before the coming of the Messiah (Jubilees 23:18; Apocalypse of Baruch 27–29). But the word occurs with no idea of birth as the pains of death (Ps. 18:6; Acts 2:24). These woes, says Jesus, are proof not of the end but of the beginning.

24:9. *"Tribulation"*[10] (θλῖψιν, see 13:21), a word common in the Acts, Epistles, and the Apocalypse for the oppression laid upon Christians.

"And you will be hated by all nations"[11] (καὶ ἔσεσθε μισούμενοι ὑπὸ πάντων τῶν ἐθνῶν). The periphrastic future passive participial phrase emphasizes the continuous process of linear action.

"Because of My name" (διὰ τὸ ὄνομά μου). The most glorious name in the world would soon be a byword of shame (Acts 5:41). The disciples would count it an honor to be dishonored for his name's sake.

24:11. *"Many false prophets will arise"*[12] (πολλοὶ ψευδοροφῆται ἐγερθήσονται). Jesus had warned against false prophets in the Sermon on the Mount (7:15).

24:12. *"Most people's love will grow cold"*[13] (ψυγήσεται ἡ ἀγάπη τῶν πολλῶν), third person singular second future passive indicative from ψύχω. To breathe cool by blowing, to grow cold, "spiritual energy blighted or chilled by a malign or poisonous wind."[14] Love of the brotherhood gives way to mutual hatred and suspicion.

24:14. *"This gospel of the kingdom shall be preached in the whole world"* (κηρυχθήσεται τοῦτο τὸ εὐαγγέλιον τῆς βασιλείας ἐν ὅλῃ τῇ οἰκουμένῃ). It will be heralded in all the inhabited world. It is not here said that all will be saved, nor must this language be given too literal and detailed an application to encompass every individual.

24:15. *"Therefore when you see the abomination of desolation"*[15] (Ὅταν οὖν ἴδητε τὸ βδέλυγμα τῆς ἐρημώσεως). This is an illusion to Daniel 9:27; 11:31; 12:11. Antiochus Epiphanes erected an altar to Zeus on the altar of Jehovah (1 Macc. 1:54, 59; 6:7; 2 Macc. 6:1–5). The desolation in the mind of Jesus is apparently the Roman army (Luke 21:20) in the temple, an application of the words of Daniel to this dread event. The verb βδελύσσομαι is "to feel nausea because of stench, to abhor, to detest." Idolatry was a stench to God (Luke 16:15; Rev. 17:4). Josephus tells us that the Romans burned the temple and offered sacrifices to their ensigns at the Eastern Gate when they proclaimed Titus emperor.[16]

Let the reader understand (ὁ ἀναγινώσκων νοείτω). This parenthesis occurs also in Mark 13:14. It is not to be supposed that Jesus used these words. They were inserted by Mark as he wrote his book, and he was followed by Matthew.

24:16. *"Then those who are in Judea must flee to the mountains"*[17] (τότε οἱ ἐν τῇ Ἰουδαίᾳ φευγέτωσαν εἰς τὰ ὄρη[18]). The mountains east of the Jordan are meant. Eusebius says that before the siege of Jerusalem the Christians actually fled to Pella at the foot of the mountains, about seventeen miles south of the Sea of Galilee.[19] They remembered the warning of Jesus and fled to safety.

24:17. *"Whoever is on the housetop must not go down to get the things out that are in his house"*[20] (ὁ ἐπὶ τοῦ δώματος μὴ καταβάτω ἆραι τὰ ἐκ τῆς οἰκίας αὐτοῦ[21]). They could flee from roof to roof and so escape, "the road of the roofs," as the rabbis called it. There was need for haste.

24:18. *"[And] whoever is in the field must not turn back to get his cloak"*[22] (καὶ ὁ ἐν τῷ ἀγρῷ μὴ ἐπιστρεψάτω ὀπίσω ἆραι τὸ ἱμάτιον αὐτοῦ[23]). The peasant left his mantle at home while at work.

24:20. *"But pray that your flight will not be in the winter, or on a Sabbath"*[24] (προσεύχεσθε δὲ ἵνα μὴ γένηται ἡ φυγὴ ὑμῶν χειμῶνος μηδὲ σαββάτῳ[25]). Χειμῶνος is a genitive of time, σαββάτῳ is a locative of time. Winter is mentioned because of the rough weather, "on a Sabbath" because some would hesitate to escape by journeying on the day of worship. Josephus gives the best illustration of the horrors foretold by Jesus in verse 21.[26]

24:22. *"[And] unless those days had been cut short"*[27] (καὶ εἰ μὴ ἐκολοβώθησαν αἱ ἡμέραι ἐκεῖναι). The verb is from κολοβός, which means "lopped off, mutilated." It is a second class condition, determined as unfulfilled. It is a prophetic figure, the future regarded as past.

"But for the sake of the elect" (διὰ δὲ τοὺς ἐκλεκτούς). See verse 31. Jesus also uses this phrase in 22:14. The siege was shortened by various historical events, such as Herod Agrippa's decision to stop strengthening of the walls, imperial orders received by the Roman invaders, the sudden arrival of Titus to finish off the rebels, and the failure of the defenders to prepare for a long siege. "Titus himself confessed that God was against the Jews, since otherwise neither his armies nor his engines would have availed against their defences."[28]

24:23. *"'Behold, here is the Christ,' or 'There He is'"*[29] (Ἰδοὺ ὧδε ὁ Χριστός, ἤ, Ὧδε). False prophets (v. 11) contributed to the nation's trouble, and false Christs (ψευδόχριστοι, cf. v. 24) would extend their own offer of a way out—rebellion to overthrow the yoke of Rome. Deluded victims raise the cries of "Lo, here," when these false Messiahs arise with their panaceas for all sorts of political, religious, moral, and spiritual ills.

24:24. *"Will show great signs and wonders"*[30] (δώσουσιν σημεῖα μεγάλα καὶ τέρατα). These are two of the three words so often used in the New Testament about the works (ἔργα) of Jesus, the other being δυνάμεις, "powers." They often occur together of the same work (John 4:48; Acts 2:22; 4:30; 2 Cor. 12:12; Heb. 2:4). Τέρας is a wonder or prodigy, δύναμις, a mighty work or power, σημεῖον, a sign of God's purpose. Miracle (*miraculum*) presents only the notion of wonder or portent. The same deed can be looked at from these different angles. But the point to note here is that mere "signs and wonders" do not of themselves prove the power is from God. These charlatans will be so skillful that they will, "if possible" (εἰ δυνατόν), lead astray the very elect. The implication is that it is not possible. People become excited and are misled and are unable to judge of results. Advertising and marketing can make full use of the credulity of people, as do spiritualistic mediums.

24:26. *"'Behold, He is in the wilderness'"*[31] ('Ιδοὺ ἐν τῇ ἐρήμῳ ἐστίν), like Simon son of Gioras.[32]

"'Behold, He is in the inner rooms'"[33] ('Ιδοὺ ἐν τοῖς ταμείοις). Like John of Giscala.[34] False Messiahs act the role of the great unseen and unknown.

24:27. *"For just as the lightning comes from the east and flashes even to the west"*[35] (ὥσπερ γὰρ ἡ ἀστραπὴ ἐξέρχεται ἀπὸ ἀνατολῶν καὶ φαίνεται ἕως δυσμῶν). Visible in contrast to the invisibility of the false Messiahs (cf. Rev. 1:7), like a flash of lightning.

24:28. *"Wherever the corpse is"*[36] (ὅπου ἐὰν ᾖ τὸ πτῶμα[37]), as in 14:12. Originally a fallen body from πίπτω, to fall, like the Latin *cadaver* from *cado*, to fall. The proverb here, as in Luke 17:37, is like that in Job 39:30; Prov. 30:17.

"There the vultures will gather" (ἐκεῖ συναχθήσονται οἱ ἀετοί). Perhaps the griffon vulture, larger than the eagle, which was often seen in the wake of an army and followed Napoleon's retreat from Russia.

24:29. *"But immediately after the tribulation of those days"*[38] (Εὐθέως δὲ μετὰ τὴν θλῖψιν τῶν ἡμερῶν ἐκείνων[39]). This word, εὐθέως, common in Mark's Gospel as εὐθύς, gives trouble if one stresses the time element. The problem is how much time intervenes between "the tribulation of those days" and the vivid symbolism of verse 29. The use of ἐν τάχει in Revelation 1:1

should give pause. Here we have a prophetic panorama like that with foreshortened perspective. The apocalyptic pictures in verse 29 also call for sober judgment. One may compare Joel's prophecy as interpreted by Peter in Acts 2:16–22. Literalism is not appropriate in interpreting apocalyptic eschatology.

24:30. *"And then the sign of the Son of Man will appear in the sky"*[40] (καὶ τότε φανήσεται τὸ σημεῖον τοῦ υἱοῦ τοῦ ἀνθρώπου ἐν οὐρανῷ[41]). Many theories for the sign have been suggested, for example a cross in the sky. A. B. Bruce sees a reference to Daniel 7:13 "one like the Son of Man" and holds that Christ himself is the sign in question (the genitive of apposition).[42] This is certainly possible.

"They will see the Son of Man coming" (ὄψονται τὸν υἱὸν τοῦ ἀνθρώπου ἐρχόμενον). It is confirmed by the rest of the verse (see 16:27; 26:64). The Jews had asked for such a sign[43] (12:38; 16:1; John 2:18).

24:31. *"And He will send forth His angels with a great trumpet"*[44] (καὶ ἀποστελεῖ τοὺς ἀγγέλους αὐτοῦ μετὰ[45] σάλπιγγος μεγάλης).[46] The trumpet was the signal to call the hosts of Israel to march. It is used in prophetic imagery (Isa. 27:13; Rev. 11:15). Clearly "the coming of the son of man is not to be identified with the judgment of Jerusalem but rather forms its preternatural background."[47]

24:32. *"When its branch has already become tender and puts forth its leaves"*[48] (ὅταν ἤδη ὁ κλάδος αὐτῆς γένηται ἁπαλὸς καὶ τὰ φύλλα ἐκφύῃ). The second verb is third person singular present active subjunctive.[49] If accented ἐκφυῇ on the last syllable, it is third person singular second aorist passive subjunctive.

24:34. *"This generation"* (ἡ γενεὰ αὕτη). The problem is whether Jesus is here referring to the destruction of Jerusalem or to the Second Coming and end of the world. If to the destruction of Jerusalem, there was a literal fulfillment. In the Old Testament, a generation was reckoned as forty years. This is the natural way to take verses 33–34,[50] "all things" meaning the same in both verses.

24:36. *"No one knows, not even the angels of heaven, nor the Son"*[51] (οὐδεὶς οἶδεν, οὐδὲ οἱ ἄγγελοι τῶν οὐρανῶν οὐδὲ ὁ υἱός[52]). Probably genuine, though absent in some ancient MSS. The idea is really involved in the words "but the Father only" (εἰ μὴ ὁ πατὴρ[53] μόνος). It is equally clear that in this verse Jesus has in mind the time of His return. He had plainly stated in verse 34 that those events (destruction of Jerusalem) would take place in that generation. He now as pointedly states that no one but the Father knows the day or the hour when these things (the Second Coming and the end of the world) will come. One may, of course, accuse Jesus of hopeless confusion or of ignorance in mixing the Second Coming into the whole chain of events. So McNeile: "It is impossible to escape the conclusion that Jesus as Man, expected the End, within the lifetime of his contemporaries."[54] But Jesus here explicitly denies that He expects anything of the kind. It is as easy to attribute ignorance to modern scholars, with their various theories about Jesus.

24:37. *"Just like the days of Noah"*[55] ($\overset{\backprime}{\omega}\sigma\pi\epsilon\rho$ $\gamma\grave{\alpha}\rho$[56] $\alpha\grave{\iota}$ $\mathring{\eta}\mu\acute{\epsilon}\rho\alpha\iota$ $\tauο\hat{\upsilon}$ $N\hat{\omega}\epsilon$). Jesus had used this imagery among the Pharisees (Luke 17:26–30). In Noah's day there was plenty of warning, but utter unpreparedness. Today, most people are indifferent about the Second Coming or they couch it in keeping with their fantasies. Few are really eager and expectant and leave to God the time and the plans.

24:38. *"They were eating and drinking"*[57] ($\mathring{\eta}\sigma\alpha\nu$ . . . $\tau\rho\acute{\omega}\gamma\omicron\nu\tau\epsilon\varsigma$ $\kappa\alpha\grave{\iota}$ $\pi\acute{\iota}\nu\omicron\nu\tau\epsilon\varsigma$), a periphrastic imperfect participial construction. The first participle means to chew raw vegetables or fruits like nuts or almonds.

24:41. *"Two women will be grinding at the mill"*[58] ($\delta\acute{\upsilon}\omicron$ $\mathring{\alpha}\lambda\acute{\eta}\theta\omicron\upsilon\sigma\alpha\iota$ $\mathring{\epsilon}\nu$ $\tau\hat{\omega}$ $\mu\acute{\upsilon}\lambda\omega$[59]). The millstone referred to here was part of a hand-mill that could be turned by women (cf. Exod. 11:5). There was a handle near the edge of the upper stone.

24:42. *"Therefore be on the alert"*[60] ($\gamma\rho\eta\gamma\omicron\rho\epsilon\hat{\iota}\tau\epsilon$ $\omicron\hat{\upsilon}\nu$). A late present imperative from the second perfect $\mathring{\epsilon}\gamma\rho\acute{\eta}\gamma\omicron\rho\alpha$ from $\mathring{\epsilon}\gamma\epsilon\acute{\iota}\rho\omega$. Keep awake, be on the watch "therefore" because of the uncertainty of the time of the Second Coming. Jesus gives a half dozen parables to enforce the point of this exhortation: (1) The Porter; (2) The Master of the House; (3) The Faithful Servant and the Evil Servants; (4) The Ten Virgins; (5) The Talents; and (6) The Sheep and the Goats. Matthew does not give The Porter (see Mark 13:35–37).

24:43. *"If the head of the house had known at what time of the night the thief was coming"*[61] ($\epsilon\grave{\iota}$ $\mathring{\eta}\delta\epsilon\iota$ $\grave{\omicron}$ $\omicron\mathring{\iota}\kappa\omicron\delta\epsilon\sigma\pi\acute{\omicron}\tau\eta\varsigma$ $\pi\omicron\acute{\iota}\alpha$ $\phi\upsilon\lambda\alpha\kappa\hat{\eta}$ $\grave{\omicron}$ $\kappa\lambda\acute{\epsilon}\pi\tau\eta\varsigma$ $\acute{\epsilon}\rho\chi\epsilon\tau\alpha\iota$). The night was divided into four watches (cf. 14:25).

"Would not have allowed his house to be broken into" ($\omicron\mathring{\upsilon}\kappa$ $\mathring{\alpha}\nu$ $\epsilon\mathring{\iota}\alpha\sigma\epsilon\nu$ $\delta\iota\omicron\rho\upsilon\chi\theta\hat{\eta}\nu\alpha\iota$[62] $\tau\grave{\eta}\nu$ $\omicron\mathring{\iota}\kappa\acute{\iota}\alpha\nu$ $\alpha\mathring{\upsilon}\tauο\hat{\upsilon}$). The thief dug through the tile roof or under the wall. The floor was dirt in houses where the poor lived.

24:44. *"For the Son of Man is coming at an hour when you do not think He will"*[63] ($\acute{\omicron}\tau\iota$ $\mathring{\eta}$ $\omicron\mathring{\upsilon}$ $\delta\omicron\kappa\epsilon\hat{\iota}\tau\epsilon$ $\acute{\omega}\rho\alpha$ $\grave{\omicron}$ $\upsilon\grave{\iota}\omicron\varsigma$ $\tauο\hat{\upsilon}$ $\mathring{\alpha}\nu\theta\rho\acute{\omega}\pi\omicron\upsilon$ $\acute{\epsilon}\rho\chi\epsilon\tau\alpha\iota$[64]). It is useless to set the day and hour for Christ's coming. It is folly to neglect it. This figure of the thief is used also by Paul concerning the unexpectedness of Christ's Second Coming (1 Thess. 5:2). See also Matthew 24:50 for the unexpectedness of the coming, with punishment for the evil servant.

24:48. *"My master is not coming for a long time'"*[65] (Χρονίζει μου ὁ κύριος[66]). That is the temptation and to give way to indulge in fleshly appetites or to pride of superior intellect. Within a generation scoffers already were denigrating the promise of the coming of Christ (2 Peter 3:4). Such people forget that God's clock is not like ours (3:8).

NOTES

1. NIV has "Jesus left the temple." TR and Maj.T have ἐξελθὼν ὁ Ἰησοῦς ἐπορεύετο ἀπὸ τοῦ ἱεροῦ.
2. Josephus, *Wars of the Jews*, 5.5.6.
3. NIV had "As Jesus was sitting." The name *Jesus* is not explicit in the Greek text but is implied.
4. NIV has "Watch out that no one deceives you."
5. Josephus, *Wars of the Jews*, 6.5.2–3.
6. NIV has "see to it that you are not alarmed."
7. A. T. Robertson, *A Grammar of the Greek New Testament in the Light of Historical Research* (Nashville: Broadman, 1934), 949.
8. NIV has "but the end is still to come."
9. NIV has "All these are the beginning of birth pains."
10. NIV has "and you will be hated by all nations because of me."
11. NIV has "persecution."
12. NIV has "many false prophets will appear."
13. NIV has "the love of most will grow cold."
14. Marvin R. Vincent, *Word Studies in the New Testament*, Vol. 1, *The Synoptic Gospels* (repr. ed., Grand Rapids: Eerdmans, 1946), 127.
15. NIV has "So when you see . . . the abomination that causes desolation."
16. Josephus, *Wars of the Jews*, 6.6.1.
17. NIV has "then let those who are in Judea flee to the mountains."
18. TR and Maj.T have the preposition ἐπί instead of εἰς.
19. Eusebius, *Church History*, 3.5.3
20. NIV has "Let no one on the roof of his house go down to take anything out of the house."
21. TR and Maj.T have καταβαινέτω ατι instead of καταβάτω ατά.
22. NIV has "Let no one in the field go back to get his cloak."
23. TR and Maj.T have the plural τὰ ἱμάται instead of the singular τὸ ἱμάτιον.
24. NIV has "Pray that your flight will not take place in winter nor on the Sabbath."
25. TR has the preposition ἐν before σαββάτῳ.
26. Josephus, *Wars of the Jews*, book 5.

27. NIV has "If those days had not been cut short."
28. Vincent, *Word Studies*, 129.
29. NIV has "Look, here is the Christ," or "There he is!"
30. NIV has "perform great signs and miracles."
31. NIV has "There he is, out in the desert."
32. Josephus, *Wars of the Jews*, 6.9.5, 7.
33. NIV has "Here he is, in the inner rooms."
34. Josephus, *Wars of the Jews*, 5.6.1.
35. NIV has "For as lightning that comes from the east is visible even to the west."
36. NIV has "Wherever there is a carcass."
37. TR and Maj.T add the conjunction $\gamma\acute{\alpha}\rho$ here.
38. NIV has "Immediately after the distress of those days."
39. TR has the acute accent rather than the circumflex in $\theta\lambda\acute{\iota}\psi\iota\nu$.
40. NIV has "At that time the sign of the Son of Man will appear in the sky."
41. TR and Maj.T have the article $\tau\hat{\omega}$ before $o\dot{\upsilon}\rho\alpha\nu\hat{\omega}$.
42. Bruce, *Expositor's*, 295.
43. Broadus, *Matthew*, 490.
44. NIV has "And he will send his angels with a loud trumpet call."
45. TR and Maj.T add the noun $\phi\omega\nu\hat{\eta}s$ here.
46. TR and Maj.T include $\phi\omega\nu\hat{\eta}s$, $\kappa\alpha\grave{\iota}$ $\dot{\alpha}\pi\sigma\sigma\tau\epsilon\lambda\epsilon\hat{\iota}$ $\tau\sigma\upsilon s$ $\dot{\alpha}\gamma\gamma\acute{\epsilon}\lambda\sigma\upsilon s$ $\alpha\dot{\upsilon}\tau\sigma\hat{\upsilon}$ $\mu\epsilon\tau\acute{\alpha}$ $\sigma\acute{\alpha}\lambda\pi\iota\gamma\gamma\sigma s$ $\phi\omega\nu\hat{\eta}s$ $\mu\epsilon\gamma\acute{\alpha}\lambda\eta s$.
47. Bruce, *Expositor's*, 296.
48. NIV has "As soon as its twigs get tender and its leaves come out."
49. In WH.
50. Bruce, *Expositor's*, 296.
51. NIV has "No one knows . . . not even the angels in heaven, nor the Son."
52. TR and Maj.T omit $o\dot{\upsilon}\delta\epsilon$ $\dot{o}$ $\upsilon\acute{\iota}\acute{o}s$.
53. TR and Maj.T add the pronoun $\mu\sigma\upsilon$ here.
54. McNeile, *Matthew*, 355.
55. NIV has "As it was in the days of Noah."
56. TR and Maj.T have the conjunction $\delta\acute{\epsilon}$ here rather than $\gamma\acute{\alpha}\rho$.
57. NIV has "people were eating and drinking."
58. NIV has "Two women will be grinding with a hand mill."
59. TR and Maj.T have $\mu\acute{\upsilon}\lambda\omega\nu\iota$.
60. NIV has "Therefore keep watch."
61. NIV has "If the owner of the house had known at what time of night the thief was coming."
62. TR and Maj.T have the infinitive $\delta\iota\sigma\rho\upsilon\gamma\hat{\eta}\nu\alpha\iota$ here rather than $\delta\iota\sigma\rho\upsilon\chi\theta\hat{\eta}\nu\alpha\iota$.

63. NIV has "when you do not expect him."
64. TR and Maj.T have a different word order $\mathring{\eta}$ ὥρᾳ οὐ δοκεῖτε.
65. NIV has "My master is staying away a long time."
66. TR and Maj.T have a different word order plus an infinitive at the end, Χρονίζει ὁ κύριός μου ἐλθεῖν.

Matthew: Chapter 25

25:1. *"Ten virgins"* (δέκα παρθένοις). There is no special point in the number ten. The scene is apparently centered round the house of the bride, to which the bridegroom is coming for the wedding festivities. Alfred Plummer places the scene near the house of the bridegroom who has gone to bring the bride home.[1] This reference to the cultural milieu is hazy now, but it is not pertinent to the point of the parable.

"Lamps" (λαμπάδας). Probably torches with a wooden staff and a dish on top in which was placed a piece of rope or cloth dipped in oil or pitch. But sometimes λαμπάς has the meaning of oil lamp (λύχνος) as in Acts 20:8. That may be the meaning here.[2]

25:3. *"They took no oil with them"*[3] (οὐκ ἔλαβον μεθ' ἑαυτῶν ἔλαιον). They probably took none at all, not realizing their lack of oil until they tried to light the torches on the arrival of the bridegroom and his party.

25:4. *"But the prudent took oil in flasks"*[4] (αἱ δὲ φρόνιμοι ἔλαβον ἔλαιον ἐν τοῖς ἀγγείοις). Ἀγγείοις is found here alone in the New Testament, although ἄγγη is found in 13:48. An extra supply was taken in these receptacles besides the oil in the dish on top of the staff.

25:5. *"They all got drowsy and began to sleep"*[5] (ἐνύσταξαν πᾶσαι καὶ ἐκάθευδον). They dropped off to sleep, nodded (ingressive aorist) and then went on sleeping (imperfect, linear action), a vivid picture drawn by the difference in the two tenses.

25:6. *"But at midnight there was a shout"*[6] (μέσης δὲ νυκτὸς κραυγὴ γέγονεν). A cry has come, a dramatic use of the present perfect (second perfect active) indicative, not the perfect for the aorist. It is not ἐστιν but γέγονεν, which emphasizes a sudden outcry rending the air. The very memory of it is preserved by this tense, with all the bustle and confusion.

"'Come out to meet him'" (ἐξέρχεσθε εἰς ἀπάντησιν [αὐτοῦ]). Or, "go out to meet him," depending on whether the cry comes from outside the house or inside where they are sleeping because of the delay. A ceremonial salutation is neatly expressed by the Greek phrase.

25:7. *"Trimmed their lamps"* (ἐκόσμησαν τὰς λαμπάδας ἑαυτῶν[7]), "put

206

in order, make ready." The lights had been out while they slept, so wicks were lit and fresh oil put in the dishes. A nineteenth-century marriage ceremony in India is described in Richard Trench's *Parables*: "After waiting two or three hours, at length near midnight it was announced, as in the very words of Scripture, 'Behold the bridegroom cometh; go ye out to meet him.'"

25:8. *"'Our lamps are going out'"* (αἱ λαμπάδες ἡμῶν σβέννυνται), third person plural present passive indicative of linear action, not aorist. When the five foolish virgins lit their lamps, they discovered the lack of oil. The sputtering, flickering, smoking wicks were a sad revelation. "And *perhaps* we are to understand that there is something in the coincidence of the lamps going out just as the Bridegroom arrived. Mere outward religion is found to have no illuminating power."[8]

25:9. *"But the prudent answered, 'No, there will not be enough for us and you too'"*[9] (ἀπεκρίθησαν δὲ αἱ φρόνιμοι λέγουσαι, Μήποτε οὐ μὴ ἀρκέσῃ ἡμῖν καὶ ὑμῖν). The elliptical construction is not easy to explain. Some MSS have οὐκ instead of οὐ μή. Even so, μήποτε has to be explained, either by supplying an imperative such as γινέσθω or by a verb of fearing such as φοβούμεθα. The latter is more likely. Either οὐκ or οὐ μή would be proper with the futuristic subjunctive ἀρκέσῃ:[10] "We are afraid that there is no possibility of there being enough for us both." Oil is denied by the wise virgins because there is not enough. "It was necessary to show that the foolish virgins could not have the consequences of their folly averted at the last moment."[11] The reply is courteous but final. The compound Greek negatives are expressive, μήποτε and οὐ μή.

25:10. *"And while they were going away"*[12] (ἀπερχομένων δὲ αὐτῶν), a genitive plural feminine present middle/passive deponent participle, genitive absolute, while they were going away, descriptive linear action.

"The door was shut" (ἐκλείσθη ἡ θύρα), third person singular effective aorist passive indicative. It was shut with finality and would stay shut.

25:11. *"Later the other virgins also came"*[13] (ὕστερον δὲ ἔρχονται καὶ αἱ λοιπαὶ παρθένοι). The way is barred to them.

"Saying, 'Lord, lord, open up for us'"[14] (λέγουσαι, Κύριε κύριε, ἄνοιξον ἡμῖν). They appeal to the bridegroom, who is now master, whether at the bride's house or his own.

25:12. *"'I do not know you'"*[15] (οὐκ οἶδα ὑμᾶς). There was no reason for special favors to be granted. They must abide the consequences of their own negligence.

25:13. *"Be on the alert then"*[16] (Γρηγορεῖτε οὖν). This is the refrain with all of these parables; lack of foresight is inexcusable. Ignorance of the time of the Second Coming does not excuse neglect. It is a reason for readiness.

25:14. *"For it is just like a man about to go on a journey"*[17] (Ὥσπερ γάρ ἄνθρωπος ἀποδημῶν). The man was on the point of going abroad, about to go away from his people (δῆμος). This word is in ancient use in this sense. An ellipse has to be supplied, "It is as when" or "The kingdom of heaven is as when." This parable of the talents is quite similar to the parable of the pounds in Luke 19:11–28. Jesus varied the story. Some scholars deny that He might do this, crediting Jesus with very little versatility.

"Entrusted his possessions to them"[18] (παρέδωκεν αὐτοῖς τὰ ὑπάρχοντα αὐτοῦ). The words "his belongings" are an accusative plural neuter present active participle, used as a substantive.

25:15. *"To one he gave five talents"* (ᾧ μὲν ἔδωκεν πέντε τάλαντα). Functioning as a demonstrative ὅ", not as the relative, a neat Greek idiom.

"Each according to his own ability" (ἑκάστῳ κατὰ τὴν ἰδίαν δύναμιν). Each had all that he was capable of handling. The use that one makes of his opportunities is the measure of his capacity for more. One talent represented a considerable amount of money at a time when a δηνάριον was a day's wage (see on 18:24).

25:16. *"Immediately"*[19] (εὐθέως[20]). The business temper of this slave is shown by his promptness.

"Traded with them"[21] (ἠργάσατο[22] ἐν αὐτοῖς). He worked, did business, traded with them (the talents). "The virgins wait, the servants work."[23]

"Gained" (ἐκέρδησεν), as in verse 17. Κέρδος means interest. This gain was a hundred percent.

25:19. *"Settled accounts with them"* (συναίρει λόγον μετ' αὐτῶν[24]), as in 18:23. G. Adolf Deissmann quotes two papyri records and a Nubian ostracon that use this very business idiom.[25] Ancient Greek writers do not show it.

25:21. *"'Enter into the joy of your master'"*[26] (εἴσελθε εἰς τὴν χαρὰν τοῦ κυρίου σου). The word χαρα, "joy," may refer to the feast that celebrated the master's return (cf. v. 23).

25:24. *"And the one also who had received the one talent came up"*[27] (προσελθὼν δὲ καὶ ὁ τὸ ἓν τάλαντον εἰληφώς). Note the nominative singular masculine perfect active participle to emphasize the fact that he still had it. In verse 20 we have ὁ . . . λαβών (nominative singular masculine aorist active participle).

"'I knew you to be a hard man'" (ἔγνων σε ὅτι σκληρὸς εἶ ἄνθρωπος). First person singular second aorist active indicative, experiential knowledge

from γινώσκω and proleptical use of σε. "A hard man": harsh, stern, rough, worse than αὐστηρός in Luke 19:21, grasping and ungenerous.

"'Gathering where you scattered no seed'" (συνάγων ὅθεν οὐ διεσκόρπισας). This scattering was of seed mixed with the chaff that blew away as wheat was winnowed.

25:26. "'You wicked, lazy slave'" (Πονηρὲ δοῦλε καὶ ὀκνηρέ). Πονηρὲ from πόνος, "hard, disturbing work," and ὀκνέω, "to be slow, poky, or slothful." WH reads this reply to the end of verse 26 as a question. It is sarcasm.

25:27. "'Then you ought to have put my money in the bank'"[28] (ἔδει σε οὖν βαλεῖν τὰ ἀργύριά μου τοῖς τραπεζίταις[29]). His very words of excuse convict him. It was a necessity (ἔδει) that he did not see. The bankers (τοῖς τραπεζίταις) were money changers or brokers who exchanged money for a fee and took investments at interest. The word is common in late Greek.

"'I would have received my money back with interest'" (ἐγὼ ἐκομισάμην ἂν τὸ ἐμὸν σὺν τόκῳ). The conclusion of a second class condition. The condition is implied: "If you had done that." Τόκῳ, "interest," is from τίκτω, to bring forth. The charge was not usury in the sense of extortion or oppression. The term *usury* originally meant simply "use." Compound interest at 6 percent doubles the principal every sixteen to seventeen years. If the interest is added to the principal, it doubles in eleven years. In the early Roman Empire, the cap on legal interest was 8 percent. Still, desperate borrowers might not find money for under 12 percent, 24 percent, or even 48 percent interest.[30] Mosaic Law did not allow Jews to charge interest against fellow Hebrews, but they could loan at interest to Gentiles (Deut. 23:19–20; Ps. 15:5).

25:30. "'Throw out the worthless slave'"[31] (τὸν ἀχρεῖον δοῦλον ἐκβάλετε[32]). "Useless" is from α privative and χρεῖος, "useful." The slave is "unprofitable." The range of meaning includes "doing harm." Doing nothing is doing harm.

25:32. "All the nations will be gathered before Him" (συναχθήσονται ἔμπροσθεν αὐτοῦ πάντα τὰ ἔθνη[33]), Jews as well as Gentiles. Some challenge this program for the general judgment as a composition by the evangelist to exalt Christ. But why should not Christ say this if he knew himself to be both Son of Man and Son of God? A "reduced" Christ has trouble with all the Gospels, not merely with the fourth Gospel, and no less with Q and Mark than with Matthew and Luke. This is a majestic picture with which to close the series of parables about readiness for the Second Coming. Here is the program when he does come. William Sanday wrote, "I am aware that doubt is thrown on this passage by some critics. But the doubt is most wanton. Where is the second brain that could have invented anything so original and so sublime as verses 35–40, 42–45?"[34]

"As the shepherd separates the sheep from the goats" (ὥσπερ ὁ ποιμὴν ἀφορίζει τὰ πρόβατα ἀπὸ τῶν ἐρίφων), a common figure in Palestine. The sheep are usually white and the goats black. The kids (ἔριφος) graze together. Goats can devastate a field of all herbage. The shepherd stands at the gate and taps the sheep to go to the right and the goats to the left.

25:34. "'Inherit the kingdom prepared for you from the foundation of the world'"[35] (κληρονομήσατε τὴν ἡτοιμασμένην ὑμῖν βασιλείαν ἀπὸ καταβολῆς κόσμου). This is the eternal purpose of the Father for his elect in all the nations. The Son of Man in verse 31 is the King, here seated on the throne in judgment.

25:36. "'Naked, and you clothed Me'"[36] (γυμνὸς καὶ περιεβάλετέ με), second person plural second aorist active indicative, "cast something around Me."

"'I was sick, and you visited Me'"[37] (ἠσθένησα καὶ ἐπεσκέψασθέ με), looked after, came to see. The English word visit is from Latin viso, video, the meaning being "go to see."

25:40. "'You did it to Me'"[38] (ἐμοὶ ἐποιήσατε). This is a dative of personal interest. Christ identifies himself with the needy and suffering. This conduct is proof of possession of love for Christ and likeness to him.

25:42. "'For I was hungry, and you gave Me nothing to eat'" (ἐπείνασα γὰρ καὶ οὐκ ἐδώκατέ μοι φαγεῖν). You did not give me anything to eat. The repetition of the negative οὐ in verses 42 and 43 is like the falling of clods on the coffin or the tomb. It is curious that Jesus says that both the sheep and the goats express surprise. Some sheep will think that they are goats and some goats will think that they are sheep.

25:46. "These will go away into eternal punishment" (ἀπελεύσονται οὗτοι εἰς κόλασιν αἰώνιον). The word κόλασιν comes from κολάζω, "to mutilate or prune." Hence those who cling to the hope of universal salvation use this phrase to mean an age-long pruning that ultimately leads to salvation of the goats. The pruning is believed disciplinary rather than penal. Aristotle makes such a distinction between μωρία (vengeance) and κόλασις. But the same adjective αἰώνιος is used with κόλασιν and ζώην. If by etymology we limit the scope of κόλασιν, we may likewise have only age-long ζώην. There is not the slightest indication in the words of Jesus that the punishment is not just as eternal as the life. If one does believe in conditional chastisement, it seems hard to imagine how a life of sin in hell might change one to accept a life of love and obedience. The word αἰώνιος (from αἰών, age; Latin aevum, aei) means without beginning, without end, or without either beginning or end. It comes as near to the idea of eternal as the Greek puts it in one word. The concept is difficult to express in language. Sometimes we have "ages of ages" ($\alpha i\tilde{\omega}\nu\epsilon\varsigma$ $\tau\tilde{\omega}\nu$ $\alpha i\dot{\omega}\nu\omega\nu$).

NOTES

1. Alfred Plummer, *An Exegetical Commentary on the Gospel According to Saint Matthew* (repr. ed., Grand Rapids: Eerdmans, 1956), 343.
2. Rutherford, *New Phrynichus.*
3. NIV has "did not take any oil with them."
4. NIV has "The wise, however, took oil in jars."
5. NIV has "they all became drowsy and fell asleep."
6. NIV has "At midnight the cry rang out."
7. TR and Maj.T have $\alpha\dot{\upsilon}\tau\tilde{\omega}\nu$ in place of $\dot{\epsilon}\alpha\upsilon\tau\tilde{\omega}\nu$.
8. Plummer, *Matthew*, 345.
9. NIV has "No, they replied, there may not be enough for both us and you."
10. Moulton, *Prolegomena*, 1.192, and A. T. Robertson, *A Grammar of the Greek New Testament in the Light of Historical Research* (Nashville: Broadman, 1934), 1161, 1174.
11. Plummer, *Matthew*, 345.
12. NIV has "But while they were on their way."
13. NIV has "Later the others also came."
14. NIV has "Sir! Sir! they said, Open the door for us."
15. NIV has "I don't know you."
16. NIV has "Therefore keep watch."
17. NIV has "Again, it will be like a man going on a journey."
18. NIV has "entrusted his property to them."
19. NIV has "at once."
20. The NIV and NASB has this in verse 16, however, the Greek text has it at the end of verse 15.
21. NIV has "put his money to work."
22. TR and Maj.T have the spelling of the verb as $\epsilon i\rho\gamma\dot{\alpha}\sigma\alpha\tau o$.
23. Marvin R. Vincent, *Word Studies in the New Testament*, Vol. 1, *The Synoptic Gospels* (repr. ed., Grand Rapids: Eerdmans, 1946), 133.
24. TR and Maj.T have a different word order, $\sigma\upsilon\nu\alpha i\rho\epsilon\iota$ $\mu\epsilon\tau'$ $\alpha\dot{\upsilon}\tau\tilde{\omega}\nu$ $\lambda\dot{o}\gamma o\nu$.
25. G. Adolf Deissmann, *Light from the Ancient East: The New Testament Illustrated by Recently Discovered Texts of the Graeco-Roman World*, trans. L. R. M. Strachan (rev. ed., Grand Rapids: Baker, 1965), 117.

26. NIV has "share your master's happiness."
27. NIV has "Then the man who had received the one talent."
28. NIV has "Well then, you should have put my money on deposit with the bankers."
29. TR and Maj.T have a different word order and reading, ἔδει οὖν σε βαλεῖν τὸ ἀργύριόν μου τοῖς τραπεζίταις.
30. Vincent, *Word Studies*, 135.
31. NIV has "throw that worthless servant outside."
32. TR has the present tense verb, ἐκβάλλετε.
33. TR and Maj.T have the third person singular verb, συναχθήσεται.
34. Sanday, *Life of Christ in Recent Research*, 182.
35. NIV has "take your inheritance, the kingdom prepared for you since the creation of the world."
36. NIV has "I needed clothes and you clothed me."
37. NIV has "I was sick and you looked after me."
38. NIV has "you did for me."

Matthew: Chapter 26

26:2. *"After two days the Passover is coming"*[1] (μετὰ δύο ἡμέρας τὸ πάσχα γίνεται), futuristic use of the present middle/passive indicative. This was probably our Tuesday evening (beginning of Jewish Wednesday). Passover began on our Thursday evening (beginning of Jewish Friday). "After two days" is just the popular mode of speech. Passover came technically on the second day from this time.

"The Son of Man is to be handed over" (ὁ υἱὸς τοῦ ἀνθρώπου παραδίδοται), another instance of the futuristic present middle/passive indicative. The same form occurs in verse 24. Thus Jesus sets a definite date for the coming crucifixion that he has predicted for six months.

26:3. *Then the chief priests and the elders of the people were gathered together*[2] (Τότε συνήχθησαν οἱ ἀρχιερεῖς[3] καὶ οἱ πρεσβύτεροι τοῦ λαοῦ). It is a meeting of the Sanhedrin as these two groups indicate (cf. 21:23).

In the court of the high priest[4] (εἰς τὴν αὐλὴν τοῦ ἀρχιερέως), the *atrium* or court around which the palace buildings were built. An informal meeting gathered in this open court. Caiaphas was high priest from A.D. 18 to 36. His father-in-law Annas had been high priest from 6 to 15. Many still referred to him by the title.

26:4. *They plotted together* (συνεβουλεύσαντο), third person plural aorist middle indicative, indicating their puzzled state of mind. They had had no trouble in finding Jesus (John 11:57). Their problem was how to "seize Jesus by stealth and kill Him"[5] (ἵνα τὸν Ἰησοῦν δόλῳ κρατήσωσιν[6] καὶ ἀποκτείνωσιν). The triumphal entry and the Tuesday debate in the temple had revealed the extent of Jesus' following, especially among the people from Galilee.

26:5. *"A riot might occur among the people"*[7] (ἵνα μὴ θόρυβος γένηται ἐν τῷ λαῷ). They feared an uprising on behalf of Jesus. Some argued that the matter must be postponed until after the feast was over and the crowds had scattered. Then they could catch him "by craft" (δόλῳ), as they would trap a wild beast.

26:6. *At the home of Simon the leper*[8] (ἐν οἰκίᾳ Σίμωνος τοῦ λεπροῦ).

213

Evidently a man who had been healed of his leprosy by Jesus gave the feast in honor of Jesus. All sorts of fantastic theories have arisen about it. Some even identify this Simon with the one in Luke 7:36–50, but *Simon* was a very common name, and the details are very different. Some hold that it was Martha's house, since she served (John 12:2) and that Simon was either the father or husband of Martha. However, Martha loved to serve, so that proves nothing. Some identify Mary of Bethany with the sinful woman in Luke 7 and even with Mary Magdalene. Neither theory has any ground.[9] John 12:1 seems to place the feast six days before Passover, while Mark 14:1–3 and Matthew 26:6 seem to place it on the Tuesday evening (Jewish Wednesday), just two days before the Passover meal. It is possible that John anticipates the date and notes the feast at Bethany at this time because he does not refer to Bethany again. If not, the order of Mark must be followed. According to the order of Mark and Matthew, this feast took place at the very time that the Sanhedrin was plotting to kill Jesus (Mark 14:1–3).

26:7. *A woman came to Him with an alabaster vial of very costly perfume*[10] (προσῆλθεν αὐτῷ γυνὴ ἔχουσα ἀλάβαστρον μύρου[11] βαρυτίμου). The flask was of alabaster, a carbonate of lime or sulphate of lime, white or yellow stone, named alabaster from the town in Egypt where it was chiefly found. It was used for expensive vials used to hold precious ointments, as is shown in works by ancient writers, plus inscriptions and papyri. Alabaster containers generally had a cylindrical form at the top, like a closed rosebud according to Pliny. Matthew does not identify the ointment (μύρου) beyond saying that it was "exceeding precious [Βαρυτίμου], of weighty value, selling at a great price." The term is used here only in the New Testament. "An alabaster of nard (μύρου) was a present for a king."[12] It was one of five presents sent by Cambyses to the King of Ethiopia.[13]

She poured it on His head (κατέχεεν ἐπὶ τῆς κεφαλῆς[14] αὐτοῦ). So says Mark 14:3, while John 12:3 says that she "anointed the feet of Jesus." She easily could have done both. The verb κατέχεεν literally means "to pour down." This unusual form is the third person singular aorist active indicative.

26:8. *"Why this waste?"* (Εἰς τί ἡ ἀπώλεια αὕτη;). They considered it total loss (ἀπώλεια), nothing but sentimental aroma. The criticism must have been a cruel shock to Mary of Bethany after she carried out such a lavish act of worship. Matthew does not tell, as John 12:4 does, that Judas made the comment, which the rest endorsed. Mark 14:5 gives an estimated price of the gift of "three hundred denarii," while Matthew 26:9 only says "for much" (πολλοῦ).

26:10. *"Why do you bother the woman?"*[15] (Τί κόπους παρέχετε τῆ γυναικί;). The phrase is not common in Greek writers, though two examples occur in the papyri for giving trouble.[16] Κόπος is from κόπτω, "to beat, smite, cut." It refers to a beating, trouble, or toil. Jesus champions Mary's act with this striking phrase. It is hard for some people to allow others liberty to express their own personalities in praise. It is easy to raise small objections to what we do not like and do not understand. Jesus said that she had done a "good deed to Me"[17] (ἔργον γὰρ καλὸν ἠργάσατο[18] εἰς ἐμέ), a beautiful deed upon Jesus himself.

26:12–13. *"She did it to prepare Me for burial"* (πρὸς τὸ ἐνταφιάσαι με ἐποίησεν). Mary alone understood what Jesus had said repeatedly about his approaching death. The disciples were so wrapped up in their own notions of a political kingdom that they failed utterly to sympathize with Jesus as he faced the cross. But Mary, with her woman's fine intuition, did begin to understand. Now she expressed her high emotions and loyalty. In John 19:40, ἐνταφιάσαι describes what Joseph of Arimathea and Nicodemus did for the body of Jesus before burial. Πρὸς τό, the infinitive of purpose, shows the intent of the act. Mary was vindicated by Jesus, and her noble deed has become "a memory of her" (εἰς μνημόσυνον αὐτῆς) as well as of Jesus.

26:15. *"What are you willing to give me. . . ?"*[19] (Τί θέλετέ μοι δοῦναι. . . ;). There was haggling in the transaction.[20] Mary and Judas are set side by side as extreme opposites, "she freely spending in love, he willing to sell his Master for money."[21] Her act of love and the rebuke of Jesus, added to other motivations, provoked Judas to his despicable deed.

"To betray Him to you?" (κἀγὼ ὑμῖν παραδώσω αὐτόν;). The use of καί with a coordinate clause is a colloquialism common in the Κοινή as in the Hebrew use of *wav*. "A colloquialism or a Hebraism, the traitor mean in style as in spirit."[22] The use of ἐγώ as part of κἀγω seems to mean, "I, though one of his disciples, will hand him over to you if you give me enough."

And they weighed out thirty pieces of silver to him[23] (οἱ δὲ ἔστησαν αὐτῷ τριάκοντα ἀργύρια). They placed the money in the balances or scales. "Coined money was in use, but the shekels may have been weighed out in antique fashion by men careful to do an iniquitous thing in the most orthodox way."[24] It is not known whether the Sanhedrin had offered a reward for the arrest of Jesus. The thirty pieces of silver is a reference to Zechariah 11:12. If a man's ox gored a servant, he had to pay this amount (Exod. 21:32). Some manuscripts have στατῆρας (staters). These thirty silver shekels were equal to 120 denarii, a worker's wages for 120 days work. A slave could be purchased for that price. The price no doubt deliberately reflected contempt for Jesus held by both the Sanhedrin and Judas.

26:16. *He began looking for a good opportunity to betray Jesus*[25] (ἐζήτει εὐκαιρίαν ἵνα αὐτὸν παραδῷ). Note the imperfect tense. Judas went at his business and stuck to it. "Judas knew how to take him by night away from the crowd."[26]

26:17. *"Where do You want us to prepare for You to eat the Passover?"*[27] (Ποῦ θέλεις ἑτοιμάσωμέν σοι φαγεῖν τὸ πάσχα;). Two feasts were combined, the Passover Feast and the Feast of Unleavened Bread. Either name was employed. The Feast of Unleavened Bread often was used to take in the entire eight-day festival.[28] Here the Passover meal is meant, although in John 18:28 it seems that the feast referred to as the Passover meal (the Last Supper) had already been observed. There is a famous controversy on the apparent disagreement between the Synoptic Gospels and the fourth Gospel on the date of this last Passover meal. My view is that the five passages in John (13:1–2, 27; 18:28; 19:14, 31) agree with the Synoptic Gospels (Matt. 26:17, 20 = Mark 14:12, 27 = Luke 22:7, 14). Rightly interpreted they indicate that Jesus ate the Passover meal at the regular time of about 6 P.M. at the beginning of 15 Nisan. The Passover lamb was slain on the afternoon of 14 Nisan and the meal eaten at sunset at the beginning of 15 Nisan. According to this view, Jesus ate the Passover meal at the regular time and died on the cross the afternoon of 15 Nisan.[29] The question of the disciples here assumes that they are to observe the regular Passover meal. Note the deliberative subjunctive ἑτοιμάσωμεν after θέλεις with ἵνα.[30]

26:18. *"Go into the city to a certain man"* (Ὑπάγετε εἰς τὴν πόλιν πρὸς τὸν δεῖνα). This is the only instance in the New Testament of this old Attic idiom for a person one cannot or does not wish to name.[31] The papyri show it for "Mr. X,"[32] and the modern Greek keeps it. Jesus may have indicated the man's name. Mark (14:13) and Luke (22:10) describe him as a man bearing a pitcher of water. Some think it may have been the home of Mary, the mother of John Mark.

"I am to keep the Passover at your house with My disciples"[33] (πρὸς σὲ ποιῶ τὸ πάσχα μετὰ τῶν μαθητῶν μου), a futuristic present indicative. The use of πρὸς σέ for "at your house" is fine Greek of the classic period. Evidently there was no surprise in this home at the command of Jesus. It was a gracious privilege to serve him thus.

26:20. *Reclining [at the table] with the twelve [disciples]* (ἀνέκειτο μετὰ τῶν δώδεκα). He was reclining, lying back on the left side on the couch with the right hand free. According to Passover custom, Jesus and the Twelve all reclined. The entire paschal lamb had to be consumed (Exod. 12:4, 43).

26:21. *"One of you will betray Me"* (εἷς ἐξ ὑμῶν παραδώσει με). This was a bolt from the blue for all except Judas, and he must have been startled to discover that Jesus knew of his treacherous bargain.

26:22. *"Surely not I, Lord?"* (Μήτι ἐγώ εἰμι, κύριε;). The negative expects the answer no. Judas bluffed by asking the same question as the others (v. 25).

26:23. *"He who dipped his hand with Me in the bowl is the one who will betray Me"*[34] (Ὁ ἐμβάψας μετ᾽ ἐμοῦ τὴν χεῖρα ἐν τῷ τρυβλίῳ[35] οὗτός με παραδώσει). They all dipped their hands, having no knives, forks, or spoons. The nominative singular masculine aorist active participle with the article simply means that the betrayer is the one who dips his hand in the dish or platter with the broth of nuts and raisins and figs into which the bread was dipped before eating. The rest still did not identify Judas still as the one on the basis of what Jesus had said. This language means that one of those who had eaten bread with him had violated the rights of hospitality by betraying him. Arab culture has always been punctilious on this point. Eating one's bread ties the hands of the host that might wish to do evil. Eating together compels friendship.

26:24. *"It would have been good for that man if he had not been born"*[36] (καλὸν ἦν αὐτῷ εἰ οὐκ ἐγεννήθη ὁ ἄνθρωπος ἐκεῖνος). Conclusion of a second class condition that is contrary to fact. Neither clause of the condition is untrue, though ἄν is not expressed. It is not needed with verbs of obligation and necessity. Some would excuse the crime of Judas, but Jesus pronounces a terrible doom. Judas heard it and apparently left the gathering at this point (John 13:31). He went on with his hellish bargain with the Sanhedrin.

26:25. *"You have said"* (Σὺ εἶπας). Judas now takes his turn to ask whether he is the betrayer. The answer of Jesus means that yes, he is.

26:26. *Jesus took some bread, and after a blessing, He broke it*[37] (λαβὼν ὁ Ἰησοῦς ἄρτον[38] καὶ εὐλογήσας ἔκλασεν[39]). The special "grace" came in the middle of the Passover meal, "as they were eating." For the institution of the supper, Jesus broke one of the Passover wafers or cakes that each might have a piece, not as a symbol of the breaking of His body as the TR has it in 1 Corinthians 11:24. The correct text there has only τὸ ὑπὲρ ὑμῶν without κλώμενον. As a matter of fact the body of Jesus was not "broken" (John 19:33), as John expressly states.

"This is My body" (τοῦτό ἐστιν τὸ σῶμά μου). The bread as a symbol

represents the body of Jesus offered for us, "a beautifully simple, pathetic, and poetic symbol of his death. . . . But some have made it 'run into fetish worship.'[40] Jesus, of course, does not mean that the bread actually becomes his body and is to be worshiped. The purpose of the memorial is to remind us of his death for our sins.

26:28. *"For this is My blood of the covenant"*[41] (τοῦτο γάρ ἐστιν τὸ αἷμά μου τῆς διαθήκης[42]). The adjective καινῆς in the TR is not genuine. The covenant is an agreement or contract between two (διά, δύο, θήκε, from τίθημι). It is used for a will (Latin, *testamentum*), an agreement that becomes operative at death (Heb. 9:15–17). Either *covenant* or *will* makes sense here. Covenant is the idea behind Hebrews 7:22; 8:8. In Hebrew culture, to make a covenant involved cutting up a sacrifice, by which the agreement was ratified (Gen. 15:9–18). Lightfoot argues that διαθήκη means "covenant" everywhere in the New Testament except in Hebrews 9:15–17. Jesus here uses the solemn words of Exodus 24:8, "the blood of the covenant" at Sinai. "My blood of the covenant" is in contrast with that. This is the New Covenant of Jeremiah 38 and Hebrews 8.

"Which is poured out for many" (τὸ περὶ πολλῶν ἐκχυννόμενον), a prophetic present passive participle. The act is symbolized by the ordinance, the purpose of Christ expressed in 20:28. There ἀντί is used and here περί.

"For forgiveness of sins"[43] (εἰς ἄφεσιν ἁμαρτιῶν). This clause is in Matthew alone but it is not to be restricted for that reason. It is the truth. This passage answers all the modern sentimentalism that finds in the teaching of Jesus only pious ethics or eschatological dreams. He had the definite conception of his death on the cross as the basis for forgiveness of sin. The purpose of the shedding of his blood of the New Covenant was precisely to remove (forgive) sins.

26:29. *"When I drink it new with you in My Father's kingdom"*[44] (ὅταν αὐτὸ πίνω μεθ' ὑμῶν καινὸν ἐν τῇ βασιλείᾳ τοῦ πατρός μου). This language rather implies that Jesus himself partook of the bread and the wine, though it is not distinctly stated. In the messianic banquet it is not necessary to suppose that Jesus means the language literally, "the fruit of the vine." Deissmann[45] gives an instance of γένημα used of the vine in a papyrus 230 B.C. The language here employed does not make it obligatory to employ wine rather than pure grape juice if one wishes the other.

26:30. *After singing a hymn*[46] (ὑμνήσαντες), the *Hallel*, part of Psalms 115–118. Apparently they did not go out at once to the Garden of Gethsemane. Jesus tarried with them in the Upper Room for the wonderful discourse and prayer in John 14–17. They may have gone out to the street after John 14:31. It was no longer considered obligatory to remain in the house after the Passover meal until morning as had been the case at the first Passover (Exod. 12:22). Jesus went out to Gethsemane, the garden of the agony, outside of Jerusalem, toward the Mount of Olives.

26:33. *"Even though all may fall away because of You, I will never fall away"*[47] (Εἰ[48] πάντες σκανδαλισθήσονται ἐν σοί, ἐγὼ οὐδέποτε σκανδαλισθήσομαι), "made to stumble," not "offended," a volitive future passive indicative. Peter ignored the prophecy of the resurrection of Jesus and the promised meeting in Galilee (v. 32). The quotation from Zechariah 13:7 made no impression on him. He was intent on showing that he was superior to the rest. Judas had turned traitor, and all were weak, especially Peter though he did not realize it.

26:34. *"Before a rooster crows"* (πρὶν ἀλέκτορα φωνῆσαι). No article in the Greek, "before a cock crows." Jesus has to make it plainer by pointing out "this night" as the time. Mark (14:30) says that Peter will deny Jesus thrice before the cock crows twice. When one cock crows in the morning, others generally follow. The period of the three denials later that night lasted over an hour. Some scholars hold that chickens were not allowed in Jerusalem by the Jews, but the Romans would have them.

26:35. *"Even if I have to die with You"* (Κἂν δέη με σὺν σοὶ ἀποθανεῖν), a third class condition. A noble speech and well meant, his profession of loyalty is made stronger by "I will never fall away" or "renounce/disown you" (οὐ μή σε ἀπαρνήσομαι). Likely embarrassed by Peter's boast, the other disciples joined in the profession of fidelity.

26:36. *Gethsemane* (Γεθσημανί[49]). The word means "oil-press or olive vat" in the Hebrew. The place (χωρίον) was an enclosed plot or estate, "garden," or orchard (κῆπος). It is called *villa* in the Vulgate for John 18:1. It was beyond the torrent Kedron at the foot of the Mount of Olives, about three-fourths of a mile from the eastern walls of Jerusalem.[50]

"Sit here while I go over there and pray" (Καθίσατε αὐτοῦ ἕως [οὗ] ἀπελθὼν ἐκεῖ προσεύξωμαι[51]). Jesus clearly pointed to the place where he would pray. Literally "there."

26:37. *He took with Him Peter and the two sons of Zebedee*[52] (παραλαβὼν τὸν Πέτρον καὶ τοὺς δύο υἱοὺς Ζεβεδαίου). Taking along, by his side (παρα-), as a mark of special favor and privilege, instead of leaving this inner circle of three (Peter, James, and John) with the other eight. The eight would serve as a sort of outer guard to watch by the gate of the garden for the coming of Judas while the three would be able to share the agony of soul already upon Jesus. They could at least give him some human sympathy, which he craved as he sought help from the Father in prayer. These three had been with Jesus on the Mount of Transfiguration and now they are with him in this supreme crisis. The grief of Christ was now severe.

Began to be grieved and distressed[53] ($\mathring{\eta}\rho\xi\alpha\tauo$ $\lambda\upsilon\pi\epsilon\mathring{\iota}\sigma\theta\alpha\iota$ $\kappa\alpha\mathaccent"705F\iota$ $\mathaccent"705F\alpha\delta\eta\mu o\nu\epsilon\mathaccent"705F\iota\nu$). The word for *distressed* is of doubtful etymology. There is an adjective $\mathaccent"705F\alpha\delta\mathaccent"0308\eta\mu os$, equal to $\mathaccent"705F\alpha\pi\acute{o}\delta\eta\mu os$, meaning "not at home," "away from home," like the German *unheimisch, unheimlich*. But whatever the etymology, the notion of intense discomfort is plain. The word $\mathaccent"705F\alpha\delta\eta\mu o\nu\epsilon\mathaccent"705F\iota\nu$ occurs in the papyri[54] of the first century, where it means "excessively concerned." In Philippians 2:26, Paul uses it of Epaphroditus. Moffatt renders it here "agitated." The word occurs sometimes with $\mathaccent"705F\alpha\pi o\rho\acute{\epsilon}\omega$, "to be at a loss as to which way to go."[55] Here Matthew has also "to be sorrowful" ($\lambda\upsilon\pi\epsilon\mathaccent"705F\iota\sigma\theta\alpha\iota$), but Mark (14:33) has the startling phrase "very distressed and troubled" ($\mathaccent"705F\epsilon\kappa\theta\alpha\mu\beta\epsilon\mathaccent"705F\iota\sigma\theta\alpha\iota$ $\kappa\alpha\mathaccent"705F\iota$ $\mathaccent"705F\alpha\delta\eta\mu o\nu\epsilon\mathaccent"705F\iota\nu$), "a feeling of terrified surprise."

26:38. *"Keep watch with Me"* ($\gamma\rho\eta\gamma o\rho\epsilon\mathaccent"705F\iota\tau\epsilon$ $\mu\epsilon\tau$' $\mathaccent"705F\epsilon\mu o\mathaccent"705F\upsilon$). This late present from the perfect $\mathaccent"705F\epsilon\gamma\rho\acute{\eta}\gamma o\rho\alpha$ means "to keep awake and not go to sleep." The hour was late and the strain had been severe, but Jesus pleaded for a bit of human sympathy as he wrestled with his Father. It did not seem too much to ask. He had put his sorrow in strong language, "to the point of death" ($\mathaccent"705F\epsilon\omega s$ $\theta\alpha\nu\acute{\alpha}\tauou$). That ought to have alarmed them.

26:39. *And He went a little beyond them*[56] ($\pi\rho o\epsilon\lambda\theta\mathaccent"705F\omega\nu$[57] $\mu\iota\kappa\rho\acute{o}\nu$). As if he could not fight the battle in their immediate presence. He was on his face, not on his knees.[58]

"Let this cup pass from Me"[59] ($\pi\alpha\rho\epsilon\lambda\theta\acute{\alpha}\tau\omega$[60] $\mathaccent"705F\alpha\pi$' $\mathaccent"705F\epsilon\mu o\mathaccent"705F\upsilon$ $\tau\mathaccent"705F o$ $\pi o\tau\acute{\eta}\rho\iota o\nu$ $\tauo\mathaccent"705F\upsilon\tauo$). The figure can mean only the approaching death. Jesus had used it of his coming death when James and John came to him with their ambitious request, "the cup which I am about to drink" (Matt. 20:22). But now the Master is about to taste the bitter dregs in the cup of death for the sin of the world. He was not afraid that he would die before the cross, though he instinctively shrank from the cup. He instantly surrendered his will to the Father's will and drank it to the full. Evidently Satan tempted Christ now to draw back from the cross. Here Jesus won the power to go on to Calvary.

26:40. *"So, you men could not keep watch with Me for one hour?"*[61] ($O\mathaccent"705F\upsilon\tau\omega s$ $o\mathaccent"705F\upsilon\kappa$ $\mathaccent"705F\iota\sigma\chi\acute{\upsilon}\sigma\alpha\tau\epsilon$ $\mu\acute{\iota}\alpha\nu$ $\mathaccent"705F\omega\rho\alpha\nu$ $\gamma\rho\eta\gamma o\rho\mathaccent"705F\eta\sigma\alpha\iota$ $\mu\epsilon\tau$' $\mathaccent"705F\epsilon\mu o\mathaccent"705F\upsilon$;). The Greek adverb ($o\mathaccent"705F\upsilon\tau\omega s$) is not interrogative or exclamatory. It means only "so or thus." There is a tone of sad disappointment at the discovery that they were asleep after the earnest plea that they keep awake (v. 38). "Did you not thus have strength enough to keep awake one hour?"

26:41. *"Keep watching and praying"*[62] (γρηγορεῖτε καὶ προσεύχεσθε). Jesus repeats the command of verse 38 with the addition of prayer and with the warning against the peril of temptation. He himself was feeling the worst of all temptations of his earthly life just then. He did not wish then to enter such "temptation," πειρασμόν, not merely a trial, as is the word's primary meaning. Thus we are to understand the prayer in Matthew 6:13 about leading (being led) into temptation. Their failure was due to weakness of the flesh, as is often the case. *Spirit* (πνεῦμα) here is the moral life (intellect, will, emotions) as opposed to the flesh (cf. Isa. 31:3; Rom. 7:25).

26:42. *"If this cannot pass away unless I drink it"*[63] (εἰ οὐ δύναται τοῦτο παρελθεῖν ἐὰν μὴ αὐτὸ πίω[64]). First class negative condition, followed by a third class negative condition with likelihood of determination. This delicate distinction accurately presents the real attitude of Jesus towards this subtle temptation.

26:43. *For their eyes were heavy* (ἦσαν γὰρ αὐτῶν οἱ ὀφθαλμοὶ βεβαρημένοι). Past perfect passive indicative periphrastic participial construction. Their eyes had been weighted down with sleep just as they had been on the Mount of Transfiguration (Luke 9:32).

26:45. *"Are you still sleeping and resting?"* (Καθεύδετε [τὸ] λοιπὸν καὶ ἀναπαύεσθε;). There is "mournful irony"[65] or reproachful concession to the words: "You may sleep and rest indefinitely so far as I am concerned; I need no longer your watchful interest."[66] Or the query may contain more sadness, as in most modern translations: "Are you still sleeping and taking your rest?" So Moffatt. This use of λοιπόν for "now or henceforth" is common in the papyri.

"The hour is at hand"[67] (ἤγγικεν ἡ ὥρα). Time for action has now come. They have missed their chance for sympathy with Jesus. He has now won the victory without their aid. "The Master's time of weakness is past; He is prepared to face the worst."[68]

"The Son of Man is being betrayed"[69] (ὁ υἱὸς τοῦ ἀνθρώπου παραδίδοται). Futuristic or inchoative (ingressive) present, the first act in the betrayal is at hand. Jesus had foreseen his "hour" for long and now he faces it bravely.

26:46. *"Let us be going"*[70] (ἄγωμεν). The traitor now comes. The eight at the gate seemed to have given no notice. Each Synoptic Gospel at this point describes Judas as εἷς τῶν δώδεκα, "one of the twelve" (cf. Matt. 26:47; Mark 14:43; Luke 22:47). This aspect of the horror of the moment is emphasized: One of the chosen twelve has done this.

"The one who betrays Me is at hand"[71] (ἤγγικεν ὁ παραδιδούς με). The same verb and tense used of the hour above, present perfect active of ἐγγίζω, *to draw near,* the very form used by John the Baptist of the coming of the kingdom of heaven (Matt. 3:2). Whether Jesus heard the approach of the betrayer with the crowd around him or saw the lights or just felt the proximity of the traitor (J. Weiss), we do not know. It matters little. The scene is pictured as it happened with lifelike power.

26:47. *While He was still speaking* (ἔτι αὐτοῦ λαλοῦντος), a genitive absolute construction. It was an electric moment as Jesus faced Judas with his horde of helpers as if he turned to meet an army.

A large crowd with swords and clubs[72] (ὄχλος πολὺς μετὰ μαχαιρῶν καὶ ξύλων). The chief priests and Pharisees had furnished Judas with a band of soldiers from the garrison in Antonia (John 18:3) and the temple police (Luke 22:52), with swords (knives) and staves (clubs). There also was a hired rabble with lanterns (John 18:3), in spite of the full moon. Judas was taking no chances of failure, for he well knew the strange power of Jesus.

26:48. *Now he who was betraying Him gave them a sign*[73] (ὁ δὲ παραδιδοὺς αὐτὸν ἔδωκεν αὐτοῖς σημεῖον), probably just before he reached the place, though Mark (14:44) has "had given" (δεδώκει), which certainly means before arrival at Gethsemane. At any rate Judas had given the leaders to understand that he would kiss (φιλήσω) Jesus in order to identify him for certain. The kiss was a common mode of greeting and Judas chose that sign and actually "kissed Him fervently" (κατεφίλησεν, v. 49), though the compound verb sometimes in the papyri has lost its intensive force. Bruce thinks that Judas was prompted by the inconsistent motives of smouldering love and cowardice.[74] At any rate this revolting ostentatious kiss is "the most terrible instance of the ἑκούσια φιλήματα ἐχθροῦ (LXX Prov. 27:6), the profuse kisses of an enemy."[75] This compound verb occurs in Luke 7:38 of the sinful woman, in Luke 15:20 of the Father's embrace of the prodigal son, and in Acts 20:37 of the Ephesian elders' affection for Paul.

26:50. *"Do what you have come for"*[76] (ἐφ᾽ ὃ πάρει[77]). Moffatt and Goodspeed take it: "Do your errand." There has been a deal of trouble over this phrase. Deissmann shows that ἐφ᾽ ὃ in late Greek has the interrogative sense of ἐπὶ τί. Therefore, it is a question.[78] The use of ἐφ᾽ ὃ for "why here" occurs on a first-century Syrian tablet. It "was current coin in the language of the people."[79] Most early translations (e.g., Old Latin and Old Syriac) frame it as a question. The Vulgate has *ad quid venisti.* Here the King James Version's "Friend, wherefore art thou come?" is more to the sense of the original than are most contemporary versions. The question exposes the pretence and shows that Jesus does not believe the paraded affection of Judas.[80]

26:51. *One of those who were with Jesus*[81] ($\epsilon\hat{\iota}_S$ τῶν μετὰ Ἰησοῦ). Like the other Synoptics, Matthew conceals the name of Peter, probably because striking someone on official judicial business was a serious matter, and Peter was still alive before 68. Writing at the end of the century, John is free to identify Peter (John 18:10). The sword or knife was one of the two that the disciples had (Luke 22:38). Bruce suggests that it was a large knife that had been used in connection with the paschal feast. Peter may have aimed to cut off the man's head, not his ear, for ὠτίον is diminutive in form, but not in sense. This servant may have led the band. His name, Malchus, is also given by John (18:10) because Peter was then dead and in no danger.

26:52. *"Put your sword back into its place"* (Ἀπόστρεψον τὴν μάχαιράν σου εἰς τὸν τόπον αὐτῆ[82]). "Turn back your sword into its place." It was a stern rebuke for Peter, who showed that he had misunderstood the teaching of Jesus in 5:39 and Luke 22:38 (cf. John 18:36). The reason given by Jesus has had innumerable illustrations in human history. The sword calls for the sword. Offensive war is given flat condemnation. The will to peace is the first step toward peace, the outlawing of war.

26:53. *"At once"* (ἄρτι), just now, at this very moment.

"Twelve legions of angels?" (δώδεκα λεγιῶνας ἀγγέλων;). Λεγιῶνας is the Greek version of a Latin word. No large numbers of Roman soldiers were in Palestine until the Jewish War began in 66, but sizable contingents were in Caesarea and housed in the tower of Antonia in Jerusalem. A full Roman legion had 6,100 foot soldiers and 726 horse soldiers in the time of Augustus. Jesus sees more than twelve legions at his command (enough for one for each disciple) and shows his undaunted courage in this crisis. The statement brings to mind the story of Elisha at Dothan (2 Kings 6:17).

26:54. *"It must happen this way"* (δεῖ γενέσθαι). Jesus sees clearly his destiny now that he has won the victory in Gethsemane.

26:55. *"As you would against a robber"*[83] (Ὡς ἐπὶ λῃστήν). As a robber, not as a thief, but a robber hiding from justice. He will be crucified between two robbers and on the very cross planned for their leader, Barabbas. They have come with no warrant for any crime, but with an armed force to seize Jesus as if He were a highway robber. Jesus reminds them that he has been sitting (imperfect, ἐκαθεζόμην) in the temple teaching. But He sees God's purpose at work for the prophets had foretold his "cup." The desertion of

Jesus by the disciples followed this rebuke of the effort of Peter. Jesus had surrendered, so the disciples fled.

26:58. *Sat down with the officers to see the outcome*[84] (ἐκάθητο μετὰ τῶν ὑπηρετῶν ἰδεῖν τὸ τέλος). Peter rallied from the panic and followed afar off (μακρόθεν), "more courageous than the rest and yet not courageous enough."[85] John the beloved disciple went on into the room where Jesus was. The rest remained outside, but Peter "sat with the officers" to see and hear, hoping to escape notice.

26:59. *The whole Council kept trying to obtain false testimony against Jesus*[86] (τὸ σύνέδριον ὅλον ἐζήτουν ψευδομαρτυρίαν κατὰ τοῦ Ἰησοῦ). Imperfect tense, kept on seeking. Judges have no right to be prosecutors, nor certainly to seek false witness and even offer bribes to get it.

26:60. *They did not find any* (οὐχ εὗρον). They found false witnesses in plenty, but no false witness that would stand any sort of test of truth.

26:61. *"'I am able to destroy the temple of God'"* (Δύναμαι καταλῦσαι τὸν ναὸν τοῦ θεοῦ). What he had said (John 2:19) referred to the temple of his body, which they would destroy and he would raise again in three days. They perverted what Jesus had said. Even so, the two witnesses disagreed in their misrepresentation (Mark 14:59).

26:63. *But Jesus kept silent*[87] (ὁ δὲ Ἰησοῦς ἐσιώπα). Third person singular imperfect active indicative. Jesus refused to answer the bluster of Caiaphas.

"I adjure You by the living God"[88] (Ἐξορκίζω σε κατὰ τοῦ θεοῦ τοῦ ζῶντος[89]). Caiaphas put Jesus on oath in order to make him incriminate himself. This was unlawful procedure in Jewish jurisprudence, but Caiaphas was desperate, for he had failed to secure any accusation that would stand. Jesus did not refuse to answer under solemn oath, clearly showing that he had not forbade the taking of oaths in courts of justice (Matt. 5:34). Caiaphas charges that Jesus claims to be the Messiah, the Son of God. To refuse to answer would be tantamount to a denial, so Jesus answers, knowing what will be made of his declaration.

26:64. *"You have said it yourself"*[90] (Σὺ εἶπας). This is a Greek affirmative reply. Mark (14:62) has it plainly, "I am" (εἰμι). But this is not all that Jesus said to Caiaphas. He states that the day will come when Jesus will be the Judge and Caiaphas the culprit. Jesus uses the prophetic language of Psalm 109:1 and Daniel 7:13. This was all that Caiaphas wanted to make his case.

26:65. *"He has blasphemed!"*[91] (Ἐβλασφήμησεν). There was no need of witnesses, for Jesus had incriminated himself by claiming under oath to be the Messiah, the Son of God. It would not be blasphemy for the real Messiah to make such a claim, but it was unthinkable to these men that Jesus might be the Messiah of Jewish hope. At the beginning of Christ's ministry, he occasionally used the word *Messiah* of himself, but he had soon ceased, for it was plain that people would take him to be a political revolutionist who would throw off the Roman yoke. If he declined that role, the Pharisees would have none of him for that was the kind of a Messiah that they desired. But the hour had come. At the Triumphal Entry Jesus let the Galilean crowds hail him as Messiah, knowing what the effect would be. Now he has made his claim and defied the high priest.

26:66. *"He deserves death!"*[92] ("Ενοχος θανάτου ἐστίν). "He is held in the bonds of death" (ἐν, ἔχω) as actually guilty, with the genitive, θανάτου. The dative expresses liability, as τῇ κρίσει and εἰς and the accusative in 5:21–22. Death was the penalty of blasphemy (Lev. 24:15). However, the vote of condemnation could not be taken at night under Jewish law. Their action also was improper since they no longer had authority to execute a criminal. The Romans had taken that power for them. But they enjoyed taking this vote as their answer to Jesus' unanswerable speeches in the temple on the dreadful Tuesday of that very week. The vote was unanimous among those who were present. Joseph of Arimathea and Nicodemus and perhaps others did not agree, but they probably did not know this proceeding was even taking place. They were under suspicion of being secret disciples of the Galilean.

26:68. *"Prophesy to us, You Christ"*[93] (Προφήτευσον ἡμῖν, Χριστέ), with a definite sneer at his claims under oath in 26:63. With the uncontrolled glee and abandon of a gang of hoodlums, these doctors of divinity insulted Jesus. They actually spat in his face, buffeted him on the neck (ἐκολάφισαν, from κόλαφος, "fist"), and struck him in the face with the palms of their hands (ἐράπισαν, from ῥάπις, *"rod"*). After the legal injustice they had already perpetrated, they gave vent to their spite and hatred by personal indignities.

26:69. *"You too were with Jesus"*[94] (Καὶ σὺ ἦσθα μετὰ Ἰησοῦ). Peter had gone *within* (ἔσω) the palace (v. 58), but sat *without* (ἔξω) the hall where the trial was going on. He was in the open central court with the servants or officers (ὑπηρετῶν, literally "under rowers," cf. v. 58) of the Sanhedrin. He could possibly see through the open door above what was going on inside. It is not plain at what stage during the Jewish trial the denials of Peter took place nor the precise order in which they came. The Gospel accounts vary. One slave girl (παιδίσκη) stepped up to Peter as he was sitting in the court and pointedly said: "You too were with Jesus the Galilean." Peter was warming himself by the fire and the light shone in his face. She probably had noticed Peter come in with John, who had gone on up into the hall of trial. Or she may have seen Peter with Jesus previously.

26:70. *"I do not know what you are talking about"* (Οὐκ οἶδα τί λέγεις). This affectation of extreme ignorance deceived no one.[95] It was an ineffective subterfuge. Dalman suggests that Peter used the Galilean Aramaean word for "know" instead of the Judean Aramaean word. That alone would have betrayed him as a Galilean.[96]

26:71. *When he had gone out to the gateway*[97] (ἐξελθόντα δὲ εἰς τὸν πυλῶνα[98]). Peter moved away to a more shadowy place, but he was not safe out here, for another maid recognized him and spoke of him as "this fellow" (οὗτος), with a gesture so those around would know whom she meant.

26:72. *And again he denied it with an oath*[99] (καὶ πάλιν ἠρνήσατο μετὰ[100] ὅρκου). This time Peter added an oath, probably falling into a habit common among the Jews at that time. He denied acquaintance with Jesus and even refers to Jesus as "the man" (τὸν ἄνθρωπον), an expression that could convey contempt, "the fellow."

26:73. *A little later the bystanders came up and said to Peter*[101] (μετὰ μικρὸν δὲ προσελθόντες οἱ ἑστῶτες εἶπον τῷ Πέτρῳ). The talk about Peter continued. Luke 22:59 states that about an hour passed. Some bystanders came up and bluntly asserted that Peter was "of a truth" (Ἀληθῶς) one of the followers of Jesus, for his speech betrayed him. Even the Revised Version retains "bewrayeth," quaint old English for "betrayeth." The Greek has it simply "makes you evident" (δῆλόν σε ποιεῖ). His dialect (λαλιά) clearly revealed that he was a Galilean. Galileans had difficulty with gutturals and Peter's phrasings even in his cursing second denial had exposed the truth to the loungers who continued to nag him.

26:74. *Then he began to curse and swear*[102] (τότε ἤρξατο καταθεματίζειν[103] καὶ ὀμνύειν). He repeated his denial with the addition of profanity, trying to prove that he was telling the truth, when they all knew that he was lying. Each repeated denial had given him away, for he could not pronounce the Judean gutturals. He called down on himself (καταθεματίζειν) imprecations in his desperate loss of self-control at his exposure.

And immediately a rooster crowed (καὶ εὐθέως ἀλέκτωρ ἐφώνησεν). No article in the Greek, just "a cock crowed" at that juncture. That startled Peter.

26:75. *And Peter remembered the word which Jesus had said*[104] (καὶ ἐμνήσθη ὁ Πέτρος τοῦ ῥήματος Ἰησοῦ[105] εἰρηκότος), a small thing, but *magna circumstantia*. He recalled the words of Jesus a few hours before (v. 34) and the proud boast that "even if I must die with You, yet will I not deny You" (v. 35). And now this triple denial was a fact. There is no extenuation for the base denials of Peter. Now he earned the dread penalty warned by Jesus in 10:33. Would Jesus deny Peter before the Father in heaven? But Peter felt sudden, immediate revulsion at his sin.

And he went out and wept bitterly (καὶ ἐξελθὼν ἔξω ἔκλαυσεν πικρῶς). Luke 22:61 adds that the Lord turned and looked upon Peter. That look brought Peter to his senses. He could not stay with the revilers of Jesus, nor did he feel worthy or able to go openly into the hall where Jesus was. So he left with a broken heart. The constative aorist here does not emphasize as clearly as does the imperfect ἔκλαιεν in Mark 14:72 the depths of his continued weeping. The tears were made all the more bitter by that look of understanding pity from Jesus. One of the tragedies of the cross is the bleeding heart of Peter. Judas was a total wreck and Peter was nearly derelict. Satan had sifted them all as wheat, but Jesus had prayed specially for Peter (Luke 22:31–32). Would Satan show that Peter was all chaff, like Judas?

NOTES

1. NIV has "the Passover is two days away."
2. NIV has "Then the chief priests and the elders of the people assembled."
3. TR and Maj.T add καὶ οἱ γραμματεῖ" here.
4. NIV has "in the palace of the high priest."
5. NIV has "to arrest Jesus in some sly way and kill him."
6. TR reverses the two words, κρατήσωσιν δόλῳ.
7. NIV has "there may be a riot among the people."
8. NIV has "in the home of a man known as Simon the Leper."
9. For proof that Mary of Bethany, Mary Magdalene, and the sinful woman of Luke 7 are different individuals, see A. T. Robertson, *Some Minor Characters in the New Testament* (repr. ed., Nashville: Broadman & Holman, 1976).
10. NIV has "a woman came to him with an alabaster jar of very expensive perfume."
11. TR and Maj.T have a different word order, ἀλάβαστρον μύρου ἔχουσα.
12. Alexander Balmain Bruce, *The Expositor's Greek Testament*, Vol. 1, *The Synoptic Gospels* (Grand Rapids: Eerdmans, 1951), 308.
13. Herodotus, *History*, 3.20.
14. TR and Maj.T have the accusative case after the preposition, ἐπὶ τὴν κεφαλήν.
15. NIV has "Why are you bothering this woman?"
16. James Hope Moulton and George Milligan, *The Vocabulary of the Greek Testament* (London: Hodder and Stoughton, 1952), 355.

17. NIV has "She has done a beautiful thing to me."
18. TR and Maj.T have a different spelling for the verb, εἰργάσατο.
19. NIV has "What are you willing to give me if I hand him over to you?"
20. Marvin R. Vincent, *Word Studies in the New Testament*, Vol. 1, *The Synoptic Gospels* (repr. ed., Grand Rapids: Eerdmans, 1946), 137.
21. Bruce, *Expositor's*, 309.
22. Ibid.
23. NIV has "So they counted out for him thirty silver coins."
24. Bruce, *Expositor's*, 310.
25. NIV has "Judas watched for an opportunity to hand him over."
26. A. T. Robertson, *Commentary on the Gospel According to Matthew* (New York: Macmillan, 1911), 255.
27. NIV has "Where do you want us to make preparations for you to eat the Passover?"
28. Josephus, *Antiquities of the Jews*, 2.15.1.
29. See A. T. Robertson, *Harmony of the Gospels for Students of the Life of Christ* (New York: Harper and Row, 1922), 279–84.
30. For the asyndeton see A. T. Robertson, *A Grammar of the Greek New Testament in the Light of Historical Research* (Nashville: Broadman, 1934), 935.
31. W. Bauer, W. F. Arndt, and F. W. Gingrich, *Greek-English Lexicon of the New Testament and Other Early Christian Literature* (Chicago: University of Chicago, 1957), 172.
32. Moulton and Milligan, *Vocabulary*, 138.
33. NIV has "I am going to celebrate the Passover with my disciples at your house."
34. NIV has "The one who has dipped his hand into the bowl with me will betray me."
35. TR and Maj.T have a different word order, ἐν τῷ τρυβλίῳ τὴν χεῖρα.
36. NIV has "It would be better for him if he had not been born."
37. NIV has "Jesus took bread, gave thanks and broke it."
38. TR and Maj.T have the article, τὸν ἄρτον.
39. TRb and Maj.T do not have the moveable ν, ἔκλασε.
40. Bruce, *Expositor's*, 1.312.
41. NIV has "This is my blood of the covenant."
42. TR and Maj.T have τοῦτο γάρ ἐστιν τὸ αἷμά μου, τὸ τῆς καινῆς διαθήκης.
43. NIV has "for the forgiveness of sins."
44. NIV has "when I drink it anew with you in my Father's kingdom."
45. G. Adolf Deissmann, *Bible Studies: Contributions, Chiefly from Papyri and Inscriptions, to the History of the Language, the Literature, and the Religion*

of Hellenistic Judaism and primitive Christianity, trans. A. Grieve. (Edinburgh: T. & T. Clark, 1901), 109f.

46. NIV has "When they had sung a hymn."
47. NIV has "Even if all fall away on account of you, I never will."
48. TR includes καί between Εἰ and πάντες.
49. TR and Maj.T have Γεθσημανη; WH has Γεθσημανεί.
50. In the 1930s, Robertson could add that "there are now eight old olive trees still standing in this enclosure. One cannot say that they are the very trees near which Jesus had his agony, but they are very old." He quotes Arthur Penrhyn Stanley, *Sinai and Palestine* (New York: W. J. Widdleton, 1865), 450, of these trees: "They will remain so long as their already protracted life is spared, the most venerable of their race on the surface of the earth. Their guarded trunks and scanty foliage will always be regarded as the most affecting of the sacred memorials in or about Jerusalem."
51. TR and Maj.T have the word order reversed, προσεύξωμαι ἐκεῖ.
52. NIV has "He took Peter and the two sons of Zebedee along with him."
53. NIV has "he began to be sorrowful and troubled."
54. P. Oxy. 2, 298, 456. Moulton and Milligan, *Vocabulary*, 9.
55. Braid Scots has it "sair putten-aboot."
56. NIV has "Going a little farther."
57. Maj.T has προσέλθων.
58. Alan Hugh McNeile, *The Gospel According to St. Matthew: The Greek Text with Introduction, Notes, and Indices* (repr. ed., Grand Rapids: Baker, 1980), 390.
59. NIV has "may this cup be taken from me.
60. TR and Maj.T have παρελθέτω.
61. NIV has "Could you men not keep watch with me for one hour?"
62. NIV has "Watch and pray."
63. NIV has "if it is not possible for this cup to be taken away unless I drink it."
64. TR and Maj.T have εἰ οὐ δύναται τοῦτο τὸ ποτήριον παρελθεῖν ἀπ᾽ ἐμοῦ ἐὰν μὴ αὐτὸ πίω.
65. Alfred Plummer, *An Exegetical Commentary on the Gospel According to Saint Matthew* (repr. ed., Grand Rapids: Eerdmans, 1956), 371.
66. Bruce, *Expositor's*, 315.
67. NIV has "the hour is near."
68. Bruce, *Expositor's*, 315.
69. NIV has "the Son of Man is betrayed."
70. NIV has "let us go."

71. NIV has "Here comes my betrayer."

72. NIV has "a large crowd armed with swords and clubs."

73. NIV has "Now the betrayer had arranged a sign with them."

74. Bruce, *Expositor's*, 316.

75. Broadus, *Matthew*, 540.

76. NIV has "do what you came for."

77. TR and Maj.T have ἐφ' ᾧ πάρει.

78. G. Adolf Deissmann, *Light from the Ancient East: The New Testament Illustrated by Recently Discovered Texts of the Graeco-Roman World*, trans. L. R. M. Strachan (rev. ed., Grand Rapids: Baker, 1965), 125–31; Robertson, *Grammar*, 725.

79. Deissmann, *Light from the Ancient East*, 129.

80. Bruce, *Expositor's*, 317.

81. NIV has "one of Jesus' companions."

82. TR and Maj.T have Ἀπόστρεψόν σου τὴν μάχαιραν εἰς τὸν τόπον αὐτῆ.

83. NIV has "Am I leading a rebellion?"

84. NIV has "sat down with the guards to see the outcome."

85. Bruce, *Expositor's*, 319.

86. NIV has "the whole Sanhedrin were looking for false evidence against Jesus."

87. NIV has "But Jesus remained silent."

88. NIV has "I charge you under oath by the living God."

89. TRs has the acute accent on σέ.

90. NIV has "Yes, it is as you say."

91. NIV has "He has spoken blasphemy!"

92. NIV has "He is worthy of death."

93. NIV has "Prophesy to us, Christ."

94. NIV has "You also were with Jesus."

95. Bruce, *Expositor's*, 321.

96. Gustaf Dalman, *The Words of Jesus, Considered in the Light of Post-Biblical Jewish Writings and the Aramaic Language* (Edinburgh: T. & T. Clark, 1902), 80f.

97. NIV has "Then he went out to the gateway."

98. TR and Maj.T have ἐξελθόντα δὲ αὐτὸν εἰς τὸν πυλῶνα.

99. NIV has "He denied it again, with an oath."

100. TR and Maj.T have the preposition spelled μεθ'.

101. NIV has "After a little while, those standing there went up to Peter and said."

102. NIV has "Then he began to call down curses on himself and he swore to them."

103.   TR has the infinitive spelled καταναθεματίζειν.
104.   NIV has "Then Peter remembered the word Jesus had spoken."
105.   TR and Maj.T have the article with the proper noun, τοῦ Ἰησοῦ.

Matthew: Chapter 27

27:1. *Now when morning came*[1] (Πρωΐας δὲ γενομένης), a genitive absolute participle construction. After dawn came, the Sanhedrin held a formal meeting to ratify the illegal trial that had been convened during the night (Mark 15:1; Luke 22:66–71). Luke gives the details of this second trial, with its condemnation of Jesus. "Conferred together" (συμβούλιον ἔλαβον) is a Latin idiom (*consilium ceperunt*) for συνεβουλεύσαντο.

27:2. *Delivered Him to Pilate the governor*[2] (παρέδωκαν Πιλάτῳ τῷ ἡγεμόνι[3]). What they had done was all form and farce. Only Pilate had the power of death, but they had greatly enjoyed the condemnation and the buffeting of Jesus, who was now in their power, bound as a condemned criminal. He was no longer the master of assemblies in the temple, able to make the Sanhedrin cower before him. He had been bound in the garden and was bound before Annas (John 18:12, 24), but may have been unbound before Caiaphas.

27:3. *He felt remorse*[4] (μεταμεληθεὶς). Probably Judas saw Jesus led away to Pilate and thus knew that the condemnation had taken place. This nominative singular masculine first aorist passive participle of μεταμέλομαι means "to be sorry afterward," like the English word *repent* from the Latin *repoenitet*, "to have pain again or afterward." The same verb, μεταμεληθεὶς in 21:29, describes the boy who became sorry for his rebellion and decided to obey. Paul uses it of his sorrow for his sharp letter to the Corinthians, a sorrow that ceased when good came of the letter (2 Cor. 7:9). When he wept bitterly, this sorrow led Peter back to Christ. It led Judas into suicidal remorse.

27:4. *"See to that yourself!"*[5] (σὺ ὄψῃ[6]). To the Sanhedrin, but not to God, nor to Jesus, Judas made a belated confession of his sin in betraying innocent blood. The Sanhedrin shared this guilt, so they ignored the "innocent or righteous blood" (αἷμα ἀθῷον or δίκαιον) and tell Judas that whatever guilt he feels is his problem. They ignore their own guilt in the matter. The use of σὺ ὄψῃ as a volitive future, equivalent to the imperative, is common in Latin (*tu videris*) but seldom seen in Greek. Occasionally Κοινή writings show it. Both Hugo Grotius and A. B. Bruce observe that the sentiment of the Sanhedrin rabbis is that of Cain.[7]

232

27:5. *He went away and hanged himself*[8] (ἀπελθὼν ἀπήγξατο), a reflexive middle. His act was sudden after he hurled the money into the sanctuary (εἰς τὸν ναὸν), the sacred enclosure where the priests were. The motives of Judas in the betrayal were mixed, as is usually the case with criminals. The money, while substantial, was not an immense sum. The figure seemed to be more of an expression of contempt, representing the price of a slave.

27:6. *"It is not lawful to put them into the temple treasury"*[9] (Οὐκ ἔξεστιν βαλεῖν αὐτὰ εἰς τὸν κορβανᾶν). Josephus also uses κορβανᾶς for the sacred treasury.[10] *Korbaʾn* is Aramaic for *gift* (δῶρον), as in Mark 7:11. Blood money would, under the restriction of Deuteronomy 23:18, pollute the treasury, so they used the money for a secular purpose. The rabbis knew how to split hairs about *korbaʾn* (Matt. 15:1–20; Mark 7:1–23), but their theology balks at this blood money.

27:7. *The Potter's Field*[11] (τὸν ἀγρὸν τοῦ κεραμέως). Grotius suggests that it was a small field where potter's clay was obtained, like a brickyard.[12] If there was another reason for the name, it is unknown. Acts 1:18 offers another perspective on the death of Judas. His body "burst open" (possibly because the bloating corpse fell from the place where he hanged himself) after he obtained the field with the wages of iniquity. While Acts 1 indicates that Judas acquired the field, Matthew 27 shows that it was done in his name by the temple administrators. Thus, "acquired," ἐκτήσατο in Acts 1, refers to the use of the blood money of Judas after he was dead. Matthew is not inconsistent with Acts 1:18–19.

27:8. *The Field of Blood* (Ἀγρὸς Αἵματος). This name was attached to it because it was the price of blood. In English and North American history, communities have established "potter's field" burial places for the indigent who had nowhere else to lie. This field became a burial ground for foreigners (εἰς ταφὴν τοῖς ξένοις, v. 7) or for Jews from elsewhere who died while in Jerusalem. In Acts 1:19, it is called *Hakeldama* or "place of blood" (Χώριον Αἵματος) because Judas's blood was shed there or because it was purchased with blood money or for both reasons.

27:9. *That which was spoken through Jeremiah the prophet* (τὸ ῥηθὲν διὰ Ἰερεμίου τοῦ προφήτου). This quotation comes mainly from Zechariah 11:13, though not in exact language. In Jeremiah 18:1–4 the prophet tells of a visit to a potter's house and in 32:6–9 of the purchase of a field. It is in Zechariah that seventeen shekels, or about thirty pieces of silver, are mentioned. Elaborate theories are offered as to why the words of Zechariah and Jeremiah are combined and attributed to Jeremiah. A similar mixing of prophetic texts occurs in

Mark 1:2–3, in which part of the quotation from Isaiah actually is from Malachi. The practice may have been, when quoting prophecies, to attribute to the more prominent. In their commentaries, John Broadus and Alan McNeile discuss the various theories.[13] Matthew has in verse 10 "the Potter's Field" (ϵἰς τὸν ἀγρὸν τοῦ κεραμέως). Zechariah "threw them to the potter in the house of the LORD" (Zech. 11:13). That language is more parallel with the language of Matthew 27:7.

27:11. *Now Jesus stood before the governor* (Ὁ δὲ Ἰησοῦς ἐστάθη ἔμπροσθεν τοῦ ἡγεμόνος). In one of the dramatic episodes of history, Jesus stands face-to-face with the Roman governor. The verb ἐστάθη, not ἔστη[14] (second aorist active), is first aorist passive and can mean "was placed" there, but He stood, rather than sat. The term ἡγεμών (from ἡγέομαι, "to lead") technically refers to a *legatus Caesaris*, an officer of the emperor, and more precisely to a *procurator*. Procurators ruled under the emperor over less important provinces than did *propraetors*, who were over more significant provinces, such as Syria. *Proconsuls* governed senatorial provinces, for example Achaia. Pilate represented Roman law in an insignificant part of the Empire.

"Are You the King of the Jews?" (Σὺ εἶ ὁ βασιλεὺς τῶν Ἰουδαίων;). This was the question that really mattered to Pilate. Matthew does not give the charges made by the Sanhedrin (Luke 23:2) nor the private interview with Pilate (John 18:28–32). If Pilate ignored the accusation that Jesus claimed to be "King of the Jews," he could be accused of disloyalty to Caesar. Rivals to caesar or would-be liberators from Rome commonly arose across the Empire. Here was one more. By his answer, "It is as you say," Jesus confesses that he is in some sense a king. Pilate has the problem of determining what sort of king this one claims to be.

27:14. *And He did not answer him with regard to even a single charge*[15] (καὶ οὐκ ἀπεκρίθη αὐτῷ πρὸς οὐδὲ ἓν ῥῆμα). Jesus refused to answer the charges of the Jews (v. 12). He continues his silence under the direct question of Pilate. The Greek is very precise and uses the double negative. This silent dignity amazed Pilate, yet he was strangely impressed.

27:17. *"Barabbas, or Jesus who is called Christ?"* (βαραββᾶν ἢ Ἰησοῦν τὸν λεγόμενον Χριστόν;). Pilate sought any loophole to escape condemning a harmless lunatic or exponent of a superstitious cult, such as he deemed Jesus to be. Obviously this was no political rival to Caesar. The Jews interpreted "Christ" for Pilate to be a claim to be King of the Jews in opposition to Caesar. So verse 15 says that Pilate took advantage of the Passover custom of releasing to the people "any one prisoner whom they wanted"[16] (ἕνα τῷ ὄχλῳ δέσμιον ὃν ἤθελον). No parallel case has been found in Roman or Jewish records, but Josephus mentions the custom.[17] Barabbas was, for some reason, a popular hero, a notable (ἐπίσημον), if notorious, prisoner. He had led an insurrection or revolution (Mark 15:7), probably against Rome. Pilate may have chosen him since he was clearly guilty of the very crime that the Jewish leaders were trying to fasten on Jesus. Yet Pilate had learned that Jesus claimed to be king in the spiritual sense. By his strategem, Pilate unwittingly compared two prisoners who represented the antagonistic forces of all time. He frames the question in an ellliptical structure: "Whom do you want me to release for you?" (Τίνα θέλετε ἀπολύσω ὑμῖν;). This is either two questions in one, an *asyndeton*, or the ellipse of ἵνα before ἀπολύσω. The same idiom occurs in verse 21. But Pilate tested both the Jews and himself with the question. The same decision has tested people ever since. Some manuscripts add the name *Jesus* to *Barabbas*, which sharpens the parallel: "Do you want *Jesus Barabbas* or *Jesus Christ?*"

27:18. *Because of envy they had handed Him over*[18] (διὰ φθόνον παρέδωκαν αὐτόν). Pilate did not have the full picture, but he knew that the Jewish leaders were jealous of the power of Jesus among the people. He may have heard of the events of the Triumphal Entry and maybe even the temple teaching.

27:19. *His wife sent him a message*[19] (ἀπέστειλεν πρὸς αὐτὸν ἡ γυνὴ αὐτοῦ). Poor Pilate became increasingly entangled with every passing moment as he hesitated. He knew he should set Jesus free, for the man had committed no crime against Caesar. Just as he was trying to enlist support for Jesus in the crowd against the schemes of the Jewish leaders, his wife sent a message about her dream concerning Jesus. She calls Jesus "that righteous Man"[20] (τῷ δικαίῳ ἐκείνῳ) and her psychic sufferings heightened Pilate's superstitious fear. Tradition names her Procla and improbably calls her a secret disciple. Her words unnerved the weak Pilate as he sat on the judgment seat (ἐπὶ τοῦ βήματος), looking down on the people.

27:20. *But the chief priests and the elders persuaded the crowds* (Οἱ δὲ ἀρχιερεῖς καὶ οἱ πρεσβύτεροι ἔπεισαν τοὺς ὄχλους). The chief priests (Sadducees) and elders (Pharisees) saw the peril of the situation and took no chances. While Pilate wavered in pressing the question, they incited the people to "to ask for themselves" (αἰτήσωνται, indirect middle ingressive aorist subjunctive), choosing Barabbas and not Jesus.

27:22. *"Then what shall I do with Jesus who is called Christ?"* (Τί οὖν ποιήσω Ἰησοῦν τὸν λεγόμενον Χριστόν;). They had asked for Barabbas under the instigation of the Sanhedrin, but Pilate pressed home the problem of

Jesus with the dim hope that they might ask for Jesus also. It is at least possible that someone who shouted "Hosannah" on the morning of the Triumphal Entry now shouted "Crucify Him!" or "Let Him be crucified" (Σταυρωθήτω). The hero of Sunday was the condemned criminal of Friday. All the while, Pilate shirks his own fearful responsibility and hides his weakness and injustice behind popular clamor and prejudice.

27:23. *"Why, what evil has He done?"*[21] (Τί γὰρ κακὸν ἐποίησεν;). This was a feeble protest by a flickering conscience. Pilate now had been goaded into arguing with a mob inflamed with passion for the blood of Jesus. This exhibition of weakness made the mob fear that Pilate might refuse to proceed.

But they kept shouting all the more[22] (οἱ δὲ περισσῶς ἔκραζον), third person singular imperfect active indicative of repeated action and vehemently. Their demand for the crucifixion of Jesus was like a gladiatorial show in which the people demanded death.

27:24. *He took water and washed his hands* (λαβὼν ὕδωρ ἀπενίψατο τὰς χεῖρας). The hand washing demonstration was Pilate's last attempt to get the crowd to think amid the hubbub (θόρυβος) that increased because of his vacillation. The verb ἀπονίζω means "to wash off," and the middle voice means that he washed his own hands as a common symbol of cleanliness. His pious claim was a slap at them.

"I am innocent of this Man's blood; see to that yourselves"[23] (Ἀθῷός εἰμι ἀπὸ τοῦ αἵματος τούτου ὑμεῖς ὄψεσθε[24]). The Jews used this symbol (Deut. 21:6; Pss. 26:6; 73:13). Alfred Plummer doubts that Pilate was thinking of his wife's message as he said these words (v. 19),[25] but I fail to see the ground for that skepticism. The false *Gospel of Peter* says that Pilate washed his hands because the Jews refused to do so.

27:25. *"His blood shall be on us and on our children"*[26] (Τὸ αἷμα αὐτοῦ ἐφ᾽ ἡμᾶς καὶ ἐπὶ τὰ τέκνα ἡμῶν). These solemn words, probably shouted by one of the leaders, show a certain consciousness and even pride of guilt. But Pilate could not wash away his own part of this guilt that easily. The water did not wash away the blood of Jesus from his hands any more than could Shakespeare's Lady Macbeth wash away the blood of Duncan that stained her as a murderess. Legend makes much of Pilate's act. It is said that in storms on Mount Pilatus in Switzerland, his ghost comes out to wash his hands in the storm clouds. The guilt of Jesus' death marked Judas, Caiaphas and the Sanhedrin, Sadducees and Pharisees, the entire Jewish people (πᾶς ὁ λαό), Pilate, and all humankind. The sins of all of us nailed Jesus to the cross. The language of the crowd has been used to excuse race hatred and contributes to the sensitivity felt by Jews toward Christians. Both sides have approached the subject of the cross with a degree of prejudice.

27:26. *But after having Jesus scourged*[27] (τὸν δὲ Ἰησοῦν φραγελλώσας), the Latin verb *flagellare*. Pilate apparently lost interest in Jesus when he discovered that he had no support. The religious leaders had been eager to get Jesus condemned before the Galileans friendly to Jesus came into the city and learned what was happening. They apparently succeeded. Scourging before crucifixion was a brutal Roman custom. It was part of the capital punishment. G. Adolf Deissmann quotes a Florentine papyrus of A.D. 85 in which G. Septimius Vegetus, governor of Egypt, says of a certain Phibion: "You have been worthy of scourging, . . . but I will give thee to the people."[28]

27:27. *Then the soldiers of the governor took Jesus into the Praetorium* (Τότε οἱ στρατιῶται τοῦ ἡγεμόνος παραλαβόντες τὸν Ἰησοῦν εἰς τὸ πραιτώριον). In Rome, the *praetorium* was the camp of the *praetorian* (from *praetor*) guard of soldiers (Phil. 1:13). In the provinces, it was the palace in which the governor resided, as the governor's palace at Caesarea in Acts 23:35. So here in Jerusalem Pilate ordered Jesus and all the band or cohort (ὅλην τὴν σπεῖραν) of soldiers to be led into the palace in front of which the judgment seat had been placed. The Latin *spira* was anything rolled into a circle like a twisted ball of thread. These Latin words are natural here in the atmosphere of the court and the military environment. The soldiers gathered for the sport of seeing the scourging. These heathen soldiers would enjoy showing their contempt for both the Jews and the condemned man.

27:28. *Put a scarlet robe on Him* (χλαμύδα κοκκίνην περιέθηκαν αὐτῷ[29]). A kind of short cloak worn by soldiers, military officers, magistrates, kings, emperors (2 Macc. 12:35),[30] a soldier's *sagum* or scarf. Carr suggests that it may have been a worn-out scarf of Pilate's.[31] The scarlet color (κοκκίνην) was a dye derived from the female insect (κέρμες) that gathered on the *ilex coccifera* found in Palestine. These dried clusters of dead insects look like berries and are crushed to form the famous dye. The word occurs in Plutarch, Epictetus, Herodas, and late papyri besides the LXX and New Testament. Mark (15:17) has "purple" (πορφυρὰν). There are various shades of purple and scarlet and it is not easy to distinguish these colors or tints. The manuscripts vary here between "stripped" (ἐκδύσαντες) and "clothed" (ἐνδύσαντες). He had been stripped for the scourging. If "clothed" is correct, the soldiers added the scarlet (purple) mantle. This scarlet mantle on Jesus was mock imitation of the royal purple.

27:29. *And after twisting together a crown of thorns, they put it on His* head[32] (καὶ πλέξαντες στέφανον ἐξ ἀκανθῶν ἐπέθηκαν ἐπὶ τῆς κεφαλῆς αὐτοῦ[33]). They wove a crown out of thorns that grew all around, probably even in the palace grounds. It is immaterial whether they were young and tender thorn bushes, as probable in the spring, or hard bushes with sharp prongs. The soldiers would not care, for they were after ridicule and mockery that caused pain. It was more like a victor's garland (στέφανον) than a royal diadem (διάδημα), but it served the purpose. So with the reed (κάλαμον), a stalk of common cane grass which served as sceptre. The soldiers were familiar with the *Ave Caesar* and copy it in their mockery of Jesus: "Hail, King of the Jews!" (Χαῖρε, βασιλεῦ τῶν Ἰουδαίων[34]). The soldiers added the insults used by the Sanhedrin (Matt. 26:67), spitting on him and smiting him with the reed. Probably Jesus had been unbound. The garments of mockery were removed before the *via dolorosa* to the cross (v. 31).

27:32. *They found a man of Cyrene named Simon, whom they pressed into service*[35] (εὖρον ἄνθρωπον Κυρηναῖον ὀνόματι Σίμωνα· Τοῦτον ἠγγάρευσαν). This word of Persian origin (ἠγγάρευσαν) was used in Matthew 5:41. There are numerous papyri examples of Ptolemaic date. The word survives in modern Greek vernacular. The soldiers draft Simon of Cyrene, a town of Libya, as a Persian courier (ἄγγαρος) and impress him into service. Probably Jesus was showing signs of physical weakness in bearing the crossbeam of his own cross, as the victims had to do. It was not a mere jest on Simon. "Gethsemane, betrayal, the ordeal of the past sleepless night, scourging, have made the flesh weak."[36] The burden of sin for the world also was breaking his heart.

To bear His cross[37] (ἵνα ἄρῃ τὸν σταυρὸν αὐτοῦ). Jesus had used the term *cross* about himself (16:24). It was a familiar enough picture under Roman rule. Jesus had foreseen and foretold this horrible form of his death (20:19; 26:2). He had heard the cry of the mob to Pilate that he be crucified (27:22) and Pilate's surrender (v. 26). He was on the way to the cross (v. 31). There were various kinds of crosses, and we do not know precisely the shape of the cross on which Jesus was crucified, though tradition is universal for the shape that has become a Christian symbol. Usually the hands were nailed to the crossbeam before it was raised and then the feet. It was not very high. The crucifixion was done by the soldiers (v. 35) in charge.

27:33. *When they came to a place called Golgotha* (ἐλθόντες εἰς τόπον λεγόμενον Γολγοθᾶ), Chaldaic or Aramaic *Gulgatha*, Hebrew *Gulgoleth*, place of a skull-shaped mount, not place of skulls. Latin Vulgate *Calvariae locus*, hence the English word *Calvary*. Tyndale misunderstood it as a place of dead men's skulls. Golgotha was outside the city.

27:34. *They gave Him wine to drink mixed with gall*[38] (ἔδωκαν αὐτῷ πιεῖν οἶνον μετὰ χολῆς μεμιγμένον). Late MSS[39] read *vinegar* (ὄξος) instead of wine, and Mark 15:23 has myrrh instead of gall. The myrrh gave the sour wine a better flavor and, like the bitter gall, had a narcotic, stupefying effect. Both elements may have been in the drink Jesus tasted but refused to drink. Women provided the drink to deaden the sense of pain, and the soldiers may have added the gall to make it disagreeable. John 18:11 comments that Jesus desired to drink to the full the cup from his Father's hand.

27:36. *They began to keep watch over Him there*[40] (ἐτήρουν αὐτὸν ἐκεῖ), imperfect tense descriptive of the task to prevent the possibility of rescue or removal of the body. These rough Roman soldiers cast lots over the garments of Christ, a piece of comedy at the foot of the cross, the tragedy of the ages.

27:37. *And above His head they put up the charge against Him*[41] (καὶ ἐπέθηκεν ἐπάνω τῆς κεφαλῆς αὐτοῦ τὴν αἰτίαν αὐτοῦ γεγραμμένην). The title (τίτλος, John 19:19) or placard of the crime (the inscription, ἡ γραφή), which was carried before the victim or hung around his neck as he walked to execution was now placed above (ἐπ' ἄνω) the head of Jesus on the projecting piece (*crux immurus*). This inscription gave the name and place of origin, "Jesus of Nazareth," and the charge on which He was convicted, "the King of the Jews" with the identification, "This is." The four reports all give the charge and vary in providing other details. The full inscription would have been, "This is Jesus of Nazareth the King of the Jews." John 19:20 notes that it was inscribed in three languages, Latin for law, Hebrew (Aramaic) for the Jews, and Greek for everybody. The accusation (charge, cause, αἰτία) correctly told the facts of condemnation.

27:38. *Two robbers were crucified with Him* (Τότε σταυροῦνται σὺν αὐτῷ δύο λῃσταί). A robber was crucified on either side of Jesus, so three crosses stood in a row (v. 38). These were robbers, not thieves (κλέπται) as in the Authorized Version (see v. 55). Interpreters have speculated that these robbers may have been members of the band led by Barabbas, on whose cross Jesus now hung, but Scripture says nothing more about them or Barabbas.

27:39. *Wagging their heads*[42] (κινοῦντες τὰς κεφαλὰς αὐτῶν), probably in mock commiseration. The Jews watch with the same malice they had demonstrated in the Sanhedrin trial.[43] "To us it may seem incredible that even his worst enemies could be guilty of anything so brutal as to hurl taunts at one suffering the agonies of crucifixion."[44] These passersby jeer (παραπορευόμενοι) at the fallen foe.

27:40. *"If You are the Son of God"* (εἰ υἱὸς εἶ τοῦ θεοῦ). More exactly, "If you are *a* son of God," the very language of the Devil to Jesus (4:3) in the early temptations. The words are now hurled at Jesus under the Devil's prompting as he hung upon the cross. There is allusion, of course, to the claim of Jesus under oath before the Sanhedrin "the Son of God" (ὁ υἱὸς τοῦ θεοῦ) and a repetition of the misrepresentation of his words about the temple of his body. It is a pitiful picture of human depravity and failure in the presence of Christ dying for sinners.

27:41. *In the same way the chief priests also, . . . were mocking Him*[45] (ὁμοίως καὶ οἱ ἀρχιερεῖς ἐμπαίζοντες[46]). "Scribes and elders" of the Sanhedrin are included. The word ἐμπαίζοντες for mocking (ἐν and παίζω, from παῖς, child) means "acting like silly children" who love to mock one another. These grave and revered seniors had given vent to their glee at the condemnation of Jesus (26:67).

27:42. *"He saved others; He cannot save Himself"*[47] (Ἄλλους ἔσωσεν, ἑαυτὸν οὐ δύναται σῶσαι). The sarcasm is true, though they do not know the significance of what they are saying. If he saved himself now, he could save no one else. The paradox is precisely the philosophy proclaimed by Jesus Himself (see 10:39).

Let Him now come down from the cross (καταβάτω νῦν ἀπὸ τοῦ σταυροῦ). He is a condemned criminal nailed to the cross with the claim of being "the King of Israel" (the Jews) over his head. They spitefully assert that they would then believe "upon Jesus" (ἐπ᾽ αὐτόν) if he came down. This plainly is untrue. Had he done so, they would have shifted their ground to some other excuse. When Jesus wrought his greatest miracles, they wanted "a sign from heaven." These "pious scoffers"[48] are like many who make factitious and arbitrary demands of Christ. His character and power and deity are plain to all who are not blinded by the god of this world. Christ will not give new proofs to the blind in heart.

27:43. *Let God rescue Him now* (ρυσάσθω νῦν εἰ θέλει αὐτόν[49]). They add the word "now" to Psalm 22:8. The point of the sneer at Christ's claim to be God's Son is again thrown at him. Surely God has the power and willingness to help his "Son." The verb θέλω here may mean "love," as in the LXX (Pss. 18:20; 41:23) or "cares for" (Moffatt).[50]

27:44. *The robbers who had been crucified with Him were also insulting Him with the same words*[51] (τὸ δ᾽ αὐτὸ καὶ οἱ λῃσταὶ οἱ συσταυρωθέντες σὺν αὐτῷ ὠνείδιζον αὐτόν[52]). "Even the robbers" (Weymouth) felt momentary superiority to Jesus as he was thus maligned by all. The inchoative (inceptive) imperfect ὠνείδιζον means that they "began to reproach him."

27:45. *Now from the sixth hour*[53] (Ἀπὸ δὲ ἕκτης ὥρας). Curiously, McNeile uses John 19:14 to say that Matthew here refers to the trial before Pilate.[54] John does set the trial at the sixth hour, but clearly he has in mind Roman time. John was writing at the close of the century, long after the Jewish War and total subjugation of Palestine. Even among the Jews, Jewish time was no longer a way of life. By Roman reckoning, the trial before Pilate was at six o'clock in the morning. According to Mark 15:25, using Jewish time, the crucifixion began at the third hour or 9 A.M. The darkness began at noon, the sixth hour Jewish time, and lasted until 3 P.M. Roman time, the ninth hour Jewish time (Mark 15:33 = Matt. 27:45 = Luke 23:44). Three hours of intense darkness is too long to be an eclipse of the sun. Luke 23:45 says only "the sun's light failing." This could have been darkness preceding the earthquake, or simply dense masses of clouds obscuring the sun. Or in some divinely guided way, nature may have cast a darkness of sorrow and sympathy over the tragedy of the dying Creator on the cross. This would literally express Paul's metaphor in Romans 8:22 that creation groans and travails under the curse.

27:46. *"My God, My God, why have You forsaken Me?"* (Θεέ μου θεέ μου, ἱνατί με ἐγκατέλιπες;). Matthew first transliterates the Aramaic, according to Vatican B, giving in Greek script the words used by Jesus: Ηλι ηλι λεμα σαβαχθανι. Some MSS give the transliteration of the Hebrew of Psalm 22:1, *Eli, Eli, lama Zaphthanei*. Matthew and Mark give only this saying of Christ on the cross. The other six occur in Luke and John. This is the only Aramaic sentence of any length preserved in Matthew, although he uses such Aramaic words as *amen, Korba'n, mammon, pascha, raca, Satan,* and *Golgotha*. The so-called Gospel of Peter preserves this saying in a Docetic (Cerinthian) form: "My power, my power, thou hast forsaken me!" Cerinthian Gnostics held that the *aeon* Christ came on the man Jesus at his baptism and left him there on the cross, so that only the man Jesus died. No other statement of Jesus so well illustrates the depth of his suffering of soul. The Sinless One felt himself regarded as sin (2 Cor. 5:21). John 3:16 comes to our relief as we see the Son of God bearing the sin of the world. This cry of desolation comes at the close of the three hours of darkness.

27:48. *And gave Him a drink*[55] (ἐπότιζεν αὐτόν), imperfect of conative (attempted but unsuccessful action) action, "offered him a drink of vinegar" on a sponge on a reed. Others interrupted this kind man, but Jesus did taste this mild stimulant, for he thirsted (John 19:28, 30).

27:49. *"Let us see whether Elijah will come to save Him"*[56] (Ἄφες ἴδωμεν εἰ ἔρχεται Ἠλίας σώσων αὐτόν). The excuse had a pious sound. They misunderstood the words of Jesus in his outcry of soul anguish. We have here one of the rare instances ($\sigma\omega\sigma\omega\nu$) of the future participle to express purpose in the New Testament, though it was a common Greek idiom. Some MSS copy here from John 19:34. It is genuine in John but completely wrecks the context for Matthew 27:50. Jesus cried with a loud voice and was not yet dead in verse 49. The addition of John 19:34 was a crass mechanical gloss by some scribe.[57]

27:50. *And yielded up His spirit*[58] ($\dot{\alpha}\phi\hat{\eta}\kappa\epsilon\nu$ $\tau\grave{o}$ $\pi\nu\epsilon\hat{u}\mu\alpha$). The loud cry may have been Psalm 31:5 as given in Luke 23:46: "Father, into Your hands I commit My spirit." John 19:30 gives "It is finished," $\tau\epsilon\tau\acute{\epsilon}\lambda\epsilon\sigma\tau\alpha\iota$, though which was actually last is not clear. Jesus did not die from slow exhaustion but with a loud cry. Matthew 27:50 speaks of a dismissing or sending back of Christ's Spirit. Mark 15:37 relates that "He breathed out" ($\dot{\epsilon}\xi\acute{\epsilon}\pi\nu\epsilon\upsilon\sigma\epsilon\nu$). John 19:30 says "He gave up His spirit" ($\pi\alpha\rho\acute{\epsilon}\delta\omega\kappa\epsilon\nu$ $\tau\grave{o}$ $\pi\nu\epsilon\hat{u}\mu\alpha$). The theme running through these variations is that Jesus acted and was not acted upon. He gave up his life because he willed it, when he willed it, and as he willed it. William Stroud, one of the first New Testament scholars to research the subject medically, considered the loud cry one of the proofs that Jesus died of a ruptured heart as a result of bearing the sin of the world.[59]

27:51. *The veil of the temple was torn in two from top to bottom*[60] ($\tau\grave{o}$ $\kappa\alpha\tau\alpha\pi\acute{\epsilon}\tau\alpha\sigma\mu\alpha$ $\tau o\hat{u}$ $\nu\alpha o\hat{u}$ $\dot{\epsilon}\sigma\chi\acute{\iota}\sigma\theta\eta$ $\dot{\alpha}\pi$' $\ddot{\alpha}\nu\omega\theta\epsilon\nu$ $\ddot{\epsilon}\omega\varsigma$ $\kappa\acute{\alpha}\tau\omega$ $\epsilon\dot{\iota}\varsigma$ $\delta\acute{u}o$[61]). Both Mark 15:38 and Luke 23:45 mention this fact. Matthew connects it with the earthquake. "The earth shook" ($\dot{\eta}$ $\gamma\hat{\eta}$ $\dot{\epsilon}\sigma\epsilon\acute{\iota}\sigma\theta\eta$). Josephus tells of a quaking in the temple before the destruction and the Talmud tells of a quaking forty years before the destruction of the temple.[62] Willoughby Allen suggests that "a cleavage in the masonry of the porch, which rent the outer veil and left the Holy Place open to view, would account for the language of the Gospels, of Josephus, and of the Talmud."[63] This veil was a most elaborately woven fabric of seventy-two twisted plaits of twenty-four threads each. The veil was sixty feet long and thirty feet wide. The rending of the veil signified the removal of the separation between God and the people.

27:52. *The tombs were opened*[64] ($\tau\grave{\alpha}$ $\mu\nu\eta\mu\epsilon\hat{\iota}\alpha$ $\dot{\alpha}\nu\epsilon\acute{\omega}\chi\theta\eta\sigma\alpha\nu$), third person plural first aorist passive indicative (double augment). The splitting of the rocks by the earthquake and the opening of tombs can be due to the earthquake. But the raising of the bodies of the dead after the resurrection of Jesus, which appeared to many in the holy city, puzzles many today who admit the actual bodily resurrection of Jesus. Some would brand all these portents as legends, since they appear in Matthew alone. Others would say that "after his resurrection" should read "after their resurrection," but that would make it conflict with Paul's description of Christ as the firstfruits of them that sleep (1 Cor. 15:20). Some say that Jesus released these spirits after his descent in hades. So it goes. We come back to miracles connected with the birth of Jesus, God's Son coming into the world. If we grant the possibility of such manifestations of God's power, there is little to disturb one here in the story of the death of God's Son.

27:54. *"Truly this was the Son of God!"* (Ἀληθῶς θεοῦ υἱὸς ἦν οὗτος). There is no article with *God* or *Son* in the Greek, so that there is no way to tell whether the soldier means "God's Son," "the son of a god" or "a Son of God." Evidently the centurion (ἑκατόνταρχος here, ruler of a hundred. The Latin is transliterated as κεντυριων in Mark 15:39.) was deeply moved by the portents he had witnessed. He had heard the several flings at Jesus for claiming to be the Son of God and may even have heard of his claim before the Sanhedrin and Pilate. How much he meant by his words we do not know, but probably he meant more than merely "a righteous man" (Luke 23:47). Tradition ascribes the name Petronius to this centurion. If he was won to trust in Christ, he came as a pagan and, like the robber who believed, was saved as Jesus hung upon the cross. All who are ever saved in truth are saved because of the death of Jesus on the cross. Whatever the state of this man's heart, the cross began to do its work at once.

27:55. *Many women were there* (δὲ ἐκεῖ γυναῖκες πολλαὶ). We have come to expect the women from Galilee to be faithful. They were last at the cross and first at the tomb. Luke 23:49 says that "all His acquaintances" (πάντες οἱ γνωστοὶ αὐτῷ) stood at a distance and saw the end. One hopes that the apostles were in that sad group. Certainly women were there. The mother of Jesus was taken away from the side of the cross by the beloved disciple to his own home (John 19:27). Matthew names three of the group by name. Mary Magdalene is mentioned as a well-known person, though not previously named in Matthew's Gospel. Certainly she is not the sinful woman of Luke 7 nor Mary of Bethany. There is another Mary, the mother of James and Joseph (Joses), who is not otherwise known to us. And then there is the mother of the sons of Zebedee (James and John), usually identified with Salome of Mark 15:40. Matthew 27:55 tells that these faithful women were "beholding from afar" (ἀπὸ μακρόθεν θεωροῦσαι). They may have drawn nearer to the cross for Mary the mother of Jesus stood beside the cross (παρὰ τῷ σταυρῷ) with Mary of Clopas and Mary Magdalene (John 19:25) before she left. They had ministered to Jesus (διακονοῦσαι αὐτῷ), and now he is dead. Matthew does not try to picture the anguish of heart of these noble women, nor does he say as Luke 23:48 of the crowd that they left the scene beating their breasts. He drops the curtain on that saddest of all tragedies as the loyal band stands watching the dead Christ on Golgotha. What hope did life now hold for them?

27:57–60. *When it was evening*[65] ('Οψίας δὲ γενομένης). This would place it between 3 P.M. and 6 P.M. It was the *preparation day* (παρασκευή), the day before the sabbath (Mark 15:42; Luke 23:54; John 31:42). Παρασκευή is the modern Greek name for Friday. The Jews were anxious that the bodies should be taken down before the Sabbath began at 6 P.M. The request of Joseph of Arimathea for the body of Jesus was a relief to Pilate and to the Jews. We know little about this member of the Sanhedrin save that his name was Joseph and that he came from Arimathea. He was wealthy and a secret disciple, who had not agreed to the death of Jesus. Probably he now wished that he had made an open profession. But he has courage now when others are cowardly and asked for the personal privilege (ἠτήσατο, middle voice, "asked for himself") of placing the body of Jesus in his new tomb. Some today identify this tomb with one of the rock tombs now visible under Gordon's Calvary. It was a mournful privilege and dignity that came to Joseph and Nicodemus (John 19:39–41) as they wrapped the body of Jesus in clean linen cloth and with proper spices placed it in this fresh (καινῷ) tomb in which no body had yet been placed. The tomb was cut in the rock (ἐλατόμησεν) for his own body, but now it was for Jesus. He rolled a great stone across the doorway to the tomb and departed. That was for safety. Two women likely remained to watch the sad ceremony. Mary Magdalene and Mary mother of James and Joseph were sitting opposite and looking on in silence.

27:63. *"Sir, we remember"*[66] (Κύριε, ἐμνήσθημεν). On Saturday, the Jewish Sabbath, the day after the preparation (see v. 62), Pilate again met with a delegation from the Sanhedrin. Ingressive aorist indicative, "we have just recalled." It is objected that the Jewish rulers would know nothing of such a prediction, but at least once, recorded in 12:40, he expressly made it to them. Some dismiss as unhistorical legend the whole story that Christ definitely foretold his resurrection on the third day. Such scholars make legendary much of the Gospels and limit Jesus to his humanity. The problem remains why the disciples forgot and the Jewish leaders remembered. That is probably due in part to the overwhelming grief of the disciples, coupled with the loss of all their hopes in a political Messiah. The nervous leaders, by contrast, still dreaded the power and popularity of Jesus though dead. They wanted to make sure of their victory and prevent any possible revival of this pernicious heresy.

"That deceiver said" (ἐκεῖνος ὁ πλάνος εἶπεν), they call him a "vagabond wanderer" (πλάνος) with a slur in the use of *that* (ἐκεῖνος), a picturesque sidelight on their intense hatred of and fear of Jesus.

27:64. *"The last deception"*[67] (ἡ ἐσχάτη πλάνη), "the last delusion, imposture" (Weymouth), "fraud" (Moffatt). Latin *error* is used in both senses, from *errare*, to go astray. The first fraud was belief in the messiahship of Jesus, the second belief in his resurrection.

27:65. *"You have a guard"*[68] (Ἔχετε κουστωδίαν), present imperative, a guard of Roman soldiers, not mere temple police. The Latin term κουστωδία occurs in an Oxyrhynchus papyrus of A.D 22.[69] "The curt permission to the Jews whom he despised is suitable in the mouth of the Roman official."[70]

"Make it as secure as you know how" (ἀσφαλίσασθε ὡς οἴδατε). "Make it secure for yourselves (ingressive aorist middle) as you know how."

27:66. *And they went and made the grave secure, and along with the guard they set a seal on the stone*[71] (οἱ δὲ πορευθέντες ἠσφαλίσαντο τὸν τάφον σφραγίσαντες τὸν λίθον μετὰ τῆς κουστωδίας). Probably a cord was stretched across the stone and sealed at each end, as in Daniel 6:17. The sealing was done in the presence of the Roman guard who were left in charge to protect this stamp of Roman authority and power. They did their best to prevent theft and the Resurrection,[72] but they overreached themselves and only provided additional witness to the fact of the empty tomb.[73]

NOTES

1. NIV has "Early in the morning."
2. NIV has "handed him over to Pilate, the governor."
3. TR and Maj.T have παρέδωκαν αὐτὸν Ποντίῳ Πιλάτῳ τῷ ἡγεμόνι; WH spells *Pilate* as Πειλάτῳ.
4. NIV has "he was seized with remorse."
5. NIV has "That's your responsibility."
6. TR and Maj.T have οὐ ὄψει.
7. Alexander Balmain Bruce, *The Expositor's Greek Testament*, Vol. 1, *The Synoptic Gospels* (Grand Rapids: Eerdmans, 1951), 323.
8. NIV has "he went away and hanged himself."
9. NIV has "It is against the law to put this into the treasury."
10. Josephus, *Wars of the Jews*, 2.9.4.
11. NIV has "the potter's field."
12. John A. Broadus, *Commentary on Matthew* (repr. ed., Grand Rapids: Kregel, 1990), 559.

13. Ibid., 560–61; see also Alan Hugh McNeile, *The Gospel According to St. Matthew: The Greek Text with Introduction, Notes, and Indices* (repr. ed., Grand Rapids: Baker, 1980), 409.

14. TR and Maj.T have the verb ἔστη.

15. NIV has "But Jesus made no reply, not even to a single charge." The name *Jesus* is not found in the Greek text.

16. NIV has "a prisoner chosen by the crowd."

17. Josephus, *Antiquities of the Jews*, 20.9.3.

18. NIV has "it was out of envy that they had handed Jesus over to him."

19. NIV has "his wife sent him this message."

20. NIV has "that innocent man."

21. NIV has "Why? What crime has he committed?"

22. NIV has "But they shouted all the louder."

23. NIV has "I am innocent of this man's blood," he said. "It is your responsibility."

24. TR and Maj.T have Ἀθῷός εἰμι ἀπὸ τοῦ αἵματος τοῦ δικαίου τούτου.

25. Alfred Plummer, *An Exegetical Commentary on the Gospel According to Saint Matthew* (repr. ed., Grand Rapids: Eerdmans, 1956), 391.

26. NIV has "Let his blood be on us and on our children!"

27. NIV has "But he had Jesus flogged."

28. G. Adolf Deissmann, *Light from the Ancient East: The New Testament Illustrated by Recently Discovered Texts of the Graeco-Roman World*, trans. L. R. M. Strachan (rev. ed., Grand Rapids: Baker, 1965), 269.

29. TR and Maj.T have a different word order, περιέθηκαν αὐτῷ χλαμύδα κοκκίνην.

30. Josephus, *Antiquities*, 5.1.10.

31. A. Carr, *The Cambridge Bible for Schools and Colleges: The Gospel According to St. Matthew* (Cambridge: Cambridge University Press, 1894), 218.

32. NIV has "and then twisted together a crown of thorns and set it on his head."

33. TR and Maj.T have the accusative case rather than the genitive case, ἐπὶ τὴν καφαλὴν αὐτοῦ.

34. TR and Maj.T have Χαῖρε, ὁ βασιλευς τῶν Ἰουδαίων.

35. NIV has "they met a man from Cyrene, named Simon, and they forced him."

36. Bruce, *Expositor's*, 328.

37. NIV has "to carry his cross."

38. NIV has "There they offered Jesus wine to drink, mixed with gall."

39. Such as TR and Maj.T.

40. NIV has "they kept watch over him there."

41. NIV has "Above his head they placed the written charge against him."

42. NIV has "shaking their heads."

43. McNeile, *Matthew*, 419.

44. Bruce, *Expositor's*, 329.

45. NIV has "In the same way the chief priests, . . . mocked him."

46. TR and Maj.T have the double conjunctions, δὲ καί.

47. NIV has "He saved others," they said, "but he can't save himself!"

48. Bruce, *Expositor's*, 330.

49. TR and Maj.T have an extra αὐτόν after νῦν.

50. "gin he cares ocht for him" says Braid Scots.

51. NIV has "In the same way the robbers who were crucified with him also heaped insults on him."

52. TR and Maj.T do not have the preposition σύν and have αὐτῷ for αὐτόν.

53. NIV has "From the sixth hour."

54. McNeile, *Matthew*, 420.

55. NIV has "and offered it to Jesus to drink."

56. NIV has "Let's see if Elijah comes to save him."

57. See full discussion in A. T. Robertson, *An Introduction to the Textual Criticism of the New Testament* (Nashville: Broadman, 1925).

58. NIV has "he gave up his spirit."

59. William Stroud, *Treatise on the Physical Cause of the Death of Christ: And Its Relation to the Principles and Practice of Christianity*, 2d ed. (London: Hamilton, Adams & Co., 1871).

60. NIV has "the curtain of the temple was torn in two from top to bottom."

61. TR and Maj.T have τὸ καταπέτασμα τοῦ ἐσχίσθη εἰς δύο ἀπὸ ἄνωθεν ἕως κάτω.

62. Josephus, *Wars of the Jews*, 6.299.

63. Willoughby G. Allen, *A Critical and Exegetical Commentary on the Gospel According to Matthew*, International Critical Commentary (Edinburgh: T. & T. Clark, 1912), 296.

64. NIV has "The tombs broke open."

65. NIV has "As evening approached."

66. NIV has "Sir," they said, "we remember."

67. NIV has "This last deception."

68. NIV has "Take a guard."

69. James Hope Moulton and George Milligan, *The Vocabulary of the Greek Testament* (London: Hodder and Stoughton, 1952), 356.

70. McNeile, *Matthew*, 429.

71. NIV has "So they went and made the tomb secure by putting a seal on the stone and posting the guard."
72. Bruce, *Expositor's*, 335.
73. Plummer, *Matthew*, 410.

Matthew: Chapter 28

28:1. *Now after the Sabbath, as it began to dawn toward the first day of the week*[1] ('Οψὲ δὲ σαββάτων, τῇ ἐπιφωσκούσῃ εἰς μίαν σαββάτων). This careful chronological statement according to Jewish days means that before the Sabbath was over, that is before 6 P.M., the women went "to look at the grave" (θεωρῆσαι τὸν τάφον). They had seen the place of burial on Friday afternoon (Matt. 27:61; Mark 15:47; Luke 23:55). They had rested on the Sabbath after preparing spices and ointments for the body of Jesus (Luke 23:56). They had endured a Sabbath of unutterable sorrow and woe. They would buy other spices after sundown, when the new day has dawned and the Sabbath is over (Mark 16:1). Both Matthew here and Luke 23:54 use *dawn*, ἐπιφώσκω, for the dawning of the twenty-four-hour day at sunset, not the dawning of the twelve-hour day at sunrise. Aramaic used the verb for "dawn" in both senses. The so-called Gospel of Peter has ἐπιφώσκω in the same sense as Matthew and Luke, as does a late papyrus. Apparently the Jewish sense of "dawn" is here expressed by this Greek verb. Some suggest that Matthew misunderstands Mark at this point, but clearly Mark is speaking of sunrise and Matthew of sunset. Why allow only one visit for the anxious women?

28:2. *A severe earthquake had occurred*[2] (σεισμὸς ἐγένετο μέγας), clearly not the earthquake of 27:51. The precise time of this earthquake is not given. It was before sunrise on the first day of the week when the women made the next visit. Matthew alone relates the coming of the angel of the Lord who rolled away the stone and was sitting upon it (ἀπεκύλισεν τὸν λίθον καὶ ἐκάθητο ἐπάνω αὐτοῦ[3]). Anyone wishing to avoid talk of these supernatural phenomena should reflect that the resurrection of Jesus is one of the great supernatural events of all time. Cornelius Lapide dares to say: "The earth, which trembled with sorrow at the Death of Christ as it were leaped for joy at His Resurrection." The angel of the Lord announced the incarnation of the Son of God and also the Resurrection. There are apparent inconsistencies in the various narratives of the resurrection and appearances of the risen Christ. We do not know enough details to definitively reconcile the accounts. Ironically, the variations strengthen the argument that these are independent witnesses to the essential fact that Jesus rose from the grave. Each writer gives the account from his own vantage point. The stone was rolled away, not to let the Lord out but to let the women in to prove the fact of the empty tomb.[4]

28:3. *His appearance was like lightning* (ἦν δὲ ἡ εἰδέα αὐτοῦ ὡς ἀστραπή). Εἰδέα for "appearance" is found only here in the New Testament.[5] Compare εἰδέα with μορφή ("form or nature") and σχῆμα ("likeness or natural form").

28:4. *The guards shook for fear of him*[6] (ἀπὸ δὲ τοῦ φόβου αὐτοῦ ἐσείσθησαν οἱ τηροῦντες). No wonder that they became as dead men and fled before the women came.

28:5. *The angel said to the women* (ἀποκριθεὶς δὲ ὁ ἄγγελος εἶπεν ταῖς γυναιξίν). According to John, Mary Magdalene left to tell Peter and John of the supposed grave robbery (John 20:1–2). The other women remained and encountered the angel (or men, Luke 24:4) about the empty tomb and the risen Christ.

"Jesus who has been crucified"[7] (Ἰησοῦν τὸν ἐσταυρωμένον), accusative masculine singular perfect passive participle, a state of completion. This he will always be. So Paul in 1 Corinthians 2:2 preaches as essential to his gospel "this one crucified" (τοῦτον ἐσταυρωμένον).

28:6. *"He is not here, for He has risen"* (οὐκ ἔστιν ὧδε, ἠγέρθη γάρ), "Jesus the risen one." This is the heart of the testimony of the angel to the women. It is what Paul wishes Timothy never to forget (2 Tim. 2:8), "Jesus Christ risen from the dead" (Ἰησοῦν Χριστὸν ἐγηγερμένον ἐκ νεκρῶν).

"Come, see the place where He was lying"[8] (δεῦτε ἴδετε τὸν τόπον ὅπου ἔκειτο). They were afraid and dazzled by the glory of the scene. Critical Greek texts do not have ὁ κύριος, as in "where the Lord was lying," but Christ is the subject of ἔκειτο. His body was not there. It will not do to say that Jesus rose in spirit and appeared alive, though his body remained in the tomb. The empty tomb is the first great fact confronting the women and later the men. Various theories were offered then as now. None of the alternatives satisfy the evidence and explain the survival of faith and hope in the disciples. The only thing to account for the changes in the people was the fact of the risen Christ, whose body was no longer in the tomb.

28:7. *"He is going ahead of you into Galilee"* (προάγει ὑμᾶς εἰς τὴν Γαλιλαίαν). Jesus did appear to the disciples in Galilee on at least two notable occasions, by the beloved lake (John 21) and on the mountain (Matt. 28:16–20). Jesus appeared to various disciples in Jerusalem on this first great Sunday, probably before the women had the opportunity to tell of the appointment in Galilee in full to the disciples. They dismissed the women's first reports as idle talk (Luke 24:11). Jesus did not say that he would not see any of them in Jerusalem. He merely made a definite appointment in Galilee, which he kept.

28:8. *They left the tomb quickly with fear and great joy*[9] (ἀπελθοῦσα[10] ταχὺ ἀπὸ τοῦ μνημείου μετὰ φόβου καὶ χαρᾶς μεγάλης). The excited women ran quickly "to report it to His disciples" (ἀπαγγεῖλαι τοῖς μαθηταῖς αὐτοῦ). They had the greatest piece of news that it was possible to have. Mark calls it fear and ecstasy. Anything seemed possible now. Mark even says that at first they told no one anything for they were afraid (Mark 16:9), the tragic close of the text of Mark in Aleph and B, our two oldest manuscripts. But these mingled emotions of ecstasy and dread need cause no surprise when all things are considered.

28:9. *Jesus met them* (Ἰησοῦς ὑπήντησεν αὐταῖς[11]), came suddenly face-to-face with them as they brooded over the message of the angel and the fact of the empty tomb (associative instrumental, αὐταῖ"; cf. 8:34; 24:1–6). Probably the lost portion of Mark's Gospel contained the story of this meeting with Jesus, which changed their fears into joy and peace. His greeting was the ordinary "Hail." They fell at his feet and held them in reverence while they worshiped him. Jesus allowed this act of worship though he forbade eager handling of his body by Mary Magdalene (John 20:17). It was a great moment of faith and cheer.

28:10. *"Do not be afraid"* (Μὴ φοβεῖσθε). They were still afraid, with mixed joy and self-consciousness in the presence of divinity. Jesus calms their excitement by repeating the charge from the angel for the disciples to meet him in Galilee. There is no special mention of Peter as in Mark 16:7, but we may be sure that this is when Jesus delivered the special message to Peter.

28:11. *Some of the guard came into the city and reported to the chief priests* (τινες τῆς κουστωδίας ἐλθόντες εἰς τὴν πόλιν ἀπήγγειλαν τοῖς ἀρχιερεῦσιν). These Roman soldiers had been placed at the disposal of the Sanhedrin. They were probably afraid also to report to Pilate and tell him what had happened. They apparently told a truthful account as far as they understood it. But were the Sanhedrin convinced of the resurrection of Jesus?

28:12. *They gave a large sum of money to the soldiers* (ἀργύρια ἱκανὰ ἔδωκαν τοῖς στρατιώταις). The use of the plural for pieces of silver (ἀργύρια) is common. The papyri have many instances of ἱκανὰ for "considerable"[12] (from ἱκάνω, "to reach to, attain to"). These pious Sanhedrists knew full well the power of bribes. They make a contract with the Roman soldiers to tell a lie about the resurrection of Jesus as they paid Judas money to betray him. They show not the slightest tendency to be convinced by the facts.

28:13. *"'His disciples came by night and stole Him away while we were asleep'"* (Οἱ μαθηταὶ αὐτοῦ νυκτὸς ἐλθόντες ἔκλεψαν αὐτὸν ἡμῶν κοιμωμένων), a genitive absolute construction. If they were asleep they would not know anything about it.

28:14. *"We will win him over and keep you out of trouble"*[13] (ἡμεῖς πείσομεν [αὐτὸν] καὶ ὑμᾶς ἀμερίμνους ποιήσομεν). They would try money also on Pilate and assume all responsibility. Hence the soldiers have no anxiety (ἀμερίμνους, α privative and μεριμνάω, "to be anxious"). They lived up to their bargain and this lie lives on through the ages. Justin[14] accuses the Jews of spreading the charge.

28:15. *This story was widely spread among the Jews*[15] (διεφημίσθη ὁ λόγος οὗτος παρὰ Ἰουδαιοις). The Sanhedrin worked diligently to excuse their disbelief.

28:17. *But some were doubtful*[16] (οἱ δὲ ἐδίστασαν), from δίς ("in two, divided in mind," cf. 14:31). The reference is not to the eleven, who were all now convinced after some doubt, but to others. Paul states that more than five hundred were present at one or more encounters with the Lord. Most of them were still alive when he wrote (1 Cor. 15:6). It is natural that some should hesitate to believe so great a thing at the first appearance of Jesus to them. Their very doubt makes it easier for us to believe. This was the mountain where Jesus had promised to meet them. This fact explains the large number present. Time and place were arranged beforehand. It was the climax of the various appearances and in Galilee where were so many believers. They worshiped (προσεκύνησαν) Jesus as had the women (Matt. 28:9).

28:18. *"All authority has been given to Me"* (Ἐδόθη μοι πᾶσα ἐξουσία), a timeless aorist.[17] Jesus came close to them (προσελθών) and made this astounding claim that he now held the completeness of God's authority. He spoke as one already in heaven with a world outlook and the resources of heaven at his command. His authority or power during his earthly life had been great (e.g., 7:29; 11:27). Now it is boundless and includes earth and heaven. The risen Christ, without money or army or governmental state, charges this band of five hundred men and women to conquer the world. He brings them to believe that the task is possible if they undertake it with serious passion and power. Pentecost is still to come, but dynamic faith rules on this mountain in Galilee.

28:19. *"Make disciples of all the nations"* (μαθητεύσατε πάντα τὰ ἔθνη), not just the Jews scattered among the Gentiles, but the Gentiles themselves in every land. They are not to do it by making Jews of them, though this point is not made plain here. It will take time for the disciples to grow into this missions *Magna Carta*. But here is the world program of the risen Christ. It should not by forgotten by those who seek to foreshorten it all by saying that Jesus expected a quick return within the lifetime of those who heard. We are to leave the timing to the Father and push on the campaign for world conquest. This program includes making disciples or learners ($\mu\alpha\theta\eta\tau\epsilon\dot{\upsilon}\sigma\alpha\tau\epsilon$) like themselves. That means evangelism in the fullest sense. Baptism is *in* ($\epsilon\dot{\iota}\varsigma$, not *into*) the name of the Trinity—Father, Son, and Holy Spirit. Objection is raised that these words are too theological to be Jesus' own, so they must not be a genuine part of the Gospel of Matthew (cf. similar language in 11:27).[18] The name of Jesus is the essential part, as is shown in the Acts. Three-fold immersion is not taught. The use of *name* ($\ddot{o}\nu o\mu\alpha$) here is common in the LXX and papyri to mean "power or authority." For the use of $\epsilon\dot{\iota}\varsigma$ with $\ddot{o}\nu o\mu\alpha$ in this sense, see Matthew 10:41f. (cf. also 12:41).

28:20. *"Teaching them to observe all that I commanded you"*[19] ($\delta\iota\delta\dot{\alpha}\sigma\kappa o\nu\tau\epsilon\varsigma$ $\alpha\dot{\upsilon}\tau o\dot{\upsilon}\varsigma$ $\tau\eta\rho\epsilon\hat{\iota}\nu$ $\pi\dot{\alpha}\nu\tau\alpha$ $\ddot{o}\sigma\alpha$ $\dot{\epsilon}\nu\epsilon\tau\epsilon\iota\lambda\dot{\alpha}\mu\eta\nu$ $\dot{\upsilon}\mu\hat{\iota}\nu$). Christians have been slow to realize the full value of religious education. The work of teaching belongs to the home and the church. Good books should be in every home, plus the reading of the Bible itself. Some overreact and put education in the place of conversion or regeneration. But teaching is a weighty part of the work of Christians.

"I am with you always" ($\dot{\epsilon}\gamma\dot{\omega}$ $\mu\epsilon\theta$' $\dot{\upsilon}\mu\hat{\omega}\nu$ $\epsilon\dot{\iota}\mu\iota$ $\pi\dot{\alpha}\sigma\alpha\varsigma$ $\tau\dot{\alpha}\varsigma$ $\dot{\eta}\mu\dot{\epsilon}\rho\alpha\varsigma$). Jesus employs the prophetic present ($\epsilon\dot{\iota}\mu\iota$, I am). He is with us all the days until he comes in glory. He is to be with the disciples when he is gone, with all the disciples, with all knowledge, with all power, with them all the days (all sorts of days of weakness, sorrows, joy, and power).

"Even to the end of the age"[20] ($\ddot{\epsilon}\omega\varsigma$ $\tau\hat{\eta}\varsigma$ $\sigma\upsilon\nu\tau\epsilon\lambda\epsilon\dot{\iota}\alpha\varsigma$ $\tauo\hat{\upsilon}$ $\alpha\dot{\iota}\hat{\omega}\nuo\varsigma$). That goal is in the unknown future. This blessed hope is not a sedative to an inactive mind and complacent conscience, but an incentive to the fullest endeavor to press on to the farthest limits of the world, that all the nations may know Christ and the power of his risen life. So Matthew's Gospel closes in a blaze of glory. Christ is conqueror in prospect and in fact. Christian history has been the fulfilment of that promise insofar as God's power works in us. The risen, all-powerful Redeemer remains with his people all the time.

NOTES

1. NIV has "After the Sabbath, at dawn on the first day of the week."
2. NIV has "There was a violent earthquake."
3. TR and Maj.T have the prepositional phrase $\dot{\alpha}\pi\dot{o}$ $\tau\hat{\eta}\varsigma$ $\theta\dot{\upsilon}\rho\alpha\varsigma$ after $\tau\dot{o}\nu$ $\lambda\dot{\iota}\theta o\nu$; TRb and Maj.T eliminate the moveable ν on the verb $\dot{\alpha}\pi\epsilon\kappa\dot{\upsilon}\lambda\iota\sigma\epsilon$.

4. Alan Hugh McNeile, *The Gospel According to St. Matthew: The Greek Text with Introduction, Notes, and Indices* (repr. ed., Grand Rapids: Baker, 1980), 430.

5. TR and Maj.T have ἰδέα here.

6. NIV has "The guards were so afraid of him that they shook."

7. NIV has "Jesus, who was crucified."

8. NIV has "Come, see the place where he lay."

9. NIV has "So the women hurried away from the tomb, afraid yet filled with joy."

10. TR and Maj.T have the participle ἐξελθοῦσαι.

11. TR has the article with the proper noun, ὁ Ἰησοῦς. TR and Maj.T have ἀπήντησεν αὐταῖ".

12. James Hope Moulton and George Milligan, *The Vocabulary of the Greek Testament* (London: Hodder and Stoughton, 1952), 302.

13. NIV has "we will satisfy him, and keep you out of trouble."

14. *Dial*, 108.

15. NIV has "this story has been widely circulated among the Jews."

16. NIV has "but some doubted."

17. A. T. Robertson, *A Grammar of the Greek New Testament in the Light of Historical Research* (Nashville: Broadman, 1934), 836f.

18. Robertson devotes a chapter to this subject in *The Christ of the Logia* (New York: Doran, 1924).

19. NIV has "teaching them to obey everything I have commanded you."

20. NIV has "to the very end of the age."

THE GOSPEL ACCORDING TO
MARK

Introduction to Mark

One of the clearest results of modern critical study of the Gospels is the early date of Mark's Gospel. Precisely how early is not definitely known, but there are leading scholars who hold that A.D. 50 is quite probable. My own views are given in detail in my *Studies in Mark's Gospel.*[1] Theodor Zahn argues that the Gospel according to Matthew was written earlier than was Mark, but there are compelling arguments not to accept this time sequence as the accurate one.[2] The framework of Mark's Gospel appears to lie behind both Matthew and Luke and nearly all of it is used by one or the other. A careful comparison of similarities and differences in content, using a harmony of the Gospels in Greek or English, suggests that Mark was available to the writers of Matthew and Luke. It is possible that Mark used some earlier collection of recorded notes or sayings that might correspond to what critics call "*Q,*" but that would only mean that the theoretical *Q* joins Mark as sources for Matthew and Luke. Whatever might be said of *Q,* Mark's work is the one that survives, despite its use by Matthew and Luke. For this preservation we are all grateful. Streeter (*The Four Gospels*[3]) has emphasized the local use of texts in preserving portions of the New Testament.

If Mark wrote in Rome, as is quite possible, his book had a powerful environment in which to take root. It has distinctive merits of its own that helped to keep it in use. It is mainly narrative and the style is direct and simple with vivid touches. It uses the historical present tense of an eyewitness. Early writers testify that Mark was the interpreter for Simon Peter, with whom he was at one time, according to Peter's own statement, either in Babylon or Rome (1 Peter 5:13). Although this Gospel is the briefest of the four, it is densely packed with details that a close associate of Jesus, such as Peter, might have used in his discourses. Mark describes green grass, flower beds (6:39), two thousand hogs (5:13), and the physical nuances that accompanied Christ's words (e.g., 3:5, 34).

Peter would have spoken in Aramaic, and Mark has more Aramaic phrases than do the other records: *Boanerges* (3:17); *Talitha cumi* (5:41); *Korbaᵓn* (7:11); *Ephphatha* (7:34); and *Abba* (14:36). The Greek is distinctively

257

vernacular κοινή, for example one-eyed (μονόφθαλμον, 9:47) as one would expect from Palestinian Jews such as Peter and Mark. There also are more Latin phrases and idioms than in the other Gospels: *centurion* (15:39); *quadrans* (12:42); *flagellare* (15:15); *speculator* (6:27); *census* (12:14); *sextarius* (7:4); and *praetorium* (15:6). C. H. Turner wonders if Mark might have written the autograph (original manuscript) in Latin. The Latin influence at least adds evidence for a writing in Rome. Some linguists hold that Mark wrote first in Aramaic, but the Aramaic feel to the text also could be explained if Mark was working from his notes of Peter's preaching in Aramaic to Jews in Rome. Mark might have written the Gospel in Rome while with Peter, who would have read the manuscript.

B. W. Bacon holds that this Gospel has a distinct Pauline flavor and may have had several recensions.[4] The *Ur-Marcus* theory no longer enjoys strong support. Mark was once a coworker with Barnabas and Paul but deserted them at Perga. Paul held this against Mark and refused to take him on the second mission tour. Barnabas took Mark, his cousin, with him and then he appeared with Simon Peter with whom he did his greatest work. When Mark made good with Barnabas and Peter, Paul rejoiced and commends him heartily to the Colossians (Col. 4:10). In the end Paul asks Timothy to bring Mark along with him to Rome, for Paul has found Mark useful for ministry. Such a reference to the man who had made such a mistake that Paul would have no more of him throws credit upon both of them.[5]

The character of the Gospel of Mark is determined largely by the scope of Peter's preaching as we see it in Acts 10:36–42, covering the period from John the Baptist to the Resurrection. There is nothing about the birth of the Baptist or of Jesus. This peculiarity of Mark's Gospel cannot be used against the narratives of the virgin birth of Jesus in Matthew and Luke, since Mark tells nothing whatever about Jesus' birth.

The closing passage in the Textus Receptus, Mark 16:9–20, is not found in the oldest Greek Manuscripts, Aleph and B, and probably is not genuine. A discussion of the evidence for this conclusion will appear at the proper place.

Henry Swete points out that Mark deals with two great themes: the ministry in Galilee (chs. 1–9) and the last week in Jerusalem (chs. 11–16). These are joined by a brief sketch of the period of withdrawal from Galilee (ch. 10). The first fourteen verses are introductory, and 16:9–20 is an appendix.

The Gospel of Mark pictures Christ in action. There is a minimum of discourse and a maximum of deed. Yet the same essential pictures of Christ appear as in the writings of Matthew, Luke, John, Paul, Peter, and the writer of

Hebrews.[6] The Jesus of Mark is the Christ of Paul. Each account has its own shading, but the same picture. Christ is Son of God and Son of Man, Lord of life and death, Worker of miracles, and Savior from sin. This Gospel is the one for children to read first and the one by which we should lay the foundation for our view of Christ. In Robertson's *Harmony of the Gospels* Mark is placed first in the framework, since Matthew, Luke, and John follow in broad outline his plan, with additions and supplemental materials.[7]

Mark throbs with life and bristles with vivid details. We see with Peter's eyes and catch almost the very look and gesture of Jesus as he moved among men in his work of healing men's bodies and saving men's souls.

NOTES

1. A. T. Robertson, *Studies in Mark's Gospel* (1919; repr ed., Nashville: Broadman, 1958).

2. Theodor Zahn, *Geschichte des neutestamentlichen Kanons* (Erlangen: 1888–92).

3. Burnett Hillman Streeter, *The Four Gospels: A Study of Origins, Treating of the Manuscript Tradition, Sources, Authorship, and Dates* (London: Macmillan, 1924).

4. Benjamin Wisner Bacon, *An Introduction to the New Testament* (London: Macmillan, 1924). Here and elsewhere in this volume, a number of higher critical theories are referred to without critique. References to them should be regarded as information that does not indicate acceptance.

5. This is shown in A. T. Robertson, *Making Good in the Ministry: A Sketch of John Mark* (1918; repr. ed., Grand Rapids: Baker, 1976).

6. As shown in A. T. Robertson, *The Christ of the Logia* (New York: Doran, 1924).

7. A. T. Robertson, *Harmony of the Gospels for Students of the Life of Christ* (New York: Harper and Row, 1922).

Mark: Chapter 1

1:1. *The beginning of the gospel* (Ἀρχὴ τοῦ εὐαγγελίου). There is no article for ἀρχή in the Greek. It is possible that the phrase served as a heading or title for the paragraph about the ministry of the Baptist or as the superscription for the whole Gospel[1] placed either by Mark or a scribe. And then "the gospel of Jesus Christ" means the message about Jesus Christ (objective genitive). The word *gospel* (εὐαγγέλιον) comes close to meaning the record itself as told by Mark. Swete notes that each writer has a different starting point (ἀρχή).[2] Mark, as the earliest form of the evangelic tradition, begins with the work of the Baptist, Matthew with the ancestry and birth of the Messiah, Luke with the birth of the Baptist, John with the preincarnate Logos, Paul with the foundation of each of the churches (Phil. 4:15).

The Son of God ([υἱοῦ θεοῦ]).[3] If this is a heading added to what Mark wrote, the heading may have existed early in two forms, one with and one without "Son of God." If Mark wrote the words, there is no reason to doubt that they are genuine since he uses such a construction elsewhere.

1:2. *In Isaiah the prophet* (ἐν τῷ Ἡσαΐᾳ τῷ προφήτῃ). The quotation comes from Malachi 3:1 and Isaiah 40:3.[4] But Isaiah is the chief of the prophets. It was common to combine quotations from different prophets in *testimonia* and *catenae* (chains of quotations). This is Mark's only prophetic quotation, although he records quotations by Jesus.[5]

1:3. *"The voice of one crying in the wilderness"*[6] (φωνὴ βοῶντος ἐν τῇ ἐρήμῳ). God is coming to his people to deliver them from their captivity in Babylon. So the prophet cries like a voice in the wilderness to make ready for the coming of God. When the committee from the Sanhedrin asked John who he was, he used this very language of Isaiah (John 1:23). He was only a voice, but that voice still echoes through the corridor of centuries.

"Make His paths straight"[7] (εὐθείας ποιεῖτε τὰς τρίβους αὐτοῦ). The wonderful Persian roads for the couriers of the king and for the king himself were much like fine automobile highways. Such roads knit together the Roman Empire. Sections of these roads survive. In this comparison Mark testifies that John had a high and holy mission as the forerunner of the Messiah.

261

1:4. *John the Baptist appeared*[8] (ἐγένετο Ἰωάννης [ὁ][9] βαπτίζων). His coming was an epoch (ἐγένετο), not a mere event (ἦν). His coming was in accordance with the prophetic picture (καθὼς, v. 2). Note that the same verb about John occurs in John 1:6. The coming of John the Baptizer was the real beginning of the spoken message about Christ. Mark describes him as "the baptizing one (ὁ βαπτίζων) in the wilderness (ἐν τῇ ἐρήμῳ)." The baptizing took place in the River Jordan (Mark 1:5, 9) in an area encompassing the wilderness of Judea.

Preaching a baptism of repentance (κηρύσσων βάπτισμα μετανοίας), heralded a repentance centered baptism (βάπτισμα, genitive genus case). See on Matthew 3:2 for discussion of *repent*, which is an exceedingly poor rendering of John's great word μετανοέω. He called upon the Jews to change their minds and to turn from their sins, "confessing their sins" (ἐξομολογούμενοι τὰς ἁμαρτίας αὐτῶν in Mark 1:5; see Matt. 3:16). The public confessions produced a profound impression, as they would now.

For the forgiveness of sins (εἰς ἄφεσιν ἁμαρτιῶν) is a difficult phrase to translate accurately. Certainly John did not mean that the baptism was the means of obtaining the forgiveness of their sins or necessary to the remission of sins. The trouble lies in the use of εἰς, which sometimes expresses purpose and at other times has no such implication (as in Matt. 10:41; 12:41). Probably "with reference to" is as good a translation as is possible. The baptism was on the basis of the repentance and confession of sin. As Paul later explained (Rom. 6:4), it pictured death to sin and resurrection to new life in Christ. The symbol was used to mark the rebirth of Gentile proselytes into full membership among the children of Abraham. John is treating the Jewish nation as a collection of pagans who need to repent, to confess their sins, and to come into the kingdom of God. The baptism in the Jordan was the objective challenge to the people.

1:5. *And all the country of Judea was going out to him*[10] (καὶ ἐξεπορεύετο πρὸς αὐτὸν πᾶσα ἡ Ἰουδαία χώρα). Third person singular imperfect middle/ passive deponent indicative describes the steady stream of people who kept coming to the baptism (ἐβαπτίζοντο, third person plural imperfect passive indicative), a wonderful sight. The baptism was literally "in the Jordan River" (ἐν τῷ Ἰορδάνῃ ποταμῷ).

1:6. *John was clothed with camel's hair*[11] (καὶ ἦν[12] ὁ Ἰωάννης[13] ἐνδεδυμένος τρίχας καμήλου). Matthew 3:4 has it a "garment" (ἔνδυμα) of camel's hair. Matthew places *garment* in the nominative singular masculine perfect passive participle with hair, its object, in the accusative feminine plural, according to common Greek idiom. It was not made of tanned skin but rough cloth woven of camel's hair. For the locusts and wild honey, see on Matthew 3:4. Dried locusts are considered palatable. The wild honey, or "mountain honey" as some versions give it ($\mu\acute{\epsilon}\lambda\iota$ $\check{\alpha}\gamma\rho\iota o\nu$), was bountiful in the clefts of rocks. Some Bedouins still make their living by gathering this wild honey out of the rocks.

1:7. *"After me One is coming who is mightier than I"*[14] ($^{"}E\rho\chi\epsilon\tau\alpha\iota$ $\acute{o}$ $\iota\sigma\chi\upsilon\rho\acute{o}\tau\epsilon\rho\acute{o}\varsigma$ $\mu o\upsilon$ $\acute{o}\pi\acute{\iota}\sigma\omega$ $\mu o\upsilon$), found in each of the Synoptics. Gould calls this language skeptical self-depreciation.[15] But John was sincere in appraising the difference in status between himself and the coming Messiah. The "thong"[16] ($\tau\grave{o}\nu$ $\iota\mu\acute{\alpha}\nu\tau\alpha$) held the sandal together. When guests came to wealthy homes a slave untied their sandles before they bathed. Mark alone gives this touch.

1:8. *"I baptized you with water"*[17] ($\acute{\epsilon}\gamma\grave{\omega}$ $\acute{\epsilon}\beta\acute{\alpha}\pi\tau\iota\sigma\alpha$ $\acute{\upsilon}\mu\hat{\alpha}\varsigma$ $\check{\upsilon}\delta\alpha\tau\iota$[18]). So Luke 3:16 has "with water." Matthew 3:11 has $\acute{\epsilon}\nu$ ("in") water and the Holy Spirit. The water baptism by John was a symbol of the spiritual baptism by Jesus.

1:9. *[Jesus] was baptized by John in the Jordan* ($\acute{\epsilon}\beta\alpha\pi\tau\acute{\iota}\sigma\theta\eta$ $\epsilon\acute{\iota}\varsigma$ $\tau\grave{o}\nu$ $^{'}I o\rho\delta\acute{\alpha}\nu\eta\nu$ $\acute{\upsilon}\pi\grave{o}$ $^{'}I\omega\acute{\alpha}\nu\nu o\upsilon$[19]). This construction follows "out of the water" ($\acute{\epsilon}\kappa$ $\tau o\hat{\upsilon}$ $\check{\upsilon}\delta\alpha\tau o\varsigma$) in verse 10, after the baptism into the Jordan. Mark is as fond of using the term *immediately* ($\epsilon\acute{\upsilon}\theta\grave{\upsilon}\varsigma$) as Matthew is of *then* ($\tau\acute{o}\tau\epsilon$).

1:10. *He saw the heavens opening*[20] ($\epsilon\hat{\iota}\delta\epsilon\nu$ $\sigma\chi\iota\zeta o\mu\acute{\epsilon}\nu o\upsilon\varsigma$ $\tau o\grave{\upsilon}\varsigma$ $o\acute{\upsilon}\rho\alpha\nu o\acute{\upsilon}\varsigma$), split like a garment (accusative plural masculine present passive participle). Jesus saw the heavens parting as he came up out of the water, a more vivid picture than "opened" in Matthew 3:16 and Luke 3:21. Evidently the Baptist saw the Holy Spirit coming down upon Jesus as a dove because his own description is quoted in John 1:32. Cerinthian Gnostics took the dove to mean the heavenly *aeon Christ* that here descended upon the man Jesus and remained with him until he was crucified, at which point it left him. They made the same sort of distinction as sometimes is attempted today between the "Jesus of history" and the "theological Christ."

1:11. *"You are My beloved Son"*[21] ($\Sigma\grave{\upsilon}$ $\epsilon\hat{\iota}$ $\acute{o}$ $\upsilon\acute{\iota}\acute{o}\varsigma$ $\mu o\upsilon$ $\acute{o}$ $\acute{\alpha}\gamma\alpha\pi\eta\tau\acute{o}\varsigma$), so Luke 3:22. Matthew 3:17 has "This is My beloved Son" ($o\hat{\upsilon}\tau\acute{o}\varsigma$ $\acute{\epsilon}\sigma\tau\iota\nu$ $\acute{o}$ $\upsilon\acute{\iota}\acute{o}\varsigma$ $\mu o\upsilon$ $\acute{o}$ $\acute{\alpha}\gamma\alpha\pi\eta\tau\acute{o}\varsigma$). Both Mark and Luke have "In You I am well-pleased" while Matthew has "in whom."

1:12. *Immediately the Spirit impelled Him*[22] ($\epsilon\acute{\upsilon}\theta\grave{\upsilon}\varsigma$ $\tau\grave{o}$ $\pi\nu\epsilon\hat{\upsilon}\mu\alpha$ $\alpha\acute{\upsilon}\tau\grave{o}\nu$ $\acute{\epsilon}\kappa\beta\acute{\alpha}\lambda\lambda\epsilon\iota$), a vivid verb, bolder than Matthew's "was led up" ($\acute{\alpha}\nu\acute{\eta}\chi\theta\eta$) and Luke's "was led" ($\mathring{\eta}\gamma\epsilon\tau o$). The same word is employed for the driving out of demons (vv. 34, 39). Mark has here "immediately" where Matthew has "then" (see on v. 9). The forty days in the wilderness were under the direct guidance of the Holy Spirit. The entire earthly life of Jesus was bound up with the Holy Spirit.

1:13. *And He was with the wild beasts*[23] (καὶ ἦν μετὰ τῶν θηρίων). Mark does not give the narrative of the three temptations found in Matthew and Luke, but he adds this little touch about the wild beasts in the wilderness. At night this rocky desert was the haunt of the wolf, the boar, the hyena, the jackal, and the leopard. It was lonely and even dangerous in its isolation. In Psalm 91:13 the promise of victory over the wild beasts comes immediately after that of angelic guardianship cited by Satan in Matthew 4:6.[24] The angels did come and "minister" (διηκόνουν), third person plural imperfect active indicative. They kept it up till he was cheered and strengthened.

1:14. *Jesus came into Galilee*[25] (ἦλθεν ὁ Ἰησοῦς εἰς τὴν Γαλιλαίαν). Mark is followed by Matthew and Luke in opening the narrative of Jesus' active ministry. Mark undoubtedly follows the preaching of Peter. But for the Fourth Gospel, we should not know of the year of work in various parts of the land (Perea, Galilee, Judea, Samaria) preceding the Galilean ministry. John supplements the Synoptic Gospels. The arrest of John influenced Jesus to depart from Judea to Galilee (John 4:1-4).

Preaching the gospel of God[26] (κηρύσσων τὸ εὐαγγέλιον τοῦ θεοῦ[27]). This is the subjective genitive, referring to the gospel that comes from God. Swete observes that repentance (μετανοία) is the keynote in the message of the Baptist as gospel (εὐαγγέλιον) is with Jesus.[28] But Jesus with John proclaimed both repentance and the arrival of the kingdom of God.

1:15. *"The time is fulfilled"*[29] (Πεπλήρωται ὁ καιρός). Mark adds these words to Matthew's report. John looks backward to the promise of the coming of the Messiah and signifies that fulfilment is near at hand (third person singular perfect passive indicative). John's theme is like Paul's "fullness of time" (πλήρωματος τοῦ χρόνου) in Galatians 4:4 and "fullness of the times" (πλήρωμα τῶν καιρῶν) in Ephesians 1:10. In Ephesians 1, he employs the word καιρός, "opportunity or crisis," as here in Mark, rather than the more general term χρόνος.

"And believe in the gospel"[30] (καὶ πιστεύετε ἐν τῷ εὐαγγελίῳ), both repent and believe in the gospel. Usually faith in Jesus as God is expected, as in John 14:1. But this crisis called for faith in the message of Jesus that the Messiah had come. He did not use here the term *Messiah*, for that term had provocative political connotations. But the kingdom of God had arrived with the presence of the King. Belief or disbelief in the message of Jesus sharply divided those who heard him. "Faith in the message was the first step; a creed

of some kind lies at the basis of confidence in the person of Christ, and the occurrence of the phrase πιστεύετε ἐν τῷ εὐαγγελίῳ in the oldest record of the teaching of our Lord is a valuable witness to this fact."[31]

1:16. *As He was going along by the Sea of Galilee*[32] (Καὶ παράγων παρὰ τὴν θάλασσαν τῆς Γαλιλαίας[33]). Mark uses παρά ("along, beside") twice and makes the picture realistic. He catches this glimpse of Christ in action.

Casting a net (ἀμφιβάλλοντας[34]), literally casting on both sides, now on one side, now on the other. Matthew 4:18 has a different phrase. Two papryi use the verb ἀμφιβάλλω, one verb absolutely for fishing as here, the other with the accusative.[35] These four disciples were fishermen (ἁλιεῖς) and were partners, as Luke 5:7 states (μετόχοις).

1:17. *"Follow Me, and I will make you become fishers of men"*[36] (Δεῦτε ὀπίσω μου, καὶ ποιήσω ὑμᾶς γενέσθαι ἁλιεῖς ἀνθρώπων). Mark has γενέσθαι, which is not in Matthew. It would be a slow and long process, but Jesus would make fishers of men out of fishermen. Fishers of men are made out of any willing to leave all to serve Christ.

1:19. *Going on a little farther*[37] (Καὶ προβὰς ὀλίγον[38]), a Marcan detail.

Mending the nets[39] (καταρτίζοντας τὰ δίκτυα). Compare this with Matthew 4:21. They were getting ready, that they might succeed better at the next haul.

1:20. *They left their father Zebedee in the boat with the hired servants*[40] (ἀφέντες τὸν πατέρα αὐτῶν Ζεβεδαῖον ἐν τῷ πλοίῳ μετὰ τῶν μισθωτῶν). Μισθός, "one hired for wages," is a very old Greek word. Zebedee and his two sons evidently had an extensive business in cooperation with Andrew and Simon (Luke 5:7, 10). Mark alone has this detail of the hired servants left with Zebedee. They left the boat and their father (Matt. 4:22) with the hired servants. The business would go on while they left all (Luke 5:11) and became permanent followers of Jesus.

1:21. *He entered the synagogue and began to teach*[41] (εἰσελθὼν εἰς τὴν συναγωγὴν ἐδίδασκεν), inchoative (ingressive) imperfect. He began to teach as soon as he entered the synagogue in Capernaum on the Sabbath. The synagogue in Capernaum afforded the best opening for Jesus. He had made Capernaum (Tell Hum) his headquarters after Nazareth rejected him (see Matt. 4:13–16; Luke 4:16-31). Ruins of an ancient Capernaum synagogue have been discovered. Jesus both taught (ἐδίδασκεν) and preached (ἐκήρυσσεν) in the Jewish synagogues as opportunity was offered by the chief or leader of the synagogue (ἀρχισυνάγωγος). The service consisted of prayer, praise, reading of Scripture, and exposition by a rabbi or competent person. Paul spoke at such meetings. Luke 4:20 describes Jesus reading then giving back the roll of Isaiah to the attendant or beadle (τῷ ὑπηρέτῃ), who saw to it that the precious manuscript remained safe. Jesus had preached for over a year when he began to teach in the Capernaum synagogue. His reputation had preceded him (v. 14).

1:22. *They were amazed at His teaching*[42] (ἐξεπλήσσοντο ἐπὶ τῇ διδαχῇ αὐτοῦ). A pictorial imperfect as in Luke 4:32 describing the amazement of the audience, "meaning strictly to strike a person out of his senses by some strong feeling, such as fear, wonder, or even joy."[43]

As one having authority, and not as the scribes[44] (ὡς ἐξουσίαν ἔχων καὶ οὐχ ὡς οἱ γραμματεῖς). Luke 4:32 has only "with authority" (ἐν ἐξουσίᾳ), while Mark has "as one having authority" (ὡς ἐξουσίαν ἔχων).[45] He struck a note not found by the rabbis. They quoted other rabbis and felt their function to be expounders of the traditions, which they hung around the necks of the people like a millstone. Their traditions and petty legalism actually transgressed God's revealed law (Mark 7:9, 13). The scribes were casuists who made false interpretations to prove their punctilious points of external etiquette to the utter neglect of spiritual reality. The people noticed at once that here was someone who got his power (authority) from God. This was unlike the authority of the scribes, who drew only on leading rabbis.[46] Matthew 7:29 describes a similar impression made on those who listened to the Sermon on the Mount. Christ's chief controversy was with the professional teachers of the oral law. His independence from the old group made a sensation in the best sense of the word. The buzz of excitement only increased with the miracle that followed the sermon.

1:23. *There was a man in their synagogue with an unclean spirit*[47] (ἦν ἐν τῇ συναγωγῇ αὐτῶν ἄνθρωπος ἐν πνεύματι ἀκαθάρτῳ). The use of ἐν ("in") relating to the evil spirit in the man is common in the Septuagint, like the Hebrew "be," but it occurs also in the papyri. It is the same idiom as "in Christ" or "in the Lord" that is common with Paul. In English we speak of our being "in love." The unclean spirit was in the man and the man in the unclean spirit, a man in the power of the unclean spirit. Luke speaks of people *having* an evil spirit (see also Matt. 22:43). *Unclean spirit* here is synonymous with *demon*. It is the idea of a spirit estranged from God (Zech. 13:2). The whole subject of demonology is difficult, but no more so than the problem of the Devil. Jesus distinguishes between the man and the unclean spirit. Usually physical or mental disease accompanied the possession by demons.

1:24. *"What business do we have with each other"*[48] (Τί ἡμῖν καὶ σοί), the same idiom in Matthew 8:29, an ethical dative. There is nothing in common between the demon and Jesus. Note use of the plural *we*. The man speaks for the demon and himself, a double personality. Note that demons recognized Jesus, while the rabbis failed to do so. Demons call Jesus "the Holy One of God" (ὁ ἅγιος τοῦ θεοῦ). The demon feared that Jesus was come to destroy him and the man in his power. In Matthew 8:29 a demon calls Jesus "Son of God." Later the disciples will call Jesus "The Holy One of God" (John 6:69). The demon cried out aloud (ἀνέκραξεν, late first aorist form, ἀνέκραγεν, common second aorist), so that all heard the strange testimony to Jesus. In various text families the man says "I know" (οἶδά) or "we know" (οἴδαμεν), the plural meant to include the demon.

1:25. *"Be quiet!"* (φιμώθητι). First aorist passive imperative of φιμόω. "Be quiet," Moffatt translates it. But it is a more vigorous word, "Be muzzled," like an ox. So literally in Deuteronomy 25:4; 1 Corinthians 9:9; and 1 Timothy 5:18. It is common in Josephus, Lucian, and the LXX (see Matt. 22:12, 34). It may be rendered "Shut up." "Shut your mouth" would be too colloquial. Vincent suggests "gagged," [49] but that is more the idea of ἐπιστομαζεῖν in Titus 1:11, "to stop the mouth."

1:26. *Throwing him into convulsions*[50] (σπαράξαν αὐτόν) or "convulsing him." Medical writers use a related English word for the rotating of the stomach. Luke 4:35 adds "when the demon had thrown him down in the midst." Mark mentions the "loud voice" (φωνῇ μεγάλῃ) or screech. It was a moment of intense excitement.

1:27. *They debated among themselves* (συζητεῖν πρὸς ἑαυτοὺς λέγοντας[51]), by look and word.

A new teaching with authority[52] (διδαχὴ καινὴ κατ᾽ ἐξουσίαν[53]). One surprise had followed another this day. The teaching was fresh (καινή), original as morning dew on the blossoms. That was a novelty in that synagogue, where only staid and stilted rabbinical rules had droned out. This new teaching charmed the people, but it would soon be rated as heresy by the rabbis. And it was "with authority" (κατ᾽ ἐξουσίαν). It is not certain whether the phrase is to be taken with "new teaching." Moffatt has it, "It's new teaching with authority behind it." Or it can be taken with the verb: "with authority commands even the unclean spirits" (καὶ τοῖς πνεύμασι τοῖς ἀκαθάρτοις ἐπιτάσσει). The position is equivocal and may be due to the fact that "Mark gives the incoherent and excited remarks of the crowd in this natural roughness."[54] But the most astonishing thing is that the demons "obey Him" (ὑπακούουσιν αὐτῷ). The people were accustomed to the use of magical formulae by exorcists

(Matt. 12:27; Acts 19:13), but here was something utterly different. Simon Magus could not understand how Simon Peter could do miracles without trickery (Acts 8:19).

1:28. *The news about Him.*[55] (ἡ ἀκοὴ αὐτοῦ), The Vulgate term used for "news" can be translated "rumor" (see Matt. 14:1; 24:6). They had no telephones, telegraphs, newspapers, or radio, but news spread quickly by word of mouth. The fame of this new teacher went "everywhere" (πανταχοῦ[56]) throughout Galilee.

1:29. *They came into the house of Simon and Andrew*[57] (ἦλθον εἰς τὴν οἰκίαν Σίμωνος καὶ Ἀνδρέου). Peter and Andrew lived together in Peter's house (Matt. 8:14) with Peter's wife and mother-in-law. Peter evidently was married before he began to follow Jesus. Later his wife accompanied him on his apostolic journeys (1 Cor. 9:5). This incident followed immediately after the service in the synagogue on the Sabbath. All the Synoptics give it. Mark heard Peter tell it as it occurred in his own house, where Jesus made his home while in Capernaum.

1:30. *Simon's mother-in-law was lying sick with a fever*[58] (ἡ δὲ πενθερὰ Σίμωνος κατέκειτο πυρέσσουσα). She lay prostrate burning with fever. Each Gospel gives individual touches to the story. Matthew 8:14 describes the woman as "lying sick in bed (βεβλημένην) with a fever." Luke 4:38 uses a more precise medical description to say she was "suffering from a high fever" (ἦν συνεχομένη πυρετῷ μεγαλῷ). Accounts mention the instant recovery, without any convalescence. Mark and Matthew 8:14–15 speak of the touch of Jesus on her hand and Luke 4:39 speaks of Jesus standing over her like a doctor in this tender scene.

1:32. *After the sun had set*[59] (ὅτε ἔδυ ὁ ἥλιος). Mark uses this picturesque phrase to expand on his statement "when evening came"[60] (Ὀψίας δὲ γενομένης, a genitive absolute, "evening having come"). Matthew has "when evening was come," Luke "when the sun was setting." The Sabbath ended at sunset, so people were at liberty to bring their sick to Jesus. The news about the casting out of the demon and the healing of Peter's mother-in-law had spread all over Capernaum. They brought a steady stream (imperfect tense, ἔφερον). Luke 4:40 adds that Jesus laid his hand on each of them as they passed by in grateful procession.

1:33 *The whole city had gathered at the door*[61] (ἦν ὅλη ἡ πόλις ἐπισυνηγμένη πρὸς τὴν θύραν[62]). Outside Peter's house, people from all around gathered, a past perfect passive periphrastic construction, double compound ἐπί and σύν. Mark alone mentions this vivid detail. He is seeing through

Peter's eyes again. Peter no doubt watched the beautiful scene with pride and gratitude as Jesus stood in the door and healed the great crowds in the glory of that sunset. He must have loved to describe this scene.

1:34. *He healed many who were ill with various diseases*[63] (ἐθεράπευσεν πολλοὺς κακῶς ἔχοντας ποικίλαις νόσοις). See on Matthew 4:24 regarding ποικίλος, meaning "many-colored or variegated." All sorts of sick folk came and were healed.

He was not permitting the demons to speak[64] (οὐκ ἤφιεν λαλεῖν τὰ δαιμόνια). He would not allow, imperfect tense of continued refusal. The reason given is that "they knew who He was" (ὅτι ᾔδεισαν αὐτόν). "To be Christ" (Χριστὸν εἶναι) is a direct reference to 1:24, when in the synagogue the demon recognized and addressed Jesus as the Holy One of God. Testimony from such a source would not help the cause of Christ with the people. He had told the other demon to be silent (see discussion of the word *demon* relating to Matt. 8:29).

1:35. *In the early morning, while it was still dark*[65] (πρωῒ ἔννυχα λίαν[66]). Luke has only "when it was day" (γενομένης ἡμέρας). Πρωῒ in Mark means the last watch of the night, from 3 A.M. to 6 A.M. (see on 6:48). Ἔννυχα λίαν means in the early part of the watch while it was still a bit dark (cf. Mark 16:2, λίαν πρωῒ).

[Jesus] got up, and left [the house] (ἀναστὰς ἐξῆλθεν), out of the house and city (ἀπῆλθεν). Ezra Gould notes that Jesus seems to retreat before his sudden popularity, to pray with the Father "that he might not be ensnared by this popularity, or in any way induced to accept the ways of ease instead of duty."[67] But Jesus also had a plan for a preaching tour of Galilee, and "He felt He could not begin too soon. He left in the night, fearing opposition from the people."[68] Jesus knew what it was to spend a whole night in prayer. He knew the blessing of prayer and the power of prayer.

And was praying there[69] (κἀκεῖ προσηύχετο). Imperfect tense picturing Jesus as praying through the early morning hours.

1:36. *Simon and his companions searched for Him*[70] (κατεδίωξεν αὐτὸν Σίμων καὶ οἱ μετ' αὐτοῦ[71]), "hunted Him out" (Moffatt), perfective use of the preposition κατά ("down to the finish"). The verb διώκω is used for the hunt of chase or pursuit. Vulgate has *persecutus est*. The personal story of Peter comes in here. "Simon's intention at least was good; the Master seemed to be losing precious opportunities and must be brought back."[72] Peter and those with him kept up the search until they found him. The message that they brought surely would bring Jesus back to Peter's house.

1:38. *"Let us go somewhere else to the towns nearby"*[73] (Ἄγωμεν ἀλλαχοῦ εἰς τὰς ἐχομένας κωμοπόλεις[74]). It was a surprising decision for Jesus to leave the eager, excited throngs in Capernaum for the country town without walls or much importance. Κωμοπόλεις, a late Greek word for "villages," is not used elsewhere in the New Testament. The use of ἐχομένας, "next," means "clinging to or next to a thing" (so in Luke 13:33; Acts 13:44; 20:15; Heb. 6:9). Text D has ἐγγύς (near).

1:39. *He went into their synagogues throughout all Galilee, preaching*[75] (ἦλθεν κηρύσσων εἰς τὰς συναγωγὰς αὐτῶν εἰς ὅλην τὴν Γαλιλαίαν[76]). We are told little about this first preaching tour of Galilee by Jesus.

1:40. *Falling on his knees*[77] ([καὶ γονυπετῶν][78]), picturesque detail omitted by some manuscripts. Luke 5:12 has "fell on his face."

1:41. *Moved with compassion*[79] (σπλαγχνισθείς), only in Mark, first aorist passive participle.

1:43. *He sternly warned him and immediately sent him away*[80] (καὶ ἐμβριμησάμενος αὐτῷ εὐθὺς[81] ἐξέβαλεν αὐτόν), an intensity to Christ's command used only in Mark. Luke 5:14 has παρήγγειλεν, "commanded." Ἐμβριμησάμενος occurs also in 14:5 and in Matthew 9:30 and John 11:38 (see on Matt. 9:30; Mark 14:5). It is a strong word for the snorting of a horse and expressed powerful emotion as Jesus stood face-to-face with leprosy, itself a symbol of sin and all its train of evils. The command to report to the priests was in accord with the Mosaic regulations (Lev. 14:2–32) and the prohibition against talking about it was to allay excitement and to avoid needless opposition.

1:44. *As a testimony to them* (εἰς μαρτύριον αὐτοῖς). Without the formal testimony of the priests, the people would not receive the leper as officially clean.

1:45. *Began to proclaim it freely*[82] (ἤρξατο κηρύσσειν πολλά). Luke 5:15 puts it, "so much the more" (μᾶλλον). One of the best ways to spread a story is to warn people not to tell it. This certainly was the case here. Soon Jesus had to stay in rural areas to avoid the crowds. Even then people kept coming to Jesus (ἤρχοντο, imperfect tense).

NOTES

1. Alexander Balmain Bruce, *The Expositor's Greek Testament*, Vol. 1, *The Synoptic Gospels* (Grand Rapids: Eerdmans, 1951), 341.

2. Henry Barclay Swete, *Commentary on Mark* (repr. ed., Grand Rapids: Kregel, 1977), 1.

3. Aleph 28, 255 omit these words, but B, D, L, have them and the great mass of the manuscripts have υἱοῦ τοῦ θεοῦ.

4. The Western and Neutral classes read "Isaiah," the Alexandrian and Syrian, "the prophets," an evident correction because part of it is from Malachi.

5. Bruce, *Expositor's*, 342.

6. NIV has "a voice of one crying in the desert."

7. NIV has "make straight paths for him."

8. NIV has "And so John came, baptizing. . . ."

9. TR and Maj.T do not include the article.

10. NIV has "The whole Judean countryside . . . went out to him."

11. NIV has "John wore clothing made of camel's hair."

12. TR and Maj.T have ἦν δέ.

13. WH spells Ἰωάνης with only one ν.

14. NIV has "After me will come one more powerful than I."

15. Ezra P. Gould, *Critical and Exegetical Commentary on the Gospel According to St. Mark* (Edinburgh: T. & T. Clark, 1896), 9.

16. NIV has "the thongs."

17. NIV has "I baptize you with water."

18. TR and Maj.T have ἐγὼ μὲν ἐβάπτισα ὑμας ἐν ὕδατι.

19. TR and Maj.T have a different word order, ἐβαπτίσθης ὑπὸ Ἰωάννου εἰς τὸν Ἰορδάνην. However, TRb and WH spell Ἰωάνου with only one ν.

20. NIV has "he saw heaven being torn open."

21. NIV has "You are my Son, whom I love."

22. NIV has "At once the Spirit sent him out into the desert."

23. NIV has "He was with the wild animals."

24. Swete, *Commentary on Mark*, 11.

25. NIV has "Jesus went into Galilee."

26. NIV has "proclaiming the good news of God."

27. TR and Maj.T have κηρύσσων τὸ εὐαγγέλιον τῆς βασιλείας τοῦ θεοῦ.

28. Swete, *Commentary on Mark*, 12.

29. NIV has "The time has come."

30. NIV has "and believe the good news."

31. Swete, *Commentary on Mark*, 16.

32. NIV has "As Jesus walked beside the Sea of Galilee."

33. TR and Maj.T have περιπατῶν δὲ παρὰ τὴν θάλασσαν τῆς Γαλιλαίας.

34. TR and Maj.T have βάλλοντας ἀμφίβληστρον.

35. James Hope Moulton and George Milligan, *The Vocabulary of the Greek Testament* (London: Hodder and Stoughton, 1952), 28.

36. NIV has "Come, follow me . . . and I will make you fishers of men."

37. NIV has "When he had gone a little farther."

38. TR and Maj. T have Καὶ προβὰς ἐκεῖθεν ὀλίγον.

39. NIV has "preparing their nets."

40. NIV has "they left their father Zebedee in the boat with the hired men."

41. NIV has "Jesus went into the synagogue and began to teach."

42. NIV has "The people were amazed at his teaching."

43. Gould, *Critical and Exegetical Commentary*, 21.

44. NIV has "not as the teachers of the law."

45. NIV has "as one who had authority."

46. According to Bruce, "Mark omits much, and is in many ways a meagre Gospel, but it makes a distinctive contribution to the evangelic history *in showing by a few realistic touches* (this one of them) *the remarkable personality of Jesus.*" Bruce, *Expositor's*, 345. Emphasis Bruce's.

47. NIV has "a man in their synagogue who was possessed by an evil spirit."

48. NIV has "What do you want with us?"

49. Vincent, *Word Studies*, 1.165.

50. NIV has "shook the man violently."

51. TR has αὐτούς rather than ἑαυτούς.

52. NIV has "A new teaching—and with authority!"

53. TR and Maj. T have τις ἡ διδαχὴ ἡ καινὴ αὕτη, ὅτι κατ᾽ ἐξουσίαν.

54. Swete, *Commentary on Mark*, 21.

55. NIV has "News about him."

56. TR and Maj.T do not include πανταχοῦ.

57. NIV has "they went with James and John to the home of Simon and Andrew."

58. NIV has "Simon's mother-in-law was in bed with a fever."

59. NIV has "after sunset."

60. NIV has "that evening."

61. NIV has "the whole town gathered at the door."

62. TR and Maj.T have a different word order, ἡ πόλις ὅλη ἐπισυνηγμένη ἦν πρὸς τὴν θύραν.

63. NIV has "Jesus healed many who had various diseases."

64. NIV has "he would not let the demons speak."

65. NIV has "Very early in the morning, while it was still dark."

66. TR and Maj.T have πρωῒ ἔννυχον λίαν.

67. Gould, *Critical and Exegetical Commentary*, 28.

68. Bruce, *Expositor's*, 347.

69. NIV has "where he prayed."

70. NIV has "Simon and his companions went to look for him."
71. TR and Maj.T have κατεδίωξαν αὐτὸν ὁ Σίμων καὶ οἱ μετ᾽ αὐτοῦ.
72. Swete, *Commentary on Mark*, 26.
73. NIV has "Let us go somewhere else—to the nearby villages."
74. TR and Maj.T do not include ἀλλαχοῦ.
75. NIV has "So he traveled throughout Galilee preaching in their synagogues."
76. TR and Maj.T have ἦν κηρύσσων ἐν ταῖς συναγωγαῖς αὐτῶν εἰς ὅλην τὴν Γαλιλαίαν.
77. NIV has "begged him on his knees."
78. Maj.T has a different spelling for γονευπετῶν.
79. NIV has "Filled with compassion."
80. NIV has "Jesus sent him away at once with a strong warning."
81. TR and Maj. T have a different spelling, εὐθέως.
82. NIV has "began to talk freely."

Mark: Chapter 2

2:1. *When He had come back to Capernaum several days afterward*[1] (Καὶ εἰσελθὼν πάλιν εἰς Καφαρναοὺμ δι' ἡμερῶν[2]). After the first tour of Galilee, Jesus returned to the city that was now headquarters for the work in Galilee. The phrase δι' ἡμερῶν means that there were two days (διά, δύο, "two") between the departure and return.

It was heard that He was at home[3] (ἠκούσθη ὅτι ἐν οἴκῳ ἐστίν[4]), for the home of Peter had become the home of Jesus. Another picture directly from Peter's discourse.[5] "It was heard" (ἠκούσθη, first aorist, passive indicative from ἀκούω, "to hear"). People spread the rumor, "He is at home, He is indoors."

2:2. *So that there was no longer room, not even near the door*[6] (ὥστε μηκέτι χωρεῖν μηδὲ τὰ πρὸς τὴν θύραν). Another graphic Markan detail is seen through Peter's eyes. The double compound intensifies the negative in Greek. The door to this house apparently opened onto the street, not a court as in larger houses. The house was packed inside, and there was a jam outside.

And He was speaking the word to them[7] (καὶ ἐλάλει αὐτοῖς τὸν λόγον). Mark's favorite tense is the descriptive imperfect (ἐλάλει). Note that λαλέω, as contrasted with λέγω ("to say"), is an onomatopoetic word with some emphasis on the sound and manner of speaking. The word is common in the vernacular papyri to indicate conversation.

2:3. *And they came*[8] (καὶ ἔχονται), a fine illustration of Mark's vivid dramatic historical present. It is preserved by Luke 5:18 but not by Matthew 9:2, which uses the imperfect.

Carried by four men[9] (αἰρόμενον ὑπὸ τεσσάρων), another picturesque Markan detail not in the others.

2:4. *Being unable to get to Him because of the crowd,*[10] *they removed the roof above Him*[11] (καὶ μὴ δυνάμενοι προσενέγκαι[12] αὐτῷ διὰ τὸν ὄχλον ἀπεστέγασαν τὴν στέγην ὅπου ἦν). "They unroofed the roof." This is the only instance of the verb ἀποστεγάζω in the New Testament, a rare word in late Greek, with no papyrus example.[13] They climbed up a stairway on the outside or ladder to the flat tile roof and dug out or broke up the tiles (the roof). There were thus tiles (διὰ τῶν κεράμων, Luke 5:19) of laths and plaster

274

and even slabs of stone stuck in for strength that had to be dug out. It is not clear where Jesus was (ὅπου ἦν), either downstairs, or upstairs, or in the quadrangle (*atrium* or *compluvium*), if the house had one. "A composition of mortar, tar, ashes and sand is spread upon the roofs, and rolled hard, and grass grows in the crevices. On the houses of the poor in the country the grass grows more freely, and goats may be seen on the roofs cropping it."[14]

They let down the pallet on which the paralytic was lying[15] (χαλῶσι τὸν κράβαττον ὅπου ὁ παραλυτικὸς κατέκειτο[16]), a historical present again ("they let down"), aorist tense in Luke 5:19 (κάθηκαν). The verb means to lower from a higher place, as from a boat. Probably the four men had a rope fastened to each corner of the pallet or poor man's bed (κράβαττου; Lat. *grabatus*, so one of Mark's Latin words). Matthew 9:2 has κλίνης, a general term for bed. Luke has κλινίδιον, "little bed or couch." Mark's word is common in the papyri and is sometimes spelled κράββατος and sometimes κράβατος, while W, Codex Washingtonius, has it κράββατον.

2:5. And Jesus seeing their faith[17] (καὶ ἰδὼν ὁ[18] Ἰησοῦς τὴν πίστιν αὐτῶν), the faith of the four friends and of the lame man himself. There is no reason for excluding the sick man's faith. They all had confidence in the power and willingness of Jesus.

"Son, your sins are forgiven" (Τέκνον, ἀφίενταί σου αἱ ἁμαρτίαι[19]), ἀφίενται, aoristic present passive.[20] So Matthew 9:3, but Luke 5:20 has the Doric perfect passive ἀφέωνται. The astonishing thing both to the paralytic and to the four friends is that Jesus forgave his sins instead of healing him.

2:6. But some of the scribes were sitting there and reasoning in their hearts[21] (ἦσαν δέ τινες τῶν γραμματέων ἐκεῖ καθήμενοι καὶ διαλογιζόμενοι ἐν ταῖς καρδίαις αὐτῶν), another of Mark's pictures through Peter's eyes. These scribes (and Pharisees, Luke 5:21) were there to cause trouble, to pick flaws in the teaching and conduct of Jesus. His popularity and power had aroused their jealousy.

2:7. "He is blaspheming" (βλασφημεῖ[22]). This is the unspoken charge in their hearts. The critics justify the charge with the conviction that God alone has the power (δύναται) to forgive sins. The word βλασφημέω means injurious speech or slander. It was, they held, blasphemy for Jesus to assume this divine prerogative. Their logic was correct. The only flaw was that they ignored the alternate possibility that a unique relation to God justified Jesus' claim. So the two forces clash on the deity of Christ Jesus. Knowing full well that he had exercised the prerogative of God in forgiving the man's sins, he proceeds to justify his claim by healing the man.

2:8. *Immediately Jesus, aware in His spirit that they were reasoning that way within themselves*[23] (καὶ εὐθὺς[24] ἐπιγνοὺς ὁ Ἰησοῦς τῷ πνεύματι αὐτοῦ ὅτι οὕτως διαλογίζονται ἐν ἑαυτοῖς). There is no indication that they spoke aloud the murmur "within themselves" (Matt. 9:3). It was not necessary, for their looks gave them away, and Jesus knew their thoughts (v. 4) and perceived their reasoning (Luke 5:22). The debate (διαλογιζόμενοι) in their hearts was written on their faces.

2:10. *"But so that you may know"* (ἵνα δὲ εἰδῆτε). The scribes could have said either of the alternatives in verse 9 with equal futility. Jesus could say either with equal effect. In fact Jesus chose the harder first, the forgiveness that they could not see. So he now performs the miracle of healing that all could see, by which all could know that he really had authority to forgive sins. He calls himself "the Son of Man," Christ's favorite self-designation, a claim to be the Messiah in terms that could not be attacked easily. He has the right and power on earth to forgive sins, here and now without waiting for the Day of Judgment.

He said to the paralytic (λέγει τῷ παραλυτικῷ). This remarkable parenthesis in the middle of the sentence occurs also in Matthew 9:6 and Luke 5:24, indication that Matthew and Luke had access to Mark's narrative. It is inconceivable that all three writers should independently have injected the same parenthesis at the same place.

2:12. *He . . . went out in the sight of everyone*[25] (ἐξῆλθεν ἔμπροσθεν πάντων[26]). Luke 5:25 follows Mark in this detail. He picked up (ἄρας) his pallet and walked and went home as Jesus had commanded him to do (Mark 2:11).

They were all amazed and were glorifying God, saying, "We have never seen anything like this" (ἐξίστασθαι, πάντας καὶ δοξάζειν τὸν θεὸν λέγοντας ὅτι Οὕτως οὐδέποτε εἴδομεν[27]). The amazing proceeding made it unnecessary for Jesus to refute the scribes further on this occasion. The amazement (ἐξίστασθαι, from which the English *ecstasy* is drawn) came because Jesus had acted with the power of God and claimed equality with God and had given evidence of His claim. For it all they glorified God.

2:13. *And He went out again by the seashore*[28] (Καὶ ἐξῆλθεν πάλιν παρὰ τὴν θάλασσαν), a pretty picture of Jesus walking by the sea and a walk that Jesus loved (Matt. 4:18; Mark 1:16). Probably Jesus went out from the crowd in Peter's house as soon as he could. It was a joy to get a whiff of fresh air by the sea. But it was not long until the crowd began to come (ἤρχετο, third person singular imperfect middle/passive deponent indicative), and Jesus was teaching them (ἐδίδασκεν, third person singular imperfect active indicative).

2:14. *As He passed by*[29] (καὶ παράγων), nominative singular masculine present active participle, "He was passing by." Jesus was constantly on the alert for opportunities to do good. An unlikely candidate for Jesus' favor was Levi (Matthew), son of Alpheus, who was sitting at the tollgate (τελώνιον) on the Great West Road from Damascus to the Mediterranean. He was a publican (τελώνης) who collected toll for Herod Antipas. The Jews hated, or at least despised, these publicans and classed them with sinners (ἁμαρτωλοί, see v. 15). The challenge of Jesus was sudden and sharp, but Levi (Matthew) was ready to respond, unlike businessmen who put off service to Christ to carry on their business. Great decisions are often made on a moment's notice.

2:16. *The scribes of the Pharisees* (οἱ γραμματεῖς τῶν Φαρισαίων;[30] cf. "their scribes" in Luke 5:30). Matthew gave a great reception (δοχὴν) in his house (Mark 2:15; Luke 5:29). These publicans and sinners not only accepted Levi's invitation, but they imitated his example "and were following [Jesus]" (καὶ ἠκολούθουν αὐτῷ). It was a scandalous crew from the standpoint of the scribes of the Pharisees, who were on hand to pick flaws. The scribes would have stood and ridiculed Jesus and the disciples in the long hall of the house, unless they stood outside, feeling too pious to go into the house of a publican. It was an offense for a Jew to eat with Gentiles, which would become a problem for early Jewish Christians (Acts 11:3). Publicans and sinners were regarded as no better than Gentiles (1 Cor. 5:11).

2:17. *"I did not come to call the righteous, but sinners"*[31] (οὐκ ἦλθον καλέσαι δικαίους ἀλλὰ ἁμαρτωλούς). For the sake of argument, Jesus accepts the claim that the Pharisees are righteous. Elsewhere (Matt. 23) He will charge that the Pharisees only wore a cloak of pride and hypocritical respectability as they extorted and devoured. The words "to repentance" (εἰς μετάνοιαν) are added in Luke 5:32. Jesus called people to repentance and new spiritual life from sin. But this claim stopped their mouths against what Jesus was doing. The well or the strong (ἰσχύοντες) are not those who need the physician in an epidemic.

2:18. *John's disciples and the Pharisees were fasting*[32] (Καὶ ἦσαν οἱ μαθηταὶ Ἰωάννου[33] καὶ οἱ Φαρισαῖοι νηστεύοντες[34]), the periphrastic imperfect, so common in Mark's vivid description. Probably Levi hosted this feast on one of the weekly fast days (the second and fifth days of the week for strict Jews). So there was a clash of viewpoints. The disciples of John sided with the Pharisees in the Jewish ceremonial ritualistic observances. John was still a prisoner in Machaerus. John was more of an ascetic than was Jesus (Matt. 9:14f; Luke

7:33–35), but neither pleased their critics. The learners or disciples (μαθηταὶ) of John had missed the spirit of their leader as they aligned with the Pharisees against Jesus. But there was no real congeniality within Pharisee formalism (οἱ μαθηταὶ Ἰωάννου καὶ οἱ μαθηταὶ τῶν Φαρισαίων). Later, Pharisees, Sadducees, and Herodians, who bitterly detested each other, made common cause against Jesus Christ. So today we find mutually hostile groups that become allies when Christians are around. See on Matthew 9:14–17 for comments. Matthew follows Mark closely.

2:19. *"The attendants of the bridegroom"*[35] (οἱ υἱοὶ τοῦ νυμφῶνος), not merely the groomsmen but the guests also, the *paranymphs* (παρανύμφοι of the old Greek). Jesus adopts the Baptist's own metaphor (John 3:29), changing "the friend of the bridegroom" (ὁ φίλος τοῦ νυμφίου) to "sons of the bridechamber." Jesus identifies himself with God in his covenant relation with Israel, the Bridegroom of the Old Testament (Hos. 2:18–20).[36] Mourning does not suit the wedding feast. Matthew, Mark, and Luke all give the three parables (Bridegroom, Unfulled Cloth, and New Wineskins) illustrating and defending the conduct of Jesus in feasting with Levi on a Jewish fast day. Luke 5:36 calls these parables. Jesus seems iconoclastic to the ecclesiastics and revolutionary in his emphasis on the spiritual instead of the ritualistic and ceremonial.

2:21. *"No one sews a patch of unshrunk cloth on an old garment"* (οὐδεὶς ἐπίβλημα ῥάκους ἀγνάφου ἐπιράπτει ἐπὶ ἱμάτιον παλαιόν[37]). The compound form of the verb is found only in Greek literature, though the uncompounded verb ῥάπτω (to sew) is common enough. For "sews upon," Matthew 9:16 and Luke 5:36 use ἐπιβάλλει, "put upon or clap upon."

2:22. *"No one puts new wine into old wineskins"*[38] (ἀλλὰ οἶνον νέον εἰς ἀσκοὺς καινούς[39]). Brooke Foss Westcott and Fenton John Anthony Hort bracket this clause in their 1881 critical text (hereafter listed as WH) as a Western noninterpolation though it is omitted only in D and some old Latin manuscripts.

2:23. *He was passing through the grainfields on the Sabbath*[40] (ἐγένετο αὐτὸν ἐν τοῖς σάββασιν παραπορεύεσθαι διὰ τῶν σπορίμων[41]), see on Matthew 12:1, so Matthew and Luke 6:1. But Mark uses παραπορεύεσθαι, "to go along beside," unless διαπορεύεσθαι (found in B, C, and D) is accepted. Perhaps now on the edge, now within the grain. Mark uses also ὁδὸν ποιεῖν, "to make a way," like the Latin *iter facere,* as if through the standing grain, "picking the heads of grain"[42] (τίλλοντες τοὺς στάχυας). Rabbis called it work in harvesting grain and preparing food. The margin of the RV has it correctly: They began to make their way plucking the ears of corn (grain, wheat, or barley, we should say). See on Matthew 12:1–8 for further discussion of this passage and its Luke 6:1–5 parallel.

2:26. *"How he entered the house of God"* (πῶς εἰσῆλθεν εἰς τὸν οἶκον τοῦ θεοῦ), the tent or tabernacle at Nob, not Solomon's temple in Jerusalem. *"In the time of Abiathar the high priest"*[43] (ἐπὶ Ἀβιαθὰρ ἀρχιερέως[44]). Reference to the time of Abiathar as high priest is a neat Greek idiom. There was confusion in the Massoretic text and in the LXX about the difference between Ahimelech (Abimelech) and Abiathar (2 Sam. 8:17), Ahimelech's son and successor (1 Sam. 21:2; 22:20). Apparently Ahimelech, not Abiathar, was high priest at this time. It is possible that both father and son bore both names (1 Sam. 22:20; 2 Sam. 8:17; 1 Chron. 18:16). Abiathar is mentioned although both were involved, as ἐπι may mean in identifying Abiathar. Ancient priests had elaborate rules for preparing the shewbread (τοὺς ἄρτους τῆς προθέσεως), the loaves of presentation, the loaves of the face or presence of God. New loaves were brought on the commencement of the Sabbath and the old bread deposited on the golden table in the porch of the sanctuary. This old bread was eaten by the priests as they came and went. This is what David ate.

2:27. *"The Sabbath was made for man"* (Τὸ σάββατον διὰ τὸν ἄνθρωπον ἐγένετο). Mark alone has this profound saying, which subordinates the Sabbath to humanity's real welfare. That the human race is in view is shown by use of a generic article with ἄνθρωπος, class from class. People were not made for the Sabbath as the rabbis seemed to think, with all their petty rules about eating an egg laid on the Sabbath or looking in the glass (see 2 Macc. 5:19 and *Mechilta* on Exod. 31:13: "The Sabbath is delivered unto you and you are not delivered unto the Sabbath"). Christianity has had to fight this battle about institutionalism. The church itself is for people, not people for the church.

2:28. *"So the Son of Man is Lord even of the Sabbath"* (ὥστε κύριός ἐστιν ὁ υἱὸς τοῦ ἀνθρώπου καὶ τοῦ σαββάτου). Mark, Matthew (12:8), and Luke (6:5) all give this as a climax in the five reasons given by Christ on the occasion for the conduct of the disciples, but Mark has the little word *even* (καί) that is not in the others. Mark thus proclaims that Jesus knew that he was making a great claim as Son of Man, the representative man. The Messiah had lordship (κύριος) even over the Sabbath. He was not slave to the Sabbath but master of it. "Even of the sabbath, so invaluable in your eyes. Lord, not to abolish, but to interpret and keep in its own place, and give it a new name."[45]

NOTES

1. NIV has "A few days later, when Jesus again entered Capernaum."
2. TR and Maj.T have καὶ πάλιν εἰσῆλθεν εἰς Καπερναοὺμ δι᾿ ἡμερῶν.
3. NIV has "the people heard that he had come home."
4. TR and Maj.T have ἠκούσθη ὅτι εἰς οἶκόν ἐστιν.
5. Some of the manuscripts have εἰς οἶκον, illustrating the practical identity in meaning of ἐν and εἰς. See A. T. Robertson, *A Grammar of the Greek New Testament in the Light of Historical Research* (Nashville: Broadman, 1934), 591–96.
6. NIV has "that there was no room left, not even outside the door."
7. NIV has "and he preached the word to them."
8. NIV has "Some men came."
9. NIV has "carried by four of them."
10. NIV has "Since they could not get him to Jesus because of the crowd."
11. NIV has "they made an opening in the roof above Jesus."
12. TR and Maj.T have προσεγγίσαι for προσενέγκαι.
13. James Hope Moulton and George Milligan, *The Vocabulary of the Greek Testament* (London: Hodder and Stoughton, 1952).
14. Vincent, *Word Studies*, 1.170.
15. NIV has "lowered the mat the paralyzed man was lying on."
16. TR and Maj.T have χαλῶσιν τὸν κράββατον ἐφ᾿ ᾧ ὁ παραλυτικὸς κατέκειτο.
17. NIV has "When Jesus saw their faith."
18. TR and Maj.T have ἰδὼν δέ.
19. TR and Maj.T have Τέκνον, ἀφέωνταί σοι αἱ ἁμαρτίαι σου.
20. Robertson, *Grammar*, 864ff.
21. NIV has "Now some teachers of the law were sitting there."
22. TR and Maj.T have βλασφημίαις.
23. NIV has "Immediately Jesus knew in his spirit that this is what they were thinking in their hearts."
24. TR and Maj.T have εὐθέως.
25. NIV has "(He) walked out in full view of them all."
26. TR and Maj.T have ἐξῆλθεν ἐναντίον πάντων.
27. TR and Maj.T have a different word order, οὐδέποτε οὕτως εἴδομεν.
28. NIV has "Once again Jesus went out beside the lake."
29. NIV has "As he walked along."
30. TR and Maj.T have οἱ γραμματεῖς καὶ οἱ Φαρισαῖοι.
31. NIV has "I have not come to call the righteous, but sinners."
32. NIV has "Now John's disciples and the Pharisees were fasting."

33. WH has the spelling Ἰωάνης.
34. TR and Maj.T have οἱ τῶν Φαρισαίων νηστεύοντες.
35. NIV has "the guests of the bridegroom."
36. Henry Barclay Swete, *Commentary on Mark* (repr. ed., Grand Rapids: Kregel, 1977), 44.
37. TR and Maj.T have καὶ οὐδεὶς ἐπίβλημα ῥάκους ἀγνάφου ἐπιρράπτει ἐπὶ ἱματίῳ παλαίῳ.
38. NIV has "No, he pours new wine into new wineskins."
39. TR and Maj.T have the additional word βλητέον at the end of the phrase.
40. NIV has "One Sabbath Jesus was going through the grainfields."
41. TR and Maj.T have a different word order, Καὶ ἐγένετο παραπορεύεσθαι αὐτὸν ἐν τοις σάββασιν διὰ τῶν σπορίμων.
42. NIV has "they began to pick some heads of grain."
43. NIV has "In the days of Abiathar the high priest."
44. TR has ἐπὶ Ἀβιάθαρ τοῦ ἀρχιερέως.
45. Alexander Balmain Bruce, *The Expositor's Greek Testament*, Vol. 1, *The Synoptic Gospels* (Grand Rapids: Eerdmans, 1951), 356.

Mark: Chapter 3

3:1. *And a man was there whose hand was withered*[1] (καὶ ἦν ἐκεῖ ἄνθρωπος ἐξηραμμένην ἔχων τὴν χεῖρα). It is a common idiom in the Greek to have the article function as a possessive. Thus, "his" hand was in a withered state, accusative singular feminine perfect passive participle (adjective ξήραν in Matthew and Luke), showing that it was not congenital, but the result of injury by accident or disease. Luke 6:6 offers the information that the *right* hand was diseased.

3:2. *They were watching Him*[2] (καὶ παρετήρουν αὐτόν), third person plural imperfect active indicative. The Pharisees were watching on the side or sly. Luke 6:7 uses the middle voice, παρετηροῦντο, to accent their personal interest in the proceedings. Wycliff rightly puts it, "They aspieden him." They played the spy on Jesus. It was the Sabbath day and in the synagogue. They were there ready to catch him in the act if he should dare to violate their rules as he had in the wheat fields. Probably the same Pharisees are present now as then.

So that they might accuse Him[3] (ἵνα κατηγορήσωσιν αὐτοῦ), so Matthew 12:10. Luke (2:7) has it "that they might find how to accuse Him" (ἵνα εὕρωσιν κατηγορεῖν αὐτοῦ). They were determined to accuse him. The Sabbath controversy offered the best opening. So they are ready for business.

3:3. *"Get up and come forward!"*[4] (Ἔγειρε εἰς τὸ μέσον[5]). Step into the middle of the room where all can see. Christ boldly defied his spying enemies. One can see the commotion among the long-bearded hypocrites at this daring act of Jesus.

3:4. *But they kept silent*[6] (οἱ δὲ ἐσιώπων), third person plural imperfect active indicative. In sullen silence and helplessness before the merciless questions of Jesus as the poor man stood there before them all. Jesus cornered them with the Sabbath-keeping alternatives between doing what is good (ἀγαθὸν ποιέω, late Greek in LXX and New Testament) or doing evil (κακοποιέω, ancient Greek word). Were they to save a life or to kill (ψυχὴν σῶσαι ἢ ἀποκτεῖναι)? The choice stood in the room before them. It was a terrible exposure.

3:5. *After looking around at them with anger*[7] (περιβλεψάμενος αὐτοὺς μετ᾽ ὀργῆς). Mark refers frequently to the emotions on Jesus' face when he looked at others (3:5, 34; 10:23; 11:11). Luke does so only in 6:10. The eyes of Jesus swept the room. Each rabbinical hypocrite felt the cut of that condemnatory glance. This indignant anger was not inconsistent with the love and pity of Jesus. Jesus knew the murder in their hearts. Anger against wrong as wrong is a sign of moral health.[8]

Grieved at their hardness of heart[9] (συλλυπούμενος ἐπὶ τῇ πωρώσει τῆς καρδίας αὐτῶν). Mark alone gives this point. The anger was tempered by grief.[10] Jesus is the Man of Sorrows. This present participle brings out the continuous state of grief, whereas the momentary angry look is expressed by the aorist participle. Their own hearts or attitudes were in a state of moral ossification (πώρωσις) like hardened hands or feet. Πῶρος was used of a kind of marble and then of the callous on fractured bones. "They were hardened by previous conceptions against this new truth."[11] See also on Matthew 12:9–14.

3:6. *The Pharisees went out and immediately began conspiring with the Herodians against Him*[12] (καὶ ἐξελθόντες οἱ Φαρισαῖοι εὐθὺς[13] μετὰ τῶν Ἡρῳδιανῶν συμβούλιον ἐδίδουν[14] κατ᾽ αὐτοῦ). The Pharisees could stand no more. Out they stalked in a rage (Luke 6:11). Outside the synagogue they took counsel (συμβούλιον ἐποίησαν) or gave counsel (συμβούλιον ἐδίδουν, as some manuscripts have it, imperfect tense, offered counsel as their solution of the problem) with their bitter enemies, the Herodians, on the Sabbath day "as to how they might destroy Him"[15] (ὅπως αὐτὸν ἀπολέσωσιν). Here was a striking illustration of the very alternatives Jesus had just laid before them, "to save life or to kill." This is the first mention of the Herodians or supporters of Herod Antipas and the Herod family rather than the Romans. The Pharisees welcomed the help of their rivals to destroy Jesus. In the presence of Jesus, they unite forces, as in Mark 8:15 and 12:13 and in Matthew 22:16.

3:7. *Jesus withdrew to the sea with His disciples*[16] (ὁ Ἰησοῦς μετὰ τῶν μαθητῶν αὐτοῦ ἀνεχώρησεν πρὸς τὴν θάλασσαν[17]). Jesus knew that "He and His would be safer by the open beach."[18] He has the disciples with him. Vincent notes that Mark mentions on eleven occasions the withdrawals of Jesus to escape his enemies, for prayer, for rest, for private conference with his disciples (1:12; 3:7; 6:31, 46; 7:24, 31; 9:2; 10:1; 14:33). But, as often, a great multitude (πολὺ πλῆθος) from Galilee followed him.

3:8. *A great number of people heard of all that He was doing*[19] (ἀκούοντες ὅσα ἐποίει[20]), nominative plural masculine present active participle, though πλῆθος is neuter singular (construction according to sense in both number and gender). This crowd by the sea came from north, south, east, and northwest. They had come from Galilee, Judea and Jerusalem, beyond Jordan (Decapolis and Perea), Tyre and Sidon, and Phoenicia. There were some even from Idumea, which is mentioned only here in the New Testament. John Hyrcanus had won this area to Palestine. Idumea was practically a part of Judea, with a Jewish population.[21] Many of these from Phoenicia and the Decapolis probably were Gentiles, who may have known only the Greek language. The fame of Jesus had spread through the regions round about. There was a jam as the crowds came to Jesus by the Sea of Galilee.

3:9. *And He told His disciples that a boat should stand ready for Him*[22] (καὶ εἶπεν τοῖς μαθηταῖς αὐτοῦ ἵνα πλοιάριον προσκαρτερῇ αὐτῷ). The boat was to keep close (note present tense subjunctive of προσκαρτερέω) to the shore in constant readiness and move as Jesus did. Whether he needed it is not told.

So that they would not crowd Him[23] (ἵνα μὴ θλίβωσιν αὐτόν). They might press or crush him. Jesus stayed with the crowds for they needed him, present subjunctive.

3:10. *All those who had afflictions pressed around Him in order to touch Him*[24] (ὥστε ἐπιπίπτειν αὐτῷ ἵνα αὐτοῦ ἅψωνται ὅσοι εἶχον μάστιγας). They were falling upon him to such an extent that it was dangerous. They were not hostile but simply intensely eager, each to be attended to by Jesus. They hoped for a cure by contact with Christ, third person plural aorist subjunctive. It was a really pathetic scene and a tremendous strain on Jesus. As many as had plagues, strokes, or scourges (here μάστιγας, "beatings, afflictions"). Our word *plague* is from πλήγη (Latin *plaga*), from πλήγνυμι, to strike a blow, common in ancient Greek in this sense. Μάστιγας has the same range of meaning (see also 5:29, 34; Luke 7:21; 2 Macc. 9:11).

3:11. *Whenever the unclean spirits saw Him*[25] (ὅταν αὐτὸν ἐθεώρουν[26]), third person plural imperfect active indicative with ὅταν of repeated action. They kept falling down before him (προσέπιπτον) and crying (ἔκραζον), and he kept charging or rebuking (ἐπετίμα) them, all imperfects. The unclean spirits or demons again recognized Jesus as the Son of God, and Jesus again charged them not to make him known. He did not wish their testimony. This ordeal is given only by Mark. Note nonfinal use of ἵνα.

3:13. *And He went up on the mountain*[27] (Καὶ ἀναβαίνει εἰς τὸ ὄρος). Luke 6:12 adds "to pray." The verb indicates a historical present so common in Mark's vivid narrative. Neither Gospel gives the name of the mountain, assuming it to be well known. It probably was not far from the lake.

And summoned those whom He Himself wanted[28] (καὶ προσκαλεῖται οὓς ἤθελεν αὐτός), emphatic use of αὐτός (Himself) at end of sentence. Whether by personal imitation or through the disciples, Jesus invites or calls to himself (προσκαλεῖται, historical middle present indicative) a select number out of the vast crowds by the sea, those whom he really wished to have with him.

And they came to Him (καὶ ἀπῆλθον πρὸς αὐτόν). Luke 6:12 states that Jesus "spent the whole night in prayer to God." It was a crisis in the ministry of Christ. This select group up in the hills probably respected the long agony of Jesus though they did not comprehend his motive. They formed a sort of spiritual bodyguard around the Master during his night vigil in the mountain.

3:14. *And He appointed twelve* (καὶ ἐποίησεν δώδεκα). This was a second selection out of those invited to the hills, made after the night of prayer (Luke 6:13). Perhaps he chose twelve to represent the elect to God from the twelve tribes of national Israel. They were to be princes in a new Israel (cf. Matt. 19:28; Luke 22:30; Rev. 21:14, 15). Luke 6:13–16 gives the list of the twelve at this point while Matthew (10:1–4) postpones until recounting how the twelve are sent out in Galilee. There is a fourth list in Acts 1:13.[29] The three groups of four begin alike (Simon, Philip, James).

[Whom He also names apostles] ([οὓς καὶ ἀποστόλους ὠνόμασεν]).[30] Jesus himself gave the name "apostle or missionary" (ἀποστέλλω, "to send") to this group of twelve. The word also is applied in the New Testament to delegates or messengers of churches (2 Cor. 8:23; Phil. 2:25), and the messenger in John 13:16. It is applied also to Paul on a par with the twelve (e.g., Gal. 1:1, 11–2:9), to Barnabas (Acts 14:14), and perhaps to Timothy and Silas (Acts 17:14–15; 1 Thess. 2:7–9; 1 Peter 5:12).

So that they would be with Him and that He could send them out to preach (ἵνα ὦσιν μετ᾽ αὐτοῦ καὶ ἵνα ἀποστέλλῃ αὐτοὺς κηρύσσειν). Mark mentions two purposes of Jesus in choosing these twelve. They would not be ready to be sent forth until they had been with Jesus for some time. One of the chief tasks of Christ was to train this group of men.[31] The very word ἀπόστολος is from ἀποστέλλω. Two infinitives express the two purposes in sending forth the apostles. They were "to preach" (κηρύσσειν, from κῆρυξ, "herald") and "to have authority to cast out the demons" (ἔχειν ἐξουσίαν ἐκβάλλειν τὰ δαιμόνια[32]). This double ministry of preaching and healing was to mark their work. The two things are, however, different, and one does not necessarily involve the other.

3:16. *Simon (to whom He gave the name Peter)* (ἐπέθηκεν ὄνομα τῷ Σίμωνι Πέτρον[33]). The Greek idiom is not so awkward as it seems in English. *Peter* is in apposition with *name* or ὄνομα (accusative). This surname Jesus gave in addition (ἐπέθηκεν) to Simon (dative case). Here then is a direct reference to what is told in John 1:42 when Jesus met Simon for the first time. Mark reflects Peter's own words. Luke 6:14 simply says, "whom He also named Peter." See on Matthew 16:18 for explanation of the names *Peter, Rock,* and *Cephas.*

3:17. *(To them He gave the name Boanerges, which means, "Sons of Thunder")* (ἐπέθηκεν αὐτοῖς ὀνόμα[τα] Βοανηργές[34] ὅ ἐστιν Υἱοὶ Βροντῆς). This Hebrew nickname is given only by Mark. It may refer to the fiery temperament revealed in Luke 9:54, when James and John wanted to call down fire on unfriendly Samaritan villages. Βοανηργές literally means "sons of tumult or thunder" in Syriac. No other epithets are given by Mark save descriptions to distinguish between men with the same names, as Simon the Cananaean (or Zealot) and Judas Iscariot, "who also betrayed Him" (v. 19). Andrew (from ἀνήρ, "a man") and Philip (Philippos, "fond of horses") are both Greek names. Matthew is a Hebrew name meaning "gift of God" (Μαθθαῖος). Thomas is Hebrew and means "Twin" (Didymus, John 11:16). There are two forms of the name of James (also Ἰάκωβος, "Jacob"). Thaddeus is another name for Lebbaeus.

3:20. *And He came home*[35] (Καὶ ἔρχεται[36] εἰς οἶκον), historical present again without an article. He comes home from the mountain, probably the house of Simon as in 1:29. Mark passes by the Sermon on the Mount given by Matthew and Luke on the mountain (plateau on the mountain in Luke). Mark's Gospel is full of action and does not undertake to tell all that Jesus did and said.

To such an extent that they could not even eat a meal[37] (ὥστε μὴ δύνασθαι αὐτοὺς μηδὲ[38] ἄρτον φαγεῖν). Not the infinitive with ὥστε. Apparently Jesus and the disciples were indoors with the great crowd in the house and at the door as in 1:33; 2:2 to which Mark refers by "again." The jam was so great that they could not rest, could not eat, and apparently Jesus could not even teach. The crowd reassembled at once upon Christ's return from the mountain.

3:21. *When His own people heard of this*[39] (καὶ ἀκούσαντες οἱ παρ' αὐτοῦ). The phrase means literally "those from the side of Him [Jesus]." It could mean another circle of disciples who had just arrived and who knew of the crowds and strain of the Galilean ministry who now come at this special juncture. But the idiom most likely means the kinspeople or family of Jesus, as is common in the LXX. Verse 31 expressly mentions "His mother and His brothers," indicating that they are "the friends" of verse 21.

"He has lost His senses"[40] (ἐξέστη), third person singular second aorist active indicative intransitive. It is a mournful spectacle to think of the mother and brothers saying this. The same charge was brought against Paul (Acts 26:24; 2 Cor. 5:13). We say that one is "out of his head." Certainly Mary did not believe that Jesus was in the power of Beelzebub, as the rabbis said (see on Matt. 9:32–34; 10:25; and 12:24 for *Beelzebub* and *Beelzebul*). The scribes from Jerusalem are trying to discount the power and prestige of Jesus (3:22). Mary probably felt that Jesus was overwrought and wished to take him home out of the excitement and strain so that he might get rest and proper food.[41] His brothers did not yet believe the pretensious claims of Jesus (John 7:5). Herod Antipas will later consider Jesus to be John the Baptist risen from death. The scribes treat him as under demonic possession. Even family and friends fear that he has a disordered mind as a result of overstrain. It was a crucial moment for Jesus, as his family or friends came to take him home, to lay hold of him (κρατῆσαι) forcibly if need be.

3:23. *Began speaking to them in parables*[42] (ἐν παραβολαῖς ἔλεγεν αὐτοῖς), in crisp pungent thrusts Jesus exposed the inconsistencies of the scribes and Pharisees. See on Matthew 13 for discussion of the word *parable* (παραβολή, "placing beside for comparison"). He begins with a retorical question about Satan to clarify his own power to cast out demons.

3:24. *"If a kingdom is divided against itself, that kingdom cannot stand"* (ἐὰν βασιλεία ἐφ' ἑαυτὴν μερισθῇ, οὐ δύναται σταθῆναι ἡ βασιλεία ἐκείνη). Short parabolic quips in verses 24–25 show that Satan cannot cast out himself (ἐκβάλλει, the very word used of casting out demons). A kingdom divided (μερισθῇ, for a mere portion) against itself and a house divided (μερισθῇ) against itself show two conditions of the third class undetermined, but with prospect of determination.

3:27. *"No one can enter the strong man's house and plunder his property"*[43] (οὐ δύναται οὐδεὶς εἰς τὴν οἰκίαν τοῦ ἰσχυροῦ εἰσελθὼν τὰ σκεύη αὐτοῦ διαρπάσαι[44]). *Plunder* is a compound verb meaning "thoroughly ransack." In a *reductio ad absurdum*, Jesus pictures Satan plundering the demons, the very tools (σκεύη) by which he carries on his business. Jesus is the conqueror of Satan, not his ally.

3:29. *"But is guilty of an eternal sin"* (ἀλλὰ ἔνοχός ἐστιν αἰωνίου ἁμαρτήματος[45]). The genitive of the penalty occurs here with ἔνοχος. In saying that Jesus had an unclean spirit (v. 30) Jesus' enemies had attributed to the Devil the work of the Holy Spirit. This is the unpardonable sin, and it can be committed today by those who call the work of Christ the work of the

Devil. Friedrich Nietzsche did so in philosophy. Those who hope for a second probation hereafter may ponder carefully how a soul that eternally sins in such an environment can never repent. That is eternal punishment. The text uses ἁμαρτήματος (sin), not κρισέως (judgment) as the *Textus Receptus* has it.

3:31. *Standing outside* (ἔξω στήκοντες[46]), a late present tense from the perfect ἔστηκα. Pathetic picture of the mother and brothers standing on the outside of the house thinking that Jesus inside is beside himself and wanting to take him home. They were crowded out.

They sent word to Him and called Him[47] (ἀπέστειλαν πρὸς αὐτὸν καλοῦντες[48] αὐτόν). They were unwilling to disclose their errand to take him home[49] and so get the crowd to pass word to Jesus on the inside, "calling Him" through others. Some manuscripts add "sisters" as seeking Jesus with the mother and brothers.

3:32. *A crowd was sitting around Him* (ἐκάθητο περὶ αὐτὸν ὄχλος[50]). They sat in a circle (κύκλῳ) around Jesus with the disciples forming a sort of inner circle.

3:34. *Looking about at those who were sitting around Him*[51] (καὶ περιβλεψάμενος τοὺς περὶ αὐτὸν κύκλῳ καθημένους[52]), another of Mark's life touches. Jesus calls those who do the will of God his mother, brothers, and sisters. This does not prove that the sisters were actually there. The brothers were hostile and that gives point to the tragic words of Jesus. One's heart goes out to Mary, who has to go back home without even seeing her wondrous Son. What did it all mean to her at this hour?

NOTES

1. NIV has "and a man with a shriveled hand was there."
2. NIV has "So they watched him closely."
3. NIV has "Some of them were looking for a reason to accuse Jesus."
4. NIV has "Stand up in front of everyone."
5. TR and Maj.T have Ἔγειραι εἰς τὸ μέσον.
6. NIV has "But they remained silent."
7. NIV has "He looked around at them in anger."
8. Ezra P. Gould, *Critical and Exegetical Commentary on the Gospel According to St. Mark* (Edinburgh: T. & T. Clark, 1896), 53.
9. NIV has "deeply distressed at their stubborn hearts."
10. Henry Barclay Swete, *Commentary on Mark* (repr. ed., Grand Rapids: Kregel, 1977), 52.

11. Gould, *Critical and Exegetical Commentary*, 53.
12. NIV has "Then the Pharisees went out and began to plot with the Herodians."
13. TR and Maj.T have εὐθέως for εὐθύς.
14. TR and Maj.T have ἐποίουν for ἐδίδουν.
15. NIV has "how they might kill Jesus."
16. NIV has "Jesus withdrew with his disciples to the lake."
17. TR and Maj.T have a different word order, καὶ ὁ Ἰησοῦς ἀνεχώρησεν μετὰ τῶν μαθητῶν αὐτοῦ πρὸς τὴν θάλασσαν. However, TRb and Maj.T do not include the moveable ν on the verb ἀνεχώρησε.
18. Swete, *Commentary on Mark*, 54.
19. NIV has "When they heard all he was doing."
20. TR and Maj.T have the aorist participle, ἀκούσαντες ὅσα ἐποίει.
21. George Adam Smith, *The Historical Geography of the Holy Land* (New York: Harper and Brothers, 1931).
22. NIV has "he told his disciples to have a small boat ready for him."
23. NIV has "to keep the people from crowding him."
24. NIV has "those with diseases were pushing forward to touch him."
25. NIV has "Whenever the evil spirits saw him."
26. TR and Maj.T have ὅταν αὐτὸν ἐθεώρει.
27. NIV has "Jesus went up on a mountainside."
28. NIV has "and called to him those he wanted."
29. See a discussion of the names of the apostles on Matthew 10:1–4 and A. T. Robertson, *Harmony of the Gospels for Students of the Life of Christ* (New York: Harper and Row, 1922), 271–73.
30. This is found in the margin of the RSV from the WH and draws on Aleph, B, C, etc. It is genuine in Luke 6:13 but not considered so here.
31. See A. B. Bruce, *The Training of the Twelve* (Grand Rapids: Kregel, 1971).
32. TR and Maj.T have ἔχειν ἐξουσίαν θεραπεύειν τὰς νόσους καὶ ἐκβάλλειν τὰ διανόνια.
33. TR and Maj.T have a different word order, καὶ ἐπέθηκεν τῷ Σίμωνι ὄνομα Πέτρον. However, TRb and Maj.T do not include the moveable ν on the verb ἐπέθηκε.
34. TR and Maj.T spell it Βοανεργές.
35. NIV has "Then Jesus entered a house."
36. TR and Maj.T have the plural ἔρχονται. TRs has this clause as part of v. 19.
37. NIV has "so that he and the disciples were not even able to eat."
38. TR and Maj.T have the negative μητέ.
39. NIV has "When his family heard about this."

40. NIV has "He is out of his mind."

41. See A. T. Robertson, *Mary the Mother of Jesus: Her Problems and Her Glory* (New York: Doran, 1925).

42. NIV has "spoke to them in parables."

43. NIV has "no one can enter a strong man's house and carry off his possessions."

44. TR and Maj.T have a different word order, οὐ δύναται οὐδεὶς τὰ σκεύη τοῦ ἰσχυροῦ, εἰσελθὼν εἰς τὴν οἰκίαν αὐτοῦ διαρπάσαι. However, Maj.T begins the clause with Οὐδεὶς δύναται.

45. TR and Maj.T have the following, ἀλλ' ἔνοχός ἐστιν αἰωνίου κρίσεως.

46. TR and Maj.T have ἔξω ἐστῶτες.

47. NIV has "they sent someone in to call him."

48. TR and Maj.T have φωνοῦντες for καλοῦντες.

49. Swete, *Commentary on Mark*, 69.

50. TR and Maj.T have a different word order, ἐκάθητο ὄχλος περὶ αὐτόν. NIV has "Then he looked at those seated in a circle around him."

51. NIV has "Then he looked at those seated around him."

52. TR and Maj.T have a different word order, καὶ περιβλεψάμενος κύκλῳ τοὺς περὶ αὐτὸν καθημένους.

Mark: Chapter 4

4:1. *A very large crowd gathered to Him*[1] (συνάγεται[2] πρὸς αὐτὸν ὄχλος πλεῖστος), a graphic pictorial present again. See the crowds pressing Jesus into the sea. He first sat by the beach (Matt. 13:1) and then a "very great multitude" (ὄχλος πλεῖστος) made him enter a boat in which he sat and taught. Jesus now frequently taught crowds on the beach (Mark 2:13; 3:7–12).

He got into a boat in the sea and sat down[3] (ὥστε αὐτὸν εἰς πλοῖον ἐμβάντα καθῆσθαι ἐν τῇ θαλάσσῃ[4]). He sat in the boat, of course, which was in the sea.

4:2. *He was teaching them*[5] (ἐδίδασκεν αὐτοὺς), an imperfect tense describing it as ongoing.

In parables[6] (ἐν παραβολαῖς), as in 3:23, only here the parables are more extended. See further discussion of Christ's use of parables on Matthew 13. Eight parables are given in Matthew 13. The parable of the lamp occurs in Mark 4:21 and Luke 8:16. Both the sower and the lamp parables are in Luke. The seed growing of itself in Mark 4:26–29 is not in Matthew or Luke. Four parables are mentioned in Mark 4:1–34 (the Sower, the Lamp, the Seed Growing of Itself, and the Mustard Seed). But Mark adds (4:34), "without a parable spake He not unto them," clearly meaning that Jesus spoke many other parables on this occasion. Matthew (13:34) makes the same statement. Manifestly, therefore, Jesus told many parables on this day, and all exegetical or dispensational theories for the number of kingdom parables quite miss the mark.

4:3. *"Listen to this!"*[7] (Ἀκούετε). It is significant that even Jesus had to ask people to listen when he spoke. See also verse 9.

4:7. *"And the thorns came up and choked it"*[8] (καὶ ἀνέβησαν αἱ ἄκανθαι καὶ συνέπνιξαν αὐτό). Πνίγω means "to strangle, throttle." Mark has the compounded form with συν- ("squeezed together"). Matthew 13:7 has ἀπέπνιξαν, "choked off."

"And it yielded no crop"[9] (καὶ καρπὸν οὐκ ἔδωκεν), in Mark alone, "barren in results."

4:8. *"As they grew and increased"*[10] (ἐδίδου καρπὸν ἀναβαίνοντα καὶ

291

αὐξανόμενα[11]), in Mark alone, a vivid detail enlarging on the continued growth implied in the imperfect "yielded fruit." It kept on yielding as it grew. Fruit is what matters.

4:10. *As soon as He was alone*[12] (ὅτε ἐγένετο κατὰ μόνας[13]), only in Mark, a vivid recollection of Peter. Mark has also "His followers, along with the twelve"[14] (οἱ περὶ αὐτὸν σὺν τοῖς δώδεκα). Matthew and Luke have simply "the disciples." The disciples did not want the multitude to see that they did not understand the teaching of Jesus.

4:11. *"To you has been given the mystery of the kingdom of God"*[15] (Ὑμῖν τὸ μυστήριον δέδοται τῆς βασιλείας τοῦ θεοῦ[16]). See on Matthew 13:11 regarding μυστήριον. It is used in this account alone in the Gospels (Mark 4:11 = Matt. 13:11 = Luke 8:10), but in Paul it occurs twenty-one times and in the Revelation four times. It also occurs frequently in the LXX for Daniel and the Apocrypha. Matthew and Luke use it in the plural and add "to know" (γνῶναι), but Mark covers a wider range than growing knowledge, the permanent possession of the mystery even before they understand it. The secret is no longer hidden from the initiated. Discipleship means initiation into the secret of God's kingdom, and it will come gradually to these men.

"But those who are outside"[17] (ἐκείνοις δὲ τοῖς ἔξω). This is peculiar to Mark, meaning those outside our circle, the uninitiated, the hostile group like the scribes and Pharisees who were charging Jesus with being in league with Beelzebub. Luke 8:10 has "to the rest" (τοῖς λοιποῖς), Matthew 13:11 simply "to them" (ἐκείνοις). Without the key, the parables are hard to understand, for parables veil the truth of the kingdom. Their truth is stated in terms of another realm. Without spiritual insight, they are unintelligible, and today they are often perverted. The parables are a condemnation on the willfully blind and hostile, while a guide and blessing to those with faith.

4:12. *"So that"* (ἵνα). Mark has the construction of the Hebrew "lest" of Isaiah 6:9f. with the subjunctive; so does Luke 8:10. Matthew 13:13 uses causal ὅτι with the indicative following the LXX. See on Matthew 13:13 for the so-called causal use of ἵνα. See Ezra Gould on Mark 4:12 for a discussion of the differences between Matthew, Mark, and Luke. He argues that Mark probably "preserves the original form of Jesus' saying."[18] God ironically commands Isaiah to harden the hearts of the people. If the notion of purpose is preserved in the use of ἵνα in Mark and Luke, there is probably some irony in the sad words of Jesus. If ἵνα is given the causative use of ὅτι in Matthew, the difficulty disappears. What is certain is that in using parables Jesus assumed God's judicial blindness of those who will not see.

"Otherwise they might return and be forgiven" (μήποτε ἐπιστρέψωσιν καὶ ἀφεθῇ αὐτοῖς). Luke does not have these difficult words, which seem in Isaiah to have an ironic turn, though Matthew 13:15 does retain them even after using ὅτι for the first part of the quotation. There is no way to make μήποτε in Mark 4:12 and Matthew 13:15 have a causal sense. It is the purpose of condemnation for willful blindness and rejection such as suits the Pharisees after their blasphemous accusation against Jesus. Jesus is pronouncing their doom in the language of Isaiah. It sounds like the dirge of the damned.

4:13. *"Do you not understand this parable?"* (Οὐκ οἴδατε τὴν παραβολὴν ταύτην). They had asked Jesus his reasons for using parables. This question implies surprise at the dullness of these who were initiated into the secret of God's kingdom. Incapacity to comprehend this parable of the sower raises doubt about all the others on this day and at all times.

4:14. *"The sower sows the word"*[19] (ὁ σπείρων τὸν λόγον σπείρει). It is not put this clearly and simply in Matthew 13:19 or Luke 8:11.

4:15. *"Where the word is sown"* (ὅπου σπείρεται ὁ λόγος), an explanatory detail only in Mark.

"Satan" (Σατανᾶς). Matthew 13:19 has "the evil one" (ὁ πονηρός) and Luke 8:12 has "the devil" (ὁ διάβολος).

"Which has been sown in them"[20] (τὸν ἐσπαρμένον εἰς αὐτούς[21]), within them, not just among them. Matthew has "in his heart."

4:19. *"The desires for other things"* (αἱ περὶ τὰ λοιπὰ ἐπιθυμίαι). All the passions or longings, sensual, worldly, "pleasures of this life" (ἡδονῶν τοῦ βίου) as Luke has it (8:14), the world of sense drowning the world of spirit. The word ἐπιθυμία is not evil in itself. One can yearn (this word) for what is high and holy (Luke 22:15; Phil. 1:23).

4:20. *"They hear the word and accept it and bear fruit"*[22] (οἵτινες ἀκούουσιν τὸν λόγον καὶ παραδέχονται καὶ καρποφοροῦσιν), same word in Matthew 13:23 and Luke 8:15. Mark gives the order from thirty, sixty, to a hundred, while Matthew 13:23 has it reversed.

4:21. *"Is it not brought to be put on the lampstand?"*[23] (οὐχ ἵνα ἐπὶ τὴν λυχνίαν τεθῇ[24]), third person singular first aorist passive subjunctive of τίθημι, with ἵνα (purpose). The lamp in the one-room house was a familiar object along with the bushel, the bed, and the lampstand. Note the article with each. Μήτι in the Greek expects the answer no.[25] To put the lamp under the bushel (μόδιον) would put it out besides giving no light. So as to the bed or table-couch (κλίνην) if it was raised above the floor and liable to be set on fire.

Some sayings were repeated by Jesus on other occasions, as shown in Matthew and Luke.

4:22. *"For nothing is hidden, except to be revealed"*[26] (οὐ γάρ ἐστιν κρυπτὸν ἐὰν μὴ ἵνα φανερωθῇ[27]), note ἐὰν μή and ἵνα. Luke 8:17 has it "that shall not be made manifest" (ὃ οὐ φανερὸν γενήσεται). Here in Mark it is stated that the temporary concealment is a means to that end of final manifestation. Those charged with the secret at this time are given the set responsibility of proclaiming it on the housetops after the ascension.[28] The hidden (κρυπτὸν) and the secret (ἀπόκρυφον) are to be revealed in due time.

4:23. *"If anyone has ears to hear, let him hear"* (εἴ τις ἔχει ὦτα ἀκούειν ἀκουέτω). Verse 23 repeats verse 9 with a conditional form instead of a relative clause. Perhaps Jesus noticed some inattention among his listeners.

4:24. *"Take care what you listen to"*[29] (Βλέπετε τί ἀκούετε). Luke 8:18 has it "how you hear" (πῶς ἀκούετε). Both are important. Some things should not be heard at all for they besmirch the mind and heart. What is worth hearing should be heard rightly and heeded.

"By your standard of measure"[30] (ἐν ᾧ μέτρῳ). See already in the Sermon on the Mount (Matt. 7:2; Luke 6:38).

4:25. *"Even what he has shall be taken away from him"* (καὶ ὃ ἔχει ἀρθήσεται ἀπ' αὐτοῦ). Luke 8:18 has *even that which he thinks that he has or seems to have* (καὶ ὃ δοκεῖ ἔχειν). It is possible that ἔχει here has the notion of acquiring. One who does not acquire soon loses what he thinks he had. This is one of the paradoxes of Jesus that repay thought and practice.

4:26. *"The kingdom of God is like a man who casts seed upon the soil"*[31] (Οὕτως ἐστὶν ἡ βασιλεία τοῦ θεοῦ ὡς[32] ἄνθρωπος βάλῃ τὸν σπόρον ἐπὶ τῆς γῆς). Note ὃ" with the aorist subjunctive without ἄν. It is a supposable case and so the subjunctive and the aorist tense because of a single instance. Blass considers this idiom "quite impossible," but it is the true text and makes good sense.[33] The more common idiom would have been ὅς ἐάν (or ἄν).

4:27. *"And he goes to bed at night and gets up by day"*[34] (καὶ καθεύδῃ καὶ ἐγείρηται νύκτα καὶ ἡμέραν), present subjunctive for continued action. So also "the seed sprouts and grows" (καὶ ὁ σπόρος βλαστᾷ[35] καὶ μηκύνηται), two late verbs. The process of growth goes on all night and all day, an accusative of time.

"How, he himself does not know"[36] (ὡς οὐκ οἶδεν αὐτός). Note position of ὡς (beginning) and αὐτός (end) of clause: Literally it is "How knows not he." Some mechanisms of plant growth still puzzle farmers and scientists, but nature's secret processes do not fail to operate because we are ignorant. This

secret and mysterious growth of the kingdom in the heart and life is the point of this beautiful parable. "When man has done his part, the actual process of growth is beyond his reach or comprehension." [37]

4:28. *"The soil produces crops by itself"*[38] (αὐτομάτη ἡ γῆ καρποφορεῖ[39]). Growth is automatic, we say. The secret of growth is in the seed. Soil, weather, and cultivation help, but the seed spontaneously works according to its nature. The word αὐτομάτη is from αὐτός ("self") and μέμαα ("desire eagerly") from obsolete μάω. The only other example of this term in the New Testament is in Acts 12:10 when the city gate opens to Peter of its own accord. "The mind is adapted to the truth, as the eye to the light." [40] So we sow the seed, God's kingdom truth, and the soil (the soul) is ready for the seed. The Holy Spirit works on the heart and uses the seed sown and makes it germinate and grow, "first the blade, then the head, then the mature grain in the head"[41] (πρῶτον χόρτον εἶτα στάχυν εἶτα πλήρης[42] σῖτον ἐν τῷ στάχυϊ). This is the order of nature and also of grace in the kingdom of God. Hence it is worthwhile to preach and teach. "This single fact creates the confidence shown by Jesus in the ultimate establishment of his kingdom in spite of the obstacles which obstruct its progress." [43]

4:29. *"But when the crop permits"*[44] (ὅταν δὲ παραδοῖ ὁ καρπός[45]), second aorist subjunctive, whenever the fruit yields itself or permits.

"He immediately puts in the sickle"[46] (εὐθὺς ἀποστέλλει τὸ δρέπανον), sends forth the sickle. The word *apostle* comes from this verb. See John 4:38: "I sent you forth to reap" (ἐγὼ ἀπέστειλα ὑμᾶς θερίζειν). *Sickle* (δρέπανον) by metonymy stands for the reapers who use it when the harvest stands ready for it (παρέστηκεν, stands by the side, present perfect indicative).

4:30. *"How shall we picture the kingdom of God?"*[47] (Πῶς[48] ὁμοιώσωμεν τὴν βασιλείαν τοῦ θεοῦ[;]), a deliberative first aorist subjunctive. This question is found only in Mark, as is the companion question that follows immediately: "By what parable shall we present it?"[49] (ἐν τίνι αὐτὴν παραβολῇ θῶμεν;[50]), a deliberative second aorist subjunctive. The graphic question draws the interest of the hearers. Luke 13:18 retains the double question. Matthew 13:31f. does not use a question, though Matthew probably is citing some of Christ's favorite sayings, teachings He often repeated.

4:31. *"Which, when sown upon the soil"* (ὃς ὅταν σπαρῇ ἐπὶ τῆς γῆς), third person singular second aorist passive subjunctive of σπείρω, alone in Mark and repeated in verse 32.

"It is smaller than all the seeds that are upon the soil"[51] (μικρότερον ὂν πάντων τῶν σπερμάτων τῶν ἐπὶ τῆς γῆς[52]), a comparative adjective with

the ablative case after it. Jesus uses hyperbole to stress that large plants can grow from a very small seed, and so will come the gradual pervasive expansive power of the kingdom of God.

4:32. *"It grows up . . . so that the birds of the air can nest under its shade"* (ἀναβαίνει . . . ὥστε δύνασθαι ὑπὸ τὴν σκιὰν αὐτοῦ τὰ πετεινὰ τοῦ οὐρανοῦ κατασκηνοῦν). The picture differs from that of Matthew 13:32, "in its branches" (ἐν τοῖς κλάδοις αὐτοῦ), but both Matthew and Mark use κατασκηνόω, "to tent or camp down, make nests in the branches in the shade or hop on the ground under the shade just like a covey of birds." In Matthew 8:20, the birds have nests (κατασκηνώσεις). The use of the mustard seed for smallness seems to have been proverbial and Jesus employs it elsewhere (Matt. 17:20; Luke 17:6).

4:33. *So far as they were able to hear it*[53] (καθὼς ἠδύναντο ἀκούειν), only in Mark, an imperfect indicative (see John 16:12 for οὐ δύνασθε βαστάζειν, "not able to bear"). There was a limit even to the use of parables before unbelievers. Christ gave the mysteries of the kingdom in this veiled parabolic form, which was the only feasible form at this stage.

4:34. *But He was explaining everything privately to His own disciples*[54] (κατ᾿ ἰδίαν δὲ τοῖς ἰδίοις μαθηταῖς[55] ἐπέλυεν πάντα). To his own (ἰδίοις) disciples in private, in distinction from the mass of people, Jesus was in the habit (imperfect tense, ἐπέλυεν) of revealing all things (πάντα) in plain language without the parabolic form used before the crowds. The verb ἐπιλύω occurs in the New Testament only here and in Acts 19:39, where the town clerk of Ephesus says of the troubles by the mob: "It shall be settled in the regular assembly" (ἐν τῇ ἐννόμῳ ἐκκλησίᾳ ἐπιλύθησεται), third person singular first future passive indicative from ἐπιλύω. The word means to give additional (ἐπί) loosening (λύω), so to explain, to make plainer, clearer, even to the point of revelation. This last is the idea of the substantive in 2 Peter 1:20 where even the RV has it: "No prophecy of Scripture is of private interpretation" (πᾶσα προφητεία γραφῆς ἰδίας ἐπιλύσεως οὐ γίνεται). Here the use of γίνεται ("comes") with the ablative case (ἐπιλύσεως) and the explanation given in verse 21 show plainly that disclosure or revelation to the prophet is what is meant, not interpretation of what the prophet said. The prophetic impulse and message came from God through the Holy Spirit. In private the further disclosures of Jesus amounted to fresh revelations concerning the mysteries of the kingdom of God.

4:35. *When evening came* (ὀψίας γενομένης), a genitive absolute. It had been a busy day. The blasphemous accusation, the visit of the mother and brothers and possibly sisters, to take him home, leaving the crowded house for the sea, the first parables by the sea, then more in the house, and now out of the house and over the sea.

"Let us go over to the other side" (Διέλθωμεν εἰς τὸ πέραν). Hortatory (volitive) subjunctive, second aorist active tense. They were on the western side and a row over to the eastern shore in the evening would be a delightful change and refreshing to the weary Christ. It was the only way to escape the crowds.

4:36. *Just as He was* (ὡς ἦν). They take Jesus along (παραλαμβάνουσιν) without previous preparation.

And other boats were with Him[56] (καὶ ἄλλα πλοῖα ἦν μετ᾽ αὐτοῦ[57]). This detail also is given only by Mark. Some people had got into boats to get close to Jesus. There was a crowd even on the lake.

4:37. *And there arose a fierce gale of wind*[58] (καὶ γίνεται λαῖλαψ μεγάλη ἀνέμου[59]). Mark includes a vivid historical present again. Matthew 8:24 has ἐγένετο ("arose") and Luke 8:23 κατέβη ("came down"). Luke has also λαῖλαψ, but Matthew σεισμὸς ("tempest"), a violent upheaval like an earthquake. Λαῖλαψ is an old word for these cyclonic gusts or storms. Luke's "came down" shows that the storm fell suddenly from Mount Hermon into the Jordan Valley and smote the Sea of Galilee violently at its depth of 682 feet below the Mediterranean Sea. The hot air at this depth draws storms down with sudden ferocity. The word occurs in the LXX of the whirlwind out of which God answered Job (Job 38:1) and in Jonah 1:4.

The waves were breaking over the boat[60] (τὰ[61] κύματα ἐπέβαλλεν εἰς τὸ πλοῖον), imperfect tense (were beating) vividly picturing the rolling over the sides of the boat "so that the boat was covered with the waves" (Matt. 8:24). Mark has it: "so much that the boat was already filling up"[62] (ὥστε ἤδη γεμίζεσθαι τὸ πλοῖον[63]), a graphic description of the plight of the disciples.

4:38. *Asleep on the cushion*[64] (ἐπὶ τὸ προσκεφάλαιον καθεύδων). Mark also mentions the cushion or bolster and the stern of the boat (ἐν τῇ πρύμνῃ). Matthew 8:24 notes that Jesus "was sleeping" (ἐκάθευδεν), Luke that "He fell asleep" (ἀφύπνωσεν, third person singular ingressive aorist active indicative). He was worn out from the toil of this day.

They woke Him[65] (ἐγείρουσιν αὐτόν[66]), so Mark's graphic historical present. Matthew and Luke both have "awoke Him." Mark has also what the others do not: "Do You not care?"[67] (οὐ μέλει σοι). They were angry and frustrated that Jesus slept through such a dangerous storm when they needed his strong arms.

"We are perishing"[68] (ἀπολλύμεθα, linear present). Precisely this form is found in Matthew 8:25 and Luke 8:24.

4:39. *He got up and rebuked the wind* (διεγερθεὶς ἐπετίμησεν τῷ ἀνέμῳ) as in Matthew 8:26 and Luke 8:24. He spoke to the sea also. All three Gospels speak of the sudden calm (γαλήνη) and the rebuke to the disciples for this lack of faith.

4:40. *"Why are you afraid?"*[69] (Τί δειλοί ἐστε;[70]). They had the Lord of the wind and the waves with them in the boat. He was still Master even if asleep in the storm.

"How is it that you have no faith?"[71] (οὔπω ἔχετε πίστιν;[72]). Not yet had they come to feel that Jesus was really Lord of nature. They had accepted his messiahship, but all the conclusions from it they had not yet drawn.

4:41. *They became very much afraid*[73] (ἐφοβήθησαν φόβον μέγαν), a cognate accusative with the first aorist passive indicative. They feared a great fear. Matthew 8:27 and Luke 8:25 mention that "they marvelled." But there was fear in it also.

"Who then is this?"[74] (Τίς ἄρα αὐτός ἐστιν[;]). No wonder that they feared if this One could command the wind and the waves at will as well as demons and drive out all diseases and speak such mysteries in parables. They were growing in their apprehension and comprehension of Jesus Christ. They had much yet to learn. There is much yet for us today to learn or seek to grow in the knowledge of our Lord Jesus Christ. This incident opened the eyes and minds of the disciples to the majesty of Jesus.

NOTES

1. NIV has "The crowd that gathered around him was so large."
2. TR and Maj.T have the verb συνήχθη.
3. NIV has "he got into a boat and sat in it on the lake."
4. TR and Maj.T have a different word order, ὥστε αὐτὸν ἐμβάντα εἰς τὸ πλοῖον καθῆσθαι ἐν τῇ θαλάσσῃ.
5. NIV has "He taught them."
6. NIV has "by parables."
7. NIV has "Listen!"
8. NIV has "which grew up and choked the plants."
9. NIV has "they did not bear grain."
10. NIV has "It came up, grew and produced a crop."
11. TR and Maj.T have the participle αὐξάνοντα.
12. NIV has "When he was alone."
13. TR and Maj.T have Ὅτε δὲ ἐγένετο κατὰ μόνας.
14. NIV has "the Twelve and the others around him."

15. NIV has "The secret of the kingdom of God has been given to you."

16. TR and Maj.T have a different word order, Ὑμῖν δέδοται γνῶναι τὸ μυστήριον τῆς βασιλείας τοῦ θεοῦ.

17. NIV has "But to those on the outside."

18. Ezra P. Gould, *Critical and Exegetical Commentary on the Gospel According to St. Mark* (Edinburgh: T. & T. Clark, 1896), 73.

19. NIV has "The farmer sows the word."

20. NIV has "that was sown in them."

21. TR and Maj.T have τὸν ἐσπαρμένον ἐν ταῖς καρδίαις αὐτῶν.

22. NIV has "Others . . . hear the word, accept it, and produce a crop."

23. NIV has "don't you put it on its stand?"

24. TR and Maj.T have the compound verb ἐπιτεθῇ for τεθῇ.

25. It is a curious instance of early textual corruption that both Aleph and B, the two oldest documents, have ὑπὸ τὴν λυχνίαν (under the lampstand) instead of ἐπὶ τὴν λυχνίαν, making shipwreck of the sense. WH places it in the margin, but that is sheer slavery to Aleph and B.

26. NIV has "For whatever is hidden is meant to be disclosed."

27. TR and Maj.T have οὐ γάρ ἐστίν τι κρυπτὸν ὅ ἐὰν μὴ φανερωθῇ. However, TRb and Maj.T do not include the moveable ν with the verb ἐστί.

28. Henry Barclay Swete, *Commentary on Mark* (repr. ed., Grand Rapids: Kregel, 1977), 82.

29. NIV has "Consider carefully what you hear."

30. NIV has "With the measure you use."

31. NIV has "This is what the kingdom of God is like. A man scatters seed on the ground."

32. TR and Maj.T have the conditional particle ἐάν after ὡς.

33. A. T. Robertson, *A Grammar of the Greek New Testament in the Light of Historical Research* (Nashville: Broadman, 1934), 968.

34. NIV has "Night and day, whether he sleeps or gets up."

35. TR and Maj.T spell the verb βλαστάνῃ instead of βλαστᾷ.

36. NIV has "though he does not know how."

37. Swete, *Commentary on Mark*, 84.

38. NIV has "All by itself the soil produces grain."

39. TR and Maj.T have the postpositive γάρ between αὐτομάτη and ἡ.

40. Gould, *Critical and Exegetical Commentary*, 80.

41. NIV has "first the stalk, then the head, then the full kernel in the head."

42. TR and Maj.T have the spelling πλήρη for πλήρης.

43. Gould, *Critical and Exegetical Commentary*, 80.

44. NIV has "As soon as the grain is ripe."
45. TR and Maj.T have the second aorist active subjunctive spelling παραδῷ for παραδοῖ.
46. NIV has "he puts the sickle to it."
47. NIV has "What shall we say the kingdom of God is like?"
48. TR and Maj.T have Τίνι for Πῶς.
49. NIV has "what parable shall we use to describe it?"
50. TR and Maj.T have ἐν ποίᾳ παραβολῇ παραβάλωμεν αὐτήν.
51. NIV has "which is the smallest seed you plant in the ground."
52. TR and Maj.T have μικρότερος πάντων τῶν σπερμάτων ἐστὶν τῶν ἐπὶ τῆς γῆς. However, TRb and Maj.T do not include the moveable ν on the verb ἐστί.
53. NIV has "as much as they could understand."
54. NIV has "But when he was alone with his disciples, he explained everything."
55. TR and Maj.T have the phrase τοῖς μαθηταῖς αὐτῶν.
56. NIV has "There were also other boats with him."
57. TR and Maj.T have καὶ ἄλλα δὲ πλοιάρια ἦν μετ᾽ αὐτοῦ.
58. NIV has "A furious squall came up."
59. TR and Maj.T have a reverse word order, ἀνέμου μεγάλη.
60. NIV has "the waves broke over the boat."
61. TR and Maj.T include the postpositive conjunction δέ.
62. NIV has "so that it was nearly swamped."
63. TR and Maj.T have ὥστε αὐτὸ ἤδη γεμίζεσθαι.
64. NIV has "sleeping on a cushion."
65. NIV has "The disciples woke him."
66. TR and Maj.T have the compound verb διεγείρουσιν αὐτόν.
67. NIV has "don't you care?"
68. NIV has "if we drown."
69. NIV has "Why are you so afraid?"
70. TR and Maj.T have Τί δειλοί ἐστε οὕτως.
71. NIV has "Do you still have no faith?"
72. TR and Maj.T have πῶς οὐκ ἔχετε πίστιν.
73. NIV has "They were terrified."
74. NIV has "Who is this?"

Mark: Chapter 5

5:1. *Into the country of the Gerasenes*[1] (εἰς τὴν χώραν τῶν Γερασηνῶν[2]), like Luke 8:26 while Matthew 8:28 has "the Gadarenes." The ruins of the village Khersa (Gerasa) probably are at this site, which is in the district of Gadara some six miles southeastward, not to the city of Gerasa some thirty miles away.

5:2. *When He got out of the boat*[3] (καὶ ἐξελθόντος αὐτοῦ ἐκ τοῦ πλοίου[4]). Immediately (εὐθύς[5]) Mark says, using the genitive absolute and then repeating αὐτῷ, associative instrumental, after ὑπήντησεν, "he met." The demoniac greeted Jesus at once. Mark and Luke 9:27 mention only one man while Matthew notes two demoniacs, perhaps one more violent than the other. Each of the Gospels has a different phrase. Mark has a man "with an unclean spirit"[6] (ἐν πνεύματι ἀκαθάρτῳ), Matthew 8:28 "two possessed with demons" (δύο διαμονιζόμενοι), Luke 8:27 "one having demons" (τις ἔχων δαιμόνια). Mark includes detail not found in Matthew or Luke (see on Matt. 8:28).

5:3. *And no one was able to bind him anymore, even with a chain* (καὶ οὐδὲ ἁλύσει οὐκέτι οὐδεὶς ἐδύνατο αὐτὸν δῆσαι[7]), instrumental case ἁλύσει, a handcuff (α privative and λύω, to loosen). This demoniac had strength to snap bonds as if he had been bound with string.

5:4. *Because he had often been bound* (διὰ τὸ αὐτὸν πολλάκις . . . δεδέσθαι), perfect passive infinitive, state of completion.

With shackles (πέδαις), from πέζα, "foot or instep." Chains bound him hand and foot to no purpose. The English plural of *foot* is *feet* (Anglo-Saxon *fot, fet*) and at one time the plural of *fetter* was *feeter*.

The chains had been torn apart by him[8] (διεσπάσθαι ὑπ' αὐτοῦ τὰς ἁλύσεις), perfect passive infinitive, drawn (σπάω) in two (δια- from the same root as δύο).

Broken in pieces[9] (συντετρῖφθαι), perfect passive infinitive again, from συντρίβω, to rub together. Rubbed together, crushed together. Perhaps the neighbors who told the story could point to broken fragments of chains and fetters. The fetters may have been cords or even wooden stocks, not chains.

No one was strong enough to subdue him (καὶ οὐδεις ἴσχυεν αὐτὸν[10]

301

δαμάσαι), third person singular imperfect active indicative. He roamed at will like a lion in the jungle.

5:5. *He was screaming . . . and gashing himself with stones*[11] (ἦν κράζων καὶ κατακόπτων ἑαυτὸν λίθοις), further vivid details by Mark. Night and day his loud scream or screech could be heard (cf. 1:26; 3:11; 9:26). The verb for cutting himself occurs here only in the New Testament, though an old verb. It means "to cut down" (perfective use of κατα-). We say "cut up, gash, or hack to pieces." Perhaps he was scarred all over with such gashes from his moments of wild frenzy night and day in the tombs and on the mountains. Periphrastic imperfect active with ἦν and the participles.

5:6. *He ran up and bowed down before Him*[12] (ἔδραμεν καὶ προσεκύνησεν αὐτῷ). "At first perhaps with hostile intentions. The onrush of the naked, yelling maniac must have tried the newly recovered confidence of the Twelve. Imagine their surprise when, on approaching, he threw himself on his knees."[13]

5:7. *"I implore You by God"*[14] (ὁκίζω σε τὸν θεόν). The demoniac calls upon Jesus with an oath (two accusatives) after a startled outcry like the one in 1:24 (see on that text). He calls Jesus "Son of the Most High God" (υἱὲ τοῦ θεοῦ τοῦ ὑψίστου), as in Luke 8:28 (cf. Gen. 14:18f.).

"Do not torment me!"[15] (μή με βασανίσῃς), prohibition with μή and the ingressive aorist subjunctive. *Torment* means to test metals or to torture (as the English colloquialism, "the third degree"). The same word occurs in all three Gospels.

5:8. *For He had been saying to him*[16] (ἔλεγεν γὰρ αὐτῷ), a progressive imperfect. Jesus had repeatedly ordered the demon to come out of the man, and the demon protested. Matthew 8:29 has "before the time" (πρὸ καιροῦ), and Luke 8:31 shows that the demons did not want to go back to the abyss (τὴν ἄβυσσον) right now. That was their real home, but they did not wish to return to the place of torment just then.

5:13. *Jesus gave them permission*[17] (καὶ ἐπέτρεψεν αὐτοῖς). These words present the crucial difficulty for interpreters. We are not told why Jesus allowed the demons to enter the hogs and destroy them instead of sending them back to the abyss. Certainly it was better for hogs to perish than men, but this loss of property raises the same problem as does loss in tornadoes and earthquakes, since they also come from God. Some have wondered also as to how one man could host so many demons. Since demons are spirit beings, without spatial dimension, that seems little more of an issue than how one demon can dwell in someone. Jesus told a story about a demon who was cast out of a man but then returned with seven worse demons and took possession (Matt. 12:43–

45). Ezra Gould thinks that the "legion of demons" is hyperbole, as in "I feel as if I were possessed by a thousand devils." This is too easy an explanation. See on Matthew 8:32 for "rushed down the steep."

And they were drowned in the sea (καὶ ἐπνίγοντο ἐν τῇ θαλάσσῃ), imperfect tense picturing graphically the disappearance of pig after pig into the sea. Luke 8:33 has ἀπεπνίγη, "choked off," a constative second aorist passive indicative, treating the herd as a whole. Matthew 8:32 merely has "perished" (ἀπέθανον).

5:14. *[They] reported it in the city and in the country*[18] (ἀπήγγειλάν[19] εἰς τὴν πόλιν καὶ εἰς τοὺς ἀγρούς). In the fields and in the city as the excited men ran, they told the tale of the destruction of the hogs. "The people came to see" (ἦλθον ἰδεῖν). "The whole city came out to meet Jesus" (Matthew 8:34). "The people went out to see what had happened" (Luke 8:35).

5:15. *They came to Jesus*[20] (καὶ ἔρχονται πρὸς τὸν Ἰησοῦν), a vivid present tense. They came to the cause of it all, "to meet Jesus" (εἰς ὑπάντησιν τῷ Ἰησοῦ, Matt. 8:34).

And observed the man who had been demon-possessed[21] (καὶ θεωροῦσιν τὸν δαιμονιζόμενον), again the vivid present tense.

And they became frightened[22] (καὶ ἐφοβήθησαν). Mark drops back to the ingressive aorist tense (passive voice). They had all been afraid of the man, but there he was, "sitting down, clothed and in his right mind"[23] (καθήμενον[24] ἱματισμένον καὶ σωφρονοῦντα). Note the participles. Luke 8:35 adds that the man was sitting "at the feet of Jesus." For a long time he had worn no clothes, according to Luke 8:27. The same Jesus had healed the wild man and destroyed the hogs.

5:17. *And they began to implore Him to leave their region*[25] (καὶ ἤρξαντο παρακαλεῖν αὐτὸν ἀπελθεῖν ἀπὸ τῶν ὁρίων αὐτῶν). Once before, the people of Nazareth had driven Jesus out of the city (Luke 4:16–31). Soon they will do it again (Matt. 13:3–58; Mark 6:1–6). In Decapolis, pagan influence was strong. The owners of the hogs cared more about the loss of property than for the man who had been healed. In the clash between business and spiritual welfare, business came first. All three Gospels tell that they asked Jesus to leave. They feared the power of Jesus and wanted no further interference in their business affairs.

5:18. *As He was getting into the boat, the man . . . was imploring Him*[26] (καὶ ἐμβαίνοντος[27] αὐτοῦ εἰς τὸ πλοῖον παρεκάλει αὐτὸν).

5:19. *"Go home to your people"*[28] ("Υπαγε εἰς τὸν οἶκόν σου πρὸς τοὺς σούς). "To your own folks" rather than "your friends." Certainly no people needed the message about Christ more than these who were begging Jesus to leave. Jesus had greatly blessed this man and so gave him the hard task of going home as a witness of new life. Several times in Galilee Jesus had forbidden those he healed to tell what he had done, but here it was different. There was no danger of too much enthusiasm for Christ in this environment.

5:20. *And he went away*[29] (καὶ ἀπῆλθεν). He did as Jesus instructed. He heralded (κηρύσσειν) or published the story all over Decapolis, and people kept on marvelling (ἐθαύμαζον, imperfect tense) at what Jesus had done. The man had a greater opportunity for Christ right in his home area than he would have had anywhere else. All knew that this once wild demoniac was a new man in Christ Jesus.

5:23. *"My little daughter"* (Τὸ θυγάτριόν μου), a diminutive of θυγάτηρ (Matt. 9:18). "This little endearing touch in the use of the diminutive is peculiar to Mark."[30]

"Is at the point of death"[31] (ἐσχάτως ἔχει). It was a tragic moment for Jairus. Matthew 9:18 has "My daughter has just died" (ἄρτι ἐτώλυσεν). Luke 8:42 has "she was dying" (αὐτὴ ἀπέθνῃσκεν, imperfect). An ellipsis before ἵνα is not uncommon, a sort of imperative use of ἵνα with the subjunctive.[32]

5:24. *And He went off with him*[33] (καὶ ἀπῆλθεν μετ᾽ αὐτοῦ), aorist tense. He went off with him promptly, but a great multitude kept following (ἠκολούθει), imperfect tense.

Pressing in on Him[34] (συνέθλιβον αὐτόν), imperfect tense again. The only occurrences of this compound in the New Testament are here and in verse 31. It was common in old Greek. Jesus could hardly move because of the jam (συνέπνιγον, Luke 8:42).

5:26. *And had endured much at the hands of many physicians*[35] (καὶ πολλὰ παθοῦσα ὑπὸ πολλῶν ἰατρῶν), a pathetic picture of a woman with a chronic case who had tried doctor after doctor.

[She] had spent all that she had (καὶ δαπανήσασα τὰ παρ᾽ αὐτῆς[36] πάντα) on treatments. For the idiom with παρά see Luke 10:7; Philippians 4:18.

[She] was not helped at all, but rather had grown worse[37] (καὶ μηδὲν ὠφεληθεῖσα ἀλλὰ μᾶλλον εἰς τὸ χεῖρον ἐλθοῦσα). Her money was gone, and the disease was gaining on her. Yet she had hope with the coming of Jesus. Matthew says nothing about her experience with the doctors. Luke 8:43 says that she "had spent all her living upon physicians and could not be healed of any." Luke the physician considers it a chronic case for which the doctors couldn't be blamed. She had a disease that they did not know how to cure. Vincent quotes a prescription in the Talmud for an issue of blood. It makes one grateful that we no longer are under the care of doctors of that era.[38]

5:28. *"If I just touch His garments"*[39] (Ἐὰν ἅψωμαι κἂν τῶν ἱματίων αὐτοῦ[40]). She was timid and did not wish to attract attention. She crept up in the crowd and touched the hem or border of his garment (κρασπέδου), according to Matthew 9:20 and Luke 8:44.

5:29. *And she felt in her body* (καὶ ἔγνω τῷ σώματι). "She knew," the verb means. She said to herself, "I am healed" (ἴαται). Ἴαται retains the perfect passive in the indirect discourse. It was a vivid moment of joy. The plague (μάστιγος) or scourge was a whip used in flagellations as was almost carried out on Paul by the Roman soldiers at Jerusalem to find out his guilt (Acts 22:24; cf. Heb. 11:26). It is an old word used for afflictions regarded as a scourge from God (see on Mark 3:10).

5:30. *Immediately Jesus, perceiving in Himself*[41] (εὐθὺς[42] ὁ Ἰησοῦς ἐπιγνοὺς ἐν ἑαυτῷ). She thought, perhaps, that the touch of Christ's garment would cure her without his knowing it, but Jesus was conscious that healing power had gone from him. The more precise meaning of the Greek idiom is, "Jesus perceiving in himself the power from go out" (τὴν ἐξ αὐτοῦ δύναμιν ἐξελθοῦσαν). The aorist participle here is a simple, timeless punctiliar, as in Luke 10:18: "I was beholding Satan fall" (Ἐθεώρουν τὸν Σατανᾶν ... πεσόντα). Πεσόντα does not mean "fallen" (πεπτωκότα), as in Revelation 9:1, nor "falling" (πίπτοντα), but simply the constative aorist "fall."[43] So Jesus means to say: "I felt in Myself the power from Me go." Scholars argue whether in this instance Jesus healed the woman by conscious will or by unconscious response when she touched his garment. We know only that Jesus was conscious that power had gone out. Luke 8:46 uses ἔγνων (personal knowledge), but Mark has ἐπιγνούς (personal and additional, clear knowledge). One may remark that no real good can be done without the outgoing of power. That is true of mother, preacher, teacher, doctor.

"Who touched My garments?"[44] (Τίς μου ἥψατο τῶν ἱματίων) More precisely, "Who touched Me on My clothes?" The Greek verb uses two genitives, of the person and of the thing. It was a dramatic moment. Later it was a common practice for the crowds to touch the hem of Christ's garments and be healed (Mark 6:56). But Jesus made a point of the woman's action. There was no magic in the garments of Jesus. Perhaps there was superstition in the woman's mind, but Jesus honored her faith, as those were honored who thought that they would be healed by Peter's shadow or Paul's handkerchief (Acts 5:15; 19:12).

5:31. *"You see the crowd pressing in on You"*[45] (Βλέπεις τὸν ὄχλον συνθλίβοντά σε, see v. 24). The disciples were amazed that Jesus was sensitive to anyone's touch in the midst of the crowd. They did not understand Jesus' utmost human sympathy for the sufferers He healed.

5:32. *And He looked around*[46] (καὶ περιεβλέπετο), an imperfect middle indicative. The answer of Jesus to the protest of the disciples was this scrutinizing gaze (see on 3:5, 34). Jesus did not need to explain that he knew the differences among the touches. [47]

5:33. *But the woman fearing and trembling, aware of what had happened to her*[48] (ἡ δὲ γυνὴ φοβηθεῖσα καὶ τρέμουσα, εἰδυῖα ὃ γέγονεν αὐτῇ[49]). These participles vividly portray the fears of this woman who tried to hide in the crowd. She heard Christ's question and felt his gaze. She had to come and confess, for something "has happened" (γέγονεν, second perfect active indicative) to her. When she knew that Jesus was aware of her, she "fell down before Him"[50] (προσέπεσεν αὐτῷ). Worship was the only proper attitude.

The whole truth (πᾶσαν τὴν ἀλήθειαν). Secrecy was no longer possible. She told "the pitiful tale of chronic misery."[51]

5:34. *"Go in peace"* (ὕπαγε εἰς εἰρήνην). She found sympathy, healing, and pardon for sins. *Peace* may have more the idea of the Hebrew *shalom*, health of body and soul. So Jesus adds, "Be healed of your affliction"[52] (ἴσθι ὑγιὴς ἀπὸ τῆς μάστιγός σου). The meaning is "Continue in wholeness and well-being."

5:35. *While He was still speaking*[53] (Ἔτι αὐτοῦ λαλοῦντος), a genitive absolute construction. This is another vivid touch in Mark and Luke 8:49. The phrase is in Genesis 29:9. Nowhere does Mark preserve better the lifelike traits of an eyewitness like Peter than in these incidents in chapter 5. At that moment, messengers from Jairus arrived to divert attention from the woman. The ruler's daughter has died (ἀπέθανεν), so "why trouble the Teacher anymore?" (τί ἔτι σκύλλεις τὸν διδάσκαλον). Jesus has raised from the dead the son of the widow of Nain (Luke 7:11–17), but people did not expect him to raise the dead. The word σκύλλω, from σκῦλον ("skin, pelt, spoils"), means "to skin, to flay," in Aeschylus. The term can mean to vex, annoy, distress (see Matt. 9:36). The middle is common in the papyri for "bother, worry," as in Luke 7:6. There was no further reason to trouble the Teacher about the girl.

5:36. *But Jesus, overhearing what was being spoken*[54] (ὁ δὲ Ἰησοῦς παρακούσας[55]). The construction can mean "not heeding" (see Matt. 18:17 and occurrences in the LXX). The sense is that of "hearing aside." Jesus overheard what was not spoken directly to him. "Jesus might overhear what was said and disregard its import."[56] Certainly he ignored the conclusion of the messengers. The present participle λαλούμενον suits the idea of overhearing.

Both Mark and Luke 8:50 testify that Jesus responded to the ruler of the synagogue (τῷ ἀρχισυναγώγῳ), "Fear not, only believe" (Μὴ φόβου, μόνον πίστευε).

5:37. *Except Peter and James and John the brother of James* (εἰ μὴ τὸν Πέτρον καὶ Ἰάκωβον καὶ Ἰωάννην[57]). The house may have been too small for the other disciples to crowd in among the family. This is the first time we see this inner circle of three set apart. They will have importance on the Mount of Transfiguration and in the Garden of Gethsemane (e.g., Mark 9:2; 14:33). Greek use of a single article for all three treats the group as a unit.

5:38. *He saw a commotion, and people loudly weeping and wailing*[58] (καὶ θεωρεῖ θόρυβον και[59] κλαίοντας καὶ ἀλαλάζοντας πολλά). Ἀλαλάζοντα has been regarded as an onomatopoetic word from Pindar down. The soldiers on entering battle cried Ἀλᾶλα. It is used of clanging cymbals (1 Cor. 13:1) and like ὀλολύζω in James 5:1. It is used of the monotonous wail of the hired mourners.

5:39. *"Why make a commotion and weep?"*[60] (Τί θορυβεῖσθε καὶ κλαίετε). Jesus had dismissed one crowd (v. 37) but finds the hired mourners making bedlam (θόρυβος) in the house. It was custom that they showed grief by their ostentatious noise. Matthew 9:23 spoke of flute players (αὐλητάς) and the hubbub of the excited throng (θορυβούμενον cf. Mark 14:2; Acts 20:1, 21:34). Mark, Matthew, and Luke all quote Jesus as saying, "The child is not dead, but sleeps." Some commentators believe Jesus meant that the child was not really dead. More likely he meant that she would not stay dead. Jesus uses a beautiful word (καθεύδει, "she is *sleeping*") for death.

5:40. *They began laughing at Him*[61] (καὶ κατεγέλων αὐτοῦ). "They jeered at him" (Weymouth). Note the imperfect tense. They kept it up. And note also κατ- (perfective use; the same words are found in Matt. 9:24 and Luke 8:53). Jesus on his part (αὐτος δέ) took charge of the situation.

He took along the child's father and mother and His own companions[62] (παραλαμβάνει τὸν πατέρα τοῦ παιδίου καὶ τὴν μητέρα καὶ τοὺς μετ' αὐτοῦ). Having put out (ἐκβαλὼν) the rest by a stern assertion of authority, as if he were master of the house, Jesus enters the chamber of death *where the child was* (ὅπου ἦν τὸ παιδίον) with only the five. The presence of some people ruins the atmosphere for spiritual work.

5:41. *"Talitha kum!"*[63] (Ταλιθα κουμ[64]). These Aramaic words were spoken by Jesus to the child. Peter remembered them and passed them to us through Mark. Mark added a Greek translation for readers who did not know Aramaic (Τὸ κοράσιον, σοὶ λέγω, ἔγειρε[65]), "Little girl, I say to you, get up!" Mark uses the diminutive κοράσιον, a little girl, from κόρη, girl.[66] Luke 8:54 has it ῾Η παῖς, ἔγειρε, "Maiden, arise." All three Gospels mention the fact that Jesus took her by the hand, a touch of life (κρατήσας τῆς χειρός), giving confidence and help.

5:42. *Immediately the girl got up and began to walk*[67] (εὐθὺς[68] ἀνέστη τὸ κοράσιον καὶ περιεπάτει), an aorist tense (a single act) followed by the imperfect (the walking went on).

For she was twelve years old (ἦν γὰρ ἐτῶν δώδεκα). The age mentioned by Mark, probably an explanation that she was old enough to walk.

And immediately they were completely astounded[69] (καὶ ἐξέστησαν [εὐθὺς[70]] ἐκστάσει μεγάλη). See on Matthew 12:23 and Mark 2:12 regarding this verb construction. Here the word is repeated in the substantive in the associative instrumental case (ἐκστάσει μεγάλη), with great ecstasy, especially on the part of the parents (Luke 8:56).

5:43. *And He gave them strict orders that no one should know about this*[71] (καὶ διεστείλατο αὐτοῖς πολλὰ ἵνα μηδεὶς γνοῖ τοῦτο), the last verb is a second aorist active subjunctive. But would they keep still about it? There was the girl besides. Mark and Luke note that Jesus ordered that food be given to the child, "something should be given her to eat" (καὶ εἶπεν δοθῆναι αὐτῇ φαγεῖν), a natural care of the Great Physician. Two infinitives here (first aorist passive and second aorist active). "She could walk and eat; not only alive, but well."[72]

NOTES

1. NIV has "to the region of the Gerasenes."
2. TR and Maj.T have the spelling Γαδαρηνῶν.
3. NIV has "When Jesus got out of the boat."
4. TR and Maj.T have the dative absolute clause, ἐξεθόντι αὐτῷ ἐκ τοῦ πλοίου.
5. TR and Maj.T have the adverb spelled εὐθέως.
6. NIV has "a man with an evil spirit."
7. TR and Maj.T have καὶ οὔτε ἁλύσεσιν οὐδεὶς ἠδύνατο αὐτὸν δῆσαι.
8. NIV has "he tore the chains apart."
9. NIV has "broke the irons on his feet."
10. TR and Maj.T have the pronoun and verb in reverse order, αὐτὸν ἴσχυεν. However, TRb and Maj.T do not include the moveable ν on the verb ἴσχυε.
11. NIV has "he would cry out and cut himself with stones."
12. NIV has "he ran and fell on his knees in front of him."
13. Henry Barclay Swete, *Commentary on Mark* (repr. ed., Grand Rapids: Kregel, 1977), 94.

14. NIV has "Swear to God."
15. NIV has "you won't torture me."
16. NIV has "For Jesus was saying to him."
17. NIV has "He gave them permission."
18. NIV has "(They) reported this in the town and countryside."
19. TR and Maj.T have the verb ἀνήγγειλαν.
20. NIV has "When they came to Jesus."
21. NIV has "they saw the man who had been possessed by the legion of demons."
22. NIV has "and they were afraid."
23. NIV has "sitting there, dressed and in his right mind."
24. TR and Maj.T include a καί after καθήμενον.
25. NIV has "Then the people began to plead with Jesus to leave their region."
26. NIV has "As Jesus was getting into the boat."
27. TR and Maj.T have the second aorist participle ἐμβάντος for the present participle ἐμβαίνοντος.
28. NIV has "Go home to your family."
29. NIV has "So the man went away."
30. Marvin Richardson Vincent, *Word Studies in the New Testament*, 4 vols. (Grand Rapids: Eerdmans, 1946), 1.188.
31. NIV has "is dying."
32. A. T. Robertson, *A Grammar of the Greek New Testament in the Light of Historical Research* (Nashville: Broadman, 1934), 943.
33. NIV has "So Jesus went with him."
34. NIV has "pressed around him."
35. NIV has "She had suffered a great deal under the care of many doctors."
36. TR has the reflexive pronoun ἑαυτῆς instead of the personal pronoun αὐτῆς.
37. NIV has "yet instead of getting better she grew worse."
38. Vincent, *Word Studies*, 1.189.
39. NIV has "If I just touch his clothes."
40. TR and Maj.T have κἂν τῶν ἱματίων αὐτοῦ ἅψωμαι.
41. NIV has "At once Jesus realized."
42. TR and Maj.T have the adverb spelled εὐθέως.
43. Robertson, *Grammar*, 684.
44. NIV has "Who touched my clothes?"
45. NIV has "You see the people crowding against you."
46. NIV has "But Jesus kept looking around."
47. Alexander Balmain Bruce, *The Expositor's Greek Testament*, Vol. 1, *The Synoptic Gospels* (Grand Rapids: Eerdmans, 1951), 375.

48. NIV has "Then the woman, knowing what had happened to her . . . trembling with fear."

49. TR and Maj.T have the preposition with the pronoun, ἐπ' αὐτῇ.

50. NIV has "fell at his feet."

51. Bruce, *Expositor's*, 376.

52. NIV has "be freed from your suffering."

53. NIV has "While Jesus was still speaking."

54. NIV has "Ignoring what they said."

55. TR and Maj.T have Ὁ δὲ Ἰησους εὐθέως ἀκούσας.

56. Bruce, *Expositor's*, 376.

57. WH has the spelling with only one ν, Ἰωάνην.

58. NIV has "Jesus saw a commotion, with people crying and wailing loudly."

59. TR and Maj.T do not include the conjunction καί between θόρυβον and κλαίοντας.

60. NIV has "Why all this commotion and wailing?"

61. NIV has "But they laughed at him."

62. NIV has "he took the child's father and mother and the disciples who were with him."

63. NIV has "Talitha koum!"

64. TR and Maj.T have Ταλιθά, κούμι; WH has Ταλειθά κούμ.

65. TR and Maj.T have the verb spelled ἔγειραι.

66. *Braid Scots* has it: "Lassie, wauken."

67. NIV has "Immediately the girl stood up and walked around."

68. TR and Maj.T have the adverb spelled εὐθέως.

69. NIV has "At this they were completely astonished."

70. TR and Maj.T do not include εὐθύς.

71. NIV has "He gave them strict orders not to let anyone know about this."

72. Bruce, *Expositor's*, 377.

Mark: Chapter 6

6:1. *[Jesus] came into His hometown*[1] (ἔδχεται εἰς τὴν πατρίδα αὐτοῦ), so Matthew 13:54. There is no real reason for identifying this visit to Nazareth with that recorded in Luke 4:16–31 at the beginning of the Galilean Ministry. He was rejected both times, but it is not incongruous that Jesus should give Nazareth a second chance. It was natural for Jesus to visit his mother, brothers, and sisters. Neither Mark nor Matthew mentions Nazareth by name at this point, but it is plain that by πατρίδα the region of Nazareth is meant. He had not lived in Bethlehem since his birth.

6:2. *He began to teach in the synagogue* (ἤρξατο διδάσκειν ἐν τῇ συναγωγῇ[2]), as was now his custom, in the synagogue on the Sabbath. The ruler of the synagogue (ἀρχισυναγώγων, Mark 5:22) would ask someone to speak whensoever he wished. The reputation of Jesus all over Galilee opened the door for him. Jesus may have gone to Nazareth for rest, but he could not resist this opportunity for service.

"Where did this man get these things?" (Πόθεν τούτῳ ταῦτα). Laconic and curt, "Whence these things to this fellow?" with a sting and a fling in their words, as the sequel shows. They continued to be amazed (ἐξεπλήσσοντο, imperfect tense passive). They challenge both the apparent wisdom (Σοφία) with which he spoke and the mighty works (or "powers," δυνάμεις) such as those (τοιαῦται) coming to pass ("repeatedly wrought," γινόμεναι, present middle/passive participle) "by His hands" (διὰ τῶν χειρῶν). They felt that there was some hocus-pocus about it. They do not deny the wisdom of his words nor the wonder of his works, but the townsmen knew Jesus, and they had never suspected that he possessed such gifts and graces.

6:3. *"Is not this the carpenter?"* (οὐχ οὗτός ἐστιν ὁ τέκτων). Matthew (13:55) calls him "the carpenter's son" (ὁ τοῦ τέκτονος υἱός). He was both. Evidently since Joseph's death he had carried on the business and was "the carpenter" of Nazareth. The word τέκτων comes from τεκεῖν, τίκτω, to beget, create, like τεχνή (craft, art). It is a very old word, from Homer down. It was originally applied to the worker in wood or builder with wood like our carpenter. Then it was used of any artisan or craftsman in metal, or in stone as

311

well as in wood and even of sculpture. Justin Martyr speaks of plows and yokes made by Jesus. In Palestine, where wood was a rare commodity, *carpenter* also meant stonemason. Jesus may have helped build some of the stone synagogues in Galilee, like that in Capernaum. But in Nazareth the people knew him, his family (no mention of Joseph), and his trade. Therefore, they discounted all that they now saw with their own eyes and heard with their own ears. This word *carpenter* "throws the only flash which falls on the continuous tenor of the first thirty years from infancy to manhood, of the life of Christ."[3] That is an exaggeration, for we have Luke 2:41–50 and "as his custom was" (Luke 4:16), to go no further. But we are grateful for Mark's realistic use of τέκτων here.

And they took offense at Him (καὶ ἐσκανδαλίζοντο ἐν αὐτῷ). As in Matthew 13:57, "took offense at Him," trapped by the σκάνδαλον because He had so recently been one of them, and they could not explain him. "The Nazarenes found their stumbling block in the person or circumstances of Jesus. He became πέτρα σκανδάλου (1 Peter 2:7, 8; Rom. 9:33) to those who disbelieved."[4] Matthew 13:57 (which see) also preserves this retort of Jesus using the proverb that a prophet lacks honor in his own country. John 4:44 records that Jesus had said the same thing on a previous return to Galilee. It is to be noted that use of the statement means that Jesus identified himself as a prophet or seer (προφήτης, a forthspeaker for God). He already had claimed to be Messiah (John 4:26 = Luke 4:21), the Son of Man with the power of God (Mark 2:10 = Matt. 9:6 = Luke 5:24), the Son of God (John 5:22). Skeptics stumble over the identity of Jesus today as did the townspeople of Nazareth.

6:4. *"In his own household "*[5] (ἐν τῇ οἰκίᾳ αὐτοῦ; see also on Matt. 13:57). Literally his own brothers disbelieved his Messianic claims (John 7:5).

6:6. *And He wondered at their unbelief*[6] (καὶ ἐθαύμαζεν διὰ τὴν ἀπιστίαν αὐτῶν), aorist tense, though WH puts the imperfect in the margin. Jesus had divine knowledge and accurate insight into the human heart, but he had human limitations in certain things that are not clear to us. He marvelled at the faith of the Roman centurion where one would not expect faith (Matt. 8:10 = Luke 7:9). Here he marvels at the lack of faith where he had a right to expect it, not merely among the Jews, but in his own hometown, among his kinspeople, even in his own home. Mary, the mother of Jesus, need not be identified with this unbelief. Puzzled, as she probably was by the ways of Jesus (Mark 3:21, 31), there is no proof that she ever doubted his messianic divinity.

And He was going around the villages teaching[7] (Καὶ περιῆγεν τὰς κώμας κύκλῳ διδάσκων). An entirely new paragraph begins with these words, as Jesus sets out on his third tour of Galilee. They should be placed with verse 7. "Jesus resumes the role of a wandering preacher in Galilee,"[8] imperfect tense, περιῆγεν.

6:7. *And began to send them out in pairs*[9] (καὶ ἤρξατο αὐτοὺς ἀποστέλλειν δύο δύο). This repetition of the numeral instead of the use of ἀνὰ δύο or κατὰ δύο is usually called a Hebraism. The Hebrew does have this idiom, but it appears in Aeschylus and Sophocles, in the vernacular κοινή (Oxyrhynchus Papyri 121), in Byzantine Greek, and in modern Greek.[10] Mark preserves the vernacular κοινή within his vivid style more clearly than do the other Gospels. The six pairs of apostles could cover Galilee in six different directions. Mark notes that he "began to send them forth" (ἤρξατο αὐτοὺς ἀποστέλλειν), aorist tense and present infinitive. This may refer simply to this particular occasion in Mark's picturesque way. The imperfect ἐδίδου means that through the tour he kept on giving them all a continuous power (authority) over unclean spirits—singled out by Mark as representing "all manner of diseases and all manner of sickness" (Matt. 10:1), "to cure diseases" (νόσους θεραπεύειν, Luke 9:1; cf. "heal," ἰᾶσθαι, Luke 9:2). They were to preach and to heal (Matt. 10:7; Luke 9:1–2). Mark does not mention preaching in the commission to the twelve on this first tour, but he states that they did preach (v. 12). They were missionaries, who were sent (ἀποστέλλειν) in harmony with their office (ἀπόστολοι).

6:8. *Except a mere staff*[11] (εἰ μὴ ῥάβδον μόνον). Every traveller and pilgrim carried his staff. A. B. Bruce thinks that Mark has preserved the meaning of Jesus more clearly than does Matthew 10:10 and Luke 9:3, in which the instruction was not to take a staff.[12] Commentators have wondered about this difference. Grotius suggests no second staff for Matthew and Luke.[13] Henry Swete considers that Matthew and Luke report "an early exaggeration of the sternness of the command."[14] "Without even a staff is the *ne plus ultra* of austere simplicity, and self-denial. Men who carry out the spirit of these precepts will not labor in vain."

6:9. *But to wear sandals*[15] (ἀλλὰ ὑποδεδεμένους σανδάλια[16]). Perfect passive participle in the accusative case as if with the infinitive πορεύεσθαι or πορευθῆναι ("to go"). Note the aorist infinitive middle, ἐνδύσασθαι (WH), but ἐνδύσησθε (aorist middle subjunctive) in the margin. Change from indirect to direct discourse common enough, not necessarily due to "disjointed notes on which the Evangelist depended."[17] Matthew 10:10 has "nor shoes" (μηδὲ ὑποδήματα), possibly preserving the distinction between "shoes" and "sandals" (worn by women in Greece and by men in the East, especially travelers). Again *extra* shoes may be the prohibition (see on Matt. 10:10).

"Do not put on two tunics"[18] ($\mu\dot{\eta}$ $\dot{\epsilon}\nu\delta\dot{\upsilon}\sigma\eta\sigma\theta\epsilon$ $\delta\dot{\upsilon}o$ $\chi\iota\tau\hat{\omega}\nu\alpha\varsigma$) may indicate the direction of Jesus' instructions regarding shoes and staff. "In general, these directions are against luxury in equipment, and also against their providing themselves with what they could procure from the hospitality of others."[19]

6:10. *"Stay there until you leave town"* ($\dot{\epsilon}\kappa\epsilon\hat{\iota}$ $\mu\dot{\epsilon}\nu\epsilon\tau\epsilon$ $\dot{\epsilon}\omega\varsigma$ $\dot{\alpha}\nu$ $\dot{\epsilon}\xi\dot{\epsilon}\lambda\theta\eta\tau\epsilon$ $\dot{\epsilon}\kappa\epsilon\hat{\iota}\theta\epsilon\nu$), so also Matthew 10:11; Luke 9:4. Only Matthew has city or village (10:11), but he mentions house in verse 12. They were to avoid a restless and dissatisfied manner and to take pains in choosing a home. It is not a prohibition against accepting invitations.

6:11. *"For a testimony against them"*[20] ($\epsilon\dot{\iota}\varsigma$ $\mu\alpha\rho\tau\dot{\upsilon}\rho\iota o\nu$ $\alpha\dot{\upsilon}\tauo\hat{\iota}\varsigma$), not in Matthew. Luke 9:5 has a variation of expression with the same translation ($\epsilon\dot{\iota}\varsigma$ $\mu\alpha\rho\tau\dot{\upsilon}\rho\iota o\nu$ $\dot{\epsilon}\pi$' $\alpha\dot{\upsilon}\tauo\dot{\upsilon}\varsigma$). The dative $\alpha\dot{\upsilon}\tauo\hat{\iota}\varsigma$ in Mark is the dative of disadvantage and really carries the same idea as $\dot{\epsilon}\pi\dot{\iota}$ in Luke. The dramatic figure of shaking "the dust off the soles of your feet" ($\dot{\epsilon}\kappa\tau\iota\nu\dot{\alpha}\xi\alpha\tau\epsilon$ $\tau\dot{o}\nu$ $\chi o\hat{\upsilon}\nu$ $\tau\dot{o}\nu$ $\dot{\upsilon}\pi o\kappa\dot{\alpha}\tau\omega$ $\tau\hat{\omega}\nu$ $\pi o\delta\hat{\omega}\nu$ $\dot{\upsilon}\mu\hat{\omega}\nu$, effective aorist imperative, Mark and Matthew). Luke 9:5 uses the present imperative $\dot{\alpha}\pi o\tau\iota\nu\dot{\alpha}\sigma\sigma\epsilon\tau\epsilon$ for "shaking off."

6:12. *They went out and preached that men should repent* ($\dot{\epsilon}\xi\epsilon\lambda\theta\dot{o}\nu\tau\epsilon\varsigma$ $\dot{\epsilon}\kappa\dot{\eta}\rho\upsilon\xi\alpha\nu$ $\ddot{\iota}\nu\alpha$ $\mu\epsilon\tau\alpha\nu o\hat{\omega}\sigma\iota\nu$[21]), constative aorist ($\dot{\epsilon}\kappa\dot{\eta}\rho\upsilon\xi\alpha\nu$), summary description. This was the message of the Baptist (Matt. 3:2) and of Jesus (Mark 1:15).

6:13. *And they were casting out many demons and were anointing with oil many sick people*[22] ($\kappa\alpha\dot{\iota}$ $\delta\alpha\iota\mu\dot{o}\nu\iota\alpha$ $\pi o\lambda\lambda\dot{\alpha}$ $\dot{\epsilon}\xi\dot{\epsilon}\beta\alpha\lambda\lambda o\nu$, $\kappa\alpha\dot{\iota}$ $\ddot{\eta}\lambda\epsilon\iota\phi o\nu$ $\dot{\epsilon}\lambda\alpha\dot{\iota}\omega$ $\pi o\lambda\lambda o\dot{\upsilon}\varsigma$ $\dot{\alpha}\rho\rho\dot{\omega}\sigma\tauo\upsilon\varsigma$ $\kappa\alpha\dot{\iota}$ $\dot{\epsilon}\theta\epsilon\rho\dot{\alpha}\pi\epsilon\upsilon o\nu$), imperfect tenses, continued repetition, alone in Mark. This is the only example in the New Testament of $\ddot{\eta}\lambda\epsilon\dot{\iota}\phi\omega$ $\dot{\epsilon}\lambda\alpha\dot{\iota}\omega$ used in connection with healing, save in James 5:14. In both cases it is possible that the use of olive oil as a medicine is the basis of the practice. See Luke 10:34 regarding the practice of pouring oil and wine upon wounds. The papyri give a number of examples of olive oil's medicinal value, both internally and externally. Often it was employed after bathing. The question remains whether $\dot{\alpha}\lambda\epsilon\dot{\iota}\phi\omega$ in Mark and James 5:14 is used wholly in a ceremonial sense or whether the application combines medicinal and symbolic virtues related to divine healing. "Traces of a ritual use of the unction of the sick appear first among Gnostic practices of the second century."[23] We have today, as in the first century, God and medicine. God through nature does the real healing when we use medicine and the doctor.

6:14. *And King Herod heard of it*[24] ($K\alpha\dot{\iota}$ $\ddot{\eta}\kappa o\upsilon\sigma\epsilon\nu$ $\dot{o}$ $\beta\alpha\sigma\iota\lambda\epsilon\dot{\upsilon}\varsigma$ $H\rho\dot{\omega}\delta\eta\varsigma$[25]). This tour of Galilee by the disciples in pairs wakened all Galilee, for the name of Jesus became known (Φανερόν) until even Herod heard of him. "A palace is late in hearing spiritual news."[26]

"And that is why these miraculous powers are at work in Him"[27] (καὶ διὰ τοῦτο ἐνεργοῦσιν αἱ δυνάμεις ἐν αὐτῷ). Herod may have reasoned that, although John had wrought no miracles (John 10:41), perhaps a John risen from the dead could. "Herod's superstition and his guilty conscience raised this ghost to plague him."[28] The English word energy descends from ἐνεργοῦσιν. It means "at work." Miraculous powers were at work in Jesus, all agreed, but they differed widely as to whether he was simply another prophet or the raised John the Baptist. Herod was perplexed (διηπόρει, see v. 20; Luke 9:7).

6:16. "John, whom I beheaded, has risen!"[29] ("Ὅν ἐγὼ ἀπεκεφάλισα Ἰωάννην, οὗτος ἠγέρθη[30]). His fears got the best of him. The late verb ἀποκεφαλίζω means to cut off the head. Herod had ordered it done and recognizes his guilt.

6:17. For Herod himself had sent and had John arrested[31] (Αὐτὸς γὰρ ὁ Ἡρῴδης ἀποστείλας ἐκράτησεν τὸν Ἰωάννην[32]). Mark breaks in at this point to give the narrative of John the Baptist's murder as the reason for Herod's fears. Mark may be close to the chronological order. News of John's death at Machaerus may have come at the close of the Galilean tour. "The tidings of the murder of the Baptist seem to have brought the recent circuit to an end."[33] The disciples of John "went out and told Jesus. Now when Jesus heard it, he withdrew from thence in a boat" (Matt. 14:12f.; see on Matt. 14:3–12).

6:18. "It is not lawful for you to have your brother's wife" (Οὐκ ἔξεστίν σοι ἔχειν τὴν γυναῖκα τοῦ ἀδελφοῦ σου). After a brother's death it was often a duty to marry his widow, but that was not justification while the brother was alive (Lev. 18:16; 20:21).

6:19. Herodias had a grudge against him[34] (ἡ δὲ Ἡρῳδιὰς ἐνεῖχεν αὐτῷ), a dative of disadvantage. Literally, she "had it in for him." No object of εἶχεν is expressed, though ὀργήν or χολόν may be implied. The tense is imperfect and aptly describes the feelings of Herodias towards this upstart prophet of the wilderness, who dared to denounce her private relations with Herod Antipas. Gould suggests that she "kept her eye on him" or kept up her hostility toward him.[35] She never let up but bided her time. See the same idiom in Genesis 49:23.

And wanted to put him to death[36] (ἤθελεν αὐτὸν ἀποκτεῖναι), imperfect again.

And could not do so[37] (καὶ οὐκ ἠδύνατο). Καὶ here has an adversative sense: She had the will but not the power to destroy John.[38]

6:20. *For Herod was afraid of John*[39] (ὁ γὰρ ʿΗρῴδης ἐφοβεῖτο τὸν Ἰωάννην[40]), imperfect tense, continual state of fear. He also feared Herodias. Between the two, Herod vacillated. He knew John was "righteous and holy" (δίκαιον καὶ ἅγιον), "so he kept him safe"[41] (καὶ συνετήρει αὐτόν), imperfect. Also, Mark said that Herod enjoyed listening to the Baptist, presumably in the prison at Machaerus. These interviews braced "his jaded mind as with a whiff of fresh air."[42] Then he saw Herodias again and was entangled anew (ἠπόρει, "lose one's way," α privative and πόρος, "way").

6:21. *A strategic day came*[43] (Καὶ γενομένης ἡμέρας εὐκαίρου), a genitive absolute. The day was "well appointed" (εὐ, "well," καιρος, "time") for the purpose of Herodias. She had laid her plans to make her husband Herod Antipas do her will with the Baptist. Γενεσίοις is locative case or associative instrumental of time. See on Matthew 14:6 for discussion of Herod's birthday.

Gave a banquet for his lords[44] *and military commanders and the leading men of Galilee* (δεῖπνον ἐποίησεν[45] τοῖς μεγιστᾶσιν αὐτοῦ καὶ τοῖς χιλιάρχος καὶ τοῖς πρώτοις τῆς Γαλιλαίας). Μεγιστᾶσιν emerges from μεγιστάν, which in turn is from μέγας, "great." The term for societal lordship is common in the LXX and later Greek (cf. Rev. 6:15; 18:23) and is also found in the papyri. The military tribunes and commanders of a thousand men (χιλιάρχος) were invited, as were grandees, magnates, nobles, the chief men of civil life (τοῖς πρώτοις τῆς Γαλιλαίας). The notable gathering included the first men of social importance and prominence on Herod's birthday.

6:22. *And when the daughter of Herodias herself* (καὶ . . . τῆς θυγατρὸς αὐτοῦ ʿΗρῳδιάδος[46]), a genitive absolute. Instead of αὐτῆς, "herself," some manuscripts read αὐτου, "his," referring to Herod Antipas (so WH). In that case the daughter of Herodias would also have the name *Herodias* as well as *Salome*, the name commonly given to her. Toward the close of the banquet, when all had partaken freely of the wine, Herodias made her daughter come in and dance (εἰσελθούσης . . . καὶ ὀρχησαμένης) "before them" (Matt. 14:6). "Such dancing was an almost unprecedented thing for women of rank, or even respectability. It was mimetic and licentious, and performed by professionals."[47] Herodias degraded her own daughter in order to carry out her set purpose against John.

She pleased Herod and his dinner guests (ἤρεσεν τῷ ʿΗρῴδῃ καὶ τοῖς συνανακειμένοις[48]). The maudlin group lounging on the divans were thrilled by the licentious dance of the half-naked princess.

6:23. *And he swore to her*[49] (καὶ ὤμοσεν αὐτῇ [πολλά][50]). The girl was of marriageable age, though called κοράσιον (cf. Esther 2:9). Salome was afterward married to Philip the Tetrarch. The swaggering oath to half of the kingdom reminds one of Esther 5:3, where Ahasuerus made a similar oath.

"Ask me for whatever you want and I will give it to you"[51] (Ὅ τι ἐάν με αἰτήσῃς δώσω σοι). The drunken Tetrarch was caught in the net of Herodias by his public promise.

6:24. *"What shall I ask for?"* (Τί αἰτήσωμαι;[52]). The girl had not been told beforehand what to ask. Matthew condenses the account, and Matthew 14:8 is not so clear. The girl's question implies by the middle voice that she is thinking of something for herself. She was, no doubt, unprepared for her mother's ghastly reply.

6:25. *Immediately she came in a hurry to the king and asked*[53] (εἰσελθοῦσα εὐθὺς μετὰ σπουδῆς πρὸς τὸν βασιλέα ἠτήσατο[54]). She was sent back hurriedly, before the king's rash mood passed and while he was still under the spell of the dancing princess. Herodias knew her game well (see on Matt. 14:8).

6:26. *He was unwilling to refuse her*[55] (οὐκ ἠθέλησεν ἀθετῆσαι αὐτήν[56]). Antipas was caught between his conscience and his environment. The environment stifled conscience.

6:27. *Immediately the king sent an executioner* (καὶ εὐθὺς ἀποστείλας ὁ βασιλεὺς σπεκουλάτορα[57]), related to the Latin *speculator*. A spy, scout, assassin, and often executioner. The word was used to refer to the bodyguard of the Roman emperor and a similar officer is in view for Herod. This henchman was used to murderous errands, and he soon delivered John's head to the damsel, apparently in the presence of all the guests. She took it to her mother. From this day, the guilt-ridden Tetrarch, slave of Herodias, had been a slave to his fears. He was haunted by the ghost of John and shudders at reports of the work of Jesus.

6:29. *They came and took away his body and laid it in a tomb*[58] (ἦλθον καὶ ἦραν τὸ πτῶμα αὐτοῦ καὶ ἔθηκεν αὐτὸ ἐν μνημείῳ[59]). It was a mournful time for the disciples of John. "They went and told Jesus" (Matt. 14:12). What else could they do?

6:30. *The apostles gathered together with Jesus*[60] (Καὶ συνάγονται οἱ ἀπόστολοι πρὸς τὸν Ἰησοῦν), a vivid historical present.

And they reported to Him all that they had done and taught (καὶ ἀπήγγειλαν αὐτῷ πάντα[61] ὅσα ἐποίησαν καὶ ὅσα ἐδίδαξαν). The Greek uses the aorist indicative, constative aorist that summed up the story of their first tour without Jesus. Jesus listened to it all (Luke 9:10). He was deeply concerned in the outcome.

6:31. *"Come away by yourselves to a secluded place and rest a while"*[62] (Δεῦτε ὑμεῖς αὐτοὶ κατ' ἰδίαν εἰς ἔρημον τόπον καὶ ἀναπαύσασθε[63] ὀλίγον). The disciples were excited and needed refreshment (ἀναπαύσασθε, middle voice, lit. "rest up"). Even Jesus felt the need for occasional change and refreshment.

They did not even have time to eat (καὶ οὐδὲ φαγεῖν εὐκαίρουν[64]), imperfect tense. Crowds were coming and going, so change was necessary.

6:32. *They went away in the boat to a secluded place by themselves*[65] (καὶ ἀπῆλθον ἐν τῷ πλοίῳ εἰς ἔρημον τόπον κατ' ἰδίαν[66]). They accepted with alacrity, and off they went.

6:33. *The people saw them going*[67] (καὶ εἶδον αὐτοὺς ὑπάγοντας). The multitude that was following Jesus was not to be put off. They recognized (ἐπέγνωσαν) Jesus and the disciples and ran around the head of the lake on foot (πεζῇ). They were waiting for Jesus when the boat came.

6:34. *Because they were like sheep without a shepherd* (ὅτι ἦσαν ὡς πρόβατα μὴ ἔχοντα ποιμένα). Matthew has these words in another context (9:36). Mark alone has them here. Μή is the usual negative for the participle in the κοινή. These excited people[68] needed both preaching and healing (Matt. 14:14 mentions healing, as does Luke 9:11), but a crowd of vigorous runners would not include many sick. The people had plenty of official leaders, but these rabbis were blind spiritual leaders of the blind. Jesus had come over for rest, but his heart was touched by the pathos of this situation.

He began to teach them many things[69] (καὶ ἤρξατο διδάσκειν αὐτοὺς πολλά). Two accusatives with the verb of teaching and the present tense of the infinitive mean that He kept it up.

6:35. *When it was already quite late*[70] (Καὶ ἤδη ὥρας πολλῆς γενομένης). Notice the genitive absolute; ὥρας is used here for daytime (so Matt. 14:15) as in Polyhbius and late Greek (lit. "Much daytime already gone"). Luke 9:12 has it "began to incline or wear away" (κλίνειν). It was after 3 P.M. Note second evening or sunset in Mark 6:47 = Matthew 14:23 = John 6:16. Sunset was approaching. The idiom is repeated at the close of the verse (see on Matt. 14:15).

6:36. *"Send them away so that they may go into the surrounding countryside and villages"* (ἀπόλυσον αὐτούς, ἵνα ἀπελθόντες εἰς τοὺς κύκλῳ ἀγροὺς καὶ κώμας). The fields (ἀγρούς) were the scattered farms (Latin, *villae*). The villages (κώμας) may have included Bethsaida Julias, which was near (Luke 9:10). The other Bethsaida was on the western side of the lake (Mark 6:45).

"Something to eat" (τί φάγωσιν). Literally, "what to eat, what they were to eat." Deliberative subjunctive retained in the indirect question.

6:38. *"Go look!"*[71] (ὑπάγετε ἴδετε[72]). John says that Jesus asked Philip to find out what food they had (John 6:5) probably after the disciples had suggested that Jesus send the crowd away as night was coming on (Mark 6:35). On this protest to his command that they feed the crowds (Mark 6:37 = Matt. 14:16 = Luke 9:13), Jesus said, "Go see what you can get hold of." Andrew reports the fact of the lad with five barley loaves and two fish (John 6:8). They had suggested before that two hundred denarii (δηναρίων διακοσίων, see on Matt. 18:28) was wholly inadequate. John's Gospel alone tells of the lad with his lunch.

6:39. *By groups* (συμπόσια συμπόσια). Distribution here is expressed by repetition, as in verse 7 (δύο δύο), instead of using ἀνά or κατά. The English word *symposium* is derivative. It originally meant a drinking party (cf. Latin *convivium*), but the term came to mean a party of guests of any kind without the notion of drinking.[73]

On the green grass (ἐπὶ τῷ χλωρῷ χόρτῳ). This is another Markan touch. It was Passover time (John 6:4) and the afternoon sun shone upon the orderly groups upon the green spring grass (see on Matt. 14:15). The grass is not green in Palestine much of the year, mainly at the Passover time. So the Synoptic Gospels have an indication of more than a one-year ministry of Jesus.[74] It is still one year before the last Passover when Jesus was crucified. The people half reclined (ἀνακλῖναι) and may have been seated like companies at tables, open at one end.

6:40. *They sat down in groups* (ἀνέπεσαν πρασιαὶ πρασιαί). The word ἀνέπεσαν means "fell up here" (English speakers have to say "fell down."). But they were arranged in groups by hundreds and by fifties. The sight would have looked like garden beds, with the many colored clothes that even men wore in the Orient. Mark again uses a repetitive construction, πρασιαὶ πρασιαὶ, in the nominative absolute as in verse 39. The alternative would have been to use ἀνά or κατά with the accusative for the idea of distribution. Peter must have recalled the color as well as order in the grouping. Food could be distributed along orderly aisles between the rows on rows of diners on the green.

6:41. *He blessed the food and broke the loaves and He kept giving them to the disciples to set before them; and He divided up the two fish among them all*[75] (εὐλόγησεν καὶ κατέκλασεν τοὺς ἄρτους καὶ ἐδίδου τοῖς μαθηταῖς [αὐτοῦ] ἵνα παρατιθῶσιν[76] αὐτοῖς, καὶ τοὺς δύο ἰχθύας ἐμέρισεν πᾶσιν). Apparently the two fish were in excess of the twelve baskets full of broken pieces of bread (see discussion of the two kinds of baskets, κοφίνος and σφύρις, on Matt. 14:20).

6:44. *There were five thousand men* (καὶ ἦσαν . . . πεντακισχίλιοι ἄνδρες). The term is gender specific rather than a generic reference to people, so men are counted, as in Matthew 14:21. The number of women present is not given. This remarkable nature miracle, which only God can work, is recorded by all four Gospels. No theories of accelerated natural processes can explain this miracle. Matthew, John, and Peter through Mark give three distinct eyewitness reports.[77]

6:45. *Go ahead of Him to the other side to Bethsaida*[78] (προάγειν εἰς τὸ πέραν πρὸς βηθσαϊδάν). Now the attention turns back to the west side of the water, to Bethsaida, not Bethsaida Julias on the eastern side (Luke 9:10).

While He Himself was sending the crowd away[79] (ἕως αὐτὸς ἀπολύει[80] τὸν ὄχλον). Matthew 14:22 has it "while He sent the crowds away"[81] (ἕως οὗ ἀπολύσῃ τοὺς ὄχλους) with the aorist subjunctive of purpose. Mark's present indicative ἀπολύει pictures Jesus as personally engaged in persuading the crowds to return home (cf. John 6:41). The crowds were excited at their free meal and in the mood to proclaim Jesus their king in a revolt against Rome. He had already told the disciples to "go ahead" (προάγειν) in the boat. He may have wanted them away from this overwrought atmosphere. The people were in danger of sedition as they gave their own political twist to the concept of the Messianic Kingdom. This was the Pharisaic conception, and it distracted from what Jesus was communicating (see on Matt. 14:22–23). It also could precipitate events leading to the Crucifixion a year before Jesus was ready for it. Jesus had helped and blessed the crowds and had lost his chance to rest. No one really understood him at this point, neither the crowds nor the disciples. Jesus needed the Father to steady him. In a sense, the Devil again tempted him with world dominion in league with the Pharisees, and the populace.

6:47. *When it was evening*[82] (ὀψίας γενομένης). The second or late evening, 6 P.M. at this season, or sunset.

He was alone on the land (καὶ αὐτὸς μόνος ἐπὶ τῆς γῆς), another Markan touch. Jesus had prayed to the Father. He is by the sea again in the late twilight. Apparently Jesus remained some hours on the beach. "It was now dark and Jesus had not yet come to them" (John 6:17).

6:48. *Seeing them straining at the oars*[83] (καὶ ἰδὼν αὐτοὺς βασανιζομένους ἐν τῷ ἐλαύνειν[84]). Βασανίζω is discussed on Mark 5:7, as well as on Matthew 4:24; 8:29. Ἐλαύνειν is literally "to drive," relating to ships or chariots, and Xenophon uses it of a marching column of soldiers. Boats were driven by oars.

At about the fourth watch of the night (περὶ τετάρτην φυλακὴν τῆς νυκτὸς), between 3 A.M. and 6 A.M. The wind was "against them" (ἐναντίος αὐτοῖς). This is "a strong wind" (John 6:18). Rowing was difficult against such a headwind, and the disciples had made little progress. They should have reached the other side long before this.

He intended to pass by them[85] (καὶ ἤθελεν παρελθεῖν αὐτούς). This detail, using the imperfect ἤθελεν, is only found in Mark.

6:49. *They supposed that it was a ghost,*[86] *and cried out*[87] (ἔδοξαν ὅτι φάντασμά ἐστιν[88] καὶ ἀνέκραξαν). Literally a shriek of terror or scream is described.

6:50. *"Take courage; it is I"* (Θαρσεῖτε, ἐγώ εἰμι). These were astounding words of cheer, coming in the darkness from someone who was walking by on the water. But now they recognized Jesus, and his voice assured them.

6:51. *They were utterly astonished*[89] (λίαν [ἐκ περισσοῦ] ἐν ἑαυτοῖς ἐξίσταντο). The full reaction is only found in Mark. Note the imperfect tense, vividly picturing the excitement. Mark passes by Peter's attempt to walk on the water. Perhaps Peter was not fond of that story.

6:52. *For they had not gained any insight from the incident of the loaves*[90] (οὐ γὰρ συνῆκαν ἐπὶ τοῖς ἄρτοις). This is the explanation of their excessive amazement, i.e., their failure to grasp the full significance of who Jesus was from the miracle of the loaves and fish. Their reasoning process (καρδία, in the general inner sense) was hardened[91] (αὐτῶν ἡ καρδία πεπωρωμένη). See on 3:5 about πώρωσις. Because of such intellectual hardness or denseness, many cannot believe in a God who can or would work miracles.

6:53. *And moored to the shore*[92] (καὶ προσωρμίσθησαν). Only here in the New Testament, though it is an old Greek verb and occurs in the papyri. Ὅρμος is the inner anchorage of a harbor, where ships lie. They cast anchor or lashed the boat to a post onshore. It was at the plain of Gennesaret, several miles south of Bethsaida. The night wind had blown them far off course.

6:54. *The people recognized Him*[93] (ἐπιγνόντες αὐτόν). They recognized Jesus, knowing fully (ἐπί) as nearly all did by now, a second aorist active participle.

6:55. *And ran about that whole country*[94] (περιέδραμον[95] ὅλην τὴν χώραν ἐκείνην). A vivid constative aorist pictures the excited pursuit of Jesus as the news spread that he was in Gennesaret.

And began to carry . . . on their pallets those who were sick[96] (καὶ ἤρξαντο ἐπὶ τοῖς κραβάττοις τοὺς κακῶς ἔχοντας περιφέρειν). The pallets were like that on which the man was let down through the roof (Mark 2:4).

To the place they heard He was[97] (ὅπου ἤκουον ὅτι ἐστίν). Third person plural imperfect tense of ἀκούω (repetition), third person singular present indicative ἐστίν retained in indirect discourse.

6:56. *Wherever He entered villages*[98] (καὶ ὅπου ἂν εἰσεπορεύετο εἰς κώμας). The imperfect indicative with ἂν is used to make a general indefinite statement with the relative adverb. See the same construction at the close of the verse, καὶ ὅσοι ἂν ἥψαντο[99] αὐτοῦ ἐσώζοντο (aorist indicative and ἂν in a relative clause), "as many as touched it (the cloak) were being cured."[100] One must enlarge the details to get an idea of the richness of the healing ministry of Jesus. We are now near the close of the Galilean ministry, when Jesus' healing mercies and the popular excitement are high.[101]

NOTES

1. NIV has Jesus "went to his hometown."
2. TR and Maj.T have a different word order, ἤρξατο ἐν τῇ συναγωγῇ διδάσκειν.
3. Frederick W. Farrar, *The Life of Christ* (repr. ed., Minneapolis: Klock and Klock, 1982).
4. Henry Barclay Swete, *Commentary on Mark* (repr. ed., Grand Rapids: Kregel, 1977), 114.
5. NIV has "in his own house."
6. NIV has "And he was amazed at their lack of faith."
7. NIV has "Then Jesus went around teaching from village to village."
8. Alexander Balmain Bruce, *The Expositor's Greek Testament*, Vol. 1, *The Synoptic Gospels* (Grand Rapids: Eerdmans, 1951), 378.
9. NIV has "he sent them out two by two."
10. G. Adolf Deissmann, *Light from the Ancient East: The New Testament Illustrated by Recently Discovered Texts of the Graeco-Roman World*, trans. L. R. M. Strachan (rev. ed., Grand Rapids: Baker, 1965), 122f.
11. NIV has "except a staff."
12. Bruce, *Expositor's*, 379.
13. Hugo Grotius, *The Truth of the Christian Religion*.
14. Swete, *Commentary on Mark*, 116.
15. NIV has "Wear sandals."
16. TR and Maj.T have ἀλλ᾽ ὑποδεδεμένους σανδάλια.
17. Swete, *Commentary on Mark*, 116–17.
18. NIV has "but not an extra tunic."
19. Ezra P. Gould, *Critical and Exegetical Commentary on the Gospel According to St. Mark* (Edinburgh: T. & T. Clark, 1896), 107.

20. NIV has "as a testimony against them."
21. TR and Maj.T have the imperfect form of the verb, ἐκήρυσσον.
22. NIV has "They drove out many demons and anointed many sick people with oil."
23. Swete, *Commentary on Mark*, 119.
24. NIV has "King Herod heard about this."
25. TR spells the proper noun without an iota subscript, Ἡρώδης.
26. John Albert Bengel, *New Testament Word Studies*, vol. 1 (repr. ed., Grand Rapids: Kregel, 1971), 334.
27. NIV has "and that is why miraculous powers are at work in him."
28. Gould, *Critical and Exegetical Commentary*, 109.
29. NIV has "John, the man I beheaded, has been raised from the dead."
30. TR and Maj.T have ὃν ἐγὼ ἀπεκεφάλισα Ἰωάννην, οὗτος ἐστιν. αὐτὸς ἠγέρθη ἐκ νεκρῶν.
31. NIV has "For Herod himself had given orders to have John arrested."
32. WH spells the proper noun with only one ν, Ἰωάνην.
33. Swete, *Commentary on Mark*, 122.
34. NIV has "So Herodias nursed a grudge against John."
35. Gould, *Critical and Exegetical Commentary*, 112.
36. NIV has "wanted to kill him."
37. NIV has "But she was not able to."
38. Swete, *Commentary on Mark*, 123.
39. NIV has "because Herod feared John."
40. WH spells the proper noun with only one ν, Ἰωάνην.
41. NIV has "and protected him."
42. Swete, *Commentary on Mark*, 124.
43. NIV has "Finally the opportune time came."
44. NIV has "for his high officials."
45. TR and Maj.T have the imperfect verb, δεῖπνον ἐποίει.
46. TR spells the proper noun without the iota subscript, Ἡρωδιάδος.
47. Gould, *Critical and Exegetical Commentary*, 113.
48. TR and Maj.T have καὶ ἀρεσάσης τῷ Ἡρώδη (Maj.T has the iota subscript, Ἡρῴδη) καὶ τοῦς συνανακειμένοις.
49. NIV has "And he promised her with an oath."
50. TR and Maj.T do not include πολλά.
51. NIV has "Whatever you ask I will give you."
52. TR and Maj.T have the future form, Τί αἰτήσομαι.
53. NIV has "At once the girl hurried in to the king with the request."

54. TR and Maj.T have the adverb spelled εὐθέως.

55. NIV has "he did not want to refuse her."

56. TR and Maj.T have a different word order, οὐκ ἠθέλησεν αὐτὴν ἀθετῆσαι.

57. TR and Maj.T have the adverb spelled εὐθέως and the last noun spelled σπεκουλάτωρα.

58. NIV has "John's disciples came and took his body and laid it in a tomb."

59. TR has the plural noun in agreement with the previous two verbs, and includes an article, ἔθηκά αὐτὸ ἐν τῷ μνημείῳ.

60. NIV has "The apostles gathered around Jesus."

61. TR and Maj.T include the conjunction καί between πάντα and ὅσα.

62. NIV has "Come with me by yourselves to a quiet place and get some rest."

63. TR and Maj.T have the present tense verb, ἀναπαύεσθε.

64. TR has a different spelling for the verb, ηὐκαίρουν.

65. NIV has "So they went away by themselves in a boat to a solitary place."

66. TR and Maj.T have καὶ ἀπῆλθον εἰς ἔρημον τόπον τῷ πλοίῳ κατ᾽ ἰδίαν.

67. NIV has "But many who saw them leaving."

68. Bruce, *Expositor's*, 383.

69. NIV has "So he began teaching them many things."

70. NIV has "By this time it was late in the day."

71. NIV has "Go and see."

72. TR and Maj.T have ὑπάγετε καὶ ἴδετε.

73. So in Plutarch and the LXX, especially 1 Maccabees.

74. Gould, *Critical and Exegetical Commentary*, 118.

75. NIV has "He gave thanks and broke the loaves. Then he gave them to the disciples to set before the people. He also divided the two fish among them all."

76. TR and Maj.T have the aorist form of the verb, παραθῶσιν.

77. Gould, *Critical and Exegetical Commentary*, 120.

78. NIV has "go on ahead of him to Bethsaida."

79. NIV has "while he dismissed the crowd."

80. TR and Maj.T have the aorist subjunctive verb, ἀπολύσῃ.

81. NIV has "while he dismissed the crowd."

82. NIV has "When evening came."

83. NIV has "He saw the disciples straining at the oars."

84. TR and Maj.T have the second aorist indicative verb εἶδεν in place of the participle.

85. NIV has "He was about to pass by them."

86. NIV has "they thought he was a ghost."

87.   NIV has "They cried out."

88.   TR and Maj.T have ἔδοξαν φάντασμα εἶναι.

89.   NIV has "They were completely amazed."

90.   NIV has "for they had not understood about the loaves."

91.   NIV has "their hearts were hardened."

92.   NIV has "and anchored there."

93.   NIV has "people recognized Jesus."

94.   NIV has "They ran throughout that whole region."

95.   TR and Maj.T have the present active participle, περιδραμόντες.

96.   NIV has "and carried the sick on mats."

97.   NIV has "to wherever they heard he was."

98.   NIV has "And wherever he went—into villages."

99.   TR and Maj.T have the imperfect form of the verb, ἥπτοντο.

100. NIV has "and all who touched him were healed."

101. Bruce, *Expositor's*, 386.

Mark: Chapter 7

7:2. *Some of His disciples were eating their bread with impure hands, that is, unwashed*[1] (τινὰς τῶν μαθητῶν αὐτοῦ ὅτι κοιναῖς χερσίν, τοῦτ᾽ ἔστιν ἀνίπτοις, ἐσθίουσιν τοὺς ἄρτους[2]). "Unwashed hands" is in the associative instrumental case. Originally κοινός meant what was common to everybody, related to the term κοινή for the Greek spoken by the common people. In later usage κοινός came also to mean, as here, what is vulgar or profane. Peter uses the term in Acts 10:14 to tell God that he has never eaten what is "common and unclean." Emissaries of the Pharisees and the scribes from Jerusalem had seen "some of the disciples" eat with hands that were ceremonially unclean, unwashed. How many disciples were observed we are not told. Henry Swete suggests that in going through the plain the disciples may have been seen eating of the bread preserved in the twelve baskets from the previous afternoon's miracle.[3] The objection raised is on ceremonial, not sanitary, grounds.

7:3. *They carefully wash their hands*[4] (πυγμῇ νίψωνται τὰς χεῖρας) is instrumental case, *with the fist*, up to the elbow, rubbing one hand and arm with the other hand clenched.[5] It could be a dry wash or rubbing of the hands without water as a ritualistic concession. The reflexive middle voice νίψωνται means their own hands. This verb is often used for parts of the body while λούω is used of the whole body (John 13:10). On the tradition of the elders, see on Matthew 15:2.

7:4. *When they come from the market place* (καὶ ἀπ᾽ ἀγορᾶς[6]). Ceremonial defilement was inevitable in public. This ἀγορά from ἀγείρω, to collect or gather, was a public forum in every town where the people gathered. The disciples already were ceremonially defiled.

They cleanse themselves[7] (βαπτίσωνται), first aorist middle subjunctive of βαπτίζω, "wash, dip, or immerse."[8] Before eating they wash the hands always. When they come from market, they take a bath before eating. Ezra Gould terms ῥαντίσωνται "a manifest emendation," to get rid of the difficulty of dipping or bathing the whole body.[9] This is not the place to enter into any controversy about the meaning of βαπτίζω, "to dip," ῥαντίζω, "to sprinkle," and ἐχχέω, "to pour," all used in the New Testament. The words have their distinctive meanings here as elsewhere. Some scribes felt a difficulty about the use of βαπτίσωνται.[10] Swete considers the immersion of beds (βαπτισμοὺς κλινῶν) "an incongruous combination."[11] But Gould says that archaeologist Alfred Edersheim "shows that the Jewish ordinance required immersions, βαπτισμοὺς, of these vessels."[12]

7:6. *"Rightly did Isaiah prophesy of you hypocrites"*[13] (Καλῶς ἐπροφήτευσεν[14] Ἡσαΐας περὶ ὑμῶν τῶν ὑποκριτῶν). Appositely here, but with ironical sarcasm in verse 9.

7:8. *"Neglecting the commandment of God"*[15] (ἀφέντες[16] τὴν ἐντολὴν τοῦ θεοῦ). Note the sharp contrast between the command of God and the traditions of men. Jesus drives a keen wedge into the Pharisaic contention. They had covered up the Word of God with oral teaching. Jesus shows that they care more for the oral teaching of the scribes and elders than for the written law of God. The Talmud gives abundant specific confirmation of the truth of this indictment.

7:9. *"You are experts at setting aside the commandment of God in order to keep your tradition"*[17] (Καλῶς ἀθετεῖτε τὴν ἐντολὴν τοῦ θεοῦ, ἵνα τὴν παράδοσιν ὑμῶν στήσητε[18]). One can almost see the scribes withering under this terrible arraignment. Its biting sarcasm cut to the bone. The evident irony should prevent literal interpretation as commendation of the Pharisaic pervasion of God's Word[19] (see Matt. 15:7).

7:11. *Corban (that is to say, given to God)*[20] (Κορβᾶν, ὅ ἐστιν, Δῶρον; see on Matt. 15:5). Mark preserves the Hebrew word for a gift or offering to God (Exod. 21:17; Lev. 20:9), indeclinable here, meaning "gift" (Δῶρον), but declinable κορβανᾶς in Matthew 27:6, meaning sacred treasury. The rabbis ("but you say . . . ," ὑμεῖς δὲ λέγετε) allowed the mere saying of this word by an unfaithful son to prevent the use of needed money for support of his father or mother. They held that after saying this, the son was prohibited from using the money for father or mother, though he still might use it for himself.

7:13. *"Thus invalidating the word of God by your tradition"*[21] (ἀκυροῦντες τὸν λόγον τοῦ θεοῦ τῇ παραδόσει ὑμῶν). See the discussion of ἀκυροῦντες on Matthew 15:6. It means "invalidating" and is a stronger word than ἀθετεῖν, "to set aside," in verse 9. Both are used in Galatians 3:15, 17. Setting aside does invalidate.

7:14. *After He called the crowd to Him again*[22] (Καὶ προσκαλεσάμενος πάλιν τὸν ὄχλον[23]), an aorist middle participle, "calling to himself." The rabbis had attacked the disciples about not washing their hands before eating.

Jesus now turned the tables on them completely and laid bare their hollow, pretentious hypocrisy.

"Listen to Me, all of you, and understand"[24] (Ἀκούσατέ μου πάντες καὶ σύνετε[25]). This is a most pointed appeal to the people to see through the chicanery of these ecclesiastics (see on Matt. 15:11).

7:17. *When He had left the crowd and entered the house*[26] (Καὶ ὅτε εἰσῆλθεν εἰς οἶκον ἀπὸ τοῦ ὄχλου). This detail in Mark alone probably shows Jesus back in Peter's house in Capernaum. To the crowd Jesus spoke the parable of *corban*, but the disciples want it interpreted (cf. 4:10ff., 33ff.). Matthew 15:15 represents Peter as spokesman, which usually seems to have been the case.

7:18. *"Are you so lacking in understanding also?"*[27] (Οὕτως καὶ ὑμεῖς ἀσύνετοί ἐστε;). See on Matthew 15:16. It was discouraging for the great Teacher if his chosen pupils were still under the spell of the Pharisaic theological outlook. His words remained a riddle to them. "They had been trained in Judaism, in which the distinction between clean and unclean is ingrained, and could not understand a statement Mark 7:21 abrogating this."[28] They had noticed that the Pharisees stumbled at the parable of Jesus (Matt. 15:12). They were stumbling themselves and did not know how to answer the Pharisees. Jesus charges the disciples with dull intellect and spiritual stupidity.

7:19. *Thus He declared all foods clean*[29] (καθαρίζων πάντα τὰ βρώματα[30]). This anacoluthon can be understood by repeating "he says" (λέγει) from verse 18. The masculine participle agrees with Jesus, the speaker. The words do not come from Jesus but are added by Mark. Peter reports this to Mark, probably mediated by vivid recollection of his own later housetop vision in Joppa, when three times he declined the Lord's invitation to kill and eat unclean animals (Acts 10:14–16). Christ's abrogation of purity laws had remained a riddle to Peter until that day. "Christ asserts that *Levitical* uncleanness, such as eating with unwashed hands, is of small importance compared with *moral* uncleanness."[31] The two chief words in both incidents, here and in Acts, are *defile* (κοινόω) and *cleanse* (καθαρίζω). "What God has cleansed do not treat as defiled" (Acts 10:15). It was a revolutionary declaration by Jesus. Peter was slow to understand it, even after the coming of the Holy Spirit at Pentecost. Jesus was amply justified in his astonished question of Mark 7:18, "Do you not understand?" (οὐ νοεῖτε[;]). They were far from comprehending this spiritual insight.

7:21. *"Out of the heart of men, proceed the evil thoughts"*[32] (ἐκ τῆς καρδίας τῶν ἀνθρώπων οἱ διαλογισμοὶ οἱ κακοὶ ἐκπορεύονται). Evil in the inner heart leads to the dreadful list of crimes: fornications[33] (πορνεῖα, usually meaning sexual sins between the unmarried); thefts (κλοπαί); murders (φόνοι);

adulteries ($\mu o\iota\chi\epsilon\hat\iota\alpha\iota$,[34] referring to sexual sins that betray the marriage covenant); coveting[35] ($\pi\lambda\epsilon o\nu\epsilon\xi\hat\iota\alpha\iota$, "craze for more and more"); wickedness[36] ($\pi o\nu\eta\rho\hat\iota\alpha\iota$, from $\pi\acute o\nu o\varsigma$, a general reference to criminality or knavery); deceit ($\delta\acute o\lambda o\varsigma$, "to lure or snare with bait"); sensuality[37] ($\dot\alpha\sigma\acute\epsilon\lambda\gamma\epsilon\iota\alpha$, reference to unrestrained sexual impulses); envy ($\dot o\phi\theta\alpha\lambda\mu\grave o\varsigma$ $\pi o\nu\eta\rho\acute o\varsigma$, "an eye that works evil" and haunts one with its gloating stare); slander ($\beta\lambda\alpha\sigma\phi\eta\mu\acute\iota\alpha$, "blasphemy, hurtful speech"); and pride ($\dot\upsilon\pi\epsilon\rho\eta\phi\alpha\nu\acute\iota\alpha$, "holding oneself above others"). The last entry on the list is "foolishness" ($\dot\alpha\phi\rho o\sigma\acute\upsilon\nu\eta$, "lack of sense"), which describes all of the others.

7:24. *Jesus got up and went away from there to the region of Tyre*[38] ($^{\prime}E\kappa\epsilon\hat\iota\theta\epsilon\nu$ $\delta\grave\epsilon$ $\dot\alpha\nu\alpha\sigma\tau\grave\alpha\varsigma$ $\dot\alpha\pi\hat\eta\lambda\theta\epsilon\nu$ $\epsilon\dot\iota\varsigma$ $\tau\grave\alpha$ $\ddot o\rho\iota\alpha$ $T\acute\upsilon\rho o\upsilon$[39]). Jesus makes the second of four withdrawals from Galilee. The first had been to the region of Bethsaida Julias in the territory of Herod Philip. This is distinctly heathen land, including the edge of Phoenicia, as well as the region of Tyre and Sidon (Matt. 15:21). He left behind the people who would crown him king, the bitter Pharisees, and the suspicion of Herod Antipas.

Yet He could not escape notice[40] ($\kappa\alpha\grave\iota$ $o\dot\upsilon\kappa$ $\dot\eta\delta\upsilon\nu\acute\eta\theta\eta$ $\lambda\alpha\theta\epsilon\hat\iota\nu$). Jesus wanted to be alone in the house after all the strain in Galilee. He craved privacy and rest in Phoenicia. Note the adversative sense of $\kappa\alpha\acute\iota$, "but. . . ."

7:25. *But after hearing of Him*[41] ($\dot\alpha\lambda\lambda^{\prime}$ $\epsilon\dot\upsilon\theta\upsilon\varsigma$ $\dot\alpha\kappa o\acute\upsilon\sigma\alpha\sigma\alpha$ ... $\pi\epsilon\rho\grave\iota$ $\alpha\dot\upsilon\tau o\hat\upsilon$[42]). Even in this heathen territory, Jesus was known. For example, people from Tyre and Sidon had been present to hear the Sermon on the Plain (Luke 6:17).

A woman whose little daughter had an unclean spirit[43] ($\gamma\upsilon\nu\grave\eta$ ... $\hat\eta\varsigma$ $\epsilon\hat\iota\chi\epsilon\nu$ $\tau\grave o$ $\theta\upsilon\gamma\acute\alpha\tau\rho\iota o\nu$ $\alpha\dot\upsilon\tau\hat\eta\varsigma$ $\pi\nu\epsilon\hat\upsilon\mu\alpha$ $\dot\alpha\kappa\acute\alpha\theta\alpha\rho\tau o\nu$). Little daughter is a diminutive with a tender touch.

7:26. *Now the woman was a Gentile, of the Syrophoenician race*[44] ($\dot\eta$ $\delta\grave\epsilon$ $\gamma\upsilon\nu\grave\eta$ $\hat\eta\nu$ $^{c}E\lambda\lambda\eta\nu\acute\iota\varsigma$, $\Sigma\upsilon\rho o\phi o\iota\nu\acute\iota\kappa\iota\sigma\sigma\alpha$[45] $\tau\hat\omega$ $\gamma\acute\epsilon\nu\epsilon\iota$). She was "a Greek in religion, a Syrian in tongue, a Phoenician in race,"[46] from Euthymius Zigabenus. She was not a Phoenician of Carthage.

She kept asking Him[47] ($\dot\eta\rho\acute\omega\tau\alpha$ $\alpha\dot\upsilon\tau\acute o\nu$). The imperfect tense indicates she persisted in seeking Jesus' attention. This verb, as in late Greek, is here used for a request, not a mere question.

7:27. *"Let the children be satisfied first"*[48] ($^{\prime}A\phi\epsilon\varsigma$ $\pi\rho\hat\omega\tau o\nu$ $\chi o\rho\tau\alpha\sigma\theta\hat\eta\nu\alpha\iota$ $\tau\grave\alpha$ $\tau\acute\epsilon\kappa\nu\alpha$). The Jews had first claim. In the third tour of Galilee, Jesus avoided the Gentiles and Samaritans (Matt. 10:5). This pattern continued to be a model. Paul was Apostle to the Gentiles, but he gave the Jew the first opportunity even as the gospel went to the world from an impartial God (Rom. 2:9–10; see on Matt. 15:24).

7:28. *"But even the dogs under the table feed on the children's crumbs"* (καὶ τὰ κυνάρια ὑποκάτω τῆς τραπέζης ἐσθίουσιν ἀπὸ τῶν ψιχίων τῶν παιδίων[49]). The persistent Gentile mother pleads her case in utter humility. Even the little dogs under the table can eat what falls from the children's plates. Little dogs, little scraps of bread (ψιχίων, diminutive of ψῖχος, "morsel"), little children (παιδία, diminutive of παῖς).[50] The woman accepts Jewish prerogatives without giving up her cry for grace. Hers is "a unique combination of faith and wit."[51] Instead of resenting Christ's words about giving the children's bread to the dogs (Gentiles) in verse 27, she instantly turned it to the advantage of her plea for her little daughter.

7:29. *"Because of this answer go"*[52] (Διὰ τοῦτον τὸν λόγον ὕπαγε). She had great faith, as Matthew 15:28 shows, and her wisdom pleased Jesus. It was worth missing his rest to answer a call like this.

7:30. *The demon having left*[53] (καὶ τὸ δαιμόνιον ἐξεληλυθός[54]). The perfect active participle expresses the state of completion. The demon was gone for good.

7:31. *Within the region of Decapolis*[55] (ἀνὰ μέσον τῶν ὁρίων Δεκαπόλεως). Jesus left Phoenicia but did not go back into Galilee. He went east of the Sea of Galilee into the region of the Greek cities of Decapolis. He thus kept out of the territory of Herod Antipas. It was in this region that he had healed the demoniac (see on 5:1).

7:32. *They brought to Him one who was deaf and spoke with difficulty*[56] (καὶ φέρουσιν αὐτῷ κωφὸν καὶ μογιλάλον[57]). This dramatic incident is found only in Mark.

7:33. *Jesus took him aside from the crowd*[58] (καὶ ἀπολαβόμενος αὐτὸν ἀπὸ τοῦ ὄχλου κατ᾽ ἰδίαν). The secrecy observed was partly to avoid agitation and partly to get the attention of the deaf and dumb demoniac. He could not hear what Jesus said. So Jesus put his fingers into his ears, spat, and touched his tongue. Mark does not say why Jesus used saliva. Some regarded spittle as therapeutic. Exorcists used it in their incantations. Whether Jesus was dealing with the man on a level he could comprehend, one does not know, but it all showed the poor man that Jesus had healed him in his own way.

7:34. *He said to him, "Ephphatha!" that is, "Be opened!"* (καὶ λέγει αὐτῷ, Εφφαθα, ὅ ἐστιν, Διανοίχθητι). This is another of Mark's Aramaic words transliterated into Greek.[59] Jesus sighed (ἐστέναξεν) as he looked up into heaven and spoke the word Εφφαθα. What he felt in the complexity of this man as deaf, dumb, and demon possessed, we do not know.

7:35. *And he began speaking plainly* (καὶ ἐλάλει ὀρθῶς). He began to speak correctly, an inceptive imperfect tense.

7:36. *The more widely they continued to proclaim it*[60] (αὐτοὶ μᾶλλον περισσότερον ἐκήρυσσον[61]). The imperfect tense indicates continued action. This is a double comparative as occurs elsewhere for emphasis as in Philippians 1:23, "much more better" (πολλοὶ μᾶλλον κρεῖσσον).[62] Human nature is a peculiar thing. The more Jesus commanded them not to tell (ὅσον δὲ αὐτοῖς διεστέλλετο), the more they told (cf. Mark 1:44–45).

7:37. "He has done all things well" (Καλῶς πάντα πεποίηκεν). The present perfect active shows the settled convictions of these people about Jesus. Their great amazement (ὑπερπερισσῶς ἐξεπλήσσοντο), imperfect passive and compound adverb, thus found expression in a vociferous championship of Jesus in this pagan land.

NOTES

1. NIV has "some of his disciples eating food with hands that were 'unclean,' that is, unwashed."

2. TR and Maj.T do not include ὅτι and in place of the last three words have ἐσθίοντας ἄρτους.

3. Henry Barclay Swete, *Commentary on Mark* (repr. ed., Grand Rapids: Kregel, 1977), 142.

4. NIV has "they give their hands a ceremonial washing."

5. The manuscript Aleph had πυκνά probably because of the difficulty about πυγμῇ (kin to Latin *pugnus*).

6. TR and Maj.T have καὶ ἀπὸ ἀγαρᾶς.

7. NIV has "they wash."

8. WH puts ῥαντίσωνται in the text, translated "sprinkle themselves" in the margin of the RV, because Aleph, B, and some of the most reliable cursives have it.

9. Ezra P. Gould, *Critical and Exegetical Commentary on the Gospel According to St. Mark* (Edinburgh: T. & T. Clark, 1896), 127.

10. The Western and Syrian classes of manuscripts add "and couches" (καὶ κλινῶν) at the end of the sentence.

11. Swete, *Commentary on Mark*, 145.

12. Gould, *Critical and Exegetical Commentary*, 127. We must let the Jewish scrupulosity stand for itself, though "and couches" is not supported by Aleph, B L D Bohairic, probably not genuine.

13. NIV has "Isaiah was right when he prophesied about you hypocrites."

14. TR and Maj.T spell the verb, προεφήτευσεν.
15. NIV has "You have let go of the commands of God."
16. TR and Maj.T have the postpositive conjunction, γάρ.
17. NIV has "You have a fine way of setting aside the commands of God in order to observe your own traditions."
18. TR and Maj.T have the verb, τηρήσητε.
19. See A. T. Robertson, *The Pharisees and Jesus* (New York: Scribner, 1920), for illustrations of the way that they placed this oral tradition above the written law.
20. NIV has "Corban (that is, a gift devoted to God)."
21. NIV has "Thus you nullify the word of God by your tradition."
22. NIV has "Again Jesus called the crowd to him."
23. TR and Maj.T have καὶ προσκαλεσάμενος πάντα τὸν λόγον.
24. NIV has "Listen to me, everyone, and understand this."
25. TR and Maj.T have the present tense verbs, Ἀκούετέ μου πάντες, καὶ συνίετε.
26. NIV has "After he had left the crowd and entered the house."
27. NIV has "Are you so dull?"
28. Gould, *Critical and Exegetical Commentary*, 131.
29. NIV has "(in saying this, Jesus declared all foods clean)."
30. TR and Maj.T have καθαρίζον πάντα τὰ βρώματα.
31. Vincent, *Word Studies*, 1.201.
32. NIV has "out of men's hearts come evil thoughts."
33. NIV has "sexual immorality."
34. TR and Maj.T have a different word order, μοιχεῖαι, πορνεῖαι, φόνοι, κλοπαί.
35. NIV has "greed."
36. NIV has "malice."
37. NIV has "lewdness."
38. NIV has "Jesus left that place and went to the vicinity of Tyre."
39. TR and Maj.T have καὶ ἐκεῖθεν ἀναστὰς ἀπῆλθεν εἰς τὰ μεθόρια Τύρου καὶ Σιδῶνος.
40. NIV has "yet he could not keep his presence secret."
41. NIV has "a woman whose little daughter was possessed by an evil spirit."
42. NIV has "In fact, as soon as she heard about him."
43. TR and Maj.T have ἀκούσασα γὰρ γυνὴ περὶ αὐτοῦ.
44. NIV has "The woman was a Greek, born in Syrian Phoenicia."
45. TR has the spelling Συροφοίνισσα.
46. Alexander Balmain Bruce, *The Expositor's Greek Testament*, Vol. 1, *The Synoptic Gospels* (Grand Rapids: Eerdmans, 1951), 390.

47. NIV has "She begged Jesus."
48. NIV has "First let the children eat all they want."
49. TR and Maj.T have καὶ γὰρ τὰ κυνάρια ὑποκάτω τῆς τραπέζης ἐσθίει ἀπὸ τῶν ψιχίων τῶν παιδίων.
50. *Braid Scots* has it: "Yet the wee dowgs aneath the table eat o' the moole the bairns."
51. Gould, *Critical and Exegetical Commentary*, 136.
52. NIV has "For such a reply, you may go."
53. NIV has "and the demon gone."
54. TR and Maj.T have εὗρεν τὸ δαιμόνιον ἐξεληλυθός, although TRb and Maj.T have the verb without the moveable ν, εὗρε.
55. NIV has "and into the region of the Decapolis."
56. NIV has "There some people brought to him a man who was deaf and could hardly talk."
57. TR and Maj.T do not include the conjunction καί between κωφόν and μογιλάλον.
58. NIV has "After he took him aside, away from the crowd."
59. *Braid Scots* has "Be thou unbarred."
60. NIV has "the more they kept talking about it."
61. TR and Maj.T have μᾶλλον περισσότερον ἐκήρυσσον.
62. A. T. Robertson, *A Grammar of the Greek New Testament in the Light of Historical Research* (Nashville: Broadman, 1934), 663f.

Mark: Chapter 8

8:1. *And they had nothing to eat*[1] (καὶ μὴ ἐχόντων τί φάγωσιν). This is a plural genitive absolute because the previous ὄχλου is a collective singular. The repetition of a nature miracle of feeding four thousand in Decapolis disturbs some modern critics, who cannot imagine how Jesus could or would perform another miracle so similar to the feeding of the five thousand near Bethsaida Julias. Both Mark and Matthew give both miracles without apology, however. They distinguish the words for baskets (κόφινος, σφύρις). Jesus later refers to both incidents, distinguishing between them (Matt. 16:9–10). Surely it is easier to conceive that Jesus wrought similar miracles than that Mark and Matthew (or even some later "redactor") made such a jumble of the business.

8:2. *"They have remained with Me now three days"*[2] (ἤδη ἡμέραι τρεῖς προσμένουσίν μοι[3]). This text preserves a curious parenthetic nominative of time[4] (see on Matt. 15:32).

8:3. *"And some of them have come from a great distance"* (καί τινες αὐτῶν ἀπὸ μακρόθεν ἤκασιν[5]). This detail appears only in Mark.

8:4. *"Here in this desolate place"*[6] (ὧδε ... ἐπ' ἐρημίας). Of all places, in this desert region in the mountains. The disciples again feel helpless. They do not rise to faith out of previous experience.

8:6. *[He] broke them, and started giving them to His disciples* (ἔκλασεν καὶ ἐδίδου τοῖς μαθηταῖς αὐτοῦ). Notice the constative aorist followed by an imperfect. The giving kept on.

To serve to them[7] (ἵνα παρατιθῶσιν[8]), a present subjunctive describing the continuous process.

8:7. *They also had a few small fish*[9] (καὶ εἶχον ἰχθύδια ὀλίγα). Mark mentions them last, as if they were served after the food, but not so in Matthew 15:36.

8:8. *And they picked up seven large baskets full of what was left over of the broken pieces*[10] (καὶ ἦραν περισσεύματα κλασμάτων ἑπτὰ σπυρίδας). The bread collected was not just the scraps or crumbs but the pieces of bread Jesus had broken but had not been used. There was an overabundance.

334

8:10. *[He] came to the district of Dalmanutha*[11] (ἦλθεν εἰς τὰ μέρη Δαλμανουθά). Matthew 15:39 calls it "the borders of Magadan." Both names are unknown elsewhere but apparently refer to the same region of Galilee, west of the lake near Tiberias. Mark uses *parts* (μέρη) in the same sense as *borders* (ὅρια) in 7:24. Matthew reverses the pattern, with *parts* in Matthew 15:21 and *borders* in 15:39. Mark has "with His disciples" (μετὰ τῶν μαθητῶν αὐτοῦ), a fact only implied in Matthew 15:39.

8:11. *The Pharisees came out and began to argue with Him*[12] (Καὶ ἐξῆλθον οἱ Φαρισαῖοι καὶ ἤρξαντο συζητεῖν αὐτῷ). At once they opened a controversy. Matthew 16:1 adds "and Sadducees," the first time these two parties appear together against Jesus (see discussion on Matt. 16:1). Pharisees and Herodians had already joined hands against Jesus in the Sabbath controversy (see on Mark 3:6). Dispute, not mere inquiry is indicated, with an associative instrumental case for αὐτῷ. They began at once and kept it up (present infinitive).

8:12. *Sighing deeply in His spirit* (ἀναστενάξας τῷ πνεύματι αὐτοῦ). This is the only instance of this compound participle in the New Testament, though it is found in the LXX. The uncompounded form is common. For example, it occurs in Mark 7:34. The preposition ἀνα- intensifies the meaning of the verb (perfective use). "The sigh seemed to come, as we say, from the bottom of his heart, the Lord's human spirit was stirred to its depths."[13] Jesus resented the settled prejudice against him and his work among the Pharisees and now also the Sadducees.

"No sign will be given to this generation" (εἰ δοθήσεται τῇ γενεᾷ ταύτῃ σημεῖον). Matthew 16:4 has simply οὐ δοθήσεται, plain negative with the future passive indicative. Mark has εἰ instead of οὐ, which is technically a conditional clause with the conclusion unexpressed,[14] really aposiopesis in imitation of the Hebrew use of *im*. This is the only instance in the New Testament, except in quotations from the LXX (Heb. 3:11; 4:3, 5). It is common in the LXX. The rabbis were splitting hairs over the miracles of Jesus as having a possible natural explanation (as some critics do today) even if by the power of Beelzebub, and those not of the sky (from heaven), which would be manifested from God. So they put up this fantastic test to Jesus, which he deeply resents. Matthew 16:4 adds "but the sign of Jonah" mentioned already by Jesus on a previous occasion (Matt. 12:39–41) at more length and to be mentioned again (Luke 11:21). But the mention of the sign of Jonah was "an absolute refusal of signs in their sense."[15] And when he did rise from the dead on the third day, the Sanhedrin refused to be convinced (see Acts 3 to 5).

8:14. *They had forgotten to take bread*[16] (ἐπελάθοντο λαβεῖν ἄρτους), *loaves*, plural.

More than one loaf (εἰ μὴ ἕνα ἄρτον), except one loaf. The details in verse 14 are found only in Mark.

8:15. *"Watch out! Beware of the leaven of the Pharisees and the leaven of Herod"*[17] (Ὁρᾶτε, βλέπετε ἀπὸ τῆς ζύμης τῶν Φαρισαίων καὶ τῆς ζύμης Ἡρῴδου[18]). The two verbs are present imperatives. Note Ἀπό and the ablative case. Ζύμης, "leaven," is from ζυμόω, "cause to rise," and occurs in Matthew 13:33 in a good sense. For the bad sense see 1 Corinthians 5:6. Jesus repeatedly charged (διεστέλλετο, imperfect indicative) the disciples, showing that the warning was needed. The disciples came out of an insidiously Pharisaic atmosphere, and they had just met it again at Dalmanutha. Note the combination of Herod with the Pharisees. This is after the agitation of Herod because of the death of the Baptist and the ministry of Jesus (Mark 6:14–29 = Matt. 14:1–12 = Luke 9:7–9). Jesus warns the disciples against "the leaven of Herod" (bad politics) and the leaven of the Pharisees and Sadducees (bad theology and also bad politics).

8:16. *They began to discuss with one another* (διελογίζοντο πρὸς ἀλλήλους). The imperfect tense indicates that they kept it up. Matthew 16:7 has ἐν ἑαυτοῖς, in themselves or among themselves.

8:17–20. Mark gives six keen questions of Jesus while Matthew 16:8–11 gives four that really include the six of Mark, running some together. The questions reveal Jesus' disappointment at the intellectual dullness of his pupils. He questions why they cannot comprehend (νοεῖτε, from νοῦς, συνίετε), asking if their dullness is caused by hardness of heart (πεπωρωμένην, perfect passive predicate participle as in Mark 6:52, which see). Haven't they been seeing and listening? Don't they remember? Christ distinguishes sharply between the two miracles of feeding the five thousand and the four thousand. He distinguishes even between two kinds of baskets (κοφίνους, σφυρίδων). The disciples should recall the number of baskets left over in either instance, twelve and seven. Jesus "administers a sharp rebuke for their preoccupation with mere temporalities, as if there were nothing higher to be thought of *than bread*."[19] "The twelve are wayside hearers, with hearts like a beaten path, into which the higher truths cannot sink so as to germinate."[20]

8:21. *"Do you not yet understand?"* (Οὔπω συνίετε;[21]), after all this rebuke and explanation. The greatest of all teachers had the greatest of all classes, but he struck a snag. Matthew 16:12 gives the result: "Then they understood that he did not say to beware of the leaven of bread, but of the teaching of the

Pharisees and Sadducees." They had once said that they understood the parables of Jesus (Matt. 13:51), but these new concepts would require more of the Teacher's patience.

8:22. *And they came to Bethsaida* (Καὶ ἔρχονται εἰς βηθσαϊδάν[22]). They returned to Bethsaida Julias, east of the Sea of Galilee and not far from the place of the feeding of the five thousand. Note the dramatic present tense for *they come* (ἔρχονται) and *they bring* (φέρουσιν). This healing of a blind man with spittle and the laying on of hands is found in Mark alone (vv. 22–26).

8:23. *He brought him out of the village*[23] (ἐξήνεγκεν[24] αὐτὸν ἔξω τῆς κώμης). Philip had enlarged Bethsaida Julias until it could be categorized as a town or even a city, but it still was popularly known as a village (vv. 23, 26). As in the case of the deaf and dumb demoniac, given alone in Mark 7:31–37, Jesus observes utmost secrecy in performing this miracle. Mark does not say why it was important for Jesus to take the man outside the town. It was the season of retirement, and Jesus is making the fourth withdrawal from Galilee. That fact may explain his reticence. Mark's account is marked by interesting details. Jesus led the blind man by the hand, put spittle on his eyes (using the poetical and Κοινή papyri word ὄμματα instead of the usual ὀφθαλμούς), and laid hands upon him. Perhaps all this served to strengthen the man's faith.

8:24. *"I see men, for I see them like trees, walking around"*[25] (Βλέπω τοὺς ἀνθρώπους, ὅτι ὡς δένδρα ὁρῶ περιπατοῦντας). This is a vivid description of dawning sight. The first level of vision was incomplete. This is the only case recounted in the Gospels where healing was not instantaneous. Mark does not explain why this miracle was so distinctive.

8:25. *He looked intently*[26] (διέβλεψεν[27]). Healing now moved to completion (effective aorist). The man's vision was completely restored (ἀπεκατέστη, second aorist, double compound and double augment), and he "began to see everything clearly" (ἐνέβλεπεν,[28] imperfect) or at a distance (τηλαυγῶς, a common Greek word from τῆλε, afar, and αὐγή, radiance, far-shining).

8:26. *He sent him to his home*[29] (ἀπέστειλεν αὐτὸν εἰς[30] οἶκον αὐτοῦ). The blind man was sent toward a joyful homecoming with his family, but he was not allowed to enter the village, so that no tumult would follow Jesus to Caesarea Philippi.

8:27. *To the villages of Caesarea Philippi*[31] (εἰς τὰς κώμας Καισαρείας τῆς Φιλίππου). Matthew 16:13 has *parts* (μέρη). This Caesarea of Philippi must be distinguished from Caesarea Maritima, which stood on the Mediterranean shore. Mark is referring not to Caesarea proper but to outlying villages of the district. This region is on a spur of Mount Hermon in Iturea, an area ruled by Herod Philip. Here Jesus was safe from Herod Antipas and the Pharisees and Sadducees. On the mountain slopes, Jesus can prepare his disciples for the crucifixion, which will occur in a little over six months.

"Who do people say that I am? (Τίνα με λέγουσιν οἱ ἄνθρωποι εἶναι;). Matthew 16:13 has "the Son of Man" in place of "I" in Mark and in Luke 9:18. The disciples had heard the same popular opinions about Jesus as had Herod Antipas (Mark 3:21, 31).

8:28. *They told Him*[32] (οἱ δὲ εἶπαν[33]). The disciples reveal how much they had been influenced by their environment as well as by direct instruction of Jesus. They knew only too well (see on Matt. 16:14, 28).

8:29. *"You are the Christ"* (Σὺ εἶ ὁ Χριστός). Mark does not give "the Son of the living God" (Matt. 16:16) or "of God" (Luke 9:20). The more complete confession is found in Matthew. Luke's language means practically the same as Matthew's, while Mark's account is the briefest. But the form in Mark gives the full idea. Mark omits praise of Peter, probably because this is Peter's own version of the incident. For criticism of the view that Matthew's narrative reflects later ecclesiastical development and the effort to justify ecclesiastical prerogatives, see on Matthew 16:16, 18. Disciples had confessed Jesus as Messiah before (thus John 1:41; 4:29; 6:69; Matt. 14:33). But Jesus had ceased to use the word Messiah to avoid the revolutionary political complications that would occur if people took his words the wrong way (John 6:14–15). Now he would see whether they understood the truth, despite opposition and defections.

8:30. *Tell no one about Him* (μηδενὶ λέγωσιν περὶ αὐτοῦ). Although he was the Christ (Matt. 16:20), it was not yet time for full declaration. That would come with triumphal entry into Jerusalem, when the very stones would have cried out, if people had remained silent (Luke 19:40).

8:31. *He began to teach them* (ἤρξατο διδάσκειν αὐτούς). Mark is fond of this idiom, but it is not a mere rhetorical device. Matthew 16:21 expressly says "from that time." The disciples had to be told about his approaching death. Their confession of faith indicated that it was a good time to begin. Death would come at the hands of the Sanhedrin (elders, chief priests, and scribes), in which Pharisees and Sadducees had about equal strength. The resurrection on the third day was mentioned, but it did not yet make an impression.

After three days rise again (μετὰ τρεῖς ἡμέρας ἀναστῆναι). Matthew 16:21 has "the third day" (τῇ τρίτῃ ἡμέρᾳ) in the locative case of point of time (so also Luke 9:22). Some demand strict interpretation of "after three days," which would be "on the fourth day," not "on the third day." Mark's phrase has the same sense as that in Matthew and Luke, or else they are hopelessly contradictory. In popular language "after three days" can and often does mean "on the third day." The fourth day is impossible.

8:32. *He was stating the matter plainly*[34] (παρρησίᾳ τὸν λόγον ἐλάλει). He held back nothing, told it all (πᾶν, all, ῥησία, from εἶπον, say), without reserve, to all of them. The imperfect tense in ἐλάλει shows that Jesus did it repeatedly. Mark does not give the great eulogy of Peter in Matthew 16:17, 19 after his confession (Mark 8:29; Matt. 16:16; Luke 9:20), but he does tell the stinging rebuke that he received from Jesus (see on Matt. 16:21, 26).

8:33. *But turning around and seeing His disciples*[35] (ὁ δὲ ἐπιστραφεὶς καὶ ἰδὼν τοὺς μαθητὰς αὐτοῦ). Peter had called Jesus off to himself (προσλαβόμενος), but Jesus quickly wheeled round on Peter (ἐπιστραφείς, only στραφείς in Matthew). In doing that the other disciples also were in plain view (this touch is found only in Mark). Hence Jesus rebukes Peter before the whole group. Peter no doubt felt that it was his duty as leader of the Twelve to remonstrate with the Master that death was not an acceptable option.[36] The others may have shared Peter's views and were watching the effect of his daring rebuke. Peter had not risen above the level of ordinary men and so was being used by Satan, whose role he was assuming. The withering rebuke was needed. The Devil had offered much the same temptation on the mountain as Peter here makes (see on Matt. 16:23).

8:34. *And He summoned the crowd with His disciples*[37] (Καὶ προσκαλεσάμενος τὸν ὄχλον σὺν τοῖς μαθηταῖς αὐτοῦ). Mark alone notes the unexpected gathering of a crowd in this remote spot near Caesarea Philippi in heathen territory. Before this crowd, Jesus explains his philosophy of life and death, which is in direct contrast to that offered by Peter and shared by the other disciples and people. Jesus gives a profound reinterpretation of life and death.

"He must deny himself" (ἀπαρνησάσθω ἑαυτόν). He must say no to himself. Note the reflexive along with the middle voice, an ingressive first aorist imperative (see on Matt. 16:24 about taking up the cross). The shadow of the cross already was on Christ and those who would follow him (Mark 8:31).

8:35. *"For My sake and the gospel's"*[38] (ἕνεκεν ἐμοῦ καὶ τοῦ εὐαγγελίου). This is found in Mark alone (see on Matt. 16:25) for this seeming paradox. Note the two senses of *life* and *save*. For the last *save* (σώσει), Matthew 16:25 has *find* (εὑρήση). A further discussion on the words *gain, profit,* and *exchange* can be found on Matthew 16:26.

8:38. *"For whoever is ashamed of Me and My words"*[39] (ὃς γὰρ ἐὰν[40] ἐπαισχυνθῇ με καὶ τοὺς ἐμοὺς λόγους), first aorist passive subjunctive with indefinite relative and ἐάν = ἄν.[41] It is not a statement about future conduct but about one's attitude toward Jesus. A Christian's conduct toward Christ determines Christ's conduct (ἐπαισχυνθήσεται, first future passive indicative). This passive verb is transitive and uses the accusative (με, αὐτόν).

"In this adulterous and sinful generation" (ἐν τῇ γενεᾷ ταύτῃ τῇ μοιχαλίδι καὶ ἁμαρτωλῷ). This is only found in Mark.

"When He comes" (ὅταν ἔλθῃ). This is an aorist active subjunctive with reference to the future second coming of Christ with the glory of the Father with his holy angels (cf. Matt. 16:27). This is a clear prediction of the final eschatological coming of Christ. This verse could not be separated from Mark 9:1 as the chapter division does. These two verses in Mark 8:38 and 9:1 form one paragraph and go together.

NOTES

1. NIV has "Since they had nothing to eat."
2. NIV has "they have already been with me three days."
3. TR has ἤδη ἡμέρας τρεῖς προσμένουσίν μοι.
4. A. T. Robertson, *A Grammar of the Greek New Testament in the Light of Historical Research* (Nashville: Broadman, 1934), 460.
5. TR and Maj.T have τινες γὰρ αὐτῶν μακρόθεν ἥκασιν.
6. NIV has "where in this remote place."
7. NIV has "to set before the people."
8. TRs has ἵνα παραθῶσιν and TRb and Maj.T have ἵνα παραθῶσι.
9. NIV has "They had a few small fish as well."
10. NIV has "the disciples picked up seven basketfuls of broken pieces that were left over."
11. NIV has "(He) went to the region of Dalmanutha."
12. NIV has "(They) began to question Jesus."
13. Henry Barclay Swete, *Commentary on Mark* (repr. ed., Grand Rapids: Kregel, 1977), 168.
14. Robertson, *Grammar*, 1024.
15. Alexander Balmain Bruce, *The Expositor's Greek Testament*, Vol. 1, *The Synoptic Gospels* (Grand Rapids: Eerdmans, 1951), 394.
16. NIV has "The disciples had forgotten to bring bread."
17. NIV has "Be careful . . . Watch out for the yeast of the Pharisees and that of Herod."
18. TR does not have the iota subscript on the proper noun, Ἡρώδου.

19. Bruce, *Expositor's*, 395.

20. Ibid.

21. TR and Maj.T have Πῶς οὐ συνίετε.

22. TR and Maj.T have the singular verb, ἔρχεται.

23. NIV has "(He) led him outside the village."

24. TR and Maj.T have a different verb, ἐξήγαγεν.

25. NIV has "I see people, they look like trees walking around."

26. NIV has "his sight was restored."

27. TR and Maj.T have ἐποίησεν αὐτὸν ἀναβλέψαι.

28. TR and Maj.T have the aorist tense, ἐνέβλεψεν. TRb and Maj.T do not include the moveable ν, ἐνέβλεψε.

29. NIV has "Jesus sent him home." The name *Jesus* is not found in the Greek text, but it certainly refers to him.

30. TR and Maj.T have the article with the preposition, εἰς τὸν οἶκον αὐτοῦ.

31. NIV has "to the villages around Caesarea Philippi."

32. NIV has "They replied."

33. TR and Maj.T have Οἱ δὲ ἀπεκρίθησαν.

34. NIV has "He spoke plainly about this."

35. NIV has "But when Jesus turned and looked at his disciples."

36. Swete, *Commentary on Mark*, 154–55.

37. NIV has "Then he called the crowd to him along with his disciples."

38. NIV has "for me and for the gospel."

39. NIV has "If anyone is ashamed of me and my words."

40. TR has ἄν for ἐάν.

41. Robertson, *Grammar*, 957–59.

Mark: Chapter 9

9:1. *"Until they see the kingdom of God after it has come with power"*[1] (ἕως ἂν ἴδωσιν τὴν βασιλείαν τοῦ θεοῦ ἐληλυθυῖαν ἐν δυνάμει). In 8:38 Jesus seems to open the subject of his second coming. Commentators frequently ask whether that subject extends into 9:1. One is reminded of Mark 13:32 = Matthew 24:36, where Jesus expressly states that only the Father knows the day or the hour of his return. Is Christ saying that the coming is so imminent that his hearers may see it? First, note that Luke has only "see the kingdom of God," while Matthew 24:30 has "see the Son of Man coming" (ἐρχόμενον, present participle, a process). Mark has "see the kingdom of God" (ἐληλυθυῖαν, perfect active participle, already come). Jesus speaks of a coming "with power." Second, Mark moves immediately to the Transfiguration on Mount Hermon—certainly a glimpse of the power reality of the kingdom. Third, the language also could apply to the coming of the Holy Spirit at Pentecost. Fourth, some have seen in Jesus' words a reference to the destruction of the temple in A.D. 70. It is open to question whether the Master is speaking of the same event in 8:38 and 9:1.

9:2. *By themselves*[2] (μόνους). This word is found only in Mark. Further discussion of the Transfiguration can be found on Matthew 17:1–8. Luke 9:28 adds "to pray" as a motive of Jesus for taking Peter, James, and John into the high mountain.

9:3. *His garments became radiant and exceedingly white*[3] (τὰ ἱμάτια αὐτοῦ ἐγένετο στίλβοντα λευκὰ λίαν). Matthew 17:2 has *white as light* (λευκὰ ὡς τὸ φῶς), Luke 9:29 *white and gleaming* (λευκὸς ἐξαστράπτων) like lightning.

As no launderer on earth can whiten them[4] (οἷα γναφεὺς ἐπὶ τῆς γῆς οὐ δύναται οὕτως[5] λευκᾶναι). Γνάφω is an old word, "to card wool." Note οὕτως, "so" white. Some manuscripts in Matthew 17:2 add ὃς χίων, "as snow." The snow-capped summit of Hermon may have been visible on this very night. For consideration of the term *transfigure* (μεταμορφόομαι), see on Matthew 17:2.

9:4. *Elijah appeared to them along with Moses*[6] (ὤφθη αὐτοῖς Ἡλίας σὺν

342

Μωϋσεῖ[7]). Matthew and Luke have "Moses and Elijah." Both, as a matter of fact, were prophets and both dealt with law. The other order is in Mark 9:5.

9:6. *For he did not know what to answer*[8] (οὐ γὰρ ἤδει τί ἀποκριθῇ[9]). This is a deliberative subjunctive retained in indirect question. But why did Peter say anything? Luke says that he spoke, "not knowing what he said," as an excuse for the inappropriateness of his remarks. Perhaps Peter felt embarrassed at having been asleep (Luke 9:32) and the Feast of Tabernacles (or Booths, σκηναί) was near. See on Matthew 17:4. Peter and the others apparently did not hear or at least did not understand then the conversation with Moses and Elijah. Luke 9:31 explains that they were talking about Jesus' coming "decease" (ἔξοδον), his "exodus or departure." They little knew the special comfort that Jesus found in these two old friends as he approached the horror of the cross—concerning which Peter recently had shown such absolute stupidity (Mark 8:32–33). On the overshadowing and the voice, see on Matthew 17:5.

9:8. *All at once they looked around*[10] (ἐξάπινα περιβλεψάμενοι). Matthew 17:8 has "lifting up their eyes." Mark is more graphic. Suddenly the cloud with Moses and Elijah was gone, and they scanned the mountainside looking for a remnant of it.

[They] saw no one with them anymore, except Jesus alone (οὐκέτι οὐδένα εἶδον ἀλλὰ τὸν Ἰησοῦν μόνον μεθ᾽ ἑαυτῶν). Mark shows their surprise. They were afraid (Matt. 17:6) before Jesus touched them.

9:9. *Until the Son of Man rose from the dead* (εἰ μὴ ὅταν ὁ υἱὸς τοῦ ἀνθρώπου ἐκ νεκρῶν ἀναστῇ). For "until," Matthew 17:9 has ἕως οὗ. The verb is third person singular second aorist active subjunctive. More precisely, Mark says "until the Son of Man *should rise*" (futuristic aorist). Luke 9:36 says merely that they "kept silent, and reported to no one in those days any of the things which they had seen." The full benefit of this high and holy secret experience would come later.

9:10. *They seized upon that statement, discussing [it] with one another*[11] (τὸν λόγον ἐκράτησαν πρὸς ἑαυτοὺς συζητοῦντες). For the first time they notice his allusion to rising from the dead (Mark 8:31).

9:12. *"Elijah does first come and restore all things"* (Ἠλίας[12] μὲν ἐλθὼν πρῶτον ἀποκαθιστάνει[13] πάντα). This late double-compound verb usually occurs in the papyri as ἀποκαθίστημι. Christ is describing the Baptist as the promised Elijah and forerunner of the Messiah (see on Matt. 17:10–13). The disciples now understood that the Baptist fulfilled the prophecy in Malachi 4:5. They had seen Elijah on the mountain, but Jesus had preceded this coming of Elijah. John had prepared the way for the Christ. Jesus patiently enlightens His dull pupils.

9:14. *And some scribes arguing with them*[14] (καὶ γραμματεῖς συζητοῦντας πρὸς αὐτούς[15]). Mark is much detailed on this incident (9:14–29) than either Matthew (17:14–20) or Luke (9:37–43). It was just like the professional scribes to take keen interest in the failure of the nine disciples to cure this poor boy. Jesus and the three come down from the mountain to see the Jewish leaders gleefully nagging and faultfinding.

9:15. *They were amazed*[16] (ἐξεθαμβήθησαν[17]), first aorist passive ingressive aorist with perfective compound ἐκ-. The sudden and opportune appearance of Jesus in the midst of the dispute, when no one was looking for him, redirected the attention of all. The people were awed for the moment and then "began running up to greet Him" (προστρέχοντες ἠσπάζοντο αὐτόν), present participle and imperfect middle deponent indicative.

9:16. *"What are you discussing with them?"*[18] (Τί συζητεῖτε πρὸς αὐτούς;). Jesus takes hold of the situation to intercede for the embarrassed nine.

9:17. *"I brought You my son"* (ἤνεγκα τὸν υἱόν μου πρὸς σέ). The father stepped up and explained the dispute in direct and simple pathos.

9:18. *"Whenever it seizes him"* (ὅπου ἐὰν[19] αὐτὸν καταλάβῃ). The English *catalepsy* is related to this term, which was used in the ancient world by Galen and Hippocrates to describe a fit. The word is very common in the papyri in various senses as in the older Greek. Each of the verbs Mark uses here helps paint a graphic picture.

"It slams him to the ground"[20] (ῥήσσει αὐτόν), convulses, rends, and tears asunder, an old and common word.

"He foams at the mouth" (ἀφρίζει). This late poetical term is found only here in the New Testament. This makes it a New Testament "hapax legomenon," meaning that this is the only occurrence of the term in the New Testament.

"Grinds his teeth"[21] (τρίζει τοὺς ὀδόντας[22]), the term *grinds* is another New Testament hapax legomenon.

"Stiffens out"[23] (ξηραίνεται), an old word for drying or withering as of grass, occurs in James 1:11.

"And they could not do it" (καὶ οὐκ ἴσχυσαν). The disciples did not have the strength (ἴσχυς) to handle this case. See Matthew 17:16 = Luke 9:40 (καὶ οὐκ ἠδυνήθησαν, first aorist passive).

9:19. *"Bring him to Me"*[24] (φέρετε αὐτὸν πρός με). The disciples' unbelief had led to this fiasco. They were part of the *faithless* (ἄπιστος, unbelieving) generation in which they lived. The word *faithless* does not mean treacherous as it does with us. But Jesus is not afraid to undertake this case. We can always come to Jesus when others fail us.

9:20. *Immediately the spirit threw him into a convulsion*[25] (τὸ πνεῦμα εὐθὺς συνεσπάραξεν αὐτόν[26]). Luke 9:42 has both ἔρρηξεν (dashed down, like Mark 9:18, ῥήσσει) and συνεσπάραξεν (convulsed). This compound with συν- (together with), strengthens the force of the verb as in συνπνίγω (4:7) and συντηρέω (6:20). The only other instance of this compound verb known is in Maximus Tyruij (second century B.C.).

He began rolling around[27] (ἐκυλίετο), imperfect passive, was rolled, a pitiful sight, a late form of the old κυλίνδω.

9:22. *"But if You can do anything"* (ἀλλ' εἴ τι δύνῃ[28]). Jesus had asked (v. 21) the history of the case like a modern physician. The father gave it and added further pathetic details about the fire and the water. The failure of the disciples had not wholly destroyed his faith in the power of Jesus, though the conditional form (first class, assuming it to be true) does suggest doubt whether the boy can be cured at all. It was a chronic and desperate case of epilepsy with the demon possession added.

"Help us" (βοήθησον ἡμῖν), an ingressive aorist imperative. Do it now. With touching tenderness he makes the boy's case his own as the Syrophoenician woman had said, "Have mercy on me" (Matt. 15:21). The leper had said: "If You will" (Mark 1:40). This father says: "If You can."

9:23. *"If You can?"* (Τὸ εἰ δύνῃ;[29]). The Greek has a neat idiom not preserved in the English translation. The article takes up the very words of the man and puts the clause in the accusative case of general reference. "As to the 'if You can,' all things can (δυνατά) to the one who believes." The word for "possible" is δυνατά, the cognate adjective of the verb δύνῃ (can). This quick turn challenges the father's faith.[30]

9:24. *The boy's father cried out*[31] (κράξας ὁ πατὴρ τοῦ παιδίου), a loud outcry and *immediately* (εὐθὺς[32]). The late manuscripts have "with tears" (μετὰ δακρύων), not in older documents.

"I do believe; help my unbelief"[33] (Πιστεύω[34] βοήθει μου τῇ ἀπιστίᾳ). This is an exact description of his mental and spiritual state. He still had faith, but craved more. Note the present imperative (continuous help) Βοήθει, while the aorist imperative (instant help) βοήθησον, is in verse 22. The word comes from βοή, a cry and θέω, to run, to run at a cry for help, a vivid picture of this father's plight.

9:25. *A crowd was rapidly gathering*[35] (ἐπισυντρέχει ὄχλος). A double compound is found here alone in the New Testament and not in the old Greek writers. Ἐπιτρέχω occurs in the papyri but not ἐπισυντρέχω. The double compound vividly describes the rapid gathering of the crowd to Jesus and the epileptic boy to see the outcome.

"*Come out of him*" (ἔξελθε ἐξ αὐτοῦ). Jesus addresses the demon as a separate being from the boy as he often does. This makes it difficult to believe that Jesus was merely indulging popular belief in a superstition. He evidently regards the demon as the cause in this case of the boy's misfortune.

9:26. *Throwing him into terrible convulsions*[36] (πολλὰ σπαράξας[37]). The compounded verb is used in verse 20.

The boy became so much like a corpse (ἐγένετο ὡσεὶ νεκρός). He became as if dead from the violence of the spasm. The demon did him all possible harm in leaving him.

9:28. *His disciples began questioning Him privately* (οἱ μαθηταὶ αὐτοῦ κατ᾽ ἰδίαν ἐπηρώτων αὐτόν[38]). Indoors the nine disciples seek an explanation for their colossal failure. They had cast out demons and healed before. Some are here puzzled over Mark's use of ὅτι as an interrogative particle meaning "why" where Matthew 17:19 has διὰ τί. Some of the manuscripts have διὰ τί here in Mark 9:28 as all do in Matthew 17:19. See also Mark 2:16 and 9:11. It is probable that in these examples ὅτι really means "why."[39] The use of ὅς as interrogative "is by no means rare in the late Greek."[40]

9:29. *"This kind cannot come out by anything but prayer"* (Τοῦτο τὸ γένος ἐν οὐδενὶ δύναται ἐξελθεῖν εἰ μὴ ἐν προσευχῇ). The addition of "and of fasting" does not appear in the two oldest Greek manuscripts (Aleph and B). It is clearly a late addition to help explain the failure. But it is needless and also untrue. Prayer is what the nine had failed to use. They were powerless because they were prayerless. Their self-complacency spelled defeat. Matthew 17:20 has "because of your little faith" (ὀλιγοπιστίαν). That is true also. They had too much faith in themselves, too little in Christ. "They had trusted to the semi-magical power with which they thought themselves invested."[41] "Spirits of such malignity were quick to discern the lack of moral power and would yield to no other."[42]

9:30. *He did not want anyone to know about it*[43] (οὐκ ἤθελεν ἵνα τις γνοῖ[44]). An imperfect tense is followed by an ingressive aorist subjunctive. He was not willing that anyone should learn it. Back in Galilee Jesus was well known, but he was avoiding public work there now (cf. 7:24). He was no longer the hero of Galilee. He had left Caesarea Philippi for Galilee.

9:31. *For He was teaching His disciples*[45] (ἐδίδασκεν γὰρ τοὺς μαθητὰς αὐτοῦ). This is an imperfect tense and the reason given for secrecy. He was renewing again definitely the prediction of his death in Jerusalem some six months ahead as he had done before (Mark 8:31 = Matt. 16:21 = Luke 9:22). Now as then Jesus foretells his resurrection "after three days" ("the third day," Matt. 17:23).

9:32. *But they did not understand this statement*[46] (οἱ δὲ ἠγνόουν τὸ ῥῆμα). This is imperfect tense, chiefly found in Paul's Epistles in the New Testament. They continued not to understand. They were agnostics on the subject of the death and Resurrection even after the transfiguration experience. As they came down from the mountain they were puzzled again over the Master's allusion to his resurrection (Mark 9:10). Matthew 17:23 notes that "they were exceeding sorry" to hear Jesus talk this way again, but Mark adds that they "were afraid to ask Him" (ἐφοβοῦντο αὐτὸν ἐπερωτῆσαι). They continued to be afraid (imperfect tense), perhaps with a bitter memory of the term *Satan* hurled at Peter when he protested the other time when Jesus spoke of his death (Mark 8:33 = Matt. 16:23). Luke 9:45 explains that "it was concealed from them," probably partly by their own preconceived ideas and prejudices.

9:33. *When He was in the house* (ἐν τῇ οἰκίᾳ γενόμενος). It was probably Peter's house in Capernaum, the home of Jesus in the city.

"What were you discussing on the way?"[47] (Τί ἐν τῇ ὁδῷ διελογίζεσθε;[48]). This is another imperfect tense. They had been disputing (v. 34), not about the coming death of the Master, but about the relative rank of each of them in the political kingdom which they were expecting him to establish. Jesus had suspected the truth about them and they had apparently kept it up in the house. See on Matthew 18:1 where the disciples are represented as bringing the dispute to Jesus while Jesus asks them about it. Probably they asked Jesus first and then he pushed the matter further and deeper to see if this had not been the occasion of the somewhat heated discussion on the way in.

9:34. *But they kept silent*[49] (οἱ δὲ ἐσιώπων). Here is another imperfect tense. Put thus to them, they felt ashamed that the Master had discovered their jealous rivalry. It was not a mere abstract query, as they put it to Jesus, but it was a canker in their hearts.

9:35. *Sitting down, He called the twelve*[50] (καθίσας ἐφώνησεν τοὺς δώδεκα). Jesus took deliberate action to handle this delicate situation. Jesus gives them the rule of greatness: "If any man would be first [πρῶτος], he shall be last [ἔσχατος] of all, and minister [διάκονος] of all." This saying of Christ, like many others, was repeated at other times (Mark 10:43f.; Matt. 23:8ff.; Luke 22:24f.).

9:36. *Taking him in His arms* (ἐναγκαλισάμενος αὐτὸ, aorist middle participle, late Greek word from ἀγκάλη as in Luke 2:28), he spoke again to the disciples. Matthew 18:2 says that he called a little child, one there in the house, perhaps Peter's child. Luke 9:47 notes that he "set him by his side."

9:37. *"Whoever receives one child like this"*[51] (Ὃς ἂν[52] ἐν τῶν τοιούτων παιδίων). Matthew 18:5 has "one such little child" and Luke 9:48 "this little child." It was an object lesson to the arrogant conceit of the twelve apostles contending for primacy. They did not learn this lesson for they will again wrangle over primacy (Mark 10:33–45 = Matt. 20:20–28), and they will be unable to comprehend easily what the attitude of Jesus was toward children (Mark 10:13–16 = Matt. 19:13–15 = Luke 18:15–17). The child was used as a rebuke to the apostles.

9:38. *"Because he was not following us"*[53] (ὅτι οὐκ ἠκολούθει ἡμῖν[54]). Note the vivid imperfect tense again. John evidently thought to change the subject from the constraint and embarrassment caused by their dispute. So he told about a case of extra zeal on his part expecting praise from Jesus. Perhaps what Jesus had just said in verse 37 raised a doubt in John's mind as to the propriety of his excessive narrowness. One needs to know the difference between loyalty to Jesus and hanging on to one's own narrow prejudices.

9:39. *"Do not hinder him"*[55] (Μὴ κωλύετε αὐτόν). Stop hindering him (Μή and the present imperative) as John had been doing.

9:40. *"For he who is not against us is for us"* (ὃς γὰρ οὐκ ἔστιν καθ' ἡμῶν, ὑπὲρ ἡμῶν ἐστιν). This profound saying throws a flood of light in every direction. The complement of this logion is that in Matthew 12:30: "He who is not with Me is against Me." Both are needed. Some people imagine that they are really for Christ who refuse to take a stand in the open with him and for him.

9:41. *"As followers of Christ"*[56] (ὅτι Χριστοῦ ἐστε). This is a predicate genitive, belong to Christ (see Rom. 8:9; 1 Cor. 1:12; 2 Cor. 10:7). That is the bond of universal brotherhood of the redeemed. It breaks over the lines of nation, race, class, sex, everything. No service is too small, even a cup of cold water, if done for Christ's sake. See on Matthew 18:6f. for discussion on stumbling-blocks for these little ones who believe on Jesus (Mark 9:42), a loving term of all believers, not just children.

9:43. *"To go into hell, into the unquenchable fire"*[57] (εἰς τὴν γέενναν, εἰς τὸ πῦρ τὸ ἄσβεστον). This is not hades, but gehenna. ἄσβεστον is alpha privative and σβέστος from σβέννυμι, which means to quench. It occurs often in Homer. This word has come directly into the English as *asbestos*, with an opposing meaning. It refers to a substance that *can quench* fire. Matthew

18:8 has "into the eternal fire." *Gehenna* referred to the Valley of Hinnom, which had been desecrated by the sacrifice of children to Moloch. It was an accursed place, used for the city garbage heap, where worms gnawed and fires burned. Gehenna is a vivid picture of eternal punishment.

9:44, 46. The oldest manuscripts do not have these two verses. They came into the text from the Western and Syrian (Byzantine) text families and repeat verse 48. Hence we lose numbers 44 and 46.

9:47. *"With one eye"* (μονόφθαλμον). This literally means "one-eyed" (see on Matt. 18:8–9). It is vernacular κοινή and condemned by the Atticists. Mark has here "kingdom of God" where Matthew 18:9 has "life."

9:48. *"Where their worm does not die"* (ὅπου ὁ σκώληξ αὐτῶν οὐ τελευτᾷ). "The worm, i.e. that preys upon the inhabitants of this dread realm."[58] Two bold figures of gehenna are combined, the gnawing worm, the burning flame. No figures of gehenna can equal the dread reality that is described (see Isa. 66:24).

9:50. *"Have salt in yourselves"* (ἔχετε ἐν ἑαυτοῖς ἅλα[59]). Jesus had called them the salt of the earth (Matt. 5:13) and had warned them against losing the saltness of the salt. If it is ἄναλον, nothing can *season* (ἀρτύω) it and it is of no use to season anything else. It is a spent force.

NOTES

1. NIV has "before they see the kingdom of God come with power."
2. NIV has "all alone."
3. NIV has "His clothes became dazzling white."
4. NIV has "whiter than anyone in the world could bleach them."
5. TR and Maj.T do not include οὕτως.
6. NIV has "there appeared before them Elijah and Moses."
7. TR has Ἠλίας and Μωυσεῖ; Maj.T has Ἠλείας and Μωσεῖ; WH has Μωσῆ.
8. NIV has "He did not know what to say."
9. TR and Maj.T have οὐ γὰρ ᾔδει τί λαλήσῃ.
10. NIV has "Suddenly, when they looked around."
11. NIV has "They kept the matter to themselves."
12. TR has Ἠλίας Ἠλίας; WH has Ἠλείας.
13. TR and Maj.T have ἀποκαθιστᾷ.
14. NIV has "and some teachers of the law arguing with them."
15. TR and Maj.T have the dative case αὐτοῖς in place of the prepositional phrase.
16. NIV has "they were overwhelmed with wonder."
17. TR and Maj.T have ἐξεθαμβήθη.

18. NIV has "What are you arguing with them about?"
19. TR and Maj.T have ἄν in place of ἐάν.
20. NIV has "it throws him to the ground."
21. NIV has "gnashes his teeth."
22. TR and Maj.T have τρίζει τοὺς ὀδόντας αὐτοῦ.
23. NIV has "becomes rigid."
24. NIV has "Bring the boy to me."
25. NIV has "it immediately threw the boy into a convulsion."
26. TR and Maj.T have εὐθέως τὸ πνεῦμα ἐσπάραξαν αὐτόν.
27. NIV has "rolled around."
28. TR and Maj.T have ἀλλ' εἴ τι δύνασαι.
29. TR and Maj.T have Τὸ εἰ δύνασαι.
30. On this use of the Greek article, see A. T. Robertson, *A Grammar of the Greek New Testament in the Light of Historical Research* (Nashville: Broadman, 1934), 766.
31. NIV has "the boy's father exclaimed."
32. TR and Maj.T have εὐθέως.
33. NIV has "I do believe; help me overcome my unbelief."
34. TR and Maj.T include the vocative after Πιστεύω, Κύριε.
35. NIV has "a crowd was running to the scene."
36. NIV has "convulsed him violently."
37. TR and Maj.T have σπαράξαν πολλά.
38. TR and Maj.T have a different word order, οἱ μαθηταὶ αὐτοῦ ἐπηρώτων αὐτὸν κατ' ἰδίαν.
39. Robertson, *Grammar*, 730.
40. G. Adolf Deissmann, *Light from the Ancient East: The New Testament Illustrated by Recently Discovered Texts of the Graeco-Roman World*, trans. L. R. M. Strachan (rev. ed., Grand Rapids: Baker, 1965), 126.
41. Henry Barclay Swete, *Commentary on Mark* (repr. ed., Grand Rapids: Kregel, 1977), 202.
42. Ibid.
43. NIV has "Jesus did not want anyone to know where they were."
44. TR and Maj.T have the verb spelled γνῷ.
45. NIV has "because he was teaching his disciples."
46. NIV has "But they did not understand what he meant."
47. NIV has "What were you arguing about on the road?"
48. TR and Maj.T have Τί ἐν τῇ ὁδῷ πρὸς ἑαυτοὺς διελογίζεσθε.
49. NIV has "But they kept quiet."

50. NIV has "Sitting down, Jesus called the twelve." Note that the name *Jesus* is not found in the Greek text, although the implied pronoun clearly refers to him.
51. NIV has "Whoever welcomes one of these little children."
52. TR and Maj.T have $\dot{\epsilon}\acute{\alpha}\nu$ in place of $\ddot{\alpha}\nu$.
53. NIV has "because he was not one of us."
54. TR and Maj.T have $\ddot{o}\varsigma$ in place of $\ddot{o}\tau\iota$.
55. NIV has "Do not stop him."
56. NIV has "because you belong to Christ."
57. NIV has "to go into hell, where the fire never goes out."
58. Ezra P. Gould, *Critical and Exegetical Commentary on the Gospel According to St. Mark* (Edinburgh: T. & T. Clark, 1896), 180.
59. TR and Maj.T have $\ddot{\alpha}\lambda\alpha\varsigma$ for $\ddot{\alpha}\lambda\alpha$.

Mark: Chapter 10

10:1. *He went from there to the region of Judea and beyond the Jordan*[1] (ἔρχεται εἰς τὰ ὅρια τῆς Ἰουδαίας [καὶ]² πέραν τοῦ Ἰορδάνου). See on Matthew 19:1 concerning this curious expression. Matthew adds "from Galilee," and Luke 17:11 says that Jesus "was passing through the midst of Samaria and Galilee" after leaving Ephraim (John 11:54). A great deal has intervened between the events at the close of Mark 9 and those in the beginning of Mark 10. For these events, see Matthew 18; Luke 9:57–18:14; and John 7–11. One-third of Luke's Gospel is devoted to this period. At the close of Mark 9, Christ's Passion was about six months away. Now in Mark 10, the crisis is but a few weeks away. Jesus has begun his last journey to Jerusalem, going north through Samaria, Galilee, across the Jordan into Perea, and back into Judea near Jericho with the Passover pilgrims from Galilee.

Crowds gathered around Him again[3] (συμπορεύονται πάλιν ὄχλοι). Note the dramatic historical present. In these caravans journeying to Jerusalem were many followers of Jesus from Galilee. Most were at least kindly disposed toward him.

According to His custom (ὡς εἰώθει). This second past perfect is used like an imperfect from εἰώθα, second perfect active.

He once more began to teach them[4] (ἐδίδασκεν αὐτούς, imperfect, no longer present tense). Jesus was teaching this moving caravan.

10:2. *Some Pharisees came up to Jesus, testing Him* (προσελθόντες Φαρισαῖοι ἐπηρώτων αὐτὸν⁵). As soon as Jesus appears in Galilee, the Pharisees attack him again (cf. 7:5; 8:11). The word ἐπηρώτων means either *testing* or tempting, but their motive was evil.[6] They had once involved the Baptist with Herod Antipas and Herodias on this subject. They may have some hopes about Jesus, or their purpose may have been to see if Jesus will be stricter than Moses taught. They knew that he had spoken in Galilee on the subject (Matt. 5:31f.).

10:3. *"What did Moses command you?"* (Τί ὑμῖν ἐνετείλατο Μωϋσῆς;⁷). Jesus at once brought up the issue concerning the teaching of Moses (Deut.

352

24:1). But Jesus goes back beyond this concession allowed by Moses to the ideal state commanded in Genesis 1:27.

10:4. *"Moses permitted a man to write a certificate of divorce and send her away"* (Ἐπέτρεψεν Μωϋσῆς[8] βιβλίον ἀποστασίου γράψαι καὶ ἀπολῦσαι). The word for "certificate" (βιβλίον) is a diminutive and means "little book," like the Latin *libellus*, from which comes our word *libel*.[9] Wycliff has it "a libel of forsaking." This same point the Pharisees raise in Matthew 19:7, showing probably that they held to the liberal view of Hillel, easy divorce for almost any cause. That was the popular view, as now (see on Matt. 19:7 for discussion of "for your hardness of heart," σκληροκαρδία). Expounding the purpose of marriage (Gen. 2:24), Jesus takes the stricter view of divorce of the school of Shammai (see on Matt. 19:1–12). Mark 10:10 notes that the disciples asked Jesus about the problem "in the house" after they had gone away from the crowd.

10:11. *"Whoever divorces his wife and marries another woman commits adultery against her"* (Ὃς ἂν ἀπολύσῃ τὴν γυναῖκα αὐτοῦ καὶ γαμήσῃ ἄλλην μοιχᾶται ἐπ᾽ αὐτήν). Mark does not give the exception "except for fornication" as in Matthew 19:9 (which see), though the point is really covered in what Mark does record. Formal divorce does not annul actual marriage consummated by the physical union. Breaking that bond does annul it.

10:12. *"If she herself divorces her husband and marries another man"* (ἐὰν αὐτὴ ἀπολύσασα τὸν ἄνδρα αὐτῆς γαμήσῃ ἄλλον[10]). This is a third class condition, a possible or supposed action, not actual or assumed. Greek and Roman law allowed a wife to divorce the husband; Jewish law did not provided for it. Herodias divorced her husband before she married Herod Antipas. So also Salome, Herod's sister, divorced her husband. A. B. Bruce and Gould think that Mark added this to the words of Jesus for the benefit of Gentiles who would hear this Roman Gospel.[11] But Jesus knew that this was standard practice throughout the Roman world. He prohibited marrying a divorced man or woman.

10:13. *They were bringing children to Him*[12] (προσέφερον αὐτῷ παιδία), an imperfect active indicative, implying repetition. So also, Luke 18:15. Matthew 19:13 has the constative aorist passive (προσηνέχθησαν). "This incident follows with singular fitness after the Lord's assertion of the sanctity of married life."[13] These children (παιδία in Mark and Matthew; βρέφη in Luke) were of various ages. They were brought to Jesus for his blessing and prayers (Matthew). The mothers had reverence for Jesus and wanted him to touch (ἅψηται) their children with the rabbinical blessing prayer for God's mercy.

10:14. *He was indignant* (ὁ Ἰησοῦς ἠγανάκτησεν). This is in Mark alone. The verb is ingressive aorist, "became indignant," and is a strong word of deep emotion (from ἀγάν and ἄχθομαι, to feel pain). The common word is found in Matthew 21:15; 26:8.

"Permit the children to come to Me"[14] (Ἄφετε τὰ παιδία ἔρχεσθαι πρός με). Mark has the infinitive ἔρχεσθαι (come) found also in Luke. Surely it ought to be a joy to parents to bring their children to Jesus, certainly to allow them to come. To hinder their coming is a crime. There are parents who will have to give answer to God for keeping their children away from Jesus.

10:15. *"Like a child"* (ὡς παιδίον). How does a little child receive the kingdom of God? The child learns to obey simply and uncomplainingly. Jesus here presents the little child with trusting and simple and loving obedience as the model for adults in coming into the kingdom. Jesus does not here say that children are in the kingdom of God because they are children.

10:16. *He took them in His arms* (ἐναγκαλισάμενος[15]), which was a distinct rebuke to the protest of the over-particular disciples. This word was already seen in 9:36. In Luke 2:28 we have the full idiom, "he took Him into his arms" (ἐδέχατο αὐτὸ εἰς τὰς ἀγκάλας). So with tenderness Jesus repeatedly "blessed" (κατευλόγει, imperfect), laying his hands upon each (τιθεὶς, present participle).

10:17. *A man ran up to Him* (προσδραμὼν εἷς). Jesus had left the house (v. 10) and was proceeding with the caravan on the way (εἰς ὁδόν) when this ruler eagerly ran and kneeled (γονυπετήσας) and was asking (ἐπηρώτα, imperfect) Jesus about his problem. Both these details are found alone in Mark.

"What shall I do to inherit eternal life?" (τί ποιήσω ἵνα ζωὴν αἰώνιον κληρονομήσω;). Matthew 19:16 has (σχῶ), that I may "get."

10:18. *"Why do you call Me good?"* (Τί με λέγεις ἀγαθόν;), so also in Luke 18:19. Matthew 19:17 has it: "Why do you ask concerning that which is good?" The young ruler was probably sincere and not simply flattering, but Jesus challenges him to define his attitude and think through its implications. Did he mean "good" (ἀγαθός) in the absolute sense applied to God? The language is not, as some skeptics suppose, a disclaimer of deity by Jesus.

10:20. *"I have kept all these things from my youth up"*[16] (ταῦτα πάντα ἐφυλαξάμην ἐκ νεότητός μου), literally, "these all."

10:21. *Looking at him, Jesus felt a love for him*[17] (ὁ δὲ Ἰησοῦς ἐμβλέψας αὐτῷ ἠγάπησεν αὐτόν). Mark alone mentions this glance of affection, ingressive aorist participle and verb. Jesus felt a particular compassion for this charming young man.

"One thing you lack" ("Εν σε ὑστερεῖ[18]). Luke 18:22 has it: "One thing you lack yet" ("Ετι ἕν σοὶ λείπει). Possibly there are two translations of the same Aramaic phrase. Matthew 19:20 quotes the young man's question, "What am I still lacking?" (Τί ἔτι ὑστέρω;). The man understands already that the basis for salvation must go beyond outward obedience to laws and regulations, but he evidently has a high view of his own morality. Jesus puts his finger on the heart of the man's own weakness in relation to the law. The verb ὑστέρω, from the adjective ὕστερος (behind), means "to be too late, to come short or lack." It is used with the accusative as here, or with the ablative, as in 2 Corinthians 11:5. TR uses it with the dative, σοί.

10:22. *He was saddened*[19] (ὁ δὲ στυγνάσας). It is found in the LXX and Polybius once and Matthew 16:3 (passage bracketed in WH). The verb is from στυγνός, sombre, gloomy, like a lowering cloud. For discussion of the related concept, "sorrowful" (λυπούμενος), see the discussion on Matthew 19:22.

10:23. *And Jesus, looking around*[20] (Καὶ περιβλεψάμενος ὁ Ἰησοῦς). This is another picture of the looks of Jesus found in Mark alone (see also Mark 3:5, 34). "To see what impression the incident had made on the Twelve."[21] "When the man was gone the Lord's eye swept the circle of the Twelve, as he drew for them the lesson of the incident."[22]

"How hard it will be" (Πῶς δυσκόλως). So in Luke 18:24. Matthew 19:23 has it: "With difficulty (δυσκόλως) shall a rich man" (see on this verse).

10:24. *The disciples were amazed at His words* (οἱ δὲ μαθηταὶ ἐθαμβοῦντο ἐπὶ τοῖς λόγοις αὐτοῦ), an imperfect passive. The look of blank astonishment on their faces at this statement was natural, for Jews regarded wealth as proof of God's special favor.

"Children, how hard it is to enter the kingdom of God" (Τέκνα, πῶς δύσκολόν ἐστιν εἰς τὴν βασιλείαν τοῦ θεοῦ εἰσελθεῖν[23]). This tender, paternal note reassures them in their perplexity.[24]

10:25. *"It is easier for a camel to go through the eye of a needle"* (εὐκοπώτερόν ἐστιν κάμηλον διὰ [τῆς] τρυμαλιᾶς [τῆς] ῥαφίδος διελθεῖν[25]). See on Matthew 19:24. Luke uses the term for a surgical needle, βελόνης. Matthew has the word ῥαφίς like Mark from ῥάπτω, to sew, and it appears in the papyri. Both Matthew and Luke employ τρήματος for "eye," from τρῆμα, "a hole or perforation."

10:26. *"Then who can be saved?"* (Καὶ τίς δύναται σωθῆναι;). Matthew 19:25 has Τίς ἄρα. Evidently καί has an inferential sense like ἄρα.

10:27. *Looking at them, Jesus said*[26] (ἐμβλέψας αὐτοῖς ὁ Ἰησοῦς λέγει), so also in Matthew 19:26. Their amazement increased.

"With people it is impossible, but not with God" (Παρὰ ἀνθρώποις ἀδύνατον, ἀλλ' οὐ παρὰ θεῷ).[27] Note the locative case with Παρά ("beside"). What is impossible *by the side of human beings* becomes possible *by the side of God*. That is the whole point and brushes aside all petty theories of a gate called a "needle's eye."

10:28. *Peter began to say to Him* (Ἤρξατο λέγειν ὁ Πέτρος αὐτῷ[28]). Peter and the others must have been struggling to remain silent about this issue of where they fit into God's new economy. Matthew 19:27 says that "Peter answered," as if the remark had been addressed to him in particular. Peter reminds Jesus of what they had left to follow him, four of them on that one day by the sea (Mark 1:20 = Matt. 4:22 = Luke 5:11). He claimed obedience to the high ideal where the rich young ruler had failed. As Jesus was now speaking of dying, Peter wanted to know what their sacrifice would mean in their lives?

10:30. *"Along with persecutions"* (μετὰ διωγμῶν). This extra touch is in Mark alone. There is a reminiscence of some of "the apocalyptic of the familiar descriptions of the blessings of the Messianic kingdom. But Jesus uses such language from the religious idiom of this time only to idealize it."[29]

The apostles soon would see a foreshadowing of their persecution. Vincent notes that Jesus omits "a hundred wives" in this list, showing that Julian the Apostate's sneer on that score was without foundation.[30]

10:31. *"But many who are first will be last, and the last, first"* (πολλοὶ δὲ ἔσονται πρῶτοι ἔσχατοι καὶ [οἱ] ἔσχατοι πρῶτοι). See on Matthew 19:30 for the use of irony and even an apparent paradox about earthly value systems in a kingdom perspective. After his boast, Peter would have felt the sting of this rebuke, even though Jesus does not address him personally.

10:32. *And they were amazed*[31] (καὶ ἐθαμβοῦντο). The imperfect tense describes the feelings of the disciples as "Jesus was walking on ahead of them" (ἦν προάγων αὐτοὺς ὁ Ἰησοῦς, periphrastic imperfect active). This unusual circumstance in itself seemed to bode no good as they traveled through Perea toward Jerusalem. In fact, "those who followed were fearful" (οἱ δὲ ἀκολουθοῦντες ἐφοβοῦντο[32]) as Jesus distanced himself from them and walked in solitude. The idiom (οἱ δέ) may not mean that *all* the disciples were afraid. "The Lord walked in advance of the Twelve with a solemnity and a determination which foreboded danger"[33] (cf. Luke 9:5). Reading the uncharacteristically solemnity in Jesus, they began to fear coming disaster.

And again He took the twelve aside (καὶ παραλαβὼν πάλιν τοὺς δώδεκα). Matthew has "apart" from the crowds, and that is what Mark also means. Note παραλαβών, taking to his side.

And began to tell them what was going to happen to Him (ἤρξατο αὐτοῖς λέγειν τὰ μέλλοντα αὐτῷ συμβαίνειν). He had spoken of his coming death at least three times before (Mark 8:31; 9:13; 9:31), and they had failed utterly to understand. Luke says that the disciples were no less befuddled this time (18:34): "They understood none of these things." Mark and Matthew show how two disciples were wholly occupied with their own selfish ambitions while Jesus was giving details of his approaching death and resurrection.

10:35. *James and John, the two sons of Zebedee, came up to [Jesus]*[34] (Καὶ προσπορεύονται αὐτῷ Ἰάκωβος καὶ Ἰωάννης[35] οἱ υἱοὶ Ζεβεδαίου). Note the dramatic present tense, literally, "And come to Him James and John." Matthew has τότε, "then," showing that the request of the two brothers with their mother followed immediately the talk of Christ's death (Matt. 20:20).

"We want" (θέλομεν), "we wish," bluntly told. Matthew says that the mother "came worshiping" (προσκυνοῦσα). The mother spoke for the sons, trying to commit Jesus to their desires before they told what they were. They behaved like spoiled children.

10:37. *"In Your glory"* (ἐν τῇ δόξῃ σου). Matthew 20:21 has "in Your kingdom." In Matthew 20, see on verse 20 for the literal interpretation of 19:28. They are looking for a grand Jewish world empire with apocalyptic features in the eschatological culmination of the Messiah's kingdom. That dream brushed aside all talk of death and resurrection as mere pessimism.

10:38. *"Or to be baptized with the baptism with which I am baptized?"* (ἢ[36] τὸ βάπτισμα ὃ ἐγὼ βαπτίζομαι βαπτισθῆναι). The cognate accusative occurs with both passive verbs. Matthew 20:22 has only the cup, but Mark has both the cup and the baptism, both referring to death. In the Garden of Gethsemane, Jesus again will refer to his death as "the cup" (Mark 14:36 = Matt. 26:39 = Luke 22:42). He had already used baptism as a figure for his death (Luke 12:50). Paul will use it in that sense several times (Rom. 6:3–6; 1 Cor. 15:29; Col. 2:12).

10:39–45. *"For even the Son of Man did not come to be served, but to serve, and to give His life a ransom for many"* (καὶ γὰρ ὁ υἱὸς τοῦ ἀνθρώπου οὐκ ἦλθεν διακονηθῆναι ἀλλὰ διακονῆσαι καὶ δοῦναι τὴν ψυχὴν αὐτοῦ λύτρον ἀντὶ πολλῶν, v. 45). See on Matthew 20:23–28 for discussion on these memorable verses, which are identical in the three Synoptics. In Mark 10:45, note the language of Jesus concerning his death as "a ransom for many" (λύτρον ἀντὶ πολλῶν). These words of the Master were not understood by the apostles on the day they heard them from Jesus, but their implications were quite clear when Peter later preached them, and Mark preserved them. Some interpreters empty these words of meaning, believing that Jesus could not have held such a conception of his death for sinners.

10:46. *And as He was leaving Jericho* (καὶ ἐκπορευομένου αὐτοῦ ἀπὸ Ἰεριχώ[37]). See on Matthew 20:29 for a discussion of this phrase and Luke 18:35, "nigh unto Jericho," with regard to the old Jericho and the new Roman town. New Jericho was over a mile south of the site of the more ancient Jericho, about five miles west of the Jordan and fifteen miles east of Jerusalem. It was near the mouth of the *Wadi Kelt*.[38]

A large crowd (ὄχλου ἱκανοῦ), often in Luke and the papyri in this sense. For the sense of "fit" for ἱκανός, see comment on Matthew 3:11.

A blind beggar[39] (τυφλὸς[40] προσαίτης). "Begging," ἐπαιτῶν, Luke 18:35 has it. All three Gospels picture him as "sitting by the road"[41] (ἐκάθητο παρὰ τὴν ὁδόν). Bartimaeus was in his regular place. Vincent quotes William Thompson concerning Ramleh: "I once walked the streets counting all that were either blind or had defective eyes, and it amounted to about one-half the male population. The women I could not count, for they are rigidly veiled."[42] The dust, the glare of the sun, and the unsanitary habits of the people all contributed to the spread of contagious eye diseases.

Bartimaeus (Βαρτιμαῖος). This is an Aramaic name like Bartholomew, *bar* meaning "son" (Heb. בַּר). His name means "the son of Timaeus," as Mark explains for people unaccustomed to Aramaic names, ὁ υἱὸς Τιμαίου. Mark focuses on this one man, who may have been known personally by some who would see the letter. Matthew does not name Bartimaeus and mentions that another beggar was involved (see on Matt. 20:30).

10:48. *Many were sternly telling him to be quiet*[43] (ἐπετίμων αὐτῷ πολλοὶ ἵνα σιωπήσῃ). The imperfect tense indicates that they kept rebuking him. The aorist tense is found in Matthew 20:31. The ingressive aorist subjunctive, σιωπήσῃ, means "become silent."

But he kept crying out all the more[44] (ὁ δὲ πολλῷ μᾶλλον ἔκραζεν). Luke 18:39 says the same. Matthew 20:31 uses the standard word for "all the more," μεῖζον.

10:49. *Jesus stopped* (στὰς ὁ Ἰησοῦς). This is a second aorist active ingressive participle as in Matthew 20:32. Luke 18:40 has σταθείς, an aorist passive participle.

"He is calling for you" (φωνεῖ σε). That was joyful news to Bartimaeus. There are vivid dramatic presents in Mark.

10:50. *Throwing aside his cloak* (ὁ δὲ ἀποβαλὼν τὸ ἱμάτιον αὐτοῦ), a second aorist active participle. He threw his outer robe in his haste.

He jumped up (ἀναπηδήσας[45]). He was leaping up, a vivid detail of Mark. 10:51. *"What do you want Me to do for you?"* (Τί σοι θέλεις ποιήσω;[46]). This is a neat Greek idiom with the aorist subjunctive without ἵνα after θέλεις.[47] *Rabboni*[48] (Ραββουνι). The Aramaic word translated Lord (Κύριε) in Matthew 20:33 and Luke 18:41. This form occurs again in John 20:16.

"I want to regain my sight!"[49] (ἵνα ἀναβλέψω). I want to recover my sight, to see again (ἀνά + βλέψω). Apparently he had once been able to see. Here ἵνα is used, although θέλω is not (cf. 10:35). The Messiah was expected to give sight to the blind (Isa. 61:1; Luke 4:18; 7:22).

10:52. *"Your faith has made you well"*[50] (ἡ πίστις σου σέσωκέν σε), a perfect active indicative. The word commonly means save and that may be the idea.

Immediately he regained his sight and began following Him (εὐθὺς ἀνέβλεψεν καὶ ἠκολούθει αὐτῷ[51]). The imperfect tense pictures joyful Bartimaeus as he followed the caravan of Jesus into the new Jericho.

NOTES

1. NIV has "Jesus then left that place and went into the region of Judea and across the Jordan." Note that the name ὁ Ἰησοῦς is not found in the Greek text but is implied.

2. TR and Maj.T have διὰ τοῦ in place of καί.

3. NIV has "crowds of people."

4. NIV has "he taught them."

5. TR and Maj.T have προσελθόντες οἱ Φαρισαῖοι ἐπηρώτησαν αὐτόν. However, Maj.T does not have the article οἱ.

6. Ezra P. Gould, *Critical and Exegetical Commentary on the Gospel According to St. Mark* (Edinburgh: T. & T. Clark, 1896), 183.

7. TR and Maj.T spell the proper noun Μωσῆς; WH spells it Μωυσῆς, both here and verse 4.

8. TR and Maj.T have a reverse order for Μωσῆς ἐπέτρεψεν. TRb and Maj.T do not include the moveable ν, ἐπέτρεψε.

9. Marvin Richardson Vincent, *Word Studies in the New Testament*, 4 vols. (Grand Rapids: Eerdmans, 1946), 1.211.

10. TR and Maj.T have ἐὰν γυνὴ ἀπολύσῃ τὸν ἄνδρα αὐτῆς καὶ γαμηθῇ ἄλλῳ.

11. Alexander Balmain Bruce, *The Expositor's Greek Testament*, Vol. 1, *The Synoptic Gospels* (Grand Rapids: Eerdmans, 1951), 409; Gould, *Commentary on Mark*, 186.

12. NIV has "People were bringing little children to Jesus." The proper noun *Jesus* is not found in the Greek text.

13. Henry Barclay Swete, *Commentary on Mark* (repr. ed., Grand Rapids: Kregel, 1977), 219.
14. NIV has "Let the little children come to me."
15. TR and Maj.T have ἐναγκαλισάμενος αὐτά.
16. NIV has "all these I have kept since I was a boy."
17. NIV has "Jesus looked at him and loved him."
18. TR and Maj.T have Ἐν σοι ὑστερεῖ.
19. NIV has "the man's face fell."
20. NIV has "Jesus looked around."
21. Bruce, *Expositor's*, 411.
22. Swete, *Commentary on Mark*, 227–28.
23. TR and Maj.T have Τέκνα, πῶς δύσκολόν ἐστιν τοὺς πεποιθότας ἐπὶ τοῖς χρήμασιν εἰς τὴν βασιλείαν τοῦ θεοῦ εἰσελθεῖν.
24. For them that trust in riches (τοὺς πεποιθότας ἐπὶ τοῖς χρήμασιν). These words do not occur in Aleph, B, Delta, Memphitic, and one Old Latin manuscript. WH omits them, evidently with the reasong that this is added to explain the difficult words of Jesus.
25. TR and Maj.T have εὐκοπώτερόν ἐστιν κάμηλον διὰ τῆς τρυμαλιᾶς τῆς ῥαφίδος εἰσελθεῖν.
26. NIV has "Jesus looked at them and said."
27. TR and Maj.T include the postpositive conjunction δέ.
28. TR and Maj.T have a different word order, ἤρξατο ὁ Πέτρος λέγειν αὐτῷ.
29. Gould, *Critical and Exegetical Commentary*, 196.
30. Vincent, *Word Studies*, 1.213.
31. NIV has "and the disciples were astonished."
32. TR and Maj.T have καὶ ἀκολουθοῦντες ἐφοβοῦντο.
33. Swete, *Commentary on Mark*, 233.
34. The Greek text does not have the proper name *Jesus*.
35. WH spells the proper noun with only one ν, Ἰωάνης.
36. TR and Maj.T have the conjunction καί in place of ἤ.
37. WH spells the proper noun Ἰερειχώ.
38. Swete, *Commentary on Mark*, 242.
39. NIV has "a blind man."
40. TR and Maj.T have the article with the noun, ὁ τυφλός.
41. NIV has "sitting by the roadside."
42. Vincent, *Word Studies*, 1.213. Vincent was quoting a Middle East traveler early in the twentieth century after a visit to Ramleh, Egypt, a village on the outskirts of Alexandria. William M. Thompson's observation of the large

number of blind in the town was told in his book *The Land and the Book: Biblical Illustrations Drawn from the Manners and Customs, the Scenes and Scenery of the Holy Land* (New York: Thomas Nelson, 1913).

43. NIV has "Many rebuked him and told him to be quiet."

44. NIV has "but he shouted all the more."

45. TR and Maj.T have ἀναστάς.

46. TR and Maj.T have a different word order, Τί θέλεις ποιήσω σοί;

47. For this asyndeton (or parataxis), see A. T. Robertson, *A Grammar of the Greek New Testament in the Light of Historical Research* (Nashville: Broadman, 1934), 430.

48. NIV has "Rabbi."

49. NIV has "I want to see."

50. NIV has "your faith has healed you."

51. TR and Maj.T have καὶ εὐθέως ἀνέβλεψε (ν), καὶ ἠκολούθει τῷ Ἰησοῦ. However TRb and Maj.T do not include the moveable ν, ἀνέβλεψε.

■ ■ ■ ■ ■ ■

Mark: Chapter 11

11:1. *Bethphage and Bethany* (ἐγγίζουσιν εἰς Ἰερουσαλὴμ εἰς βηθφαγὴ καὶ βηθανίαν[1]). The two towns are listed together here and in Luke 19:29, though Matthew 21:1 mentions only Bethphage (see on Matt. 21:1).

11:2. *"Immediately as you enter it"*[2] (εὐθὺς εἰσπορευόμενοι[3]), a present middle/passive deponent participle is also found in Luke 19:30.

"You will find a colt tied there" (εὑρήσετε πῶλον δεδεμένον). Matthew 21:2 speaks of the donkey (ὄνον) also.

"On which no one yet has ever sat"[4] (ἐφ᾽ ὃν οὐδεὶς οὔπω ἀνθρώπων ἐκάθισεν).

11:3. *"'The Lord has need it'"* (Ὁ κύριος αὐτοῦ χρείαν ἔχει), so also Matthew and Luke. See on Matthew 21:3 for discussion of this word applied to Jesus by himself.

"Immediately he will send it back here" (εὐθὺς αὐτὸν ἀποστέλλει πάλιν ὧδε[5]). Note the present indicative in a futuristic sense. Matthew 21:3 has the future ἀποστελεῖ.

11:4. *They went away and found a colt tied at the door, outside in the street* (ἀπῆλθον καὶ εὗρον πῶλον δεδεμένον πρὸς θύραν ἔξω ἐπὶ τοῦ ἀμφόδου[6]), a carefully drawn picture. The colt was outside the house in the street, but fastened (bound, perfect passive participle) to the door. "The better class of houses were built about an open court, from which a passage way under the house led to the street outside. It was at this outside opening to the street that the colt was tied."[7] The word ἀμφόδου (from ἄμφω, both, and ὁδός, road) is difficult. It apparently means a road that winds around a thing, a crooked street, as most of them were (cf. Straight Street at Damascus in Acts 9:11). The term occurs only here in the New Testament besides D in Acts 19:28.

And they untied it (καὶ λύουσιν αὐτόν). Note the dramatic historical present tense. Perhaps Peter was one of those sent this time, as he was later (Luke 22:8). If so, that explains Mark's vivid details.

11:5. *Some of the bystanders*[8] (καί τινες τῶν ἐκεῖ ἑστηκότων), a genitive plural perfect active participle meaning bystanders. Luke 19:33 terms them

362

"the owners thereof" (οἱ κύριοι αὐτοῦ), the lords or masters of the colt. They make a natural protest.

11:7. *They brought the colt to Jesus* (φέρουσιν τὸν πῶλον πρὸς τὸν Ἰησοῦν[9]). The historical present is again used. The owners acquiesced as Jesus had predicted. They must have been followers who considered Jesus their "Lord" (v. 3).

11:8. *And others spread leafy branches*[10] (ἄλλοι δὲ στιβάδας[11]), a litter of leaves and rushes from the fields. Matthew 21:8 has κλάδους, from κλάω, to break, branches broken or cut from trees. John 12:13 uses the branches of the palm trees (τὰ βαία τῶν φοινίκων), "the feathery fronds forming the tufted crown of the tree."[12] People among the throng found individual ways to do obeisance to Jesus (see on Matt. 21:4–9). By His deliberate conduct, Jesus was publicly proclaiming himself to be the Messiah. At last his "hour" has come. The excited crowds in front (οἱ προάγοντες) and behind (οἱ ἀκολούθουντες) fully realize the significance of it all. Hence their unrestrained enthusiasm. They expect that Jesus will now set up his rule in opposition to that of Caesar. Rome will be driven from Palestine, conquering the world for the Jews.

11:11. *Looking around at everything* (περιβλεψάμενος πάντα). Another Markan detail is found in this aorist middle participle. Mark does not correspond with Luke 19:39–55 or with Matthew 21:10–17. But it is all implied in this swift glance at the temple before he went out to Bethany with the twelve, "since it was already late" (ὀψίας ἤδη οὔσης τῆς ὥρας), a genitive absolute, "the hour being already late."

11:12. *The next day* (τῇ ἐπαύριον). Matthew 21:18 has "early" (πρωὶ), which tends to refer to the fourth watch of the night (before 6 A.M.). This was Monday morning, after Sunday's entry into Jerusalem.

11:13. *He went to see if perhaps He would find anything on it*[13] (ἦλθεν εἰ ἄρα τι εὑρήσει ἐν αὐτῇ[14]). This use of εἰ and the future indicative for purpose ("to see if . . . ," a sort of indirect question) as in Acts 8:22; 17:27. Jesus was hungry. Perhaps he had had no food on the night before after the excitement and strain of the entry into Jerusalem. The early figs in Palestine do not get ripe before May or June; the late crop comes in August. It was not the season of figs, Mark notes. But this precocious tree in a sheltered spot had put out leaves as a sign of fruit. It had promise without performance.

11:14. *"May no one ever eat fruit from you again!"* (Μηκέτι εἰς τὸν αἰῶνα ἐκ σοῦ μηδεὶς καρπὸν φάγοι[15]). The verb φάγοι is in the second aorist active optative. It is a wish for the future that in its negative form constitutes a curse upon the tree. Matthew 21:19 has the aorist subjunctive, which amounts to a prohibition. Jesus probably spoke Aramaic on this occasion.

And His disciples were listening[16] (καὶ ἤκουον οἱ μαθηταὶ αὐτοῦ). They listened in evident amazement. After all, it was not the fault of the fig tree that it had put out leaves. Fruit trees often begin to blossom during a warm spell, only to be nipped by frost when the weather becomes seasonable once more.

11:15. *Began to drive out those who were buying and selling in the temple* (ἤρξατο ἐκβάλλειν τοὺς[17] πωλοῦντας καὶ τοὺς ἀγοράζοντας ἐν τῷ ἱερῷ). Mark is fond of "began." See on Matthew 21:12–14 for discussion of this second cleansing of the temple in relation to the first (cf. John 2:14–17).

Overturned the tables of the money changers (τραπέζας τῶν κολλυβιστῶν . . . κατέστρεψεν). See on Matthew 21:12.

11:16. *He would not permit anyone to carry merchandise through the temple* (οὐκ ἤφιεν ἵνα τις διενέγκη σκεῦος διὰ τοῦ ἱεροῦ). Temple authorities had prohibited using the outer court of the temple as a shortcut between the city and the Mount of Olives, but the rule was neglected. All sorts of irreverent conduct was going on, and the spirit of Jesus stirred. This item is given only in Mark. Note use of ἵνα after ἤφιεν (imperfect tense) instead of the infinitive (the usual construction).

11:17. *" 'My house shall be called a house of prayer for all the nations' "* ('Ο οἶκός μου οἶκος προσευχῆς κληθήσεται πᾶσιν τοῖς ἔθνεσιν). In Mark Jesus combines the statements of Isaiah 56:7 and Jeremiah 7:11. The people shared the guilt of the temple authorities in desecrating the part of God's house of prayer in which Gentiles could worship. Jesus exercises messianic authority to smite this political and financial abuse. His denunciation had business and international political implications.

11:18. *And began seeking how to destroy Him*[18] (καὶ ἐζήτουν πῶς αὐτὸν ἀπολέσωσιν[19]). The imperfect indicative sets forth a continuous attitude and endeavor. Note the deliberative subjunctive with πῶς, retained in an indirect question. Sadducees (chief priests) and Pharisees (scribes) all resent the claims of Jesus and join forces to kill him. See discussion on Mark 3:6 of the Pharisee-Herodian plot to kill Jesus. At the seat of Pharisee-Sadducee power, Christ initiates the final crisis by declaring God's controversy with the religious powers.

For they were afraid of Him (ἐφοβοῦντο γὰρ αὐτόν). This is the imperfect middle/passive deponent indicative. In planning his death, they are cautious. Jesus has power among the people.

The whole crowd was astonished at His teaching (πᾶς γὰρ[20] ὁ ὄχλος ἐξεπλήσσετο ἐπὶ τῇ διδαχῇ αὐτοῦ), an imperfect passive. That people who see and hear Jesus in the temple look to him as the Messiah heightens the fear of the Sanhedrin.

11:19. *When evening came* (ὅταν[21] ὀψὲ ἐγένετο), literally, "whenever evening came on" or more exactly "whenever it became late." The use of ὅταν (ὅτε ἄν) with the aorist indicative is like ὅπου ἄν with the imperfect indicative (εἰσεπορεύετο) and ὅσοι ἄν with the aorist indicative (ἥψαντο) in Mark 6:56. As here, use of ἄν *usually* makes the clause more indefinite. In a linguistic irony of Greek, occasionally this construction makes action *more definite*. The interpretation of a more indefinite time frame goes with Luke 21:37. Luke has the accusative of extent of time, "the days," "the nights." The imperfect tense *they would go* (ἐξεπορεύοντο) out of the city suggests "whenever" as the meaning in Mark 11:19.

11:20. *As they were passing by in the morning*[22] (παραπορευόμενοι πρωΐ[23]), the next morning. They went to their evening lodging by the lower road up the Mount of Olives and came down each morning by the steeper, more direct way. Hence they passed on their morning route the tree Jesus had cursed. Matthew 21:20 does not separate the two mornings as does Mark.

Withered from the roots up (ἐξηραμμένην ἐκ ῥιζῶν). Mark alone gives this detail with ἐξηραμμένην, a perfect passive supplementary participle from ξηραίνω.

11:21. *Being reminded, Peter said to Him*[24] (καὶ ἀναμνησθεὶς ὁ Πέτρος λέγει αὐτῷ). This is a first aorist participle and found only in Mark as part of Peter's story.

"Look, the fig tree which You cursed has withered" (ἴδε ἡ συκῆ ἣν κατηράσω ἐξήρανται). Peter remarks about what Jesus has done to the fig tree by his authority. A note of reproach might be attached to these words, but Jesus ignores any such motivation and makes a point about faith.

11:22. *"Have faith in God"* (Ἔχετε πίστιν θεοῦ). This is the objective genitive θεοῦ, as in Romans 3:22, 26, and Galatians 2:26. Jesus uses the prompt fulfillment of his curse on the fig tree to teach the power of faith (see on Matt. 21:21).

11:23. *"And does not doubt in his heart"* (καὶ μὴ διακριθῇ ἐν τῇ καρδίᾳ αὐτοῦ). The verb has in view a divided judgment (διά from δύο, "two," and κρίνω, "to judge"). Jesus means a wavering doublemindedness, not a single act of doubt (διακριθῇ).

"What he says is going to happen" (ὃ λαλεῖ γίνεται[25]), a futuristic present middle/passive deponent indicative.

11:24. *"Believe that you have received them"* (πιστεύετε ὅτι ἐλάβετε[26]). The test of faith is utter confidence in a fulfilment that has not yet occurred. Ἐλάβετε is second aorist active indicative, antecedent in time to πιστεύετε, unless it be considered the timeless aorist when it is simultaneous with it. For an example of this aorist of immediate consequence, see John 15:6.

11:25. *"Whenever you stand praying"* (ὅταν στήκετε προσευχόμενοι). Note the use of ὅταν as in verse 19. Jesus does not mean that standing is the only proper posture in which to pray.

"So that your Father who is in heaven will also forgive you your transgressions" (ἵνα καὶ ὁ πατὴρ ὑμῶν ὁ ἐν τοῖς οὐρανοῖς ἀφῇ ὑμῖν τὰ παραπτώματα ὑμῶν). Evidently God's willingness to forgive is limited by our willingness to forgive others. This is a solemn thought for all who pray (see on Matt. 6:12, 14–15).[27]

11:27. *The chief priests and the scribes and the elders came to Him* (ἔρχονται πρὸς αὐτὸν οἱ ἀρχιερεῖς καὶ οἱ γραμματεῖς καὶ οἱ πρεσβύτεροι). Note the article with each separate group, as in Luke 20:1 and Matthew 21:23. These three classes were in the Sanhedrin. This is a large representative committee of the Sanhedrin sent to confront Jesus in a formal attack upon his authority for cleansing the temple and teaching in it.

11:28. *"By what authority are You doing these things?"* (Ἐν ποίᾳ ἐξουσίᾳ ταῦτα ποιεῖς;). This question, recorded in all three Synoptics, was appropriate (see on Matt. 21:23–27). Note the present subjunctive, ἵνα ταῦτα ποιῇς, "that You keep on doing these things."

11:30. *"Answer Me"*[28] (ἀποκρίθητέ μοι). This sharp demand for a reply is recorded only in Mark (see v. 29). Jesus does not dodge the question. Rather he shows that this is the central issue—an attitude that defines the religious leaders' failure to understand either John or Jesus. They rejected the source of John's authority, and now they reject the innate authority of Jesus as Messiah.

11:31. *"If we say"* (Ἐὰν εἴπωμεν). This is a third-class condition with the aorist active subjunctive. The alternatives are sharply presented in their secret conclave. It is the committee that must dodge Jesus' question because they are thinking in terms only of political expediency, rather than a truth. From that perspective, they are thrust upon a dilemma. They see only too well where Jesus is heading. They are trapped by their attempt to break Christ's popular authority.

11:32. *"But shall we say"*[29] (ἀλλὰ εἴπωμεν . . . ;[30]). This is a deliberative subjunctive with an aorist active subjunctive. It is possible to supply ἐάν as a condition, based upon its conditional use in verse 31. So Matthew 21:26 and

Luke 20:6 use it. But in Mark the structure continues rugged after "from men" with anacoluthon or even aposiopesis—"they feared the people" Mark adds. Matthew has it: "We fear the multitude." Luke puts it: "all the people will stone us." All three authors demonstrate the widely accepted view that John is a prophet. Mark's "verily" is ὄντως, "really or actually." Jewish authorities feared the dead John as much as did Herod Antipas. John's martyrdom had deepened his hold on the people. Disrespect toward his memory might raise a storm.[31]

11:33. *"We do not know"* (Οὐκ οἴδαμεν). Their self-declared ignorance is a refusal to take a stand about the Baptist as the forerunner of Christ. Jesus, however, is not ready to allow them to escape with their admission of defeat.

NOTES

1. TR and Maj.T both have this form.
2. NIV has "just as you enter it."
3. TR and Maj.T have εὐθέως εἰσπορευόμενοι.
4. NIV has "which no one has ever ridden."
5. TR and Maj.T have εὐθέως αὐτὸν ἀποστελεῖ ὧδε.
6. TR and Maj.T have Ἀπῆλθον δὲ καὶ εὗρον τὸν πῶλον δεδεμένον πρὸς τὴν θύραν ἔξω ἐπὶ τοῦ ἀμφόδου.
7. Ezra P. Gould, *Critical and Exegetical Commentary on the Gospel According to St. Mark* (Edinburgh: T. & T. Clark, 1896), 207.
8. NIV has "some people standing there."
9. TR and Maj.T have the aorist verb ἤγαγον.
10. NIV has "while others spread branches."
11. TR and Maj.T have ἄλλοι δὲ στοιβάδας.
12. Marvin Richardson Vincent, *Word Studies in the New Testament*, 4 vols. (Grand Rapids: Eerdmans, 1946), 1.214.
13. NIV has "he went to find out if it had any fruit."
14. TR and Maj.T have ἦλθεν εἰ ἄρα εὑρήσει τι ἐν αυτῇ.
15. TR and Maj.T have a different word order, Μηκέτι ἐκ σοῦ εἰς τὸν αἰῶνα μηδεὶς καρπὸν φάγοι.
16. NIV has "And his disciples heard him say it."
17. TR and Maj.T do not include the article τούς.
18. NIV has "and began looking for a way to kill him."
19. TR has the future tense verb, ἀπολέσουσιν.
20. TR and Maj.T have ὅτι πᾶς in place of πᾶς γάρ.
21. TR and Maj.T have ὅτε in place of ὅταν.

22. NIV has "In the morning, as they went along."

23. TR and Maj.T have the reverse word order, πρωὶ Παραπορευόμενοι.

24. NIV has "Peter remembered and said to Jesus." The proper name *Jesus* is not found in the Greek text, but the pronoun certainly refers to him.

25. TR and Maj.T have ἃ λέγει γίνεται.

26. TR and Maj.T have πιστεύετε ὅτι λαμβάνετε.

27. Mark 11:26 is omitted in WH. The RV puts it in a footnote. NASB puts this verse in brackets with a footnote. NIV puts the verse in a footnote without explanation.

28. NIV has "Tell me."

29. NIV has "But if we say.".

30. TR has ἀλλ᾽ ἐὰν εἴπωμεν. Maj.T has Ἀλλ᾽ εἴπωμεν.

31. Henry Barclay Swete, *Commentary on Mark* (repr. ed., Grand Rapids: Kregel, 1977), 264.

Mark: Chapter 12

12:1. *And He began to speak to them in parables* (Καὶ ἤρξατο αὐτοῖς ἐν παραβολαῖς λαλεῖν[1]). The common Markan idiom does not mean that this was the beginning of Christ's use of parables (see 4:2). Rather, his teaching on this occasion now turned to parable. "The circumstances called forth the parabolic mood, that of one whose heart is chilled, and whose spirit is saddened by a sense of loneliness, and who, retiring within himself, by a process of reflection, frames for his thoughts forms which half conceal, half reveal them."[2] Mark does not record all the parable content of this attack on the religious leaders. Matthew sets in this context the parable of the two sons (21:28–32) and the marriage feast of the king's son (22:1–14). Mark uses the parable of the wicked husbandmen (cf. Matt. 21:33–46 = Luke 20:9–19). Matthew 21:33 calls the vineyard owner "a householder" (οἰκοδεσπότης).

"And dug a vat under the wine press" (ὤρυξεν ὑπολήνιον). This noun is found only here in the New Testament, although it is common in the LXX and in late Greek. Matthew 21:33 has λῆνον, "wine press." This is the vessel or trough under the winepress on the hillside to catch the juice when the grapes were trodden. The Romans called it *lacus* and Wycliff *dalf* (both meaning "lake"). See on Matthew 21:33.

"And rented it out to vine-growers"[3] (καὶ ἐξέδετο[4] αὐτὸν γεωργοῖς). These are workers in the ground, tillers of the soil.

12:2. *"At the harvest time"* (τῷ καιρῷ). It was the season for fruits.

"He sent a slave"[5] (ἀπέστειλεν . . . δοῦλον), a bondslave. Matthew 21:34 has plural *servants*.

"In order to receive some of the produce of the vineyard from the vine-growers"[6] (ἵνα παρὰ τῶν γεωργῶν λάβῃ ἀπὸ τῶν καρπῶν τοῦ ἀμπελῶνος[7]). This is a purpose clause with the second aorist subjunctive. Matthew 21:34 has the infinitive λαβεῖν, a purpose infinitive.

12:4. *"And they wounded him in the head"*[8] (κἀκεῖνον ἐκεφαλίωσαν[9]). This is an old verb (κεφαλαίω), "to bring under heads (κεφαλή), to summarize, then to hit on the head." It is found only here in the New Testament.

12:5. *"Beating some and killing others"* (οὓς μὲν δέροντες οὓς δὲ

369

ἀποκτέννοντες[10]). This distributive use of the demonstrative appears also in Matthew 21:35 in the singular. Originally δέρω in Homer meant "to skin, to flay," then "to smite, to beat." Ἀποκτένοντες is a form of the -μι verb (ἀποκτέννυμι) and means "to kill off."

12:6. *"He had one more to send, a beloved son"* (ἕνα εἶχεν υἱὸν ἀγαπητόν[11]). Luke 20:13 has "my beloved son" (τὸν υἱόν μου τὸν ἀγαπητόν). Jesus evidently has in mind the language of the Father to him at his baptism (Matt. 3:17 = Mark 1:11 = Luke 3:22).

"He sent him last of all to them" (ἀπέστειλεν αὐτὸν ἔσχατον πρὸς αὐτούς). This is found only in Mark. See the discussion of "reverence" on Matthew 21:37.

12:7. *"But those vine-growers said to one another"*[12] (ἐκεῖνοι δὲ οἱ γεωργοὶ πρὸς ἑαυτοὺς εἶπαν[13]). This phrase is found only in Mark. Luke 20:14 has "with one another" (πρὸς ἀλλήλους), a reciprocal instead of a reflexive pronoun.

12:8. *"They took him, and killed him and threw him out of the vineyard"* (καὶ λαβόντες ἀπέκτειναν αὐτόν καὶ ἐξέβαλον αὐτὸν ἔξω τοῦ ἀμπελῶνος[14]). Matthew and Luke reverse the order, "cast forth and killed."

12:10. *"Have you not even read this Scripture"* (οὐδὲ τὴν γραφὴν ταύτην ἀνέγνωτε). Jesus quotes Psalm 118:22–23 (see on Matt. 21:42).

12:11. *"'This came about from the Lord'"*[15] (παρὰ κυρίου ἐγένετο αὕτη). The feminine in the LXX may refer to κεφαλή (head) or may be a translated Hebraism. The Hebrew original זאת (this thing) in Psalm 118:23 otherwise would be translated by the neuter τοῦτο.

12:12. *For they understood that He spoke the parable against them* (ἔγνωσαν γὰρ ὅτι πρὸς αὐτοὺς τὴν παραβολὴν εἶπεν). The parabolic quotation from the psalm regarding the rejected stone, combined with the story of the wicked husbandmen, could have only one application. Matthew 21:43–45 shows that Jesus made certain that the people got his point. The Sanhedrin representatives were so angry that they almost tried to seize him right there. But the people were more enthusiastic than ever. The religious leaders went off in disgust, after they suffered through the parable of the king's son (Matt. 22:1–14).

12:13. *In order to trap Him in a statement*[16] (ἵνα αὐτὸν ἀγρεύσωσιν λόγῳ), an ingressive aorist subjunctive. The verb, from ἄγρα (*a hunt* or *catching*), appears in the LXX and papyri but here alone in the New Testament. Luke 20:20 has the same idea, literally "that they may take hold of his speech" (ἐπιλάβωνται αὐτοῦ λόγον), while Matthew 22:15 uses "to trap" (παγιδεύσωσιν; see on Matt. 22:15). The scribes and Pharisees had tried this before. Mark and Matthew note the combination of Pharisees and Herodians, as Mark did in 3:6. Matthew speaks of "disciples" or pupils of the Pharisees, while Luke calls them "spies" (ἐγκαθέτους).

12:15. *"Shall we pay or shall we not pay?"* (δῶμεν ἢ μὴ δῶμεν;).[17] Mark alone repeats the question in this sharp form. The deliberative subjunctive is the aorist tense active voice. For discussion of the flattery by these theological students, see on Matthew 22:16–22.

Knowing their hypocrisy (ὁ δὲ εἰδὼς αὐτῶν τὴν ὑπόκρισιν). Matthew 22:18 has "But Jesus perceived their malice" (γνοὺς δὲ ὁ Ἰεσοῦς τὴν πονηρίαν αὐτῶν). These sly, shrewd young men did not deceive Jesus.

12:17. *And they were amazed at Him* (καὶ ἐξεθαύμαζον ἐπ᾽ αὐτῷ[18]), the imperfect tense with perfective use of the preposition ἐξ. Both Matthew and Luke use the ingressive aorist. Luke 20:16 adds that they "held their peace" (ἐσίγησαν), while Matthew 22:22 notes that they "went their way" (ἀπῆλθαν, "went off or away").

12:18. *Some Sadducees . . . came to Jesus* (ἔρχονται Σαδδουκαῖοι πρὸς αὐτόν). Note the dramatic historical present. The Pharisees and Herodians had had their turn after the formal committee of the Sanhedrin had been routed. The Sadducees now would show their intellectual superiority over these raw theologians (see on Matt. 22:23–33). The Sadducees tried to score against Jesus and at the same time air their disbelief in a resurrection.

12:19. *"Moses wrote"* (Μωϋσῆς ἔγραψεν[19]). The same form is found in Luke 20:28 (see Gen. 38:8; Deut. 25:5f.). Matthew 22:24 has "said" (εἶπεν).

12:20. *"And the first took a wife"*[20] (καὶ ὁ πρῶτος ἔλαβεν γυναῖκα). Luke 20:29 has λαβὼν γυναῖκα. Matthew 22:25 has "married" (γήμας).

12:22. *"Last of all the woman died also"* (ἔσχατον πάντων καὶ ἡ γυνὴ ἀπέθανεν[21]). Note the adverbial use of ἔσχατον.

12:23. *"For all seven had married her"* (οἱ γὰρ ἑπτὰ ἔσχον αὐτὴν γυναῖκα). This is a predicate accusative in apposition with "her" (αὐτήν). Luke has the same, but Matthew 22:28 merely has "had her" (ἔσχον αὐτήν), a constative aorist active indicative.

12:24. *"Is this not the reason you are mistaken?"*[22] (Οὐ διὰ τοῦτο πλανᾶσθε... ;). Mark puts it as a question with ου, expecting the affirmative answer. Matthew 22:29 puts it as a positive assertion: "You are." Πλανάομαι is "to wander astray" (cf. the English *planet*). Jude 13 refers to those who would lead Christians into sin as "wandering stars," ἀστέρες πλανῆται. The concept corresponds to the Latine *errare* (cf. *err, error*).

"That you do not understand the Scriptures"[23] (μὴ εἰδότες τὰς γραφάς). Sadducees posed as men of superior intelligence and knowledge, in opposition to the traditionalists among the Pharisees with their oral law. Yet these intellectuals were ignorant of the Scriptures as the real source of truth.

"Or the power of God" (μηδὲ τὴν δύναμιν τοῦ θεοῦ). Ignorance of God's revealed Word accompanies ignorance of the being and attributes of God (cf. 1 Cor. 15:34).

12:25. *"For when they rise from the dead"*[24] (ὅταν γὰρ ἐκ νεκρῶν ἀναστῶσιν), a second aorist active subjunctive with ὅταν (ὅτε plus ἄν). Matthew 22:30 has it "in the resurrection," Luke 20:35 "to attain to the resurrection." The Sadducees were actually defeating only the Pharisees' errant view that the future resurrection body would perform marriage functions. The Sadducees knew their opponents' views but not the source of truth, so they revealed their own ignorance of what God had said about the resurrection body and the future life, in which marriage would be replaced by something greater.

"But are like angels in heaven" (ἀλλ᾽ εἰσὶν ὡς ἄγγελοι ἐν[25] τοῖς οὐρανοῖς). See on Matthew 22:30. Luke 20:36 has "equal to the angels" (ἰσάγγελοι). Equality with angels means that humans are delivered from mortality and its consequences.[26] Angels are directly created, not procreated.

12:26. *"In the passage about the burning bush"*[27] (ἐπὶ τοῦ βάτου[28]). This technical use of ἐπί is good Greek for "in the matter of or in the passage about." βάτος is masculine here and feminine in Luke 20:37. The reference is to Exodus 3:3–6.

12:27. *"You are greatly mistaken"* (πολὺ πλανᾶσθε). Only in Mark, a solemn and severe statement of the importance Christ gives to the Resurrection.[29]

12:28. *One of the scribes came and heard them arguing*[30] (Καὶ προσελθὼν εἷς τῶν γραμματέων ἀκούσας αὐτῶν συζητούντων[31]). The victory of Christ over the Sadducees pleased Pharisees who had come back with mixed emotions as Jesus put the Sadducees in their place (Matt. 22:34). Luke 20:39 represents one of the scribes as commending Jesus for his wise reply to the Sadducees. Mark puts this scribe in a favorable light, "recognizing that He had answered them [the Sadducees] well"[32] (ἰδὼν ὅτι καλῶς ἀπεκρίθη αὐτοῖς ἐπηρώτησεν αὐτόν[33]). Matthew 22:35 shows that the question also had a sinister motive. The lawyer (νομικὸς) was "tempting" (πειράζων). He perhaps understood that the Rabbi surpassed the Pharisees as a champion of truth, though his task was to snare him in untruth.

"What commandment is the foremost of all?"[34] (Ποία ἐστὶν ἐντολὴ πρώτη

πάντων;[35]), the first in rank and importance. See the discussion of *great* (μεγαλή), the term used in Matthew 22:36. Probably Jesus was speaking in Aramaic. *First* and *great* are indistinguishable concepts in Greek. Mark quotes Deuteronomy 6:4–5 and Leviticus 19:18 from the LXX. Matthew 22:40 adds Jesus' summary: "On these two commandments hangs (κρέμαται) the whole law and the prophets."

12:32. *The scribe said to Him*[36] (καὶ εἶπεν αὐτῷ ὁ γραμματεύς). Mark alone gives the reply of the scribe, who repeats what Jesus had said about the first and the second commandments and adds 1 Samuel 15:22 about love as superior to whole burnt offerings.

"Right"[37] (Καλῶς). It is not to be taken with "said" (εἶπες) as the RV has it, following Wycliff. Probably καλῶς (well) is exclamatory: "Fine, Teacher; You have *truly* stated . . ." (ἐπ᾽ ἀληθείας).

12:34. *Intelligently*[38] (νουνεχῶς), from νοῦς, "intellect," and ἔχω, "to have." Using the mind to good effect is what the adverb means; it is used only here in the New Testament. The man was wise to understand the central eternal issues.

"Not far" (Οὐ μακράν). The critical attitude of the lawyer had melted into genuine enthusiasm at the reply of Jesus. His love for God's truth and openness to Jesus showed a purity of heart that went beyond mere intellectual facts about the kingdom of God.

After that, no one would venture to ask Him any more questions[39] (καὶ οὐδεὶς οὐκέτι ἐτόλμα αὐτὸν ἐπερωτῆσαι). Note the double negative. The debate was closed (ἐτόλμα, imperfect tense, dared). Jesus was complete victor on every side.

12:35. *"How is it that the scribes say"* (Πῶς λέγουσιν οἱ γραμματεῖς). The opponents of Jesus are silenced, but he answers them and goes on teaching (διδάσκων) in the temple, as before the attacks began that morning (11:27). The scribes no longer dared to question Jesus, but he had a question to put to them "while the Pharisees were gathered together" (Matt. 22:41). Christ's question is not a conundrum or scriptural puzzle.[40] He points out a theological difficulty that is solved in his person and work.[41] The scribes all taught that the Messiah would be the son of David (John 7:41). The people in the triumphal entry had acclaimed Jesus as the son of David (Matt. 21:9). But the rabbis overlooked the fact that David in Psalm 110:1 called the Messiah his Lord also. Joint deity and humanity of the Messiah is the only plausible answer to this problem. Matthew 22:45 observes that "no one was able to answer Him a word."

12:37. *And the large crowd enjoyed listening to Him*[42] (καὶ [ὁ] πολὺς ὄχλος ἤκουεν αὐτοῦ ἡδέως), literally, the "much multitude." A huge crowd listened (imperfect tense) to him gladly. Mark alone has this item. The Sanhedrin had begun the formal attack that morning to destroy the influence that Jesus had shown since the Triumphal Entry. Instead, their attacks had drawn the crowds even closer to him.

12:38. *"Beware of the scribes"*[43] (Βλέπετε ἀπὸ τῶν γραμματέων). Jesus now warns the multitudes and his disciples (Matt. 23:1) about the scribes and the Pharisees, although scribes and Pharisees were present to hear his denunciation. Mark (14:38–40) gives a mere summary sketch of this bold indictment, which is preserved in more detail in Matthew 23. Luke 20:45–47 follows Mark closely. See Matthew 8:15 for this same use of βλέπετε ἀπὸ with the ablative. It is usually called a translation Hebraism, a usage based on the translation from Aramaic into Greek that is not found with βλέπω in the older Greek. However, the papyri give it as a vivid vernacular idiom. "Beware of the Jews" (βλέπε σάτον ἀπὸ τῶν Ἰουδαίων).[44]

"Respectful greetings in the market places" (ἀσπασμοὺς ἐν ταῖς ἀγοραῖς). The pride of the pompous scribes is itemized by Mark: They walk around in long robes[45] (ἐν στολαῖς περιπατεῖν), stoles, the dress of kings and priests. The people can see their dignity and give them respect.

12:39. *"And chief seats in the synagogues"*[46] (καὶ πρωτοκαθεδρίας ἐν ταῖς συναγωγαῖς). This is a mark of special piety; they took seats up in front, the better to be seen and admired.

"And places of honor at banquets" (καὶ πρωτοκλισίας ἐν τοῖς δείπνοις), recognizing proper rank and station. Even the disciples fall victims to this desire for precedence at table (Luke 22:24).

12:40. *"Who devour widows' houses"* (οἱ κατεσθίοντες τὰς οἰκίας τῶν χηρῶν). This is a new sentence in the nominative. Such men inveigled widows into giving their homes to the temple, then took the dwellings for themselves.

"And for appearance's sake offer long prayers"[47] (καὶ προφάσει μακρὰ προσευχόμενοι). Προφάσει is an instrumental case of the word πρόφημι, from which the English word "prophet" derives. The related word προφαίνω means "to show forth." Here the meaning is that of pretentious piety that promotes personal glory and steals from widows.

"These will receive greater condemnation"[48] (οὗτοι λήμψονται[49] περισσότερον κρίμα), "more abundant condemnation."

12:41. *And He sat down opposite the treasury*[50] (Καὶ καθίσας κατέναντι τοῦ γαζοφυλακίου[51]). The storm is over. The Pharisees, Sadducees, Herodians, and scribes have slunk away. Mark draws this immortal picture of the weary

Christ sitting by the treasury (a compound word in the LXX joining γάζα, the Persian word for "treasure," and φυλακή, "guard").

Began observing[52] *how the people were putting money into the treasury*[53] (ἐθεώρει πῶς ὁ ὄχλος βάλλει χαλκὸν εἰς τὸ γαζοφυλάκιον). Imperfect tense, "He was watching."

12:42. *A poor widow came* (καὶ ἐλθοῦσα μία χήρα πτωχὴ). The πτωχός was in direst financial straits, the extreme opposite of the wealthy who had been pouring in their offerings. The money given by such an impoverished person was copper.

Two small copper coins (ἔβαλεν λεπτὰ δύο). Λεπτός means "peeled or stripped" and so very thin. Two λεπτά were about two-fifths of a cent.[54]

12:43. *Calling His disciples to Him* (καὶ προσκαλεσάμενος τοὺς μαθητὰς αὐτοῦ), an indirect middle voice. He gets the disciples' attention. If this comes immediately after his denunciation of the scribes and Pharisees, the disciples may have slipped away in puzzlement and fear at the ferocity of his words. He now gives a practical application of the kingdom values he has been defending.

"This poor widow put in more than all the contributors to the treasury" (ἡ χήρα αὕτη ἡ πτωχὴ πλεῖον πάντων ἔβαλεν τῶν βαλλόντων εἰς τὸ γαζοφυλάκιον[55]). It may mean, "more than all the rich put together."

12:44. *"Put in all she owned"*[56] (πάντα ὅσα εἶχεν ἔβαλεν), imperfect tense followed by the aorist tense, in sharp contrast.

"All she had to live on" (ὅλον τὸν βίον αὐτῆς). Her livelihood, not her life.

NOTES

1. TR and Maj.T have the infinitive λέγειν.
2. Alexander Balmain Bruce, *The Expositor's Greek Testament*, Vol. 1, *The Synoptic Gospels* (Grand Rapids: Eerdmans, 1951), 420.
3. NIV has "Then he rented the vineyard to some farmers."
4. TR and Maj.T have ἐξέδοτο.
5. NIV has "he sent a servant."
6. NIV has "to collect from them some of the fruit of the vineyard."
7. TR has the plural articular noun, τῶν καρπῶν.
8. NIV has "they struck this man on the head."
9. TR and Maj.T have κἀκεῖνον λιθοβολήσαντες ἐκεφαλαίωσαν.
10. TR and Maj.T have τοὺς μὲν δέροντες, τοὺς δὲ ἀποκτείνοντες.
11. TR and Maj.T have ἕνα υἱὸν ἔχων ἀγαπητὸν αὐτοῦ.
12. NIV has "But the tenants said to one another."

13. TR and Maj.T have a different spelling for the verb and a different word order, ἐκεῖνοι δὲ οἱ γεωργοὶ πρὸς ἑαυτοὺς εἶπαν.

14. TR and Maj.T have a καὶ λαβόντες αὐτὸν ἀπέκτειναν καὶ ἐξέβαλον ἔξω τοῦ ἀμπελῶνος.

15. NIV has "the Lord has done this."

16. NIV has "to catch him in his words."

17. This question is found in 12:14 in the Greek text, but 12:15 in NASB and NIV.

18. TR and Maj.T have καὶ ἐθαύμασαν ἐπ᾽ αὐτῷ.

19. TR and Maj.T have the spelling Μωσῆς; WH has Μωυσῆς.

20. NIV has "The first one married."

21. TR and Maj.T have ἐσχάτη πάντων ἀπέθανεν καὶ ἡ γυνή; however, the verb in TRb and Maj.T do not include the moveable ν, ἀπέθανε.

22. NIV has "Are you not in error."

23. NIV has "because you do not know the Scriptures."

24. NIV has "When the dead rise."

25. TR and Maj.T include the article οἱ before the preposition ἐν.

26. Henry Barclay Swete, *Commentary on Mark* (repr. ed., Grand Rapids: Kregel, 1977), 281.

27. NIV has "in the account of the bush."

28. TR has ἐπὶ τῆς βάτου.

29. Bruce, *Expositor's*, 424.

30. NIV has "One of the teachers of the law came and heard them debating."

31. WH spells the participle συνζητούντων.

32. NIV has "Noticing that Jesus had given them a good answer."

33. TR and Maj.T have εἰδὼς ὅτι καλῶς αὐτοῖς ἀπεκρίθη, ἐπηρώτησεν.

34. NIV has "Of all the commandments, which is the most important?"

35. TR and Maj.T have a different word order, Ποία ἐστὶν πρώτη πασῶν ἐντολη. However, TRb and Maj.T do not include the moveable ν on ἐστί.

36. NIV has "the man replied."

37. NIV has "You are right."

38. NIV has "wisely."

39. NIV has "And from then on no one dared ask him any more questions."

40. Ezra P. Gould, *Critical and Exegetical Commentary on the Gospel According to St. Mark* (Edinburgh: T. & T. Clark, 1896), 234.

41. Swete, *Commentary on Mark*, 288.

42. NIV has "The large crowd listened to him with delight."

43. NIV has "Watch out for the teachers of the law."

44. Berl. G. U. 1079. A.D. 41. See A. T. Robertson, *A Grammar of the Greek New*

Testament in the Light of Historical Research (Nashville: Broadman, 1934), 577.

45. NIV has "to walk around in flowing robes."
46. NIV has "and have the most important seats in the synagogues."
47. NIV has "and for a show make lengthy prayers."
48. NIV has "Such men will be punished most severely."
49. TR and Maj.T spell the verb without the μ, λήψονται.
50. NIV has "Jesus sat down opposite the place where the offerings were put."
51. TR and Maj.T include the explicit subject, Καὶ καθίσας ὁ Ἰησους κατέναντι τοῦ γαζοφυλακίου.
52. NIV has "watched."
53. NIV has "the crowd putting their money into the temple treasury."
54. NIV has "worth only a fraction of a penny."
55. TR and Maj.T have ἡ χήρα αὕτη ἡ πτωχὴ πλεῖον πάντων βέβληκεν τῶν βαλόντων εἰς τὸ γαζοφυλάκιον; however, TRb and Maj.T do not include the moveable ν on βέβληκε.
56. NIV has "put in everything."

Mark: Chapter 13

13:1. *"Teacher, behold what wonderful stones and what wonderful buildings"*[1] (Διδάσκαλε, ἴδε ποταποὶ λίθοι καὶ ποταπαὶ οἰκοδομαί). Matthew 24:1 and Luke 21:5 tell of the comment, but Mark alone gives the precise words. Perhaps Peter himself[2] sought by a pleasant observation to lighten the mood after the serious hours in the temple. Josephus[3] speaks of the great size of these stones and the beauty of the buildings. Some of these stones at the southeastern and southwestern angles survive and measure from twenty to forty feet long and weigh a hundred tons each. Jesus and the disciples had observed them at each visit to the temple.

13:2. *"Do you see these great buildings?"* (Βλέπεις ταύτας τὰς μεγάλας οἰκοδομάς;). Jesus fully appreciates their greatness and beauty—which will make what he is predicting about their utter demolition (καταλυθῇ) all the more remarkable.[4] Only the foundation stones and bits of wall would remain after Jerusalem fell in A.D. 70.

13:3. *Opposite the temple, Peter and James and John and Andrew were questioning Him privately* (κατέναντι τοῦ ἱεροῦ ἐπηρώτα αὐτὸν κατ᾽ ἰδίαν Πέτρος καὶ Ἰάκωβος καὶ Ἰωάννης καὶ Ἀνδρέας[5]). On the Mount of Olives, in full view of the temple that they had been discussing, the four disciples, named only in Mark, evidently had been discussing Jesus' strange comment. Such radical destruction, they decided, could apply only to the end of time. They drew Jesus aside to ask about it, although the rest surely drew up as the Lord began his eschatological discourse.

13:4. *"Tell us, when will these things be?"*[6] (Εἰπὸν ἡμῖν πότε ταῦτα ἔσται[7]). English translations generally punctuates this as a direct question, but the Greek suggests an indirect inquiry. The disciples ask about the *when* (πότε) and the *what* (τί τὸ σημεῖον) of the sign of Christ's return. Matthew 24:3 includes "the sign of Your coming and the end of the world," indicating that these events are joined in their thinking. See a fuller discussion of the interpretation of this discourse on Matthew 24:3. This chapter in Mark is often called "the little apocalypse." Some modern scholars have had the notion that a Jewish apocalypse is adapted by Mark and incorrectly attributed to Jesus. Many believe Jesus or the Gospel writers or editors made a grave error on this subject. The view adopted in the discussion in Matthew is that Jesus blended in one picture his death and the destruction of Jerusalem within that generation. The Second Coming and end of the world are typified by the destruction of Jerusalem in A.D. 70. The lines between these topics are not sharply drawn, and it is not possible to dogmatically separate Jesus' words into topical categories. This is the longest discourse preserved in Mark. Peter and Mark may have given it in order to warn[8] readers about the coming catastrophe of Jerusalem. Indeed, few if any Christians were caught in Jerusalem by the Romans because the church well understood what was to occur there. Both Matthew 24 and Luke 21:5–36 follow the general line of Mark 13. Matthew 24:43 to 25:46 adds parables Jesus used to illustrate the point.

13:5. *"See to it that no one misleads you"*[9] (Βλέπετε μή τις ὑμᾶς πλανήσῃ). These are the same words as in Matthew 24:4. Luke 21:8 has it "that you be not led astray" (μὴ πλανηθῆτε). This word πλανάω (our *planet*) is a bold one. This warning runs through the whole discussion and remains pertinent. About the coming of false Christs and the details in verses 6–8, see on Matthew 24:5–8. In spite of Jesus' warning, people have sought continually to apply his teaching to their own calamities.

13:7. *"Those things must take place"*[10] (δεῖ γενέσθαι[11]). Already there had been genocidal outbreaks against the Jews in Alexandria, Seleucia, Jamnia, and elsewhere. More than fifty thousand had been slaughtered. Caligula, Claudius, and Nero all would threaten the Jews, even before the actual Jewish War (A.D. 65–71) and the destruction of the city and temple by Titus in 70. In the years between this prophecy by Jesus in 29 or 30 and the destruction of Jerusalem, there would be major earthquakes in Crete (46 or 47), Tome (51), Apamaia in Phrygia (60), and Campania (63). Four famines ravaged the reign of Claudius in 41–54. One of them in Judea is alluded to in Acts 11:28.[12] Tacitus describes killer storms at Campania in 65.[13]

13:9. *"But be on your guard"*[14] (βλέπετε δὲ ὑμεῖς ἑαυτούς). Only in Mark, but it is a dominant note of warning all through the discourse. Note ὑμεῖς, very emphatic.

"For they will deliver you to the courts"[15] (παραδώσουσιν ὑμᾶς εἰς συνέδρια[16]). This is the same noun used of the Sanhedrin in Jerusalem. These local councils (συν, ἑδρα, sitting together) were modeled after that in Jerusalem.

"You will be flogged in the synagogues" (εἰς συναγωγὰς δαρήσεσθε), second future passive indicative second person plural. The word δέρω means

"to flay or skin." Aristophanes uses the term in the softer colloquial sense of "beat," as do the κοινή papyri.

"You will stand before governors and kings for My sake, as a testimony to them"[17] (ἡγεμόνων καὶ βασιλέων σταθήσεσθε ἕνεκεν ἐμοῦ εἰς μαρτύριον αὐτοῖς). They would be heard by Gentile rulers as well as Jewish councils.

13:10. *"The gospel must first be preached to all the nations"* (καὶ εἰς πάντα τὰ ἔθνη πρῶτον δεῖ[18] κηρυχθῆναι τὸ εὐαγγέλιον). This is only found in Mark. It is interesting to note that Paul in Colossians 1:6, 23 claims even before the destruction of Jerusalem that the gospel has spread all over the world.

13:11. *"Do not worry beforehand about what you are to say"* (μὴ προμεριμνᾶτε τί λαλήσητε). The negative with a present imperative makes a general prohibition or habit. Jesus is not referring to preaching but to defenses made before these councils and governors. A typical example is seen in the courage and skill of Peter and John before the Sanhedrin in Acts 4. The verb μεριμνάω is from μερίζω, "to be drawn in opposite directions, to be distracted." See on Matthew 6:25. They are to face fearlessly those in high places who are seeking to overthrow the preaching of the gospel. These words have been used by lazy preachers to excuse their failure to prepare sermons. That is not the sort of reliance upon the Holy Spirit that Jesus is describing (cf. John 14–16).

13:13. *"But the one who endures to the end"*[19] (ὁ δὲ ὑπομείνας εἰς τέλος). Note this aorist participle with the future verb. The idea is true to the etymology of the word, remaining under (ὑπομένω) until the end. Jesus previously had predicted divisions in families (Luke 12:52–53; 14:26).

"He will be saved" (οὗτος σωθήσεται). Jesus means final salvation (effective aoristic future passive), not initial salvation.

13:14. *"Standing where it should not be"*[20] (ἑστηκότα ὅπου οὐ δεῖ[21]). Matthew 24:15 has "standing in the holy place" (ἑστὸς ἐν τόπῳ ἁγίῳ), neuter and agreeing with βδέλυγμα (abomination), the very phrase applied in 1 Maccabees 1:54 to the altar to Zeus erected by Antiochus Epiphanes where the altar to Jehovah was. Mark personifies the abomination as personal (masculine), while Luke 21:20 defines it by reference to the armies (of Rome, as it turned out). So the words of Daniel find a second fulfilment, Rome taking the place of Syria.[22] See on Matthew 24:15 for this phrase and the parenthesis inserted in the words of Jesus ("Let him that reads understand"). See also on Matthew 24:16–25 for discussion of details in Mark 13:14–22.

13:16. *"In the field"* (εἰς τὸν ἀγρὸν). Matthew 24:18 has ἐν τῷ ἀγρῷ, showing identical use of εἰς with the accusative and ἐν with the locative.

13:19. *"Which God created"* (ἣν ἔκτισεν ὁ θεὸς[23]). Note this amplification to the quotation from Daniel 12:1.

13:20. *"Whom He chose"* (οὓς ἐξελέξατο). This is the indirect aorist middle indicative, found in Mark alone. He explains the sovereign choice of God in the end by and for himself.

13:22. *"In order to lead astray"*[24] (πρὸς τὸ ἀποπλανᾶν[25]). "With a view to leading off" (πρὸς + infinitive). Matthew 24:24 has ὥστε πλανῆσαι, "so as to lead off."

13:23. *"But take heed"*[26] (ὑμεῖς δὲ βλέπετε). Gullibility is no mark of a saint or of piety. Note the emphatic first position of "you," ὑμεῖς. Credulity ranks no higher than scepticism. God gave us our wits for self-protection. Christ has warned us beforehand.

13:24. *"The sun will be darkened"* (ὁ ἥλιος σκοτισθήσεται), a future passive indicative. These figures come from the prophets (Isa. 13:9–10; Ezek. 32:7–8; Joel 2:1–2, 10–11; Amos 8:9; Zeph. 1:14–16; Zech. 12:12). This prophetic imagery, with its apocalyptic symbols, deals in metaphor rather than literal narrative. Peter in Acts 2:15–21 applies Joel's prophecy about the sun and moon to events on the Day of Pentecost. See on Matthew 24:29–31 for details of verses 24–27.

13:25. *"And the stars will be falling from heaven"*[27] (καὶ οἱ ἀστέρες ἔσονται ἐκ τοῦ οὐρανοῦ πίπτοντες[28]), a periphrastic future indicative, ἔσονται, with a present active participle, πίπτοντες.

13:27. *"Will gather together His elect"* (ἐπισυνάξει τοὺς ἐκλεκτοὺς [αὐτοῦ]). This is the purpose of God through the ages.

"From the farthest end of the earth to the farthest end of heaven" (ἀπ᾿ ἄκρου γῆς ἕως ἄκρου οὐρανοῦ). The Greek is very brief, "from the tip of earth to the tip of heaven." This precise phrase occurs nowhere else in Scripture.

13:29. *"When you see these things happening"* (ὅταν ἴδητε ταῦτα[29] γινόμενα), a present middle/passive deponent participle, linear action. See on Matthew 24:32–36 for details of the parable of the fig tree.

13:32. *"Nor the Son"* (οὐδὲ ὁ υἱός). This disclaimer of knowledge naturally interpreted applies to the Second Coming, not to the destruction of Jerusalem in A.D. 70, which Jesus had set definitely in the time frame of that generation.

13:34. *"Commanded the doorkeeper to stay on the alert"*[30] (τῷ θυρωρῷ ἐνετείλατο ἵνα γρηγορῇ). The porter or doorkeeper, as well as all the rest, are to keep watch (present subjunctive). This parable of the porter is found only in Mark. Our ignorance of the time of the Master's return calls us to be alert and eagerly ready, not indifferent or fanatic.

13:35. *"In the evening, at midnight, or when the rooster crows, or in the morning"* (ἢ ὀψὲ ἢ μεσονύκτιον[31] ἢ ἀλεκτοροφωνίας [cock-crowing] ἢ πρωΐ). The night was divided into these four watches.

13:37. *"Be on the alert"*[32] (γρηγορεῖτε). "Be on the watch," a present imperative of a verb meaning, "to be awake." Stay awake till the Lord comes.

NOTES

1. NIV has "Look, Teacher! What massive stones! What magnificent buildings!"
2. Henry Barclay Swete, *Commentary on Mark* (repr. ed., Grand Rapids: Kregel, 1977), 295.
3. Josephus, *Antiquities of the Jews*, 15.11.3.
4. NIV has "thrown down."
5. TR and Maj.T have ἐπηρώτων αὐτὸν κατ' ἰδίαν.
6. NIV has "Tell us, when will these things happen?"
7. TR and Maj.T have Εἰπὲ ἡμῖν πότε ταῦτα ἔσται;
8. Alexander Balmain Bruce, *The Expositor's Greek Testament*, Vol. 1, *The Synoptic Gospels* (Grand Rapids: Eerdmans, 1951), 428.
9. NIV has "Watch out that no one deceives you."
10. NIV has "Such things must happen."
11. TR and Maj.T have the postpositive conjunction included, δεῖ γὰρ γενέσθαι.
12. Marvin Richardson Vincent, *Word Studies in the New Testament*, 4 vols. (repr. ed., Grand Rapids: Eerdmans, 1946), 1.222.
13. Tacitus, *Annals*, 15.10–13.
14. NIV has "You must be on your guard."
15. NIV has "You will be handed over to the local councils."
16. TR and Maj.T include the postpositive conjunction, παραδώσουσιν γὰρ ὑμᾶς εἰς συνέδρια.
17. NIV has "you will stand before governors and kings as witnesses to them."
18. TR and Maj.T have the reverse order for δεῖ πρῶτον.
19. NIV has "but he who stands firm to the end."
20. NIV has "standing where it does not belong."
21. TRs has ἑστὸς ὅπου οὐ δεῖ; TRb and Maj.T have ἑστὼς ὅπου οὐ δεῖ.
22. Swete, *Commentary on Mark*, 304.
23. TR and Maj.T have ἧς ἔκτισεν ὁ θεός.
24. NIV has "to deceive."
25. TR has the iota subscript with the infinitive, ἀποπλανᾶν.
26. NIV has "So be on your guard."
27. NIV has "the stars will fall from the sky."

28. TR and Maj.T have καὶ οἱ ἀστέρες τοῦ οὐρανοῦ ἔσονται ἐκπίπτοντες.
29. TR and Maj.T have the reverse order for the verb and demonstrative pronoun, ταῦτα ἴδητε.
30. NIV has "tells the one at the door to keep watch."
31. TR and Maj.T have μεσυννυκτίου.
32. NIV has "Watch!"

Mark: Chapter 14

14:1. *Now the Passover and Unleavened Bread were two days away* (Ἦν δὲ τὸ πάσχα καὶ τὰ ἄζυμα μετὰ δύο ἡμέρας). This was Tuesday evening as Westerners now count time. By Jewish reckoning, the date changed at 6 P.M. The evening hours belonged to the same date as the following daylight hours. In Matthew 26:2, Jesus says that this same Tuesday by modern reckoning is two days before he will be crucified. John mentions five items that superficially contradict the Synoptic accounts of this week. There is no contradiction, but rather Western confusion as to Jewish terminology regarding Friday and the holiday period.[1] Mark speaks of "the Passover and the Unleavened Bread." These two names designated an eight-day feast period. Sometimes "Passover" specifically refers to the first day, but Jews observed no sharp distinction between that first night and the entire eight days.

The chief priests and the scribes were seeking how to seize Him by stealth and kill Him[2] (ἐζήτουν οἱ ἀρχιερεῖς καὶ οἱ γραμματεῖς πῶς αὐτὸν ἐν δόλῳ κρατήσαντες ἀποκτείνωσιν). The imperfect tense indicates they were still at it, though prevented so far.

14:2. *"Not during the festival"*[3] (Μὴ ἐν τῇ ἑορτῇ). They had planned to kill him at the feast (John 11:57), but the Triumphal Entry and their defeat at the great debate with Jesus at the temple this very morning forced a decision to wait until after the feast. They feared Jesus' influence over the masses (see on Matt. 26:47).

14:3. *Reclining at the table* (κατακειμένου αὐτοῦ). Matthew 26:7 uses ἀνακειμένου, both words meaning reclining or leaning down or up or back. They are in the genitive absolute construction. See on Matthew 26:6–13 for differentiation between this event and that described in Luke 7:36–50.

Very costly perfume of pure nard (μύρου νάρδου πιστικῆς πολυτελοῦς). Use of πιστικῆς and νάρδου occurs only here and in John 12:3. The adjective is common enough in the older Greek and appears in the papyri to describe something as genuine or unadulterated. That seems to be the idea. The word *spikenard* is from the Vulgate *nardi spicati*, likely from the Old Latin *nardi pistici*.

384

She broke the vial and poured it over His head[4] (συντρίψασα τὴν ἀλάβαστρον κατέχεεν αὐτοῦ τῆς κεφαλῆς[5]). This is only recorded in Mark. Probably she broke the narrow neck of the vase that held the ointment.

14:5. *"For this perfume might have been sold for over three hundred denarii"*[6] (ἠδύνατο γὰρ τοῦτο τὸ μύρον πραθῆναι ἐπάνω δηναρίων τριακοσίων[7]). John also sets the value at three hundred denarii, while Matthew has "for much."

And they were scolding her[8] (καὶ ἐνεβριμῶντο αὐτῇ). The imperfect tense of this striking word is used of the snorting of horses and seen already in Mark 1:43; 11:38. It occurs in the LXX in the sense of anger, as here (Dan. 11:30). Judas made the complaint against Mary of Bethany (see John 12:4), but all the apostles joined in the chorus of criticism of the wasteful extravagance.

14:8. *"She has done what she could"* (ὃ ἔσχεν ἐποίησεν[9]). This is recorded alone in Mark. Note the two aorists. Literally, "what she had she did." Mary could not comprehend the Lord's death, but she at least showed her sympathy with him and some understanding of the coming tragedy. After all of Jesus' teaching of his coming death, she at some level understood what her critics had not.

"She has anointed My body beforehand for the burial"[10] (προέλαβεν μυρίσαι τὸ σῶμά μου εἰς τὸν ἐνταφιασμόν[11]). Literally, "she took beforehand to anoint My body for the burial." She anticipated the event. This is Christ's justification of her noble deed. Matthew 26:12 also speaks of the burial preparation by Mary, using the verb ἐνταφιάσαι.

14:9. *"In memory of her"* (εἰς μνημόσυνον αὐτῆς), so also in Matthew 26:13. Mausoleums and "permanent" memorials crumble, but this monument to Jesus continues to fill the world with fragrance.

14:10. *Then Judas Iscariot, who was one of the twelve* (Καὶ Ἰούδας Ἰσκαριὼθ ὁ εἷς τῶν δώδεκα[12]). Note the article here, "the one of the twelve," while Matthew has only εἷς, "one." Some have held that Mark here calls Judas the primary one among the twelve. Rather he means to call attention to the idea that he was *the one* among the twelve who did this deed.

14:11. *They were glad when they heard this*[13] (οἱ δὲ ἀκούσαντες ἐχάρησαν). No doubt the rabbis looked on the treachery of Judas as a veritable dispensation of providence, amply justifying their plots against Jesus.

And he began seeking how to betray Him at an opportune time[14] (καὶ ἐζήτει πῶς αὐτὸν εὐκαίρως παραδοῖ[15]). This was the whole point of the offer of Judas. He claimed that he knew enough of the habits of Jesus to enable them to catch him "in the absence of the multitude" (Luke 22:6). They need not wait for Passover to end and the crowds to leave. For discussion of the motives of Judas, see on Matthew 26:15. Mark merely notes the promise of "money," while Matthew mentions "thirty pieces of silver" (Zech. 11:12), the price of a slave.

14:12. *When the Passover lamb was being sacrificed*[16] (ὅτε τὸ πάσχα ἔθυον). The imperfect tense indicates a customary practice here. The paschal lamb (note πάσχα) was slain at 6 P.M., the beginning of the fifteenth of the month (Exod. 12:6), but the preparations were made beforehand on the fourteenth (Thursday). See on Matthew 26:17 for the discussion of "eat the Passover."

14:13. *He sent two of His disciples* (ἀποστέλλει δύο τῶν μαθητῶν αὐτοῦ). Luke 22:8 names Peter and John.

"And a man will meet you carrying a pitcher of water"[17] (ἀπαντήσει ὑμῖν ἄνθρωπος κεράμιον ὕδατος βαστάζων). This item is also in Luke but not in Matthew.

14:14. *"Say to the owner of the house"* (εἴπατε τῷ οἰκοδεσπότῃ). This is a nonclassical word, but it is found in the late papyri. It means "master (despot) of the house" or "householder." The usual Greek has two separate words, οἴκου δεσπότης (master of the house).

"Where is My guest room" (Ποῦ ἐστιν τὸ κατάλυμά μου[18]). It is found in the LXX, papyri, and modern Greek for a lodging place or inn, as in Luke 2:7 or guest chamber as here.

"In which I may eat the Passover with My disciples?" (ὅπου τὸ πάσχα μετὰ τῶν μαθητῶν μου φάγω;). This is a futuristic aorist subjunctive with ὅπου.

14:15. *"And he himself"* (καὶ αὐτὸς), emphatic pronoun.

"Will show you a large upper room" (ὑμῖν δείξει ἀνάγαιον), anything above ground, and particularly upstairs as here. It is found in this account and in Luke 22:12. Jesus wishes to observe this last feast with his disciples alone, not with others, as was often done. Evidently this friend of Jesus would understand.

"Furnished" (ἐστρωμένον), a perfect passive participle of στρώννυμι, a state of readiness. "Strewed with carpets, and with couches properly spread."[19]

14:17. *He came with the twelve*[20] (ἔρχεται μετὰ τῶν δώδεκα). Note the dramatic historical present. It is assumed that Jesus is observing Passover at the traditional time and hour, at 6 P.M. at the beginning of the fifteenth. This would have corresponded to the modern Western Thursday evening, though it was the beginning of the Jewish Friday. Mark and Matthew note the time as evening and identify it with the regular Passover meal.

14:18. *As they were reclining at the table* (ἀνακειμένων αὐτῶν). These verbs seldom have been translated properly. Even Leonardo da Vinci in his immortal painting of the Last Supper has Jesus and his apostles sitting, not reclining. If he understood the truth, he took artistic license to place the supper in his own cultural dining tradition.

"One who is eating with Me" (ὁ ἐσθίων μετ᾽ ἐμοῦ). See Psalm 4:9. To this day, Arab tradition demands that one must not mistreat guests who have broken bread in one's home.

14:20. *"It is one of the twelve, one who dips with Me in the bowl"* [21] (Εἷς τῶν δώδεκα[22] ὁ ἐμβαπτόμενος μετ᾽ ἐμοῦ εἰς τὸ τρύβλιον[23]). It is as bad as that. The sign that Jesus gave, "one who dips with Me in the bowl," escaped the notice of all. Jesus gave the sop to Judas who understood perfectly that Jesus was aware of his purpose (see on Matt. 26:21–24).

14:23–25. *When He had taken a cup*[24] (λαβὼν ποτήριον[25]). It was probably the ordinary wine of the country mixed with two-thirds water, though the word for wine (οἶνος) is not used in the Gospels but "the fruit of the vine" (ἐκ τοῦ γενήματος τῆς ἀμπέλου) in verse 25. See Matthew 26:26–29 for discussion of important details. Mark and Matthew give substantially the same account of the institution of the Supper by Jesus, while Luke 22:17–20 agrees closely with 1 Corinthians 11:23–26 where Paul claims to have obtained his account by direct revelation from the Lord Jesus.

14:26. *After singing a hymn*[26] (ὑμνήσαντες). See on Matthew 26:30.

14:29. *"Even though all may fall away, yet I will not"*[27] (Εἰ καὶ πάντες σκανδαλισθήσονται, ἀλλ᾽ οὐκ ἐγὼ[28]). Mark records Peter's boast of loyalty even though all desert him. All the Gospels tell it (see on Matt. 26:33).

14:30. *"Before a rooster crows twice"* (πρὶν ἢ δὶς ἀλέκτορα φωνῆσαι). This detail is found only in Mark. One crowing is always the signal for more. The Fayum papyrus agrees with Mark in having δίς. The cock's crow marks the third watch of the night (see on Mark 13:35).

14:31. *But Peter kept saying insistently*[29] (ὁ δὲ ἐκπερισσῶς ἐλάλει[30]). This strong compounded adverb is found only in Mark and probably preserves Peter's own statement of the remark. For further discussion of the boast of Peter, see on Matthew 26:35.

14:32. *They came to a place named Gethsemane*[31] (ἔρχονται εἰς χωρίον οὗ τὸ ὄνομα Γεθσημανί[32]). Literally, "whose name was." Regarding Gethsemane, see on Matthew 26:36.

"Sit here until I have prayed"[33] (Καθίσατε ὧδε ἕως προσεύξωμαι). The aorist subjunctive with ἕως is really with purpose involved, a common idiom. Matthew adds "go over there" (ἀπέλθων ἐκεῖ).

14:33. *And began to be very distressed and troubled* (καὶ ἤρξατο ἐκθαμβεῖσθαι καὶ ἀδημονεῖν). Matthew 26:37 can be translated "grieved or sorrowful and very distressed." See on 26:37 for ἀδημονεῖν. Mark alone uses ἐκθαμβεῖσθαι, here and in 9:15.[34] The verb θαμβέω occurs in 10:32 to describe the disciples' amazement as they contemplated the look on Jesus' face as he went toward Jerusalem. Now Jesus himself feels amazement as he directly faces his own struggle in the Garden of Gethsemane. He wins the victory over himself in Gethsemane, and then he can endure the loss, despising the shame. But for the moment, he is rather amazed at the feelings welling up within his human nature, and he is so very homesick for heaven. "Long as He had foreseen the Passion, when it came clearly into view its terror exceeded His anticipations."[35] "He learned from what He suffered" (Heb. 5:8). This new experience enriched the human soul of Jesus.

14:35. *And fell to the ground* (καὶ . . . ἔπιπτεν ἐπὶ τῆς γῆς[36]). The descriptive imperfect makes one see him fall. Matthew has the aorist ἔπεσεν.

And began to pray (καὶ προσηύχετο). The imperfect tense indicates praying repeatedly or it may mean an inchoative sense of prayer's inception, as "He *began* to pray." Either makes good sense.

The hour might pass Him by[37] (παρέλθῃ ἀπ᾽ αὐτοῦ ἡ ὥρα). Jesus had long looked forward to this "hour" and had often mentioned it (John 7:30; 8:20; 12:23, 27; 13:1; see on v. 41). Now he experiences the immensity of human dread, a trait that all can understand.

14:36. *"Abba! Father!"* (Αββα ὁ πατήρ). The first word is Aramaic and the second is Greek. This is not a case of translation. Jesus could have used both terms, as Paul does in Galatians 4:6. Perhaps Paul was remembering his own childhood prayers in a home suspended between Hebrew and Greek cultures.

"Remove this cup from Me" (παρένεγκε τὸ ποτήριον τοῦτο ἀπ᾽ ἐμοῦ). About Jesus' meaning regarding "the cup," see on Matthew 26:39. It is not possible to take the language of Jesus to mean that he was afraid that he might die before he came to the cross. He was heard (Heb. 5:7–8) and helped to submit to the Father's will as he does instantly.

"Yet not what I will" (ἀλλ᾽ οὐ τί ἐγὼ θέλω). Matthew has "as" (ὡς). We see the humanity of Jesus in its fullness both in the temptations and in Gethsemane, but without sin each time. And this was the severest of all the temptations, to draw back from the cross. The victory over self brought surrender to the Father's will.

14:37. *"Simon, are you asleep?"* (Σίμων, καθεύδεις;). It is the old name, not the new name, *Peter*. Already his boasted loyalty was failing in the hour of crisis. Jesus knows the weakness of human flesh (see on Matt. 26:41).

14:40. *For their eyes were very heavy* (ἦσαν γὰρ αὐτῶν οἱ ὀφθαλμοὶ καταβαρυνόμενοι[38]). This is the perfective use of κατα- with the participle. Matthew has the simple verb. Mark's word is only here in the New Testament and is rare in Greek writers. Mark has the vivid present passive participle, while Matthew has the perfect passive βεβαρημένοι.

And they did not know what to answer Him (καὶ οὐκ ἤδεισαν τί ἀποκριθῶσιν αὐτῷ[39]). The deliberative subjunctive is retained in the indirect question only in Mark and reminds one of the similar embarrassment of these same three disciples on the Mount of Transfiguration (9:6). On both occasions weakness of the flesh prevented their real sympathy with Jesus in his highest and deepest experiences. "Both their shame and their drowsiness would make them dumb."[40]

14:41. *"It is enough"* (ἀπέχει), alone in Mark. This impersonal use is rare and has puzzled expositors. The papyri furnish many examples of the term referring to a receipt for payment in full.[41] See also Matthew 6:2, 5; Luke 6:24; and Philippians 4:18 for the notion of payment in full. It is used here by Jesus in an ironical sense. There was no need to further reprove the disciples for their failure to watch with him. "This is no time for a lengthened exposure of the faults of friends; the enemy is at the gate."[42] See on Matthew 26:45 the description of the approach of Judas.

14:43. *Who were from the chief priests and the scribes and the elders* (παρὰ τῶν ἀρχιερέων καὶ τῶν γραμματέων καὶ τῶν πρεσβυτέρων). Mark adds this item, while John 18:3 mentions "Pharisees." It was evidently a committee of the Sanhedrin, the group with whom Judas had struck his bargain (Matt. 26:3 = Mark 14:1 = Luke 22:2). See discussion of the betrayal and arrest on Matthew 26:47–56.

14:44. *Now he who was betraying Him had given them a signal*[43] (δεδώκει δὲ ὁ παραδιδοὺς αὐτὸν σύσσημον αὐτοῖς). This is a common word in the ancient Greek for an arranged signal. It is here only in the New Testament. Matthew 26:48 has σημεῖον, sign. The signal was the kiss, a contemptible desecration of a friendly salutation.

"Seize Him and lead Him away under guard"[44] (κρατήσατε αὐτὸν καὶ ἀπάγετε[45] ἀσφαλῶς). This is only in Mark. Judas wished no slip to occur. Only John 18:4–9 tells of the fear that made the armed mob fall back when Jesus challenged them.

14:47. *But one of those who stood by drew his sword* (εἷς δέ [τις] τῶν παρεστηκότων σπασάμενος τὴν μάχαιραν). Only John 18:10, written after Peter's death, says that it was Peter who tried to kill the chief priest's servant

Malchus. Nor does Mark record the rebuke Jesus gives to Peter (see on Matt. 26:52–54).

14:48. *"As you would against a robber?"*[46] ($^{\prime}\Omega_S \, \dot{\epsilon}\pi\grave{\iota} \, \lambda\eta\sigma\tau\dot{\eta}\nu. \, . \, . \, ;$). Highway robbers like Barabbas were common. Zealots might regard them as antiauthoritarian heroes. Jesus soon will take a robber's cross in the place of Barabbas.

14:51. *A young man was following Him* ($\nu\epsilon\alpha\nu\acute{\iota}\sigma\kappa\sigma_S \, \tau\iota_S \, \sigma\upsilon\nu\eta\kappa\sigma\lambda\sigma\acute{\upsilon}\theta\epsilon\iota \, \alpha\dot{\upsilon}\tau\hat{\omega}^{47}$). This incident is unique to Mark, and it is easy to speculate that Mark himself may have been the young man. He was the son of Jesus' follower Mary (Acts 12:12). It could have been Mark's house in which Jesus and the disciples celebrated Passover. The curious lad might have followed Jesus to the Garden and gets caught up in the unfolding events at the arrest. This is an argument from silence, for if Mark is not the one being described, the point of this anecdote is hard to see. The story does present a touch of real-life experience of the sort that accompanies such momentous experiences. The young man was following (imperfect tense) Jesus.

Wearing nothing but a linen sheet ($\dot{o} \, \delta\dot{\epsilon} \, \kappa\alpha\tau\alpha\lambda\iota\pi\grave{\omega}\nu \, \tau\grave{\eta}\nu \, \sigma\iota\nu\delta\acute{o}\nu\alpha$). It was fine linen cloth such as might be used for wrapping the dead (Matt. 27:59 = Mark 15:46 = Luke 23:53). In this instance it could have been a bedsheet or what the boy might have worn to bed.

They seized him ($\kappa\rho\alpha\tau\sigma\hat{\upsilon}\sigma\iota\nu \, \alpha\dot{\upsilon}\tau\acute{o}\nu$). Note the vivid dramatic present, literally, "They seize him."

14:54. *Peter had followed Him at a distance* ($\kappa\alpha\grave{\iota} \, \dot{o} \, \Pi\acute{\epsilon}\tau\rho\sigma_S \, \dot{\alpha}\pi\grave{o} \, \mu\alpha\kappa\rho\acute{o}\theta\epsilon\nu \, \dot{\eta}\kappa\sigma\lambda\sigma\acute{\upsilon}\theta\eta\sigma\epsilon\nu \, \alpha\dot{\upsilon}\tau\hat{\omega}$). Mark uses the constative aorist $\dot{\eta}\kappa\sigma\lambda\sigma\acute{\upsilon}\theta\eta\sigma\epsilon\nu$, where Matthew 26:58 and Luke 22:54 have the picturesque imperfect, $\dot{\eta}\kappa\sigma\lambda\sigma\acute{\upsilon}\theta\epsilon\iota$, "was following." Possibly Mark did not care to dwell on the picture of Peter furtively following at a distance, not bold enough to take an open stand with Christ as did the beloved disciple did, yet unable to remain away with the other disciples.

And he was sitting with the officers[48] ($\kappa\alpha\grave{\iota} \, \mathring{\eta}\nu \, \sigma\upsilon\gamma\kappa\alpha\theta\acute{\eta}\mu\epsilon\nu\sigma_S^{49} \, \mu\epsilon\tau\grave{\alpha} \, \tau\hat{\omega}\nu \, \dot{\upsilon}\pi\eta\rho\epsilon\tau\hat{\omega}\nu$), a periphrastic imperfect middle pictures Peter as making himself at home in the shadows among the officers. John 18:25 describes Peter as standing $\dot{\epsilon}\sigma\tau\acute{\omega}_S$. In his restless, weary agitation he could not settle into any position.

And warming himself at the fire ($\kappa\alpha\grave{\iota} \, \theta\epsilon\rho\mu\alpha\iota\nu\acute{o}\mu\epsilon\nu\sigma_S \, \pi\rho\grave{o}_S \, \tau\grave{o} \, \phi\hat{\omega}_S$), a reflexive middle. Firelight illuminated Peter's face. He was not so hidden as he supposed.

14:56. *Many were giving false testimony against Him* ($\pi\sigma\lambda\lambda\sigma\grave{\iota} \, \gamma\grave{\alpha}\rho$

ἐψευδομαρτύρουν κατ' αὐτοῦ). The imperfect tense indicates repeated action. No two witnesses bore agreeing testimony as was required to justify a capital sentence according to the Law (see Deut. 19:15). Note the imperfects in verses 55–57 to indicate repeated failures.

But their testimony was not consistent[50] (καὶ ἴσαι αἱ μαρτυρίαι οὐκ ἦσαν). Literally, the testimonies were not "equal." They did not agree on essential points.

14:57. Some stood up and began to give false testimony against Him (καί τινες ἀναστάντες ἐψευδομαρτύρουν κατ' αὐτοῦ). In desperation, some attempted once more (conative imperfect).

14:58. "'I will destroy this temple made with hands'"[51] (Ἐγὼ καταλύσω τὸν ναὸν τοῦτον τὸν χειροποίητον), in Mark alone. The negative form ἀχειροποίητον occurs elsewhere only in 2 Corinthians 5:1 and Colossians 2:11. In Hebrews 9:11 the negative οὐ is used with the positive form. A real λόγιον of Jesus underlies this perversion of his teaching. Mark and Matthew do not quote the witnesses precisely alike. Perhaps they quoted Jesus differently and therein is part of the disagreement, for Mark adds verse 59, which is not in Matthew, "And not even in this respect was their testimony consistent," repeating the point of verse 57. Henry Swete observes that Jesus, as a matter of fact, did do what the witnesses said. "His death destroyed the old order, and His resurrection created the new."[52] But these witnesses did not mean that. The only recorded saying of Jesus that is at all like this is in John 2:19. There he referred to the temple of his body, though no one understood his meaning at the time.

14:60. The high priest stood up (καὶ ἀναστὰς ὁ ἀρχιερεὺς εἰς μέσον[53]). For greater solemnity, he arose to make up for the lack of evidence with bluster. The high priest stepped into the midst to attack Jesus by vehement questions (see on Matt. 26:59–68).

14:61. But He kept silent (ὁ δὲ ἐσιώπα). Matthew has it, "You have spoken," which is equivalent of the affirmative. But Mark's statement is definite. See on Matthew 26:64–68 for the claims of Jesus and the conduct of Caiaphas.

14:64. And they all condemned Him to be deserving of death (οἱ δὲ πάντες κατέκριναν αὐτὸν ἔνοχον εἶναι θανάτου[54]). This would mean that only the anti-Jesus contingent of the Sanhedrin had been gathered. Joseph of Arimathea was not present since he did not consent to the death of Jesus (Luke 23:51). Nicodemus probably was not invited because of his previous sympathy with Jesus (John 7:50). All who were present voted for the death of Jesus.

14:65. And to blindfold Him (καὶ περικαλύπτειν αὐτοῦ τὸ πρόσωπον[55]).

They put a veil around his face. This is not found in Matthew, but in Luke 22:64 where the RV translates περικαλύψαντες by "blindfolded." All three Gospels record the jeering demand of the Sanhedrin: "Prophesy" (προφήτευσον). Matthew and Luke add that they demanded that Jesus tell who struck him while he was blindfolded. Mark adds "the officers" (see v. 54) of the Sanhedrin, referring to Roman lictors or sergeants-at-arms who had arrested Jesus in Gethsemane and who still had him in their charge (οἱ συνέχοντες αὐτόν, Luke 22:63). Matthew 26:67 alludes to their treatment of Jesus without identifying these tormentors.

And the officers received Him with slaps in the face[56] (καὶ οἱ ὑπηρέται ῥαπίσμασιν αὐτὸν ἔλαβον[57]). The verb ῥαπίζω in Matthew 26:67 originally meant to smite with a rod. In late writers it comes to mean to slap the face with the palm of the hands. The same thing is true of the substantive ῥάπισμα used here. A papyrus of the sixth century A.D. uses the term to refer to a facial scar resulting from a blow.[58] It is in the instrumental case. "They caught him with blows,"[59] suggests for the unusual ἔλαβον in this sense. "With rods" is, of course, possible, since lictors carried rods. It was a gross indignity.

14:66. *As Peter was below in the courtyard* (Καὶ ὄντος τοῦ Πέτρου κάτω ἐν τῇ αὐλῇ[60]). This implies that Jesus was upstairs when the Sanhedrin met. Matthew 26:69 has it "outside in the courtyard" (ἔξω ἐν τῇ αὐλῇ). The open court was outside the rooms and below.

14:67. *And seeing Peter warming himself* (καὶ ἰδοῦσα τὸν Πέτρον θερμαινόμενον). Mark mentions this fact about Peter twice (14:54, 67) as does John (18:18, 25). He was twice beside the fire. It is difficult to relate clearly the three denials. Each time several women and men may have joined in.

"You also were with Jesus the Nazarene" (Καὶ σὺ μετὰ τοῦ Ναζαρηνοῦ ἦσθα τοῦ Ἰησοῦ[61]). In Matthew 26:69 it is "the Galilean." A number were probably speaking, each saying something different.

14:68. *"I neither know nor understand what you are talking about"* (Οὔτε οἶδα οὔτε ἐπίσταμαι σὺ τί λέγεις[62]). This denial is fuller in Mark, briefest in John. This can be understood as a direct question.

And he went out onto the porch[63] (καὶ ἐξῆλθεν ἔξω εἰς τὸ προαύλιον), a term used only here in the New Testament. Plato uses it of a prelude on a flute. It occurs also in the plural for preparations of the day before the wedding. Here it means the entryway to the court. Matthew 26:71 has πυλῶνα, a common word for gate or front porch. A reference to a first cock's crow ([καὶ ἀλέκτωρ ἐφώνησεν])in verse 68 is found only in late manuscripts and should not be regarded as genuine.[64] Mark alone alludes to the cock crowing twice, in verses 30 and 72.

14:69–70. *And began once more to say to the bystanders*[65] (καὶ . . . ἤρξατο πάλιν λέγειν τοῖς παρεστῶσιν[66]). This talk about Peter was overheard. "This fellow (οὗτος) is one of them." So in verse 70 the talk is directly to Peter as in Matthew 26:73, but in Luke 22:59 it is about him. Soon the bystanders (οἱ παρεστῶτες) join in the accusation (cf. Matt. 26:73). John 18:26 seems to record the climax of this exchange (see on Matt. 26:69–70).

14:71. *But he began to curse and to swear*[67] (ὁ δὲ ἤρξατο ἀναθεματίζειν καὶ ὀμνύναι[68]). Note the connection to the English *anathema* from ἀνάθεμα. This word originally meant simply "an offering," but the nuance was added of "something devoted to destruction or accursed."[69] A distinction between the meanings that can be observed in the New Testament was common in the κοινή. Matthew 26:74 has Καταθεματίζειν, which is a New Testament hapax legomenon but common in the LXX. This meaning is to call down curses on oneself if the thing said is not true.

14:72. *And Peter remembered* (καὶ ἀνεμνήσθη ὁ Πέτρος). Matthew 26:75 has the uncompounded verb ἐμνήσθη, while Luke 22:61 has a compound, ὑπερεμνήσθη, "was reminded."

And he began to weep[70] (καὶ ἐπιβαλὼν ἔκλαιεν). The second aorist active participle of ἐπιβάλλω is used in an absolute sense, though there is a reference to τὸ ῥῆμα above, the word of Jesus, and the idiom involves τὸν νοῦν. Thus, the meaning is "to put the mind upon something." In Luke 15:12 there is another absolute use with a different sense.[71] Ἔκλαιεν is inchoative (inceptive) imperfect, "began to weep." Matthew 26:75 has the ingressive aorist ἔκλαυσεν, "burst into tears."

NOTES

1. See the discussion on Matthew 26:17 and A. T. Robertson, *Harmony of the Gospels for Students of the Life of Christ* (New York: Harper and Row, 1922), 279–84.
2. NIV has "the chief priests and the teachers of the law were looking for some sly way to arrest Jesus and kill him."
3. NIV has "not during the Feast."
4. NIV has "She broke the jar and poured the perfume on his head."
5. TR and Maj.T have συντρίψασα τὸ ἀλάβαστρον κατέχεεν αὐτοῦ κατὰ τῆς κεφαλῆς.
6. NIV has "It could have been sold for more than a year's wages."

7. TR and Maj.T have ἠδύνατο γὰρ τοῦτο πραθῆναι ἐπάνω τριακοσίων δηναρίων.

8. NIV has "And they rebuked her harshly."

9. TR and Maj.T have ὃ εἶχεν αὕτη ἐποίησεν. However, TRb and Maj.T do not include the moveable ν on the second verb ἐποίησε.

10. NIV has "She poured perfume on my body beforehand to prepare for my burial."

11. TR and Maj.T have προέλαβεν μυρίσαι μου τὸ σῶμα εἰς τὸν ἐνταφιασμόν.

12. TR and Maj.T have Καὶ ὁ Ἰούδας ὁ Ἰσκαριώτης, εἰς τῶν δώδεκα.

13. NIV has "they were delighted to hear this."

14. NIV has "So he watched for an opportunity to hand him over."

15. TR and Maj.T have καὶ ἐζήτει τοῖς εὐκαίρως αὐτὸν παραδῷ.

16. NIV has "when it was customary to sacrifice the Passover lamb."

17. NIV has "a man carrying a jar of water will meet you."

18. TR and Maj.T do not include the personal pronoun μου. TRb and Maj.T do not include the moveable ν on the verb ἐστι.

19. Marvin Richardson Vincent, *Word Studies in the New Testament*, 4 vols. (repr. ed., Grand Rapids: Eerdmans, 1946), 1.227.

20. NIV has "Jesus arrived with the twelve."

21. NIV has "one who dips bread into the bowl with me."

22. TR and Maj.T have Εἷς ἐκ τῶν δώδεκα.

23. TR accents the noun on the penult rather than the antepenult, Τρυβλίον.

24. NIV has "Then he took the cup."

25. TR and Maj.T have λαβὼν τὸ ποτήριον.

26. NIV has "When they had sung a hymn."

27. NIV has "Even if all fall away, I will not."

28. TR and Maj.T reverse the first two words, Καὶ εἰ.

29. NIV has "But Peter insisted emphatically."

30. TR and Maj.T have Ὁ δὲ ἐκ περισσοῦ ἔλεγεν μᾶλλον. However, TRb and Maj.T do not include the moveable ν on the verb ἔλεγε.

31. NIV has "They went to a place called Gethsemane."

32. TR and Maj.T spell the proper noun, Γεθσημανῆ; WH spells it Γεθσημανεῖ.

33. NIV has "Sit here while I pray."

34. A papyrus example is given in James Hope Moulton and George Milligan, *The Vocabulary of the Greek Testament* (London: Hodder and Stoughton, 1952), 194.

35. Henry Barclay Swete, *Commentary on Mark* (repr. ed., Grand Rapids: Kregel, 1977), 342.

36. TR and Maj.T have the aorist form of the verb, ἔπεσεν.

37. NIV has "the hour might pass from him."

38. TR and Maj.T have ἦσαν γὰρ οἱ ὀφθαλμοὶ αὐτῶν βεβαρημένοι.

39. TR and Maj.T have a different word order, καὶ οὐκ καὶ οὐκ ἤδεισαν τί αὐτῷ ἀποκριθῶσιν. However, TRb and Maj.T do not include the moveable ν on the verb ἀποκριθῶσι.

40. Ezra P. Gould *Critical and Exegetical Commentary on the Gospel According to St. Mark* (Edinburgh: T. & T. Clark, 1896), 271.

41. Moulton and Milligan, *Vocabulary*, 57–58; G. Adolf Deissmann, *Light from the Ancient East: The New Testament Illustrated by Recently Discovered Texts of the Graeco-Roman World*, trans. L. R. M. Strachan (rev. ed., Grand Rapids: Baker, 1965), 110–12.

42. Swete, *Commentary on Mark*, 348.

43. NIV has "Now the betrayer had arranged a signal with them."

44. NIV has "arrest him and lead away under guard."

45. TR and Maj.T have the aorist form of the verb ἀπαγάγετε.

46. NIV has "Am I leading a rebellion?"

47. TR has the imperfect verb, εἷς τις νανίσκος ἠκολούθει αὐτῷ; Maj.T has the aorist tense verb, εἷς τις νεανίσκος ἠκολούθησεν αὐτῷ.

48. NIV has "There he sat with the guards."

49. WH has the spelling for the participle, συνκαθήμενος.

50. NIV has "but their statements did not agree."

51. NIV has "I will destroy this manmade temple."

52. Swete, *Commentary on Mark*, 357.

53. TR has the article with the object of the preposition, εἰς τὸ μέσον.

54. TR and Maj.T have the adjective and infinitive in reverse order, εἶναι ἔνοχον.

55. TR and Maj.T have καὶ περικαλύπτειν τὸ πρόσωπον αὐτοῦ.

56. NIV has "And the guards took him and beat him."

57. TR and Maj.T have the imperfect tense verb, ἔβαλλον.

58. Moulton and Milligan, *Vocabulary*, 563.

59. Swete, *Commentary on Mark*, 362.

60. TR and Maj.T have καὶ ὄντος τοῦ Πέτρου ἐν τῇ αὐλῇ κάτω.

61. TR and Maj.T do not include the article and reverses the order of Ἰησοῦ ἦσθα.

62. TR and Maj.T have Οὐκ οἶδα οὐδὲ ἐπίσταμαι τί σὺ λέγεις.

63. NIV has "and went out into the entryway."

64. This is omitted by Aleph B L Sinaitic Syriac. It is genuine in verse 72 where "the second time" (ἐκ δευτέρου) occurs also. It is possible that because of verse 72 it crept into verse 68.

65. NIV has "she said again to those standing around."
66. TR and Maj.T have πάλιν ἤρξατο λέγειν τοῖς παρεστηκόσιν.
67. NIV has "He began to call down curses on himself, and he swore to them."
68. TR has the present tense infinitive, ὀμνύειν.
69. Deissmann, *Light from the Ancient East*, 95–96, has found examples at Megara of ἀνάθεμα in the sense of curse.
70. NIV has "And he broke down and wept."
71. Moulton, *Grammar, Prolegomena*, 1.131, quotes a Ptolemaic papyrus Tb P 50, where ἐπιβαλών probably means "set to," put his mind on.

■ ■ ■ ■ ■

Mark: Chapter 15

15:1. *Early in the morning*[1] (πρωί). This is the ratification meeting after daybreak. See on Matthew 26:1–5.

Held a consultation[2] (συμβούλιον ποιήσαντες).[3] The late and rare word συμβούλιον is like the Latin *consilium*. Some texts have ἑτοιμάσαντες. If that is the correct text, the idea would be rather to prepare a concerted plan of action.[4] But their night action had been illegal, so they reconvened after dawn, as described in Luke 22:66–71. Luke does not record the illegal night trial.

Binding Jesus[5] (δήσαντες τὸν Ἰησοῦν). He was bound on his arrest (John 18:12), and Annas sent him bound to Caiaphas (v. 24). Now he is bound again as he is sent to Pilate (Mark 15:1 = Matt. 27:2). By implication, he was unbound while before Annas, Caiaphas, and the Sanhedrin.

15:2. *"Are You the King of the Jews?"* (Σὺ εἶ ὁ βασιλεὺς τῶν Ἰουδαίων;). This is the only charge made by the Sanhedrin that Pilate notices (Luke 23:2). Whether Pilate believes this charge, he must pay attention to it. He does not want to be accused of passing over a potential revolutionary. After interviewing Jesus, as told in John 18:28–32, Pilate is convinced that he is dealing with a harmless religious fanatic (see on Matt. 26:11).

"It is as you say"[6] (Σὺ λέγεις). Mark records only this affirmation, while John 18:34–37 tells of a second, fuller conference between Pilate and Jesus. "Here, as in the trial before the Sanhedrin, this is the one question that Jesus answers. It is the only question on which his own testimony is important and necessary."[7] The Jews were out on the pavement or sidewalk outside the palace while Pilate came out to them from above on the balcony (John 18:28f.) and had his interviews with Jesus on the inside, calling Jesus to him (John 18:33).

15:3. *The chief priests began to accuse Him harshly*[8] (καὶ κατηγόρουν αὐτοῦ οἱ ἀρχιερεῖς πολλά). The imperfect tense suggests repeated accusations besides those they had already made. The verb is commonly used for speaking against something or someone before a court (κατά and ἀγορεύω). It is used with the genitive of the person and the accusative of the thing.

397

15:5. *So Pilate was amazed* (ὥστε θαυμάζειν τὸν Πιλᾶτον[9]). Pilate saw the envy of the accusers and was sure of Jesus' innocence (Mark 15:10). He hoped that Jesus would answer these charges and so relieve him of the burden. He marvelled at the prisoner's self-control.

15:6. *He used to release for them any one prisoner* (ἀπέλυεν αὐτοῖς ἕνα δέσμιον). The imperfect tense of customary action is used. Matthew 27:15 has the verb εἰώθει ("was accustomed to").

Whom they requested[10] (ὃν παρῃτοῦντο). The imperfect tense expresses that the people were accustomed to taking part in this holiday release custom.

15:7. *Barabbas had been imprisoned with the insurrectionists* (ἦν . . . Βαραββᾶς μετὰ τῶν στασιαστῶν[11] δεδεμένος). Barabbas seems to have been a desperate criminal, possibly a leader in the insurrection (ἐν τῇ στάσει) against Rome. This was the very thing that the Jews at Bethsaida Julias had wanted Jesus to lead (John 6:15). Pilate must have assumed that the religious leaders would not choose a man who was truly incendiary over one who was falsely charged with the same crime.

Who had committed murder in the insurrection (οἵτινες ἐν τῇ στάσει φόνον πεποιήκεισαν). The priests and people actually chose a murderer in preference to Jesus.

15:8. *As he had been accustomed to do for them*[12] (καθὼς ἐποίει αὐτοῖς[13]), the imperfect of customary action again with the dative case.

15:9. *"Do you want me to release for you the King of the Jews?"* (Θέλετε ἀπολύσω ὑμῖν τὸν βασιλέα τῶν Ἰουδαίων;). That phrase from this charge sharpened the contrast between Jesus and Barabbas, which is declared bluntly in Matthew 27:17 "Barabbas or Jesus who is called Christ" (see on Matt. 27:17).

15:10. *For he was aware*[14] (ἐγίνωσκεν γάρ). The imperfect tense indicates that Pilate's initial impression about the nature of the case was being confirmed. The truth was dawning on him. Both Mark and Matthew give "envy" (φθόνον) as the primary motive of the Sanhedrin. Pilate probably had heard of the popularity of Jesus. Surely his officers had reported the Triumphal Entry and he may have heard of the temple teaching.

Had handed Him over[15] (παραδεδώκεισαν). Past perfect indicative without an augment. Matthew 27:18 has the first aorist (kappa aorist) indicative παρέδωκαν, not preserving the distinction made by Mark.

15:11. *But the chief priests stirred up the crowd* (οἱ δὲ ἀρχιερεῖς ἀνέσεισαν τὸν ὄχλον). The leaders shook up the crowd like an earthquake (σεισμός). Matthew 27:20 uses the weaker effective aorist indicative ἔπεισαν, meaning "persuaded." The priests and scribes had amazing success. These were not the same pilgrims who had followed Jesus into Jerusalem or who had listened to his teaching in the temple. The plan of Judas and the Sanhedrin was to get the thing over before Jesus' Galilean sympathizers arose. "It was a case of regulars against an irregular, of priests against prophet."[16] "But Barabbas, as described by Mark, represented a popular passion, which was stronger than any sympathy they might have for so unworldly a character as Jesus—the passion for *political liberty*."[17] "What unprincipled characters they were! They accuse Jesus to Pilate of political ambition, and they recommend Barabbas to the people for the same reason."[18] The Sanhedrin would say to the people that Jesus had already abdicated his kingly claims while to Pilate they went on accusing him of treason to Ceasar.

To ask him to release Barabbas for them instead (ἵνα μᾶλλον τὸν Βαραββᾶν ἀπολύσῃ αὐτοῖς), instead of Jesus.

15:12. *"Then what shall I do with Him whom you call the King of the Jews?"* (Τί οὖν [θέλετε] ποιήσω [ὅν λέγετε] τὸν Βασιλέα[19] τῶν Ἰουδαίων;). Pilate rubs it in on the Jews (cf. v. 9). "Then," οὖν, means "since you have chosen Barabbas instead of Jesus."

15:13. *"Crucify Him!"* (Σταύρωσον αὐτόν). Luke 23:21 repeats the verb. Matthew 27:22 has it, "Let Him be crucified." There was a chorus and a hubbub of confused voices all demanding crucifixion for Christ (see on Matt. 27:23).

15:15. *Wishing to satisfy the crowd* (Βουλόμενος τῷ ὄχλῳ τὸ ἱκανὸν ποιῆσαι). This is a Greek version of the Latin idiom *satisfacere alicui*, "to do what is sufficient to remove one's ground of complaint." This same phrase occurs in Polybius, Appian, Diogenes Laertes, and in late papyri.[20] Pilate was becoming afraid of what this crowd might do now that they were so completely under the control of the Sanhedrin. He feared what they might tell Caesar about him. See on Matthew 27:26 for discussion of the scourging.

15:16. *The soldiers took Him away into the palace (that is, the Praetorium)* (Οἱ δὲ στρατιῶται ἀπήγαγον αὐτὸν ἔσω τῆς αὐλῆς, ὅ ἐστιν πραιτώριον). This was the palace of the Roman provincial governor. In Philippians 1:13 it means the Praetorian Guard in Rome. Mark mentions "the court" (τῆς αὐλῆς) inside of the palace into which the people passed from the street through the foyer. See further on Matthew 27:26 about the "band."

15:17. *They dressed Him up in purple*[21] (καὶ ἐνδιδύσκουσιν[22] αὐτὸν πορφύραν). See on Matthew 27:28 for discussion of the scarlet robe and crown of thorns.

15:19. *And kneeling and bowing before Him*[23] (καὶ τιθέντες τὰ γόνατα προσεκύνουν αὐτῷ), in mockery. The imperfect tense is used as well with ἔτυπτον (smote) and ἐνέπτυον (did spit on). Jesus suffered repeated indignities.

15:20. *And they led Him out to crucify Him* (καὶ ἐξάγουσιν αὐτὸν ἵνα σταυρώσωσιν αὐτόν). Note the vivid historical present after the imperfects in verse 19.

15:21. *They pressed into service a passer-by* (Καὶ ἀγγαρεύουσιν παράγοντά). Note the dramatic historical present indicative again where Matthew 27:32 has the aorist. For discussion of this Persian word, see on Matthew 5:41 and 27:32.

Coming from the country (ἐρχόμενον ἀπ᾽ ἀγροῦ). Hence Simon met the procession. Mark adds that he was "the father of Alexander and Rufus." Paul mentions a Rufus in Romans 16:13, but this was a common name. See on Matthew 27:32 for a discussion of cross-bearing by criminals. Luke 23:26 adds "after Jesus" (ὄπισθεν τοῦ Ἰησοῦ). But Jesus bore his own cross till he was relieved of it, and he walked in front of his own cross for the rest of the way.

15:22. *Then they brought Him to the place Golgotha* (καὶ φέρουσιν αὐτὸν ἐπὶ τὸν Γολγοθᾶν τόπον[24]). Note the historical present again. See on Matthew 27:33 for discussion of Golgotha.[25]

15:23. *They tried to give Him wine mixed with myrrh* (καὶ ἐδίδουν αὐτῷ ἐσμυρνισμένον οἶνον[26]). Note the imperfect tense where Matthew has the aorist ἔδωκαν. The participle ἐσμυρνισμένον means flavored with myrrh, myrrhed wine. It is not inconsistent with Matthew 27:34 "mingled with gall."

But He did not take it (ὃς δὲ[27] οὐκ ἔλαβεν[28]). Note the demonstrative ὃς with δέ. Matthew has it that Jesus was not willing to take it. Mark's statement is that he refused it.

15:24. *Casting lots for them to decide what each man should take*[29] (βάλλοντες κλῆρον ἐπ᾽ αὐτὰ τίς τί ἄρῃ). This is found only in Mark. Note the double interrogative, Who? What? The verb ἄρῃ is first aorist active deliberative subjunctive retained in the indirect question. The details in Mark 15:24 to 32 are followed closely by Matthew 27:35–44. See there for discussion of details.

15:25. *It was the third hour when they crucified Him* (ἦν δὲ ὥρα τρίτη καὶ ἐσταύρωσαν αὐτόν). This is Jewish time and would be 9 A.M. The trial before Pilate was at 6 A.M., the sixth hour according to Roman time. See John 19:14.

15:26. *The inscription of the charge against Him*[30] (καὶ ἦν ἡ ἐπιγραφὴ τῆς αἰτίας αὐτοῦ ἐπιγεγραμμένη). This "epigraph" was the writing upon the top of the cross. Luke 23:38 has this same word, but Matthew 27:37 has "accusation" (αἰτίαν). See Matthew for discussion. John 19:19 has "title" (τίτλον).

15:32. *"Now come down from the cross"* (καταβάτω νῦν ἀπὸ τοῦ σταυροῦ), now that he is nailed to the cross.

"So that we may see and believe" (ἵνα ἴδωμεν καὶ πιστεύσωμεν). Note the aorist subjunctive of purpose with ἵνα. They use almost the very language of Jesus in their ridicule, words that they had heard him use in his appeals to men to see and believe.

Those who were crucified with Him were also insulting Him[31] (καὶ οἱ συνεσταυρωμένοι σὺν αὐτῷ ὠνείδιζον αὐτόν). Note the imperfect tense, they did it several times. The story of the robber who turned to Christ on the cross is told in Luke 23:39–43.

15:33. *When the sixth hour came* (Καὶ γενομένης ὥρας ἕκτης[32]), that is noon, Jewish time, as the third hour was 9 A.M. (see on v. 25 and on Matt. 27:45). This is also given by Luke (23:44). Mark gives the Aramaic transliteration, as does B in Matthew 27 (see on Matt. 27:45).

15:34. *"Why have You forsaken Me?"* (εἰς τί ἐγκατέλιπές με;[33]). We are not able to enter into the fullness of the desolation felt by Jesus at this moment as the Father regarded him as sin (2 Cor. 5:21). This desolation was the deepest suffering. He did not cease to be the Son of God, which would be impossible.

15:35. *"Behold, He is calling for Elijah"* (Ἴδε Ἠλίαν φωνεῖ[34]). They misunderstood Ελωι ("my God") to be *Elijah*.

15:36. *"Let us see whether Elijah will come to take Him down"* (Ἄφετε ἴδωμεν εἰ ἔρχεται Ἠλίας[35] καθελεῖν αὐτόν). See on Matthew 27:49, which has "to save Him" (σώσων).

15:37. *Breathed His last* (ἐξέπνευσεν). See on Matthew 27:50, which has "yielded up His spirit." Mark uses ἐξέπνευσεν again in verse 39.

15:39. *The centurion* (ὁ κεντυρίων). In the New Testament, this word is used only here and in verse 44.

Who was standing right in front of Him (ὁ παρεστηκὼς ἐξ ἐναντίας αὐτοῦ). This description is alone in Mark, picturing the centurion "watching Jesus." See on Matthew 27:54 for discussion of his testimony of Jesus as "the Son of God," or probably according to the centurian's Roman polytheism, "the Son of [a] god."

15:40. *And Salome* (καὶ Σαλώμη). She was apparently the "mother of the sons of Zebedee" (Matt. 27:56).

15:41. *They used to follow Him and minister to Him*[36] (ἠκολούθουν αὐτῷ καὶ διηκόνουν αὐτῷ). Two imperfects describe the long ministry of these three women and many other women in Galilee (Luke 8:1–3).

Who came up with Him to Jerusalem (αἱ συναναβᾶσαι αὐτῷ εἰς Ἱεροσόλυμα). This summary description in Mark is paralleled in Matthew 27:55f. and Luke 23:49. These faithful women saw the dreadful end to all their hopes as they stood watch at the cross.

15:42. *It was the preparation day* (ἦν παρασκευή), the day before the Sabbath (προσάββατον). By modern Western reckoning it was Friday. Sabbath would begin at 6 P.M. (see on Matt. 27:57). To avoid bringing uncleanness to the day of worship, the Jews had already taken steps to get the bodies removed (John 19:31).

15:43. *A prominent member of the Council* (εὐσχήμων βουλευτής), a high member of the Sanhedrin, a man who was rich (Matt. 27:57).

Who himself was waiting for the kingdom of God (ὃς καὶ αὐτὸς ἦν προσδεχόμενος τὴν βασιλείαν τοῦ θεοῦ), a periphrastic imperfect construction (see Luke 23:5). It is the verb used by Luke of Simeon and Anna (2:25, 38). Matthew 27:57 calls him "Jesus' disciple," while John 19:38 adds "secretly for fear of the Jews." He may have taken no public stand for Jesus until now.

He gathered up courage[37] (τολμήσας), an aorist (ingressive) active participle, becoming bold. It is to the glory of Joseph and Nicodemus, secret disciples of Jesus, that they took a bold stand when the rest were in terror and dismay.

15:44. *Pilate wondered if He was dead by this time*[38] (ὁ δὲ Πιλᾶτος[39] ἐθαύμασεν εἰ ἤδη τέθνηκεν). The perfect active indicative with εἰ after a verb of wondering is a classical idiom, a kind of indirect question as we say, "I wonder if. . . ." The point was surprise that Jesus could already be dead, for death by crucifixion could take days. This detail occurs only in Mark.

He questioned him as to whether He was already dead[40] (ἐπηρώτησεν αὐτὸν εἰ πάλαι[41] ἀπέθανεν[42]). Mark does not tell the request of the Jews to break the legs of the three to hasten death before the start of the Sabbath (John 19:31–37). Pilate wanted to make sure that Jesus was actually dead by official report. Mark wanted his readers to clearly understand that Jesus' death was definite. He did not revive later in the tomb.

15:45. *He granted the body to Joseph* (ἐδωρήσατο τὸ πτῶμα τῷ Ἰωσήφ[43]). Crucified bodies usually were exposed in the city garbage heap, but Pilate would be glad to turn this body over to Joseph, given the fuss about its disposition from the Jewish leaders. Here alone, πτῶμα (cadaver, corpse) is applied to the body of Jesus. $\Sigma\hat{\omega}\mu\alpha$ is the term used in Matthew 27:59; Luke 23:53; and John 19:40.

15:46. *Wrapped Him in the linen cloth* ($\dot{\epsilon}\nu\dot{\epsilon}\dot{\iota}\lambda\eta\sigma\epsilon\nu$ $\tau\hat{\eta}$ $\sigma\iota\nu\delta\acute{o}\nu\iota$). This verb is a New Testament hapax legomenon, just as $\dot{\epsilon}\nu\tau\upsilon\lambda\acute{\iota}\sigma\sigma\omega$ is only in Matthew 27:59; Luke 23:53; and John 20:7. These verbs occur in the papyri, Plutarch, and other late Greek literature, and either can be translated "to wrap, wind, roll in." The body of Jesus was wound in the linen cloth brought by Joseph, and the hundred pounds of spices brought by Nicodemus (John 19:39) for burying were placed in the folds of the linen and the linen was bound around the body by strips of cloth (John 19:40). The time was short before the Sabbath began and these two reverently laid the body of the Master in Joseph's new tomb, which had been hewn out of a rock. The perfect passive participle ($\lambda\epsilon\lambda\alpha\tau\omega\mu\eta\mu\dot{\epsilon}\nu\omega\nu$) is from $\lambda\alpha\tau\acute{o}\mu\omega\varsigma$, a stonecutter ($\lambda\hat{\omega}\varsigma$, "stone"; $\tau\dot{\epsilon}\mu\nu\omega$, "to cut"; see on Matt. 27:57–60). Luke 23:53 and John 19:41 also tell of the new tomb of Joseph.

And he rolled a stone against the entrance of the tomb ($\kappa\alpha\grave{\iota}$ $\pi\rho\omega\sigma\epsilon\kappa\acute{\upsilon}\lambda\iota\sigma\epsilon\nu$ $\lambda\acute{\iota}\theta\omega\nu$ $\dot{\epsilon}\pi\grave{\iota}$ $\tau\grave{\eta}\nu$ $\theta\acute{\upsilon}\rho\alpha\nu$ $\tau\omega\hat{\upsilon}$ $\mu\nu\eta\mu\epsilon\acute{\iota}\omega\upsilon$). Matthew has the dative $\tau\hat{\eta}$ $\theta\acute{\upsilon}\rho\alpha$ without $\dot{\epsilon}\pi\acute{\iota}$ and adds the adjective "great" ($\mu\dot{\epsilon}\gamma\alpha\nu$).

15:47. *Were looking*[44] ($\dot{\epsilon}\theta\epsilon\acute{\omega}\rho\omega\upsilon\nu$). The imperfect tense pictures the two Marys "sitting over against the sepulchre" (Matt. 27:61) and watching in silence as the shadows fell upon all their hopes and dreams. Apparently these two remained after the other women who had been beholding from afar the melancholy end (Mark 15:40) had left and "were watching the actions of Joseph and Nicodemus."[45] They surely saw the body of Jesus carried and knew where it was laid ($\tau\dot{\epsilon}\theta\epsilon\iota\tau\alpha\iota$, perfect passive indicative, state of completion). "It is evident that they constituted themselves a party of observation."[46]

NOTES

1. NIV has "Very early in the morning."
2. NIV has "reached a decision."
3. So WH, Vulgate *consilium facientej*, though this 1881 critical text gives $\dot{\epsilon}\tau\omega\iota\mu\dot{\alpha}\sigma\alpha\nu\tau\epsilon\varsigma$ in the margin.
4. Ezra P. Gould, *Critical and Exegetical Commentary on the Gospel According to St. Mark* (Edinburgh: T. & T. Clark, 1896), 283.
5. NIV has "They bound Jesus."
6. NIV has "Yes, it is as you say."
7. Gould, *Critical Exegitical Commentary*, 283.
8. NIV has "The chief priests accused him of many things."

9. TR accents the proper noun $\Pi\iota\lambda\acute{\alpha}\tau o\nu$; WH spells it $\Pi\epsilon\iota\lambda\hat{\alpha}\tau o\nu$.

10. NIV has "whom the people requested."

11. TR and Maj.T have the participle spelled as such, $\sigma\upsilon\sigma\tau\alpha\sigma\iota\alpha\sigma\tau\hat{\omega}\nu$.

12. NIV has "to do for them what he usually did."

13. TR and Maj.T have $\kappa\alpha\theta\grave{\omega}\varsigma$ $\dot{\alpha}\epsilon\grave{\iota}$ $\dot{\epsilon}\pi o\acute{\iota}\epsilon\iota$ $\alpha\grave{\upsilon}\tau o\hat{\iota}\varsigma$.

14. NIV has "knowing."

15. NIV has "had handed Jesus over."

16. Gould, *Critical and Exegetical Commentary,* 286.

17. Alexander Balmain Bruce, *The Expositor's Greek Testament*, Vol. 1, *The Synoptic Gospels* (Grand Rapids: Eerdmans, 1951), 447.

18. Ibid.

19. TR and Maj.T do not include the article with $\beta\alpha\sigma\iota\lambda\acute{\epsilon}\alpha$.

20. James Hope Moulton and George Milligan, *The Vocabulary of the Greek Testament* (London: Hodder and Stoughton, 1952), 302.

21. NIV has "They put a purple robe on him."

22. TR and Maj.T have the verb $\dot{\epsilon}\nu\delta\acute{\upsilon}o\upsilon\sigma\iota\nu$.

23. NIV has "Falling on their knees, they paid homage to him."

24. TR and Maj.T have the prepositional phrase without the article, $\dot{\epsilon}\pi\grave{\iota}$ $\Gamma\alpha\lambda\gamma o\theta\hat{\alpha}$.

25. At the time these word studies were published, the 1885 identification of Golgotha by General Charles Gordon, was widely accepted. General Gordon's identification of this location was based on his own theological understanding of Old Testament typology and a misunderstanding of where the city walls stood at the time of Christ. Dr. Robertson accepted the assumptions of the time. It is now certain that Golgotha was not at "Gordon's Calvary." The actual location remains uncertain, but was probably in the vicinity of the Church of the Holy Sepulchre.

26 TR and Maj.T include the infinitive $\pi\iota\epsilon\hat{\iota}\nu$ between $\alpha\grave{\upsilon}\tau\hat{\omega}$ and $\dot{\epsilon}\sigma\mu\upsilon\rho\nu\iota\sigma\mu\acute{\epsilon}\nu o\nu$.

27. TR and Maj.T have $\acute{o}$ $\delta\acute{\epsilon}$ in place of $o\varsigma$ $\delta\acute{\epsilon}$.

28. TR and Maj.T do not include the moveable ν on the verb $\acute{\epsilon}\lambda\alpha\beta\epsilon$.

29. NIV has "they cast lots, to see what each would get."

30. NIV has "The written notice of the charge against him."

31. NIV has "Those crucified with him also heaped insults on him."

32. TR and Maj.T have $\Gamma\epsilon\nu o\mu\acute{\epsilon}\nu\eta\varsigma$ $\delta\grave{\epsilon}$ $\H{\omega}\rho\alpha\varsigma$ $\H{\epsilon}\kappa\tau\eta\varsigma$.

33. TR and Maj.T have $\epsilon\grave{\iota}\varsigma$ $\tau\acute{o}$ $\mu\epsilon$ $\dot{\epsilon}\gamma\kappa\alpha\tau\acute{\epsilon}\lambda\iota\pi\epsilon\varsigma$. Some MSS give $\dot{\omega}\delta\epsilon\acute{\iota}\delta\iota\sigma\alpha\varsigma$ (reproached) for the verb.

34. TRs has $\dot{}I\delta o\acute{\upsilon}$, $\dot{}H\lambda\acute{\iota}\alpha\nu$ $\phi\omega\nu\epsilon\hat{\iota}$; TRb and Maj.T have $\dot{}I\delta o\acute{\upsilon}$, $\dot{}H\lambda\acute{\iota}\alpha\nu$ $\phi\omega\nu\epsilon\hat{\iota}$; WH has $\dot{}I\delta\epsilon$, $\dot{}H\lambda\epsilon\acute{\iota}\alpha\nu$ $\phi\omega\nu\epsilon\hat{\iota}$.

35. TRs has $\dot{}H\lambda\acute{\iota}\alpha\varsigma$; WH has $\dot{}H\lambda\epsilon\acute{\iota}\alpha\varsigma$.

36. NIV has "these women had followed him and cared for his needs."
37. NIV has "went boldly."
38. NIV has "Pilate was surprised to hear that he was already dead."
39. TR accents the proper noun as follows, Πιλάτος; WH spells it Πειλᾶτος.
40. NIV has "he asked him if Jesus had already died."
41. BD read ἤδη (already) again instead of πάλαι (a long time).
42. TRb and Maj.T do not include the moveable ν on the verb ἀπέθανε.
43. TR and Maj.T have ἐδωρήσατο τὸ σῶμα τῷ Ἰωσήφ.
44. NIV has "saw."
45. Henry Barclay Swete, *Commentary on Mark* (repr. ed., Grand Rapids: Kregel, 1977), 394.
46. Gould, *Critical and Exegetical Commentary*, 298.

Mark: Chapter 16

16:1. *When the Sabbath was over* (Καὶ διαγενομένου τοῦ σαββάτου), a genitive absolute, the Sabbath having come in between and is now over. For this sense of the verb see Acts 25:13; 27:9. It was therefore after sunset.

Bought spices (ἠγόρασαν ἀρώματα), as Nicodemus did on the day of the burial (John 19:40). Ezra Gould denies that the Jews were familiar with the embalming process of Egypt,[1] but at any rate it was to be a reverential anointing (ἵνα ἐλθοῦσαι ἀλείψωσιν αὐτόν) of the body of Jesus with spices. They could buy them after sundown. Salome is in the group again, as in Mark 15:40. See on Matthew 28:1 for discussion of "late on the Sabbath day" and the visit of the women to the tomb before sundown. They had returned from the tomb after the watching late Friday afternoon and had prepared spices (Luke 23:56). Now they secured a fresh supply.

16:2. *When the sun had risen*[2] (ἀνατείλαντος τοῦ ἡλίου), a genitive absolute aorist participle.[3] Luke 24:1 has it "at early dawn" (ὄρθρου βαθέως) and John 20:1 "while it was yet dark." It was some two miles from Bethany to the tomb. Mark himself gives both notes of time, "very early" (λίαν πρωῒ) and "when the sun had risen." Probably they started while it was still dark. The sun was coming up when they arrived at the tomb. All three mention that it was on the first day of the week when the women arrived. The body of Jesus was buried late on Friday, before the Sabbath began at sunset. Luke 23:54 makes this clear. The women rested on the Sabbath (Luke 23:56) and set out in the early morning of what is now Sunday. Some have been disturbed that Jesus did not remain in the grave three full days—seventy-two hours. But Jesus had said that he would rise *on the third day*. That is precisely what happened. He was buried on Friday afternoon. He was risen on Sunday morning. If he had really remained in the tomb a full three days, it would have been on the fourth day by Jewish reckoning. The occasional phrase "after three days" is a vernacular idiom common in all languages and not meant to be precise. We can readily understand "after three days" in the sense of "on the third day." It is impossible to understand "on the third day" to mean on the fourth day.[4]

406

16:3. *"Who will roll away the stone for us?"* (Τίς ἀποκυλίσει ἡμῖν τὸν λίθον . . . ;). This is the opposite of προσκυλίω in 15:46. In verse 4 "the stone had been rolled away" (ἀποκεκύλισται ὁ λίθος, perfect passive indicative) occurs also. Both verbs occur in κοινή texts and in the papyri. Clearly the women have no anticipation that Jesus might rise from death. They were raising more mundane issues (ἔλεγον, imperfect) as they walked along.

16:4. *Looking up, they saw*[5] (ἀναβλέψασαι θεωροῦσιν). With downcast eyes and heavy hearts[6] they have walked up the hill, but now they see that the problem is solved, for the stone lies rolled back. Mark uses his vividly dramatic historical present tense with "behold." Luke 24:2 has the usual aorist "found."

Although it was extremely large[7] (ἦν γὰρ μέγας σφόδρα). Mark adds a detail about the size of the stone to heighten the impact of this surprising sight.

16:5. *Entering the tomb*[8] (καὶ εἰσελθοῦσαι εἰς τὸ μνημεῖον). This is told also in Luke 24:3, although it is not mentioned by Matthew.

They saw a young man (εἶδον νεανίσκον), an angel in Matthew 28:5, two men in Luke 24. These variations in details show differences in perspective and can all be reconciled when studied within the flow of events of that morning. These differences also show the independence of the narratives and strengthen evidence that the Resurrection was a historical event experienced in time and space by witnesses. The angel sat upon the stone (Matt. 28:2), outside. Mark says that another young man was "sitting at the right" (καθήμενον ἐν τοῖς δεξιοῖς) inside the tomb. Luke mentions that at one point both men stood inside with the witnesses (Luke 24:4).

Wearing a white robe[9] (περιβεβλημένον στολὴν λευκήν), a perfect passive participle with the accusative case of the thing retained (verb of clothing). Luke 24:4 has "in dazzling apparel."

And they were amazed[10] (καὶ ἐξεθαμβήθησαν). They were utterly (ἐξ in composition) amazed. Luke 24:5 has it "terrified." Matthew 28:3–4 describes the raiment as being white as snow, so impressive that the watchers shook "and became like dead men." This was before the arrival of the women. Matthew, Mark, and Luke do not mention the sudden departure of Mary Magdalene to tell Peter and John that there had been a grave robbery (John 20:1–10).

16:6. *"Do not be amazed"*[11] (Μὴ ἐκθαμβεῖσθε). The angel noted their amazement (v. 5) and reassures them.

"The Nazarene" (τὸν Ναζαρηνόν), used only in Mark, to identify Jesus to the women.

"Who has been crucified" (τὸν ἐσταυρωμένον). This is also in Matthew 28:5. This description of his shame has become his crown of glory. So it would be for Paul (Gal. 6:14), and for all who look to the crucified and risen Christ as Savior and Lord.

"He has risen" (ἠγέρθη), a first aorist passive indicative, denoting the simple fact of what had occurred. In 1 Corinthians 15:4 Paul uses the perfect passive indicative ἐγήγερται to emphasize the permanent state that Jesus remains risen.

"Behold, here is the place"[12] (ἴδε ὁ τόπος). Ἴδε is used as an interjection with no effect on the case (nominative). In Matthew 28:6 ἴδετε is the verb with the accusative.[13]

16:7. *And Peter* (καὶ τῷ Πέτρῳ). This is only in Mark, showing that Peter remembered gratefully this special personal message from the risen Christ. Later in the day Jesus will appear also to Peter, an event that changed doubt to certainty with the apostles (Luke 24:34; 1 Cor. 15:5). See on Matthew 28:7 for discussion of the promised meeting in Galilee.

16:8. *Trembling and astonishment had gripped them*[14] (εἶχεν[15] γὰρ αὐτὰς τρόμος καὶ ἔκστασις). The imperfect tense indicates more exactly, "held them; was holding them fast." Mark has ἔκτασις, which comes into English as *ecstasy*, while Matthew 28:8 has "with fear and great joy," which see for discussion. Clearly and naturally their emotions were mixed.

They said nothing to anyone (οὐδενὶ οὐδὲν εἶπαν[16]). This excitement was too great for ordinary conversation. Matthew 28:8 notes that they "ran to bring his disciples word." Hushed to silence, their feet had wings as they flew on.

For they were afraid[17] (ἐφοβοῦντο γάρ), imperfect tense. The continued wondering fear explains their continued silence.[18]

16:9. *Now after He had risen early on the first day of the week* (Ἀναστὰς δὲ πρωὶ πρώτῃ σαββάτου). It is probable that this note of time goes with "risen" (ἀναστάς), though it makes good sense with "appeared" (ἐφάνη). Jesus is not mentioned by name, though he is clearly meant. Mark uses μιᾷ in verse 2, but πρώτῃ in 14:12 and the plural σαββάτων in verse 2, though the singular here.

First (πρῶτον). Note the definite statement that Jesus *appeared* (ἐφάνη) to Mary Magdalene first of all. The verb ἐφάνη (second aorist passive of φαίνω) is here alone of the risen Christ (cf. Ἠλίας ἐφάνη, Luke 9:8), the usual verb being ὤφθη (Luke 24:34; 1 Cor. 15:5ff.).

From whom[19] (παρ' ἧς[20]). This is the only instance of παρά with the casting out of demons, ἐκ being the usual preposition (1:25–26; 5:8; 7:26, 29; 9:25).

He had cast out seven demons (ἐκβεβλήκει ἑπτὰ δαιμόνια). This description of Mary Magdalene is like that in Luke 8:2 and seems strange in Mark at
this point, described as a new character, though mentioned by Mark three
times just before (15:40, 47; 16:1). The appearance to Mary Magdalene is
given in full by John (20:11–18).

16:10. *She* (ἐκείνη). This is the only instance of this pronoun in Mark,
though it is a good Greek idiom (see John 19:35). See verses 11 and 20.

Went (πορευθεῖσα), a first aorist passive deponent participle. This is a common word for going, but in Mark it has occurred so far only in 9:30 in the
uncompounded form. It occurs also in verses 12 and 15.

Reported to those who had been with Him (ἀπήγγειλεν τοῖς μετ᾽ αὐτοῦ
γενομένοις). This phrase for the disciples occurs here alone in Mark and the
other Gospels if the disciples are meant. The differing Greek forms suggest
that another hand than Mark's has penned for this closing portion of verses 9
through 20.

While they were mourning and weeping (πενθοῦσι καὶ κλαίουσιν). Present
active participles in the dative plural agreeing with τοῖς . . . γενομένοις and
describing the pathos of the disciples in their utter bereavement and woe.

16:11. *They refused to believe it*[21] (ἠπίστησαν). This verb is common in
the ancient Greek, but rare in the New Testament and again in verse 16 but
nowhere else in Mark. The usual New Testament word is ἀπειθέω. Luke 24:11
uses ἠπίστουν of the disbelief of the report of Mary Magdalene and the other
women. The verb ἐθεάθη (from θεάομαι) occurs only here and in verse 14 in
Mark.

16:12. *After that*[22] (Μετὰ δὲ ταῦτα), only here in Mark. Luke tells us that
it was on the same day (24:13).

He appeared in a different form[23] (ἐφανερώθη ἐν ἑτέρᾳ μορφῇ). This was
not a μεταμόρφωσις or transfiguration like that described in 9:2. Luke explains that they were prevented from recognizing Jesus (Luke 24:16; see 24:13–
32).

16:13. *But they did not believe them either* (οὐδὲ ἐκείνοις ἐπίστευσαν).
The men fared no better than the women. But Luke's report of the two on the
way to Emmaus is to the effect that they met a hearty welcome in Jerusalem
(Luke 24:33–35). This shows the independence of the two narratives on this
point. Some still discredited all the resurrection stories, just as later on the
mountain in Galilee some would doubt (Matt. 28:17).

16:14. *Afterward He appeared to the eleven themselves*[24] (Ὕστερον [δὲ[25]]
ἀνακειμένοις αὐτοῖς τοῖς ἕνδεκα ἐφανερώθη). Both terms, eleven and twelve

(John 20:24), occur after the death of Judas. Others were present on this first Sunday evening according to Luke 24:33. "Afterward" (ὕστερον) is here alone in Mark, though it is common in Matthew.

He reproached them[26] (ὠνείδισεν). They were guilty of unbelief[27] (ἀπιστίαν) and hardness of heart[28] (σκληροκαρδίαν). Doubt is not necessarily a mark of intellectual superiority. One must steer between credulity and doubt. Luke explains how the disciples were upset by the sudden appearance of Christ and were unable to believe the evidence of their own senses (24:38–43).

16:15. *"Preach the gospel to all creation"* (κηρύξατε τὸ εὐαγγέλιον πάσῃ τῇ κτίσει). This commission in Mark is probably another version of the missionary *Magna Carta* in Matthew 28:16–20, which was spoken on the mountain in Galilee. One commission already has been given by Christ (John 20:21–23). The third appears in Luke 24:44–49 = Acts 1:3–8.

16:16. *"And has been baptized"* (καὶ βαπτισθείς). The omission of *baptized* with *disbelieved* would seem to show that Jesus does not make baptism essential to salvation. Condemnation rests on disbelief, not on a lack of baptism. So salvation rests on belief. Baptism is merely the picture of the new life not the means of securing it. Even if the text does connect baptism with salvation, its questionable canonicity could not outweigh other undisputable texts that clearly teach that faith alone (not the work of baptism) is requisite for salvation.

16:17. *"They will speak with new tongues"* (γλώσσαις λαλήσουσιν καιναῖς).[29] We have seen the casting out of demons in the ministry of Jesus. However, speaking with tongues comes in the apostolic era (Acts 2:3f.; 10:46; 19:6; 1 Cor. 12:28; 14.).

16:18. *"They will pick up serpents"*[30] (ὄφεις ἀροῦσιν). Jesus had said something like this in Luke 10:19, and Paul was unharmed by the serpent in Malta (Acts 28:3–6).

"If they drink any deadly poison" (κἂν θανάσιμόν τι πίωσιν). This is the only New Testament instance of the old Greek word θανάσιμος ("deadly"). James 3:8 has θανατηφόρος ("deathbearing"). A. B. Bruce considers these verses in Mark "a great lapse from the high level of Matthew's version of the farewell words of Jesus" and holds that "taking up venomous serpents and drinking deadly poison seem to introduce us into the twilight of apocryphal story."[31] The great doubt concerning the genuineness of these verses (fairly conclusive proof against them in my opinion) renders it unwise to take these verses as the foundation for doctrine or practice unless supported by other genuine portions of the New Testament.

16:19. *He was received up into heaven*[32] (ἀνελήμφθη εἰς τὸν οὐρανόν), a first aorist passive indicative. Luke gives the fact of the Ascension twice, once in his Gospel (Luke 24:50f.) and once in Acts 1:9–11. The Ascension in Mark took place after Jesus spoke to the disciples, not in Galilee (16:15–18), nor on the first or second Sunday evening in Jerusalem. We should not know when it took place nor where but for Luke, who locates it on Olivet (Luke 24:50) after forty days (Acts 1:3) and so after the return from Galilee (Matt. 28:16).

Sat down at the right hand of God (ἐκάθισεν ἐκ δεξιῶν τοῦ θεοῦ). Henry Swete notes that the author "passes beyond the field of history into that of theology," but Jesus' action as He leaves human history is a fact with much scriptural backing (Acts 7:55f.; Rom. 8:34; Eph. 1:20; Col. 3:1; Heb. 1:3; 8:1; 10:12; 12:2; 1 Peter 3:22; Rev. 3:21).

16:20. *Everywhere* (πανταχοῦ). This is found once in Luke.[33]

While the Lord worked with them (τοῦ κυρίου συνεργοῦντος), a genitive absolute construction. This participle is not in the Gospels elsewhere, nor is βεβαιοῦντος, nor the compound ἐπακολουθούντων. Such constructions are found in Paul's Epistles.

NOTES

1. Ezra P. Gould, *Critical and Exegetical Commentary on the Gospel According to St. Mark* (Edinburgh: T. & T. Clark, 1896), 299.
2. NIV has "just after sunrise."
3. Some MSS read ἀνατέλλοντος, a present participle.
4. See A. T. Robertson, *Harmony of the Gospels for Students of the Life of Christ* (New York: Harper and Row, 1922), 289–91.
5. NIV has "when they looked up, they saw."
6. Alexander Balmain Bruce, *The Expositor's Greek Testament*, Vol. 1, *The Synoptic Gospels* (Grand Rapids: Eerdmans, 1951), 453.
7. NIV has "which was very large."
8. NIV has "As they entered the tomb."
9. NIV has "dressed in a white robe."
10. NIV has "and they were alarmed."
11. NIV has "Don't be alarmed."
12. NIV has "See the place."
13. See A. T. Robertson, *A Grammar of the Greek New Testament in the Light of Historical Research* (Nashville: Broadman, 1934), 302.
14. NIV has "Trembling and bewildered."
15. TR and Maj.T have the postpositive conjunction δέ in place of γάρ. TRb and Maj.T do not include the moveable ν on the verb εἶχε.

16. TR and Maj.T spell the verb εἶπον.

17. NIV has "because they were afraid."

18. At this point Aleph and B, the two oldest Greek manuscripts of the New Testament, stop with this verse. Three Armenian MSS also end here. Some documents (cursive 274 and Old Latin k) have a shorter ending than the usual long one. The great mass of the documents have the long ending seen in the English versions. Some have both the long and the short endings, like L, Ψ, 0112, 099, 579, two Bohairic MSS; the Harklean Syriac (long one in the text, short one in the Greek margin). One Armenian MSS (at Edschmiadzin) gives the long ending and attributes it to Ariston (possibly the Aristion of Papias). W (the Washington Codex) has an additional verse in the long ending. So the facts are very complicated but argue strongly against the genuineness of verses 9 to 20 of Mark 16. There is little in these verses not in Matthew 28. It is difficult to believe that Mark ended his Gospel with verse 8 unless he was interrupted. A leaf or column may have been torn off at the end of the papyrus roll. The loss of the ending was treated in various ways. Some documents left it alone. Some added one ending, some another, some added both. A full discussion of the facts is found in the last chapter of A. T. Robertson, *Studies in Mark's Gospel* (1919; repr. ed., Nashville: Broadman, 1958) and in Robertson's *An Introduction to the Textual Criticism of the New Testament* (Nashville: Broadman, 1925), 214–16.

19. NIV has "out of whom."

20. TR and Maj.T have ἀφ' ἧς.

21. NIV has "they did not believe it."

22. NIV has "Afterward."

23. NIV has "Jesus appeared in a different form."

24. NIV has "Later Jesus appeared to the Eleven."

25. TR and Maj.T do not include the conjunction δέ.

26. NIV has "he rebuked them."

27. NIV has "lack of faith."

28. NIV has "their stubborn refusal."

29. WH puts καιναῖς in the margin.

30. NIV has "they will pick up snakes."

31. Bruce, *Expositor's*.

32. NIV has "he was taken up into heaven."

33. WH gives the alternative ending found in L: "And they announced briefly to Peter and those around him all the things enjoined. And after these things Jesus himself also sent forth through them from the east even unto the west the holy and incorruptible proclamation of the eternal salvation."